Contents

Advisory Editors

Richard S. K. Barnes
Department of Zoology
University of Cambridge

David E. Hanke
Botany School
University of Cambridge

Harry J. Hudson
Botany School
University of Cambridge

Development Editor

Steve M. Read
Department of Biochemistry
University of Cambridge

Picture researcher

Marion Jowett

Indexer

Joan Daniels

Contributors

John E. Almond
Department of Earth Sciences
University of Cambridge

W. Brad Amos
Department of Zoology
University of Cambridge

Peter Andrews
Department of Anthropology
British Museum
(Natural History)

Richard S. K. Barnes
Department of Zoology
University of Cambridge

Hilary B. Birks
22 Rutherford Road
Cambridge

Giles R. M. Courtice
Botany School
University of Cambridge

David W. T. Crompton
Department of Parasitology
Molteno Institute
University of Cambridge

Dianne Edwards
Department of Plant Science
University College, Cardiff

Kenneth J. Edwards
Department of Applied
Biology
University of Cambridge

S. Keith Eltringham
Department of
Applied Biology
University of Cambridge

William A. Foster
Department of Zoology
University of Cambridge

Adrian Friday
Department of Zoology
University of Cambridge

David E. Hanke
Botany School
University of Cambridge

Paul H. Harvey
School of Biological Sciences
University of Sussex

Harry J. Hudson
Botany School
University of Cambridge

David S. Ingram
Botany School
University of Cambridge

Christine M. Janis
Division of Biology
and Medicine
Brown University
Providence, Rhode Island

J. Michael Lock
Pembroke House
30 High Street
Milton, Cambridge

John A. Lucas
Department of Botany
University of Nottingham

Roger B. Moreton
Department of Zoology
University of Cambridge

E. Marjorie Northcote
Department of Zoology
University of Cambridge

Philip Oliver
Department of Genetics
University of Cambridge

Leslie Orgel
The Salk Institute
San Diego, California

Robert J. Paxton
School of Biological Sciences
University of Sussex

Steve M. Read
Department of Biochemistry
University of Cambridge

Philip H. Rubery
Department of Biochemistry
University of Cambridge

David B. Sattelle
Department of Zoology
University of Cambridge

Peter D. Sell
Botany School
University of Cambridge

Anthony J. Stuart
Department of Zoology
University of Cambridge

Brian A Whitton
Department of Botany
University of Durham

Pat Willmer
Department of Zoology
University of Oxford

Foreword

The human species must always have been interested in the living organisms with which it shares this planet: primarily for strictly practical reasons, as gatherers and hunters, then as cultivators and pastoralists, and subsequently in attempts to understand more completely the world, the origin of the human species, and its fate.

For at least 2000 years attempts have been made to discover the relationships between living things, and in particular to classify the always increasing number of plants and animals known, from the few hundred familiar to Aristotle and Theophrastus, to the thousands known to Ray and von Linné (Linnaeus), and the millions which are currently studied with the sophistication of modern technology. In addition, the question of the origin of life on this planet has taxed the imagination since remote antiquity. Scientific explanations have ranged from Aristotle's hypotheses of spontaneous generation by natural forces, to the not totally dissimilar ideas of some modern scientists based on the production of simple organic compounds by electrical discharge in mixtures of gases, with the more complex organic molecules arising in what J.B.S. Haldane has termed the 'hot dilute soup' of primaeval oceans. This curiosity about the origins and variety of life has led to what is arguably one of the greatest revolutions in human thought, Charles Darwin's theory of organic evolution by natural selection, and the accumulated knowledge concerning the other organisms with which we share this planet has provided insight into our own nature and emphasised the dangers that threaten the human species.

It is a current conceit, and one frequently encountered in forewords of this kind, that we live in the age of 'the revolution in biology'. In one sense this is quite untrue, as some of the biological advances of early ages, such as Pasteur's dismissal of the theory of spontaneous generation of life, or Darwin's demonstration of the existence of organic evolution and his discovery of its mechanism, were in concept truly more revolutionary than any recent advances in biological knowledge. It is the impact of modern technology on the detailed elucidation of living processes that is currently revolutionary. In particular, the ability to study living cells as physicochemical systems has led to the recent spectacular growth of biophysics and molecular genetics. This growth will undoubtedly have an increasing effect on many aspects of human life, ranging from the sophisticated control of our own bodily processes to dramatic changes in our methods of production of food and fuel. Despite its successes, however, the molecular approach can make only limited contributions to the elucid-ation of the mechanisms by which organisms function as integrated units and interact as communities and populations. The understanding of such complex levels of organisation as the behaviour of animals and the human mind involves concepts of high order which modern biologists are only beginning to attempt to formulate. The final implications of this research cannot yet even be imagined.

To attempt to summarise in a single volume the available information on the living organisms which inhabit, or have inhabited, the earth is, if not impossible, certainly a daunting task. The two very obvious reasons why this should be so are the extreme complexity and the enormous diversity of such organisms. Fortunately the molecular and biochemical approaches to living systems have tended to emphasise the essential similarities of the mechanisms involved in basic cellular processes such as genetic inheritance, metabolism and growth, although even this apparent unity may be illusory and a consequence of the way that we choose to look at these processes. With an appropriate viewpoint, however, it is possible and useful to compare the basic cellular functions of different organisms, such as sea-weeds and orchids, or eels and apes. Such broad comparisons become progressively less useful when applied to tissues and to organs, and at these levels of organisation it may be more profitable to consider specialised aspects of cellular function and, in particular, the transfer of information between cells. The understanding of the integrative functions of such information transfer is now one of the central biological problems, for example in developmental biology, and will undoubtedly become an essential factor in our understanding of the neural basis of animal behaviour and of our own mental processes.

This *Encyclopedia* describes a hierarchy of interactions or, perhaps better, a hierarchy of environments: the various controlled environments within the cell, the immediate extracellular environment provided for the cells within tissues, the environments provided for the tissues by their organisation into organs and then for the organ systems within organisms, and finally the components, both physical and biological, of the external environment of the whole organism. The adaptations of plants and animals to their environments, and their relations with other organisms within these environments, are central features of this book. This emphasis is very much a product of its time; it both reflects the current concern with the accelerating rate at which the environment is being exploited and destroyed, and is a natural stage in the development of the sciences of life.

J.E. Treherne

Mixed tropical riverine forest in the gorge of the Nyamugasani River, Queen Elizabeth National Park, Western Uganda.

Introduction

The most striking feature of any natural assemblage of living things is the great diversity of size and form of the micro-organisms, plants and animals within it. This diversity is perhaps most obvious in the teeming jungles of the rain-forests of the tropical regions of the world, but on closer examination is found to be almost as great in habitats as different as temperate woodlands, the continental deserts, the vast oceans which cover the greater part of the earth's surface and, perhaps surprisingly, many of the altered environments created by agriculture, industry and the building of cities.

Close observation of the natural world has, in many instances, led to major advances in biological thinking. Darwin's theory of evolution by natural selection, for example, which revolutionised biology in the nineteenth century, arose as a result of a lifetime's detailed observation of plants and animals. The observational approach of the naturalist has continued into the present century, and today is perhaps more important than ever as the activities of the human species lead to the modification or destruction of more and more habitats and the extinction of an ever-growing number of species, many of which are, and may remain, unknown to science.

The approach of the naturalist, the observer, is however limited and, although an essential prerequisite for most forms of investigation, is not sufficient to explain all the complexities of biological organisation. In the historical development of the life sciences the descriptive approach has, in most fields, been augmented by a more critical experimental tradition: the recognition that to understand the properties of the living world it is necessary to frame the right questions and to ask them in such a way that answers may be obtained with some conviction.

The experimental tradition in modern biology developed much earlier in studies of animals than in studies of plants. Walters, in *The Shaping of Cambridge Botany* (Cambridge University Press, 1981), suggested that this may have come about because, although modern botany and zoology both had their origins in medicine, the function of the botanists was accurately to describe and identify all plants, or 'herbs', for use as therapeutic agents, whereas zoology developed from comparative studies of both human anatomy **and** physiology. Thus the zoologist was more likely than the botanist to consider **together** both observation and experiment. It was not until the twentieth century, however, that the experimental approach gathered momentum in biology as a whole, and it is important to recognise that even now the enterprise is only trivially complete, despite the fact that as a result of modern developments in molecular biology it is already possible for the human species to modify other organisms genetically in ways quite unconsidered just a few years ago.

The Cambridge Encyclopedia of Life Sciences surveys the current state of knowledge in biology, thus providing a synthesis which draws both on the observations of the naturalist tradition and on the findings of the experimental approach which has arisen from it. Studies of micro-organisms, plants and animals remained largely as separate strands of research until comparatively recently, when advances in cell biology emphasised the ubiquity of basic cellular structures and metabolic processes in **all** living things. It is at the level of the cell, therefore, that the *Encyclopedia* begins, examining the ways in which cells are constructed, how their biochemistry and biophysics are organised and controlled, how cells reproduce, and how they differentiate to perform specific functions. Some organisms, such as bacteria and many microscopic plants and animals, consist of one cell only. Others are composed of more cells and range in complexity from algae to flowering plants and vertebrate animals containing many millions of cells differentiated in a variety of ways to perform numerous different functions. Consideration is next given, therefore, to the principles underlying the control of growth, development, physiology and reproduction of both unicellular and multicellular organisms. The discussions of behaviour and ecology which follow place organisms, including the human species, in the context of the living world as a whole and show how they interact with one another and with the environment to form assemblies and communities.

This analysis of the principles and processes of biology provides a firm foundation for a survey of the diversity of organisms within the major environments of the earth: marine, coastal, terrestrial and freshwater. The physical and climatic features of these environments are described, and the major assemblages of living organisms within them are presented, with consideration being given to the structural and physiological variations that enable such organisms to succeed in spite of the variety of stresses placed upon them. Also, where appropriate, the impact of the human species on environments is discussed. Finally, cells and multicellular organisms are considered as environments themselves, for parasites and pathogens.

Having dealt with the present-day living world, the *Encyclopedia* turns to evolution, a topic which has been and remains a constant source of debate among scientists and laymen alike. The controversial theories of the origin of life are examined, the forces of selection and extinction which may have led to the present-day flora and fauna are discussed through reference to the fossil record and to modern observation and experiment, and the origin of the human species itself is considered.

The Cambridge Encyclopedia of Life Sciences is not a natural history cataloguing the living world, it does not attempt to argue a case for or against biological conservation, nor does it consider the yet greater ethical problems which arise from the genetic manipulation of cells. Instead, the *Encyclopedia* seeks to present biology as a science, and in addition constitutes a plea for considering all biological phenomena as indissolubly linked, a circumstance which underlies both the frustration and the fascination felt by all life scientists.

Adrian Friday
David S. Ingram

Part one
Processes and organisation

Some of the most difficult problems in biology are those involving levels of organisation. How, for example, is the genetic message encoded in each organism unpacked and interpreted in a disciplined manner during development to give rise to the whole organism? How are changes in the genetic material sometimes incorporated in all members of a descendent population? How do the interactions of individual nerve cells confer upon a nervous system the ability to interpret the messages of the sense organs and to coordinate complex behaviour patterns?

In the first chapters of this volume the basic chemical processes of living organisms are described, together with the principles of genetic inheritance at the molecular level and at the level of the organism. The ways in which the bodies of multicellular plants and animals are constructed can often be understood by analogy with the concepts of engineering: highly sophisticated solutions to problems of engineering design frequently turn out already to have evolved in the natural world. The ways in which the components of living systems interact have parallels in other sciences and it is clear that, whatever peculiar properties living systems might possess, they developed of necessity, in accord with the laws of physics and chemistry.

Animals, being for the most part possessed of nervous systems and being more mobile than plants, exhibit behaviour patterns. A recent field of progress in biology has dealt with the social interactions within and between animal species. This and some of the concepts of behavioural ecology, recognising the ways in which animal behaviour is affected by environmental factors, form the subject of a further chapter in Part One.

A further level of interaction among and between the species of plants and animals is considered in the chapter dealing with the principles of ecology. Again, organisms must work within the constraints of the physical factors in their external as well as their internal environments, but they will often interact also with other organisms.

The basic principles of plant and animal design recur again and again in those succeeding parts of this book dealing with the diversity of organisms in environments worldwide and with the patterns and processes of evolution.

Scanning electron micrograph of the head of the flour moth (Ephestia kuhniella) *showing the compound eye and coiled proboscis (x 84).*

1 The Cell

1.1 BASIC THEMES OF LIVING ORGANISMS

By far the greatest number of living organisms on the earth are single cells, micro-organisms invisible to the naked eye. The majority of micro-organisms are bacteria, which have a simple internal structure enclosed within a single limiting cell membrane called a **plasma membrane**. This membrane has the important function of enabling the cell to maintain an internal molecular composition which is completely different from that of the medium in which it lives. The membrane is selective in the types of molecule which it allows to enter and to leave the cell, and indeed some substances may be actively accumulated from the medium. The genetic material of bacterial cells is not contained in a true nucleus bounded by a nuclear membrane, and such organisms are described as **prokaryotic** (Fig. 1.1). The other major group of prokaryotic organisms is the blue-green algae.

In contrast, **eukaryotic** cells are organised in a fundamentally different way; within their bounding plasma membrane they are internally divided into discrete membrane-bounded compartments, and their genetic material is held in a **nucleus** bounded by a nuclear membrane. The nucleus is surrounded by the rest of the cellular contents, the **cytosol** (or cytoplasm) and the **organelles** this contains. Some types of eukaryotes, such as protozoa and yeasts, are free-living micro-organisms (see section 2.1), but eukaryotic cells are also the building blocks from which the familiar multicellular organisms, plants, fungi and animals, are constructed (see sections 2.2 to 2.4 and Fig. 1.1). In a multicellular organism the individual cells are dependent on each other, and have become structurally and functionally differentiated to perform various specialised roles necessary for the whole organism.

The protoplasm of prokaryotes (their internal contents) relies, as far as is known, simply on diffusion for mixing of the molecules it contains. The time needed for transport by diffusion increases, however, in proportion to the square of the distance to be travelled, and this relationship restricts the size of prokaryotic cells; the volume of a typical bacterium is about 1 cubic micrometre. In contrast, eukaryotes have evolved a stirring mechanism called protoplasmic streaming which enables effective communication to be maintained within the cytoplasm of much larger cells: typical volumes are about 2000 to 4000 cubic micrometres for a liver cell or root meristem cell, although plant cells that contain large central vacuoles can be much larger.

Although the structural organisation of prokaryotic and eukaryotic cells is so different, the basic tasks which the cells must perform are the same and are covered by two key themes of cell biology: energy conservation and transfer, and information flow.

Energy conservation and transfer

It is convenient to distinguish two types of process from an energetic point of view: those that occur spontaneously, and those that need the expenditure of energy to drive them. Thus a car freewheels downhill, but needs to be driven uphill; and a waterfall requires no input of energy to the water, while a geyser needs the water to come into contact with hot rocks. Similarly, sugar is readily oxidised and broken down by cells, while photosynthesis to produce sugar from carbon dioxide and water is carried out by green plants using the free energy of sunlight. A thermodynamic quantity called **free energy** (or Gibbs free energy) describes the energy released during spontaneous processes and the use of energy by energy-requiring processes. Free energy is measured in joules; 1 joule will heat 1 gram of water by about $0.25\,°C$. 'Free' energy means that the energy is available to do work; it is not equivalent to heat: in essence, work stimulates organised motion and heat stimulates random motion. If a process that releases free energy can be coupled mechanistically to another process that will not occur without a supply of free energy, coupled so that one cannot happen without the other, then a proportion of the free energy released by the first, 'downhill', process can be used to do work by driving the second process energetically 'uphill'; except under ideal conditions, however, some of the free energy will be dissipated as heat.

It is this type of coupling of processes that enables living organisms to function. Cells are able to use the free energy available from the metabolic breakdown (**catabolism**) of complex food molecules, such as sugars or fats, to drive energy-requiring processes like the biosynthesis (**anabolism**) of proteins, nucleic acids, polysaccharides and other polymers from their subunits. Highly specific catalysts called enzymes (see section 1.3) are biochemical devices that enable the coupling of energy-yielding and energy-requiring processes to occur. Energy released from catabolic reactions (and, in photosynthetic organisms, energy trapped during the excitation of chlorophyll by light, see section 1.3) is funnelled to drive the 'uphill' formation of the key biochemical intermediate adenosine triphosphate (ATP) from adenosine diphosphate (ADP) and inorganic phosphate. The formation of 1 mole of ATP requires an input of free energy of about 60 kilojoules under prevailing cellular concentrations of reactants and products (a 'mole' of ATP contains 6×10^{23} molecules of ATP, the same number as there are atoms of carbon in 12 grams of the isotope carbon-12), and thus if it is then hydrolysed back to ADP and inorganic phosphate a corresponding amount of free energy will be released. Coupling of the hydrolysis of ATP to a step of an energetically unfavourable synthetic process, by the mechanism of the particular enzyme that catalyses that step, means that some of the free energy from ATP hydrolysis that would have been released is instead used to drive the synthetic process in a direction that would otherwise not occur.

ATP molecules are the common unit of energy exchange in

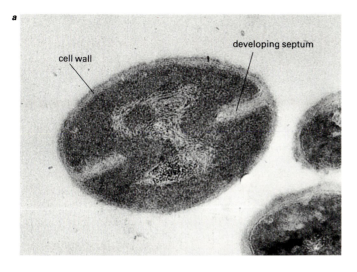

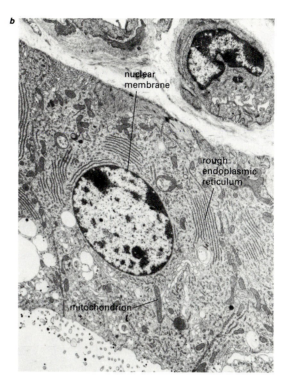

Fig. 1.1 (a) A prokaryotic cell. Electron micrograph of a dividing bacterium (Staphylococcus aureus) (x 42000). (b) A eukaryotic cell. Electron micrograph of a secretory epithelial cell from the mammary tissue of a cow (x 3600).

the cell, able to link diverse biochemical reactions because of the mechanisms of the enzymes that catalyse these reactions, and ATP is often thought of metaphorically as the energy currency of the cell. It enables energetic assets to be transferred from food materials to build the cell's own structure and to power other functions such as cytoplasmic streaming. Gradients of concentration of various ions across membranes, for example of sodium and potassium ions across the plasma membrane (see section 1.4) or of hydrogen ions across the mitochondrial inner membranes, and electric potential gradients across membranes, are also used to store energy and to do useful work. These metabolic interconversions will be described in more detail in section 1.3.

Information flow

A unicellular organism is capable of growth, of changing its activities in response to environmental signals, and of reproduction. In multicellular organisms, the cells become differentiated (see section 1.6) and can receive signals (mechanical, chemical and/or electrical) from other cells in the organism as well as from the external environment (see section 1.4 and pages 89–94); only a few of the individual cells of the organism, the cells constituting the **germ-line**, are carried over to form the members of the next generation when the organism reproduces.

The characteristics that distinguish one type of organism from another are due to differences in the properties of their proteins. Proteins are a versatile class of macromolecule, and can, for example, function as highly specific catalysts (enzymes and membrane-bound carriers), antibodies, intercellular messengers (hormones like insulin), and structural components of cells and tissues; the structure of the other major macromolecular components of tissues, carbohydrates, depends upon the nature of the enzyme proteins synthesising the carbohydrate molecules. The properties of a protein depend ultimately

upon the sequence of amino-acids that comprise it, and the information content required to specify a particular organism is that needed to specify the sequence of amino-acids in its proteins. This is stored in coded form in deoxyribonucleic acid (DNA, see section 3.1).

DNA is a polymer of four different types of subunit, called nucleotides, which are assembled one by one during biosynthesis. Each nucleotide contains a particular nitrogenous base, and the sequence in which these bases occur along the DNA molecule constitutes the heritable information of the cell. At the mitotic division of a cell nucleus which precedes cell division, each daughter cell obtains a copy of the DNA identical to that of its parent (see section 1.5). Except for any mutation, a spontaneous change in the sequence of bases in the DNA (see section 3.1), the total nuclear information content of an asexually reproducing population is thus conserved; the process of sexual reproduction, however, includes mechanisms by which a rearrangement of this genetic information occurs (see sections 1.5 and 3.2).

There are two aspects of the actual utilisation of the genetic 'blueprint' encoded in DNA. First, there has to be a mechanism for making the encoded information real in terms of molecular transformations and interactions. Secondly, since DNA contains a variety of pieces of information that a cell can call on throughout its life, there must be control mechanisms to allow the expression of this information to be selective (see section 3.1). For the first aspect, DNA programmes the biosynthesis of proteins, by specifying the order of the 20 different types of amino-acid in each protein from the sequence of bases in particular sections of the DNA molecule. A region of the DNA containing a piece of information that can affect the properties of an organism, by programming the synthesis of a protein, is called a **gene**. The second aspect, the control of gene expression, demands mechanisms for switching particular genes on and off in response to regulatory signals. In prokaryotes these signals are usually provided by the nutritional status of the

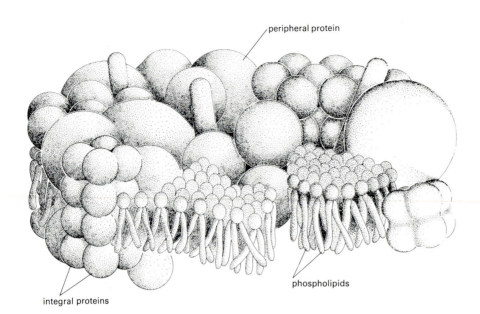

peripheral protein

integral proteins

phospholipids

Fig. 1.2. Model of the mitochondrial membrane. Most membranes consist of a phospholipid bilayer with proteins scattered in and on it. The mitochondrial membrane has a very high content of protein and here the lipid bilayer fills the gaps between the proteins.

growth environment of the organism. For example, the presence of a particular type of potential food molecule may switch on the synthesis of enzymes needed to metabolise that nutrient, while the absence of key nutrients may trigger the organism to produce the proteins required to form a cyst and become dormant.

The adaptation of eukaryotes to environmental changes, and the wider issues of cell differentiation in the multicellular eukaryotic organisms (see section 1.6) are much more complicated problems to resolve at the molecular level, largely because the organisation and expression of the genetic material of eukaryotes is formidably complex in comparison with that of prokaryotes (see section 3.1). Nevertheless, the receipt of signals from the environment and from other cells of the multicellular organism, and the implementation of these signals in terms of altered cellular activity including differential gene expression, is taken to be responsible for morphogenesis and differentiation in eukaryotes just as in prokaryotes.

1.2 FINE STRUCTURE OF CELLS

Introduction

The chemical composition and function of subcellular structures are studied in biochemistry, while observations with the electron microscope give information about the shape and arrangement of these structures.

Biochemistry

The atoms inside living systems are organised to various extents. Almost all are covalently bonded in extremely precise groups to form molecules, but these molecules vary enormously in size. Large molecules are stable and of precise shapes, but this is achieved at the expense of the speed of chemical reactions. The largest molecules are of deoxyribonucleic acid, DNA (see section 3.1), the function of which is to preserve in a stable form, through many generations, all the precise instruc-

tions for building the cell. The metabolism of living cells also needs the chaos of small molecules in solution, and the molecules undergoing frenetic chemical transformation to supply the cell with energy are among the smallest in the cell (see section 1.3).

The structures of the cell are built up of molecules of intermediate sizes: lipids and proteins. They link up with each other via reversible forms of attachment which, though much weaker than covalent bonds, are present in large numbers to compensate for this. The most important of these weak interactions is the tendency for non-polar groups (groups soluble in organic solvents) to be pushed together in water and to be excluded from the aqueous phases of the cell, just as oil spontaneously separates from water; other reversible linkages include attractions between groups with opposite electric charges, and 'hydrogen bonds' similar to the bonds between water molecules.

The structural lipids of the cell, called phospholipids, all consist of a polar, water-soluble head end, covalently linked to two long, parallel-sided, non-polar tails. The tails do not dissolve in water and thus tails of different lipid molecules lie side by side and end to end, but the heads dissolve in the aqueous phase, so that the phospholipid comes to form sheets that are two molecules thick (Fig. 1.2). Each sheet is a **membrane**. Sheets of membrane are unstable at their edges, and these coalesce, converting the sheet to a seamless bag called a vesicle.

Each living cell is contained by such a seamless coat of membrane, the **plasma membrane**. Inside eukaryotic cells (see section 1.1), membranes enclose regions of specialised function, called **organelles** by analogy with organs of specialised function in animals. Many functions are carried out in the region called the **cytosol** (or cytoplasm) that is outside the organelles but enclosed within the plasma membrane.

The complex folding of the chain of covalently linked amino-acids during the synthesis of proteins similarly involves the exclusion of non-polar sections of the protein chain from water into the interior of the molecule, while polar groups are pulled outwards until the chain settles to a stable arrangement.

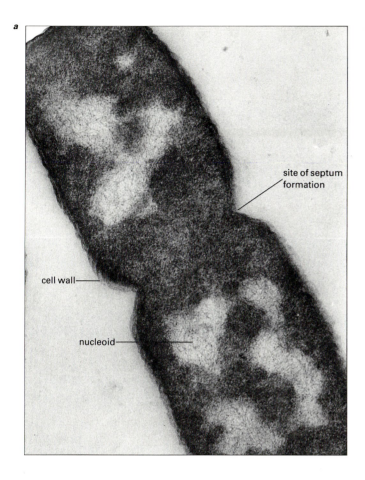

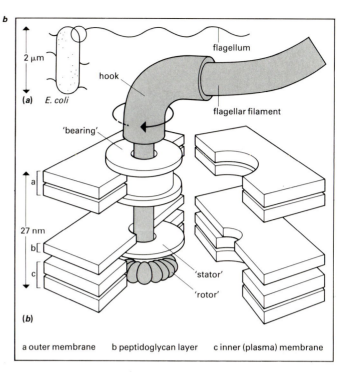

Fig. 1.3. (a) Transmission electron micrograph of a thin section of the bacterium Escherichia coli (x 60000). (b) The component parts of the bacterial flagellum, a structure unique in living organisms in that it revolves like the wheel of a car. Driven by a 'motor' inside the cell, the spinning 'drive-shaft' is set in a molecular scale 'sealed bearing'.

(Proteins found in a non-polar environment, such as the inside of a lipid membrane, have polar interiors and non-polar exteriors.) For some proteins it is not possible to tuck away all the non-polar regions, and hydrophobic patches remain on the surface of the folded protein; when such proteins meet in the polar aqueous environment, they will be pushed against each other, becoming the subunits of 'multimeric' protein complexes. Multisubunit proteins vary tremendously in their size and complexity depending on the numbers and shapes of their subunits, their hydrophobic patches and any other bonding groups. Structures made up of protein molecules can be internally complex in spite of being relatively small, such as ribosomes, or can be composed of just a few types of subunit even though their final structure is huge, such as microtubules. The structures that support the nucleic acid in chromatin and in viruses assemble by these types of protein–protein interactions.

The presence of particular bonding regions on their surface can also result in proteins being pushed into the surface of membranes, which become studded with these **extrinsic** (or **peripheral**) components. Extrinsic proteins diffusing over the membrane surface can associate with each other to form chains or aggregates (Fig. 1.2). Some proteins are inserted into a membrane as they are synthesised, and fold in the non-polar environment. These **intrinsic** (or **integral**) membrane proteins often function to communicate between the two aqueous regions separated by the membrane, for example by transporting polar substances across membranes or by relaying external signals into the cell (see sections 1.3 and 1.4).

Membranes, therefore, are barriers to non-selective movement of polar molecules, and divide the cell into compartments between which any movement of ions, sugars and other polar molecules is strictly controlled by membrane proteins; the water molecule is in fact small enough to slip through the lipid bilayers fairly effectively by itself. Membranes also provide the hydrophobic environment needed for certain reactions, such as in the synthesis of non-polar molecules and in electron transport (see section 1.3).

Electron microscopy

Most intracellular structures are considerably smaller than the wavelength of light, and can only be seen by electron microscopy. This requires the different features of the cell to be loaded with electron-opaque elements to be visible in the beam of electrons. The commonest technique is to view thin slices (some 200 to 300 nanometres thick) of killed preserved cells, stained with heavy elements like osmium, lead or uranium, and embedded in polyester resin to stiffen the material so that it can be sliced thinly.

Such **thin sections** provide a two-dimensional view only. A widely used method which generates pictures also containing information on the third dimension involves breaking rapidly frozen tissue, and then making an accurate picture (called a replica) of the fracture surface in heavy metal by coating it from the side with platinum vaporised in a vacuum. The planes of weakness followed by the fracture run between the lipid layers in each membrane, these being no longer squeezed together by liquid water. The replica is then viewed in the electron microscope. A modification of this **freeze-fracture** technique is to sublime some of the ice from the fracture face before making the replica, thereby revealing features on membrane surfaces previously submerged under ice. This technique is called **freeze-etch**.

Surface features on, for example, isolated organelles and viruses can be seen in great detail when the interstices between the features are flooded with a solution of phosphotungstic acid, which highlights unstained prominences: this technique is called **negative staining**.

Cell structures

Nuclear structures

Prokaryotes have a central area, the **nucleoid** (Fig. 1.3) containing the compactly folded circular molecule of DNA, but it is not isolated from the rest of the cell by any membrane. The distinguishing feature of eukaryotic cells is the nucleus, the central membrane-bounded organelle containing virtually all the DNA of the cell. The single circle of DNA in a prokaryote is a copy of the complete information for survival of that species, which in eukaryotes is distributed among the chromosomes, a number of linear pieces of DNA only visible as discrete entities during cell division (see section 1.5). Another feature of eukaryotic DNA is that the molecule, which is negatively charged, is wrapped around a series of protein particles each consisting of eight positively charged protein molecules, to form a structure resembling a string of beads. The positively charged proteins are called **histones**, and the individual beads **nucleosomes**. The nucleosomes are drawn closer together by another type of histone molecule to form threads of **chromatin** 10 to 30 nanometres across (see section 3.1). The nucleus is surrounded by two concentric membranes barely separated by a perinuclear space (Fig. 1.4). Part of the chromatin is thickly draped over the inside of the inner nuclear membrane, to which it is attached at intervals by a framework of extrinsic proteins, the nuclear lamina. Different proteins stabilise complex pores through both nuclear membranes. The dinoflagellates, unicellular algae which were the commonest plants in seas in the Palaeozoic era, are intermediate in having a typically eukaryotic nuclear membrane surrounding histone-free nucleoids that are typically prokaryotic.

Nuclei contain one or more large, densely staining bodies not bounded by a membrane, called **nucleoli**; these are the site of synthesis of the RNA backbone of ribosomes and sites of assembly of proteins on to the ribosomal RNA.

Cytoplasmic structures

Ribosomes (Fig. 1.4) are cytoplasmic particles about 30 nanometres across, and are precisely organised, containing over 50 different protein subunits around a core of RNA molecules. Each ribosome can translate faithfully into protein the information in specific RNA copies of portions of the DNA (messenger RNA) (see section 3.1). Ribosomes are electron-dense in thin sections of cells viewed in the electron microscope, but are not seen by freeze-etch techniques. In prokaryotic cells they fill up the space between the nucleoid and the plasma membrane. Eukaryotic ribosomes are slightly larger than prokaryotic ribosomes, and are located outside the nucleus, both free in the cytoplasm and attached to the cytoplasmic face of both the outer nuclear membrane and a system of membranes, called the **endoplasmic reticulum**, that extends through the rest of the cell. The ribosomes may be arranged in groups called polysomes; each polysome consists of a number of ribosomes at various stages of translating one messenger RNA molecule.

The endoplasmic reticulum encloses a narrow space, the lumen, that is connected to the perinuclear space, and the endoplasmic reticulum itself is chemically very similar to nuclear membrane. Ribosomes attached to the endoplasmic reticulum synthesise integral membrane proteins which stay in the membrane, and also synthesise proteins for export which move through this membrane into the lumen. The amount of endoplasmic reticulum is much greater in cells actively exporting proteins, and its shape varies from closely packed concentric sheets to thinly dispersed tubes. Regions that become loaded with newly synthesised protein break up into small vesicles which fuse with the Golgi apparatus, or are linked to it via tubular connections.

Each **Golgi body** is a stack of flattened membranous vesicles, like a pile of hollow pancakes, firmly cemented to one another. Each vesicle, or cisterna, travels through the stack as vesicles from the endoplasmic reticulum fuse to form new cisternae at one face of the stack. As it passes through the Golgi body, the lipid composition of the cisterna membrane is altered, many of the protein and some of the lipid components have sugars linked covalently to them, and, from around its rim each cisterna alternately balloons out and dimples in until opposing dimples fuse, releasing vesicles called Golgi vesicles. In animal cells the Golgi bodies are located together and form a network in which groups of vesicles are interlinked by stacks of cisternae. The network is called the Golgi complex and each component stack a dictyosome.

Proteins destined for export are secreted by exocytosis, fusion of the Golgi vesicle with the plasma membrane. Alternatively the contents of the Golgi vesicle can be secreted internally by fusion with lysosomes.

Lysosomes are small vesicles containing hydrolytic enzymes capable of breaking down proteins, lipids and nucleic acids to low-molecular-weight components. They are involved in the autodigestion of cellular structures, and in the digestion of material brought into the cell by phagocytosis, in which the plasma membrane invaginates to capture a small amount of extracellular material.

Lysosomes occur in animal cells (Fig. 1.4). If there is an equivalent in plant cells it is the **vacuole** (Fig. 1.5), a very large vesicle which fills most of the cell and contains a dilute, acidic sap, a solution chiefly of potassium malate, with a profuse

Fig. 1.4. (a) Diagram of a
generalised animal cell,
showing its component parts
and their distribution within
the cell.
(b) – (d) Transmission electron
micrographs of thin sections.
(b) An oblique section
through the surface of a
protozoon, Tetrahymena,
showing the structure of cilia
at a series of points along this
organelle (x 96 000). (c) From
a cell of the intestinal
epithelium of a pig, showing
microvilli, surface projections
supported by an internal
framework of actin (x 2240).
(d) From a cell of rat liver,
often thought of as 'typical'
animal tissue.

a

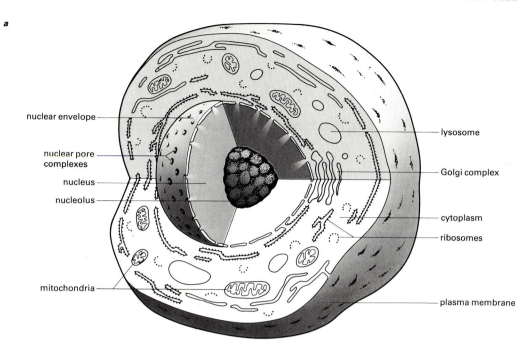

- nuclear envelope
- nuclear pore complexes
- nucleus
- nucleolus
- mitochondria
- lysosome
- Golgi complex
- cytoplasm
- ribosomes
- plasma membrane

b

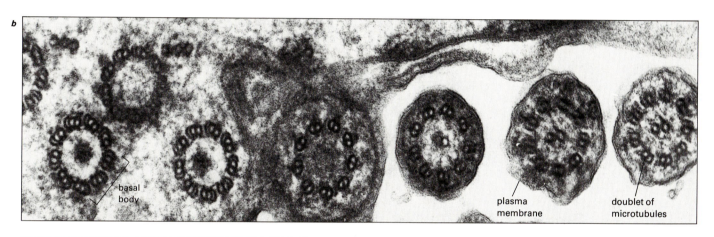

- basal body
- plasma membrane
- doublet of microtubules

c

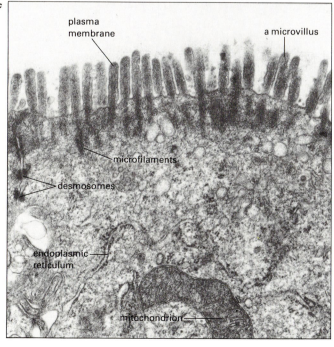

- plasma membrane
- a microvillus
- microfilaments
- desmosomes
- endoplasmic reticulum
- mitochondrion

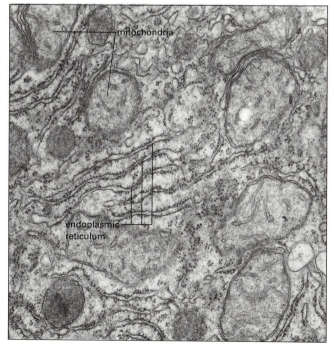

- mitochondria
- endoplasmic reticulum

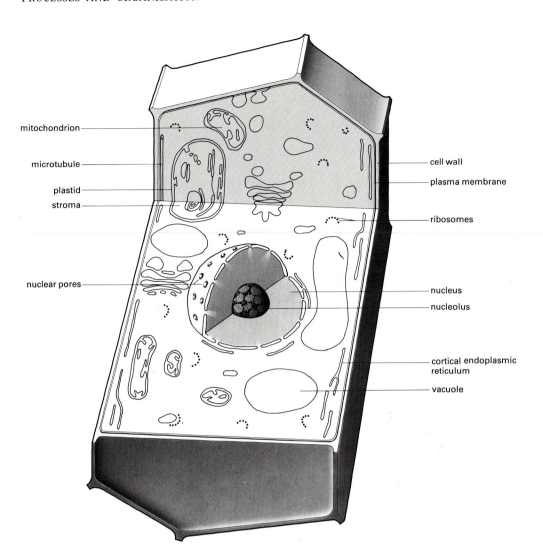

mitochondrion

microtubule

plastid

stroma

nuclear pores

cell wall

plasma membrane

ribosomes

nucleus

nucleolus

cortical endoplasmic reticulum

vacuole

variety of hydrolytic enzymes, phenolic compounds and other organic substances.

Plastids are unique to plant cells. The most important plastids are **chloroplasts** (Fig. 1.5), the organelles which trap the energy of solar radiation (see section 1.3). Chloroplasts exist within an envelope of two membranes separated only by a narrow space, and contain a complex system of chlorophyll-rich, flattened membrane sacks, the thylakoids, piled like coins into stacks, called grana, and floating in an enzyme-rich solution, the stroma. The grana are interconnected via sheets of paired membranes, called stromal lamellae, which enclose a narrow space continuous with the lumen (internal space) of the thylakoids. As well as metabolic enzymes, the stroma contains circles of histone-free DNA coding for some of the chloroplast proteins; there are also prokaryotic-type ribosomes and all the enzymic machinery for protein synthesis in the chloroplast. The similarity between chloroplasts and the prokaryotic blue-green algae, the chlorophyll of which is associated with single thylakoids derived from the plasma membrane, suggests that chloroplasts originated as free-living prokaryotes which have become modified to live inside another cell.

Under illuminated conditions, chloroplasts are produced by growth and division of other chloroplasts. They can also develop from small simple, double-membrane vesicles, called proplastids which in non-photosynthesising cells fill with stored starch, becoming amyloplasts. During development,

chloroplasts can also fill with brightly coloured yellow, orange or red pigments, and so convert to chromoplasts.

Mitochondria (Fig. 1.4) resemble chloroplasts in having a double-membrane envelope enclosing an enzyme-rich matrix, histone-free circles of DNA, ribosomes different from those of the cytoplasm, the capacity to grow and divide, and the ability to make some of their own proteins. The principal function of mitochondria is to generate the energy-rich molecule ATP (see sections 1.1 and 1.3) by the oxidation of pyruvate, itself the end product of oxidation of glucose in the cytoplasm, and by the oxidation of fats, but they also play a major part in the synthesis of lipids, and of amino-acids for proteins.

These functions are carried out by the enzymes of the matrix and by the highly organised and protein-rich inner membrane, which projects into the matrix as folds or fingers called cristae enabling large amounts of mitochondrial inner membrane to be packed into each mitochondrion, and increasing the interface of the membrane with the matrix. The inner membrane provides the insulation required for electron transfer, and a barrier across which the gradient of hydrogen ions is established (see section 1.3). The enzyme complex, called ATPase, which converts the energy of this chemical and electrical gradient into the energy of chemical bonds in ATP can be seen in the electron microscope in negatively stained preparations of the inner membranes, as structures resembling lollipops and projecting into the matrix. While each chloroplast

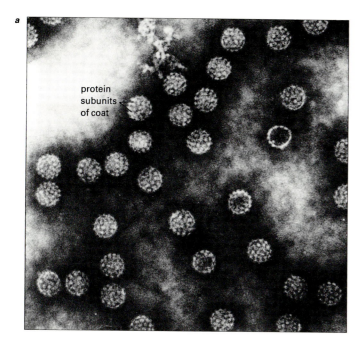

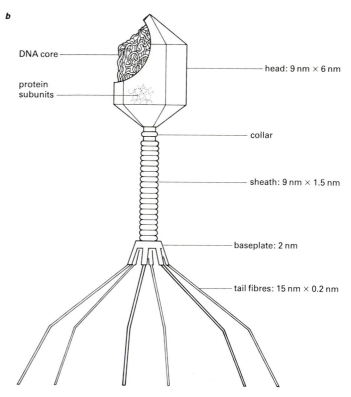

Fig. 1.6. (a) Transmission electron micrograph of a negative stain preparation of wart virus (× 135000). (b) The component parts of a 'T-even' bacteriophage, structurally the most complex of all viruses.

remains a discrete body with a distinct shape throughout its life, mitochondria are irregularly shaped and often fuse to form networks which spread through the cell and break up again.

One group of subcellular structures is assembled from proteins in the absence of lipids, as in ribosomes, but forming long rods. Their job is to provide a skeleton for the eukaryotic cell, which gives it shape and allows its parts to move relative to each other, similar to the role of the skeleton in vertebrates. This **cytoskeleton** is not a permanent construction, however, and can be disassembled and re-assembled with speed.

The largest of these structures are the **microtubules** (Fig. 1.5), which are 25 nanometres wide and composed of 13 long rows of subunits associating in parallel to form thin tubes. The subunits are the protein tubulin. Relative to its neighbours each row is staggered somewhat, so that in surface view there is a helical pattern of subunits around the tube. Microtubules can rapidly assemble from their subunits, growing from patches of cytoplasm called microtubule-organising centres that are featureless in the electron microscope. Extension takes place preferentially at one end of each microtubule, and disassembly occurs at the opposite end.

All cells have a network of microtubules near the plasma membrane, the cortical microtubules, which contribute to cell shape, especially in unicellular organisms. In addition, microtubules provide a framework on which chromosomes move during mitosis (see section 1.5), and a framework on which other microtubules move during the motion of eukaryotic flagella and cilia.

Flagella (Fig. 1.4) and **cilia** are structures that extend out like hairs from the surface of some cells. Commonly, flagella are very long (around 100 micrometres), few in number and propel cells along by wriggling sinuously. Cilia are short (20 micrometres long), thickly clustered, and either propel cells or move the surrounding liquid past them by repeatedly whipping back-

wards and flipping forwards. Inside a sheath of plasma membrane, cilia and flagella contain a precise framework of microtubules, nine doublets of microtubules forming a tube enclosing two central single microtubules. This whole arrangement is stabilised by links between all the components, and active sliding of doublet microtubules relative to other doublet microtubules forces the structure to bend. Each flagellum or cilium always grows out from a basal body just inside the plasma membrane. The basal body consists of nine short (0.5 micrometres long) triplets of microtubules arranged in the same way, and normally arises by budding from existing basal bodies, although basal bodies can form in a microtubule-organising centre.

The flagellum of prokaryotic cells consists of strands of protein subunits, and is rotated as a whole at its base, driving the cell along the same way as does the screw of a ship (see Fig. 1.3).

Microfilaments are 6 nanometres wide and are composed of two rows of subunits twisted helically around each other lengthways. The subunits are the protein actin. Microfilaments provide a framework for cytoplasmic streaming in conjunction with the protein myosin and, in a much more organised manner, are involved in muscle contraction (see section 1.4). Each microfilament has a distinct polarity, and movement along it is in one direction only. A network of microfilaments near the plasma membrane contributes to the cytoskeleton; the surface projections of the plasma membrane called microvilli are stabilised by microfilaments without microtubules (Fig. 1.4).

Intermediate filaments are 10 nanometres wide and are a heterogeneous collection of cytoskeletal components not involved in motility. Various proteins are involved, including keratin, the component of hair. Filaments of the protein desmin anchor desmosomes, junctions between the plasma membranes of adjoining animal cells that hold the cells together (Fig. 1.14).

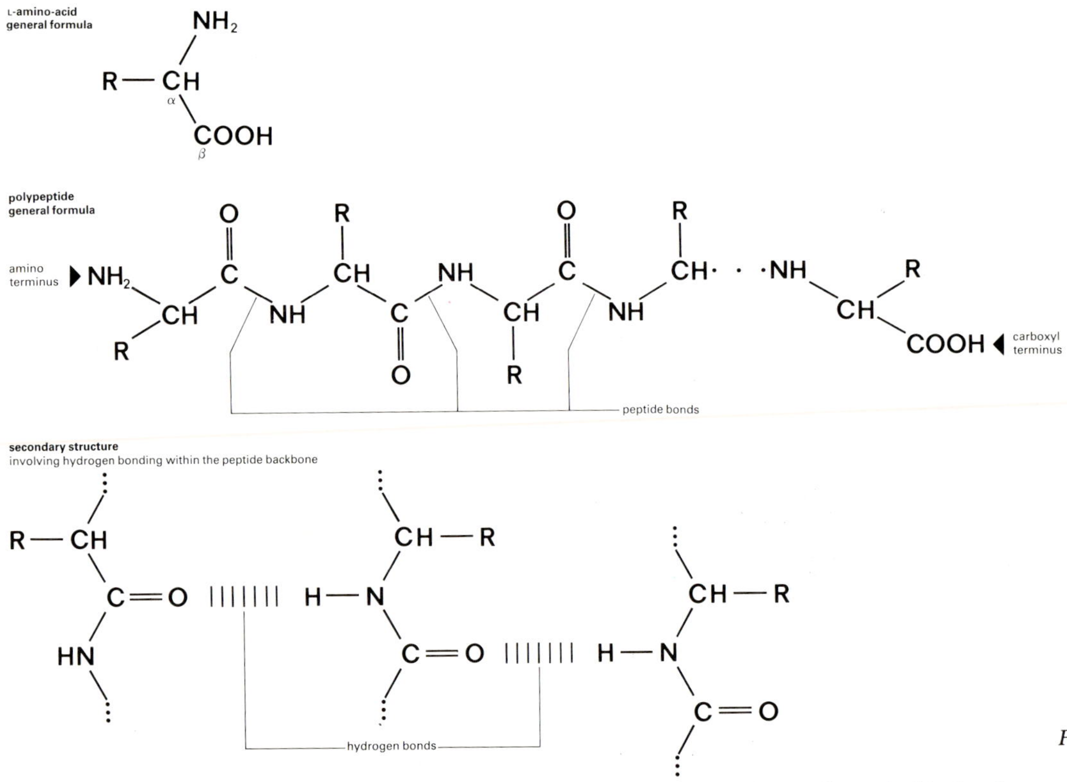

L-amino-acid
general formula

$$\begin{array}{c} NH_2 \\ | \\ R - CH \\ {}_\alpha \; | \\ COOH \\ {}_\beta \end{array}$$

polypeptide
general formula

amino
terminus ▶ NH_2 ⋯ peptide bonds ⋯ $COOH$ ◀ carboxyl
terminus

secondary structure
involving hydrogen bonding within the peptide backbone

hydrogen bonds

Fig. 1.7. Protein structure.

Extracellular structures

The outer surface of the plasma membrane is rich in glycolipids and glycoproteins, the sugar units of which form a thin, stainable layer, the glycocalyx, around animal cells. The distribution of glycoproteins over the surface of the plasma membrane is controlled by their attachment to the underlying cytoskeleton.

Prokaryotic cells (see Fig. 1.3) are always entirely surrounded by a shell of chemically complex, composite material, the **cell wall**; this consists of chains of polymerised amino-sugars, each chain covalently linked to the next via short peptides to form a vast molecular net. This is capable of opposing the tendency of the bacterial cell to swell and burst due to the high concentrations of solutes inside the cell drawing in water by osmosis. Many prokaryotic cells also have a slimy layer, the capsule, on the outside of the wall.

Plant cells (Fig. 1.5) are also always surrounded by a cell wall which, as in prokaryotes, buffers changes in hydrostatic pressure within the cell to maintain a constant volume; plant cells grow by making their cell wall extensible and so responsive to pressure changes occurring inside the cell. The wall also determines the cell shape in plants, and provides the major contribution to the integrity and rigidity of multicellular tissues such as wood.

Plant cell walls are a composite material like reinforced concrete, consisting of stiff, inextensible rods set in a featureless matrix. The rods are linear chains of cellulose, a polymer of glucose, crystallised into long microfibrils 2 nanometres wide. While the cell is growing the matrix is a watery gel of acidic polysaccharides, but when cell growth is complete the spaces between the microfibrils are more firmly packed with other polysaccharides. Plant cell walls comprise a large part of plant material, but being polysaccharide they contain very little nitrogen, which is reserved for more important uses than merely maintaining structure. There is, however, a glycoprotein in the wall, and this is characterised by being rich in the modified amino-acid hydroxyproline.

Animal cells, in contrast to plant cells, operate at constant hydrostatic pressure, accommodating an influx of water by volume changes in the short term, or by secretion in the long term. The extracellular material in animal tissues is present solely to maintain the integrity, and sometimes the rigidity, of the multicellular tissues. The extent of the extracellular material varies from the thin film joining the two halves of a desmosome, through the sheets of material that support individual layers of cells (basement layers of epithelia), to the great thicknesses of cartilage and bone in which individual cells are widely scattered.

As in plants, extracellular material in animals is reinforced with rods, consisting in animals of collagen, triple helices of a hydroxyproline-rich glycoprotein crystallised into long fibres 1.5 nanometres wide. The matrix is a watery gel of glycosaminoglycans, acidic sulphated polymers of amino-sugars and other sugars, linked into a polypeptide backbone to form **proteoglycan**. A high proportion of matrix gives a soft material, such as cartilage, and a high proportion of fibrillar component gives a hard material, such as tendon.

Viruses

Viruses are completely parasitic on eukaryotic or prokaryotic cells (see section 10.2) and outside the host they exist as inert, crystalline arrangements of protein subunits coating a core of nucleic acid. Inside the host, the coat is removed and the nucleic acid reprogrammes the synthetic machinery of the host cell into making viruses. Viruses of prokaryotic cells are known as 'phages': bacteriophages infect bacteria, and cyanophages infect blue-green algae.

There is a variety of shapes and styles of virus (Fig. 1.6). The nucleic acid can be RNA or DNA, single-stranded or double-stranded (see section 3.1), circular or linear, and intact or in

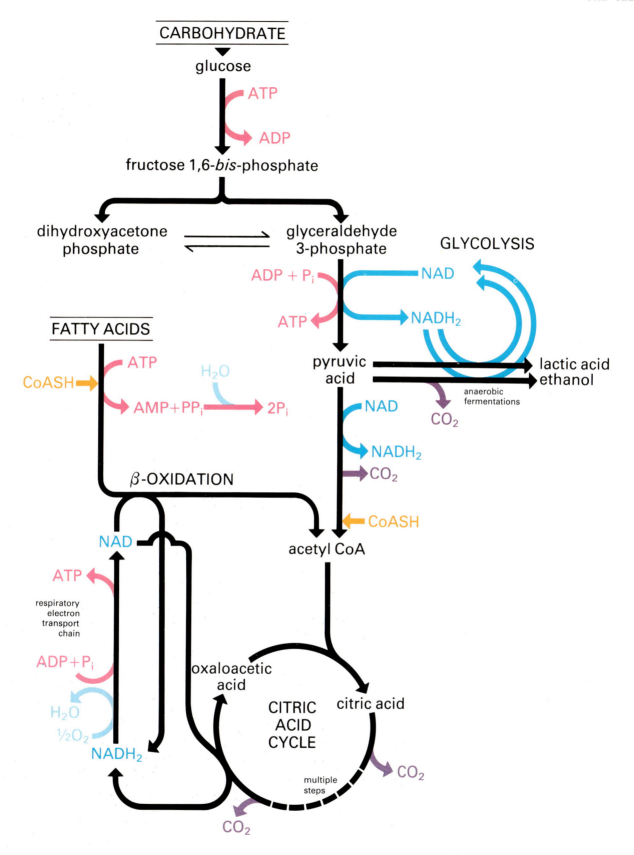

Fig. 1.8. Schematic outline of carbohydrate and fat catabolism. Production of acetyl-CoA from glucose via glycolysis, and from fatty acids by β-oxidation; oxidation of acetyl-CoA to carbon dioxide and water by the citric acid cycle and respiratory chain. A phosphate ester group is shown as Ⓟ in structural formulae.

pieces. For most viruses the protein coat is simple, consisting of a few kinds of protein assembled to form icosahedral or long cylindrical shells. In some viruses the coat proteins assemble around the nucleic acid, while in others the coat proteins assemble around scaffolding proteins which leave the coat before the nucleic acid fills it. Some viruses of animals become enveloped in a portion of the plasma membrane as they leave the host cell.

The most complex viruses known are the 'T-even' bacteriophages. Attached by a collar to the DNA-containing head is a tubular contractile mid-piece, capable of injecting the DNA into the bacterial cell. At the distal (further) end of the sheath is a base plate to which are attached six tail fibres; these recognise and bind to bacterial cell walls, and activate contraction of the mid-piece. The whole assembly is made up of 40 different proteins, and 13 different scaffolding proteins are used in its construction.

1.3 METABOLIC PROCESSES

Across the range of living organisms there is a uniformity in the biochemical strategies of the major degradative and biosynthetic pathways of metabolism. The mechanisms by which the fluxes through these pathways are controlled, and their spatial organisation in the cell, may differ significantly among micro-organisms, animals and plants. Nevertheless the particular sequence of enzyme-catalysed reactions and chemical transformations that are involved in a major metabolic pathway, for example the complete oxidation of glucose to carbon dioxide and water, a process requiring 19 steps, remains essentially constant in these different organisms. The main **catabolic** (degradative) and **anabolic** (synthetic) pathways, and their energetic coupling, are complicated, and are only outlined in part here. A large number of steps is needed in many pathways as individual enzymes can only perform simple chemistry, and also, for catabolic pathways, because some of the free energy released during the breakdown of complex molecules can be trapped as the energy of ATP molecules if the breakdown occurs in discrete steps (see section 1.1).

Metabolism can be best appreciated through the underlying chemical logic of the individual steps, recognising the structures of the intermediates involved instead of their names. Metabolic pathways can generally be dissected in a number of different ways to reveal the nature of the changes that occur along them. Among the important features are the **flow of carbon atoms**, and whether an intermediate in the pathway has gained or lost any; the **energetics** of each particular reaction, whether cleavage of ATP is necessary or whether instead sufficient free energy is available to allow ATP synthesis; and the balance of oxidation and reduction, if those processes are involved, using particular biological oxidising or reducing agents that must be regenerated in some way. The **pattern** of chemical transformations is of interest, for enzymes

in quite different metabolic pathways can use analogous ways of dealing with analogous chemical problems. The physiological **context** of the pathway must also always be considered, especially regarding the factors that control the rate of flow of material through it for a particular type of cell or organism.

Proteins, enzymes and cofactors

Proteins are biopolymers made from about 20 different types of amino-acid which, except for proline, have the general formula $R—CH(NH_2)—COOH$ (see Fig. 1.7). The R— group attached to the α-carbon atom is called the amino-acid side-chain, and specifies the particular amino-acid; it may be polar (hydrophilic, with a high affinity for water, whether charged or uncharged) or non-polar (hydrophobic, tending to avoid water). The amino-acids are linked in a linear sequence by covalent bonds between their α-amino ($—NH_2$) and carboxyl ($—COOH$) groups; these amide linkages are called **peptide bonds**. A typically sized protein may contain about 500 amino-acid residues, and have a relative molecular mass of around 60 000.

The biological properties of proteins depend on how their linear **primary sequence** of amino-acids (which is specified genetically, see section 3.1) folds in three dimensions into the structure of maximum stability in their environment. The folding pattern, and thus the shape of the molecule, is largely determed by weak non-covalent hydrogen bonds and hydrophobic interactions, which form and break readily at physiological temperatures, so allowing the protein to change shape in response to changing conditions. Both certain individual amino-acid side-chains and the peptide links can participate in hydrogen bonding. Some proteins contain extensive regions of regular helical or sheet-like conformation, termed **secondary structure**, which are formed by a regular pattern of hydrogen bonding within the peptide backbone (see Fig. 1.7).

Enzymes are proteins that are remarkably effective and specific catalysts. They allow chemical reactions to proceed, from the reactants (known as **substrates**) to the products, under physiological conditions which would not otherwise permit the reaction to occur in any realistic time. The rate of the catalysed reaction is different from the rate of the uncatalysed reaction because the chemical environment of the substrate when it is bound to the surface of the protein is different from that in free solution. The substrate is bound to a particular site on the enzyme, called the **active site**. The high specificity of enzymes, for example their ability to distinguish between pairs of optical isomers, is achieved by a close match between the structure of the substrate and the contours of the active site. Since proteins are generally not rigid, some enzymes are able to fold around their substrates after the initial binding. Typical enzyme-catalysed reactions include hydrolysis, transfer of a phosphate group from ATP to acceptors like glucose, and transfer of electrons or hydrogen atoms from one molecule to another.

When each enzyme molecule in a population is dealing with a substrate molecule, the enzyme is said to be saturated and is working at its maximum velocity (V_{max}): no enzyme molecules are unoccupied. The substrate concentration needed to achieve half this maximum velocity is called the Michaelis constant (K_m), and is an important characteristic of the enzyme. For many enzymes, the Michaelis constant is about the same as the physiological concentration of the substrate, and the rate of the reaction catalysed by the enzyme is then able to alter in response to changes in the substrate concentration.

The values of both the Michaelis constant and the maximum velocity of an enzyme can be altered by the presence of activators and inhibitors, some of which may be important for metabolic control. Also, the catalytic properties of the enzyme may be altered by modification of certain amino-acid side-chains, for example by addition of a phosphate ester group. An enzyme in a metabolic pathway that has a low maximum velocity relative to the enzymes supplying its substrate and removing its product is potentially capable of limiting the flux through the pathway as a whole, and such rate-limiting steps are often control points, as altering the kinetic parameters of that enzyme will change the rate at which the whole metabolic pathway is operating. In practice, most pathways are controlled at several reactions, and there may be no clear single rate-limiting step.

Many enzymes require the presence of other non-protein substances to catalyse a reaction successfully. These are known collectively as **cofactors**, and are subdivided into prosthetic groups, which are tightly bound to the enzyme, and coenzymes, which are not. Examples of cofactors range from metal ions such as calcium to large organic molecules like haem rings. Some of the most important cofactors, including nicotinamide adenine dinucleotide (NAD) and its close analogue NADP, mediate oxidation/reduction reactions. Both of these nucleotides are coenzymes, and since they are cofactors for many different enzymes catalysing redox reactions they can link two reactions together by diffusing between the different enzymes.

Catabolic processes: oxidation of carbohydrate and fat

Glucose is a major fuel source for many organisms. In mammals it is the main circulating blood sugar, but in insects and plants it first has to be released from a disaccharide (trehalose in insects and sucrose in plants) that is the form in which sugar is transported in their vascular system. Potential fuel molecules entering cells can either be oxidised to yield energy in the form of ATP or, if food intake exceeds current energy requirements, they can be stored as energy-reserve molecules. Storage molecules are usually fat and polysaccharide (typically glycogen in animals and starch in plants), and these reserves are broken down and metabolised in the oxidative pathways when there is a high demand for energy.

Oxidation of glucose

After glucose is taken into a cell, and before any major chemical transformation has taken place, it is first modified by addition of a phosphate group to give glucose 6-phosphate. The donor of the phosphate group is not simply inorganic phosphate, which would not be energetically feasible, but rather ATP, which is cleaved to ADP in the process. This coupling of the phosphorylation of glucose to the cleavage of the terminal bond in ATP drives the reaction towards the formation of glucose 6-phosphate (see section 1.1). The phosphorylation traps the glucose inside the cell, because charged molecules such as glucose 6-phosphate do not readily cross membranes, and it also provides a chemical 'handle' for subsequent reactions.

Glucose 6-phosphate is at a metabolic branch-point that can lead either to storage as polysaccharide or to oxidation. The metabolic pathway for oxidation of glucose, **respiration**, is outlined in Fig. 1.8; it takes place in two stages. The first stage is **glycolysis**, which occurs in the cytoplasm in eukaryotes and can occur in the absence of oxygen (anaerobically). It splits the six-carbon glucose molecule into two three-carbon molecules of pyruvic acid (or rather the ionised form pyruvate). In aerobic respiration the pyruvate is converted to carbon dioxide and water by the second stage of oxidation, the **citric acid cycle** (the Krebs cycle), which requires oxygen. In eukaryotes, the enzymes of the citric acid cycle are found in the mitochondria, and thus to be completely metabolised pyruvate must first cross the mitochondrial membrane. If oxygen is limiting, as in rapidly contracting muscle or in yeast growing anaerobically, the citric acid cycle cannot function, and the amount of energy that can be obtained from each molecule of glucose, measured as the number of ATP molecules produced, is greatly reduced. Under these conditions, the products of glycolysis must be removed for this pathway to continue to function.

The production of pyruvate from glucose includes an oxidation step, with two reducing equivalents being transferred to an acceptor molecule, an oxidising agent which thereby becomes reduced, and which is the coenzyme NAD. NAD, like other cofactors, is present only in small amounts in cells, and therefore if glycolysis is to continue under anaerobic conditions there must be a way of not just removing the product pyruvate, but also of converting the reduced form of NAD ($NADH_2$) back to the oxidised form (NAD); under aerobic conditions the $NADH_2$ can pass its reducing equivalents into the mitochondrion for oxidation at the expense of oxygen, producing three ATP molecules. In anaerobic muscle cells, $NADH_2$ is reoxidised by pyruvate itself, which is reduced to lactate and excreted to the blood; in yeast the pyruvate is first decarboxylated to acetaldehyde (ethanal) which is then reduced to ethanol by $NADH_2$, a fermentation reaction which is the basis of wine and beer production.

Overall, glycolysis under anaerobic conditions produces two molecules of lactate (or two of ethanol and two of carbon dioxide), and two molecules of ATP from every molecule of

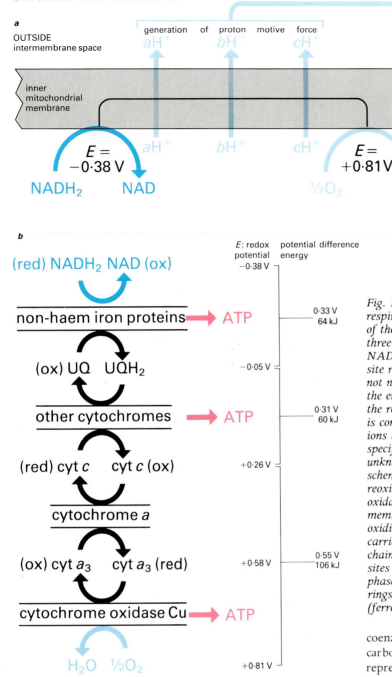

a

OUTSIDE
intermembrane space

generation of proton motive force

aH^+ bH^+ cH^+

inner
mitochondrial
membrane

aH^+ bH^+ cH^+

$E = -0.38\ V$

$E = +0.81\ V$

$NADH_2$ NAD

$\frac{1}{2}O_2$ H_2O

ATPase

3 ADP   3 ATP
$+3\ P_i$ $+3\ H_2O$

$2H^+$ ions

b

(red) $NADH_2$ NAD (ox)

non-haem iron proteins ⟶ ATP

(ox) UQ UQH_2

other cytochromes ⟶ ATP

(red) cyt c cyt c (ox)

cytochrome a

(ox) cyt a_3 cyt a_3 (red)

cytochrome oxidase Cu ⟶ ATP

H_2O $\frac{1}{2}O_2$

E: redox potential	potential difference energy
$-0.38\ V$	
	$0.33\ V$ / $64\ kJ$
$-0.05\ V$	
	$0.31\ V$ / $60\ kJ$
$+0.26\ V$	
$+0.58\ V$	$0.55\ V$ / $106\ kJ$
$+0.81\ V$	

red: reduced form   ox: oxidised form
UQ: ubiquinone   cyt: cytochrome

Fig. 1.9. (a) Oxidative phosphorylation by the mitochondrial respiratory chain (see part b). Hydrogen ions are pumped out of the central matrix compartment of the mitochondrion at three sites when a pair of reducing equivalents passes from $NADH_2$ to oxygen. The number of hydrogen ions pumped per site remains controversial but is between two and four and is not necessarily the same at each site. The sites correspond to the energetic gaps in the respiratory chain. The energy stored in the resulting chemical and electrical gradient of hydrogen ions is conserved and converted to ATP by allowing the hydrogen ions to return to the matrix energetically downhill, through a specific protein channel; the movement is coupled by an unknown mechanism to enzymatic ATP synthesis. (b) A schematic view of the mitochondrial respiratory chain. The reoxidation of $NADH_2$ by oxygen occurs via a sequence of oxidation–reduction carriers located in the inner mitochondrial membrane, grouped into blocks of increasingly positive oxidising strength as measured by their redox potentials. The carriers constitute the 'respiratory chain' or 'electron transport chain'. Sufficient free energy to make ATP is released at three sites in the chain. Ubiquinone is a quinone soluble in the lipid phase of the membrane. Cytochromes are proteins with haem rings containing iron which can cycle between the Fe(II) (ferrous) and Fe(III) (ferric) states.

coenzymes; the oxaloacetate can now accept another two-carbon fragment from acetyl-CoA, and each turn of the cycle represents the oxidation of a two-carbon fragment to carbon dioxide. Three of the reduced coenzyme molecules are $NADH_2$, while the fourth is flavin adenine dinucleotide ($FADH_2$ when reduced), and their reoxidation consumes oxygen but yields altogether 14 molecules of ATP; a further molecule of ATP is generated directly in the citric acid cycle.

Overall, the complete aerobic oxidation of glucose in the cell is coupled to the formation of 38 molecules of ATP. Since the chemical combustion of 1 mole of glucose produces 2900 kilojoules of energy under standard conditions, about 70% of the available energy in the glucose can be calculated as being temporarily stored as ATP (see Fig. 1.8).

Oxidation of fat

Fats are also an important fuel source, notably for mammals, but fat in the diet is generally stored as reserves of triglyceride (triacylglycerol, fatty-acid esters of glycerol) in adipose tissue. Fats can also be synthesised from carbohydrate via glycolysis to

glucose used, allowing for the initial input of ATP to phosphorylate the glucose. In aerobic conditions, the pyruvate then enters the mitochondrion for complete oxidation, which yields a much larger quantity of ATP.

In preparation for entry into the citric acid cycle, the pyruvate is oxidatively decarboxylated in the mitochondrion, reducing NAD to $NADH_2$, losing one carbon atom as carbon dioxide, and being converted to acetyl-CoA, the acetyl thio-ester derivative of a cofactor called Coenzyme A. This reactive two-carbon acetyl group enters the citric acid cycle by combining with oxaloacetate, a four-carbon dicarboxylic acid, to form citrate, a six-carbon tricarboxylic acid (Fig. 1.8). The reactions of the citric acid cycle then turn citrate back into oxaloacetate with the loss of two carbon dioxide molecules, and include four oxidative steps involving the reduction of

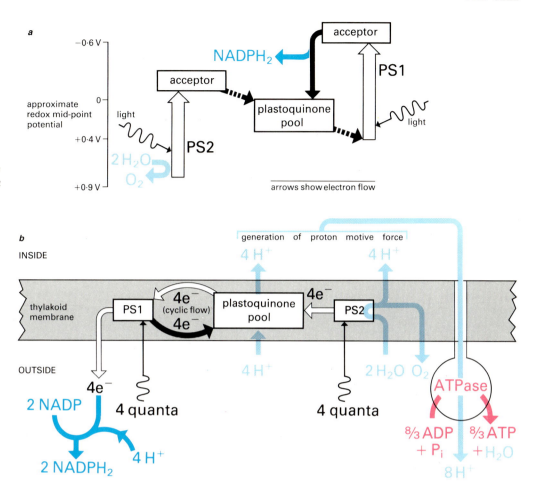

Fig. 1.10. (a) Outline 'Z'-scheme for electron flow in photosynthesis by green plants. The series of arrows shows chains of unspecified intermediates. The light-driven transfer of electrons from water to NADP is called non-cyclic electron flow and is accompanied by the evolution of oxygen. The two photosystems are connected by a chain of oxidation–reduction carriers that enable the reduced electron acceptor of photosystem 2 to supply electrons to the light-generated oxidising agent produced from photosystem 1. Plastoquinones resemble mitochondrial ubiquinone. (b) Scheme based on the chemiosmotic hypothesis to show movements of hydrogen ions and synthesis of ATP accompanying light-driven electron flow through the Z-scheme. Movement of hydrogen ions associated with cyclic electron flow could provide further ATP without generation of oxygen and $NADPH_2$.

acetyl-CoA which, in the presence of high circulating levels of the hormone insulin, does not exclusively enter the citric acid cycle but can also be carried out of the mitochondrion to the cytoplasm where fatty acids and then triglycerides are made. Free fatty acids are not stored since they are potentially toxic.

When fats are mobilised, free fatty acids are released from adipose tissue, bind to a blood protein, and are conveyed to tissues that will oxidise them. Most of these fatty acids contain 16 or 18 carbon atoms, and they are dismembered in mitochondria by breaking two-carbon fragments repeatedly off one end, producing numbers of acetyl-CoA molecules which are then oxidised in the citric acid cycle. To make an acetyl-CoA fragment from a $—CH_2—CH_2—$group in a fatty acid involves the reduction of NAD and FAD to $NADH_2$ and $FADH_2$, and reoxidation of these cofactors by oxygen yields five molecules of ATP for each acetyl-CoA produced. Since the acetyl-CoA itself yields 12 molecules of ATP on oxidation via the citric acid cycle, triglycerides are an excellent energy store, and a molecule of tripalmitoyl-glycerol (with three 16-carbon fatty acids and one three-carbon glycerol moiety) yields 410 molecules of ATP. Fat is a more efficient energy store than are glucose polymers because the carbon atoms in the fat are more reduced.

The central metabolic role of the citric acid cycle

The citric acid cycle is the hub of metabolism. It enables both carbohydrate and fat, after conversion to the common intermediate acetyl-CoA, to be oxidised by the same machinery; also, the breakdown of amino-acids produces some molecules that feed into the cycle. The citric acid cycle is not only concerned with catabolic processes, however. Several of its intermediates serve as biosynthetic precursors, particularly for the formation of amino-acids and haem rings, and citrate is the molecule that carries acetyl groups out of the mitochondrion for cytoplasmic fat synthesis. This dual role appears to raise a problem: for if citric acid cycle intermediates are removed into biosynthetic pathways then they cannot also be reconverted to oxaloacetate to allow oxidation of acetyl-CoA to continue; the catalytic nature of the cycle intermediates in the breakdown of acetyl-CoA appears to be disrupted. This difficulty is circumvented by the existence of other reactions which directly maintain the supply of oxaloacetate and so keep the cycle turning; an important example is the addition of carbon dioxide to pyruvate to make oxaloacetate (Fig. 1.8).

Generation of ATP: the respiratory chain and oxidative phosphorylation

The oxidation of reduced cofactors such as $NADH_2$ by oxygen releases large quantities of energy. To enable efficient coupling of this oxidation to synthesis of ATP, the reaction occurs in a **respiratory chain** as a number of steps (Fig. 1.9). In each step, one intermediate reduces the next member of the chain, itself being oxidised, the intermediates along the chain having an increasing power as oxidising agents until the sequence terminates with molecular oxygen being reduced to water. The members of the respiratory chain include the initial cofactor NAD, supplied in its reduced form from many enzymes, then flavoproteins and quinones which carry two reducing equivalents, and non-haem iron proteins and cytochromes which can only carry one reducing equivalent. The coordination of the eventual reduction of molecular oxygen to two molecules of water, requiring four reducing equivalents, is an important unsolved biochemical problem.

All the components of the respiratory chain are found either on the surface of, or buried inside, the mitochondrial inner membrane in eukaryotes, and the plasma membrane in bacteria. The mechanism of **oxidative phosphorylation**, by which the sequential oxidation–reduction reactions are coupled to the synthesis of ATP rather than being wasted as heat, remains controversial, but the most widely accepted view is the **chemiosmotic hypothesis** of Mitchell (Fig. 1.9). During the passage of reducing equivalents down the chain, hydrogen ions (protons, but of course hydrated in aqueous solution) are pumped out of the mitochondrion across the closed inner membrane. This sets up a chemical gradient of hydrogen ion concentration, and an electrical gradient because the hydrogen ions are positively charged; together, these represent a store of energy analogous to an electric battery. The hydrogen ions can move back across the membrane through an enzyme complex that couples the synthesis of ATP from ADP and inorganic phosphate to the energy provided by moving hydrogen ions down their electrochemical gradient. The enzyme complex is, confusingly, called ATPase. Any leakage of hydrogen ions back through the membrane at other sites allows respiration to continue but uncouples it from phosphorylation.

Photosynthesis

The absorption and use of light

In green plants photosynthesis uses the energy of sunlight to perform a reaction that appears to be the reverse of respiration. Respiration converts sugar and oxygen into carbon dioxide and water, releasing free energy, while photosynthesis reduces atmospheric carbon dioxide to carbohydrate, oxidising water to oxygen which is released into the atmosphere. The mechanisms of the two processes are, however, quite different. A transfer of four reducing equivalents is required per molecule of oxygen evolved or of carbon dioxide fixed.

The primary photochemical event, the **light reaction**, is known to be charge-separation in the green pigment molecule chlorophyll. Absorption of a quantum of light leads to excitation of an electron in the chlorophyll molecule and its transfer to an initial acceptor on a time-scale of picoseconds (10^{-12} seconds), leaving an oxidised chlorophyll molecule. All subsequent processes are independent of light, and involve generation of ATP and $NADPH_2$, which provide the assimilatory power to drive the biochemical pathway of fixation of carbon dioxide. Reduction of the oxidised chlorophyll molecule indirectly by water leads to evolution of oxygen, and reoxidation of the primary electron acceptor ultimately leads to reduction of NADP. This concept of a primary photochemical

separation of oxidising and reducing agents originated with Van Niel in the 1920s, and formed the basis for modern development of the subject.

The pigment molecules (various chlorophylls, and accessory pigments such as the yellow carotenoids) are organised on the internal membranes of the chloroplast (see section 1.2) into photosynthetic units, comprised of antenna regions that absorb light, and reaction centres into which the energy of light absorbed in antenna regions is funnelled. Reaction centres are characterised by chlorophyll molecules in a special environment, and only these become oxidised by loss of the excited electron to an acceptor.

The quantitative relationship between the energy available from light and the energy needed for assimilation of carbon dioxide and evolution of oxygen can be used to distinguish various possible mechanisms of photosynthesis. For green plants, light of wavelengths roughly of 400 nanometres (blue) to 700 nanometres (red to far-red) is effective in photosynthesis, to varying extents, while in some photosynthetic bacteria radiation in the near-infrared up to 1100 nanometres is used. A single quantum of red light of wavelength 680 nanometres, near the absorption maximum of chlorophyll, contains 2.9×10^{-19} joules of energy, and a mole of these quanta has 175 kilojoules of energy. The four-equivalent assimilation of 1 mole of carbon dioxide and the evolution of 1 mole of oxygen requires 470 kilojoules, and if four quanta of red light were to drive this then the process would be 67% efficient; the accepted consensus, however, is that eight to ten quanta are required, giving a much more realistic energy efficiency in view of the large number of metabolic 'dark' steps that follow the primary photochemistry. A figure of eight quanta of light per mole of oxygen evolved can be measured in experiments using light-flashes of sufficiently short duration to turn over the photosystems only once, and since the charge-separation produced in a single photochemical system does not provide enough energy for transfer of a reducing equivalent from water to NADP, a more complex scheme is needed.

In green plants and blue-green algae, two different light reactions in two separate photosystems cooperate in parallel quantum processes to span this energy gap (Fig. 1.10). In photosynthetic bacteria, however, stronger reducing agents than water are used (such as hydrogen sulphide or hydrogen), oxygen is not evolved, and a single light reaction suffices.

Photosystem 2 of green plants, which uses light of wavelength below 680 nanometres, generates a strong oxidising agent ($P680^+$) which can release oxygen from water, and a relatively weak reducing agent. Photosystem 1 can use longer wavelengths of light, and generates a relatively weak oxidising agent ($P700^+$) but a strong reducing agent that ultimately reduces NADP. P680 and P700 refer to chlorophyll molecules in particular environments at the reaction centres, numbered according to their wavelengths of maximum absorption. The two photosystems are connected by a chain of redox carriers which, in a downhill dark process, allows the weak reducing agent formed by photosystem 2 to reduce the weak oxidising agent formed by photosystem 1. The overall effect is to use two quanta of light to drive reducing equivalents from water to NADP, accompanied by the evolution of oxygen. This **Z-scheme**, so called because of its shape, is outlined in Fig. 1.10; the central redox carrier chain has similarities to the mitochondrial respiratory chain (see Fig. 1.9).

As in mitochondria, passage of electrons from photosystem 2 to photosystem 1, through this chain of redox carriers, is accompanied by movement of hydrogen ions across a membrane, in this case from the stroma of the chloroplast into the thylakoids. The conversion of two molecules of water to oxygen also releases hydrogen ions inside the thylakoids. Discharge of the resulting electrochemical gradient of hydrogen ions through an ATPase enzyme is coupled to synthesis of ATP. The overall stoichiometry of the scheme is that eight quanta of light are absorbed for each molecule of oxygen evolved, generating two molecules of $NADPH_2$ and transferring eight protons to the inside of the thylakoid membranes, which then allows the synthesis of $2\frac{2}{3}$ molecules of ATP; the energy of red light of wavelength 680 nanometres is conserved as $NADPH_2$ and ATP with an efficiency of about 38%. Since fixation of one molecule of carbon dioxide by the Calvin cycle (see below) requires three molecules of ATP and two of $NADPH_2$, there appears to be a short-fall in the amount of ATP made. This may be remedied by a process of cyclic electron flow using photosystem 1 only, which produces ATP but neither $NADPH_2$ nor oxygen.

The assimilation of carbon dioxide

Carbon dioxide is fixed in the stroma of the chloroplasts, and uses a reductive pathway known as the **Calvin cycle**. The key enzyme in this is ribulose *bis*-phosphate carboxylase (RuBPCase), which adds carbon dioxide to ribulose *bis*-phosphate, a five-carbon sugar bearing two phosphate ester groups; two three-carbon fragments of 3-phosphoglyceric acid are produced. The overall carbon balance is shown in Fig. 1.11. Each molecule of 3-phosphoglycerate is reduced to glyceraldehyde 3-phosphate using one molecule of $NADPH_2$ and one of ATP, and five out of every six glyceraldehyde 3-phosphate molecules are rearranged in a sequence of reactions to give three ribulose 5-phosphate molecules that are then phosphorylated by ATP to regenerate ribulose *bis*-phosphate. The overall process therefore requires, for each molecule of carbon dioxide fixed, the expenditure of two molecules of $NADPH_2$ and three of ATP, produced by the conversion of light to chemical energy. The sixth glyceraldehyde 3-phosphate molecule, which was not recycled, represents the three molecules of carbon dioxide that were fixed, and moves into the cytoplasm where it is further metabolised, principally by conversion to sucrose which is exported from the leaf to fuel other parts of the plant (see section 2.2). Chloroplasts are however very versatile biosynthetically, and the carbon dioxide fixed as 3-phos-

phoglycerate is incorporated into a wide range of compounds, with certain amino-acids being formed particularly quickly.

RuBPCase is the most abundant protein on the earth, and forms about 50% of the total protein in leaves. This is because it is a very inefficient enzyme and also has a low affinity for carbon dioxide in relation to its atmospheric concentration; and the large amount of RuBPCase is needed to maintain a sufficient rate of fixation of carbon dioxide, with the enzyme making up in quantity what it lacks in catalytic effectiveness. An important group of plants, called C_4-plants (see section 2.2), are well adapted to high temperatures and bright sunlight, and have evolved a mechanism to trap carbon dioxide more efficiently. Carbon dioxide is first fixed in mesophyll cells near the leaf surface by phospho-*enol*-pyruvate carboxylase, an enzyme with a high affinity for carbon dioxide, and the carbon dioxide is liberated again after transport of the fixation products to the cells of the bundle sheath further inside the leaf, to produce a high local concentration matching the properties of the RuBPCase enzyme in the bundle-sheath cells. In some C_4-plants the chloroplasts of the bundle-sheath cells have no photosystem 2, only performing cyclic photophosphorylation, and thus evolving no oxygen which is an inhibitor of RuBPCase; this allows a still higher rate of fixation of carbon dioxide.

Biosynthesis

Biosynthesis of small molecules

Photosynthetic green plants can synthesise all their own constituents given a supply of light, carbon dioxide, water and inorganic minerals like nitrogen and phosphorus; this is an **autotrophic** ('self-feeding') type of nutrition. Many microorganisms are also remarkably versatile and can live on simple molecules as sources of carbon; the central pathways of glycolysis and related sugar interconversions, and the citric acid cycle, then provide intermediates to feed into many of the complex metabolic routes required. In contrast, animals have to (and are able to) rely on a nutritionally complex diet of other organisms and have synthetic capabilities that are far more restricted, and a **heterotrophic** ('other-feeding') type of nutrition; in particular, they cannot synthesise many types of aromatic and branched-chain carbon compounds. The precursors of many complex cofactors like NAD must therefore be supplied as vitamins in the diet, and this dependence on the biosynthetic capabilities of other organisms extends to some amino-acids and particular types of unsaturated fatty acid.

Biosynthesis of polymers

A mechanism common to the assembly of the various types of polymer found in living systems is the use of an activated form of the monomeric building blocks, that donates in a 'downhill' reaction a monomeric unit to some type of acceptor that is either the polymer itself or on which the polymer is being built up. The energy of ATP or its equivalent is used in the synthesis of the activated donor species.

As an example, the inputs of energy and information for synthesis of glycogen will be considered. Glycogen is a highly and randomly branched polymer of glucose, used as a short-term energy and carbon store in liver and muscle. The monomers of α-D-glucose (a particular stereoisomer of glucose) are linked via their carbon atoms numbers 1 and 4, and about one in 12 residues initiates a branch by an α-(1 → 6) link.

Making an α-(1 → 4) link simply by addition of glucose to glycogen, and eliminating water, is not energetically feasible, as the equilibrium of the reaction lies far to the side of the hydrolysis of glycogen. Instead, an activated form of glucose called uridine-diphosphoglucose, UDPGlc, is used as a donor. Synthesis of UDPGlc requires glucose, energy supplied by ATP, and a similar nucleotide called UTP in which the base uracil replaces the adenine of ATP. UDPGlc can then react with glycogen, adding its glucose residue to the non-reducing end of the glycogen polymer and releasing uridine diphosphate (UDP); this reaction releases sufficient free energy to go to completion. The UDP released is rephosphorylated to UTP by ATP so that overall two high-energy phosphate bonds are needed to drive the addition of glucose to glycogen energetically 'uphill'.

There is a very active pyrophosphatase enzyme in the cell, and since the cleavage of inorganic pyrophosphate to give two molecules of inorganic phosphate releases a large amount of free energy it occurs irreversibly. This strongly favours any reaction that releases pyrophosphate, including in this case the synthesis of UDPGlc from UTP and glucose 1-phosphate.

A branching enzyme introduces the branches into glycogen, transferring a short chain of (1 → 4)-linked residues from a growing point to a nearby internal glucose residue, conserving the energy of the (1 → 4) bond it breaks to form the (1 → 6) link. The specificity of two enzymes thus provides sufficient information to build the characteristic structure of glycogen, and in general, for more complex polysaccharides with more than one type of monomer, the sequence and branching pattern result from the specificity of the enzymes that catalyse the synthesis of each particular polysaccharide.

Nucleic acids and proteins are also assembled from activated donors, nucleoside triphosphates and aminoacyl-transfer RNA molecules, respectively, but in contrast to polysaccharides the information for the sequence in which different types of each monomer are assembled is specified by a template: generally DNA in the case of nucleic acids, and messenger RNA for protein synthesis (see section 3.1). Proteins can be modified after the synthesis of their polypeptide chain to form **glycoproteins** by the sequential addition of various different sugars in a process that does not use a template; many proteins, especially those on the cell surface, are glycoproteins.

Turnover of macromolecules

Macromolecules do not last forever. The level of a particular protein, for example, depends on the balance between the rate of its biosynthesis and the rate of its degradation by proteolytic enzymes. Even DNA, which until recently was regarded as a highly stable molecule, undergoes sequence rearrangement and repair of damage. Protein turnover increases the flexibility of the cell in altering the levels of particular enzymes in response to control signals, and both the rates of synthesis and of degradation can be modulated. This is particularly important for multicellular eukaryotes; most of their cells do not divide and so, unlike bacteria, they cannot dilute out over several generations an unwanted enzyme that is no longer being synthesised. Different proteins turn over at different rates, but both the selectivity of protein degradation, and the control of its rate, are little understood. The differential stabilities of different messenger RNA molecules are even less well understood. In addition, the fat deposited in the adipose tissue of mammals is known to undergo rapid metabolic turnover.

Strategies of metabolic regulation

The flow of metabolites through the different pathways in the cell needs to be controlled, for example in the partition of dietary carbohydrate between glycogen storage and glycolysis, and in the channelling of acetyl-CoA derived from glucose into the citric acid cycle or to biosynthesis of fat. Pathways tend to be regulated at branch-points, and it is found that the enzymes that limit the rate of whole sections of the pathway often occur at such positions. Any change in the catalytic activity of these enzymes will alter the flux through the whole metabolic pathway, and **rate-determining enzymes** are often found to be activated or inhibited by alterations in the levels of small molecules that bind to the enzyme and alter its catalytic activity. Feedback inhibition by the end products of a pathway is particularly common: for example, citrate inhibits glycolysis at its rate-determining step, the reaction catalysed by the enzyme phosphofructokinase (see Fig. 1.8). The ratios of ADP to ATP, and of adenosine monophosphate (AMP) to ATP, are also important metabolic signals, high values signifying a demand for energy and activating (as one example) phosphofructokinase, so increasing glycolytic flux and the production of ATP. Conversely, relatively high ATP levels tend to inhibit the flow through energy-yielding pathways.

Regulatory enzymes can also be rapidly converted between active and inactive forms by addition or loss of covalent groups, such as phosphate ester residues, often in indirect response to a hormonal signal. This can produce larger changes in activity than can simple binding of small activators or inhibitors, and the breakdown of both fat and carbohydrate energy stores, as stimulated by the hormones glucagon and adrenaline, is controlled largely in this way; the hormone causes an increase in the intracellular levels of a 'second

Fig. 1.11. Schematic outline of the Calvin cycle. Carbon dioxide is assimilated in the stroma of chloroplasts by addition to ribulose bis-phosphate to give two molecules of 3-phosphoglyceric acid. The diagram shows the overall carbon balance for the fixation of three molecules of carbon dioxide; one three-carbon fragment is retained as fixed carbon while the others are converted back to ribulose bis-phosphate. Energy is required in the form of ATP and NADPH$_2$, which are generated in the light reactions (Fig. 1.10).

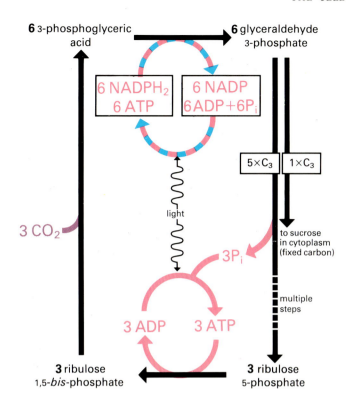

messenger' molecule, which stimulates the phosphorylation and activation of enzymes to break down glycogen and triglyceride. Over a longer time-scale (hours to days), the actual number of particular protein molecules can be changed by altering their rates of biosynthesis or degradation, again often in response to hormonal or dietary changes.

The compartmentation of the eukaryotic cell also offers important opportunities for regulation. For example, oxidation of fatty acids in animals occurs in mitochondria, while synthesis of fatty acids takes place in the cytoplasm; yet the precursor for fat synthesis, acetyl-CoA, is made in the mitochondria, and fatty acids for breakdown enter the cell from the bloodstream and must traverse the cytoplasm to the mitochondria. For either oxidation or synthesis to occur, one set of enzymes must be activated and the other set inhibited to prevent wasteful cycling of material, but there must also be movement of precursors and products across membrane barriers, and since such transport is catalysed by membrane proteins, there are possibilities for regulation analogous to the control of enzymes. Thus, the uptake of fatty acids into the mitochondrion for oxidation is found to be inhibited by malonyl-CoA, levels of which are high in the cytoplasm only during conditions when fatty acids are being synthesised; and in general the pathways of breakdown and of synthesis for a particular class of molecule are reciprocally controlled, so that one of these pathways is predominant in particular physiological conditions.

1.4 CELLULAR PHYSIOLOGY AND BIOPHYSICS

This section considers some of the physical properties of eukaryotic cells, their basic physiological processes, and the means by which cells in a multicellular organism communicate with each other, so that their functions can be properly coordinated.

Biophysical properties of membranes

Nearly all physiological processes depend on **membranes**. As well as the **plasma membrane** that separates the cell from its surroundings, in the eukaryotic cell there are membranes separating different intracellular compartments from each other, so that different chemical constituents can be concentrated where they are needed. Membranes also bind many of the enzyme molecules that carry out cellular metabolism. The physical and chemical properties of membranes have been extensively studied both in whole cells and in fragments isolated by centrifuging cell homogenates.

Most is known about the plasma membrane of animal cells, but other cell membranes generally appear similar in composition, containing two layers of lipid molecules with embed-

ded proteins (see section 1.2). Although the ratio of lipid to protein, the nature of the lipid and protein molecules, and the strength and fluidity of membranes can differ, their general properties can be assumed not to be strikingly different from those of the animal plasma membrane.

The plasma membrane regulates the passage of substances into and out of the cell. Its **permeability**, the ease with which different substances pass through it, can be measured by following the uptake of radioactively labelled material into a sample of cells: it is found that small non-polar molecules, soluble in organic solvents, are found to pass through quite easily, while polar, water-soluble molecules, like sugars, amino-acids and water, cross much more slowly. Secondly, the permeability of membranes to water-soluble substances is found to be highly selective. Inorganic salts that exist as charged ions in solution pass even less readily than water, and there are large differences in the permeabilities to ions of similar size and charge. For example, muscle cells are generally quite permeable to negatively charged ions (anions), whereas nerve cells are almost impermeable to these; and nearly all cells are selectively permeable to potassium ions, the ratio of potassium to sodium permeability sometimes approaching 100:1 despite the fact that the hydrated ions differ in diameter by only 30%.

The explanation is that the lipid centre of membranes is highly impermeable to all polar molecules, and these are only able to cross the membrane freely, and in both directions, where specialised proteins are embedded in the lipid matrix. Some proteins straddle the membrane, forming water-filled channels or pores through which water and ions can move. These pores might have electrostatically charged linings, due to the arrangement of polar amino-acids in the protein (see section 1.2), so that ions of the opposite charge could be attracted into the pore; the selectivity would then depend on the charge and the size of the channel. That such a mechanism is possible is shown by experiments with polypeptide antibiotics, such as gramicidin, which can dissolve in artificial membranes and produce a selective permeability to particular ions.

Movement of charged ions across a membrane constitutes an electric current, so the ionic permeability of a membrane can also be measured indirectly from the conductance of the membrane (or its reciprocal, the resistance). The electrical properties of cell membranes are usually measured by inserting one or more microelectrodes into the cell; these are glass capillaries drawn out to a fine tip, less than 1 micrometre in diameter, and filled with a concentrated salt solution (usually 3 molar potassium chloride) as a conductor. Microelectrode recordings have been made from many kinds of cells, including nerve and muscle cells, gland cells and even protozoans. A square centimetre of cell membrane will have a resistance usually of the order of a few thousand ohms, about 10 million times the resistance of an equally thick layer of saline solution; due to the hydrophobic lipid bilayer, membranes are excellent insulators. The membrane also has a measurable capacitance, generally 1 to 2 microfarads per square centimetre.

Cell membranes are essentially fluid structures: although the lipid molecules are arrayed in a more or less orderly fashion in the bilayer (see section 1.2), they retain a limited lateral mobility within the bilayer, so that the embedded proteins can move around and adopt the molecular configuration dictated by electrostatic and other weak forces between their different parts. This fluidity is essential for the proper functioning of membrane proteins: if cells are cooled so that the lipids crystallise into a rigid array, the proteins cease to function. One feature in the adaptation of organisms to life at low temperatures is the incorporation of more unsaturated fatty acids into the membrane lipid. With their bent hydrocarbon chains, these interfere with the packing of the lipid molecules, lowering the temperature at which a rigid array begins to form. Cholesterol and other sterols also have this effect, and are important constituents of plasma membranes.

Because it is semi-fluid, the plasma membrane is flexible, and cannot itself contribute to the shape of the cell; many cells contain a network of internal fibres, the **cytoskeleton**, which link together different parts of the cell and keep it in shape, as well as preserving a more or less orderly distribution of membrane proteins (see section 1.2). The plasma membrane of red blood cells is very tough, retaining its overall shape even when all the lipid has been removed, because a particularly well-developed cytoskeleton lies immediately beneath it. Plasma membranes are also incapable of withstanding much tension. Most animal cells are thus obliged to exist with an internal concentration of solutes very little different from that outside: otherwise, water would gradually enter or leave by osmosis, leading to bursting or collapse of the cell. Plant cells are exceptions to this; swelling is prevented by the rigid cellulose wall, and the hydrostatic pressure inside cells, their **turgidity**, is often responsible for maintaining the shape of parts of the plant. Some protozoans that live in very dilute environments balance the constant osmotic influx of water by

using energy to export the surplus via a specialised organelle known as a contractile vacuole.

Ion pumps

Although the plasma membrane cannot prevent water movements, its low permeability to ions does enable the cell to maintain an internal ionic environment quite different from the surrounding solution. Nearly all cells are rich in potassium and organic anions and relatively poor in sodium and chloride, whereas the solution bathing the cells can contain mainly sodium chloride, for example in osmoconforming marine animals (see pages 83–5). Thus there are gradients of concentration of individual ions across the plasma membrane which the cell can use like a battery, as a source of energy to drive the transport of useful substances, and to power special processes such as the nerve action potential.

The concentration gradients of ions, together with the selective ionic permeability of the cell membrane, also give rise to an electrostatic potential difference across the cell membrane. Potassium ions tend to escape from the cytoplasm down their own concentration gradient, but the anions in the cell are mainly organic and cannot cross the membrane. Sodium ions cannot enter at all rapidly because the plasma membrane is much more permeable to potassium than to sodium (in other words, sodium ions are excluded from the potassium-selective channels), so that as soon as a few potassium ions leave, the inside of the cell acquires a net negative charge which tends to attract potassium ions back in. When the electrostatic potential difference balances the concentration gradient there is no net movement of potassium, and this state is called a **Donnan equilibrium**. At this point the electrostatic potential is the equilibrium potential for potassium ions, and is proportional to the logarithm of the ratio of the external potassium concentration to the internal potassium concentration.

Microelectrode recordings show that all cells have this negative **resting potential**, varying from about -20 millivolts (inside red blood cells) to -120 millivolts (inside the giant alga *Chara*). In practice, the membrane always has a finite permeability to other ions, notably sodium, but also chloride. Thus the resting potential is never quite as negative as predicted from the ratio of the measured internal and external potassium concentrations, and there is a constant slow replacement of intracellular potassium by sodium from outside. This gradual run-down can be seen in poisoned cells, and may take from minutes to hours depending on the size of the cell. In living cells it has to be prevented by using metabolic energy to drive sodium ions out of the cell, against the electrical and concentration gradients. The chief mechanism responsible for this **active transport** is the sodium–potassium exchange pump, which was first demonstrated in giant nerve cell axons, but has been much studied in red blood cells. The action of this pump is to drive sodium ions out of the cell in exchange for potassium, and it is an enzyme that hydrolyses ATP (an ATPase), but it only does so if sodium ions are present at the inner surface of the membrane and potassium ions at the outside. The detailed mechanism by which hydrolysis of ATP is coupled to specific movements of ions is not well understood; the ATPase enzyme is probably a channel-forming protein, the configuration of which changes when ATP is hydrolysed in such a way that ions are shunted through the channel. The numbers of sodium and potassium ions transported are not necessarily equal. In cells where the ratio has been measured it is 3 sodium expelled: 2 potassium taken up:1 ATP hydrolysed. The result is a net loss of cations from the cell, which may help to balance the osmotic effect of nutrient uptake, and also in some cells causes a measurable increase in the electrostatic potential when the pump is active. The sodium–potassium pump is probably a universal feature of animal cells, but so far it has not been found in plant cells, which appear to regulate their ion content simply by uptake of potassium ions.

Cells also need to regulate their levels of calcium and their pH. The intracellular level of free ionic calcium is important for the control of many processes and is normally kept very low, below 1 micromolar, so that a pump is needed to balance the inward leakage of calcium across the plasma membrane. This pump is a calcium-stimulated ATPase, which probably works in a similar way to the sodium–potassium ATPase.

Regulation of the intracellular pH is more complex, involving more than one type of hydrogen-ion pump. Exchange of intracellular chloride ions with bicarbonate (hydrogen carbonate) ions from the outside solution also helps to regulate intracellular pH, as well as keeping a low level of intracellular chloride, which is important for some nerve cells. Active transport of chloride is the main mechanism of secretion of hydrochloric acid in the stomach, and is also important in fish which regulate their acid/base balance through the gills. Plant cells regulate their cytoplasmic pH by excretion of hydrogen ions or hydroxyl ions from the roots, and by a biochemical buffering mechanism by which carbon dioxide is fixed into carboxylic acid groups to lower the pH, and these acids are decarboxylated to raise it.

As well as these general types of ion pump, specialised active transport mechanisms are found in many tissues. Epithelia lining salivary glands, sweat glands, kidney tubules and the large intestine transport water by first pumping ions across the cells. This sets up a gradient of osmotic pressure which causes a passive movement of water across the epithelial cells, the net result being that a salt solution is pumped across the epithelium.

Cells also need to take up organic nutrients such as sugars and amino-acids. This is done by coupling their uptake to the energy of the concentration gradient of sodium. Glucose, for example, binds to a membrane protein which also binds extracellular sodium; the protein then changes conformation and both the glucose and the sodium enter the cell; glucose will continue to be accumulated up a concentration gradient of glucose, because the sodium that the structure of the protein also requires to be transported is moving down its own concentration gradient. The inward movement of sodium across plasma membranes is thus the means by which a single metabolic process, the sodium–potassium pump, is used in animals to drive indirectly a whole series of other transport processes; in plants the hydrogen-ion concentration gradient across the plasma membrane, driven by proton-pumping, is used in the same way (see section 2.2).

Communication between cells

Communication between cells and organs is essential if an organism is to function properly, and is achieved in a variety of ways. The most obvious and rapid means in animals is through the nervous system (see pages 88–9), which uses the properties of the plasma membrane and its ion pumps to conduct electrical impulses between different parts of the elongated nerve cell, but for short-range communication, and for long-term signals within the body, chemical methods are often used.

Nervous conduction

Messages in the nervous system are in the form of trains of identical electrical pulses called nerve impulses or **action potentials**, which travel at speeds of 1 to 100 metres per second depending on the size of the nerve fibre. Action potentials can be recorded outside the nerve using a pair of wires and a high-gain amplifier. With a whole nerve, overlapping signals from many fibres are seen; sometimes a single fibre (the **axon** or long process from a single nerve cell, see pages 88–9) can be isolated, as in Fig. 1.12. Larger nerve fibres (10 micrometres or more in diameter) can be penetrated with a microelectrode. The negative resting potential of the cell is shown (usually −50 to −70 millivolts), and the electrode records the action potential as a transient reversal of this membrane potential, lasting typically 1 or 2 milliseconds (Fig. 1.12). Some invertebrates have exceptionally large nerve fibres called **giant axons**; in the squid the giant axon is up to 1 millimetre in diameter, so that electrodes can be pushed down its length through a cut end.

At rest, the membrane of the axon is selectively permeable to potassium ions; but if it is slightly depolarised, channels selective for sodium begin to open. Sodium ions rush in down their own concentration gradient and down the electric potential gradient, further depolarising the membrane and making it even more permeable to sodium, producing a runaway effect which quickly drives the membrane potential towards a positive value sufficient to prevent further entry of sodium down its concentration gradient. The opening of the sodium channels is only transient, however: soon they pass into an inactivated state, halting the influx of sodium, and at the same time the permeability of the membrane to potassium is increased. Potassium ions leave the axon down their concentration gradient, restoring the membrane potential to its resting

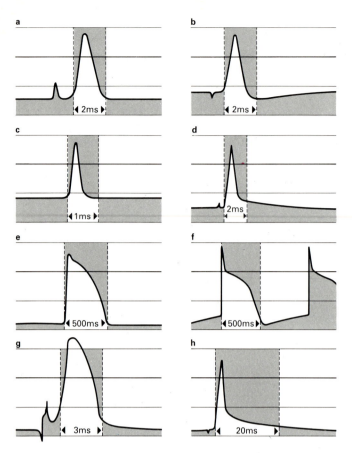

Fig. 1.12. Intracellular resting and action potentials. The bold horizontal lines show zero potential, with those above and below representing + 50 millivolts and − 50 millivolts, respectively. In some cases a stimulation artifact precedes the action potential. (a) Squid axon in situ at 8.5°C; (b) isolated squid axon at 12.5°C; (c) cat myelinated fibre; (d) cat spinal cord motoneuron cell body; (e) frog heart muscle fibre; (f) sheep's heart Purkinje fibre; (g) electroplate in electric organ of electric eel (Electrophorus electricus); (h) frog sartorius muscle fibre.

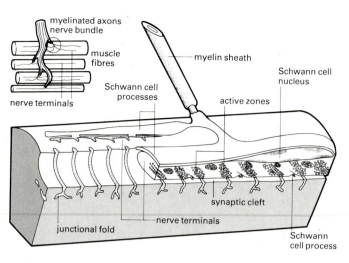

Fig. 1.13. Neuromuscular junction of the frog. Synaptic vesicles are clustered in active zones where transmitter is released into the synaptic cleft. Schwann cell processes run between the nerve terminal and the synaptic membrane.

negative-inside value. Movements of calcium ions are found to play an important part in the molecular mechanisms of these permeability changes.

The action potential has the property of travelling along a nerve fibre. The influx of sodium ions constitutes an electric current entering the active region of the axon. This current spreads lengthways through the cytoplasm of the axon, adding positive charge to local neighbouring regions, which thus become depolarised, which in turn triggers a rise in their sodium permeability, and the whole sequence is followed at the new site. The action potential is thus propagated along the axon without changing in size or shape. The speed of its propagation depends on how far ahead of the peak the local circuits of current spread: in larger axons the current spreads further, because there is less electrical resistance in the thicker cylinder of cytoplasm, so the action potential travels faster. This is why some animals have developed giant axons, which are used in very rapid escape responses.

In a complex nervous system, however, there is not room for many very large axons: vertebrates have solved the problem of

increasing the speed of transmission by providing extra insulation around each axon in the form of a **myelin sheath**, a spiral wrapping of many insulating layers of the membrane of special adjacent cells called Schwann cells, and covering the axon all along its length except for regularly spaced gaps called nodes of Ranvier. The local circuit current ahead of the action potential is forced to spread inside the axon until it reaches the next node, so that the action potential jumps from node to node. The distance between the nodes is commonly about 1 millimetre, and thus the speed of conduction is much increased. For example, a myelinated nerve fibre of 20 micrometres diameter in the cat conducts at 100 metres per second, whereas the squid giant axon, which is 25 or more times as large, conducts at only 25 metres per second. All but the smallest nerve fibres in vertebrates carry a myelin sheath: its white colour is responsible for the pale appearance of the spinal cord and inner parts of the brain. Several diseases, such as multiple sclerosis, are known which cause disruption of the myelin sheath, with severe consequences.

The maximum frequency at which action potentials can travel down an axon depends on how fast the sodium channels recover from their inactivated state after the restoration of the resting membrane potential; while the sodium channels are closed no further action potential can be transmitted, and the nerve fibre is said to be in a refractory state. For most vertebrate axons this maximum frequency is about 200 impulses a second, though some auditory neurons and the nerves of some electric fish can conduct up to 1200 impulses in one second.

Conduction of the action potential, and reactivation of the nerve fibre, require no active input of energy: the permeability changes and ion movements are linked to metabolism only indirectly through the sodium–potassium pump, which sets up and maintains the concentration gradients of sodium and potassium; these gradients are only very slightly reduced each time an action potential moves down the axon.

As well as nerve cells, some muscle cells can also conduct action potentials along their membranes. Striated ('voluntary') muscles of vertebrates have action potentials similar to those in nerves (Fig. 1.12), so that a whole muscle fibre can contract in

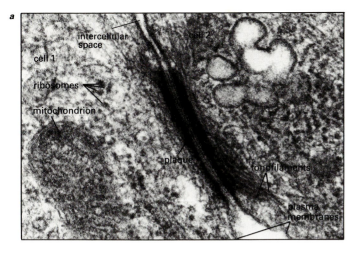

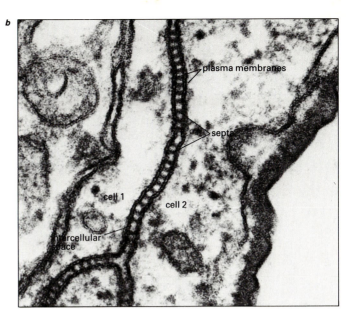

Fig. 1.14. Cell junctions. (a) A desmosome in the mammary gland of a goat (x 75000). (b) A septate junction in the tracheolar epithelium of a locust eye (x 132000).

response to an action potential reaching it at a single nerve ending. Heart muscle has a more complex action potential (Fig. 1.12), involving influx of both sodium and calcium ions, and the heart also has a special pacemaker region, which initiates action potentials at regular intervals. Smooth ('involuntary') muscles, like those controlling movement of the internal organs, and most muscles in invertebrates, do not have self-propagating action potentials, and rely on the presence of nerve endings distributed all over each fibre.

Chemical communication between cells

Once initiated in a nerve fibre, an action potential will propagate along the entire length of that fibre. Except in a few special cases requiring extreme speed or tight coupling between groups of cells, the potential will not cross directly into any neighbouring cells. Instead, transmission between adjacent nerve cells, and between adjacent nerve and muscle cells, takes place chemically at specialised junctions called **chemical synapses**. Here the membranes of the pre-synaptic and post-synaptic cells are separated by a synaptic cleft some 50 nanometres wide. Even though the intercellular space is so narrow, the high electrical resistance of the post-synaptic membrane prevents current from the pre-synaptic cell from entering the post-synaptic cell directly. Instead, electrical events in the pre-synaptic cell cause it to release a transmitter substance, which diffuses rapidly across the cleft and interacts with a receptor protein in the post-synaptic membrane, causing this membrane to change its ionic permeability. The result is a transient change in the membrane potential of the post-synaptic cell, either initiating an action potential in it or altering contractile activity. Chemical synapses also occur between nerve and gland cells, where nervous activity causes the release of secretions.

Much of our knowledge of synapses is derived from microelectrode experiments, beginning with work on vertebrate **neuromuscular junctions** (Fig. 1.13), though it seems that many synapses between nerve cells operate similarly. The transmitter at the vertebrate neuromuscular synapse is acetylcholine, which is concentrated within the terminal of the pre-synaptic cell in membrane-bound vesicles, some 5 to 6

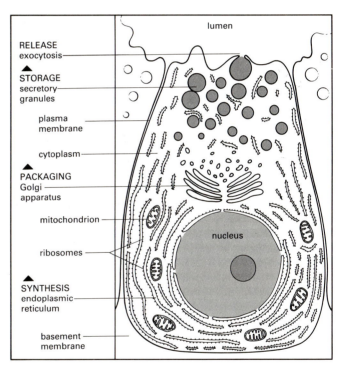

Fig. 1.15. Protein secretion by an exocrine cell of the mammalian pancreas.

nanometres in diameter, each containing several thousand molecules of acetylcholine. Arrival of a nerve impulse allows entry of calcium ions into the terminal, which is the trigger for synchronous emptying of many vesicles (about 300 in the case of the neuromuscular junction) into the synaptic cleft. Each acetylcholine molecule that diffuses to reach the post-synaptic membrane combines reversibly with a receptor protein, opening a channel which allows sodium, potassium, and possibly other cations to cross the membrane. The result is a depolarisation called an **excitatory post-synaptic potential**. A number of snake venoms, including α-bungarotoxin, act by poisoning the receptor protein for acetylcholine, and have been used to study details of the interaction.

31

Release of neurotransmitter from the pre-synaptic terminal is a transient event, so that the lifetime of the excitatory post-synaptic potential is determined by how long it takes for the transmitter to disappear from the synaptic cleft. This process is accelerated by the enzyme acetylcholinesterase, but nevertheless the post-synaptic potential lasts some 3 to 5 milliseconds, much longer than does the pre-synaptic action potential.

Acetylcholine is not the only synaptic transmitter: γ-aminobutyric acid (GABA), noradrenaline (norepinephrine) and adrenaline (epinephrine) are also important neurotransmitters, and their actions at different types of synapse have been characterised. As well as excitation, some transmitters, including acetylcholine, can produce inhibition in the post-synaptic cell, depending on the nature of the response of the receptors; receptors that open channels permeable to potassium or chloride ions make the post-synaptic cell hyperpolarised and inhibit any excitatory potential.

Chemical transmission across synapses is fast, with a delay of only 1 millisecond at the neuromuscular junction, for example; it is unidirectional; and it may result either in excitation or in inhibition. Also, although in the neuromuscular junction a pre-synaptic action potential almost always results in an excitatory post-synaptic potential sufficiently large to trigger a muscle action potential, and hence a twitch-contraction, in many nerve–nerve synapses this is not so, and the post-synaptic cell will not fire unless several excitatory potentials are generated in quick succession so that they add up or 'summate'. Thus a single neuron can integrate the inputs from the many excitatory and inhibitory synapses, translating the result into its own particular electrical activity or lack of activity. This integrative property of the synapse is of crucial importance in the nervous system.

Communication by chemical synapses occurs only between certain specialised cells, but it is now known that many animal cells possess a more direct means of communication via intercellular structures called **gap-junctions** (Fig. 1.14). These are found in most organised tissues, and appear in the electron microscope as localised areas where the plasma membranes of two cells are in close apposition, the intercellular space being narrowed to about 2 nanometres and bridged by a dense polygonal lattice of proteinaceous particles of 8 to 9 nanometres diameter, each of which forms a channel of about 1.5 nanometres in diameter directly connecting the cytoplasm of the two cells. Such intercellular junctions are especially well developed in epithelial tissues (such as salivary glands), where injection experiments show that, consistent with the observed size of the pore, ions and small molecules (up to a relative molecular mass of about 1900) can pass freely from cell to cell, and microelectrode recordings from adjacent pairs of cells confirm that there is a high degree of electrical communication between them. The degree of coupling between any given two cells is not constant, but varies during their development, and is probably regulated by the level of free ionic calcium inside the cells.

Direct cell-to-cell communication may be important in the nourishment of specialised cells and in the synchronisation of cellular development within a tissue, as for example in the exchange of amino-acids, proteins, nucleotides and nerve growth factor that have been observed between neurons and their associated glial cells, and in secretory tissues it helps to ensure a concerted response of the whole epithelium to an outside stimulus. A special case is found in **electrical synapses** within the nervous system, where gap-junctions allow action potentials to be transmitted directly from cell to cell, sometimes in either direction.

In plant tissues, extensive cytoplasmic connections approximately 20 to 40 nanometres in diameter, called **plasmodesmata**, are common between cells. Ions taken up by the root surface move through to the centre of the root via these connections; large cytoplasmic connections occur between pollen mother cells undergoing synchronised meiosis; and the highest density of cytoplasmic connections is between meristematic initials (see section 2.2). Some cells are cut off from those around them and have no connections, for example stomatal guard cells, megaspores and zygotes. For others, plasmodesmata are formed only to specific adjacent cells, for example sieve elements are connected only to their companion cells.

Chemical communication is not limited to adjacent cells. At longer ranges within an organism cells communicate by means of **hormones**, which in animals are bloodborne chemicals released by gland cells and include peptides (for example insulin) and steroids (for example cortisol) (see pages 92–4). These primary chemical messengers are recognised by specific receptor sites on plasma membranes, and their binding there initiates events that transmit the stimulus along or through the membrane, such as modification of ionic conductance (just as in the synapse) or of enzymic activity leading to changes in the level of intracellular 'second messengers', such as calcium ions or cyclic AMP, which act upon and alter the metabolism of the target cell. Calcium ions are a common second messenger, and are particularly effective because their free concentration in cytoplasm is normally very low. A very small influx or release of calcium ions from intracellular stores bound to protein can dramatically affect the free calcium ionic concentration, amplifying a weak hormonal signal. In plants, stable growth-regulators of low relative molecular mass, such as auxins and cytokinins, are analogous to steroid hormones, and coordinate growth and development. They travel through the plant in the tissues that transport sugars, salts and water. Auxins are unique in that they also travel in their own polar transport system from shoot to root, which ensures the polarity of growth and regeneration of plant tissue. An even longer-range form of chemical communication is provided by **pheromones**, messenger chemicals that travel from one organism to another of the same species and induce behavioural changes. Examples of pheromones are the sex attractants of butterflies and moths.

Fig. 1.16. Structure of vertebrate striated muscle.

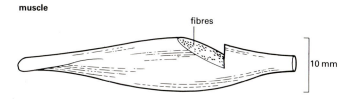

muscle

fibres

10 mm

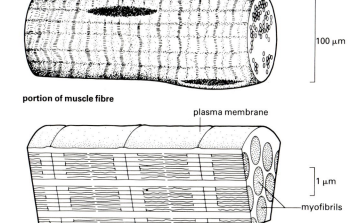

muscle fibre

nucleus   plasma membrane

100 μm

portion of muscle fibre

plasma membrane

1 μm

myofibrils

portion of isolated myofibril

a appearance under phase contrast

one sarcomere

Z disk   H zone   Z disk
I band   A band   I band

b as seen in EM, showing myofilaments

Z   M line   Z

thick filament
thin filament

Secretion and transport within cells

Many important substances are secreted from cells, including hormones, digestive enzymes and extracellular structural materials such as connective tissue fibres and the cell walls of plants and bacteria. This process of **secretion** begins with chemical synthesis of the product that is to be secreted, which is then transported to a storage site within the cell, and ends with its release through the plasma membrane in response to the appropriate external signal. The process has been studied in most detail for secretion of proteins such as trypsinogen by the pancreas (Fig. 1.15), but the same general sequence of events is found in all secreting cells.

Protein molecules are synthesised on ribosomes bound to the endoplasmic reticulum (see section 1.2); as the polypeptide chain grows, its initial amino-acid sequence, the 'leader' or 'signal' sequence, binds to a receptor protein and moves the ribosome and the growing polypeptide to a site on the surface of the endoplasmic reticulum membrane. The terminus of the polypeptide chain is then transported across the membrane, and on the far side a peptidase enzyme cleaves off the leader sequence of amino-acids from the remainder of the polypeptide chain. As the molecule grows it is gradually pulled through into the enclosed space within the endoplasmic reticulum by the process of folding into a three-dimensional protein structure. When completed, the synthesised protein molecules detach from the ribosomes, and move from the endoplasmic reticulum towards the **Golgi apparatus**, where they become enclosed in small membranous vesicles that form by budding of the membrane. The exact mechanism of this transport is not known, but it requires energy in the form of ATP. The contents of the vesicles are concentrated in the Golgi apparatus by extraction of water, and the vesicles are then stored in the cytoplasm; the number of cytoplasmic vesicles at any one moment depends on the steady rate of synthesis of the secreted material and its intermittent rate of secretion.

Release of secreted material occurs by fusion of the vesicles with the plasma membrane, which allows the contents of the vesicle to flow out into the extracellular space. The trigger for release is a rise in the intracellular concentration of free calcium ions, itself caused by the interaction of an external stimulant, whether a hormone or a neurotransmitter molecule, with a specific membrane receptor; ATP is also required for release. This type of release mechanism is called **exocytosis**, and is an important way for large molecules to cross the plasma membrane without impairing the selective permeability of this membrane to ions and small molecules.

Cellular movement and muscle contraction

The molecular mechanisms of cellular movements are beginning to be understood through a combination of ultrastructural, biochemical and biophysical investigations. The most obvious example of mechanical movement in cells is muscle contraction, but all animal and a few plant cells exhibit some form of motility at some stage in their development, and several distinct mechanisms can be recognised. Examples include the lashing of flagella (the motile organelles of spermatozoa and many unicellular organisms), the beating of cilia in the lining of the respiratory tract, the directed movements of cell contents by protoplasmic streaming, and the meanderings of cells undergoing amoeboid movement.

The best-understood type of cellular movement is the contraction of vertebrate skeletal muscle. Each muscle fibre (Fig. 1.16) is a multinucleate cell composed of **myofibrils** about 1 micrometre in diameter, containing mitochondria (for supply of energy in the form of ATP) and a highly ordered, hexagonal array of protein filaments. The filaments do not extend the

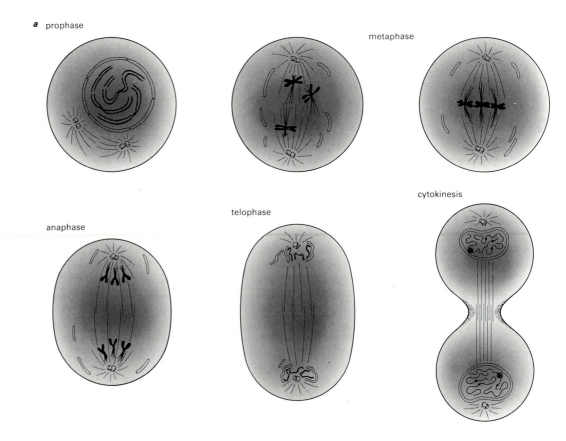

whole length of the myofibril, but are arranged end-to-end in units called **sarcomeres**, each of about 2.5 micrometres long when relaxed, and separated by disc-like structures called **Z-lines**. The sarcomeres in adjacent myofibrils are usually in register, giving the muscle fibre its striated appearance when viewed with the light microscope. In the electron microscope, two layers of filaments can be distinguished: thin filaments are attached to the Z-lines and consist mostly of the protein actin, plus controlling elements such as the calcium-binding protein troponin; and thick filaments occupy the central part of the sarcomere and consist of myosin. Each myosin molecule has a long tail, and a head-group that projects from the thick filament and has ATP-splitting activity. The myosin molecules are arranged symmetrically, with their tails pointing towards the centre of each filament, and their heads about 40 nanometres apart.

The myofibril contracts by a mechanism based on sliding filaments, as shown by studies on the properties of the isolated proteins and filaments, as well as by physical and diffraction measurements on muscle cells. An action potential, triggered at the neuromuscular junction, is conducted over the surface of the muscle cell by a series of tubular indentations of its plasma membrane called the sarcotubules. This action potential causes release of calcium ions from the sarcoplasmic reticulum, which in turn changes the configuration of the thin filaments, exposing regularly spaced actin sites able to bind to the myosin heads on the thick filaments, and this draws the filaments together. The myosin heads then undergo a conformational change linked to hydrolysis of ATP, causing them to pull longitudinally on the thin filaments. The bond between actin and myosin is then broken, and the cycle repeated using the next adjacent binding site on the thin filament. The filaments thus slide relative to one another, reducing the length of each

sarcomere, and the whole muscle fibre contracts by a series of 40-nanometre steps.

After the action potential has passed, calcium ions are taken up again from the cytoplasm by the sarcoplasmic reticulum and, as the cytoplasmic concentration of calcium ions falls below 1 micromolar, the myosin binding sites on the thin filaments disappear, and the two sets of filaments are free to slide out again; the fibre relaxes. Thus, each action potential produces a single twitch-contraction, lasting typically about one-tenth of a second.

Mechanisms based on the sliding of filaments relative to each other are common to many types of cell movement. Thus actin and myosin are widely distributed in protozoa, plants, fungi and animal cells, although myosin is never found in such high concentrations as in muscle, or in such high concentrations as actin, and the actin and myosin are generally not organised into fibrils as they are in muscle cells. There is evidence that actin filaments play a key role in the internal streaming movements of plant cells, notably in the giant algae *Nitella* and *Chara*, and in the contractile mechanism that is the basis of the amoeboid movement exhibited by a variety of animal cells. A sliding-filament mechanism is also responsible for the bending of cilia and flagella: the proteins involved here are tubulin and the ATPase dynein, which are arranged in pairs of microtubules around the periphery of the organelle, connected by other proteins to each other and to a central pair of microtubules.

A more unusual role for actin has been demonstrated in the acrosome, a structure at the tip of spermatozoa. During fertilisation, the rapid polymerisation of actin into filaments forms a projection that extends through and pierces the outer coat of the egg cell.

Not all forms of motility involve sliding filaments and the

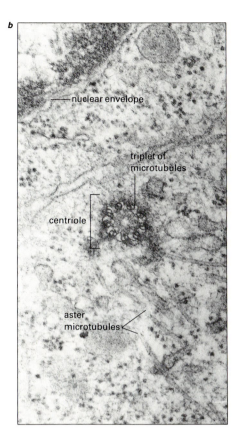

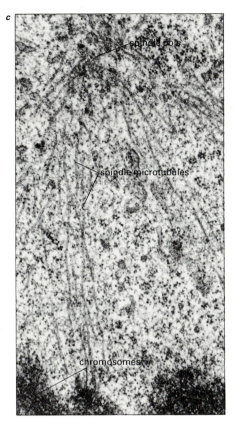

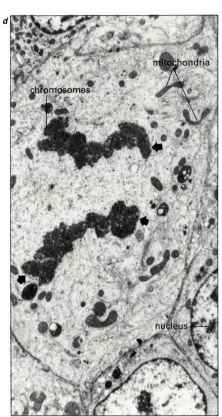

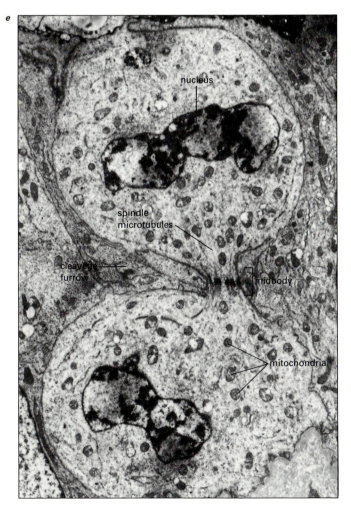

Fig. 1.17. (a) Diagrams of an animal cell at successive stages in mitosis. (b) – (d) Transmission electron micrographs of thin sections. (b) From a white blood cell of sheep, showing the structure of a centriole with its associated aster of microtubules (x 60000). (c) From a cell in an early embryo of a mouse, showing one half of the mitotic spindle in early anaphase, i.e. just as the chromosomes begin to move to the spindle poles (x 30000). (d) From sheep placenta, showing the first stages in the reassembly of the nuclear envelope during telophase, which begins with the attachment (arrowed) of flattened membrane sacs to the chromosomes (x 1000). (e) A late stage in cytokinesis in a cell of the epithelium of the uterus of a sheep (x 5600).

direct consumption of ATP. For example, the flagella of bacteria use a hydrogen-ion gradient to rotate a helical shaft composed of a single type of protein (flagellin), and various contractile fibres (myonemes and spasmonemes) of protozoa rely on a change in the degree of structural order in their protein constituents induced by calcium ions. Energy for these processes is derived from concentration gradients, which must be returned to their previous levels and maintained there by active metabolism during periods when the organelle is relaxed.

1.5 CELL DIVISION

Cell division is an ordered sequence of events generating at least two complete cells from one original cell. Most commonly, the product cells are genetically identical to each other and to the parent cell, as in **mitotic cell division**. Mitotic cell division is used for the multiplication of individuals in unicellular eukaryotes, and during processes of growth and maintenance in multicellular organisms.

A special type of cell division, in which the cells produced have only half the genetic material of the parent cell, is known as **meiotic cell division** and forms part of a mechanism for shuffling the genetic material to generate individuals with new combinations of genes. Meiotic cell division takes place at special stages in the life-cycle and in multicellular organisms takes place only in cells destined to contribute to new individuals.

Cell division in prokaryotes

Replication of the circular DNA molecule of prokaryotes precedes division into two cells. After replication (see section 3.1), the two copies are moved to opposite ends of the cell, attached to the plasma membrane (and possibly also to the cell wall outside this). A flange of cell wall and membrane grows inwards across the middle of the original cell, like the closing of an iris diaphragm, and when complete in the centre forms the cross-wall or **septum** separating the two new cells.

The control of cell division in prokaryotes is not understood and has only been studied in the enteric (gut) bacterium *Escherichia coli*, where cell division has three distinct phases. The DNA is replicated in the C-period, and this always takes 40 minutes. This is followed by the D-period, a fixed 20 minutes between the end of replication and the completion of septum formation. Completion of DNA replication is necessary for entry into the D-period. The period between formation of the septum and the initiation of the next round of DNA replication is a gap called the I-period. This is of variable duration, shortening with increasing rate of growth of the cells. In bacteria, successive cycles of cell division can be telescoped into each other by initiating a fresh round of DNA replication before the previous round is completed.

Mitotic cell division

The overall pattern of mitotic cell division in eukaryotic cells resembles cell division in prokaryotes. The replication of the original DNA to form two copies (see section 3.1), in the synthesis or S-phase, precedes division of the nucleus into two (**mitosis**), and this is then followed by separation of the cytoplasm into two daughter cells (**cytokinesis**). Except in the formation of multinucleate cells, cytokinesis follows immediately after mitosis, but there may be a period before the next S-phase, termed G1 (gap one) and equivalent to the prokaryotic I-period, and there is a period between the end of S-phase and mitosis, termed G2 (gap two) and equivalent to the prokaryotic D-period. The full sequence is referred to as the **cell cycle**. Successive eukaryotic cell cycles are never telescoped into one another as can occur in prokaryotes. The significance of the cell cycle in development is discussed in section 1.6.

Mitosis

A fixed sequence of events in mitosis ensures that the doubled number of chromosomes is divided accurately into two separate complete sets. The events occur in four successive phases, named prophase, metaphase, anaphase and telophase (Fig. 1.17). The non-mitotic phases of the cell cycle are collectively known as **interphase**, and entry into **prophase** begins with the rearrangement ('condensation') of the featureless interphase nuclear material, the **chromatin**, into its component lengths, each piece or **chromosome** being compactly wound into a discrete bundle visible in the light microscope. The two copies of each chromosome made in S-phase remain attached to each other (in this stage they are known as **sister chromatids**), so each bundle is a double structure. There is a fixed site on each chromosome for this mutual attachment of sister chromatids, the **centromere**, at which the bundle becomes narrower. At the centromere, each sister chromatid develops a ball-like (in most plants) or disc-like (in animal cells and some algae) structure, termed a **kinetochore**, on the opposite side from its attachment to its sister. The kinetochore is the structure that will join the chromatids to the mitotic **spindle**, the framework of microtubules (see section 1.2) that enables the movement of sister chromatids to opposite ends of the cell.

The mitotic spindle is assembled just outside the nucleus during prophase. In animals cells the microtubules grow out of a 'microtubule-organising centre' from amorphous (structureless) material surrounding a pair of **centrioles**, cellular organelles that enigmatically are always found oriented at right-angles to each other. Before prophase the microtubules are short, and the arrangement is termed an **aster**. During G1 each cell has one pair of centrioles, found in a depression in the nuclear membrane, but during S-phase a new centriole grows out from a site close to one side of each member of the original pair. In prophase the aster splits in two, the two new pairs of centrioles move apart as microtubules between them grow, until they reach opposite ends of the nucleus and are separated by the full-sized mitotic spindle.

Algae generally use centrioles to form the spindle, but they are absent from other plant cells. Instead the microtubules that are present underneath all of the plasma membrane in interphase first reorganise at the beginning of prophase into a densely packed collar around the cell, inside that part of the wall where the new cross-wall will, much later, fuse with the old wall. This pre-prophase band of microtubules then disappears as the spindle microtubules form over the surface of the nucleus, which they do in the shape of an open-ended barrel with an amorphous 'microtubule-organising centre' covering each end.

The transition between prophase and the next phase, **metaphase**, is marked by the fragmentation of the double membrane around the nucleus (see section 1.2) into scattered flattened vesicles. The nucleus is destabilised as a result of the

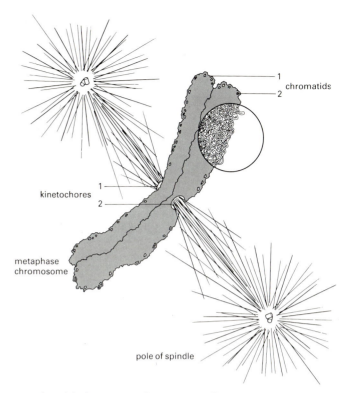

Fig. 1.18. Diagram of a pair of chromatids at mitotic metaphase in an animal cell. The chromatid microtubules are oriented with their polymerising ends attached to the kinetochores. During chromosome movement these microtubules become shorter. In contrast, the spindle microtubules are oriented with their depolymerising ends attached to the spindle pole and during chromosome movement these microtubules become longer. Polymerisation at the end distant from the spindle pole contributes to the movement apart of the spindle poles.

phosphorylation of structural proteins which hold together the membrane, the nuclear pore complexes and chromatin. Spindle microtubules invade the region now occupied by the condensed chromosomes. At the same time, microtubules appear, attached to the opposite-facing kinetochores of each chromosome, and now that the membrane barrier separating them has gone the pairs of chromatids and the mitotic spindle can interact. First, each chromosome is dragged by the kinetochores of its chromatids to the equator of the spindle, where it is rocked and jockeyed until each pair of kinetochores is aligned on the equator so that the two kinetochores of each pair face opposite poles of the spindle. Then there is a rapid and synchronised splitting apart, at the centromere of each chromosome, of the union between the sister chromatids.

This beginning of the separation of the sister chromatids defines the start of **anaphase**, during which the sister chromatids move completely apart. Their separation is partly due to movement of the kinetochore towards the spindle poles, dragging the rest of the chromatid behind, and partly due to the spindle poles themselves moving further apart. As soon as the sister chromatids are separated they become the chromosomes of the daughter cells. The shortening of the kinetochore microtubules may be due to depolymerisation at their unattached ends (Fig. 1.18). The force for the movement apart of the poles of the spindle is generated between the two sets of the spindle microtubules where they overlap at the equator, supplemented by polymerisation of microtubules at the growing ends to maintain the overlap as the sets slide further apart.

The mechanism of chromosome separation is of basic importance, and yet among the more primitive eukaryotes there is a wide variation in the extent to which these different processes contribute to the movement. It appears that movement apart of the spindle poles by growth of the spindle microtubules was the basis of the earliest mechanisms, and the effectiveness of this has been increased during evolution by kinetochore movement towards the poles as a result of depolymerisation shortening the kinetochore microtubules, and by active sliding apart of the sets of spindle microtubules.

The arrival of the chromosomes at the spindle poles denotes the boundary between anaphase and **telophase**, which is essentially prophase run in reverse. The structural proteins of the nuclear membrane are dephosphorylated and this structure reforms around the chromosomes as these lose their condensed structure. RNA synthesis, which had ceased altogether by the end of prophase, recommences and the nucleolus reforms.

Cytokinesis

By late telophase, the last remnants of the spindle microtubules are the interdigitating growing ends sited at what was the equatorial plane of the spindle. Small vesicles and amorphous material, visible with the electron microscope after staining the sample with heavy-metal cations, collect around the microtubules in this region, forming a structure known as the **mid-body** in animal cells where the amorphous matrix usually predominates, and as the **phragmoplast** in plant cells where the vesicles are much more numerous.

In animal cells, division of the cytoplasm is usually achieved by a process known as **cleavage**. The plasma membrane indents to form a valley around the cell, outside the spindle equator. This cleavage furrow first appears in anaphase, and is drawn in ever more deeply by the contraction of a ring of microfilaments (see section 1.2) that lies in the cytoplasm beneath the deepest point in the valley. There is usually a pause after the cleavage furrow reaches the mid-body before the two cells are finally separated.

Animal cells dividing in a block sometimes split by fusion of the vesicles in the mid-body into two sheets of membrane, and it is essentially this process that occurs in cells of multicellular plants except red algae. In plant cells, vesicles containing the matrix material of the cell wall are produced by the Golgi bodies (see section 1.2) and accumulate as part of the phragmoplast. They begin to fuse in the equatorial plane of the spindle to form a flat disc-like vesicle, the **cell-plate**, which grows by fusing more vesicles at its edges until it reaches and fuses with the internal surface of the plasma membrane at the region which was once the site of the pre-prophase band of microtubules.

In summary, the cell's complement of DNA is duplicated in S-phase, and in mitosis the two copies of every DNA molecule are separated with precision to opposite ends of the cell. The cytoplasm is divided into two portions, each associated with one of the two ends of the original cell. Some cellular organelles, such as mitochondria and plastids, only increase in numbers within the cell by division of pre-existing organelles of these types, and the proteins for new ribosomes are synthesised only by already formed ribosomes; the random distribution of the organelles of the mother cell ensures that both daughter cells contain representatives of all such structures.

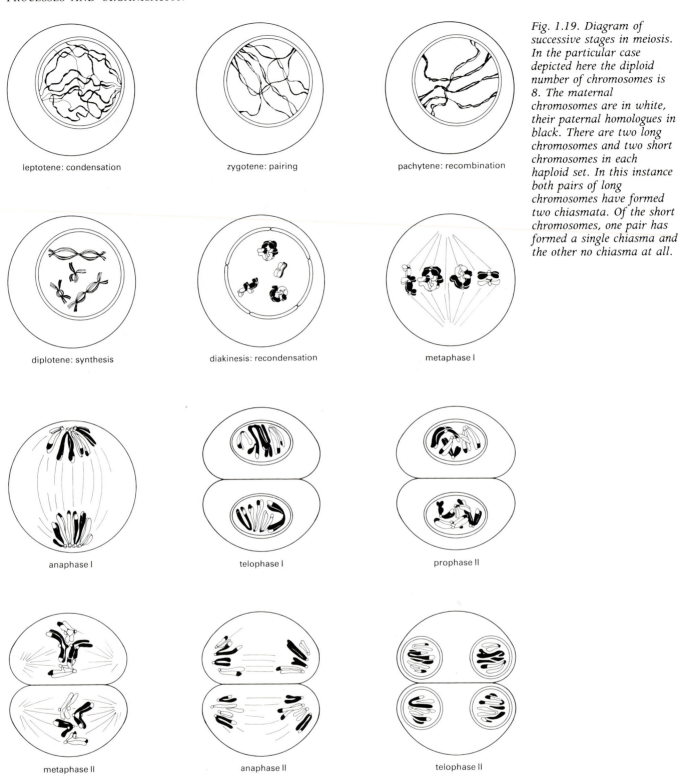

leptotene: condensation

zygotene: pairing

pachytene: recombination

diplotene: synthesis

diakinesis: recondensation

metaphase I

anaphase I

telophase I

prophase II

metaphase II

anaphase II

telophase II

Fig. 1.19. Diagram of successive stages in meiosis. In the particular case depicted here the diploid number of chromosomes is 8. The maternal chromosomes are in white, their paternal homologues in black. There are two long chromosomes and two short chromosomes in each haploid set. In this instance both pairs of long chromosomes have formed two chiasmata. Of the short chromosomes, one pair has formed a single chiasma and the other no chiasma at all.

Meiotic cell division

A haploid cell is a cell with only one version of the complete instructions for the survival of the organism, only one version of each of its chromosomes. A diploid cell has two different complete versions of these instructions, the result of a past fusion between haploid cells of two different individuals, one 'maternal' and one 'paternal', and in a diploid cell each chromosome is represented twice (see section 3.2). If the

number of chromosomes in the haploid set is n, then the diploid cells each have $2n$ chromosomes. The mitotic cell cycle is a system for maintaining the cell's complement of DNA, whether this is one or two versions of the complete instructions, by doubling each chromosome during replication then dividing it into its two constituent sister chromatids while producing two cells from one. All the chromosomes of a diploid cell are copied in S-phase, so that in G2, just before mitosis, the cell has four times the content of DNA of a haploid cell in G1; during mitosis this DNA is distributed so that each daughter cell receives one copy of both the maternal and paternal versions, as the two members of a pair of chromatids are arranged independently on the equator of the mitotic spindle and each pair splits into two identical chromosomes.

Meiosis is a system for mixing the components of the two versions of the complete instructions; it involves the replicated but undivided diploid cell, and the DNA is then shared out between four daughter cells each of which receives one copy of a new and different version of the complete instructions. Because each of the four products has only one version of the complete instructions, these cells are haploid. There are two functions of meiosis. First, it generates new combinations of sections of chromosomes and new sets of whole chromosomes, thereby providing the variety of different types in the population that is the raw material of evolution. Secondly, meiosis converts diploid cells into haploid cells, a necessary preliminary to the creation of new combinations of the new haploid versions by fusion of haploid cells from different individuals, to reform the diploid condition in the process of sexual reproduction.

A meiotic cell division consists of two modified mitotic cell cycles in sequence (Fig. 1.19). The first cycle has a greatly modified prophase, and achieves the mixing of the maternal and paternal sets of instructions. The second cycle is modified only by the omission of its S-phase, ensuring the reduction down to the haploid content of DNA.

The first meiotic prophase (**prophase I**) usually takes longer than all the other stages put together (Fig. 1.19). It is conventionally divided into five substages. In **leptotene**, the chromosomes condense, much as they do in mitosis except that sister chromatids cannot be distinguished and the ends of the chromosomes are attached to the inside surface of the nuclear membrane.

Zygotene is the stage when chromosomes come together in pairs. Each chromosome has two representatives or **homologues**, one from the maternal set and one from the paternal set. They contain different versions of instructions, encoded in DNA, for carrying out the same functions, and the ordering of genes for different functions along the length of the chromosome is the same in both homologues. Each homologous pair comes to lie together, exactly aligned along the length of their chromosomes, often beginning this apposition at the ends, which have located each other by moving in the plane of the nuclear membrane. This longitudinal alignment of homologous chromosomes is initiated by proteins which bind in a chain down one side of each homologue, and these two protein chains become cross-linked by other proteins, forming a ladder-like structure between the homologues. The matching of the chromosomal genes is exact, so that a loop is formed if a substantial length of DNA in one homologue has been inverted relative to the equivalent section of the other homologue. Each pair of homologues is known as a **bivalent**.

Once this exact apposition is completed, the nucleus is said to be in **pachytene**, the stage at which the chromosomes look thickest. It is during pachytene that the new combinations of sections of maternal and paternal chromosomes are constructed by crossing-over (see section 3.2). At a few randomly distributed sites on each chromosome, the DNA in both homologues is cut and two new joinings made across the gap between them. The homologues are now physically linked by two DNA double-helices, a connection known as a **chiasma** and joining maternal and paternal DNA. Each homologue has thus exchanged some part of its genetic material with its partner's version of the genes for the same function.

The end of pachytene is marked by the disassembly of the protein complex linking the homologous chromosomes, and the homologues relax away from each other except where they are joined by a chiasma. The association between sister chromatids lapses and this stage is called **diplotene**. It is also known as the synthesis stage, since, when the meiosis leads to the production of a large egg cell, the chromosomes decondense at this stage and are actively transcribed, and the cytoplasm accumulates large amounts of reserve foodstuffs. Developing eggs may arrest meiosis at this stage for long periods, sometimes years.

Recondensation and apparent repulsion between the centromeres mark the beginning of the last stage of prophase, **diakinesis**. The chiasmata slip to the ends of the very highly condensed chromosomes, and this changes the shape of the bivalents to noughts (if they have two chiasmata) and crosses (if they have one chiasma) (Fig. 1.19). A spindle forms to the outside of the nuclear membrane, and this membrane fragments at the start of **metaphase I**.

Each chromosome develops the usual two kinetochores, one on each chromatid at the centromere. However, in meiotic prophase the kinetochores occur not on opposite sides of the sister chromatids as in mitotic prophase but close together on the side facing away from the other homologous chromosome of the bivalent. The paired kinetochores of a single homologue both connect through to the same spindle pole. These associations are made as the bivalents come to lie at the equator of the spindle, rocking and swinging as they orient so that the centromeres of the two homologous chromosomes face opposite poles. The randomness of this process, each bivalent orienting itself on the spindle independently from its neighbours, ensures that the homologues facing any one pole are a mixture of maternal and paternal chromosomes.

Anaphase I is triggered not by the division of the centromere as in mitosis, but by a removal of the close association between those parts of sister chromatids that lie further from the centromere than do the chiasmata. Each of the two groups of chromosomes, which have moved to opposite ends of the first meiotic spindle by **telophase I**, consists of the full haploid complement of chromatid pairs, as in a haploid cell just before mitosis. However, each of these complete haploid sets is made up of a mixture of maternal and paternal chromatid pairs, and the members of each pair of chromatids are not completely identical, as they are at mitosis, because of the exchanges which took place between maternal and paternal homologues at pachytene.

The extent of the gap between the two meiotic divisions varies in different organisms, from the length of a normal interphase (normal, that is, but for the absence of DNA synthesis) to an abbreviated version in which telophase I is omitted, the spindle splits longitudinally and **metaphase II** follows directly.

By the time that the chromatid pairs are associated with the equators of the spindles in metaphase II, the two kinetochores have moved to opposite sides of the centromere as in mitosis, and subsequent stages of meiosis follow exactly as in mitosis (Fig. 1.19). The product is four haploid cells which are all genetically different.

1.6 CELL DIFFERENTIATION AND MORPHOGENESIS

Differentiation

In unicellular organisms, the single cell is versatile and carries out all the functions required for the survival and spread of the species. For prokaryotes this versatility is essentially biochemical, with a whole range of different inducible enzymes to deal with the particular nutrient supplied. The few structural specialisations of prokaryotes include a flagellum for motility, and sex pili for exchange of genetic information. Unicellular eukaryotes, on the other hand, often show detailed and intricate structural specialisation of parts of their cytoplasm for motility, feeding and perception of physiologically important parameters from the environment, such as light (see section 2.1). The disposition about the cell of these specialised parts is usually fixed in a pattern; for example, the rows of cilia on the ciliate *Paramecium* beat with a fixed polarity, giving the cell an anterior and a posterior end.

At the same time, unicellular eukaryotes, which reproduce by cell division to give new individuals, must be able to hand on their specialised cytoplasmic structures to the new individuals. In a number of cases these structures replicate themselves rather than being synthesised anew in the daughter cells; thus the number of rows of cilia on a *Paramecium* is inherited strictly via the cytoplasm, and is not affected by, for instance, nuclear exchange during conjugation (mating) in this animal. The advantages of this form of inheritance are that the polarised pattern of cytoplasmic structures is maintained throughout, and the expression of specialised functions is not interrupted by reproduction.

In multicellular organisms, the individual cells can share out the variety of functions required for survival and dispersal, and so each is able to become increasingly specialised and therefore increasingly efficient at its particular task (see

sections 2.2 to 2.4). It is generally observed that specialised cells do not divide, except in special cases such as regeneration after wounding, and even then the more highly specialised types such as nerves and plant sieve-tubes do not recommence division. Cell proliferation in multicellular organisms itself becomes a specialised function, carried out by **stem cells** in animals and by **meristematic initials** in plants, and other specialised functions are only expressed in the progeny of these cells. So, unlike unicellular organisms, the machinery responsible for the specialised functions of cells in multicellular organisms is not continuously maintained from generation to generation, but always develops anew. By the process of **differentiation** cells become different from the dividing, undifferentiated, cells which gave rise to them, and also become different from cells that develop other specialised functions.

The two major aspects to the differentiated state are biochemical specialisation and structural specialisation. Only a selected range of proteins is present in differentiated cells, due apparently to selective expression of the genetic information necessary to make protein, the result of processes going on inside the nucleus. Structural specialisation involves the organisation of cell structures in the cytoplasm into fixed patterns, which determine both the shape of the cell and its pattern of deposition of extracellular material; the chemical nature of the extracellular material, such as the cell wall in plants, is determined by biochemical specialisation.

As an example, in mammalian bone marrow the erythroid stem cells divide to generate a series of cell types culminating in the final erythrocyte (red blood cell), which is structurally specialised by having an elastic hoop of microtubules (see section 1.2) under its plasma membrane, and biochemically specialised by its high content of the oxygen-transporting protein haemoglobin. In the formation of xylem tissue in plants (see section 2.2), some of the cells generated by divisions of the meristematic initials cease dividing and become structurally specialised in that the bundles of microtubules present under the plasma membrane organise into a hooped pattern. This pattern precedes the identical hooped pattern in which massive amounts of cellulose are later deposited just outside the plasma membrane. The cells become biochemically specialised in that they synthesise the enzyme phenylalanine-ammonia lyase to catalyse the first step in the synthesis of the cell-wall polymer lignin, which is laid down to strengthen the wall.

The differentiated state

Little is known of the basis for the permanence of the fixed patterns of structure in the cytoplasm of differentiated cells, except that the cytoskeleton provides the framework to which particular molecules, subcellular structures and organelles, the positions of which were labile before differentiation, become fixed. For example, the single-celled zygotes of fucoid algae (see section 2.2) have no intrinsic thallus-to-rhizoid polarity, but

Fig. 1.20. Diagram of an experiment establishing that nuclei from tissues in a tadpole have not lost any of the information necessary for the development of the whole animal. When genetically marked nuclei isolated from the intestinal epithelium are microinjected into an egg whose nucleus has been destroyed, adult frogs can be produced, albeit at low frequency (2%).

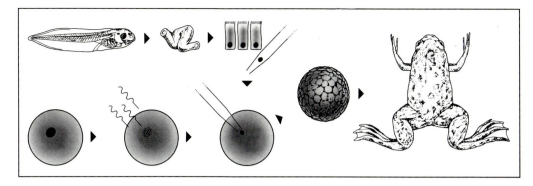

this is established by anchoring calcium-ion pumps and sodium-ion pumps in the plasma membrane to the cytoskeleton at one end of the cell.

It is also not known how each type of differentiated cell maintains a different and characteristic content of proteins. It seems certain, though, that the mechanism does not involve the irreversible loss of the genes for those proteins which are not present. Differentiated parenchymatous and mesophyll cells from several plant species can be excised from the plants, cultured in special solutions, and will develop back into complete plants. When a nucleus from the intestinal epithelium of a frog tadpole (*Xenopus*) is injected into a frog egg cell from which the nucleus has been removed, a fertile adult genetically identical to the source of the nucleus can be obtained (Fig. 1.20). The differentiated plant cell and the animal nucleus therefore still have in a retrievable form all the genetic information needed to produce all other cell types of their particular organism. The cells are thus said to be **totipotent**.

The nature of the masking that prevents the unwanted information from being expressed in other differentiated cell types is largely a mystery, and the evidence points to a range of different mechanisms. Much of the genetic material is present as heterochromatin, which is highly condensed and not transcribed (see section 3.1), and the proportion of the chromatin which is in this form increases from very little in embryonic cells to a major fraction in highly specialised cells. Also, the degree to which cytosine residues in portions of DNA are not methylated correlates in a general way with the degree of activity of the genes concerned, and the incorporation into DNA of chemical analogues of cytosine which cannot be methylated can, in cultured mammalian cells, reverse the inactivation of genes. Lastly, studies of the way that the genes for mating-type are expressed in yeast indicate that genes can remain unexpressed until they are transposed (moved within the chromosome) to a site adjacent to a promoter sequence for transcription.

The process of differentiation

Since the molecular nature of the differentiated state is essentially uncharacterised, the process of differentiation is even more difficult to understand, but nevertheless some of its characteristics can be described. Evidence from a wide range of sources suggests that there are two consecutive phases to differentiation. In the final phase, variously known as 'terminal' or 'overt' differentiation, the specialised function of the cell type is fully expressed, but in the preceding phase, while proteins and structures specific for that cell-type are not yet elaborated, the cells are stably committed to the eventual production of that particular cell type or a related set of cell types. The process whereby a stable commitment to a particular differentiation is achieved is known as **determination**.

For example, there are stem cells in bone marrow that are able to generate all the different types of blood cell; they are said to be **pluripotent**, but are already determined to the extent that they do not generate non-blood cells. The choice of which type of blood cell these stem cells become depends on their environment. One of the cell types generated by the stem cells is only able to give rise to granulocytes and macrophages (kinds of white blood cell), a further restriction of developmental choice. A specific glycoprotein synthesised in response to infection stimulates this white cell precursor to divide and differentiate. The magnitude of this same signal also influences the choice of fates for these cells, in that higher concentrations of the glycoprotein produce a higher ratio of granulocytes to macrophages. Differentiation of the stem cells into red blood cells is promoted by another glycoprotein, erythropoietin, produced by the kidney in amounts related to the content of red cells in the blood at any one time. The products of stem cell divisions do not become sensitive to erythropoietin until after they are determined to turn into red cells; committed red cell precursors, at twelve and at six cell cycles (see section 1.5) prior to terminal differentiation, respond to erythropoietin by proliferation to form more of the same type of precursor.

First, therefore, determination is a gradual process, a sequence of choices from a progressively narrower range of alternative cell types, leading up to a single type at terminal differentiation. Secondly, the determined state is stable, and this state can be 'replicated' in cell division and passed on to daughter cells. Both the pattern of heterochromatin in chromosomes and the pattern of methylation of cytosine residues in DNA share these features of gradually changing through differentiation, and of being stable through cell division.

Thirdly, individual steps in the progress towards terminal differentiation may be associated with particular cell cycles. For example, when the phloem sieve-tubes of a vascular bundle in the stem of a *Coleus* plant (see section 2.2) are damaged, nearby parenchyma cells re-differentiate to form transport channels, bypassing the damaged section. Exactly four mitotic cycles precede the terminal differentiation into phloem. Cycle one generates a phloem precursor cell and another parenchyma cell. The phloem precursor cell divides in cycle two, creating two equally competent phloem precursor cells. One or both of these divides to give rise to a phloem parenchyma cell and a pre-phloem cell. The pre-phloem cell then divides to form two cells which differentiate, one into a sieve-element and the other into a companion cell. Mitotic cell divisions that give rise to cells of identical developmental potential (as in cycle two in this example) are termed **proliferative**. Cycles one, three and four are called **fate-determining** or **quantal** mitoses.

Within individual cell cycles, developmental decisions seem to be restricted to particular phases (see section 1.5). The cells of the mouse mammary epithelium arrest in late G1 phase at sexual maturity. They respond to the hormones insulin, hydrocortisone and prolactin by re-entering the cell cycle, and only after they have passed early G1 in the presence of these hormones are they able to respond to the same hormonal signal by synthesising milk proteins. Mesophyll cells from *Zinnia* leaves differentiate into xylem in response to the plant growth substance auxin, and there appears to be a stage in G1 through which cells that have been induced by the auxin to re-enter mitotic cycles must pass in the presence of auxin in order to differentiate as xylem.

Fourthly, a number of different stages leading up to terminal differentiation can all be triggered by the same signal, which implies that the machinery for translating the signal into the developmental response is different at the different stages. A reasonable, but unproven, hypothesis is that specific alterations to the signal-translating machinery take place at fixed stages in certain cell cycles. Natural selection has favoured the establishment of links between a signal and the final pattern of differentiation that results, and so whole sequences of stages of differentiation have become tied to particular signals associated with single events in the life of the organism, such as birth, infection or loss of blood. In plants, auxin accumulates at sites of damage, and sucrose bleeds from damaged sieve-tubes. The ratio of auxin to sucrose determines the pathway of subsequent differentiation; thus re-differentiating parenchyma cells form xylem tissue where this ratio is high, and phloem tissue where it is low.

Finally, the process of terminal differentiation is often not so much a discrete phase following determination and preceding a particular active physiological role for the cell, but instead can be an extended and gradual process: responding to signals, by altering the pattern of production of proteins, can continue throughout the life of the cell. For example, fully differentiated hen oviduct cells respond to the steroid hormone oestrogen by synthesising ovalbumin, the protein of the egg-white, to coat the yolk as this descends the oviduct. In this case the hormone binds to a protein receptor, enabling it to bind to the chromatin and promote the transcription of the ovalbumin gene. The synthesis of this particular receptor protein will have been an important part of determination. Further, many differentiated cells are pre-programmed for eventual senescence and death, a developmental sequence which in plants is initiated and maintained in response to the growth substance ethene.

Morphogenesis

Morphogenesis means the formation of shape, and an important aspect of morphogenesis is how the number, size and shape of cells, and their attachment to each other, together create the bulk shape of tissues, organs and individuals. This process, however, is complicated by the intricate pattern of cellular differentiation which accompanies it.

Morphogenesis is very different in animals and plants. An individual plant invades the environment opportunistically, to maximise the efficiency of exploitation of light, carbon dioxide and minerals: the final shape of the plant can be tailored to match the characteristics of its particular site. Each individual thus begins from a minimal structure, which is able to function because the physiological relations between cells, between tissues and between organs are very simple. The rest of plant morphogenesis mostly consists of adding more of the same simple structures in positions optimal for the survival of the individual.

In contrast, the more familiar animal types, arthropods and vertebrates, survive due to their versatile and highly responsive physiologies, the products of finely tuned interlocking processes of such precision that if any one of the complex of organs does not function, the result is generally fatal. Morphogenesis leads to the whole organism complete in each detail, and the entire process therefore has to be compressed into a short, and in consequence intense, phase at the beginning of the life-cycle; in this vulnerable, non-functioning developmental stage, the **embryo** is protected and fuelled by the fully functional previous generation.

Morphogenetic processes

Cell division is an obvious prerequisite for morphogenesis. Morphogenesis in plants (see Fig. 2.8) is largely a matter of controlling the distribution and activity of zones of mitotic activity, termed **meristems**, and within each meristem of controlling the pattern, the intensity and the orientation of the cell divisions. Cell division does not so frequently determine the final shape of the organism in animal development because initially animal cells are not confined to fixed positions as they are in plants. However, the outgrowth of limb buds in vertebrate embryos proceeds by the accumulation of cells generated by cell division in the tip of the bud.

Cell expansion is the other principal means by which the shape of plant parts can be generated. The orientation of cytoplasmic microtubules under the plasma membrane determines the orientation of the inextensible cellulose microfibrils in the wall outside. Hydrostatic pressure is exerted in all directions on the wall by the turgid protoplast, and expansion occurs predominantly in the most extensible direction, at right angles to the predominant orientation of cell-wall microfibrils. Controlled patterns of cell expansion are the basis of stem and root elongation, and of the morphogenesis of epidermises, palisade and spongy mesophyll layers in the leaf.

Cell shape in animal cells can be adjusted at any time by reorganising the cytoskeleton of cytoplasmic microtubules under the plasma membrane, and by contractile bundles of microfilaments (see section 1.2). Changes in cell shape occur

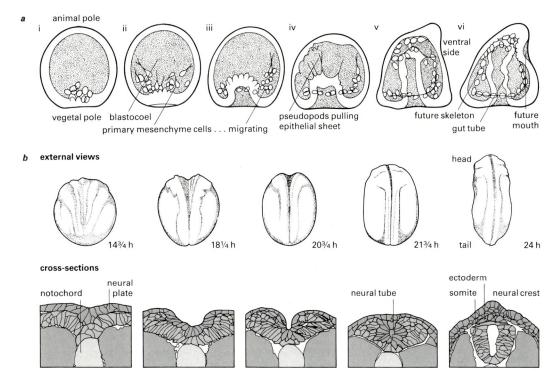

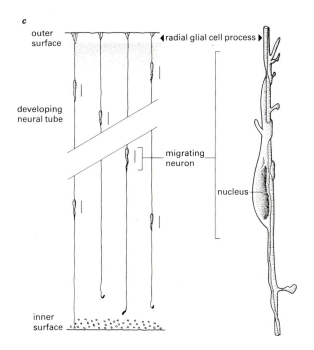

throughout morphogenesis, but their effect is most dramatic in a sheet of cells firmly attached to each other; this is the mechanism for the earliest stages of gastrulation during embryonic development (see section 2.4.10) and, later, in vertebrate embryos, for the infolding of the neural plate to create the neural tube (Fig. 1.21).

Cell adhesion between animal cells can show a high degree of specificity. For example, digestion of surface proteins under mild conditions allows the cells of the various tissues of a vertebrate embryo to separate, and if left alone then the cells later re-aggregate; if separate cells from different tissues are mixed, they re-aggregate only with others from the same tissue, and in the case of amphibian gastrulae the dissociated cells re-aggregate so as to restore the original three layers of the gastrula in their original positions. Firm bonding between cells is due to desmosome junctions (see section 1.4), and these unions may be formed between cells in a group or sheet of cells sharing common ancestry, or between cells of independent origins in the embryo which have come to adhere specifically to each other after a period of cell movement.

Cell movements during development are typical of animals but not at all of plants. For example, the muscles of vertebrate limbs are composed of cells which migrated into the limb buds as undifferentiated but fully determined cells, appearing at that stage identical to the native cells of the limb bud that subsequently differentiate into connective tissue. In some cases, the determined cells may be carried passively for a part of the way: in chicks the germ cells, the stem cells for the gametes, travel in the bloodstream to the site of the gonads, and stem cells for the blood cells are carried to the bone marrow in the same way. For developing nerve cells it is only a slender extension of the cell, and not the whole cell, that invades other tissues. In all cases, though, successful migration is terminated by specific adhesion to the other cells, which from then on maintains the correct pattern of different cell types.

In these migrations, some cells take clearly organised routes. For example, in vertebrates, the neural crest, the thin strip of

Fig. 1.21. Examples of morphogenetic processes in animal development. (a) Gastrulation in a sea-urchin embryo. A change in cell shape at one end of the hollow blastula initiates the process of inversion. Changes in cell–cell adhesion lead to the primary mesenchyme cells breaking loose. (b) The sequence of events during neurulation in vertebrate embryos. A change in cell shape along a line on the dorsal ectoderm results in the formation of a groove, the sides of which fuse to create the neural tube. (c) Immature motor neuron cells finding their way to the surface of the spinal cord by migrating specifically along the surfaces of glial cells.

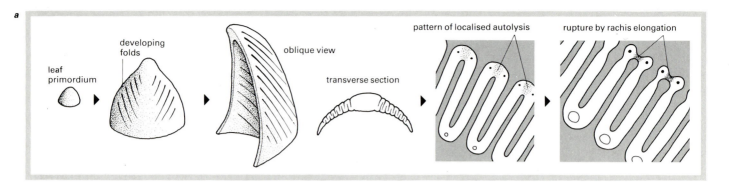

Fig. 1.22. Palm leaves develop from a sheet of tissue which buckles into a series of parallel ridges as it grows. Localised cell death along the crest of each ridge divides the leaf up into leaflets. The photograph shows an immature leaf, in which the leaflets are still folded as a solid, vertical rod of tissue, together with an opened 'palmate' leaf.

process of providing nerve connections to muscle cells, cell death is used to remove redundancy: there are enough neurons initially in contact with muscle cells to ensure that each muscle cell has several nerve cells supplying it; the subsequent death of all except one of the neurons reduces this figure to exactly one neuron only for each muscle cell. Correction by cell death is thus possible even after specific adhesion has taken place.

Programmed cell death, often of whole groups of cells, is widely used in morphogenesis. The immature palm leaf is a continuous sheet of cells, and it is literally cut into strips by lines of localised cell death to form the individual leaflets of the mature leaf (Fig. 1.22). On a smaller scale, and in all plants, cells in the leaf mesophyll next to developing guard cells die to create the substomatal chamber. In vertebrates localised cell death in a sheet of cells creates the spaces between the digits of hands and feet.

The control of morphogenetic processes

In developing animals and plants, each cell follows a sequence of morphogenetic processes. The model sequence, a basic pattern which can be modified in different ways, is for plants cell division, then cell expansion, then cell death or differentiation; and for animals it is cell division, then cell migration, then cell adhesion, then changes in cell shape, then cell death or differentiation. In the formation of any one cell type some of these stages may be either missing or extended, or even repeated. The central problem for understanding morphogenesis is to determine how each sequence is controlled for each cell type, and how the separate sequences are coordinated between cells at successively higher levels of multicellular organisation up to the level of the whole organism.

The types of control may be classified in the broadest possible way into those events which follow one another automatically, without reference to any influence outside the cell (**autonomous** or **intrinsic** control), and those events which occur in response to signals originating outside the cell (**extrinsic** control).

Some organisms rely very heavily on a set internal programme of development to generate fixed numbers of the different cell types. The control and coordination of this is achieved by a precise linking of the sequence of development

epithelium covering the dorsal side of the neural tube, generates cells which migrate and form, among other types, peripheral neurons and the pigment cells called melanocytes. If an embryo of an albino mouse at an early stage of its development is disaggregated into its component cells, and these are then allowed to re-aggregate mixed with the cells from an embryo of a brown mouse, the result is a mouse with tissues which are a mixture of the two genetically different types: this is called a **chimaera**. The patches of white and brown coat in the chimaeric mouse occur as broad stripes running around the body from the dorsal midline to the ventral midline, indicating the fixed direction followed by the migrating neural crest cells. While for some cells the direction of migration is fixed by the cells over which they move (immature motor neuron cells migrate to the surface of the spinal cord along the length of highly elongated glial cells), other cells use the polarity of the extracellular matrix that was fixed into it by the cells which laid the matrix down (migrating fibroblasts follow the orientation of the protein fibronectin in matrix material).

Cell death is a further source of selectivity for migrating cells. Cells which have failed to adhere correctly to their specific site die, for example germ cells in the chick which are carried in the bloodstream to all sorts of unsuitable sites; all the cells die except those that attach at the genital ridges. In the

Fig. 1.23. To show that insect egg cytoplasm contains factors which determine the fate of cells of the subsequent generation, cytoplasm from the posterior pole of egg 1 is transferred to the anterior end of egg 2. The cells which form at the anterior end of the egg do not normally contribute to gametes, but cells from the anterior end of egg 2, when transferred to the posterior end of a genetically marked embryo, can be shown to give rise to some of the gametes of this third individual.

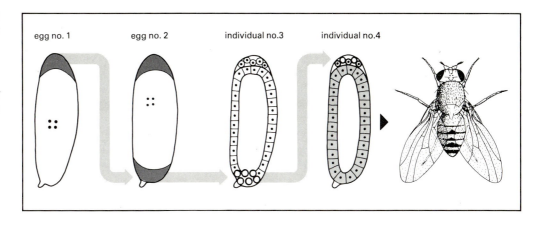

egg no. 1   egg no. 2   individual no.3   individual no.4

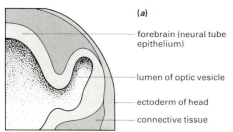
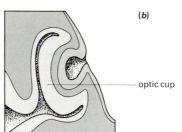
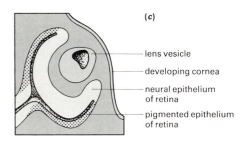

(a)

forebrain (neural tube epithelium)

lumen of optic vesicle

ectoderm of head

connective tissue

(b)

optic cup

(c)

lens vesicle

developing cornea

neural epithelium of retina

pigmented epithelium of retina

Fig. 1.24. The formation of the lens in the development of the vertebrate eye, an example of the control of morphogenetic processes by induction. The optic cup, an extension of the neural tube and therefore derived from ectoderm, induces ectoderm at the surface close to it to invaginate, internalising the ectodermal epithelium as a vesicle which becomes the lens.

to the succession of cell cycles, and the fate of each cell is determined solely by its pedigree. This 'cell lineage' mechanism is often found in 'lower' animals, organisms with a very precise arrangement of rather few cells, for example ctenophores (comb-jellies) and nematode worms. For almost all the somatic cells (cells not in the germ-line) of a nematode, destruction of neighbouring cells does not affect the subsequent development of the remaining cells. This kind of developmental system, unable to self-correct, is one of the characteristics of 'lower' organisms, and it is not used extensively in large, more complex animals; it is clearly unsuitable for plants, which respond so sensitively and precisely to the environment during their development. However, short terminal morphogenetic sequences forming small features of fixed size, such as the formation of epidermal hairs in plants (and insects), are frequently controlled by cell lineage only. Small-scale patterning can be generated with high precision by this system, for example the distribution of stomata on the leaves of grasses and cereals.

If the information that guides the developmental decisions does not come from outside the cell, and each generation of cells has to make different decisions to progress towards terminal differentiation, then developmental information has to be supplied to the daughter cells by each previous generation of cells. The influence of a previous generation has been most thoroughly investigated for eggs. The nuclear transplant experiments on Xenopus show that it is the cytoplasm of the egg, and not the nucleus of the newly formed zygote, that controls the earliest stages of embryogenesis. The influence of this maternal cytoplasm is best established, in both amphibians and insects, in the determination of some cells as the potentially immortal germ-line, while the rest become the somatic cells. For

example, in eggs of the fruit fly Drosophila, only nuclei which migrate to and form cells with the cytoplasm from the posterior pole of the egg contribute to the germ-line (Fig. 1.23). This special cytoplasm, the pole-plasm or germ-plasm, can be transferred to the anterior pole of the egg of a genetically marked fly, and the cells which form at this anterior end when transferred to the posterior end of a third egg give rise to viable gametes when egg number three has become an adult fly; therefore the germ-plasm specifically instructs the nucleus to form germ cells (Fig. 1.23).

The **mosaic** theory proposes that the cytoplasm of insect and amphibian eggs is a fixed mosaic of patches of such instructions, each patch prescribing a different fate for the cells of the embryo that are formed in that portion of the egg cytoplasm. However, except in the case of cells of the germ-line, developmental mutations that affect specific types of cell in the embryo are generally found to be inherited equally from the maternal and paternal lines, rather than solely from the female parent that synthesises the egg cytoplasm. It is thus thought unlikely that mosaic development will turn out to be used extensively in these animals. In mammalian eggs, there is no evidence for autonomous determinants located in particular places in the cytoplasm. When a four-celled embryo for a white mouse was disaggregated and the individual cells recombined with cells from embryos of black mice, three perfect chimaeric mice were recovered and cells from the 'white' embryo contributed to the germ-line in all three.

Types of control extrinsic to the cells concerned are most obvious where a 'hormone' is involved, for example in the complex sequence of the metamorphosis of a tadpole into a frog, which is controlled and coordinated by thyroid hormone. The system of linking long and complex developmental

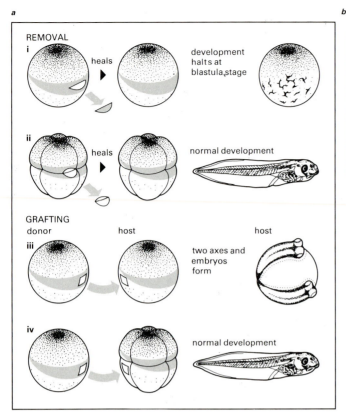

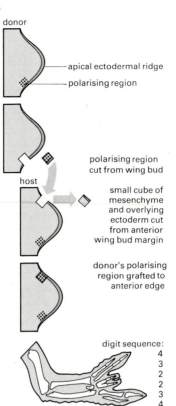

Fig. 1.25. Diagrams to show (a) the effects on the development of amphibian embryos of the grey crescent, and (b) the effects on vertebrate limb bud development of the polarising region, both examples of the control of morphogenetic processes by reference points. At an early stage, i.e. before the eight-cell stage, the grey crescent determines the longitudinal polarity of the rest of the embryo. The polarising region is found at the posterior edge of the limb bud and produces developmental information which determines the anterioposterior polarity of the limb.

sequences to a chemical signal, often where these sequences include different or paradoxical responses from different tissues with changing patterns of response, is extensively used in plants to link developmental responses to the environment; for example, in birch seedlings increased availability of nutrients is signalled by increased levels of cytokinins, to which leaf cells respond by delaying the onset of senescence but to which dormant bud meristems respond by re-entering mitotic cycles.

Information from outside the cell may be in the form of a guiding physical surface, or the chemical nature of the surface of adjacent cells, or may even be in an inorganic form that requires to be translated into an intracellular signal. The red-light signals that induce morphogenesis in those cells of dark-grown seedlings that are above ground level act by changing cytoplasmic levels of calcium ions. The two primary axes of symmetry of the amphibian embryo are established in the spherically symmetrical egg from effectively arbitrary parameters such as the direction of gravity (which determines the dorsiventral axis) and the position of entry of the successful sperm (which determines the anterio-posterior axis). Use of these arbitrary parameters is termed 'symmetry-breaking'.

Examples of one group of cells influencing the developmental fate of another group close by ('induction') are common, especially in vertebrate embryogenesis (Fig. 1.24). Usually the effect will operate across an artificially inserted filter, and is thus due to a chemical signal, but in some cases, such as formation of tubules in the kidney, cell contact is required. Induction may be involved in actual determination of the nature of the fate of the cells, or may merely permit their subsequent development to proceed.

Certain entities act as 'reference points' for morphogenesis, arising at fixed sites and appearing to generate developmental signals; the grey crescent of amphibian eggs is an example. If

this small area of cytoplasm is removed from the egg the longitudinal axis of symmetry of the embryo never forms, while grafting in an extra grey crescent induces a second axis of symmetry and produces a double embryo (Fig. 1.25). Another example of a reference point is the polarising region of a vertebrate limb bud, a group of a few hundred cells at its posterior edge. An extra polarising region grafted into the anterior edge of the limb bud results in a deformed limb composed of two posterior halves and with mirror-image symmetry. Since the polarising region from the posterior edge of a chick wing bud induces a deformed leg when implanted in the anterior edge of a leg bud, these cells are thought to be the source of a gradient of purely **positional information**. From the value of this signal in their vicinity, limb-bud cells will not be influenced as to which specialised type of limb to form, but rather which portion of the determined limb to form (Fig. 1.25).

The role of determination in development seems to be to set the nature of the response to an extrinsic signal, enabling the cell to progress along its determined pathway, by responding in a different manner from its previous response or from the response of other cells although sometimes the signal may be unchanged. If tissue from the proximal region (the region nearest the body) of a chick leg bud is grafted onto the distal end (the region furthest from the body) of a wing bud, then the grafted cells generate the structures of the distal end of a leg: thus, at the time of the transplant, these cells were determined with respect to the type of limb they were to make, but were not yet determined as to the proximal versus the distal parts of that limb (Fig. 1.25).

The gradual nature of determination is also demonstrated by the results of a 'clonal analysis' of fruit fly development (Fig. 1.26). Imaginal discs are pockets of undifferentiated tissue scattered around the larva, each of which will develop into a structure of the adult fly. Individual cells in the discs can be

Fig. 1.26. Diagrams to illustrate the contribution of larval imaginal discs to an adult fruit fly. These groups of undifferentiated cells are situated in different parts of the larva. In the pupa, larval tissues autolyse and each structure of the adult fly (imago) is formed by development of an imaginal disc.

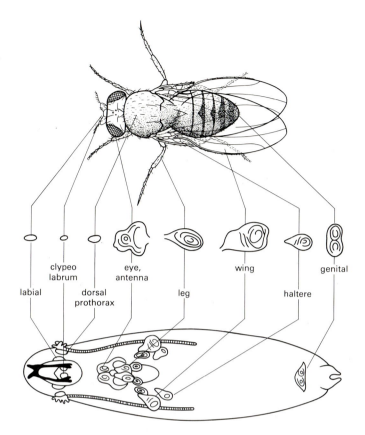

genetically marked at fixed times in their development: larvae heterozygous for particular genes (see section 3.1) are irradiated with X-rays to induce exchange of chromatids, which results in the next two daughter cells being homozygous, one for each variant of the gene. Each mutated cell then gives rise to a patch of mutant tissue. For the most part the perimeter of each patch is irregular, but the edges of patches at particular sites, such as near the middle of the wing, always appear smooth and straight, in this case at an invisible midline separating the anterior and posterior halves of the wing. Developmentally, the two halves of the wing are said to be separate **compartments**, and the midline is a boundary between them. A number of developmental mutants of *Drosophila* are known in which the type of organ found in a compartment is changed for another type of organ (homoeotic mutants), for example the 'engrailed' mutation which converts tissue in the posterior compartments of both wings and legs to the anterior form of the particular limb. This implies that, in wild-type flies, different genes are active in the posterior and anterior compartments of limbs. Interestingly, when the clonal patches in the posterior compartments of the wing or leg have the 'engrailed' phenotype, they are not curtailed by the boundary: they lack a property, almost certainly that of specific adhesion of posterior wing cells to each other, which normally keeps anterior and posterior wing cells apart (Fig. 1.26).

Rigid compartments like these probably will not be found for vertebrate embryos, as no clear-cut homoeotic mutants are known and the extensive use of long-distance migrations complicates the picture. Nevertheless, a common framework for morphogenesis is emerging which will be applicable to multicellular organisms. Groups of cells, within fields of not more than a hundred or so cells, choose one of just a few options open to them at any one stage, in the light of information from elements of the previous stage. The group of cells then becomes committed to that choice by the process of determination, which involves a stable, intrinsic alteration in the morphogenetic properties of the group of cells, such as specific cell–cell adhesion. As a consequence of determination, subgroups of cells will be created. Each subgroup may proliferate, or may alter the pattern of developmental information, or both. The subgroups will be further subdivided at subsequent stages in the series of stages until the full complexity of types is achieved, whereupon terminal differentiation can be initiated. Some system of this type is common even to plants, where the fields of extrinsic signals for leaf and flower morphogenesis are set up across apical meristems of only a few hundred cells, and stable commitment to each successive phase of morphogenesis involves a small group of cells, called the primordium.

Further reading

Alberts, B., Bray, D., Lewis, J., Raff, M., Roberts, K. and Watson, J.D. *Molecular biology of the cell.* London & New York: Garland, 1983.

Clayton, R.K. *Photosynthesis: Physical mechanisms and chemical patterns.* Cambridge: Cambridge University Press, 1980.

Metzler, D.E. *Biochemistry: The chemical reactions of living cells.* London: Academic Press, 1977.

Newsholme, E.A. and Start, C. *Regulation in metabolism.* Chichester: Wiley, 1973.

Stewart, A.D. and Hunt, D.M. *The genetic basis of development.* Glasgow & London: Blackie, 1982.

Stryer, L. *Biochemistry.* (2nd edn) San Francisco: W.H. Freeman, 1981.

Szekely, M. *From DNA to protein: The transfer of genetic information.* New York: Macmillan, 1980.

Wolfe, S.L. *Biology of the cell.* (2nd edn) Belmont: Wadsworth, 1981.

2 The Organism

2.1 UNICELLULAR ORGANISMS

Eukaryotic cells contain a number of intracellular structures, each for a specialised function, and in this way differ from prokaryotic cells such as bacteria and blue-green algae (see section 1.2). The structures responsible for carrying out the central core of metabolism, such as nuclei and mitochondria, do not vary much throughout living organisms. Other intracellular structures, however, vary much more in biochemical activity, like the secretory endomembrane system, or in shape, like the cytoskeleton: the versatility of the cytoskeleton is the basis for the astonishing diversity of shapes and functional appendages of eukaryotic cells.

The earliest eukaryotes are believed to have been single cells carrying out all the functions necessary for life. Some of their descendants have remained unicellular at all stages of their life-cycle, while many others have diversified into the range of multicellular organisms seen today (see sections 2.2 to 2.4). It would, however, be a mistake to assume that modern unicells are relics of an early stage in evolution: although many still have primitive and less efficient mechanisms for some vital processes, such as nuclear division, hundreds of millions of years of selection have refined their more adaptive features. Unicellular organisms often display an intricate precision of cytoskeleton and secreted structures which is not found in cells forming part of multicellular creatures.

The different unicellular organisms, or **protists**, are grouped according to the nature of their appendages. The amoeboid, or sarcodine, forms have protruding portions of the cell cytoplasm, called pseudopodia, which can be retracted or extended as required for locomotion and feeding. Forms with flagella are grouped as flagellates, and those with cilia as ciliates.

The **flagellates** are a very heterogeneous group, and include types that are probably closest of all unicellular organisms to the earliest forms of eukaryotic life. They show a range of different types of plastid, and of mitosis and meiosis, kinds of nuclear division that are fundamental to the eukaryotic level of organisation (see section 1.5). In dinoflagellates and euglenids, the nuclear membrane remains intact during mitosis, and dinoflagellates have chromosomes without histones, each chromosome resembling a prokaryotic nucleoid. Although all flagellates can live heterotrophically, many have chloroplasts and therefore can use sunlight as a source of energy. A number of different groups of flagellates, such as euglenids and dinoflagellates, include both such plant–animal types and also wholly animal types; these organisms may be classified in the plant kingdom with the unicellular algae, or else in the animal kingdom with unicellular animals (Protozoa).

The range of structural forms of flagellates is very wide. The flagellum, of which there are usually one to five per cell, may be variously modified by the inclusion of extra structural material inside, or hairs or scales attached to the outside. The membrane around the flagellum may be extended laterally as a thin flap, the trailing edge of which adheres to the outside of the plasma membrane to form an 'undulating membrane'. Some forms bear an exoskeleton of secreted scales. Dinoflagellates have an endoskeleton of cellulose or silica plates contained in vesicles just under the plasma membrane, and in euglenids the cortical cytoskeleton forms a tough, flexible 'pellicle'.

Apart from the various groups of flagellates, few unicellular organisms are plants: even the primitive prokaryotic blue-green algae (see page 50) almost always grow as filaments or sheets of cells. Also, since a simple physiology suffices for an autotrophic lifestyle, unicellular plants have not evolved much intracellular complexity. The most important group of unicellular plants is the diatoms, found both in freshwater and in the sea, which are responsible for an estimated 20 to 25% of the net primary production of the earth. Diatoms are golden-brown algae, and are related to a group of flagellates with similar plastids. Each diatom lives inside an exquisitely patterned pill-box shell made of silica, and daughter cells inherit either the lid or the box from the parent cell, but in both cases use it as a lid of a new, complete box. In consequence, each successive generation is smaller than the previous one, until a round of sexual reproduction restores the maximum size. Diatoms can live heterotrophically, and many move by a curious gliding mechanism, leaving a trail of mucilage behind them. The other unicellular plants are all chlorophyte green algae (see page 50), with plastids and cell walls like those of terrestrial plants. Green unicellular algae include the predominantly freshwater desmids, shaped like a rigid butterfly with outstretched wings, and *Acetabularia*, the most complex of unicellular plants. The nucleus of *Acetabularia* remains in the basal part of the cell, which is specialised for anchorage to the substratum, and the rest of the cell forms a 'trunk' 2 to 5 centimetres high bearing whorls of photosynthetic 'branches', which themselves branch into fine 'twigs'.

A number of **amoeboid** forms are similar to different flagellate types, having pseudopodia and flagella. The famous *Amoeba proteus* is exceptional in that it is naked, though it is protected by a tough cytoskeletal pellicle. Most amoebae construct around themselves a shell, called a 'test', with apertures for the broad pseudopodia. The test consists in some species of precisely interlocking sculptured scales, and in others of cemented sand grains. Foraminiferans add chambers progressively to their test, and produce filamentous pseudopodia in the shape of a net for trapping food. The floating radiolarians and the bottom-dwelling heliozoans have an internal skeleton of silica, and tapering, needle-like pseudopodia several hundred micrometres long, stiffened by cross-linked microtubules.

The most elaborate and complex unicellular organisms are the **ciliates**. The cilia are precisely arranged, and are firmly anchored to an intricate meshwork of cytoskeletal filaments that form a tough pellicle. The arrays of cilia, used for locomotion, usually form longitudinal rows; in a number of species some cilia are closely grouped, and adhere to form

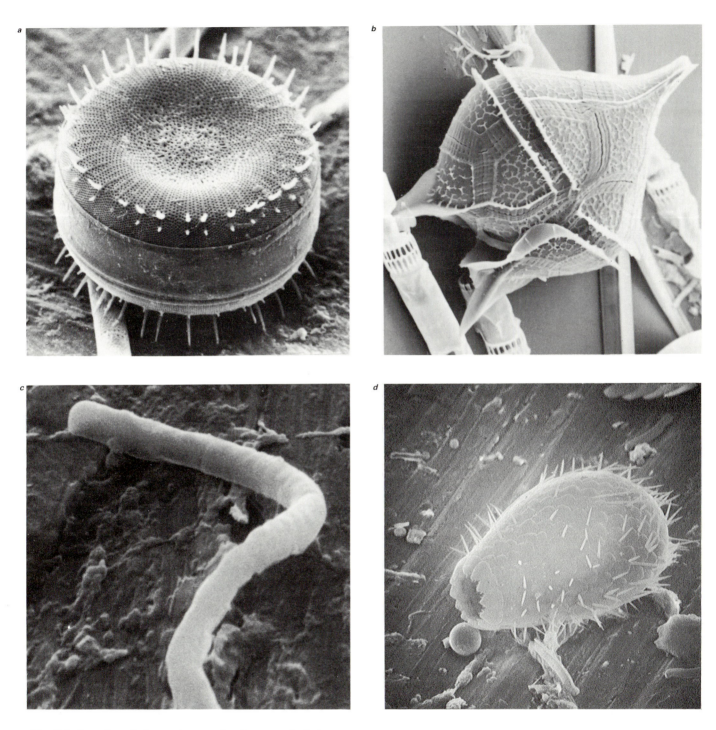

Fig. 2.1. Scanning electron micrographs of some unicellular organisms. (a) The diatom Stephanodiscus (x 2730). (b) The dinoflagellate Protoperidinium (x 1040). (c) Cells of the bacterium Bacillus megaterium (x 9000). (d) The shell of the testate amoeba Euglyphus ciliata, a protozoan (x 400 000).

bundles which enable the animal to jump.

The complexities of the pellicle in ciliates, and also in some of the flagellates, restrict certain functions to fixed sites on the surface of the cell. Unicellular organisms living in freshwater have to excrete the excess water that enters by osmosis, and in amoebae a vesicle of dilute solution moves around the cell, coalescing with smaller vesicles and eventually fusing with the plasma membrane. In the ciliate *Paramecium*, a large 'contractile vacuole' opens to the outside by a pore at a fixed site, and is supplied with fluid by contractile canals which connect with the endoplasmic reticulum. Entry of food, and the expulsion of undigested remains, are restricted to fixed sites, and complex arrays of cilia are involved in feeding. In rows between the rows of cilia are sites for the secretion of mucus or, in some species, for aggressive dischargeable darts. Such elaborate structures at fixed sites require special mechanisms to enable them to be duplicated at cell division.

Some ciliates are sessile, stalked animals that use their cilia to waft food towards them. The suctorial ciliates only have cilia in the earliest stages of their life-cycle: they have evolved tentacles capable of adhering to and sucking out the cytoplasm of prey animals. A number of ciliates, and some flagellates, are active carnivores, seeking out and pursuing other animals, and are capable of performing complex patterns of behaviour.

Most unicellular organisms either contain a nucleus that is polyploid (containing many copies of the genetic material), such as radiolarians and the larger diatoms, or have more than one nucleus, such as ciliates. The increase in the content of DNA in the cell achieved in these ways enables unicells to produce the extra quantities of RNA needed to supply the amount of cytoplasm associated with a large cell and the elaboration of specialised structures. Most unicellular organisms are very large by comparison with the cells typical of multicellular animals. Typical prokaryotic cells and cells of multicellular animals are sufficiently small for diffusion to distribute materials efficiently within them, but unicellular animals use streaming of their cytoplasm for internal transport, as do the comparatively large cells of unicellular and multicellular plants.

Even the most complex unicells have a mass measured in micrograms, and are therefore relatively susceptible to any environmental change. Although many can survive desiccation, all require liquid water to be active, and so are confined to the sea, freshwater or the soil. Large numbers of cells grouped together as multicellular organisms are not limited in size by the efficiency of intracellular processes, and can create their own internal environment favourable for the cells and protected from the outside environment. This internal environment of multicellular organisms is another site in which unicellular organisms can grow, and many are parasites. The agents of sleeping sickness and of Chagas' disease are flagellates (*Trypanosoma*), and amoebic dysentery is caused by *Entamoeba histolytica*.

Multicellular organisms that have no specialisation of their constituent cells are at a **colonial** level of organisation, but these are few in numbers and in types: specialisation, either within a unicellular organism or of the various cells in a multicellular organism, is the secret of efficiency. Present-day unicells have become specialised intracellularly, with a precise organisation of their cytoskeleton and membranes. The ancestors of modern multicellular organisms followed another evolutionary route, in which different portions of their genetic material became selectively expressed in different, specialised cells in the same individual, a process requiring the evolution of precise intercellular coordination of gene expression. In consequence they have evolved a larger scale of size and complexity than any unicellular organism.

2.2 PLANTS

Introduction

Plant groups

The distinct groupings within the diversity of plant types are shown in Fig. 2.2.

The simplest forms of plant belong to groups which occur chiefly in the sea, the **algae**, but there is a far wider variety of plant structure, multicellular organisation and life-cycle in the algae than in all other types of plant. Algae are normally classified according to the structure of their cells because this grouping coincides with grouping according to the chemistry of photosynthetic pigments, of storage polysaccharides, and of cell-wall polysaccharides, although it does separate types with similar levels of organisation and types with similar life-cycles. Thus, the same levels of organisation and life-cycles appear to have evolved separately in different groups.

The groups of algae with multicellular forms are as follows; they all use chlorophyll-*a* as their primary photosynthetic pigment. Blue-green algae (**cyanophytes** or **cyanobacteria**) are prokaryotic (see section 1.1), but share with the eukaryotic red algae (**rhodophytes**) the photosynthetic pigments phycocyanin (blue-green) and phycoerythrin (red), and a glycogen-like storage polysaccharide. Red algae have no flagella, and have reproductive structures curiously similar to those of ascomycete fungi (see section 2.3). Brown algae (**phaeophytes**) are coloured by the photosynthetic pigment fucoxanthin and have laminarin as a storage polysaccharide. Agar is a polysaccharide of the matrix of the cell wall that is unique to red algae, while the chemically very different polysaccharides alginate and fucoidan are unique to brown algae. The green algae (**chlorophytes**) resemble terrestrial plants in having chlorophyll-*b* as an accessory photosynthetic pigment and in storing starch, which they do, uniquely for algae, inside the plastid. There is very little variation in the type of chloroplast among terrestrial plants, and the algal group from which they evolved was probably the green algae, a predominantly freshwater group.

Terrestrial plants, as opposed to algae, are classified into types on the basis of similar levels of structural organisation and life-cycles. Mosses and liverworts (**bryophytes**) have negligible amounts of the transport ('vascular') tissues xylem and phloem, and the organs that produce gametes are so small as to be considered hidden: hence 'cryptogams' as the name for the group to which bryophytes belong. Cryptogams possessing vascular tissue are grouped separately into ferns, horsetails and clubmosses, and are called **pteridophytes**. The remaining vascular plants produce seeds and are termed **spermatophytes**; they are distinguished by whether the seed is exposed during its development (**gymnosperms**) or is buried in the tissues of a flower (**angiosperms**). There are two distinct

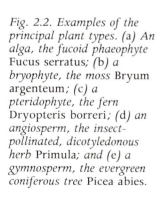

Fig. 2.2. Examples of the principal plant types. (a) An alga, the fucoid phaeophyte Fucus serratus; *(b) a bryophyte, the moss* Bryum argenteum; *(c) a pteridophyte, the fern* Dryopteris borreri; *(d) an angiosperm, the insect-pollinated, dicotyledonous herb* Primula; *and (e) a gymnosperm, the evergreen coniferous tree* Picea abies.

groups with the angiosperm organisation: those with parallel leaf veins, fibrous roots and a single seed-leaf (**monocoty-ledons**), and those with a net of leaf veins, a taproot and two rudimentary leaves on each embryo in the seed (**dicotyledons**).

Plant forms

The structures of plants of these various groups have evolved to improve the efficiency of photoautotrophy, which is the conversion of light, carbon dioxide, water and mineral ions by plants into more plants. Within the individual cells, the squeezing out of the cytoplasm into a thin film between the central vacuole and the cell wall enables plants to generate and support, cheaply and quickly, a large surface of living cytoplasm for absorbing these raw materials. The advantages of this design of the plant cell are such that it is used in all plants, which therefore have to cope with the limitations, such as rigid immobility, of life in a wooden box. When the local environment changes most animals have the option of moving, but plants have to adapt to the change, usually by an altered pattern of growth and development. Cell movements within the animal body are used extensively in animal development, but the multicellular structures of plants can only be shaped by controlling the direction and distribution of cell divisions. Plants can also selectively remove part of the plant body, and cell death with digestion of the cell contents is used in the process of forming the shape of plants and to produce empty cells with special functions, such as xylem vessels.

The simplest plants are unicellular, and sister cells produced by division escape from the mother cell wall, which must be split or digested at every cell division. In colonial algae, which are not truly multicellular, the wall of the parent cell may be temporarily retained in a gelatinised form which allows discs or hollow spheres to be built up. The simplest truly multicellular structure, where the wall of the parent cell is retained and augmented, is a filament, and results from restricting cell division to a single plane. This pattern has become more sophisticated by differentiation of a basal holdfast and by exclusively apical cell division, or may be elaborated by branching which involves scattered or occasional changes in the plane of cell division. The most complex filamentous systems are a horizontal system of filaments attached to the substrate and producing some vertical branches. Restricting cell division to two planes generates thin sheets, as in the green alga *Ulva*, sea-lettuce. Complex structures in the red algae are built up of large numbers of branching filaments growing alongside each other and then establishing cytoplasmic connections between originally seperate filaments. This 'pseudo-parenchymatous' construction resembles that of some fungal structures (see section 2.3). Truly **parenchymatous growth** involves controlled cell division in three dimensions, and is used to form the solid tissue of some brown algae and of all terrestrial plants.

Plant physiology

The subsequent discussions of this section first follow atoms from the inanimate world through their assembly, driven by solar energy, into more plant parts. The pattern of construction of the parts of the green plant, and modifications to this pattern for coping with the environment and progress through the life-cycle are then explained. Finally, the contribution of different types of life-cycle to the survival of species is assessed.

Leaves

In algae and in many bryophytes almost all the illuminated tissues carry out photosynthesis. More complex plants have restricted this process to organs specialised to carry it out with high efficiency, the leaves. The mature leaf is a chemical workshop within the plant factory, collecting light from the sun, water drawn from the roots via the stems, and carbon dioxide from the atmosphere, and then processing these raw materials into sugars which are exported to supply energy and carbon frameworks for all the other parts of the plant.

Collecting light

The upper layers of the leaf (see Fig. 2.3) process incoming solar radiation. The light first passes through a transparent **cuticle**, which in desert plants like *Yucca* and *Agave* contains chemicals that absorb destructive ultraviolet light of wavelengths between 280 and 320 nanometres. Next is a layer of non-photosynthetic cells, the **epidermis**, which in flowering plants contains flavonoid pigments to filter out longer wavelength ultraviolet light (320–400 nanometres). Finally, under these protective layers, are the photosynthetic cells of the **palisade** layer, which forms part of the **mesophyll** tissue lying between the lower and upper epidermises. The palisade layer is usually one or two cells thick, and the cells are arranged in it like the pile of a carpet. The only leaf components absorbing photosynthetically active radiation are the photosynthetic pigments found in the chloroplasts. As well as chlorophylls, which absorb red and blue light, marine algae have accessory pigments which absorb green and yellow light (fucoxanthin in brown algae and phycoerythrin in red algae) and pass the energy on to chlorophylls. Silt-laden coastal sea-water absorbs light strongly, and fucoxanthin and phycoerythrin enable the algae to use low levels of light more efficiently.

A number of features of leaves regulate the amount of photosynthetically active radiation collected (Fig. 2.4). The surface of the cuticle is often matt to reduce loss by reflection, and the development of the leaf generates a thin, flat structure with a maximal area for absorbing light. Mature leaves turn to face the light by differential growth between the leaf blade and its attachment to the stem. Finally, since the light transmitted through a single leaf is often not sufficient to allow a leaf underneath to make enough sugar to export, leaves are moved

Fig. 2.3. Diagram to show the structure and disposition of tissues within a typical, photosynthetic leaf.

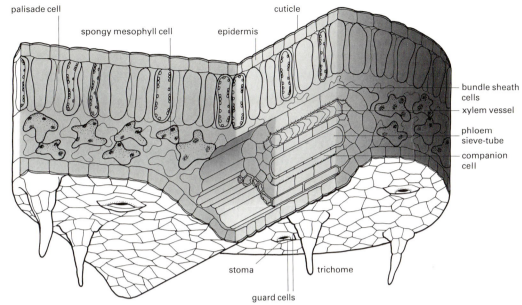

out of the shade of other leaves, by the same differential growth, to form a pattern called a leaf mosaic.

The development of leaves that grow in the shade changes to suit such a position. Structural changes in shade leaves include an increased surface area, resulting from expansion of the epidermal cells, and a decreased thickness, resulting both from reduced palisade cell expansion and from a reduced number of palisade cell layers. Physiological changes in shade leaves include an increase in the number of light-harvesting chlorophyll molecules per reaction centre (see section 1.3); red algae growing in deeper water similarly increase their content of phycoerythrin. This increased area for, and efficiency of, collecting light in the shade leaf results in a similar rate of fixation of carbon dioxide per molecule of the enzyme that fixes it (ribulose *bis*-phosphate carboxylase, see section 1.3) to that found in a sun leaf growing in a much higher light intensity. In some plants, such as many trees, leaf development can adapt to a wide range of light intensities, but the leaves of crop plants are always suited only to high intensities of light.

Collecting water

Liquid water enters the plant at the roots, but the force bringing it in and then up to the leaves is generated in the leaves. Except when the air is saturated with water vapour or when the temperature is too low, the movement of water from leaves to the atmosphere, **transpiration**, is irreversible, and the steep gradient in the concentration of water causes rapid diffusion of water molecules from within the leaf to the atmosphere. The rate of this movement fluctuates widely because of fluctuations in the temperature of the leaf and in the water content of the air, and to prevent desiccation the leaf must be able to control water loss.

The structure of leaves has evolved to achieve this control (Fig. 2.3). The photosynthetic tissue, in the mesophyll, is sandwiched between two epidermal layers of tightly joined cells. The outside surfaces of the epidermises are each coated with a cuticle of flexible cutin, a polyester of long-chain fatty-acids, which is impregnated with waterproof oils and waxes. So that water vapour can leave the leaf, these epidermes are perforated by **stomata**. The aperture of each stoma is 10

Fig. 2.4. An Australian eucalypt with vertically hanging foliage, an adaptation to constantly high light intensities. These leaves present the minimum area to the sun at midday when the intensity of solar radiation is highest.

53

micrometres across, and water loss can be restricted by its partial or complete closure. The mechanism controlling the size of the stomatal aperture involves a pair of long cells, the **guard cells**, which are separated by a slit which forms the stomatal pore. The concentration of salts in the vacuoles of the guard cells can be increased or decreased by exchange with neighbouring cells, and water follows the salt by osmosis, causing the guard cells to expand or contract. The structure of the guard-cell walls is such that as they expand the pore opens, and as they contract the pore closes. It has been shown in broad-bean leaves that as the mesophyll cells lose turgidity they synthesise abscisic acid, to which the stomata respond by closing, thus conserving water.

Collecting carbon dioxide

In contrast to the supplies of light and water, the concentration of carbon dioxide available to a leaf is constant at 0.03% by volume of the atmosphere at the leaf surface. Carbon dioxide is brought in by diffusion down a concentration gradient, but this gradient is feeble because of the low concentration of carbon dioxide in the air. The structure of the pathway by which carbon dioxide enters the leaf (Fig. 2.3) has evolved to enable this process to be as efficient as possible.

Air movements are necessary to replenish the carbon dioxide in a luxuriant canopy of leaves. Even when air is moving rapidly, as on a windy day, a boundary layer of still air is held by friction over the leaf surface. Irregularities like ribs, occasional large hairs and protruding guard cells break up the smooth flow of air, creating turbulent eddies which erode the boundary layer of still air. The crinkles and wavy edges of fronds of large sea-weeds (kelps) perform the same function in flowing water.

Carbon dioxide cannot diffuse through the cuticle, and so the stomata must be open for it to be taken up. Stomata are spaced at distances ten times their maximal pore diameter, which gives the maximum rate of diffusion of carbon dioxide per unit area of pore: diffusion through a perforated barrier is assisted by lateral diffusion towards the rim of each pore provided that the pores are not so close together that the lateral effects begin to cancel out. While the cuticularised epidermis that covers all the leaf surface except for the stomatal apertures reduces by about 100-fold the area through which carbon dioxide can enter, this is almost compensated for by the increase in the rate of diffusion per unit area of stomatal aperture because the stomata are small pores at the optimal spacing for a molecule with the diffusion constant of carbon dioxide. Thus when the stomata are open the epidermis is virtually no barrier to carbon dioxide entry, and the rate of diffusion of carbon dioxide through open stomata into the leaf is not highly dependent on the actual size of the stomatal apertures.

For most types of leaf, the stomata are almost all in the lower epidermis, and inside the leaf the mesophyll cells are arranged so as to hinder as little as possible the diffusion of carbon dioxide to the photosynthetic palisade layer. Between the palisade and the lower epidermis, the mesophyll cells are irregularly shaped with large, gas-filled intercellular spaces, forming the **spongy mesophyll**; the largest air spaces are the substomatal cavities, each one located just inside a stoma. The overall result is that each stoma feeds a 100-micrometre cube of leaf tissue with carbon dioxide through a branching 'tree' of air spaces. Similar geometries occur in the lungs and tracheae of animals, and this arrangement reduces the length of the diffusion pathway by reducing its complexity.

Carbon dioxide diffuses through the final section of the pathway, from cell surface to enzymes, in solution. The rate of diffusion is 10 000 times slower through a liquid than through a gas, but the leaf geometry corrects for this so that the time taken for a given amount of carbon dioxide to move through the liquid section of the pathway is the same as that taken through the gaseous section. This is achieved by shortening the length of the liquid section roughly 1000-fold relative to the gaseous section (palisade cell walls are only about 0.2 micrometres thick, and the chloroplasts are packed close against them), and by increasing the area through which carbon dioxide diffuses in solution relative to the area through which it diffuses as a gas (the total area of mesophyll cell walls exposed to the gas phase is 15 to 40 times the area of one side of the leaf).

Overall, the structure of a leaf is such that, with no moving parts, carbon dioxide is delivered to the enzyme that fixes it (ribulose *bis*-phosphate carboxylase) at 50 to 80% of its level in the atmosphere. Normally, with open stomata, it is the activity of this enzyme, and not the rate of entry of carbon dioxide, which puts a limit on the rate of fixation of carbon. If the stomata are closed, however, such as to reduce water loss, then the rate of carbon dioxide uptake will limit photosynthesis in the light, and excessively low concentrations of carbon dioxide have been shown to cause stomata to open.

Balancing inputs and outputs in the leaf

Loss of water from leaves occurs only through stomata but, because water diffuses more rapidly than does carbon dioxide, the spacing of the stomata in the epidermis is not at the optimal value that it is for carbon dioxide, and loss of water occurs at a rate roughly proportional to the area of the stomatal apertures. When stomata are wide open, the actual stomatal aperture does not limit the uptake of carbon dioxide and thus, as open stomata begin to close water loss is reduced without affecting carbon dioxide gain nearly so much. The ratio of water molecules lost to carbon dioxide molecules gained through wide-open stomata is twice as large as that ratio for barely open stomata: wide-open stomata lose approximately 340 molecules of water for each molecule of carbon dioxide gained, whereas just-open stomata lose approximately 160 molecules of water for each molecule of carbon dioxide gained.

Trimming water loss like this is an adaptive feature of the

Fig. 2.5. Transmission electron micrograph of a thin section through sycamore stem showing ultrastructural details of cells of the phloem (x 6400).

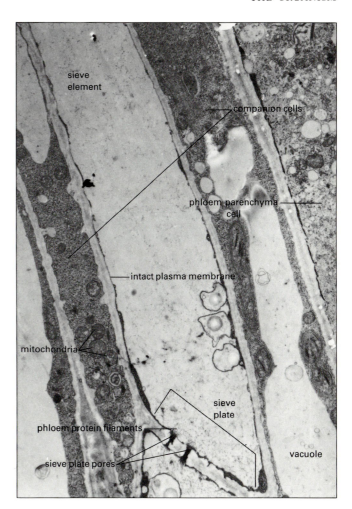

specialised group of plants called C_4-plants, which grow in dry, well-illuminated regions. Their mechanism for concentrating carbon dioxide at the ribulose *bis*-phosphate carboxylase enzyme, using light energy and four-carbon acids as carriers of carbon dioxide, results in much lower levels of carbon dioxide in the gas phase of the leaf, allowing a high rate of inward diffusion of carbon dioxide even when the stomata are partially shut, which reduces water loss even more effectively. Another photosynthetic mechanism which reduces even further the amount of water lost per molecule of carbon dioxide fixed is Crassulacean Acid Metabolism (CAM), which is found in succulent plants. Water losses are small in CAM-plants because the stomata open for uptake of carbon dioxide only in the cold hours of darkness. Photosynthesis and the fixation of carbon dioxide into sugars in the Calvin cycle (see section 1.3) can continue during the day, even though the stomata are closed then, because the carbon dioxide taken up by night is stored as a four-carbon acid, and this store is used to regenerate carbon dioxide inside the leaf or stem by day. Although biochemically similar to the adaptation of C_4-plants, the rate of carbon fixation in CAM-plants is severely limited by the capacity of the internal store of four-carbon acids in the vacuoles, and so their productivity is low, in marked contrast to C_4-plants which are highly productive in environments of high light intensity. C_4-plants include a number of tropical 'super-crops' such as maize, sorghum, millet and sugar-cane, while CAM is practised by slow-growing succulents of inhospitable arid regions.

In collecting photosynthetically active radiation, leaves cannot help also intercepting infrared radiation, which heats them, and a number of features have evolved to relieve this heat load (Fig. 2.4). Although leaves absorb light strongly in the photosynthetically active range, there is a dramatic change at a wavelength of about 700 nanometres to a very weak absorption at longer wavelengths (the near-infrared), reducing the heat load. White cuticles reduce absorption by increasing reflection, and are characteristic of plants of habitats with high light intensity, such as alpine, sea-shore and desert plants. In very high light intensities, growth movements may turn mature leaves edge-on to the light; some eucalypts and acacias, adapted to constantly intense light, have leaves permanently orientated vertically so that they are always edge-on to the midday sun. When water is available, cooling the leaf by opening the stomata and allowing evaporation is widely used; when water is limited, stomata are closed and heat can only be lost by convection. Plants adapted to this situation have many small leaves to increase convective heat loss: for example, the thin needles of conifers lose heat by convection highly efficiently, which compensates for the high absorption of infrared radiation by these opaque structures.

Overall control of the metabolism of the leaf lies with the stomata. Guard cells respond not just to abscisic acid and inadequate carbon dioxide, but also to blue light, and they can be influenced by endogenous circadian rhythms. The function of guard cells is to optimise carbon dioxide uptake, water loss and leaf temperature. These individual objectives may conflict, and the guard cells then have to balance them, taking account of the other adaptations of that plant. As a result, guard-cell behaviour is complex, and different in different plants, and is best interpreted in terms of the strategy of each particular plant.

Transport and the role of roots

The plasma membrane is a very effective and selective barrier to movement of sugars and ions, and a less effective, but still appreciable, barrier to water flow. It isolates from each other two major routes, or compartments, involved in transport within the plant. **Apoplast** is the region outside plasma membranes, that is, the cell walls and intercellular spaces; **symplast** is the region inside the plasma membranes, consisting of all the cytoplasms joined via the intercellular connections called plasmodesmata (see section 1.4). The materials transported in bulk around the plant include sugars from leaf to root and from leaf to growing tip, which occurs in tissues of the **phloem**, and water and mineral ions from root to leaf and from root to growing tip, which occurs in tissues of the **xylem**.

Phloem transport from the leaf

Sugar is synthesised by mature leaves in a form that they cannot use, commonly sucrose, and it leaves the palisade cells and accumulates in the apoplast of the leaf. From here it is actively taken up into the symplast by the cells of the phloem tissue (Fig. 2.5).

The phloem cells active in transport are the **sieve-elements** connected end-to-end to form a long conduit, the sieve-tube. Each sieve-element is a large cell that generally has lost its nucleus, and the contents of which have liquefied within an intact plasma membrane. Movement between contiguous sieve-elements is through sieve-pores, grossly enlarged plasmodesmata that perforate the end-walls of the sieve-elements. These end-walls are known as sieve-plates, and half the area of a sieve-plate is pores. Each sieve-element has extensive cytoplasmic connections to a sister cell, the **companion cell**, which is packed with organelles and is metabolically highly active. Although both types of cell contain a high concentration of sucrose, this sugar continues to be pumped in vigorously from the apoplast. Proton pumps in the plasma membrane, using the chemical energy of ATP (see section 1.1), push protons out of the symplast, and sucrose is carried back into the symplast with these protons on a proton–sucrose co-transporter. In some herbaceous angiosperms, companion cells in the leaf increase the area of the plasma membrane available for loading sucrose by having many finger-like protrusions of the cell wall into the cytoplasm, an arrangement analogous to the microvilli of animals.

Sucrose is present at 20 to 30% by mass inside the sieve-tube, in osmotic contact with the very dilute solution in the apoplast, causing the hydrostatic pressure on the inside of the sieve-element wall to be very high (20 to 30 atmospheres, 2 to 3 megapascals). The sieve-element can hold this pressure because it has a thick wall rich in cellulose, a polymer of great tensile strength arranged here like the hoops of a barrel. Also, sieve-tubes have no plasmodesmata through which the pressure could be released, except to the equally sucrose-rich companion cell.

All parts of the plant, such as roots, fruit or growing meristems, are 'plumbed in' to the phloem system, from which they take sucrose as needed. At such sinks the hydrostatic pressure inside the sieve-elements is reduced by this offloading of the osmotically active sucrose, giving hydrostatic pressure gradients along sieve-tubes between mature leaves and sinks. Measurements of these gradients vary between 0.5 and 5 atmospheres per metre (50 and 500 kilopascals per metre), and the gradients drive the liquid contents of the sieve-tubes at speeds of around 50 centimetres per hour. The energy for this transport is supplied by the leaf as ATP to the proton pumps which cause accumulation of sucrose in the symplast of the phloem. There is as yet no convincing evidence for additional mechanisms of energising the transport occurring along the sieve-tubes.

Damage to these high-pressure conduits in plants would cause bleeding, as in vertebrates. On release of pressure, filaments of phloem-protein held in the sieve-tube surge out, clog the sieve-plates and form a clot. The same pores are then tightly plugged within minutes by enzymic synthesis in the wall of a polysaccharide called callose.

The phloem transport system probably evolved before the xylem, which transports water. Brown algae use cells similar to sieve-tubes to send photosynthesised material down from illuminated fronds to sustain the holdfast in the murk below. The sugar transported in these sea-weeds is mannitol, not sucrose as in most plants. Mannitol is also used in the angiosperm family Oleaceae (including olive, ash and lilac), while sorbitol is used in the Rosaceae (including roses, apples and plums). These chemical alternatives to the sugars of cellular metabolism are used specially for transport, enabling the pattern of their formation, pumping, compartmentation and breakdown to be controlled separately from the metabolism of individual cells, and to suit instead the needs of an osmotic pressure pump; vertebrate animals can use glucose, a metabolically active sugar, for transport of carbon and of energy because they have a mechanical pressure pump, the heart.

The pumping of protons out of the phloem symplast makes the liquid of the sieve-tube alkaline, pH 8.0 to 8.5. This limits the capacity of the phloem to transport iron, calcium, manganese and copper ions, and they are said to be 'phloem-immobile'. Supplies of these to tissues are augmented by ions arriving apoplastically from the nearest xylem conduit, and deficiencies of these minerals show first in young leaves not actively transpiring.

In vascular plants, a major site for offloading of phloem is down in the roots, where sucrose is transferred, in the symplast, out to the **cortex** of young roots (the outer tissues around the central vascular bundle or **stele**, see Fig. 2.6) to supply energy for sorting, collecting and processing of the mineral elements during uptake by the plant.

Uptake of ions by the root

The photosynthetic parts of algae are directly bathed in mineral-rich water and carry out mineral uptake; their basal structures are for anchorage. In more complex plants with aerial photosynthetic structures, the basal parts, roots, have taken over the function of uptake of mineral ions.

Roots present an enormous surface area to the soil solution for the efficient uptake of ions. Off the main roots branch short-lived 'feeder' roots which are continuously renewed, reinvading the same soil. Also, epidermal cells grow a long hair-like extension, called a **root hair**, which increases the external surface area of the cell 30-fold. The total area presented to the soil at any moment by a single 4-month-old rye plant has been estimated at 630 square metres, a square 82 feet by 82 feet! But, like feeder roots, root hairs are ephemeral, so that the area of contact between root and soil over a period of time is many times greater than this figure. Ions from the soil solution diffuse freely through the cell walls of the whole root cortex, so the potential area of plasma membrane for uptake of ions is many times greater than the area of root surface.

In plants growing in the soil root-hair elongation is commonly suppressed, and roots are infected with endomycorrhizal fungi (see sections 2.3 and 10.1). In this fungus–root association, the fungus extends from the soil into cortical cells and benefits the plant by transferring minerals from the soil into the root; the fungus benefits by obtaining sugars from the root.

The potassium ion (K^+) is the mineral ion present in highest concentrations in plants as the chief cation in vacuoles, causing water to be retained osmotically and generating turgor, and it is also the principal electrolyte of cytoplasm. The sodium ion (Na^+) can substitute for the potassium ion in the vacuole, but is toxic in cytoplasm. In soil, potassium ions are held electrostatically on polyanionic surfaces of clay and humus particles, but exchange freely on to polyanionic cell-wall polymers. Uptake of potassium ions from low external concentrations is by a high-affinity potassium-ion pump in the plasma membrane, powered directly by hydrolysis of ATP and discriminating against sodium ions. At high external potassium-ion concentrations, a high-capacity uptake system can also operate: potassium and sodium ions are driven up their concentration gradients across the plasma membrane by the presence of a steeper electrical gradient (-100 millivolts (mV) inside) generated by pumping out hydrogen ions (H^+, hydrated protons). Uptake of the ammonium cation (NH_4^+) also occurs on a high-affinity pump, resembling that for uptake of potassium ions but with a high specificity for ammonium ions.

Nitrogen, phosphorus and sulphur atoms are covalently linked into and onto carbon skeletons to make the organic molecules of living systems. In soil they occur chiefly as insoluble remnants of those systems, and they are released by the action of micro-organisms. For nitrogen, the ammonium ion is the first stage to accumulate and, except on acid soils where there are fewer nitrifying bacteria, this is all oxidised to nitrate (NO_3^-) within a few days. Sulphur must similarly undergo bacterial oxidation to sulphate (SO_4^{2-}) before uptake into plants. Organic phospho-groups are hydrolysed to release inorganic phosphate ($H_2PO_4^-$ and HPO_4^{2-}, together called P_i).

The nitrate is very soluble and thus freely available in soil, and nitrifying bacteria in the soil normally fix enough nitrogen gas to ensure sufficient nitrates for plant growth. Only in waterlogged soil where there is not enough oxygen for these bacteria does nitrogen become limiting for plants. An increased availability of nitrate ions causes roots to increase their capacity for uptake of nitrates. Inorganic phosphate and sulphate ions are largely immobilised in soil by strong adsorption on clay micelles or as insoluble salts of divalent and trivalent cations. The plant's requirements for sulphate are modest and the anion is common, so it does not matter that only a small fraction of the total soil content of sulphate ions is available, but phosphate is a major nutrient and the ions are in short supply in natural soils. The poor mobility of phosphate ions in soils means that they do not diffuse to the root at an appreciable rate, as do nitrate ions, and roots have to keep growing to continue to find phosphate to take up. When the availability of phosphate ions is very low, mycorrhizal plants are not so severely affected because the fungus is better at phosphate-ion uptake and storage than are the roots. There are separate high-affinity and low-affinity uptake mechanisms for phosphate ions, and a high-affinity uptake mechanism for sulphate ions.

All the divalent and trivalent cations taken up, such as magnesium, calcium and zinc ions, activate specific enzymes; and the transition metals iron, copper, manganese and molybdenum also take part in oxidation–reduction reactions. Except for calcium, magnesium and iron the requirement is small, and so the remainder are called 'trace' nutrients. The calcium ion (Ca^{2+}) is the major counter-ion for cell-wall polyanions; the magnesium ion (Mg^{2+}) is a component of chlorophyll and the principal divalent cation in cytoplasm; and iron is used in many electron-transport proteins including ferredoxin and the cytochromes (see Fig. 1.9).

In fertile soils, calcium ions predominate on the polyanionic surfaces of clay and humus particles. They can be displaced by hydrogen ions, so countering any local increase in acidity. The level of calcium ions in the soil, which varies widely, therefore determines the soil pH on which the availability of all divalent and trivalent metals depends. At an alkaline pH these metals precipitate, reducing the availability of phosphate ions, while at acidic pHs they are very soluble and leach away. There is an uptake system for divalent cations for which all these metal ions seem to compete. Except on special soils deficient in or superabundant in particular metals, this competition does not seem to cause problems. However, a low rate of uptake of iron can limit growth even in ordinary soils because, as for phosphates, the plant's need for this nutrient is great and, except on acid soils, the availability of iron is low; the roots of 'iron-efficient' plants increase the availability of iron, in part by secreting hydrogen ions.

As potassium ions, sodium ions and ammonium ions are pumped in, sugars are converted to organic acids to provide a counter-anion (malate$^-$) plus hydrogen ions to pump out, to maintain electrical neutrality. Most phosphate ions are covalently bound to organic molecules on uptake, but nitrate and sulphate ions have to be reduced before incorporation as amino (—NH_2) and sulphydryl (—SH) groups. Nitrite ions (NO_2^-) are produced in the cytoplasm by nitrate reductase, and the synthesis of this enzyme is induced by nitrate ions. The reductions of nitrite and sulphate ions occur inside plastids. For most plants on natural soils some of the nitrate ions are reduced in the roots and some in the leaves, but all the sulphate ions are reduced in the leaves.

Provision of the reducing power for the reduction of nitrate ions in roots requires sugar, but phosphorylating ADP to provide ATP for uptake of ions also requires oxygen. Respiration in roots depends on oxygen from the atmosphere diffusing through the soil gas phase, or through the plant in a network of gas-filled intercellular spaces extending down into the root cortex.

The total supply of mineral ions in the soil fluctuates widely due to evaporation, rainfall and irregularities in the distribution, composition and size of decomposing objects. Roots buffer the plant over lean periods, as their high-capacity low-affinity uptake systems and massive storage in the vacuoles of the cortical cells (making up 70% of the root volume) maximise the ability of the roots to make use of large quantities of ions when these suddenly become available.

To the inside of the absorptive cortex there is a single layer of cells, the **endodermis**, which forms a cylindrical sheath around the core of the root, the stele, and isolates the inner (stelar) apoplast, which contains a rich solution of selected ions, from the outer (cortical) apoplast, which approximates in composition to the soil solution; this prevents the ions leaking back out. This isolation is achieved by impregnating the radial walls of the endodermal cells with suberin, a waterproof and ion-proof polyester similar to cutin, in a band distributed so as to seal the interface between the cell walls of the cortex and stele: the 'Casparian band'. The minerals collected by the whole cortex move, together with water, through the endodermis in the symplast and into the living cells of the stele.

Only a section of the root near the tip exports minerals to the xylem in this way. Very close to the tip, before xylem and endodermis are formed, the ions absorbed from the soil are used for growth of the root, while further back along the root, behind the uptake zone, the outermost cortical cells become a suberised protective exodermis, isolating the cortex from the soil solution.

Xylem transport from the root

The conduits up to the leaves are cells of the xylem tissue. The contents of these cells, including the plasma membrane, have autolysed, and so they exchange freely with the liquid in the stelar cell walls, which is a rich solution of mineral ions from still-living xylem cells. The solution contains organic acid anions, including the chelating agent citrate to keep divalent and polyvalent cations in solution; the pH of 5.5 to 5.7 prevents any precipitation. The contents of the xylem conduits move upwards because the liquid is under tension, evaporation of water from the leaf surface (transpiration) providing a force that is communicated to the roots via an unbroken thread of liquid. The process depends on strong bonds preventing the column of water snapping (the tensile strength of water is, amazingly, 10% of that of copper wire), and on the water holding onto the inner surface of the conduit.

In angiosperms the conduits are **xylem vessels**, made of cells 0.2 millimetres wide called vessel members, the end-walls of which are digested to leave an open tube or column up to several metres long. The interior of the tube is prevented from collapsing and is held open against tension exerted on the walls by the adhering liquid contents, by ribs of cellulose sealed rigid in an incompressible matrix of lignin. Removal of the end-walls

of vessel members in angiosperms is an advance on the xylem system of other plants, which have autolysed, lignin-braced cells called **tracheids** but with the passage from tracheid to tracheid being through windows of unlignified wall. Gymnosperm tracheids are a few millimetres long, and only a tenth the width of angiosperm vessels, and so their resistance to water flow is much greater even without considering the intervention of end-walls.

Since it is about a million times easier to pull water through vessels than across living tissue, the rate of transport to the leaf is increased by minimising the extent to which water has to travel through the mesophyll. Mesophyll is thus packed with fine veins (3.8 metres of them in a single beech leaf), and no cell is more than six cells from a vein that is sufficiently fine to be able to offload.

Fine leaf veins are sheathed in a single layer of living cells, the **bundle sheath**, tightly fitted to seal the vein (see Fig. 2.3). In some advanced angiosperms the inner walls of the bundle sheath cells have similar finger-like ingrowths to those of the leaf companion cells, providing a three- to ten-fold increase in the area of plasma membrane for uptake of ions into the bundle sheath from the xylem apoplast; such cells are termed **transfer cells**. The bundle sheath is so effective a 'kidney' for the absorption of ions that solutes from the stelar apoplast hardly spread at all into mesophyll cell walls, even though in leaves there is no Casparian band around the stele.

The mineral ions are thus taken into the symplast of leaves and the water is drawn out to the evaporative surface of mesophyll cells, travelling part of the way in cell walls and the rest of the way through the symplast.

Growth and development

Primary growth

The products of mature leaves and roots arrive via stems at the centres of growth in the plant for assembly into more leaves, roots and stems. The process of forming these tissues is known as **primary growth**. In macroscopic plants of parenchymatous construction (that is, produced by controlled cell division in three dimensions), specialised zones, **meristems**, carry out cell division for growth. The most efficient siting of new organs for collecting light (shoots) and minerals (roots) favours extension of the plant at its periphery, that is, at the apex of each axis.

The organs specialised to carry out apical growth are apical meristems. Each is a small dome (0.1 to 0.25 millimetres across) of a few thousand cells, comprising a single central cell (in fucoid brown algae, bryophytes and pteridophytes) or a group of cells (in gymnosperms and angiosperms) dividing slowly, and outer and basal layers of cells, called **initials**, dividing rapidly to add to the axis. In angiosperm roots the central cells, called the quiescent centre, determine the shape of the axis and regenerate the initials after damage, while in shoots the central

Fig. 2.6. *Diagram of a longitudinal section through the tip of a root to show the sequence of development of the primary tissue of the root.*

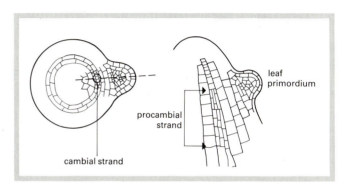

Fig. 2.7. *Diagrams showing how in the shoot apex the pattern of formation of leaf primordia determines the pattern of vascular tissue.*

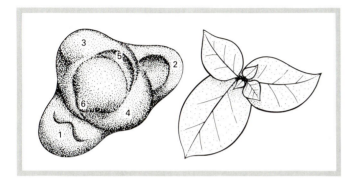

cells have a role in organisation but not in regeneration. By controlling the planes and rates of cell division, the apical meristem moves outward on top of a solid rod of cells. Cell division ceases first in the centre and at the surface of this rod, leaving a hollow cylinder of cells still dividing (hollow not because it is full of air, but because the cells inside it are not dividing), and these dividing cells form the specialised transport cells.

Root tips show a reasonably clear pattern of a zone of cell division, followed by a zone of cell expansion and, further back, by a zone in which specialised functions develop, a process known as differentiation. While cells continue to divide they remain small, but once they cease to be halved in size at frequent intervals the increase in volume is uninterrupted. Wide vessels, metaxylem, form in the centre of the root, and are produced early so as to have achieved their full size by the time this part of the root has begun to export material. The hollow cylinder of dividing cells becomes a cylinder of strands of dividing cells. Alternate strands become phloem and protoxylem, this latter developing rapidly, with small vessels, to operate until the metaxylem is functional. The phloem functions first, however, to service growing tissues that are not yet exporting. Over the apical end of the meristem is a root cap of constantly eroded, constantly regenerated, slime-secreting cells, which eases the passage of the soft apical dome through the soil (Fig. 2.6).

This simple pattern of primary growth in the root is complicated in the shoot by the development of leaves (Fig. 2.7). Each leaf begins as a bump, called a **primordium**, on the sloping side of the meristematic dome, pushed out by a local but deep-seated intensification of growth as the apical meristem begins to produce more meristems. The position of each primordium is influenced by the apical dome and nearby primordia, so that each leaf arises in the same relative position to the previous leaf, to form a pattern characteristic of the particular species (its **phyllotaxis**). This is often a spiral in which eight leaves complete five turns and so minimise self-shading.

Inside the axis, under each primordium, longitudinal cell divisions are stimulated in the cells of the hollow cylinder, an influence which extends a short way down forming a 'procambial strand' ('cambium' describes a meristematic region of vascular tissue). As primordia accumulate, the hollow cylinder is converted to procambial strands, each of which will form xylem and phloem. In the shoot, therefore, the pattern of transport tissues is fixed by the leaves these tissues will service.

Leaves are formed by a sequence of meristems with fixed life-spans ('determinate' meristems) (Fig. 2.8), beginning with a superficially located apical meristem in which cell division stops when a tiny peg, 1 millimetre long, has formed. Next, cells down either side of the length of this peg begin to divide, growing out as the rim of a thin plate of five to six cell layers, the marginal meristem. The peg becomes the midrib of the leaf and the plate becomes the leaf blade. The final seven to ten cell layers form in a wave of divisions from tip to base.

An inherited programme restricting the duration or distribution of these meristems controls the shape of the leaf, so that for conifer needles, for example, marginal meristem activity is very limited. Compound leaves of ferns and of many dicotyledons form by restricting the marginal meristem to isolated sites along the peg, each of which generates a subunit of the leaf.

Although the conventional meristem sequence is followed by some monocotyledons, grasses and lilies for example, in the other monocotyledons there are extra meristematic phases (Fig. 2.8). The marginal meristem ceases activity after the primordium base has encircled the apical dome, and a new 'abaxial meristem' on the upper, outer surface (abaxial means 'away from the axis') makes radially symmetrical leaf tissue on a sheath with distinct outer and inner faces formed by the basal 'sheathing meristem'. The abaxial meristem may make the bulk of the leaf as in onions and rushes, or no more than its stubby tip as in tulips and bananas. Suppression of the marginal meristem in these monocotyledons has led to an alternative system for forming compound leaves, by which parts of a leaf autolyse leaving gaps at appropriate sites, as in the 'Swiss cheese plant' *Monstera* and all palms. Autolysis is similarly used to generate the compound fronds of laminarian brown algae.

Cell expansion follows production of the cells by division. The layers of mesophyll which stop expanding first are pulled apart, forming the spongy mesophyll. Whole cells autolyse to make the substomatal cavity. Expansion is completed first in the tip, passing down to the leaf stalk or petiole, if this is present, and in which it may persist for positional adjustment of the leaf. To connect each developing leaf to the transport network, a meristematic strand is induced which grows down towards the top of the procambial strand for that leaf (Fig. 2.7), and the base of the procambial strand makes contact laterally with older strands. Phloem develops first up these meristematic strands, but xylem differentiation follows the pattern of progress of the procambial strand.

Various meristematic zones throughout the stem are responsible for general increases in size. In dicotyledons there is a sudden increase in length, delayed in rosette plants, and this occurs due to a 'sub-apical' meristem. In grasses, stem lengthening activity persists, confined to a band just above the site of leaf attachment; these 'intercalary meristems' also occur at the base of grass leaves where they reduce damage caused by grazing. They are also a feature of laminarian sea-weeds, the new fronds of which arise between the old fronds and the stipe (stem). Monocotyledons concentrate the cell divisions for thickening the stem in a collar of tissue, the 'primary thickening meristem', just below the slender apical dome, and xylem and phloem crossing this and crossing the intercalary meristems are being constantly stretched, destroyed and replaced.

Special cells are responsible for transport and support functions in expanding tissues. The ribs in protoxylem vessels are separate rings or an extensible spiral. Phloem is supported by fibres, cells which extend at their ends, boring between expanding cells while their middle section fills with an inextensible cellulose wall. Under the epidermis, there are collenchyma cells with very thick walls of alternating layers of cellulose, for support, and pectin, to allow the wall to extend in concert with surrounding cells.

Detailed finishing touches to the development of primary tissue are made by **meristemoids**, tiny meristems scattered over the epidermis: isolated cells recommence cell division and then differentiate to guard cells, multicellular hairs or glands.

The pattern of shape-determining cell divisions within apical and leaf meristems is under an unknown and strictly internal control. The whole shoot apical meristem will only function if the rest of the plant supplies it with one or more of the plant growth regulators, in this case auxin, cytokinin and gibberellin, the actual requirements depending on the particular species. Almost all natural **auxin** is indol-3-yl-acetic acid, synthesised in dividing cells and autolysing xylem, and exported from the shoot tip towards the root through parenchyma cells of the stele by a mechanism of directional ('polar') transport at 1 centimetre per hour. The major **cytokinin** is *trans*-zeatin, made in dividing cells and exported from the root. The predominant active natural **gibberellins** are a variety of gibberellic acids (GA_1, GA_4 and GA_7), probably made in developing plastids and exported from young leaves; the exact gibberellin present depends on the particular species of plant.

Developing leaves influence the developing stem that will support them by exporting auxin and gibberellin to that stem. The subapical meristem responds to gibberellin by increased cell division, and cell expansion in the stem is dependent on, though not normally limited by, a supply of auxin. Expansion of stem cells is also promoted by gibberellin in plants such as grasses and composites. The differentiation into fibres by cells that are preprogrammed to do so is triggered by auxin and gibberellin together. Roots influence leaf development in that in some plants their export of cytokinin increases with the supply of minerals, and cytokinin stimulates expansion of leaf cells.

Primary growth is linked to a variety of other important environmental signals, including wind, light and wounding. Winds and obstacles increase the synthesis of **ethene**. This gaseous plant growth regulator converts longitudinal cell expansion into radial cell expansion to produce a short, stress-resistant axis.

Cell expansion can be influenced to turn the axis back to the vertical (**gravitropism**, sensitivity to gravity) or parallel to the light (**phototropism**, sensitivity to light, in this case blue light). The cells which are sensitive to gravity and to the direction of blue light are the root caps in roots, the bundle sheath for controlling leaf orientation, and in stems often the endodermis. The sensory apparatus lies in plastids: for geotropism special amyloplasts (starch-storing plastids) which fall to the bottom of the cell, unlike normal amyloplasts which retain a fixed position, and for phototropism yellow chromoplasts; but the actual processes involved remain a mystery.

Plants detect other plants overhead by monitoring light in the near-infrared using a coloured protein, phytochrome, that has two forms (P_r and P_{fr}) mutually interconvertible by red light (optimal wavelength 660 nanometres, but in general light shorter than 700 nanometres, producing P_{fr} from P_r) and far-red light (optimal wavelength 740 nanometres, but in general light longer than 700 nanometres, producing P_r from P_{fr}). The transparency of leaves to far-red light, which ensures that they remain cool, causes the light under leaves to be enriched in far-red. Developing leaves respond to this far-red enrichment by producing a decreased number of stomata; they respond to red light by increasing the number of stomata, which allows them

Fig. 2.8. Diagrams illustrating the sequences of meristematic phases involved in generating: (a) simple leaves of dicotyledons, grasses and lilies; (b) the leaves of other monocotyledons; and (c) compound leaves of dicotyledons.

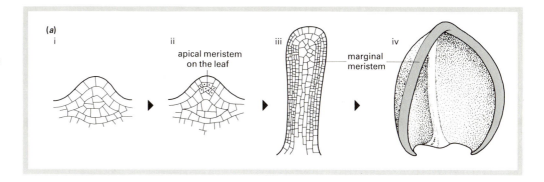

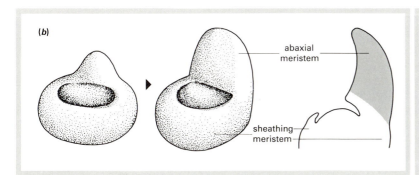

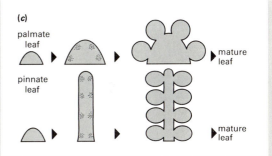

the potentially higher rates of photosynthesis and cooling needed in an unshaded position.

Wounds and damage interrupt polar transport of auxin, and almost all cells are programmed to revert to mitotic cell division in response to the local accumulation of auxin which results; the wound thus becomes filled with disorganised tissue, called callus, which subsequently differentiates to restore the original functions, completing the regeneration sequence.

Secondary growth

Meristems dormant in the primary tissue of vascular plants can be re-activated in a variety of ways in a programme of further expansion known as **secondary growth**.

As individual axes extend outwards by their primary growth, they get further apart; branching fills the gaps. In lower parenchymatous plants, such as fucoid sea-weeds, liverworts and many ferns, the apical meristem can reorganise to form two. In other plants, however, dormant meristems in the axis recommence activity when signalled by, for example, damage to the apical shoot, or by local concentrations of mineral nutrients, or by some internal programme. Dormant meristems for shoot branches are on the surface of the axis so as to be able to intercept local increases in light intensity; root branches begin deep inside the root as outgrowths of the stele.

Patterns of branching differ between individual species, and there is no single control mechanism. A common pattern is for dormant shoot buds to contain inhibitors, including **abscisic acid**. The buds break down these inhibitors, and grow out, when the stream of auxin brought by polar transport is reduced, such as by removal of the apical shoot. The dominance of the apical shoot is sensitive to the supply of nutrients through the intermediate link of cytokinins, which relax it, and apical dominance is more severe in conditions of water stress when abscisic acid synthesis increases. In contrast, lateral root

formation is stimulated by auxin arriving by polar transport, communicating the need for increased services for the expanding shoot.

When axes are taxed by accumulating leaves and branches, they either sprawl and sprout extra, 'adventitious', roots to supply the extra minerals and water or, in living gymnosperms and woody angiosperms, they initiate a developmental programme called 'secondary thickening' for increasing the support, and supply of vascular tissue, to the axes. Palms adopt an alternative strategy of thickening, using the primary thickening meristem, before the stem elongates.

In secondary thickening, cells between xylem and phloem and between the vascular strands recommence mitotic cell division, recreating the hollow cylinder of dividing cells, now termed the **vascular cambium**. Its meristematic initials are already full-sized except in the radial dimension, and they expand in this dimension after dividing lengthways to add cells inwards to the xylem and outwards to the phloem. Wood is secondary xylem, and mostly consists of dead tracheids (gymnosperms) or vessels (angiosperms). Radial incursions of blocks of living cells, known as rays from the pattern on cross-sections of tree trunks, booby-trap old vessels with antifungal blockages, called tyloses, and with chemicals toxic to fungi. Ray initials are small and divide more slowly than the surrounding cambium, but this is compensated for by extended radial elongation of the developing ray cell.

Accumulation of xylem cells inside the ring of cambium stretches this ring. In some species, cambial cells are divided by a radially oriented cell plate, adding to the ring of initials to accommodate the expansion in circumference. This is a 'storied' cambium. In other species the pointed ends of the initials elongate, pushing their way between other initials to give a 'fusiform' cambium. Wood from a fusiform cambium is less regular in its internal structure and is therefore less likely to split along lines of weakness.

The layers of cells to the outside of the vascular cambium are stretched even more by the secondary growth, and their protection requires the constant regeneration of an increasingly more extensive skin of cork, which is made of tightly fitted square cells with heavily suberinised walls. The cork-forming meristem is separate and exterior to the vascular cambium. In some species it keeps pace with internal expansion and the bark is smooth; alternatively, outer layers are abandoned at intervals with new cork cambia starting further in, causing the bark to be rough. To allow oxygen to get to the living tissues under the cork, scattered patches of cork cambium produce round, loose-fitting cells, erupting through the surface of the bark, as ventilation structures called lenticels.

Like elongation, secondary thickening in the stem seems to be coupled to the growth of the foliage the stem will be sustaining. Cambial cell division depends on a supply of auxin and gibberellin. Gibberellin produced in the plastids promotes the differentiation of phloem to transport the sugars these plastids will export, while auxin from the rest of the developing shoot promotes the differentiation of xylem to support and supply this shoot. Vascular cambium in the root, like branching of roots, is activated by polarly transported auxin.

Transformation

When a cell differentiates, its biochemistry and structure undergo a shift to a new stable pattern, the result of changing over to using a new set of genes for programming the cell (see sections 1.6 and 3.1). When this shift affects large groups of cells simultaneously, as in whole organs, meristems or individual organisms, they are said to **transform**. Transformation is used in the construction of parts of the plant body, so that, for example, the apical meristems of branches transform to the determinate state (in which their subsequent activity is restricted) to make feeder roots, or to make 'short shoots' in pines and fruit trees. As they constitute large-scale transitions in activity, transformation events also steer the plant through the phases of its life-cycle, either under the control of internal programming or in response to the environment.

For seed plants, the first transformation occurs when the embryo enters dormancy. The accumulation of inhibitors from the surrounding tissue, including abscisic acid, contributes to the transition. In many species embryos subsequently resume growth when the inhibitors are no longer present, while in other species the embryos refuse to germinate unless they receive a particular sequence of signals. This innate dormancy is a transformed state which evolved to ensure that germination is restricted to a suitable environment for survival of the species. Competence to process the signals is acquired on soaking the dry seeds, and prolonged chilling, red light, alternating temperature and the nitrate anion are commonly used as environmental signals. The nature of the sensors in the seed is unknown, except for phytochrome in the case of light.

There is evidence that a correct sequence of signals brings about increased levels of active cytokinins, or gibberellins, or both, which transform the embryo back to an active state.

The next important transformation for the plant is into the flowering state, a two-stage process involving the transformation (induction) of the youngest mature leaf into a state of competence to transform shoot meristems into flowers. When the process is cued by the environment a variety of signals may be processed by the leaf, such as prolonged chilling or the length of the night (photoperiodism). In photoperiodic induction, the connection between the light signal, picked up by phytochrome, and induction is limited by internal physiological 'clocks' to pre-set times. One type of clock, started at dawn and running for 24 hours (a circadian rhythm), reinforces another which is started at dusk and runs for a shorter period characteristic for each plant. Phytochrome is converted enzymatically to the P_r form in the dark, and the P_{fr} form is then generated by light at dawn. At the measured time after nightfall, and not until then, the presence of any of the P_{fr} form of phytochrome will block the induction of the leaf, and this induction may need several long nights to complete. There are two groups of plants: autumn-flowering 'short-day' plants in which the induced leaves transform the plant from the non-flowering state to the flowering state, and spring-flowering 'long-day' plants in which the induced leaves transform the plant from the flowering state to the non-flowering state.

The mechanism by which the induced leaf influences shoot meristems is obscure. There is evidence that the production of growth-regulator chemicals by the leaf, or the redistribution by the leaf of growth substances from the roots, is altered in ways that are complex and that differ between species just as the control of flowering does. Transformation of shoot meristems to flowers involves transition to the determinate state, production of whorls of primordia, and their transformation, often under the influence of growth regulators, to male or female flower parts, petals, sepals and so on.

Control of the formation of dormant buds in woody species is similar. The leaf is transformed in response to the environment, usually to drought or long nights, and then it transforms leaf primordia, which then develop as bud scales, and shoot apical meristems, so that these become innately dormant. Transforming dormant buds back into active meristems involves signals similar to those for germination, for example prolonged chilling for many winter buds.

The ultimate transformation for any part of the plant is into **senescence**, which is not simply the sudden ceasing of life but is a coordinated synthesis of new enzymes for a self-regulating programme of autolysis and mobilisation of materials from the senescing part, terminating in its release from the rest of the plant at a precise site in a process known as **abscission**. A similar sequence occurs in fruit tissues during ripening, being the sequel to the expansion of the fruit, a self-regulating programme signalled in most plants by growth substances supplied by the pollen at pollination. Transformation into senescence is in response to declining levels of auxin, cytokinin and gibberellin (and increased levels of abscisic acid where it is a response to drought). The progress of subsequent events is accelerated by ethene, produced at high rates by senescing and ripening tissue; the ethene activates cell expansion and dissolution of the cell wall in mature abscission zones, the sites of abscission.

In some species, the whole plant enters the senescence programme, usually after setting seed, and the signal for this transformation appears to come from the seeds. Such 'monocarpic' plants (dying after a single flowering) are mostly annuals and biennials, but spectacular examples of this phenomenon in perennials include bamboos and some large tropical trees.

Life-cycles

Among plants, especially algae, there is a variety of life-cycles, and some of these are very complex. The complexity occurs because a number of functions have to be fitted into the cycle, as well as allowing accumulation of material by biosynthesis and growth. The most important of these functions are the scattering of more individuals to spread the species, and the exchange of genetic information between individuals to create new variants so that the species may adapt. Dispersal and adaptation both increase the chance that the species will survive. Although sessile multicellular forms are most successful for competitive exploitation of the rich environment of land masses and their coasts, being sessile is incompatible with the scattering of individuals and the exchange of genetic information. So, the sessile state of multicellular plants could only evolve at limited stages of the life-cycle, these being separated by forms capable of the functions of dispersal and genetic exchange.

Free-living unicellular forms still carry out dispersal for simple plants, and are termed **spores**. In many aquatic algae flagella have been retained, and such spores are called zoospores. The cycle of production of spores, their dispersal, attachment, and subsequent development into a sessile multicellular individual is widespread among algae. Because exchange of genes between individuals is not involved this is asexual reproduction. Simple cycles involving portions of sessile plant bodies modified for dispersal and regeneration are found frequently throughout the plant kingdom, for example underground stems in bracken and tubers in potatoes, and such cycles are termed vegetative reproduction.

Free-living cells involved in genetic exchange are known as **gametes**, and are haploid (see section 1.5). While spores are developmentally primed to attach themselves to the substratum, gametes are primed to attach themselves to another gamete, to fuse and to form a diploid cell (the **zygote**), and then to attach to the substratum before developing into a new sessile individual. Somewhere after the diploid zygote and before the production of haploid gametes by the new individual there must be a meiotic cell division (see section 1.5). In charophyte

and filamentous green algae, the zygote itself undergoes meiosis and so the entire sessile phase is haploid. In the fucoid group of brown algae meiosis immediately precedes gamete production (as it does in animals) and so the sessile phase is diploid.

In the laminarian brown algae, many green algae, the red algae, bryophytes and pteridophytes, the sexual cycle is elaborated by inserting an obligatory phase of proliferation by spores. These spores are products of meiotic divisions on a diploid sessile form (the **sporophyte**) and they develop into a haploid sessile form (the **gametophyte**) that produces gametes by mitosis. The zygotes from fusion of these gametes develop into sporophytes, and the cycle is called an **alternation of generations** between sporophyte and gametophyte (Fig. 3.6).

Selection for more efficient progress through the life-cycle operates continuously on the members of all groups of plants. Similar advances appear to have occurred separately in different groups, suggesting that there are only a few ways to improve the life-cycle, and the adaptations found in gametes, sessile forms and spores can be considered to a certain extent independently of their particular plant type.

Gametes

The simpler green algae (such as *Ulva* and *Cladophora*) and brown algae (such as *Ectocarpus*) produce biflagellate gametes all of which look identical within each species (**isogamy**), although chemical differences between gametes of a species must exist because only two from different individuals will fuse.

Selection favours gametes containing the most food reserves because this provides the best start for the next sessile stage, but selection also favours gametes with the least food because these can move most efficiently. The best solution is for a species to produce both types of gamete, but to ensure that each gamete fuses only with a gamete of the opposite type: hence sexual differences evolved. In less extreme examples of such specialisation, the larger, 'female' gamete still has flagella and moves (**anisogamy**): this type is found, for example, in the brown alga *Cutleria* and the siphonaceous green algae. In all but these simplest plants, however, the female gamete is a completely non-motile egg (**oogamy**), for example in the fucoid brown algae.

With substantial investments in fewer, larger eggs, selection favours types in which the egg cells are protected during development (Fig. 2.9). In fucoids and some red algae they develop in a pit, called a conceptacle, sunk into the tissue of the frond, and in charophyte green algae protective cells grow over each egg. The female gamete of mosses and ferns develops in the bottom of a bag-shaped organ with a long, narrow neck, the archegonium, which in ferns is sunk into surrounding tissue.

Because the mature egg is a non-motile gamete and no longer transfers between individuals, selection favours types in which it is not released when mature, as it is in fucoids, but is retained

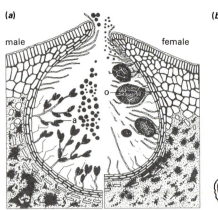

(a) male female

o
a

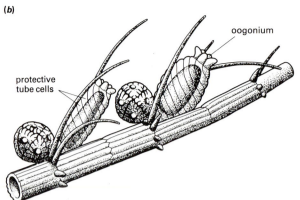

(b) oogonium

protective tube cells

Fig. 2.9. Examples of protection afforded to egg cells during their development: (a) in fucoid phaeophyte algae where both types of gamete develop in pits, 'conceptacles', sunk into the tissue of the frond; and (b) in charophyte green algae where, although the female gametes still develop in a superficial position, protective cells grow over the outer surface of each egg.

for safety on the sessile form, as occurs in red algae and charophyte green algae. In charophytes the successfully fertilised zygote is released, but in red algae there is first an extra proliferative phase in which the zygote divides to generate diploid spores called carpospores, which are released.

The logical extension of minimising the risk of losing material invested in eggs is for the subsequent sessile form derived from the zygote to be retained on the parent sessile form, an option only available to types with more than one sessile phase so that there will still be some means of dispersal. This type of life-cycle has been adopted by laminarians, mosses and ferns, and their diploid sporophyte grows out of the haploid gametophyte; the spores produced by meiosis from the sporophyte are now the only forms carrying out dispersal.

Sessile forms

There are many examples of life-cycles in which the gametophyte and sporophyte are similar (isomorphic alternation of generations) in the green algae (such as *Ulva*), brown algae (such as *Dictyota*) and red algae (such as *Rhodymenia*). The advantages of strict alternation of generations in these cases are not obvious. In many of the larger and more elaborate types, however, these two phases are specialised and differ markedly from each other (heteromorphic alternation of generations).

Sometimes the bulk of the biosynthetic accumulation and development occurs in the haploid gametophyte, as for the brown alga *Cutleria*. With evolution towards retention of egg, zygote and sporophyte on the gametophyte, the biosynthetic function of the sporophyte may be completely lost and its function is then solely to produce the spores for dispersal, as in bryophytes and in the red alga *Phyllophora truncata*; the sporophyte generation of *Phyllophora* is reduced to 'warts' on the gametophyte.

Alternatively, the diploid sporophyte may be responsible for the bulk of photosynthetic production as in laminarian seaweeds, ferns and the seed plants (gymnosperms and angiosperms). One reason why it is this alternative that has given rise to the most complex and efficient forms is that diploid organisms are superior to haploid types in their evolutionary adaptability, because genetic variation that has no immediate selective advantage can in diploids be stored concealed from selection as recessive genes, for future adaptive use (see section 3.2). In the seed plants the haploid sessile phase has been eliminated from the life-cycle (in fucoids too there is only diploid tissue). Another reason for the larger size of the diploid form may be specialisation of the two sessile phases, so that

gametophytes carry out efficient exchange of gametes, and sporophytes carry out efficient dispersal of spores. Laminarian gametophytes are tiny threads forming a dense felt close to the sea floor, and large numbers of genetically different individuals very close to each other in a sheltered site make for efficient transfer of flagellate gametes with minimal self-fertilisation or loss. The spores, by contrast, are dispersed into moving water from large, comparatively widely separated sporophytes (the kelps). Similarly, in ferns, liquid water is required for the flagellate male gametes to move between individual gametophytes, and as this process is thus restricted to a film close to the substratum the gametophytes are equally low-growing.

In some plants, specialisation of the gametophytes extends to the type of gametes produced. Even morphologically isogamous types may have two types of gametophyte, distinguishable because the gametes they produce fuse only with those from the opposite type; *Ulva* is an example. The brown alga *Dictyota* is oogamous, and male gametes and eggs are produced on separate individuals. Such gametophytes are said to be unisexual; among land plants, horsetails have unisexual gametophytes.

Spores

The same disruptive selection that operates on gametes, for large food stores and also for high mobility, also operates on spores (Fig. 2.10). Provided the sporophyte is sufficiently robust to live in moving water this medium will disperse even comparatively large propagules, such as fucoid zygotes. The sporophyte of the brown alga *Dictyota* produces large, non-flagellate spores, in groups of four (tetraspores) after meiosis, for passive dispersal; production of tetraspores is a characteristic of red algae. Alternatively, in minimising the gametophyte that grows from the spores, laminarians have reduced the need for a large food store in the spores and these have remained small (and flagellate). The tiny spores of land plants are dispersed passively through the air by various agencies such as wind or insects, protected by a tough, waterproof coat of sporopollenin.

Although the gametophyte phase in clubmosses, horsetails, ferns and their allies is very inferior to the sporophyte in size and organisation, it is generally still free-living and usually bisexual (each gametophyte producing both male and female gametes). However some pteridophytes retain the tiny gametophyte within the protection of the spore coat (endospory), growing out only for transfer of male gametes. Such gametophytes, unable to photosynthesise within the spore coat, must

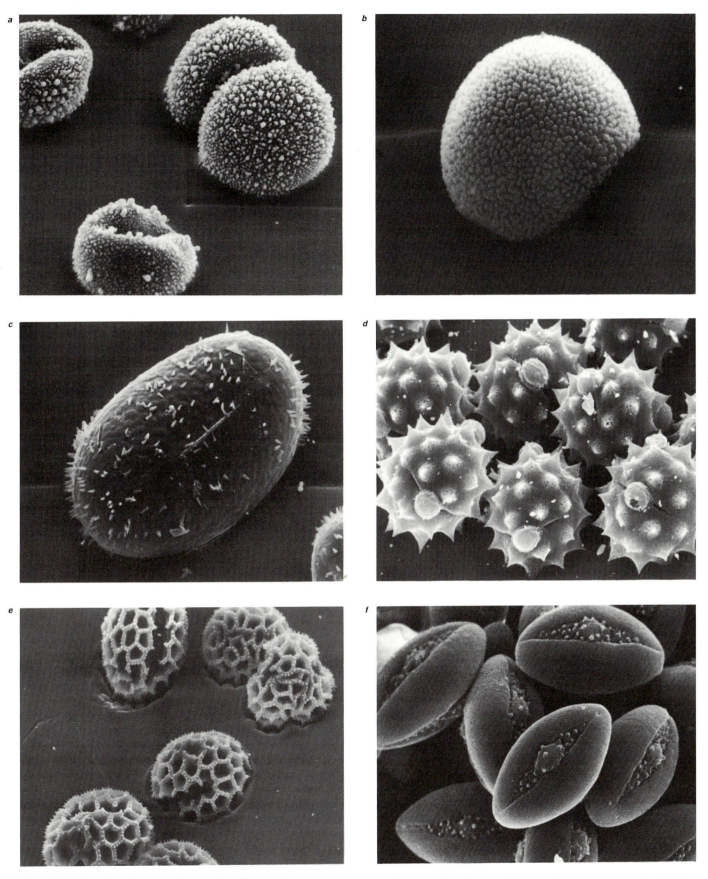

Fig. 2.10. Scanning electron micrographs of spores from different plant types: from the mosses Polytrichum gracile *(×1650) (a) and* funaria *(×3500) (b), from the fern* Polypodium *(×1100) (c), pollen (microspores) from the angiosperm dicotyledons.* Chrysanthemum mycoais *(×1225) (d), Armeria maritima, thrift (×400) (e) and* Aesculus hippocastranum, *horsechestnut (×1250) (f).*

be provisioned with reserves in the spore by the previous generation, for the task of supplying the initial materials required for the next generation. Again, however, stored food in the spore would restrict its mobility required for dispersion. The problem has been solved in the same way that it was solved in the case of gametes. Spores are dimorphic (a state called **heterospory**, which is always found combined with unisexual gametophytes) in all endosporic types: quillworts, *Selaginella* (both related to clubmosses), and two very distinct groups of aquatic ferns. All have evolved ponderous **megaspores** which develop into female gametophytes, and tiny, dispersible **microspores** which develop into male gametophytes releasing just a few gametes in close proximity to the egg. The dispersibility of spores is used in these cases for providing exchange of gametes, instead of for scattering individuals as it is in mosses and ferns, and liberates the exchange of genotypes from the severe limitations of short-range, flagellar motion through liquid.

The final step in the process of modifying the life-cycle towards minimal risk is the retention of the megaspore on the parent sporophyte until the egg in the gametophyte it contains is safely fertilised; the sporophyte of the next generation can in consequence receive further food materials from the parent sporophyte and can then be dispersed in a unit, the **seed**, containing this stored food. The chief distinction between the two groups of seed plants, gymnosperms and angiosperms, is in the degree of protection given to the developing megaspore. Megaspores develop in a blob of tissue, the nucellus, which is protected by layers of cells which grow up around it, the integuments. The whole assemblage is called an **ovule**. Male gametes are released from the microspore when this reaches the ovule, and in most cases the ovule goes on to become the unit of dispersal. Plants in which ovules are freely exposed at the surface of the plant are termed gymnosperms ('naked seed'); in other plants, angiosperms ('encased seed'), the ovules are hidden away, protected inside hollow envelopes, the carpels, made by fusing leaf-like organs along their edges.

In gymnosperms, the microspores (pollen) arrive at the nucellus through a hole, the micropyle, left during the development of the integuments. The egg cells, the female gametes, are each contained in an archegonium, a bag-shaped organ with a narrow neck, located at the apical end of the female gametophyte, and after pollination tissues between the micropyle and the archegonia liquefy, allowing male gametes released in this 'pollen chamber' to gain access to the eggs. In the cycads and *Ginkgo* the male gametes are motile and analogous to sperm, but in conifers and yews (and angiosperms) they are without flagella and are carried to the egg in an outgrowth of the microspore, the pollen tube. Fertilised eggs develop into small embryo sporophytes, usually with many seed-leaves (cotyledons), and the integuments differentiate into the seed coat (testa) before the seed is shed. The haploid tissue of the gametophyte, the prothallus, acts as a food store for the sporophyte embryo on germination of the seed.

In angiosperms the pollen tube has to penetrate the wall of the carpel to reach an ovule, and this occurs at a special receptive surface, the stigma. The gametophyte generation is minimal. The haploid nucleus of the megaspore divides only three times, forming eight nuclei, of which two fuse to form a diploid nucleus and the six others acquire plasma membranes and feeble cell walls. Just one of these cells, the central member of a trio of cells at the micropylar end of the gametophyte, acts as the female gamete. The microspore and its pollen tube make up the male gametophyte, consisting of a small haploid cell inside a larger haploid cell. The small cell divides mitotically once and, on release from the pollen tube into the liquid remains of another of the micropylar trio of female cells, one male gamete fuses with the egg cell; the other male gamete fuses with the plasma membrane around the diploid fusion-nucleus of the female gametophyte, forming a triploid cell when the nuclei fuse. This 'double fertilisation' creates, as well as a zygote, a triploid tissue (endosperm) which in many species provides food for the seed. As in gymnosperms, the developing embryo enters a dormant state at a rudimentary stage while the propagule, which in some species includes parts of the carpel as well as the ovule, is dispersed.

While the use of air currents for transfer of the microspore has been retained by gymnosperms, many types of angiosperm have evolved symbiotic associations with animals, and these take some of the biosynthetic production of plants, in the form of pollen or sugars secreted as nectar, in exchange for acting as vectors for the pollen. A plethora of complex accessory structures, the **flower**, around the carpels and the microspore-producing stamens, has evolved to improve the efficiency of transfer. Animals are also among the many agents used by different types of seed plant for dispersal of individuals in the form of seeds, often in return for soft, sugar-laden and attractively coloured fruit tissues which develop around the seeds.

Conclusions

The angiosperm state in plants is comparable to internal fertilisation, followed by vivipary, in animals. This life-cycle has evolved by stages from the alternation of generations of marine algae as an increasingly efficient adaptation to the drying aerial environment of terrestrial life. One reason for the great variety of life-cycles in plants is that, like any adaptation, each is a different compromise between the limitations imposed by the nature of the preceding forms (for example, the red algae have no flagella and thus their male gametes have to be passively dispersed) and selection for greater efficiency. Because the nature of selection is different in different environments, this is also responsible for differences in the life-cycle adopted. For example, the life-cycle of fucoid brown algae is an adaptation to life in the intertidal zone, and makes use of the pattern of the tides: gametes are released at low tide when they will find each other easily in the thin surface film of water, and a little later the zygotes produced are efficiently dispersed in the vigorous tidal onrush of moving water. Other brown algae that are established in deeper water, such as the laminarians, have different ways of achieving sessile growth, the dispersal of individuals and the exchange of genetic information. The life-cycle of each species of plant is adapted to the nature of its environment.

2.3 FUNGI

Introduction

Many distinctive features set the fungi apart from both animals and plants, and they merit classification in a kingdom of their own. Unlike green plants, fungi cannot use the energy of light to synthesise organic materials from carbon dioxide and water, and instead require a preformed source of organic carbon; they are thus **heterotrophs**. Unlike animals, they cannot ingest solids but obtain their nutrients by absorbing soluble organic and inorganic compounds from the environment. Free-living fungi are called **saprotrophs**; there are also **mutualistic** and **parasitic** fungi that live in close association with other organisms (see Chapter 10). Fungi grow on a vast range of chemical substances (their substrates) in many different ecological systems, and play an essential part in recycling organic matter (see section 5.4).

The life-cycles of fungi show unique characteristics. Many exhibit two separate but contemporaneous states, a sexual state reproducing by spores produced following nuclear fusion and meiosis, and an asexual state reproducing by spores produced following mitotic nuclear divisions (see section 1.5). The states are distinguished by the types of spore they produce, and constitute different phases in the life-cycle of the organism. Fungal classification is based on the types of spore produced and the characteristics of the life-cycle, although the chemistry of the cell wall is becoming increasingly useful in distinguishing different groups.

Table 2.1 *Distribution of fungi in Ainsworth and Bisby's Dictionary of the fungi (1971)*

		No. of species
'Real fungi'	Mastigomycotina	1100
	Zygomycotina	610
	Ascomycotina	15000
	Basidiomycotina	12000
	Deuteromycotina	15000
	TOTAL	43710
Lichens		18000
	GRAND TOTAL	61710

Percentage of all fungi which are lichenised = 29%

Some 44000 species of fungi have been described, with another 18000 species associating with algae as lichens (Table 2.1). The true fungi or Eumycota are customarily divided into five subdivisions, the Mastigomycotina, Zygomycotina, Ascomycotina, Basidiomycotina and Deuteromycotina. The Deuteromycotina was originally set up for fungi which were found only to produce asexual ('imperfect') spores, and thus also called the Fungi Imperfecti, but for some of these a sexual state has now been discovered already classified in the Ascomycotina or Basidiomycotina and with a different Latin name! The Deuteromycotina is now considered to be an artificial assemblage, containing fungi probably derived from members of the Ascomycotina and Basidiomycotina that have lost the ability to reproduce sexually or have a sexual phase that has either not been discovered or at least has not been connected to the asexual phase.

The vegetative body of fungi (that part which is not reproductive structure) may consist of a single spherical or ellipsoidal cell (Fig. 2.11). This is typical of the yeasts, but is also found in the yeast-like phases of other fungi and in some members of the Chytridiales (a group of the Mastigomycotina). In many chytrids and in the related Blastocladiales there is in addition a specialised system, extending from the central cell body, of extremely narrow and delicate, highly branched, tapering filaments which do not contain any cross-walls. These filaments are called rhizoids, and function in attachment and absorption.

In by far the majority of fungi, however, the vegetative phase consists of highly branched, cylindrical filaments called **hyphae**, which make up a mat or web called the **mycelium** (Fig. 2.11). These hyphae may or may not contain cross-walls (**septa**). The full exploitation of this simple organisation of the fungal body has contributed a great deal to the ecological diversity and success of fungi, and the morphological simplicity of their vegetative phase contrasts markedly with the range and complexity of structures seen in other filamentous groups, such as the red algae, and indeed with the relatively complex fungal reproductive structures.

Hyphal growth

Like the cells of plants (see section 2.2), the fungal cell is completely surrounded by a wall. The hyphae of different fungi appear superficially very similar in being branched, thin-walled tubes, but they differ greatly in wall composition and structure, in the number, type and position of their nuclei, and in the type of septa if these are present. These differences are believed to indicate that the fungal life has evolved independently a number of different times.

Hyphal walls contain 80 to 90% polysaccharide, 1 to 15% protein and 2 to 10% lipid (by dry mass). Many different types of polysaccharide may be present. The walls of most fungi contain some chitin, a β-$(1 \rightarrow 4)$-linked polymer of N-acetylglucosamine, making up anything from 3 to 60% of the

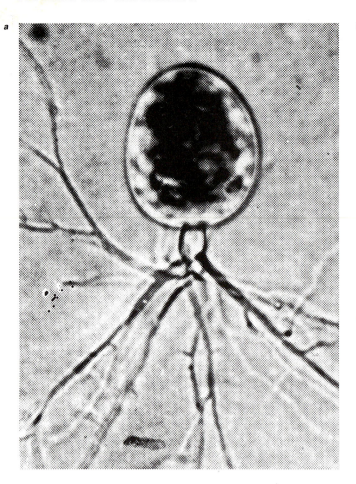

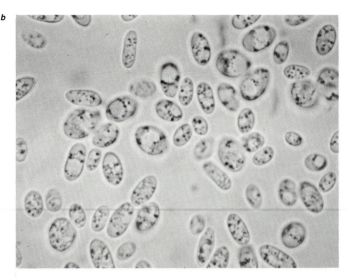

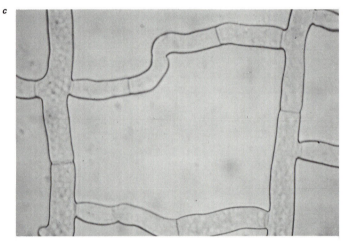

Fig. 2.11. Fungal growth-forms. (a) A chytrid. (b) Single cells of a yeast. (c) Mycelial hyphae.

wall. Chitin is usually associated with β-$(1 \to 3)$-linked and β-$(1 \to 6)$-linked polymers of glucose (glucans); the Oomycetes (a group of the Mastigomycotina) contain a microfibrillar β-$(1 \to 4)$-linked glucan, that is, cellulose. Many yeast cell walls contain substantial amounts of polymers of mannose. Cell-wall chemistry is used in the classification of the various fungal groups, but also distinguishes the fungi from other living organisms: fungal walls are quite different from those of bacteria or algae.

The walls, however varied their components, give rigidity, stability and shape to fungal hyphae, and alterations in the patterns of cell-wall construction allow fungi to produce a great variety of reproductive structures and spores. Hyphal walls normally appear homogeneous in section under the light microscope, but ultra-thin sections examined with an electron microscope reveal a layering in their structure. The hyphal wall has a distinct microfibrillar texture on the inner face, and an amorphous (structureless) appearance on the outer one, usually with many layers between. The microfibrillar components, often regarded as the major skeletal elements of the wall, are cellulose and/or chitin, and are embedded in the amorphous components, which are the more varied glucans. The protein present may assist in locking together these two phases. Wall structure and composition for *Neurospora* are illustrated in Fig.

2.12; the wall of *Neurospora* is unusual in having, behind the active tip, a network of glycoprotein between the inner fibrillar layer and outer amorphous one.

Hyphal growth is markedly polarised and occurs only by extension at the extreme apex, a fact which is very important for the mechanics of fungal growth. This type of growth can be demonstrated simply by measuring at different time intervals the distance from the hyphal tip to the first septum or to the first branch, and the distance between subsequent septa or branches once these have been formed. The increase in volume is achieved solely by extension at the hyphal tip, in a zone usually less than 20 micrometres long and called the **extension zone**, where the wall is not rigid. Even within this zone, the cell wall is at its most extensible close to the hyphal tip. Protoplasm for growth, however, is synthesised by a considerable length of the hypha behind the tip. This region, called the **peripheral growth zone**, may be 1 to 2 millimetres long, and active streaming of the hyphal contents takes newly synthesised material to the hyphal tip.

A physical pressure inside the hypha appears to be necessary for elongation, and is probably the driving force for this process. Due to the high powers of absorption of the hypha, the internal concentration of solutes is much greater than that of the environment, so water enters by osmosis and a

Fig. 2.12. Diagrammatic representation of the principal layers of the hyphal wall of Neurospora.

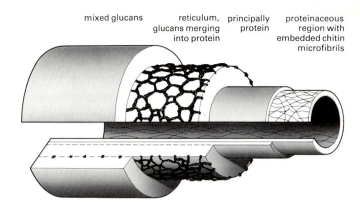

mixed glucans   reticulum,   principally   proteinaceous
glucans merging   protein   region with
into protein   embedded chitin
microfibrils

considerable hydrostatic pressure develops inside the hypha. This pressure, the **turgor pressure**, may be 4 to 8 atmospheres (0.4 to 0.8 megapascals) exerted outwards on the wall by the hyphal contents and can readily be seen when the wall is punctured or damaged, as the contents pour out. The application of highly concentrated sugar or salt solutions to hyphal apices withdraws the water from them, and elongation rapidly stops. Growth is resumed when turgor is restored after dilution of the outside medium. Turgor pressure therefore appears to be the driving force for wall extension. Soft new wall material is added at the hyphal tip and behind the apex the wall is made more rigid, presumably by cross-linking of the wall polysaccharides; this ensures that the internal pressure causes elongation only at the apex. Tip extension allows fungi to grow very rapidly across solid surfaces, sometimes at rates exceeding 1 millimetre per hour.

Two other features of hyphae are of particular importance in their growth through three-dimensional substrates: hyphae branch, and they secrete enzymes which hydrolyse the substrate externally. Branches arise successively at some distance behind the tip, from parts of the wall which have ceased extending and have attained their maximum rigidity. At the site of a branch, controlled partial dissolution of a minute area of the wall occurs, presumably by the action of degradative enzymes, the high turgor pressure from within the hypha causes the wall to bulge out, and a branch apex is created.

On a flat surface, the mycelium develops with a leading major hypha and a series of branches to either side. The leading hypha continuously extends into uncolonised substrate, and grows at a more rapid rate than do its branches. These branches are growing into regions of the substrate that have already been partially colonised and are less favourable for growth since, for example, nutrients have already been removed. When a spore germinates, a series of leading hyphae grow out from this initial common point. Their dominance over the lateral branches that are produced weakens as some primary branches reach the uncolonised parts of the substrate between the leading hyphae, so filling in gaps in the margin. A more or less circular colony thus develops; such growth within a three-dimensional substrate leads to a spherical colony.

Dense and regular branching allows the fungus to penetrate the substrate thoroughly and to remove all the nutrients from it. In addition, both the complex branching and the rigid nature of the wall behind the apex ensure that the older parts of the mycelium are firmly anchored, and the tip can thus exert considerable forward mechanical pressure.

Fungi produce and secrete to the outside of the cell enzymes which break down the substrates on which the fungi are growing. This releases soluble nutrients, which are absorbed and used for growth, and also softens or erodes the substrate, greatly assisting penetration by the hyphal tips. The narrow hyphae of filamentous fungi present a very large surface area to the substrate in relation to their volume. This is advantageous in the exploitation of any bulky substrate, like wood, leaf litter or soil, as many physiological processes depend on surface area, including the secretion of degradative enzymes, the absorption of the products of their action, and the absorption of materials in short supply such as mineral ions in the soil.

Possession of a large surface area also has its disadvantages, as it increases the susceptibility to injury by adverse environmental factors, particularly desiccation. The survival of the mycelium depends upon the maintenance of a high degree of humidity and some free moisture in the external environment. Most hyphae, not having a cuticle, are very susceptible to desiccation. This is perhaps why most fungi grow immersed in their substrate, and why those which grow exposed to the atmosphere often have walls waterproofed with pigmented melanins.

As the hyphal tips grow on, the older parts of the hyphae behind become vacuolated and finally empty, dead and sealed off by septa. The individual cells or compartments die as a result of the exhaustion of the external food supply coupled with the accumulation of toxic metabolites. If a fungus had an unlimited surface area to colonise, it would come to consist of a peripheral ring of actively growing hyphae producing more tips by branching, so increasing continuously in diameter and tapping new sources of nutrients, but at the same time gradually ageing and dying off behind.

Cross-walls in hyphae

The major taxonomic dichotomy in the fungi is between the subdivisions Mastigomycotina and Zygomycotina on the one hand, and Ascomycotina, Basidiomycotina and Deuteromycotina on the other. Members of the two former groups do not produce any complex reproductive structures around their spores, whereas the majority of the others do. In addition, the filamentous Mastigomycotina and Zygomycotina have hyphae which are typically **aseptate**, that is they lack cross-walls. Their hyphae contain many nuclei produced by mitosis, but there is no cell division and no walls are produced; this type of organisation is called **coenocytic**. Complete septa do occur in these fungi, but usually only to cut off reproductive structures or evacuated or injured parts of the hyphae. Fungi in the other three groups have septa dividing their hyphae into compartments, but the septa are perforated.

In the Ascomycotina and most Deuteromycotina each septum grows inwards from the wall, like an iris diaphragm, but a small central hole is left, 0.05 to 0.5 micrometres in diameter (Fig. 2.13). This allows cytoplasmic continuity, and also migration of nuclei. Such hyphae are thus not made up of independent cells, but are really coenocytes with incomplete

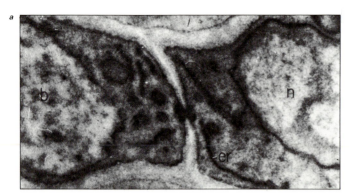

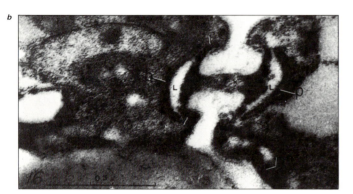

Fig. 2.13. Septal structure. Longitudinal sections of a single hypha and septum in individuals of the Ascomycotina (a) and Basidiomycotina (b).

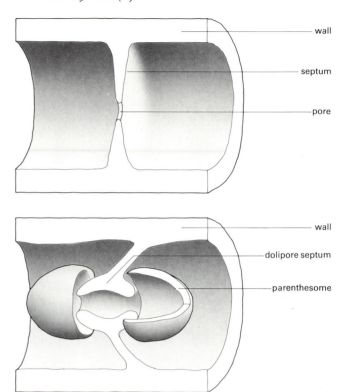

septa, not true cell walls produced from a central plate at cell division (see section 1.5). In many members of the Basidiomycotina the pore is not a simple hole but is flanged to produce an elongated channel, which may be loosely capped at one end by a crescent-shaped structure, the septal pore cap. The whole structure is only visible with the electron microscope. The channel is 0.1 to 0.2 micrometres in diameter and again allows cytoplasmic continuity. These modes of formation of transverse walls in Ascomycotina, Basidiomycotina and Deuteromycotina suggest that the distinction between aseptate and septate hyphae is not very profound, and the presence of pores in the septa implies that there is little physiological distinction either.

The septa give rigidity to hyphae by bracing the walls such that they can more effectively withstand pressures from either within or without. The fact that the pores can relatively easily be blocked also prevents excessive loss of contents when hyphae are damaged and the walls punctured or burst. However, the main function of septa may be to allow hyphae to undergo differentiation to produce a variety of different cell types adjacent to each other, such as the skeletal and binding hyphae in polypores.

Fungal reproductive structures

Fungi reproduce both asexually and sexually by spores. Many spores serve to disperse the fungus, others act as resting spores which allow the fungus to survive an unfavourable period, and some spores fulfil both functions. Spores produced by sexual reproduction (that is, by nuclear fusion followed by meiosis) serve as a source of genetic variation in the population. Subdivisions within the fungi are based on the nature of the

spores formed, especially the sexual ones, and the range of types found is illustrated in Fig. 2.14.

In most of the Ascomycotina and Basidiomycotina, hyphae become aggregated to form microscopic or macroscopic reproductive structures called **ascocarps** and **basidiocarps**, which are often reasonably solid and strong. These contain many individual **asci** or **basidia**, cells or groups of cells producing sexual spores. Basidiocarps exceed all other reproductive structures in the fungi in their range of size and complexity, and this is achieved by differentiation of the hyphae into different types, aggregation, branching, fusion and swelling of the hyphae, and thickening of their walls. Two examples from the Hymenomycetes (members of the Basidiomycotina), the fleshy ephemeral agaric and the more durable long-lived bracket polypore, will serve to illustrate some of this range.

The Agaricales or agarics are the mushrooms and toadstools; there is no scientific distinction between these two common names. The basidiocarp develops from the buried mycelium and is in the form of a disc-shaped or dome-shaped cap held aloft by a stalk, like a miniature umbrella. The basidia line vertical radiating wedge-shaped gills (as in *Amanita*), or sometimes tubes (as in *Boletus*) or less frequently spines (as in *Hydnum*), under the cap. The development of such basidiocarps is extraordinarily variable, but this remarkably constant final form seems to be governed by a number of factors, most of which relate to the properties of the individual basidium. The basidium discharges its spores violently a distance of 0.1 to 0.2 millimetres, such that they clear the other basidia and then fall vertically but do not hit the opposite gill (or tube-face or spine). The stalk supports the cap and provides a space between the cap and the ground so that the falling spores are caught in the turbulent air and carried away. The

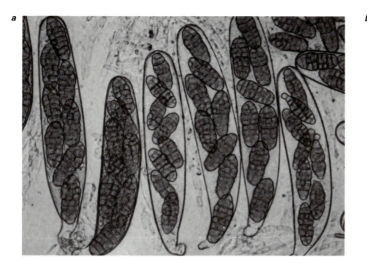

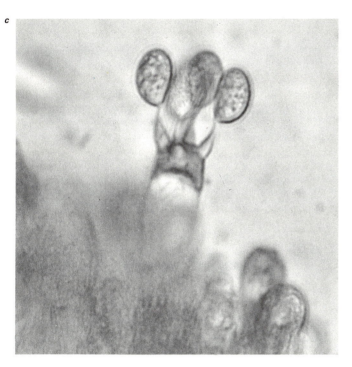

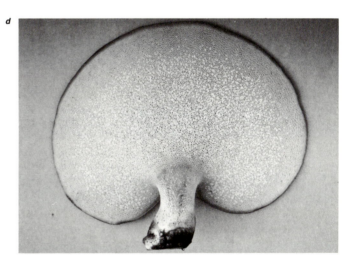

Fig. 2.14. Reproductive structures. (a) Asci and ascospores of Pleospora herbarum. *(b) A morel, an ascocarp of* Morchella esculenta. *(c) Basidiospores on a basidium. (d) Underside of the bracket polypore* Polyporus squamosus, *showing tubes and attachment stalk. (e) Conidia of* Cladosporium.

basidia cannot function if they are covered by a film of water, since they are not sufficiently powerful to project their spores through water. The cap thus also provides a shelter for the basidia, protecting them from rain. The basidia, however, can only discharge their spores properly when they are turgid (swollen with water), which requires that the ambient air be almost saturated with water vapour; if the relative humidity falls much below saturation, spore discharge almost ceases. The closely packed gills (or spines or narrow tubes) help to maintain constantly high humidities around the basidia, and the spore-bearing layer is then less susceptible to fluctuations in the humidity of the outside air. Finally, unlike tubes which are fused to each other, gills and spines hang freely and can reorientate somewhat if the whole basidiocarp tilts.

The agarics show little differentiation of their hyphae in their stalk and cap. The stalk must possess some supporting framework and have tissue conducting water or nutrients up to the basidia, but these tissues are not morphologically distinct. Some hyphae may be wider, more elongate and less branched than others, but there is little other visible modification. Such fleshy agarics are usually short-lived, and rely mainly on the turgidity of their hyphae for support, rather than developing any distinct mechanical tissue. Under dry atmospheric conditions most lose water rapidly and shrivel, and spore discharge ceases; they do not recover on return to more humid conditions. The reliance on turgidity for spore development and discharge, and for support, may explain why mushrooms and toadstools are mainly restricted in their appearance to the damper days of autumn. Most are frost-sensitive and disappear with the first frosts of late autumn.

The basidiocarps of the Aphyllophorales, the bracket fungi or polypores, are different from those of the Agaricales in being often membranous, leathery, corky or even woody in texture. They normally function for a longer period than do most agarics, and some, such as those of *Ganoderma adspersum*, are perennial. In these, three different types of hypha may be recognised: generative, skeletal and binding hyphae. **Generative** hyphae are ubiquitous ordinary hyphae, thin-walled, branched and septate. In the basidiocarp they give rise to the two other kinds of hypha. **Skeletal** hyphae are thick-walled, with a narrow internal cavity, non-septate and usually unbranched. They are of unlimited growth and are strengthening structures giving rigidity and support to the basidiocarp. **Binding** hyphae are of limited growth, very thick-walled, relatively narrow, rarely septate and are highly and irregularly branched. They develop some way behind the growing margin. Thus in these basidiocarps generative hyphae provide the ground network, skeletal hyphae provide the firm constructional framework, and the binding hyphae firmly lock these two types together. The resultant structure can be enormously strong and is often impossible to break by hand.

Very few polypores are centrally stalked like an agaric. Most are restricted to woody substrates, and arise on a tree-trunk or branch above the ground. Some have a short lateral stalk for attachment, but most are attached broadly along their base and are fan-like or bracket-like in form. The basidia underneath are protected from rain, and the spores fall into the turbulent air. The majority of polypores have their basidia lining tubes which are fused together and which thus cannot individually readjust to the vertical if knocked or tilted. In *Ganoderma adspersum* the tubes are very long and narrow, being over 10 millimetres in length but only 0.1 millimetre in internal diameter; for spores to be successfully released from the basidia lining the tubes, the tubes must be accurately aligned to the vertical. A tilt of a mere $2°$ from vertical would mean that over 70% of the spores would fail to escape. Accurate alignment is achieved initially by the growing tubes responding sensitively to gravity, and is maintained both by the broad attachment of the bracket to the

tree and by the rigidity afforded by the packed skeletal and binding hyphae. The less rigid basidiocarps, especially those with a lateral stalk, have wider and shorter tubes which permit a greater degree of tilt to occur without preventing the escape of most of the spores.

These kinds of structure may release 3000 million spores over the course of one summer, and are the most highly developed fungal structures known, but even so are constructed of hyphal filaments showing amazingly little variety of cell type.

2.4 ANIMALS

Animal architecture

Animal life exists in an enormous variety of forms, and evidence from fossils indicates that there has been even greater diversity through the course of evolution. At a first glance the possibilities for animal design seem unlimited, yet the very fact that we are able to classify animals suggests that groups of animals share certain common features, giving a limited number of basic **body plans** around which they have been built (Fig. 2.15). Evolution of new types of organisation has to start with the body plans of existing organisms, and, furthermore, within these relatively few blueprints for design in the animal kingdom there are extra restrictions imposed by the interactions of size, shape and habitat; there are no microscopic mammals, or gigantic insects, and we do not expect birds to live permanently under water or octopuses to be successful on land. Clearly there must be some fundamental limits to what can be done with the biological materials that are available, and, before the structures and working mechanisms found in animals are described, the principles underlying these questions of **animal architecture** will be considered.

Probably the single most important organising principle for an animal is its size. A very small animal has much less scope for complexity, having nowhere to put the elaborate tissues and organs on which a larger creature depends. The lower limit to size is a sac of unit membrane just able to enclose a strand of nucleic acid and enough ribosomes to make perhaps 50 essential polypeptides (see section 1.1), and this limit is probably approached by certain mycoplasms about 0.3 micrometres in diameter. Most of the familiar multicellular animals are much larger than this, and the range of their mass covers about 13 orders of magnitude, up to the largest whales which weigh 100 tonnes and are 30 metres long.

Organisms of large size have a greater capacity for internal specialisation. More cellular organelles can be accommodated within a larger cell, and in a multicellular (metazoan) organism different cells can take on different functions. However, an increase in size may be viewed also as a disadvantage in some respects, in that it brings about a need for complexity and specialisation and imposes different constraints from those of being small. The simplest and smallest animals, the unicellular protozoans, are just as successful in biological terms as are much larger, multicellular, creatures: habitats are available for the whole range of sizes of animal, and animals have evolved different types of adaptation in accord with their different sizes.

The first consequence of increasing size relates to supplying and servicing each cell. If the habitat of the animal is aquatic, nutrients, wastes and respiratory gases can be simply exchanged by diffusion of molecules across the cell membranes, but as the bulk of the organism increases then the path to the innermost cells will become too great for diffusion to occur rapidly, wastes will accumulate faster than they can be disposed of, and these cells will become starved of oxygen and food. In practice, the size limit for a solid ball of cells is about 0.8 millimetres radius. If the organism has a gut this limit is increased as the internal gut surfaces can service the inner cells, but a size limit of 1 to 2 millimetres is still imposed and is characteristic of those phyla which have a solid body (without internal cavities). For these animals, an increased size can be achieved only by keeping the surface-area-to-volume ratio high, either by forming folded flattened sheets of cells (like the sponges and coelenterates, where each part of the body is only two cells thick), or by adopting an overall flattened form with a maximum thickness not greater than that compatible with diffusion (like the platyhelminths, the flatworms). Any greater bulk requires possession of a fluid circulatory system, so that convection can supplement simple diffusion, supplying nutrients or gases and acting as a sink for wastes; by far the majority of multicellular organisms have evolved this solution.

Some of the possibilities are illustrated in Fig. 2.15. The simplest arrangement is to have an **open circulation**, where a fluid-filled body cavity within the body bathes the inner cells, and the fluid is kept circulating by the animal's own movements. This is similar to the condition of larger coelenterates such as sea-anemones, although their 'body cavity' is in fact topologically a virtually enclosed part of the outside world. A true **body cavity** is enclosed within layers of cells, and usually within the **mesoderm**, when it is called a **coelom**. (The mesoderm is the middle layer of cells that makes up the bulk of an animal's tissues and lies between the outer layer of cells, the **ectoderm**, and the inner layer of cells lining the gut, the **endoderm**.) Open circulatory systems are characteristic of many of the invertebrate phyla, including most of the worms and the molluscs and arthropods, although the cavities have different embryological origins in the various groups (see pages 96–7). However, the undirected and relatively sluggish flow of such a system is still inadequate for animals which are very large, or of moderate size but very active, and such cases require a separate, **closed**, circulatory system with blood pumped round in vessels. The functions and mechanisms of different circulatory systems are considered on pages 76–9.

Another consequence of increasing size is the need to support the animal, and usually also to permit it to move. Unicells may move by the action of cilia or flagella, or by the

flow of protoplasm, but these mechanisms become inadequate for large multicellular organisms; cilia, for example, would collapse under the weight of anything larger than a flatworm moving over a substrate, and could not generate enough force to move large animals in open water even if their surface was completely covered with cilia. All larger creatures require muscles, and muscles in turn require a skeleton to work against. For multicellular animals, therefore, support and locomotion are intimately linked.

Methods of achieving support may be very broadly classified as hydrostatic skeletons and stiff skeletons (Fig. 2.16). The **hydrostatic skeleton** merely requires an enclosed and incompressible volume of fluid against which muscles can work, and this is provided by the body cavity. Usually there are two sets of muscles, running circularly around and longitudinally along the worm-like body, and so acting in opposition (antagonistically) to each other; in the nematode worms, however, and in certain parts of other animals where the resistance to change of shape is high, longitudinal or circular muscles alone may suffice. In many cases, the earthworm being a familiar example, the hydrostatic skeleton and the muscles are arranged in segments. This helps to localise the changes in pressure caused by muscular contraction, so reducing the amount of energy required and it may permit finer control of movements by peristalsis, which is where each segment moves fractionally out of phase with the adjacent segment so that a wave of contraction passes along the body. This arrangement is suitable for continuous burrowers like the earthworm. In other cases, an unsegmented hydrostatic skeleton allows for grosser changes in shape and may be particularly useful for intermittent burrowers, especially in soft substrates. In a few special situations, localised hydrostatic systems occur, such as the water-vascular system of echinoderms like sea-urchins and star-fish, which permits stepping movements of the tube-feet seen on the underside of the animal.

Stiff skeletons are an alternative to hydrostatic skeletons, or rather an addition since few animals are without any hydrostatic support from their own body fluid. Regions of hardened material are incorporated into the body, with muscles arranged usually in antagonistic pairs to pull against them. These skeletons are generally made of fibrous proteins such as collagen, or of chitin, a carbohydrate polymer of amino-sugars, laid down in a protein matrix. The organic component is commonly either impregnated with a mineral such as calcium carbonate, calcium phosphate or silica, or it is chemically cross-linked with itself, to increase mechanical strength. Stiff skeletons may be external, such as the **exoskeleton** of arthropods and most molluscs, or internal, as in vertebrates and the echinoderms (Fig. 2.16). Exoskeletons may be incomplete, as in molluscan shells which can grow continuously at the edges, or may entirely enclose the body as in arthropods; in the latter case the skeletons must be periodically moulted to permit growth. Animals with internal skeletons (**endoskeletons**) still require an external covering, usually termed the skin, and this

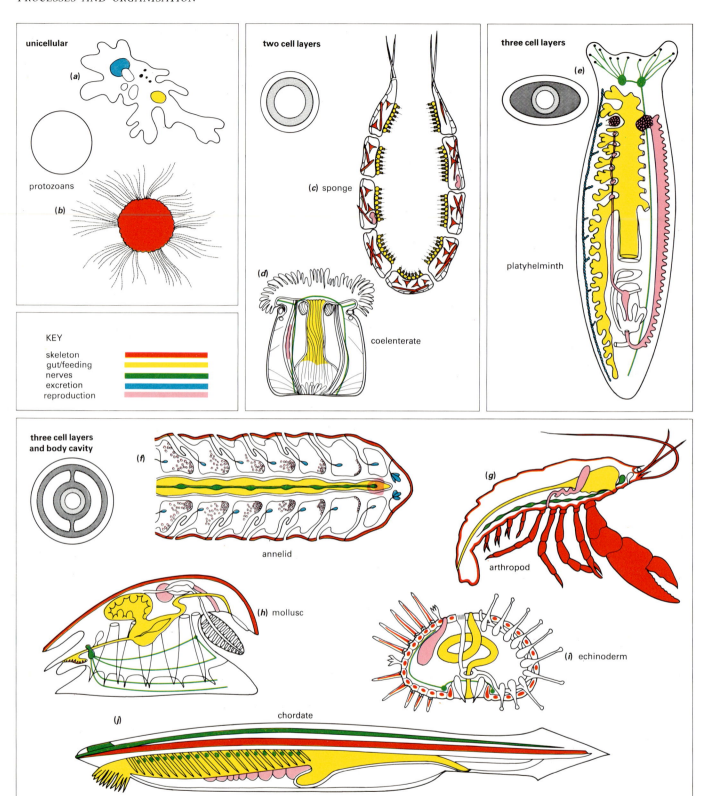

Fig. 2.15. Basic body plans of animals.

too may be quite tough and in many groups bears secondary non-living structures such as scales, hairs or feathers, for protection or insulation. All stiff skeletons provide scope for joints and true limbs to develop, and so fundamentally change the type of locomotion. Jointed limbs permit finely graded levering motions against a substrate, and so are particularly suited for life on land, and the capacity for stiff skeletons to produce flapping wings for flight is another successful adapt-

Fig. 2.16. Skeletal systems usually involve hydrostatic support by fluids, through canal systems (a) or an extensive body cavity (b); but in many cases stiff skeletal supports are added, either externally as shells or cuticles (c,e) or as internal ossicles (d) or bones (f).

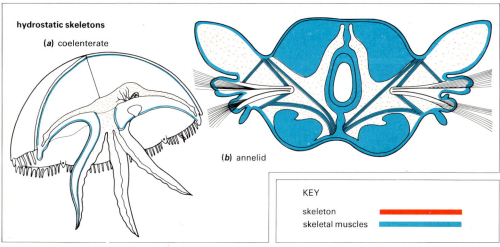

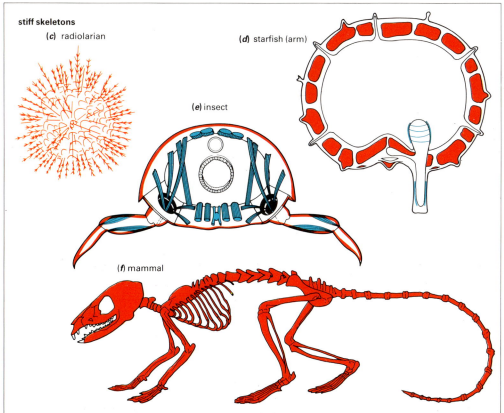

ation of terrestrial rather than marine organisms. Possession of joints also creates a good mechanical advantage, so allowing faster and less energetically expensive movements, with the body lifted off the ground to reduce friction; speed and dexterity can therefore improve considerably.

The different types of stiff skeletons, exoskeletons and endoskeletons, have their own particular advantages and limitations, which are again related to size. A small animal needs relatively little thickness of hard material to coat itself with a layer that will support it adequately, whereas a large animal would require disproportionately large quantities of exoskeleton to support its bulk and this external covering would be excessively heavy. For large animals, a system of internal jointed rods is a better solution in terms of economy of

building materials. Stiff skeletons also have protective functions, and an external covering provides good mechanical and physical protection for a small creature, because tubes are less susceptible to cracking and buckling than are rods of the same mass. However, larger animals have a high inertia and may be severely damaged by collision; for them, an external covering would be endangered by impact, whereas an endoskeleton cushioned by surrounding soft tissues would be less likely to crack. Vertebrates combine the advantages of both types of skeleton, by having a cushioned internal framework, together with an almost external covering around critical organs, in the form of the skull and rib-cage.

Hence, for reasons of support and protection, small exoskeletons and large endoskeletons may provide the best solutions, and the larger arthropods are of a comparable size to the smaller vertebrates in a particular habitat: for example compare the lobster with a small marine fish, or a locust with a pigmy shrew. The different properties of the two kinds of skeleton are accentuated in hostile environments such as dry land because of physiological problems. For small animals the problems of a large surface-area-to-volume ratio are then critical, especially in terms of losses of water and salts, so that an exoskeleton rendered as impermeable as possible is extremely desirable, which accounts for much of the extraordinary success of the small terrestrial insects.

A large body, with a circulatory fluid system and the means of support and locomotion, has a third major problem due to size, this being the coordination and regulation of the increasingly complex biological apparatus. The tissue fluids must be supplied with enough food and oxygen to maintain all the cells, so that specialisation of the gut and feeding apparatus, and perhaps of a metabolic centre such as the liver, together with the elaboration of respiratory surfaces, may be required. Similarly, carbon dioxide and nitrogenous wastes must be specifically disposed of before they can accumulate to damaging levels, so that excretory mechanisms will be needed. Hence much of the space provided by a body cavity must become filled by the specialised tissues and organs that are so typical of the higher animals. Many of these systems are considered in more detail below.

Besides regulating the composition of the body fluids to sustain individual cells, all the different biological systems of an animal must be coordinated and kept in step with changes in the outside world. This requires both perception of these changes and response to them. Hence, large and complex animals have developed a sensory and nervous system to mediate short-term changes, and a longer-term set of chemical controls (see pages 88–94). The most critical and complex event requiring coordination in an animal's life is reproduction (see pages 94–7), and again certain fundamental similarities underlie the apparent diversity of animal life.

Two critical factors besides size act as constraints on animal architecture. First, the phylogenetic (evolutionary) relations of a species are the primary determinant of its form, giving a certain basic body plan, and no matter how much this is altered during embryological development it can be used as a diagnostic feature for classification. However, it is not always easy in practice to define the evolutionary relationships of animals, and apparently similar forms may have evolved convergently to a very similar body plan as a solution to a set of common problems. Secondly, within a group accepted as having a single evolutionary origin, there are oddities which have either lost or have exaggerated some of the characteristic features of their relatives as an adaptation to different ways of life; ecological factors may be regarded as another principle determining design. For example, the structure and complexity of excretory organs differ for marine, freshwater and terrestrial animals; feeding apparatus varies with food; and all kinds of changes of

form and physiology may occur in an animal which develops a parasitic or colonial way of life. Differences may be found even within one individual as it changes from larva to adult if the habits and habitats of the two stages differ sufficiently. Thus the particular mode of existence of an individual species, together with the phylogenetic and dimensional factors already discussed, are recurring features in the detailed consideration of form and function.

Circulation

A system of circulating body fluid is necessary for an increased body size, and an enclosed volume of fluid performs a number of general functions. These are: the transport of food materials from the gut to tissues, often via storage organs; the transport of excretory products from tissues to specific detoxifying centres and/or excretory organs; the transport of gases to and from respiratory surfaces and tissues; the transport of chemical messengers (hormones); the transport of blood cells, for defence, coagulation and other reactions; the transport of metabolic heat for dissipation at the body surfaces, or of environmental heat to the tissues; support, as an incompressible hydrostatic skeleton; and the transmission of forces and pressures for locomotion, for protrusion of certain parts of the body, and for ultrafiltration in excretory systems.

These functions pertain to an enormous range of biological processes, so that a circulatory system is in many ways the key to all the other aspects of the physiology of larger animals. The six transport functions given above all contribute to **homeostasis**, the maintenance of a stable environment around all the cells of the body, allowing each to function optimally and without any stresses imposed as the animal's external environment fluctuates. The last two functions listed permit independent movement within that environment, so that extreme conditions can be avoided.

Given the diversity of functions for circulating body fluids, it is not surprising that a great range of structural arrangements occurs, and open and closed systems represent the ends of a continuum. Most groups of small marine invertebrates have an open system, with the fluid simply present in a large cavity between layers of cells and tissues and with no particular mechanism to keep the liquid circulating. For somewhat larger animals, and for smaller forms that are very active, this may prove inadequate, with the flow being too sluggish to supply nutrients and oxygen. One solution is an open system aided by a few vessels; often a contractile heart expands and draws in blood from the main cavity, and then forces blood out through a limited number of arteries during contraction. Such arteries are normally directed to the most metabolically active tissues, including the respiratory surface, the excretory organs and the brain. From there the blood returns to the open system. In very large or active animals this will not suffice and the system becomes completely enclosed in vessels, so that the fluid can be pumped under pressure by peristaltic contractions in the tube walls, and blood is supplied according to the changing needs of each muscle or organ. Animals with such closed circulatory systems are relatively rather rare, though they include many familiar forms, such as the vertebrates.

The diversity of animal circulatory systems is shown in Fig. 2.17. Even within some large protozoans a form of circulation occurs, with protoplasm flowing in fixed directions to distribute nutrients from the gullet. In those groups of animals with only two layers of cells, namely sponges and coelenterates, each cell is usually close enough to the environment for direct exchange of molecules. In addition, flow is aided in sponges by currents created by flagellate cells, and in coelenterates by muscular churning of the gut contents or by forcing fluids through channels within the jelly-like non-cellular bulk of some of the larger jet-propelled medusae (jelly-fish).

Some of the animals with three layers of cells have no circulatory system, although the blind-ending gut of flatworms may help in distributing metabolites. In most of these phyla, however, a circulatory system is present within the mesoderm, in the middle layer of body tissues. For many worm-like groups this is a simple open cavity, and its transport functions, especially for respiratory exchange, may be limited. In the nemertine and annelid worms a closed blood system is present, and in the annelids the network of vessels has an important respiratory function with capillaries extending to the surface or to specialised gills for gas exchange. Vessels also supply the simple brains of such worms, and usually each segment also has blood vessels to the nephridia, the excretory organs. However, there are exceptions to the circulatory plan shown for annelids in Fig. 2.17, as one group, the leeches, has reverted to an open-plan system of loosely connected blood sinuses, perhaps because their blood-sucking habit means that leeches need to be able to change their body volume greatly at feeding times and this is incompatible with a rigidly organised arrangement of vessels.

In the familiar invertebrate groups of molluscs and arthropods, the circulatory system is essentially open and the fluid is described as **haemolymph**. In smaller organisms in these two phyla there are no vessels at all, or perhaps only a peristaltic dorsal heart or contractile vessel (aorta) to aid movement of the haemolymph; this applies to many aquatic gastropod and bivalve molluscs, to the small planktonic crustaceans, to most insects, and to nearly all larval stages. However, representatives of these groups which are larger and/or fairly active have progressively more enclosed vascular systems, as may be seen in the familiar shrimps and crabs, in the largest active insects such as bees and moths, and above all in the most active molluscs, the cephalopods. This final group, which includes large predators such as the squid and octopus, has a completely closed blood system, with a main heart and accessory (branchial) hearts to keep a good bloodflow through the gills.

Other animals that may have both open and closed components in their circulation are the echinoderms such as sea-urchins and star-fish. These have a very curious array of vascular systems; not only is there a large body cavity which supplies and drains most of the cells, but there are two or even three other separate sets of tubes running within the body, each performing some of the functions already discussed. Perhaps most important is the water-vascular system, forming a closed hydrostatic system operating the tube-feet. The tube-feet are involved in respiration, as well as in locomotion and feeding.

Finally, within the chordates there are several small and sedentary forms having no real closed circulation, notably the adult tunicates (the sea-squirts). Most of the chordates, however, are vertebrates, and exhibit the familiar enclosed blood system with an elaborate ventral pumping heart and close association with respiratory organs. In fish there is a single loop to the circulation, whereas in mammals the circulation is double, the heart acting as two separate pumps, one to the lungs and one to the rest of the tissues; this permits a lower blood pressure in the lungs. The vertebrates show a functionally graded series of circulatory plans (Fig. 2.13), either a single or a double pump occurring in different reptiles. In all cases, though, there are major blood vessels running to the gut and liver, to the kidneys, and to the head, as well as to the main locomotory muscles; the blood runs forward ventrally and backward dorsally, in contrast to the directions of flow in invertebrates.

The circulatory system of a vertebrate has a number of components upon which its success depends. Tissues are supplied by thick-walled muscular arteries, branching into finer arterioles and ultimately into networks of capillaries. These vary in density according to the metabolic activity of particular tissues, and the diffusion path from them to the active cells can be kept very small. After passage through the capillaries most of the blood is channelled into venules and then returns to the heart through the veins. These are thinner walled and less muscular than are the arteries, being more distant from the pumping heart and so working at a lower pressure. Some fluid continually leaks through the walls of the capillaries into the spaces around the cells, and is collected from there into lymph vessels which provide a parallel circulation system, though without a separate pumping heart, and ultimately this fluid is returned to the blood.

The heart forms the pump for the whole vertebrate circulatory system, and in mammals consists of four chambers (see Fig. 2.18). The smaller, right side receives deoxygenated venous blood from the body into the right atrium, pumping it on to the lungs via the right ventricle, while the left atrium receives newly oxygenated blood from the lungs and pumps it to the body through the very muscular left ventricle. The two ventricles contract strongly, almost in synchrony, to force the blood out through the arteries. The specialised cardiac muscle can maintain an inherent contraction without repeated external nervous stimulation, though the heart rate is controlled by a pacemaker region of muscle tissue which can be regulated by

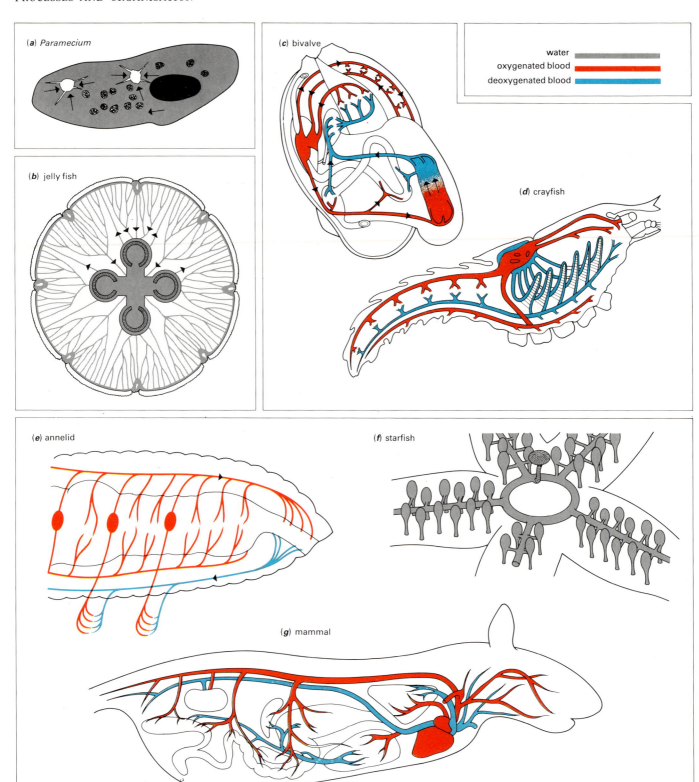

(a) Paramecium

(b) jelly fish

(c) bivalve

water
oxygenated blood
deoxygenated blood

(d) crayfish

(e) annelid

(f) starfish

(g) mammal

Fig. 2.17. Circulatory systems have many different functions reflected in their diverse patterns, which range from cytoplasmic flow (a) and channelling of sea water (b) to haemocoelic systems (c,d) where blood flows only partly in vessels, and to the completely closed systems (e–g) of annelids, echinoderms and vertebrates.

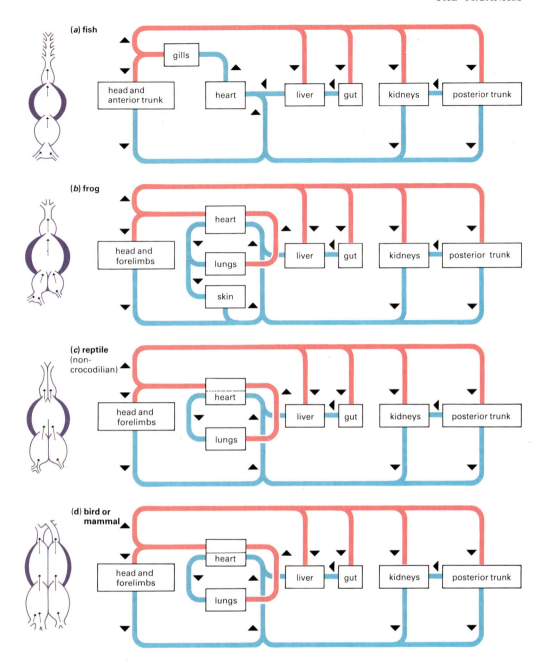

Fig. 2.18. Heart structures and circulatory plans in vertebrates. Most fish (a) have single circuit flow; amphibia and reptiles (b,c) show intermediate arrangements; but only mammals and birds (d) have fully divided hearts and dual-circuit flow. Red denotes oxygenated blood; blue deoxygenated blood.

nervous input, so allowing the heart's activities to be correlated with the needs of the tissues.

The final component of the circulatory system is of course the blood itself. It is largely water, providing a non-viscous transport medium with good solvent properties, but also contains mineral ions, foodstuffs, metabolites, hormones, and proteins with transport functions. In most animals, and certainly all vertebrates, dissolved gases are also carried, and in many cases a respiratory pigment which can bind and transport gases is then present. Where this is so, the composition of the blood may have to be closely regulated and kept at a stable pH and ion and nutrient concentration, since the function of the pigments can be critically affected by changes in the medium. However, in some animals the blood has hardly any respiratory function and so can be much more variable with respect to volume, pressure and the concentrations of dissolved substances; this is particularly true of the insects, which obtain oxygen through ingrowing air-filled tubes called tracheae, and

an adaptable open circulation of their haemolymph may be especially appropriate for these small terrestrial animals.

The circulating fluids of animals nearly always contain cells in addition to the dissolved chemicals. In vertebrates the respiratory pigment is enclosed in special **red blood cells**. In contrast, **white blood cells** are found in nearly all groups, including vertebrates, and function in the defence of the organism, both against invasion by parasites, pathogens and noxious chemicals, and against physical damage such as wounding.

Respiration

The term respiration refers both to the process of cellular oxidation of foodstuffs to provide readily available energy (see section 1.3), and to the uptake and disposal of gases and their transport within the body; it is with this latter that this section is concerned. On this larger scale, respiration involves the uptake of oxygen and the disposal of carbon dioxide, these being the gases needed for, and produced by, the underlying cellular metabolism. Gases diffuse rather slowly through liquids, and not sufficiently fast to reach respiring cells unless the supplying medium is in intimate contact with the cell membranes. Hence, all animals larger than a few millimetres require a means of distributing gases to the inner cells of their bodies, and generally also have some elaboration of the body surfaces to facilitate gas exchange with the environment.

Very small invertebrates can achieve sufficient uptake of oxygen across their body surfaces to respire without needing special organs. This applies to the two-layered coelenterates and sponges, and to several of the phyla of worms, where body-cavity fluids may help to distribute gases; direct diffusion also suffices for the echinoderms, although their tube-feet often have an accessory respiratory role. In annelid worms, gases may again be simply exchanged across the outer layers, the cuticle and epidermis, but these are specifically supplied with blood vessels (vascularised) and gases are carried in solution in the blood. For many annelids, however, either because they are highly active or because they are encased in tubes, simple respiration through the skin is inadequate and examples of respiratory specialisation are found. Some aquatic annelids such as the ragworm (*Nereis*) have vascularised gills on each segment, while many of the tube-living forms have a fan of gill filaments at the mouth end of the tube.

Efficient respiration requires a large, moist surface, externally in contact with oxygenated fluid and internally well supplied with blood vessels. This can be achieved either by subdivided, frilly extensions of tissue out from the body, or by a subdivided space forming a pocket in the body. Generally the former solution is termed a **gill** and the latter a **lung** (see Figs 2.19 and 2.20). Gills are very suitable for an aquatic animal, because they can be supported by the buoyant medium and because deoxygenated blood can flow as a counter-current to the flow of oxygen-rich water to give maximum rates of exchange. Lungs are a much better answer for terrestrial animals, partly because gills would collapse unless provided with skeletal struts, but also because the actual exchanging surfaces can be kept moist more readily if contained within a body, and loss of water can be a problem for land animals. Water naturally contains less oxygen per litre than does air, and gases also diffuse more slowly when in solution; therefore, to prevent stagnation and oxygen starvation, aquatic respiration requires a better provision for good flow over the exchanging surfaces than does respiration on land, and this can be more easily achieved with projecting gills than with forced tidal flow into and out of a lung. Hence, the nature of the habitat is the critical determinant of the form of the respiratory apparatus found in the larger representatives of major animal groups.

In molluscs there is a considerable diversity of respiratory structures. Marine forms, including most of the bivalves and many gastropods, have one pair or several pairs of gills made up of many fine filaments bearing cilia, and often of great structural complexity; some actually use these gills for filter-feeding as well. Cephalopods, which are all marine, also have paired gills, with branchial hearts boosting the blood flow. Terrestrial molluscs, such as snails and slugs, have lost their gills and instead respire across the surfaces of a highly vascularised internal cavity (lung), opening to the air through an opening called the pneumostome. Some freshwater snails, which probably returned to water from land, use the same structural solution as terrestrial snails.

Respiration in the arthropods is again largely determined by their habitat. Nearly all marine forms, including crustaceans and the king-crabs, have feathery gills covered with a very thin layer of permeable exoskeleton, and usually arranged segmentally above the legs; in some of the larger forms like crabs, however, and in woodlice, the gills are tucked under a flap of the cuticle and are hardly visible externally (see Fig. 2.19). Among the truly terrestrial arthropods, most of the arachnids, including the spiders, have internal multileaved structures called **lung-books**, and the millipedes, centipedes and insects have a system of internal **tracheae**, which are included in the definition of lungs but should perhaps be given a special status of their own. Tracheae are cuticle-lined tubes, branching inwards from segmentally arranged pores or spiracles (these are usually closable by valves), and forming eventually a network of fine tracheoles which penetrate all the tissues and even individual cells. Compressible air sacs may also be present to increase storage volume, to provide insulation and buoyancy, and to allow the whole system to be ventilated by pumping actions of the abdominal muscles. This respiratory arrangement seems particularly appropriate for small and active terrestrial animals, and provides sufficient oxygen even for insect flight muscles, the most metabolically active tissue known. It also allows a return to water, and many aquatic insect larvae have accessory gills extending from the abdomen and connecting to the air-filled tracheal network.

A tracheal system would probably be inadequate for a large terrestrial creature, and within the vertebrates there is a progressive loss of gills and development of lungs associated with the change of habitat from water to land. The vertebrate lung is believed to have been developed from the forerunner of the swim bladder that is found in modern fish. Most fish have conventional gills directly exposed to the water and supplied by complex arteries, the branchial arteries; but in some a simple sac arising from the gut forms a buoyancy device, and in the higher vertebrates this is replaced by a paired and subdivided sac supplied with blood vessels. In amphibians these lungs are of simple structure, as these animals also respire extensively through their skin and lack the rib or diaphragm muscles which could aid ventilation. In reptiles and mammals the lungs are made up of blind-ending sacs or alveoli, with a complex blood supply and associated musculature, while in birds the lung is finely subdivided into tubes called bronchi, allowing continuous flow of air through the lung. Some lizards and most birds

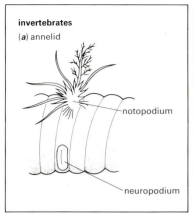

invertebrates

(*a*) annelid

notopodium

neuropodium

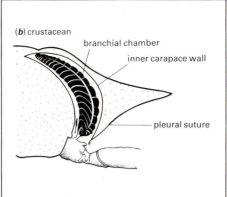

(*b*) crustacean

branchial chamber

inner carapace wall

pleural suture

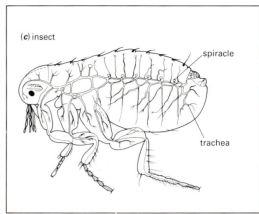

(*c*) insect

spiracle

trachea

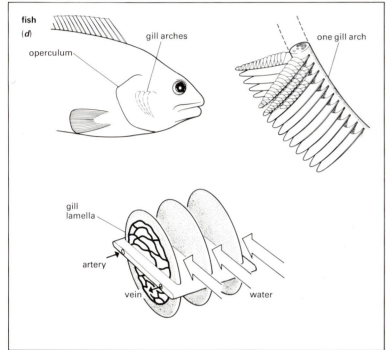

fish

(*d*)

operculum

gill arches

one gill arch

gill lamella

artery

vein

water

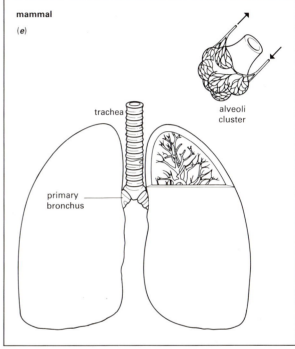

mammal

(*e*)

trachea

alveoli cluster

primary bronchus

Fig. 2.19. Respiratory mechanisms. Aquatic invertebrates and fish (a,b,d) have gills, with large surfaces protruding into the aerating water, while terrestrial solutions involve air being drawn into the body, via tracheal tubes (c) or lungs (e).

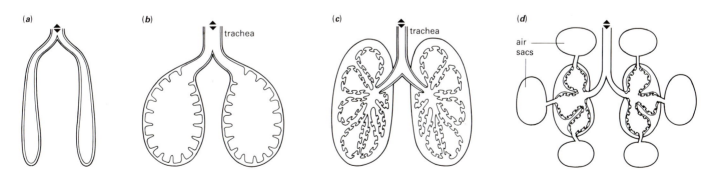

(*a*) (*b*) trachea (*c*) trachea (*d*) air sacs

Fig. 2.20. Increasing complexity of lung structure in terrestrial vertebrates, shown schematically. All systems have tidal flow except the bird lung(d),which permits some through-flow using air sacs like bellows.

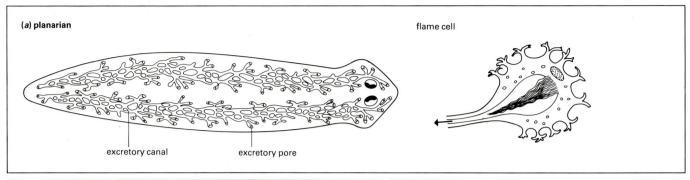

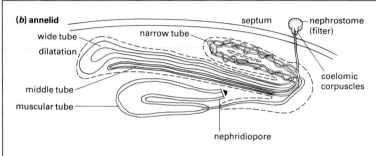

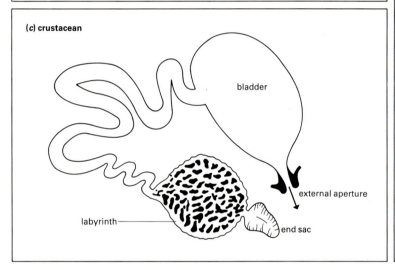

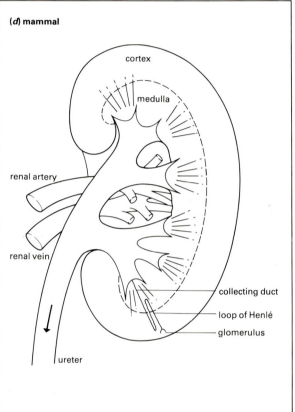

Fig. 2.21. Excretory systems in the animal kingdom. Small creatures without body cavities have many scattered flame cells (a), but most larger animals have fewer organs, two per segment in annelids (b) or one pair for the whole body as in (c) and (d). Length and complexity of the tubules are always greater in the freshwater and terrestrial forms shown here than in their marine relatives.

have air sacs as well, acting like bellows to give a more complete exchange of air in the lungs at each breath.

In mammals the lungs are very large and complex organs lying in the thorax. Air is drawn in and forced out through the nose and mouth by movements of the ribs and diaphragm. Blood is supplied from the pulmonary circulation and each alveolus is in intimate contact with blood capillaries, so that gases have only to diffuse a short distance. The total moist alveolar surface in humans may be as much as 100 square metres. Carbon dioxide passes out directly from the blood, and oxygen in from the air, because both are moving from high to low concentrations, and exchange of gases is very efficient. The lung system of higher vertebrates is also highly adaptable,

allowing birds to fly to 10000 metres above sea-level and aquatic mammals to dive down to nearly 1200 metres.

Respiration also concerns the supply of oxygen to active tissues once it is inside the body. In smaller animals it is simply dissolved in the blood, and in insects the tracheae take gaseous oxygen direct to the tissues so that no further bulk transport is needed. In a creature the size of a human, however, the cells require about 250 millilitres of oxygen per minute, and blood would have to circulate through the heart at 180 litres per minute if the oxygen were in simple solution. In fact blood flows at only about 5 litres per minute in humans, since the presence of haemoglobin in the red blood cells allows more gas to be carried. This pigment carries both oxygen and carbon

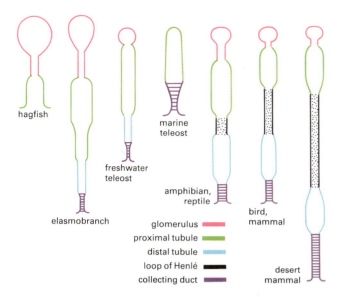

Fig. 2.22. *Kidney tubules in vertebrates: the more difficult the environment, the longer the tubule becomes (see text).*

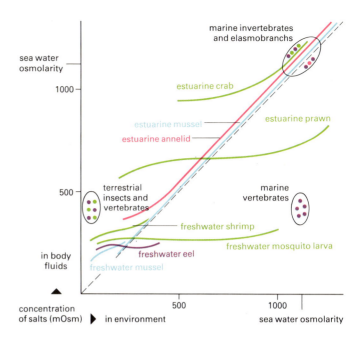

Fig. 2.23. *Regulation of body fluids in animals. Marine invertebrates are usually in equilibrium with their surroundings, while estuarine and freshwater animals show varying degrees of osmoregulation as the environmental concentration changes: estuarine mussels and annelids may allow their body fluids to dilute markedly (osmoconforming), while mosquito larvae and estuarine prawns are particularly good at keeping their body fluids constant. Marine vertebrates probably evolved from freshwater forms and have continued to osmoregulate at low blood concentrations, and a similar concentration has persisted in groups which have become terrestrial.*

dioxide; 100 millilitres of blood with haemoglobin can transport 20 millilitres of oxygen and about 50 millilitres of carbon dioxide, whereas the blood fluids alone would carry only 0.25 millilitres and 2.7 millilitres, respectively. The oxygen is reversibly attached to the iron atom at the centre of the haemoglobin molecule, causing arterial blood to be brighter red than venous blood in which the haemoglobin has lost its oxygen. The gas is released to any tissue where oxygen is lacking, and carbon dioxide is taken up in its place, mostly in the form of the bicarbonate (hydrogen carbonate, HCO_3^-) ion.

Haemoglobin is only one of several blood pigments found in animals, though it is much the commonest (see Table 2.2). In smaller invertebrates it is dissolved in the blood. For the larger forms needing proportionately more haemoglobin, this would make the fluid too viscous, and the pigment is packed in the red blood cells, where its potentially toxic iron can be safely contained. Other pigments contain different metals with which oxygen can combine, and so have different colours. The bluish colour of the blood of many molluscs is usually due to a pigment

called haemocyanin; the possession of this less efficient pigment may be one reason why the cephalopods, in many ways the most advanced of the invertebrates, are so restricted in their habitat.

Body fluids: water, salts and excretion

Regulation of the water content of the body is a major requirement for most animals. In marine invertebrates the total concentration of the cell contents is similar to sea-water, giving a negligible osmotic gradient and little movement of water, but most other animals have to regulate their water content to some degree. Marine vertebrates are nearly always more dilute than their surroundings, perhaps indicating an evolutionary history in freshwater, and they must thus take steps to avoid loss of water. Present-day freshwater animals have the opposite problem, with a high rate of inward diffusion of water, and this water must be expelled to avoid dilution and bursting. Terrestrial species have a critical need to avoid loss both of water and of solutes. Although the skins or cuticles of animals help to control these problems, a good deal of osmotic regulation is usually performed by what are generally termed excretory organs.

Whereas in sea-water the principal positively charged ion (cation) is sodium, in most cells it is potassium, and both magnesium and sulphate are less concentrated in cells than in the sea. Hence all cells, even in marine animals, have to expend some energy in regulating their ionic compositions. In a

Table 2.2 *Respiratory pigments in animals*

Pigment	Nature and relative molecular mass	Occurrence	
Haemoglobin	Iron–porphyrin protein complex 17000–3000000 (68000 in most vertebrates)	Most vertebrates Some polychaetes A few echinoderms, flatworms, insects, protozoans Even occasionally in plants	In cells In cells or in solution
Chlorocruorin	Iron–porphyrin protein complex 2500000–3000000	Some polychaetes	Always in solution
Haemerythrin	Iron-containing protein 60000–150000	Some sipunculids, priapulids, brachiopods, polychaetes	Always in cells
Haemocyanin	Copper-containing protein 300000–9000000	Many molluscs Some crustaceans	Always in solution

multicellular animal this energy requirement can be reduced by setting up an internal environment: the blood. The task of regulating the ionic concentrations around most of the cells is then delegated to a few specialised areas, and ionic regulation becomes a second function of the excretory organs.

The third and most familiar function of excretory organs is ridding the body of nitrogenous waste. A certain amount of nitrogen-containing material comes from the repair of the tissues that is continually carried out in multicellular animals, but most of it comes from the digestive processes. All proteins eaten in the diet are broken down into amino-acids, which are fed into the normal metabolic pathways after removal of the amino group as free ammonia. Ammonia is highly toxic, and must not be allowed to accumulate; but it is also a small and highly soluble molecule, so that for many small aquatic animals it can simply be allowed to diffuse out of the body across the skin and gill surfaces and be dissipated in the environment. In such cases, the excretory organs may have little role in the disposal of nitrogenous waste. Terrestrial animals, however, do not enjoy the large supplies of water required to excrete ammonia. In many land animals, ammonia is combined with the equally undesirable carbon dioxide, forming urea. This is only slightly toxic and is also moderately soluble, and so some water is required for its elimination; as an excretory product it is a compromise. Urea is the main waste material of larger land animals, such as the mammals. For a smaller creature even this limited necessity for water loss cannot be tolerated, and in birds, reptiles and insects uric acid is used instead. Uric acid is non-toxic and very poorly soluble; when water is removed, uric acid precipitates as a sludge of crystals. This permits very dry urine to be produced, and even allows the retention of excretory wastes in the body: some insects merely deposit uric acid salts in their cuticles or elsewhere through their life, and many hatchling birds leave a deposit of uric acid behind in their shells. Thus both the functions of the excretory organs and the nature of the excretory products depend upon the habitat and the size of a particular animal.

For the smallest marine animals, whether unicellular or multicellular, no specific organs of excretion are required, and each cell attends to its own ionic regulation. In small freshwater animals, however, water must be continually expelled, and in unicells and in sponges an organelle known as the **contractile vacuole** is commonly found. This vacuole fills with fluid from the surrounding cytoplasm, the fluid is diluted by the active removal of ions and is periodically ejected to the environment, giving a net loss of water. The few freshwater representatives of the coelenterates have no such vacuole nor any other observed means for removing the inevitable influx of water, and their method of osmoregulation remains uncertain.

Within the rest of the animal kingdom there are only two main types of excretory organ, although the affinities of individual cases may not always be easy to trace. One type, known as a **nephridium** (Fig. 2.21), forms as an infolding of the animal's ectoderm, and has an intracellular duct lined with cilia. In its simplest form, as the flame-cell of flatworms, rotifers and nemertine worms, the organ is a blind-ending tube; fluid is drawn in as a filtrate from the body to the inner cavity, or lumen, and is then swept out through the duct by beating cilia. In other animals, the tube has an open end connecting with the body cavity via a ciliated funnel and in close contact with blood vessels, so filtering the body fluids. This arrangement is found in some annelids, and in many larval invertebrates. The second main type of excretory organ, known as a **coelomoduct** (Fig. 2.21), arises from the mesoderm lining the body cavity, working its way outwards and having an intercellular duct. In many cases it also serves as a duct for the reproductive system to transport germ cells to the outside. This type of organ occurs in the higher invertebrate groups, notably the molluscs and crustaceans, and in the vertebrates as the kidney. The annelid worms can be seen as a transition group, since some have a true coelomoduct and others have a structure which is a fusion of a nephridium and a coelomoduct.

The excretory organs of most flatworms, annelids and crustaceans are largely concerned with regulating water content. Thus, freshwater flatworms have far more flame cells than do their estuarine and marine relatives, which often have none, and freshwater crayfish have much longer ducts to their excretory organs (known as green glands) than do marine prawns or lobsters. This trend of increase in number or length of excretory organs as the salinity decreases is common to all groups, and is principally a means of increasing the surface area for ionic regulation. The fluid which passes into the organ is initially simply a filtrate of the body fluid. Within the organ, ions can be removed from or secreted into the urine as this passes down the tube, and the longer the tube the greater the change of concentration, compared to the initial filtrate, which can be effected.

The same principle can be seen in the vertebrate kidney. This organ is made up of many individual tubules (**nephrons**), each acting as a separate filtering unit, and consisting of a **glomerulus** producing an ultrafiltrate of the blood, and a **tubule** which modifies this filtrate. The proximal tubule (nearer the glomerulus) reabsorbs salts and some organic solutes, while the distal tubule (further along) reabsorbs more salts and may also reabsorb water, as may the terminal collecting duct. The length and complexity of these tubules is correlated with the severity of the osmotic problems faced by each animal (Fig. 2.22). The hagfish is unique among vertebrates in having blood about as concentrated as sea water; it has little need for water regulation, and so the nephrons are short. Other fish have rather dilute blood, about 30% as concentrated in terms of ions as is the sea; they must therefore osmoregulate to retain water if they are marine, or osmoregulate to lose excess water and retain salts if they live in freshwater. One solution, found in the marine cartilaginous fish such as sharks and rays, is to make up the deficit in ionic concentration of the blood with organic compounds, especially urea, so that the kidney has less osmotic work to do; the tubules remain relatively simple. Marine bony fish, on the other hand, do not accumulate urea and must instead recover the water they lose to the sea; they thus drink sea water, but thereby also ingest excess sodium chloride, and removal of this excess salt is largely done by active secretion from the gills as the kidney of bony fish is not adapted to produce concentrated salt solutions. In freshwater, bony fish tend to take up water continuously, and remedy this both by producing a very dilute urine and also by actively taking up some salts through their gills.

The problems for the remaining vertebrates are essentially those of retention of water, though larval amphibians produce a dilute urine and take up salt through their skin or gills like fish. In adult amphibians, and in reptiles, birds and mammals, the kidney becomes increasingly important as an excretory and regulatory centre, and an additional region appears in the kidney tubule between its proximal and distal parts. In most reptiles this new region is short, and urine cannot be made more concentrated than the blood, but in birds and mammals of dry habitats it may be very long and forms a hairpin shape called the loop of Henlé. It operates to remove water and to produce a very concentrated urine, up to 25 times the concentration of blood plasma. In lizards, and some birds, urine from the kidney is relatively dilute, and water conservation is effected instead in a region called the cloaca at the end of the collecting duct, to leave a paste of uric acid. Some marine representatives of these groups also have nasal salt glands to excrete excess salts that enter in the diet. Thus, as in other groups, the whole process of excretion and osmotic regulation is a complex balance of mechanisms, with skin, gills and gut often involved at least as much as the actual excretory organ itself.

The insects have a novel solution to the problem of water balance, using organs unrelated to nephridia or coelomoducts and which produce a fluid by secretion rather than by ultrafiltration. These organs are the **Malpighian tubules**, blind-ending tubes leading off the midgut; in cooperation with the rectum they can produce an extremely dry paste of uric acid salts. Again the mechanism is best developed in inhabitants of dry areas, where a counter-current system helps the removal of water. Water regulation in insects is aided by the impermeability of the cuticle, which can even in some cases take up water from unsaturated air, by a mechanism still poorly understood.

Most terrestrial animals thus have complex mechanisms to keep their blood and cell contents at constant concentrations, while for most marine invertebrates the external environment is constant and equable and the cells have few such problems. For freshwater and estuarine animals, however, the environment may change radically (see Chapters 7 and 9). In these cases the animal either regulates according to need, using up energy at the gill or excretory surfaces (osmoregulating, as do terrestrial animals), or it passively tolerates the changes, leaving each cell to cope with the osmotic stress (osmoconforming, as in simple marine invertebrates) (Fig. 2.23).

Nutrition and digestion

All organisms require food, to provide materials and energy for maintenance and repair of tissues, for work, and for growth. Unlike green plants, animals cannot synthesise their own foods and so must find suitable foodstuffs. The process of feeding therefore includes locating, capturing, ingesting and finally digesting correct foods to fulfil all the animal's needs.

An animal's nutritional requirements are surprisingly exacting. All animals must take in carbohydrates, lipids of various sorts, proteins containing enough of the essential amino-acids that the tissue of the animal cannot synthesise, water, many inorganic salts including some trace elements, and certain vitamins. Once inside the body, the bulk foods of carbohydrate, lipid and protein are broken down by digestive enzymes, respectively, to glucose, glycerol and fatty acids, and amino-acids. These simpler molecules are ultimately absorbed by the cells.

Only a limited number of food resources satisfy these rather elaborate needs. Some animals ingest food items that are small relative to their own bodies (**microphagy**), usually by filtering suspended microscopic plants and animals from the aquatic medium. Other animals feed on large pieces of living plant or animal matter as herbivores or carnivores (**macrophagy**), and a third group feed on liquids derived from other living organisms. Each type of feeding requires its own specialisations, and imposes particular limitations on the structure of the animal concerned.

A great many invertebrates are aquatic and microphagous, and use an extraordinary array of devices to filter out the edible micro-organisms. These often involve finely divided ciliated surfaces, forming a fine net to trap particles as the cilia create a gentle water current. The feeding cells of sponges, the gill crowns of sedentary annelid worms, and the gills of most bivalve molluscs are of this type. Other animals, especially tunicates (sea-squirts) and some gastropod molluscs, filter-feed using sheets of mucus (see Fig. 6.11). There are also examples of animals using parts of the body hardened by a skeleton as filters: the complex bristles (setae) on the limbs of many crustaceans, the gill rakers of fish such as the herring and basking shark, the beak of the flamingo and the sieve-plates of baleen whales are all used to strain food particles from water. Finally many micro-organisms are also microphagous, ingesting other tiny creatures whole by engulfing them in a digestive vacuole. For all such microphagous animals the food is already finely divided and so digestion is relatively simple, and often occurs inside cells without the need to pour out digestive enzymes into a complex gut.

For macrophagous animals the problems are very different. Some animals feed on large inactive masses, unselectively swallowing detritus and extracting useful organic matter from it; earthworms are an example. Most others either feed on green plants or catch animals. Feeding on stationary green plants is in fact rather difficult, because most animals are unable to digest

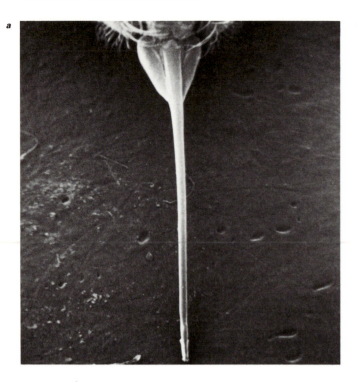

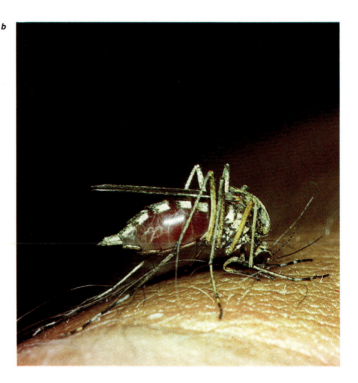

Fig. 2.24. (a) Scanning electron micrograph of the proboscis of a blood-sucking tsetse fly (Glossina). (b) Female mosquito (Aedes) feeding; the red colour of the blood meal can be clearly seen in her extended abdomen.

the cellulose cell walls and only small soluble materials which can leave the plant cells are available to them. Only three groups of animals have proved notably successful at coping with plant tissues as their sole foodstuffs: the gastropod molluscs, which have a rasping toothed radula in their mouths; some orders of insects, with sharp mandibles to cut and crush the green tissues; and certain mammals, with grinding molar teeth. In most of these cases, and in a few other specialist animals, mechanical crushing of the plants is aided by chemical methods, and almost always the cellulase enzyme required is provided by symbiotic micro-organisms living in the gut (see section 5.4). Some of the specialist herbivores, especially insects, also have complex mechanisms to find particular types of plant, homing in by scent to the chemical components of their favoured foodstuff.

Feeding on other animals presents fewer digestive problems. Vertebrate carnivores often capture and swallow prey whole, and the possession of stinging nematoblast cells on their tentacles allows coelenterates to do this too. Alternatively, the carnivore may grasp its prey in limbs or jaws and break pieces off to swallow, usually requiring some hard skeletal parts around the mouth to achieve mechanical breakdown; teeth and the mandibles of insects are obvious examples, but jaws and beak-like structures are also found in many polychaete worms and in cephalopod molluscs.

For macrophagous organisms, whether detritus-feeders, herbivores or carnivores, the gut usually becomes diversified. There is a fairly standard structure to such animal guts, with a mouth, an oral cavity, an oesophagus leading into the body, a crop for storage or a thickened gizzard for extra mechanical maceration, a stomach and intestine for progressive enzymic degradation and absorption, and a rectum for further uptake of nutrients, salts or water prior to defaecation through an anus.

Fluids are the third possible type of food, and many available fluids have nutritional value. Occasionally they are deliberately offered as food, for example the floral nectar taken by insects, birds and bats, but more commonly fluid-feeding involves being a parasite, sucking from the phloem and xylem of plants as do aphids, or taking fluid from the blood system of other animals as is the case for mosquitoes, ticks and leeches (see Fig. 2.24). Thus elaborate mouthparts for piercing may be developed, and pumps to suck with, and a very extensible body may also be required if food comes in large but infrequent amounts. Spiders and star-fish are also liquid-feeders, but achieve this by applying digestive enzymes to their prey. The enzymes are injected through the spider's mouthparts, or poured out from the star-fish's everted stomach. In both cases the resultant 'soup' of digested matter can then be lapped or sucked up. Internal parasites are also usually liquid-feeders (see section 10.2). Tapeworms, for example, have lost their digestive tracts completely, and simply absorb through their skin predigested material from the guts of their hosts. This is another example of the observed structure being determined as much by the habits of the animal as by its evolutionary history.

By whatever means food may be obtained, there is little variation in the biochemical processes of digestion that ultimately make it useful and available to cells, and enzymes very similar to those familiar from vertebrate studies are found in the guts and cells of a wide range of invertebrates. Thus, proteins are generally broken down by enzymes allied to the stomach pepsin and the intestinal trypsin of mammals, fats are attacked by lipase, and carbohydrates by amylase and related enzymes. One of the major differences, though, is the site where this digestion occurs. It is not simply that intracellular digestion in protozoans progressively changes to complex extracellular digestion in the gut of mammals. Rather, microphagous creatures, whether sponges or whales, digest most of their ingested foodstuffs within cells and the structure of their gut

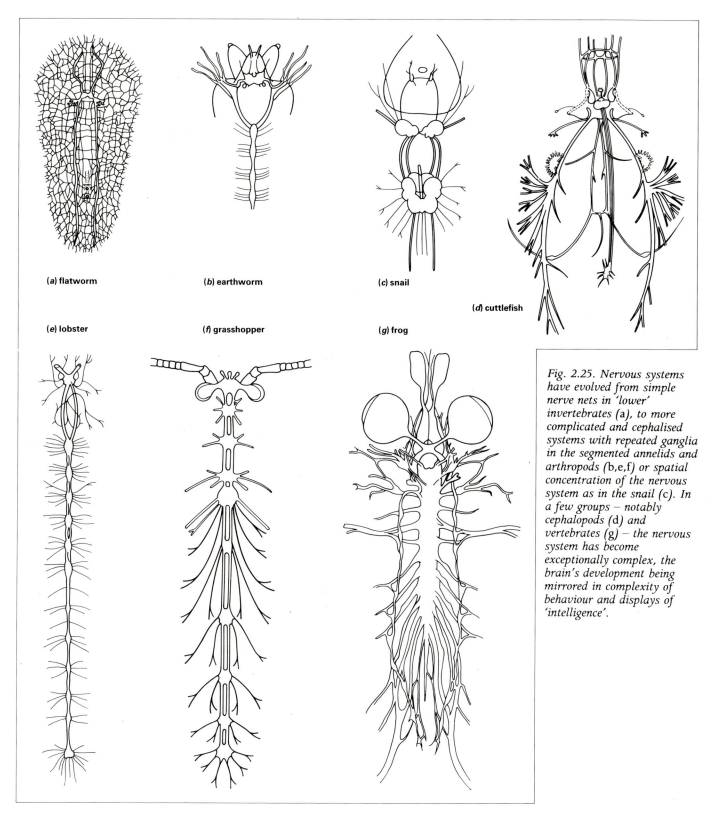

(a) flatworm

(b) earthworm

(c) snail

(d) cuttlefish

(e) lobster

(f) grasshopper

(g) frog

Fig. 2.25. Nervous systems have evolved from simple nerve nets in 'lower' invertebrates (a), to more complicated and cephalised systems with repeated ganglia in the segmented annelids and arthropods (b,e,f) or spatial concentration of the nervous system as in the snail (c). In a few groups – notably cephalopods (d) and vertebrates (g) – the nervous system has become exceptionally complex, the brain's development being mirrored in complexity of behaviour and displays of 'intelligence'.

can be simple, while macrophagous animals need more elaborate mechanisms within their digestive tract and use different areas of this for digesting and absorbing each type of food, secreting particular enzymes at particular places, and providing the right chemical environments in which the enzymes can work optimally. The two processes of extracellular and intracellular digestion are, however, rarely mutually exclusive, and extracellular digestion in the gut often serves to break up the food material into sufficiently small fragments for individual cells to take in and complete the digestion intracellularly.

Energetics, temperature and homeostasis

One of the main functions of feeding is to provide energy, and in most animals the intake of food is well adjusted to the expenditure of energy. During physically active periods extra food is ingested, while during rest periods or dormancy animals may not feed at all, their metabolism running slowly on stored foods. The metabolic rate (the energy expended per unit time) is therefore a useful indicator of how a particular animal is functioning, and it is often measured as the rate of consumption of oxygen, since releasing the energy stored in foods via the chemical intermediary ATP requires molecular oxygen (see section 1.2). Different animals have very different rates of use of oxygen, and different tissues also vary widely; muscles, excretory organs and the brain may be very demanding. Furthermore, the nature of the fuel needed in different parts may vary; for example, while most mammalian tissues will metabolise fatty acids, the brain must be supplied with glucose even though glucose releases less energy per mole.

Metabolic rate and energetics are very dependent on the size of an animal, smaller creatures having higher energy consumptions per unit mass. This is probably because so many physiological processes are related to surfaces: the uptake of gases, diffusion from blood to tissues, food uptake in the intestine, and so on. As the volume of an animal increases, the ratio of surface area to volume falls, and many processes become slower.

Regulation of body temperature is a physiological process very closely related to size, and it has often been given as the explanation for the relation between body size and metabolic rate for mammals and birds. Temperature regulation is intimately connected with energetics, because all metabolic processes generate heat. Birds, mammals and a few other terrestrial animals such as some large insects are **endothermic**, specifically able to generate large quantities of heat inside their bodies; this internal heat can be retained by insulating fur or feathers, rendering these animals warm-blooded with a relatively high and roughly constant body temperature, which only drops close to that of the environment during predetermined times of inactivity such as hibernation. In smaller animals, however, surface area is so large relative to the volume of tissue generating energy that the heat is dissipated rapidly to the surroundings. Such animals are **ectotherms**, gaining their warmth primarily from external heat sources, and controlling this by behavioural means such as sun-basking; lizards and butterflies are common examples. Even for endotherms, keeping warm by retaining metabolic heat is very difficult unless the body is large, and small mammals therefore have to have a very rapid metabolism, using up a large proportion of their food intake simply to maintain their body temperatures. If a mouse possessed a metabolic rate as low as that of a cow it would need fur about 20 centimetres thick to maintain its body temperature! Although keeping warm is energetically expensive for endotherms, especially if they are small, it means they can be active at all times of day and night in most climates, using food sources when other animals are cold and sluggish. Ectothermic animals can be fully active only within quite narrow temperature limits.

Temperature regulation is only one aspect of the phenomenon called **homeostasis**: the process of keeping a constant internal environment. Many physiological mechanisms contribute to this, whether the internal environment considered is the extracellular fluid, the body cavity or the blood. Foods are absorbed into these compartments from the gut, and are stored if in excess: ions and water are regulated by the kidneys; and the levels of the dissolved gases are maintained according to the tissues' needs by regulating flow at the respiratory surfaces. All these processes are necessary because cells work best in certain defined physiological conditions of acidity, temperature, and concentrations of ions and organic compounds, as particularly do the enzymes which regulate cellular reactions. The more efficiently an animal can regulate all aspects of its body fluids, the more it becomes independent of external circumstances, and the better able to exploit a wide range of environments or a particular previously inhospitable habitat. This is especially so for land animals, since aquatic habitats are generally more stable in time and space, and birds and mammals have developed particularly effective homeostatic regulatory mechanisms.

Nervous systems

Because of the complexity of their physiological systems, all animals require a means of coordinating their activities and of adjusting their responses to external events. Animals therefore respond to stimuli, whether from within their bodies or from the outside world. All cells are 'irritable' to some extent, and in unicellular animals the cell is both the **receptor** receiving the stimulus, and the **effector** carrying out the response. In some invertebrates, epithelial (skin) cells may retain this dual sensory and effector function, as do the musculo-epithelial cells of coelenterates. In most multicellular creatures, however, there is also a true nervous system, in which nerve cells link specialised sensory receptors to effector cells such as muscles or glands. The nervous system is primarily a communication network, but this function is augmented in several ways: it can be a sorting mechanism, selecting useful information from the enormous range of stimuli impinging on the animal; an integrating centre for these different sensory inputs; a decision-making system; a generator of spontaneous patterns of activity; and, in advanced nervous systems, an information store or memory from which selected pieces of information can be retrieved.

All of these functions are performed by **neurons**, the cells from which nervous tissues are made and which have specially developed properties of nervous conduction (see section 1.4). Neurons come in many different forms, but their basic structure and function are the same in all animals, and the complexity of a given nervous system is related simply to the way these units are linked together, at points called **synapses**. Communication between a neuron and an adjacent cell across a synapse involves diffusion of chemical transmitter molecules between two closely opposed membranes. Each neuron has a **cell body**, and usually one or more long processes or **axons** extending from this, either arising from a sensory cell or extending to an effector cell. In lower invertebrates there are generally several axons per cell body, forming a multipolar neuron, whereas in higher invertebrates and vertebrates the neurons are often monopolar, and integrative interneurons in the central portions of the nervous system may have no axons at all, connecting only to nearby neurons. Apart from axons, most nerve cells also have branching **dendrites**, tree-like processes which pick up the electric signals from adjacent cells; dendrites are therefore particularly well developed for the central interneurons.

Nervous systems also contain other types of cells, usually termed **glial cells**, which form sheaths around the neurons. These insulate the neurons from each other, help to increase the speed of their conduction and to maintain their ionic environment, and may direct their growth to ensure that neurons link up in the correct manner.

From these simple structural units are constructed the vast range of nervous systems encountered in multicellular animals. Some examples of the patterns of nervous systems are given in Fig. 2.25. In radially symmetrical animals, such as coelenterates and echinoderms, there is a diffuse **nerve net** over the whole body, although in many coelenterates there may be longitudinal tracts of nerves to help withdrawal of tentacles, and there is a dense ring of nerves round the mouth in an echinoderm. In bilaterally symmetrical animals the tendency to concentrate the nervous system into tracts is clearer, and most invertebrates have a ventral **nerve cord**, generally formed from a fusing of two or more embryonic nerve cords. In the segmented groups, each segment of the animal commonly possesses a concentration of cell bodies called a **ganglion**, which contains many synapses, and the axons to and from receptors and effectors are arranged segmentally in a repeating pattern. Particularly in higher arthropods, the segmental ganglia fuse into larger structures, and some flies have only one thoracic and one abdominal ganglion in addition to the brain at the front of the body. Unsegmented invertebrates like molluscs contain fewer ganglia although the anterior cerebral ganglion is exceptionally well developed in the cephalopod molluscs.

In vertebrates the nervous system is again segmentally arranged, with the nerves from the dorsal spinal cord associated with muscles in each segment; the segmentation in this group becomes however much less apparent as the integrative role of the brain increases. The nerve cords of vertebrates and invertebrates are differently sited, being, respectively, dorsal and ventral, and also have contrasting organisation: in invertebrates the cell bodies of neurons are arranged in the periphery of the ganglia, while in vertebrates the cell bodies form a central core, the grey matter. This core contains many interneurons and the simplest vertebrate responses, like reflex arcs, are mediated here without involvement of the higher centres of the brain. Most of the sensory inputs, however, are directed onwards via the axons of the outer white matter, and travel to the brain where an appropriate response is initiated.

The vertebrate brain is an extraordinarily complicated organ, yet it consists of the same basic components as does any other nervous tissue. The brain can be divided into three sections, and the evolution of these is traced in Fig. 2.26. In the mammalian brain the cortex and forebrain have become pre-eminent, and the association of different areas of the brain with particular senses and with motor control is precisely known; the development of each zone varies according to the particular lifestyle and sensory needs of each animal species.

Much of the vertebrate body is also served by a further set of nerves, the **autonomic nervous system**, through cranial and spinal nerve tracts (Fig. 2.27). These form a separate control mechanism for the internal organs of the body, over which there is usually little voluntary control. The whole body is thus coordinated by parallel and interrelated sets of nervous pathways, and its activities can be regulated in accordance with changing needs.

Senses and perception

Coordination of the activities of an animal with events in its environment requires that information about these external events be perceived and passed on in a usable form to the animal's effectors. Sensory receptors, whether neurons or epithelial cells secondarily connected to nerves, transduce various types of energy from the external world into the pulses of electrical energy used by the nervous system of the animal. Receptors are usually specialised, by their structure or by the properties of their membranes, to respond to only one form of energy, and are therefore classified as, for example, mechanical, chemical or photic (light) receptors. The information sent on from the receptor to the central nervous system also depends on how a stimulus is coded, in terms of strength and frequency of the nervous signal, and on whether the receptor cell is **tonic** (responding only to the onset or ending of a stimulus) or **phasic** (responding throughout the duration of a stimulus). Furthermore, some receptors respond to changes in a stimulus actually emitted by an animal, as with the echo-locating signals of bats, whales and dolphins or the electrical fields generated by electric fish. There is therefore considerable scope for specialisation in sensory systems.

Mechanoreceptors provide information concerning a range of sensations including movement, tension, pressure, balance and vibration (including sound); these sensations can be produced by the weight of the body, the relative movement of its parts, or the direct impact of the environment on the animal's surfaces. Most such receptors respond to stimuli at fairly low frequencies, whether the receptors are external tactile (touch) sensors or internal **proprioceptors** such as those sensing the tension in muscles. The higher ranges of frequency are called sound and are detected only by special auditory organs.

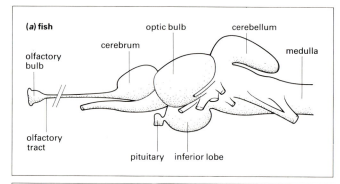

(a) fish

olfactory bulb, cerebrum, optic bulb, cerebellum, medulla, olfactory tract, pituitary, inferior lobe

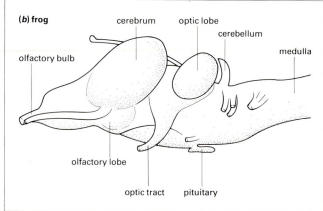

(b) frog

olfactory bulb, cerebrum, optic lobe, cerebellum, medulla, olfactory lobe, optic tract, pituitary

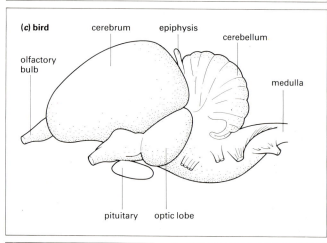

(c) bird

olfactory bulb, cerebrum, epiphysis, cerebellum, medulla, pituitary, optic lobe

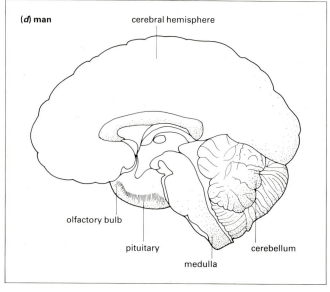

(d) man

cerebral hemisphere, olfactory bulb, pituitary, medulla, cerebellum

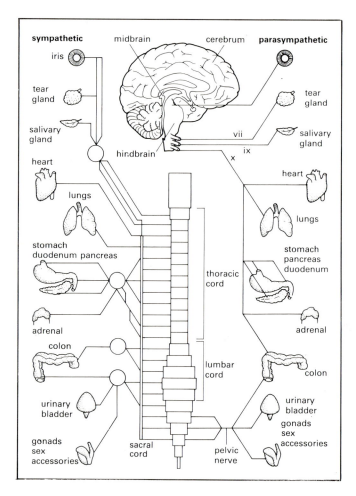

sympathetic, midbrain, cerebrum, parasympathetic, iris, tear gland, salivary gland, heart, lungs, stomach duodenum pancreas, adrenal, colon, urinary bladder, gonads sex accessories, hindbrain, thoracic cord, lumbar cord, sacral cord, vii, ix, x, tear gland, salivary gland, heart, lungs, stomach pancreas duodenum, adrenal, colon, urinary bladder, gonads sex accessories, pelvic nerve

Fig. 2.26. (left) Development of the brain in vertebrate evolution; the cerebrum becomes ever more important and the relative contribution of sensory areas varies according to lifestyle.

Fig. 2.27. (above) The autonomic (involuntary) nervous system in mammals, controlling most glands, organs and smooth muscles. The sympathetic nervous effects (raised heart rate and blood pressure, dilated pupils, erection of hair and sweating) are similar to those of the hormone adrenaline, while parasympathetic effects (especially those from vagal nerve X) are directly opposite.

Simple tactile receptors occur in almost all multicellular animals, and even protozoans have a sense of touch in their cell membrane. For most creatures the sensors are bristles or hairs, responding physically as the hair is moved. Insect exoskeletons are covered with sensory bristles, each sitting within a socket in the cuticle, while the skin of a mammal has a wide range of mechanoreceptors responding to different types of touch or pressure, especially the fingertips and around the mouth and genitals. Proprioceptors give a sense of position and movement both at joints and within muscles: the muscle spindles in vertebrates are specialised muscle fibres which send impulses to the spinal cord when they are stretched, giving information about the load on the muscle; arthropods contain similar stretch receptors in their muscles, and all other animals must have similar receptors in their locomotory muscles. Reception of tension is also important in the rectum and bladder of many animals, and in the oviducts, signalling when the organ is full and its contents ready for release. Mechanoreceptors for

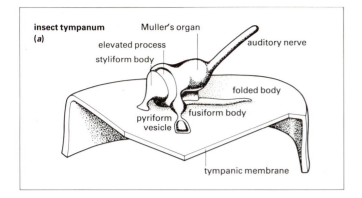

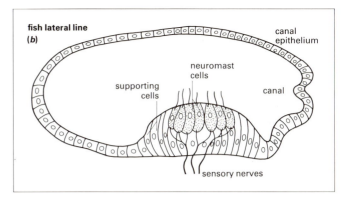

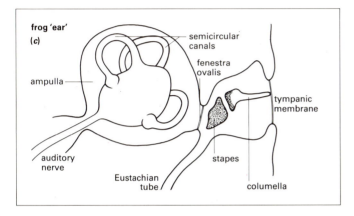

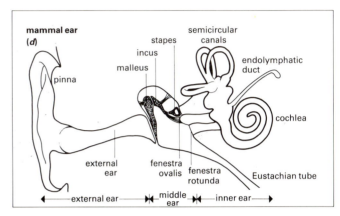

Fig. 2.28. The structure of ears and related sensory systems (position and vibration detectors) in insects and vertebrates.

equilibrium or balance also occur in most animals, whether they are aquatic or terrestrial, and often work on the simple principle of a statocyst. This is a dense particle enclosed in a fluid and acting upon a number of sensory hairs: coelenterates and flatworms have such structures, as do many arthropods, and even the semicircular canals of the vertebrate ear work in a similar manner.

The most elaborate mechanoreceptors are those responsible for hearing, and their complexity tends to increase as the whole animal becomes more complex (Fig. 2.28); in fact few invertebrates have a true sense of hearing. The insects are exceptions, and some have tympanal organs on their thorax, abdomen or legs, consisting of a thin drum of cuticle with a number of attached sensory neurons located in different planes. In the vertebrates, the lateral-line system of fish is a simple detector of vibrations, while the vertebrate ear evolved originally as an organ of equilibrium. The cochlea of the inner ear, which detects sound with an elaborately tuned vibratory basilar membrane to which sense cells are attached, is scarcely apparent in the fish and quite small in reptiles and birds, only reaching full development in the mammals; the middle ear, which transmits and amplifies sound from the environment, first appears in the amphibians and the outer ear, which collects and directs sound, is only apparent in mammals. The ear of terrestrial mammals is an extraordinarily elaborate hearing organ, and is exceptionally discriminative of the frequency, amplitude and direction of sound.

Chemoreceptors are a second very important class of animal sensors, and again range from the general sensitivity of the membranes of protozoans up to the complex organs of the mammalian nose and tongue or the insect antenna. In many cases the receptor itself is an exposed membrane to which the stimulating molecules can bind, either in solution as tastes, or as airborne scents. There may be complex receptor sites to pick up particularly relevant chemicals from the environment, and thus confer specificity on the response. Chemicals which elicit responses in animals are important in many facets of life, including communication by pheromones for finding mates (see page 94), location of prey or hosts, and recognition of plant foods. In insects chemical senses are particularly well developed, with receptors located on fine bristles, pores in the cuticle or on the elaborate antennae. There are also many internal chemoreceptors in animals, especially where homeostasis is critical, detecting changes in the composition or concentration of body fluids and initiating appropriate physiological feedbacks.

Photoreceptors are light-sensitive cells and exist in almost all animals (Fig. 2.29). Protozoans will usually move away from light sources, and in some species such as *Euglena* there are specialised pigmented eye-spots. In multicellular animals sensitivity becomes increasingly concentrated in special cells, either located singly within the epidermis, or grouped as photoreceptive organs as in the annelid worms and flatworms. In the less complex animals these organs cannot form images, as they have no lens, and are usually disc-shaped clusters of sensitive cells responding principally to the direction from which light is received. Many animals with this type of receptor also retain an overall sensitivity of the epidermis to light. In more complex animals lenses are present and the structures can be termed eyes. There are two main types of animal eye, the camera eye of cephalopod molluscs and vertebrates, and the compound eye of arthropods.

The **camera eye** as found in vertebrates is very elaborate, with a complete set of monopolar receptors, the rods and cones, forming the retina onto which the lens casts a focused image. In humans each eye contains about 125 million rods, and about 6.5 million cones responsible for colour vision. In the arthropod **compound eye** (Fig. 2.30) there are many separate visual units, or **ommatidia**, the number per eye ranging from a few up to several thousand according to the lifestyle of the species concerned. Each ommatidium has six to eight monopolar neurons, a simple lens made out of cuticle, and a sheath of pigment, and so acts as an independent, but crude, image-receiving system. Of these two types of eye, the camera eye can produce one complete image on the retina and gives great visual acuity, whereas the compound eye produces a mosaic of many images but can be extremely sensitive to movement and to flickering light sources. Either type of eye can be adapted for colour vision by using modified pigments to absorb light of different wavelengths.

For all visual systems so far analysed, the primary reception of light depends on a visual pigment called rhodopsin. This molecule is a conjugate of retinene, derived from vitamin A, and a protein called opsin, and the association between these breaks down when light is received, the retinene molecule then changing its shape slightly to trigger the electrical impulses in the receptor membrane.

Apart from the three most obvious types of sensor discussed above, animals may respond to other forms of energy, some less familiar to the sensory world of humans. Many creatures have a thermal sense, responding both to environmental temperature changes and to their body temperature. In mammals the skin has thermal sensors, and there are also receptors in the brain-stem which function to maintain a constant body temperature. Some animals also have an electrical sense, responding to changes in the electrical field around them; certain fish use modified muscle cells to generate a powerful field around themselves, and detect with their lateral-line apparatus changes in this field caused by nearby objects. Other animals have a magnetic sense and can navigate successfully without any other cues; the physiology of this ability is not yet clearly elucidated, but some degree of magnetic sense has been claimed for creatures as diverse as bacteria, snails, bees and pigeons.

One of the most important features of the sensory apparatus of an animal, made up of these numerous possible types of sense organ, is that it is fitted to the needs and habits of that particular animal. Thus, for example, internal parasites generally have very few receptors of any sort; animals living in deep waters or burrows lack eyes but have elaborate chemical, tactile and auditory organs; and active terrestrial predators have prominent eyes with binocular vision, together with powerful senses of hearing and smell. An examination of the array of sensors, and of the relative importance of the associated integrative centres in the nervous system, can

therefore provide important clues about the ways particular animals live.

Hormonal control

Sensory mechanisms, nervous systems and effectors such as muscles, are the most obvious means by which animals regulate their activities in relation to the environment, and together these provide a coordinating network which can respond very specifically and very quickly, sometimes within a few milliseconds of a stimulus. However, many biological processes occurring over a slower time-scale also need to be controlled

Table 2.3 *Principal hormones in mammals*

Hormone	Source	Chemical nature	Major functions
Digestion and metabolism			
Secretin	Duodenum	Peptide	Secretion of pancreatic juice
Gastrin	Stomach	Peptide	Secretion of gastric juice
Insulin	Pancreas	Peptide	Control of blood glucose levels, via liver
Glucagon	Pancreas	Peptide	
Noradrenaline	Adrenal medulla	Tyrosine derivative	Blood distribution, blood glucose levels
Thyroxine	Thyroid	Tyrosine derivative	Increased metabolic rate
Corticosterone	Adrenal cortex	Steroid	Carbohydrate metabolism
Water and salt balance			
Vasopressin (= antidiuretic hormone, ADH)	Hypothalamus	Peptide	Water resorption in kidney
Aldosterone	Adrenal cortex	Steroid	Sodium metabolism and excretion
Growth			
Parathormone	Parathyroid	Peptide	Regulation of calcium and bone growth
Calcitonin	Thyroid	Peptide	
Growth hormone	Pituitary	Peptide	Growth, via liver metabolism
Androgens	Adrenal cortex	Steroid	Post-puberty growth, especially in males
Reproduction			
Follicle stimulating hormone (FSH)	Pituitary	Peptide	Development of ovarian follicles and seminiferous tubules
Luteinising hormone (LH)	Pituitary	Peptide	Conversion of follicle to corpus luteum, control of progesterone
Oestrogen	Ovary	Steroid	Sexual characters and cycle of females
Progesterone	Ovary	Steroid	
Prolactin	Pituitary	Peptide	Milk production
Testosterone	Testis	Steroid	Male sexual characters
Oxytocin	Hypothalamus	Peptide	Uterine contraction, milk release

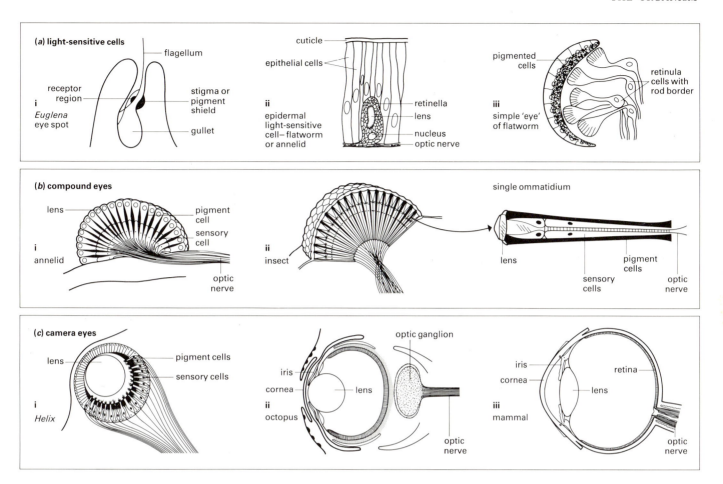

Fig. 2.29. *Photoreceptors range from simple light-sensitive cells (a) in smaller invertebrates to the more familiar 'eyes', whether compound assemblages (b) of many simple units, especially common in arthropods, or camera eyes with discriminatory retinas (c), best known in the octopus and in vertebrates.*

and integrated, and most animals therefore have a second coordinating system that relies on chemical rather than electrical signals. These chemicals are the **hormones**, released from special (endocrine) glands in the body to circulate in the body fluids and to exert their effects on the various distant cells or organs equipped with appropriate receptor sites.

There is in fact no absolute distinction between nervous and hormonal systems, because nerves also rely on chemical transmission at most synapses (see section 1.4), and many hormones are released as a result of nervous stimulation of the cells that contain them, a process called neurosecretion. Any single control system may involve more than one of these components, interacting by positive and negative feedbacks, and will also involve chemical control processes inside cells (see section 1.3).

Hormones have been far better studied in mammals than in any other group of animals, and at least 50 substances from a variety of glands are known to have hormonal effects in man (Fig. 2.31). Some of the more important ones, together with their sources and effects, are given in Table 2.3. These hormones can be fairly readily classified according to function, and in mammals the four main categories relate to digestion and metabolism, to osmoregulation, to growth and bone morphology, and to reproduction. Involved in controlling diges-

tion and metabolism are secretin and gastrin which regulate the flow of digestive juices in the gut, insulin, glucagon and noradrenaline which affect sugar uptake and usage, and thyroxine and the adrenal corticoids which control the metabolic rate of the body. In the osmoregulatory group vasopressin and aldosterone are most important, because they regulate the permeability and capacity for ionic uptake of the kidney nephrons, so determining the overall water content of the animal. Growth hormone, thyroxine, the androgens and the calcium-regulating hormones parathyroid hormone and calcitonin, are the most obvious regulators of the body form and size, and generally act over a longer time-scale than do the chemicals governing other physiological processes. The fourth group, controlling reproduction, is particularly complex, and a battery of hormones is responsible for regulating the reproductive cycle and pregnancy in the female mammal.

In spite of the great variety of mammalian hormones and of their actions, they fall chemically into only three groups. These are the steroid hormones, the peptides and proteins, and the tyrosine derivatives. In many vertebrate control systems, the primary hormone is a peptide or protein, arising by neurosecretion from the hypothalamus and pituitary complex, which is the organising centre for hormonal and nervous integration. The primary hormones from this highly complicated centre act

Fig. 2.30. Head of the dragonfly Cordulegaster boltonii, showing the large compound eyes.

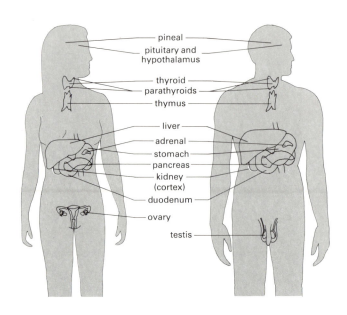

Fig. 2.31. Endocrine (hormonal) glands in the human species.

in turn on other glands to produce secondary hormones, and feedback control loops are often incorporated to prevent excessive effects and provide fine tuning of the control mechanisms.

In invertebrates the connection between nervous and hormonal systems is even more marked, and secretion of most of the chemical messengers identified is under nervous control. Since the bodies of invertebrates are often less highly organised than are those of vertebrates, invertebrates probably have fewer hormones, and most vertebrate hormones have no effect when introduced into an invertebrate body. Organs for secretion of hormones have been clearly identified in molluscs, annelid worms, arthropods and tunicates (sea-squirts), and the products associated with these are, in most cases, related to morphogenesis and sexual maturation. This is particularly well studied in the process whereby insect larvae are transformed into adults (metamorphosis), where two main hormones, juvenile hormone and ecdysone, act. An analogous control mechanism occurs when crustaceans moult their exoskeletons, when a sinus gland in the eyestalk corresponds to the insect's corpus cardiacum and a 'Y'-shaped organ in the head corresponds to the insect's prothoracic gland. In both groups there are also reproductive hormones, particularly in the female, though in insects the main control is again exerted by the chemical known as juvenile hormone, which in the adult is no longer required to regulate the expression of juvenile characters in the epidermis and cuticle. A few other arthropod hormones, controlling such physiological processes as secretion in the Malpighian tubules and heart rate, are known.

In many other groups of invertebrates there are no readily identifiable endocrine organs, but there are scattered neurosecretory cells and these seem to affect growth and reproductive processes. In a number of cases these also have significant effects in controlling colour change, affecting the distribution of pigment in the epidermis; hormonal control of this phenomenon is less frequently encountered in the higher vertebrates.

Pheromones are chemical messengers passing between individuals, and they may act as sex attractants, trail markers, alarm signals and aggregation signals. They have been most studied in insects, which rely heavily on chemical sensors and pheromonal communication, especially in the social insects (ants, bees and termites). Pheromones are also important in coelenterates, molluscs, annelid worms and echinoderms, and are probably common to all animal groups. In aquatic invertebrates they are an important regulator of spawning behaviour, and in vertebrates too they help to coordinate mating processes by triggering nervous impulses from the nose to the regulatory hypothalamus. In the human species pheromones also exist and have behavioural effects, although these may be over-ridden by voluntary, socially determined mechanisms.

Reproduction and embryology

A species can only become established in a particular habitat if enough individuals have structural and physiological adaptations for survival there to maturity, and are then able to reproduce. Adaptation of the reproductive processes is therefore an essential component of a species' strategy for survival.

Organisms can reproduce either asexually or sexually (see section 3.2). In **asexual reproduction** two or more identical units are created from one, by simple division as in protozoans, or by budding leading to fragmentation or colony formation in many coelenterates, flatworms and tunicates (sea-squirts). In some higher animals a form of asexual reproduction occurs by development of unfertilised (female) eggs, a process known as parthenogenesis, which is very familiar in insects such as aphids. All these mechanisms permit the numbers of

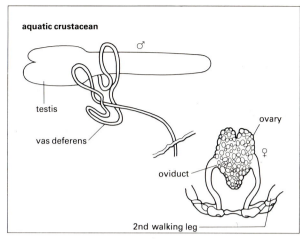

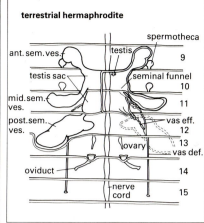

Fig. 2.32. Reproductive systems usually reflect an animal's habitat; aquatic forms can disperse sperm and eggs freely, but terrestrial animals must copulate. The female often stores male gametes in a spermatheca and has accessory glands to provide eggs with a protective covering before laying.

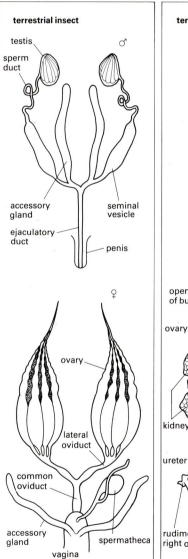

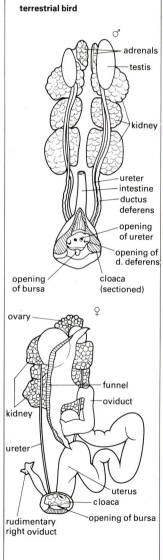

individuals to increasé very rapidly, allowing quick exploitation of suitable habitats and food sources. In **sexual reproduction**, two haploid reproductive cells or gametes from different individuals fuse together to form the diploid condition (see section 1.5), thus involving a mixing of genetic material in the reproductive process. Most multicellular forms of life reproduce sexually at least once during their life-times, and many unicellular organisms also have forms of sexual fusion.

Since sexual reproduction involves the fusion of two small and relatively unprotected germ cells, it must take place in an aqueous medium, and much of the complexity of animal reproductive systems is designed to achieve this, allowing the male **sperm** to swim to the female **egg** and providing fluid in which the fertilised egg can develop. Hence the habitat of a species has a critical effect on the reproductive process, since only aquatic animals can shed their sperm and eggs directly into their environment. Terrestrial forms must protect their gametes at all stages, and generally require fertilisation to occur inside the body of the female (internal fertilisation); this demands a much more careful regulation of the timing of gamete production, of the location of mates, and of copulation itself, as well as controls on post-fertilisation physiology and behaviour.

In aquatic invertebrates sperm and eggs are generally liberated at random into the environment and fertilisation is external. Both male and female reproductive systems can therefore be very simple, requiring only sperm-producing and egg-producing tissues with few accessory structures (Fig. 2.32). However, many of the gametes are likely to be wasted, and a very large number must therefore be produced to achieve a few fertilisations. Some aquatic animals compromise by producing fewer gametes, investing the eggs with a certain amount of stored food as yolk, and ensuring a higher frequency of fertilisation by a close association of male and female before and during release of the gametes. Many freshwater creatures adopt this strategy, and in some cases the fertilised eggs are then sheltered in a brood pouch by the female, since very small eggs and larvae would be subjected to particularly severe physiological stresses in the dilute medium of freshwater.

In terrestrial animals the difficulties of fertilisation must be overcome internally, requiring accessory organs for transfer-

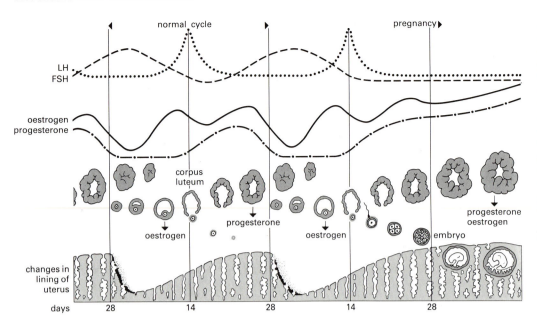

Fig. 2.33. Hormonal changes during the primate menstrual cycle and pregnancy. FSH promotes maturation of the ovarian egg follicles, which secrete oestrogen to prepare the uterus walls and to cause a surge of LH. LH then causes the corpus luteum (still in the ovary) to secrete progesterone. Only if the egg has been fertilised and implants does the progesterone secretion persist, to allow full pregnancy; otherwise it declines and menstruation is triggered.

ring and accepting the sperm. The subsequent hazards for the developing eggs may be overcome in three possible ways: by returning to water for spawning, as do most amphibians; by enclosing the fertilised eggs in a waterproof case, to produce the familiar shelled eggs of birds, reptiles, insects and spiders; or by retaining the eggs within the body until they hatch. The third process occurs in some viviparous reptiles and in insects which give birth to live young, but is most familiar in the placental mammals where the embryo is retained within the maternal uterus, fed and protected until it is large enough and sufficiently developed for independent existence. This is clearly an immensely complicated process compared to the simple external fertilisation, hatching and growth of marine invertebrates, and the reproductive organs, associated structures and behavioural responses of mammals are correspondingly elaborate.

Similarly, a very complex system of chemical regulation is necessary to coordinate the female reproductive (oestrous) cycle and the events during pregnancy; these are summarised in Fig. 2.33. Nevertheless, the advantages of such an involved process are evident. Very few gametes need to be produced to ensure fertilisation, and the embryo is given the maximum possible chance of survival, often being protected by maternal care after birth.

In all multicellular animals the two critical components in reproduction are the two gametes, sperm and egg. These are usually produced in **testes** and **ovaries** in separate male and female sexes, although some animals, such as snails, are hermaphrodite, and both sperm and ovum are produced by an organ called an ovotestis. The sperm is invariably the motile gamete, usually having a tail conferring this motility and containing an axial filament analogous to that of a flagellum, a middle piece with a coiled mechanism to inject the nucleus of the sperm, and a head piece containing this nucleus and also serving for attachment to the egg. The sperm of different animals differ in size and shape, and in a few cases are amoeboid rather than bearing a tail. The eggs are non-motile and less complex than sperm, differing between animals principally in their size and relative investment of nutritive yolk.

After the fusion of the sperm nucleus with that of the egg, the initial stages of animal embryology show a remarkable degree of similarity in nearly all groups, with the exception of the sponges which probably diverged very early from other multicellular creatures during evolution. Within the rest of the multicellular animals, unless the egg is heavily endowed with yolk, the early process of development is basically as set out in Fig. 2.34. This involves progression through a hollow ball of cells, the **blastula**, to a two-layered **gastrula** stage formed by invagination, and with a subsequent addition of the mesoderm as a third cell layer in most groups. Thus the three main cell lineages are created: **ectoderm**, giving rise to the skin, nervous system and sense organs; **mesoderm**, which forms most of the tissues; and **endoderm**, forming the gut and digestive glands.

Even at this early stage however a divergence into two different groups of animals is discernible, and this is regarded as a fundamental evolutionary dichotomy. The first group, the **Protostomia** (from 'primary mouth'), includes flatworms, annelid worms, molluscs and arthropods, and in these the opening in the gastrula formed by an invagination process, the blastopore, becomes the mouth of the animal, with a separate opening usually appearing later as the anus; these animals also show similarities in the way the dividing egg splits (cleavage) at the four-cell stage and beyond, and in the manner of formation of the body cavity. The second group, **Deuterostomia** (from 'secondary mouth'), includes the echinoderms, hemichordates and chordates, and in these the initial opening in the gastrula does not form the mouth but generally becomes the anus, with a mouth appearing secondarily elsewhere in the developing mass of cells; again members of this second group show similar patterns of cell cleavage. For the invertebrates, therefore, there may be two clear embryological groups, with the vertebrate evolutionary stem being most nearly related to the echinoderms.

The dichotomy, though by no means absolute, is also reflected in the later embryology of the different groups by the forms of the larvae that are produced. Larval forms are of course themselves an adaptation to a particular environment, and are therefore often highly modified, but at least in marine animals the simple planktonic larval stages can be traced to one of two basic patterns, and there are particularly clear resemblances between annelids, molluscs and crustaceans at this stage. Similarly the larvae of echinoderms can be related to those of

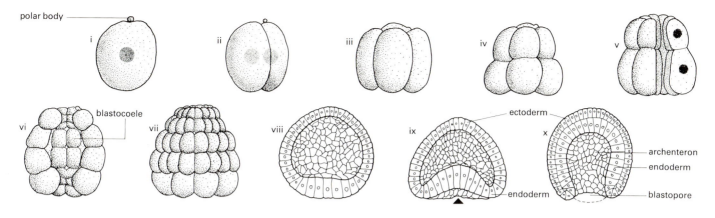

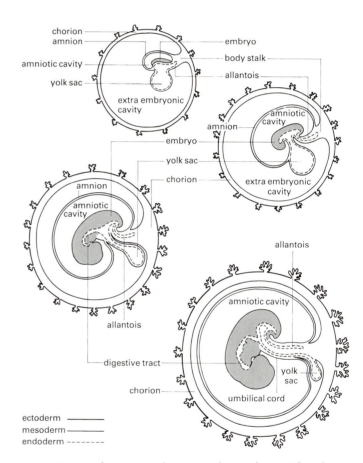

Fig. 2.34. Early development of an embryo, showing the production of a blastula (vi) and then a gastrula (ix).

the hemichordate acorn worms, the adults of which in turn resemble the tadpole larvae of tunicates, and vertebrates.

The later stages of embryology, during which tissues and organs form, inevitably become more diverse as animals adopt their adult forms, and this is especially so for terrestrial animals and others which produce large yolky eggs. In the insects, for example, there is only cleavage of the superficial layers of cells around a central core of yolk and development after hatching is greatly modified by the different demands of larvae, pupae and adults. The same complications may apply to land-living molluscs, worms and arachnids. The later embryology of the vertebrates is usually determined by the deposits of extracellular yolk and the need to keep the endodermis in close proximity to this, and in the reptiles, birds and mammals the classic course of development is even further obscured by the presence of a complex array of protective membranes surrounding the embryo. In mammals these help to anchor the progeny to the mother's uterus, and the need for large quantities of yolk is lost as the maternal blood supplies nutrients across the placenta (Fig. 2.35).

The control of these diverse embryological processes, from fertilisation through to the formation of organs, poses a number of problems for chemical coordination. During development the original cell's genetic content must be directed and modified, by repressing certain genes in some cells and allowing their full expression in others, and the processes by which the DNA of the genes can be either masked or exposed for expression are only just becoming clear. Furthermore, the reactions of cells to other cells must be controlled to ensure the correct spatial and physiological relationships of the different tissues. This again seems to be a case of chemical control, with cells growing and dividing as determined by local gradients of chemical concentration (see section 1.6). In some cases, successive regions of the newly forming body organise the development of neighbouring tissues. The eventual form of the body is thus correctly and sequentially controlled by the products of genetic machinery derived from the two original gametes, and the new individual shows the characteristics of form and physiology appropriate to its habitat and lifestyle.

Fig. 2.35. Development of the mammalian embryo within the placental membranes: the amnion and chorion grow out and enfold the embryo, while the allantois and yolk sac connect with the digestive tract, though their primitively absorptive roles are largely taken over by the placental blood supply.

Further reading

Bold, H.C. and Wynne, M.J. *Introduction to the algae.* Englewood Cliffs: Prentice-Hall, 1978.

Chapman, G. *Body fluids.* SIB no. 8. London: Edward Arnold, 1967.

Corner, E.J.H. *The life of plants.* London: Weidenfeld and Nicholson, 1964.

Currey, J.D. *Animal skeletons.* SIB no. 22. London: Edward Arnold, 1970.

Eckert, R. and Randall, D. *Animal physiology.* San Francisco: W.H. Freeman, 1978.

Ingold, C.T. *Biology of fungi.* (4th edn) London: Hutchinson, 1979.

McNeill Alexander, R. *Size and shape.* SIB no. 29. London: Edward Arnold, 1971.

Morton, J. *Guts.* SIB no. 7. London: Edward Arnold, 1967.

Raven, P.H., Evert, R.F. and Curtis, H. *Biology of plants.* (3rd edn) New York: Worth, 1981.

Ray, P.M., Steeves, T.A. and Fultz, S.A. *Botany.* Philadelphia: Saunders, 1983.

Round, F.E. *The ecology of algae.* Cambridge: Cambridge University Press, 1981.

Salisbury, F.B. and Ross, C.W. *Plant physiology.* (2nd edn) Belmont: Wadsworth, 1978.

Schmidt-Nielsen, K. *How animals work.* Cambridge: Cambridge University Press, 1972.

Schmidt-Nielsen, K. *Animal physiology: Adaptation and environment.* (2nd edn) Cambridge: Cambridge University Press, 1979.

Sleigh, M.A. *The biology of Protozoa.* London: Edward Arnold, 1973.

Usherwood, P.N.R. *Nervous systems.* SIB no. 36. London: Edward Arnold, 1973.

Webster, J. *Introduction to fungi.* (2nd edn) Cambridge: Cambridge University Press, 1980.

Wells, M.J. *Lower animals.* London: World University Library, 1968.

3 Genetics

3.1 MOLECULAR GENETICS

Molecular genetics is the study of the macromolecules that contain the information necessary for the development and continued growth of an organism, and which are passed on from generation to generation. The subject includes the structures of these molecules, their organisation, and the mechanisms by which the information they contain is expressed in a regulated way within the cell and throughout the life-cycle of each individual. Molecular genetics makes use of the techniques of the chemist and biochemist, and the logic of the geneticist, to attempt to provide an understanding of these biological phenomena.

The genetic material

One of the characteristics which define cells and organisms as being alive is their ability to reproduce. The offspring produced are similar or identical to their parents because they possess the ability to make the same kinds of proteins as did their parents, in a similar and precisely controlled way throughout their life-cycles. These characters inherited from parents are said to be heritable or **genetic**. The nature of every protein is governed by its own particular sequence of amino-acids, but proteins cannot produce identical copies of themselves; some blueprint is required, some way of storing the information to construct an organism and then expressing it as protein synthesis. This blueprint is the genetic information held in the structures called chromosomes in each cell (see page 14). These chromosomes are copied, and the original chromosomes and the copies are passed to daughter cells during cell division (see section 1.5).

Chromosomes contain proteins and a substance called deoxyribonucleic acid (DNA). These DNA molecules are responsible for the heritable characteristics of a cell or organism, and thus are the genetic material. DNA is a nucleic acid, a long linear polymer of individual units called nucleotides, and a single DNA molecule is contained within each chromosome. Each nucleotide contains a sugar, a nitrogenous base, and a phosphate group; the phosphate groups are responsible for the acidic nature of the molecule. In DNA the sugar is deoxyribose, and in the other nucleic acid found in cells (ribonucleic acid, RNA) the sugar is ribose. RNA differs from DNA in other ways too, because some RNA is constantly being synthesised and degraded, and thus it is much more metabolically active than is DNA. DNA is found within cell nuclei, and in certain semi-autonomous cell organelles such as mitochondria and chloroplasts, in characteristic and very precise quantities; it is never degraded, and is accurately copied before each cell division. This copying process is called **replication**, and is the molecular process responsible for the transmission of the genetic information from generation to generation.

The information that is encoded in the structure of the DNA molecules is known as the **genotype**, and has to be expressed as the observed characteristics of the cell or organism, the **phenotype**. In order that the particular items of information required at any moment are carried from the DNA in the nucleus to the cytoplasm where protein synthesis occurs, some intermediate carrier molecule is required, and this role is fulfilled by one particular type of RNA. RNA is synthesised in the nucleus by copying the sequence of nucleotides in portions of the DNA, a process called **transcription**. Some RNA remains in the nucleus and some is rapidly degraded, but three remaining types of RNA move to the cytoplasm. One of these is messenger RNA (**mRNA**), the direct communication between DNA and protein: mRNA molecules contain sequences synthesised as a copy of the sequence of those parts of the DNA which code for protein. The copying in the cytoplasm of the information presented as a sequence of nucleotides in mRNA, into a sequence of amino-acids in protein, is a change of language, a step called **translation**. The code for translation is supplied by another set of RNA molecules (transfer RNA, **tRNA**), and the structural support and enzymes for protein synthesis are the **ribosomes**, structures containing protein and the third sort of cytoplasmic RNA, the ribosomal RNA (**rRNA**). Whereas cytoplasmic mRNA is continually being degraded, the tRNA and rRNA live much longer as they function to translate all the different sorts of mRNA molecules into proteins.

This fundamental pattern to the flow of information in living organisms, illustrated in Fig. 3.1, was called the Central Dogma by Crick. This does not of course mean that other processes are not possible, merely that they are considered unlikely on all the current evidence. Some of the RNA-viruses are in fact known to copy their RNA chromosome back into DNA at a certain stage of their life-cycle, using an enzyme called reverse transcriptase. There is also a small but growing body of evidence that sequences called pseudogenes, in the DNA of mammals, may have resulted from the copying of mRNA molecules back into DNA, although the importance of this in our genetic history is quite unknown.

Fig. 3.1. The Central Dogma.

Structure of nucleic acids

There are four types of nitrogenous bases in the nucleotides of DNA: two purines, adenine and guanine, and two smaller pyrimidines, cytosine and thymine. The backbone of the DNA molecule consists of alternating deoxyribose sugars and phosphate groups, and a base is attached to each sugar (Fig. 3.2). The positions of the two bonds to phosphate on the sugar ring are different, and give a direction to the DNA chain, which has 5'-

a

Fig. 3.2. The organisation of DNA. (a) A two-dimensional representation of one strand of the helix. The bases protruding from the sugar-phosphate backbone are linked by hydrogen bonds to the complementary bases in the second strand. The four bases found in DNA are shown in (b).

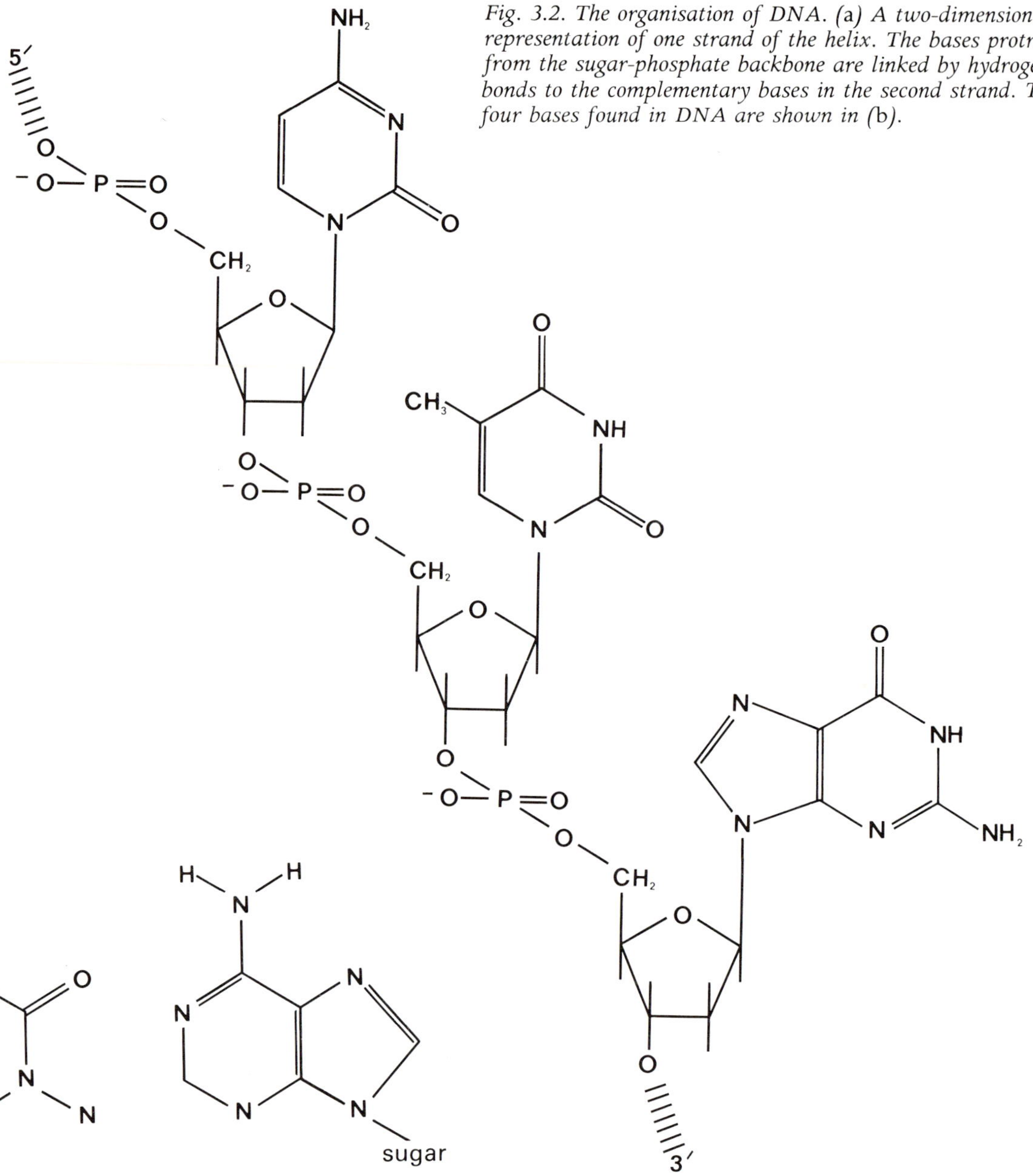

b

thymine

adenine

cytosine

guanine

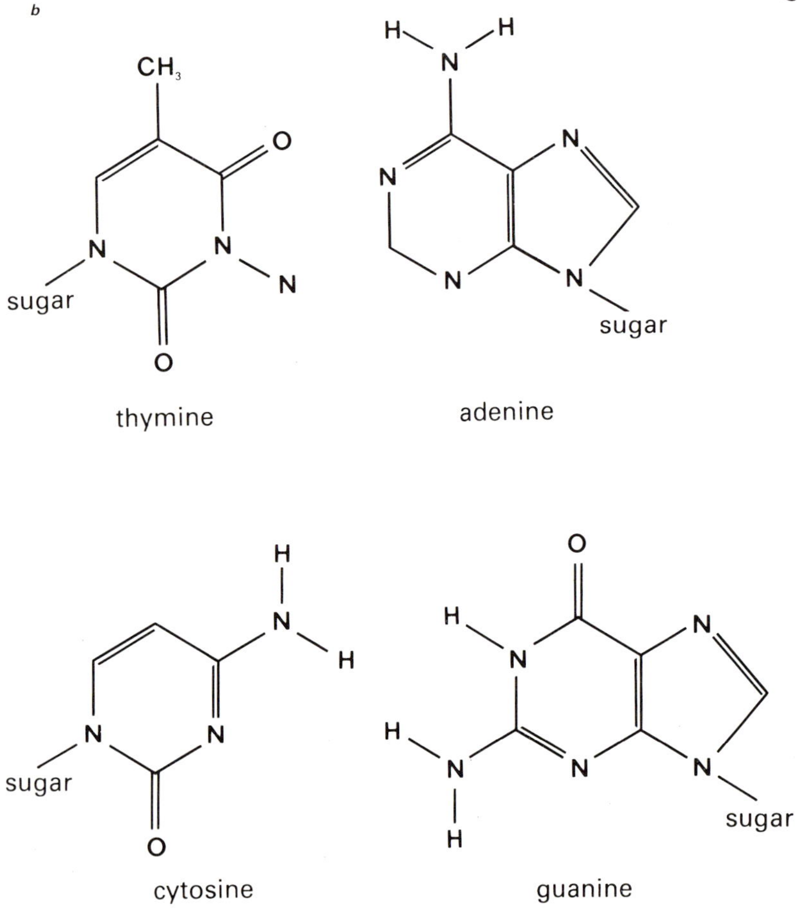

phosphate and 3′-hydroxyl ends; the internal bonding is said to be 5′→3′.

A study of X-ray diffraction patterns of crystals of DNA by both Wilkins and Franklin and Watson and Crick enabled the structure of DNA to be deduced. Molecular models constructed from these data showed that the most plausible structure was a double helix with the two sugar–phosphate backbones on the outside, in contact with the aqueous environment, and with the bases inside, lying flat and facing each other across the axis of the helix (Fig. 3.2). Adenine must be paired with thymine, and guanine with cytosine, as no other arrangements of bases could fit within the distance fixed by the rigid backbone of the helix. This explained the observation by Chargaff that the nuclei of all cells contain equal amounts of guanine and cytosine, and likewise equal amounts of adenine and thymine. The two DNA strands are oriented so that they have their chemical directions opposite to one another and the helix is said to be 'anti-parallel'. Within the cell nucleus, however, the ionic environment may be very different from that in crystals of DNA and, moreover, the DNA is bound to proteins, so that it is possible that short stretches of nuclear DNA, particularly those regions with a high guanine and cytosine content, may have structures locally different from the traditional double helix.

The double-helical nature of DNA means that the molecule is a relatively rigid rod, and also that the chemically reactive bases are concealed within the molecule. The processes of replication and transcription therefore require that the two strands of DNA be separated to allow reaction and pairing with incoming bases. This strand separation is catalysed by proteins which can bind to, and stabilise, the single-stranded DNA. RNA, which is more metabolically active, is predominantly single-stranded, although there are regions of double-strand due to base-pairing having occurred between two parts of the same molecule which has folded back on itself (Fig. 3.3). RNA also has a slightly different sugar in its backbone from DNA, and the base uracil replaces thymine. These changes cause the double-stranded regions of RNA to be less rigid than double-stranded DNA, more readily unwound, and more accessible to enzymes recognising specific sequences of bases. Secondary structure, as this base-pairing between different parts of one nucleic acid molecule is called, is important in maintaining the three-dimensional structure of RNA molecules, such as tRNA, and in general for providing a three-dimensional structure for interaction with and recognition by proteins. RNA molecules are also much shorter than those of DNA, as each is copied from only a minute portion of the total DNA.

A single liver cell contains 2 millimetres of DNA, 100 times greater in length than the whole cell. This DNA therefore has to be condensed and packaged in a highly ordered fashion to fit into the nucleus. When the DNA is extracted from the cells of higher organisms, certain basic proteins, named histones, are found associated with it; the complex of DNA and histones is called **chromatin**. This has a repeating, beaded, structure (Fig. 3.3), with an octamer of histones making the bead, around

which is coiled a length of DNA containing 200 base-pairs. One such bead is known as a nucleosome, and a further single histone molecule acts as a link to the next nucleosome. The double-stranded DNA is itself helical, and so when twisted twice around each nucleosome it becomes further, 'super-helically', coiled. The nucleosomes are themselves stacked one upon another, again helically, into a structure called a solenoid, to give a further degree of packing. The thickness of the resultant fibril, 25 nanometres, is about the same as that of the fine DNA strand seen in eukaryote interphase nuclei in the electron microscope.

The eukaryotes are organisms with a true nucleus separated from the cytoplasm by a double membrane and containing many pairs of long linear chromosomes: four pairs in fruit flies, 50 pairs in goldfish, and 23 pairs in humans. The single circular chromosome in prokaryotes such as bacteria is not separated from the cytoplasm of the bacterial cell, and protein synthesis can occur on a molecule of bacterial mRNA while this is still being transcribed from the DNA; bacterial DNA is simply associated with one type of structural protein. Viruses contain RNA or DNA as their genetic material (see pages 18–20), and this is covered with protein in the viral particle for protection during transmission between hosts. Viroids, which cause a variety of diseases of plants (see page 280), consist only of a single circular strand of RNA, base-pairing in places with itself but without any protective coat or envelope.

The bacterial chromosome also has a relatively simple genetic structure. The DNA of prokaryotes, and of other simple organisms like fungi, consists almost entirely of unique sequences coding for protein (a unique sequence is one which appears only once in the whole of the genome of the organism, considering the haploid genome for higher organisms). The genes in bacteria are separated only by relatively short non-coding sequences which are not transcribed or translated. This compactly organised chromosome allows bacteria to control efficiently the expression of their genes, and permits replication to be rapid. The pressure for a small chromosome is taken to an extreme in viruses, which need to pack their DNA inside a protein coat, and several examples have been found in which a particular piece of viral DNA may be part of more than one gene, where adjacent genes overlap in the chromosome.

Higher organisms can make more proteins than can bacteria, and therefore have many more genes: 10000 to 15000 have been estimated for mammals, whereas bacteria may have only 4000 to 5000. However, the total amount of DNA present in eukaryotes is usually 100 to 1000 times that required for the total protein-coding capacity. The DNA of higher organisms contains of course the unique sequences coding for protein, but there are also two other classes of sequence, known as the highly repeated sequences (1000 to 1 million copies of each in the genome) and the moderately repeated sequences (20 to 100 copies of each in the genome). None of the highly repeated DNA is transcribed, and some is concentrated in structurally distinct regions at the ends and the centres of the chromosomes, where

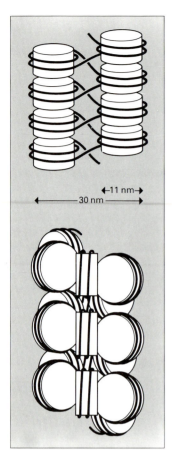

Fig. 3.3. Proposed models for the higher order structure of DNA. Double strands of DNA are wrapped around histones, forming nucleosomes, which are packed together to give a strand of chromatin.

it is believed to have a role in the mechanics of chromosome pairing at cell division. Some of the moderately repeated sequences are closely interspersed with the coding sequences, and are transcribed into RNA molecules which are degraded without leaving the nucleus. Some of the intervening sequences that are present within the majority of eukaryote genes are examples of this type of sequence, but in general the relationship of the repeated sequences in the DNA to the unique sequences is not well understood.

Replication

Each time a cell divides, it provides an accurate copy of its DNA molecules for its daughter cells. Replication is this process of copying the parental DNA, and it occurs at a particular point in the cycle of cell growth, division, and further growth.

The pairing of bases in the double-helical structure of DNA allows the parental strands to serve as a template for the order of nucleotides in the new strands and two new double helices are generated by unwinding and then copying the parental strands. Meselsohn and Stahl showed that each daughter helix contained one complete strand of the parental DNA and one newly synthesised strand; this method of replication is called 'semi-conservative'. Because the two strands of the parental DNA helix run in opposite directions ($5' \rightarrow 3'$ and $3' \rightarrow 5'$), it would seem that the enzyme synthesising DNA would have to work in both these directions. However, the DNA polymerase

enzymes are found only to be able to synthesise new DNA in a $5' \rightarrow 3'$ direction, and it is thus thought that one strand of the DNA is synthesised continuously and that the other is synthesised backwards in short pieces (Fig. 3.4), these pieces being subsequently joined together by another enzyme called DNA ligase.

The site of initiation of synthesis of DNA is known as the origin of replication; bacteria contain only one such site on their single chromosome, but eukaryotes have many at intervals along each of their chromosomes. Elongation of the growing DNA chains proceeds away from the origin in both directions along the chromosome, creating two replication forks. This continues until a sequence of bases is reached that constitutes the terminus of replication.

Many errors are possible in this process, such as the insertion of an incorrect base opposite the parental strand, or the deletion or addition of bases. Some of these mutations may have no effect on the phenotypic characteristics of the next generation, if for example they occur in a region of the DNA not coding for protein, or make no significant change in the properties of a protein, but many will be deleterious for the cell or organism, resulting in a faulty protein molecule. The replication machinery contains a number of sophisticated mechanisms to reduce its error rate, and to correct the errors that do happen ('proof-reading'). Replication of bacterial chromosomes occurs with very high fidelity, with about one error per hundred million bases copied, which is less than one error on average when the whole chromosome of *Escherichia coli* is replicated. The slow production of variation that does occur through uncorrected errors in replication provides part of the material on which natural selection works.

Transcription

During transcription the sequence of deoxyribonucleotides in sections of the DNA is copied into the complementary sequence of ribonucleotides in RNA molecules, guanosine for cytidine, adenosine for thymidine, cytidine for guanosine, and uridine for adenine. The synthesis of RNA is catalysed by the enzyme DNA-dependent RNA polymerase, a large molecule consisting of several different subunits. In prokaryotic cells there is only one type of RNA polymerase, but in eukaryotic cells there are three, each producing a different class of RNA. The products of transcription are single-stranded RNA molecules of differing lengths and life-spans; these molecules are much more metabolically active than is the DNA, and are continually being degraded and resynthesised. All the RNA made in mitochondria and chloroplasts functions there, but three different types of RNA leave the cell nucleus for the cytoplasm.

The major RNA component of the cell is ribosomal RNA (rRNA), a structural component of the ribosome, the cytoplasmic particle which translates the coded message from the nucleus into the sequences of proteins. Ribosomes contain two subunits of different sizes, each subunit having one major

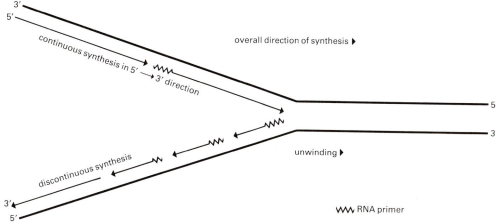

Fig. 3.4. A diagrammatic representation of the replication of DNA.

overall direction of synthesis ▶

continuous synthesis in 5' → 3' direction

unwinding ▶

discontinuous synthesis

3'
5'

5'
3'

3'
5'

ᴡᴡᴡ RNA primer

strand of rRNA, and the rRNA is relatively stable. The other stable type of RNA is transfer RNA (tRNA), which is involved with the selection of amino-acids during protein synthesis. The third type of RNA is messenger RNA (mRNA): this short-lived species carries information from the DNA to the site of protein synthesis, the ribosomes where the sequences of nucleotides in a portion of each mRNA molecule are translated into the sequences of amino-acids in proteins. The ribosomes are involved in the synthesis of proteins only as directed by the mRNA.

The unit of hereditary information is the **gene**; this is a portion of the DNA containing the sequences coding for a particular protein and the associated regulatory sequences. The set of genes of an organism is called its **genome**. The detailed structure of a gene can be analysed by mapping the order of all the mutations found to occur within it; two separate mutations in the same gene are able to recombine by crossing-over at meiosis (see section 1.5), and the more readily two particular mutations recombine then the further apart they are within the gene. Yanofsky found the order of the mutations within the gene coding for a subunit of the tryptophan synthetase enzyme in *Escherichia coli*, and in addition he worked out the sequence of amino-acids in the protein produced by each mutant and found the position of the altered amino-acid. The order of the mutations in the gene was the same as that in the protein for which it coded, showing that the gene and its product were co-linear. Using modern experimental techniques, the sequences of bases in long stretches of DNA can easily be determined, and since RNA can be copied experimentally into DNA many RNA molecules have been sequenced too. The structures of many genes and their transcripts have been determined, both from these techniques and from the more classical genetic analyses.

In both prokaryotes and eukaryotes the central portion of the mRNA molecule is co-linear with the mature protein product: the sequence of bases from the start to the end of the coding region in the mRNA directly gives the whole of the sequence of amino-acids in the protein. However, the regions at either end of the mRNA molecule do not code for protein, but carry information concerned with, for example, binding of ribosomes and ageing of the mRNA molecule. Sequences in the DNA on both sides of the portion transcribed into RNA are involved in, for example, controlling the binding of the RNA polymerase at one end, and the termination of transcription at the other; mutations in these regions of the DNA affect the rate

of these processes but not the actual sequence of the RNA produced.

When the RNA polymerase molecule has initiated transcription, it then reads along the DNA, making RNA continuously until it reaches the termination site. In prokaryotes this primary RNA product is the final RNA molecule ready for translation. In eukaryotes, however, the structure of a gene is considerably more complicated than in prokaryotes and it can contain many different sequences which are transcribed into RNA but which do not code for protein. The RNA polymerase copies into RNA all the sequences of DNA between the initiation and termination sites for transcription, but these 'primary transcripts' are considerably longer than is the final mRNA exported from the nucleus to the cytoplasm: they form a kind of RNA known as heterogeneous nuclear RNA (**hnRNA**). This has a wide range of sizes (hence 'heterogeneous') and a short half-life (several minutes only) within the nucleus. The sequences removed from an hnRNA molecule in making the final mRNA are called intervening sequences; these do not code for a sequence of amino-acids, and the eukaryote gene typically consists of coding regions interspersed with intervening non-coding sequences. Portions of the final protein molecule may thus have been coded for by stretches of DNA at some distance from each other in the genome, as the intervening sequences range in length from 50 to several thousand nucleotides and may constitute a greater length of DNA in the gene than do the coding sequences. Of the eukaryote genes studied so far, only the genes for interferon and the histones have no intervening sequences, while the gene for collagen, an important structural protein in connective tissue, has more than 50.

The fully processed eukaryotic mRNA, as found in the cytoplasm, has in addition particular sequences at the 5'-end and the 3'-end. The sequence added on to the 5'-end, called the 'cap', may protect the mRNA from degradation, and aid the ribosome in recognising the molecule. At the 3'-end is a stretch of adenylate residues, a poly-A 'tail', which can be between 20 and 200 residues long and is thought to be involved in the transport of the mRNA from the nucleus, and in maintaining its stability in the cytoplasm.

The precise site of initiation can be found from comparing the sequence of the DNA template and the primary RNA transcript. Mutations that alter the activity of a gene, by decreasing or increasing the rate at which it is transcribed, are used to define the promoter site, the site of interaction of the newly bound RNA polymerase with the DNA. The promoter sequence on the DNA is asymmetric and determines the direction and strand on which transcription is to occur. The site of binding of the RNA polymerase to the DNA can also be determined directly by sequencing those DNA fragments that are protected from enzymatic digestion by being bound to the polymerase. In all, 40 to 60 nucleotides are involved in the determination of the promoter site, which is located on the DNA before the first nucleotide that is to be transcribed.

In bacteria, which have no nucleus and in which translation of the mRNA into protein can commence while the mRNA is itself still being transcribed (Fig. 3.5), the amount of a particular protein in the cell has often been directly related to the activity of the promoter for the gene for that protein. A highly active promoter, which binds many RNA polymerase molecules and makes many copies of the mRNA from that gene, is said to have a high initiation frequency. The promoter sequences on the DNA of viruses are often initiators of very high affinity, thus altering the pattern of protein synthesis of the infected cell in favour of the viral proteins.

The bacterial RNA polymerase will transcribe the gene until it comes to a sequence which instructs it to terminate RNA synthesis and hence to fall off the DNA. The actual signal received by the RNA polymerase appears not to be on the DNA itself, but to be on the newly made RNA which at this point contains a sequence (copied of course from the DNA) that can double back on itself and form a hairpin loop. A stretch of uridine residues is also present, and these two features seem to constitute the signal for termination of transcription, although another protein factor called ρ is sometimes required.

The processes of initiation and termination of transcription are less well understood in higher organisms than they are in bacteria, and are generally more complex: for example, the position of the promoter site with respect to the site of initiation of transcription can vary from gene to gene. In one way, however, bacteria are more complicated. Each eukaryote mRNA only contains the coding sequence for one protein, and ribosomes only need to bind to the 5′-end of the mRNA and find the single site of initiation of protein synthesis. Prokaryotic mRNAs, however, may be **polycistronic**, containing the coding sequences for many proteins, and initiation of translation can therefore occur at a number of sites within the mRNA. Polycistronic mRNA molecules are found because, in bacteria, genes of related function are often clustered together under the control of a single promoter, for example the genes for all the enzymes responsible for biosynthesis of histidine. This allows the coordinated regulation of the amounts of these proteins, as alteration of the activity of the single promoter will change the rate at which they all are synthesised. In this example, the presence of excess histidine causes a repressor protein to bind to the promoter sequence and to physically prevent transcription of these genes, while when the cells lack histidine the repressor protein cannot bind to the promoter site and transcription of the genes for histidine synthesis occurs. In

eukaryotes, however, control of the amounts of proteins made is not so obviously mediated simply by altering the rates of transcription of their genes.

Translation

Protein synthesis occurs in the cytoplasm of all cells on the ribosomal particles. Ribosomes contain approximately equal amounts of RNA and protein by mass, having a large and small subunit each consisting of a major strand of rRNA and 20 to 40 different protein molecules. The rRNAs provide the structural support for the various ribosomal proteins, as well as an ability to recognise particular sequences on mRNA and tRNA molecules by base-pairing with these. The ribosomal proteins are enzymes which together perform the very complex reaction of accurate translation of the sequence of bases on mRNA into a sequence of amino-acids in protein. Ribosomes are remarkably homogeneous in composition within any one species, but prokaryotes and eukaryotes contain ribosomes of distinctly different sizes. The ribosomes of eukaryotic organelles (mitochondria and chloroplasts) resemble those found in prokaryotes rather than the ribosomes of the eukaryote cytoplasm.

There are 20 different amino-acids commonly found in proteins, and an arrangement of the four different bases in the mRNA (and in the original DNA) must be able to specify at least these 20 units of information. This is achieved by using three adjacent bases to code for each amino-acid. From the four bases it is possible to make 64 possible triplets of bases, or **codons**, and 61 of these have been found to code for the insertion of an amino-acid into protein; some common amino-acids are therefore inserted opposite more than one possible codon on the mRNA. The three remaining codons are used as full-stops, terminating the synthesis of protein at that point on the mRNA. The genetic code (the assignment of triplets of bases to amino-acids) is virtually universal, in that almost all organisms use an identical code. Since the sequence of bases in the mRNA is read in threes, it is essential for the ribosome to initiate translation at exactly the correct place on the mRNA, because if it starts just one base away then a completely different sequence of subsequent triplets, and hence amino-acids, results.

Except for the three 'stop' codons, each codon on the mRNA has a corresponding amino-acid and a corresponding tRNA molecule. It is the tRNA that translates the triplets of bases into amino-acids, as each tRNA molecule binds at one end to the codon on the mRNA and carries a particular amino-acid at the other end. All tRNA molecules have a characteristic secondary structure, and an exposed part, the anti-codon loop, carries a triplet of bases complementary to the codon in the mRNA to which the tRNA binds. Cytoplasmic enzymes recognise each tRNA molecule and load it with its particular amino-acid; the charged tRNA then binds to the mRNA when this contains the appropriate codon. A sequence of amino-acids thus arrives at the ribosome, and the enzymes on this then join the amino-acids together to make the protein molecule.

Fig. 3.5. The organisation of prokaryotic and eukaryotic genes and their relations to the resultant messenger RNAs.

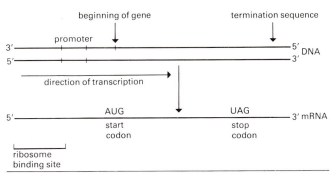

PROKARYOTIC GENE TRANSCRIPTION

EUKARYOTIC GENE TRANSCRIPTION

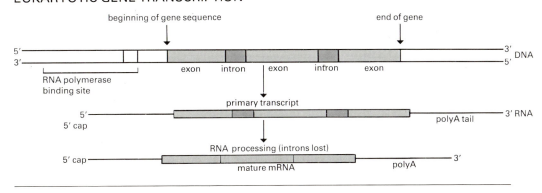

The first amino-acid incorporated into each protein is methionine, or a special derivative of it, and thus the initiation codon for translation is always the codon for methionine, adenine–uracil–guanine (AUG). The nucleotide sequences on the mRNA leading up to the initiator AUG are non-coding sequences, but are important in recognising and binding the ribosome. In prokaryotes there is homology between the non-coding sequence in the mRNA and a sequence on the rRNA of the small ribosomal subunit, allowing the ribosome to recognise that part of the mRNA molecule and to bind adjacent to the AUG codon from which translation is to be initiated. In eukaryotes there is no such specific binding to an rRNA, but instead the cap structure at the 5′-end of the mRNA molecule directs the binding of the ribosome, and the AUG codon from which translation is initiated is the first available one in the molecule.

The ribosome then advances codon by codon along the mRNA, in a 5′ → 3′ direction, binding tRNA molecules in order and linking the amino-acids these bring in to form the growing protein chain. When the ribosome arrives at one of the codons which do not code for any amino-acid, the ribosome dissociates from the mRNA and the completed protein molecule is released into the cytoplasm.

The process of translation has to occur with a high degree of accuracy, for otherwise many faulty protein molecules would be produced, and 'proof-reading', checking that a reaction has been performed correctly and reversing it if an error has been introduced, occurs at two stages in translation. The requirement for accuracy is not however as stringent as in replication, as errors at translation do not become permanently incorporated in the genetic material.

The level of any protein in a cell depends upon many factors, including the amount of its mRNA in the cell and the rate of degradation of the final protein molecule. However, the intrinsic rate of initiation by ribosomes on mRNA is also important: those mRNAs with high affinities for ribosomes will make proportionately more of their products than do other mRNAs to which ribosomes bind only poorly. In both transcription and translation, the rates of elongation for different genes and mRNAs are constant, and it is changes in the rates of initiation of transcription and translation that are responsible for the varying amounts of proteins found. The mRNAs for viruses are generally characterised by very high affinities for ribosomes, so that substantial amounts of viral protein are made in infected cells even though minute levels of the viral mRNAs have to compete with all the mRNA molecules of the host.

Many proteins are simply released from cytoplasmic ribosomes on completion of translation, as the cytoplasm is the cellular compartment in which these proteins are required. However, cells also secrete proteins, exporting them across the cell membrane (see page 33), and, in eukaryote cells, protein destined to function within the various internal membrane systems of the cells must also be transported there. A proportion of the ribosomes of a eukaryotic cell is attached to the endoplasmic reticulum (or, in a bacterial cell without internal membranes, to the plasma membrane), and the proteins which these ribosomes are translating pass directly across the membrane. The initial sequence of amino-acids of such proteins constitute a special signal directing the ribosome to bind to a site on the membrane and to pass the growing protein chain through. Once on the other side of the membrane, this leading sequence on the protein is removed by an enzyme, and the remainder of the protein is transported to its final destination.

The genes for such secreted proteins are therefore the best examples of genetic information being much more than a sequence of bases in DNA coding for the sequence of amino-acids in the final protein. The gene in the DNA contains sequences responsible for binding the RNA polymerase enzyme at the correct place and with an affinity determined by the amount of mRNA required, and in higher organisms the actual sequence of bases that is to form the mRNA is interspersed with intervening sequences which must be removed before export of the mRNA to the cytoplasm. The final mRNA molecule includes sequences at the 5′-end responsible for ribosome recognition and binding, and non-coding sequences at the 3′-end of the mRNA. Even the protein chain produced may have some sequences removed during its processing and transport. At all these stages, regulation of the rate of synthesis of the protein can occur.

3.2 GENETICS OF ORGANISMS

Reproduction

An outstanding property of all living organisms is that they are capable of reproduction. Individuals of a given species produce offspring of the same species, and in this sense reproduction is highly conservative. At the same time, variation between individuals within a species is often hereditary; and the progeny of two differing individuals may include some offspring which resemble one of their parents, some which do not, and some which combine features from both parents in new ways.

The genetic make-up of an individual is called its **genotype** while its physical and biological properties are referred to as its **phenotype**; in most organisms, differences in genotype are detected only as heritable differences in phenotype. Cells contain many enzymes, some of which are concerned with metabolising the large number of chemicals that the cell or tissue uses for growth. One of the first steps in understanding the action of genes was the 'one gene–one enzyme hypothesis': namely, that most genes code for one polypeptide chain with a specific enzymic function. Different versions of a particular gene, such as might arise by mutation (see below), are called **alleles** of that gene.

The evidence that hereditary information is carried in DNA has been described above. Replication of the DNA molecule, the exact copying of its chemical sequence of bases and hence of the genetic information that the DNA contains, provides a basis for the conservative aspects of heredity. For example, bacteria can reproduce by a process in which the single piece of DNA they contain is replicated, the cell divides, and each daughter cell receives one copy of the DNA. The daughter cells are genetically identical to the original parental bacterium, as will be members of successive generations, unless a **mutation** occurs. Mutation is an alteration in the nucleic acid sequence, either as a substitution of individual bases for others in certain positions, or as a deletion or addition of bases in the sequence. In nature, mutations in any one given gene are usually very infrequent, occurring in higher organisms at a rate of about one in a hundred thousand generations.

Mutations occur randomly, in that the likelihood of a change of sequence occurring is not related to the effects of that change. A change in one of the bases in a particular codon (a triplet of bases coding for one amino-acid, see section 3.1) may possibly lead to a new codon specifying the same amino-acid, because of the redundancy of the genetic code. However, the altered codon will more probably code for a different amino-acid from the 20 available. Some amino-acid substitutions of this kind do not affect the function of the enzyme significantly, but most destroy the function altogether. Since the mutation will only be detected if enzyme function is altered, the change in phenotype caused by the majority of mutations detected in genes of this kind is due to loss of gene function. Loss of activity of an enzyme in a biochemical pathway may, if this loss is not lethal to the organism, lead to a recognisably mutant phenotype in cells carrying the mutant gene. For example, the normal form of the enzyme may catalyse one of the biochemical steps involved in the production of an essential amino-acid from simpler precursors. The mutant cells will be able to grow only if they are supplied with this amino-acid from outside. This is typical of many mutant strains of bacteria and fungi and collectively they are called **nutritional mutants**.

There are several factors which make the inheritance of variation in higher organisms more complicated than is the case in bacteria. First, eukaryotic cells are more complex in structure than are prokaryotic cells like bacteria. The genes of eukaryotes are carried in linear sequence on the DNA, as are those of bacteria, but the DNA of eukaryotes is associated with several proteins in a complex structure called a **chromosome**. The genetic material of almost all eukaryotes studied to date is divided among more than one chromosome: there are 23 pairs of chromosomes in man, for example, and 10 pairs in maize. Eukaryotic cells have a special compartment, the nucleus, in which their chromosomes are contained (see section 1.2).

Secondly, many higher organisms are multicellular, and as a result are physiologically complex in ways that bacteria are not: phenomena like the production of different tissues in a body of cells (differentiation, see section 1.6), and development and ageing of an individual, are features unique to multicellular organisation. Even so, with a few exceptions, each cell of a multicellular organism carries in its nucleus a complete set of the genetic information possessed by the individual. Even the eukaryotes that are single cells are physiologically more complex than bacteria.

There is a third, and genetically most significant, difference between prokaryotes and eukaryotes: higher organisms often reproduce by sexual means, while bacteria do so very rarely if at all. The type of cell division already described for bacteria also takes place with eukaryotic cells; it is called **mitosis** (see section 1.5) and it leads to the production of daughter cells almost always identical genetically to the original cell. Growth and development of multicellular organisms occurs by this type of cell division. In single-celled organisms, the new cells produced by this means are new individuals, and this **asexual** (vegetative) **reproduction** is also possible in some multicellular organisms too.

In contrast, **sexual reproduction** involves two special cells called **gametes**, which may come from different individuals of the species, and which fuse to form a **zygote**. New individuals then arise from the zygote. The nucleus of the zygote is produced by fusion of the nuclei of the two gametes, and thus contains the genetic information from both the gametes. It does not, however, possess twice as much genetic information as is found in a typical cell of the parents, because the gametes are produced by a special type of cell division called **meiosis**, which results in their carrying only one chromosome from each pair and thus half the amount of genetic information carried by the original cell of the parent from which they were derived (see section 1.5).

The human species, like other mammals, reproduces only by sexual reproduction. The gametes are the sperm and the egg (ovum), and the zygote is the fertilised ovum from which the embryo, and ultimately the adult, develops by mitotic cell divisions. Some species can use both types of reproduction. The wild varieties of potato (certain *Solanum* species) reproduce asexually by budding from the 'eyes' of the tuber, but can also produce flowers and set seed. Vegetative reproduction is of great importance in horticulture and agriculture in the production of large numbers of genetically identical plants, and sexual reproduction has often become a rare process in cultivated varieties; in some crop species, artificial means of propagation such as tissue culture can be used.

The physiological complexity of higher organisms means that, beyond the general processes of transcription and translation (see section 3.1), much less is known about the molecular details of the actions of their genes compared with those of the bacterium *Escherichia coli*, although the products of the individual genes concerned with specifying metabolic enzymes in higher organisms are thought to play a role similar to that of their bacterial equivalents.

Overall, the phenotype of any individual is due to the interaction of its genotype with the environment during the whole course of its development. However, even when the molecular details of this process are unknown, much can be learned about the genetic basis of hereditary differences: the molecular basis of heredity was discovered long after its genetic basis was first analysed. The critical proof of the genetic explanations outlined below was only obtained by studying patterns of inheritance, even though these patterns of inheritance are now described as the consequence of the way in which DNA behaves in cells and organisms.

Chromosome behaviour during the life-cycle

In many organisms, the chromosomes can be observed with the light microscope, but normally only in cells which are undergoing division. With appropriate preparation and staining, the chromosomes appear as rod-like or ribbon-like structures in dividing cells. In such preparations individual chromosomes can often be distinguished, because they display consistent peculiarities of size or structure (Fig. 1.17). In this way, it has been shown that the chromosomes are persistent structures, their number and size being characteristic of the species concerned. The genetic information in each cell of a multicellular organism (in each case a complete copy of the information the individual carries) is packaged in a set of chromosomes of exactly the same number and size as that of every other cell of members of that species. Much has also been learned about how the chromosomes behave during the two types of cell division (see section 1.5).

Chromosomes are only visible in stained preparations of cells undergoing division, because when the cell divides the chromosomes, which are normally spread out into strands too thin to be seen with the light microscope, condense into shorter, thicker structures which can be observed.

When the chromosomes first become visible in the nucleus of a cell about to undergo mitotic cell division, they are already double along their length, except at the **centromere**, the region where the spindle fibres are attached. This is visual evidence that they have been copied, and their DNA replicated (see section 3.1). The two components of a replicated chromosome, which when separate will each become a chromosome, are called **chromatids**. Each chromatid corresponds to one double helix of DNA. This process of duplication of DNA into two copies, for each of the chromosomes of the organism, and separation of these copies at mitosis into different daughter cells, leads to the production of two daughter cells genetically identical to the parent cell.

Meiosis, however, consists of two sequential cell divisions in which the chromosomes, after they have replicated, first associate into their pairs; the first division separates the members of each pair of replicated chromosomes into two cells, which thus each contain half the number of chromosomes of the original cell, and these then undergo a division just like mitosis, with separation of the chromatids of each replicated chromosome, to yield four cells in all. These progeny cells either act as gametes or produce gametes by mitotic divisions.

During the period in meiosis when the chromosomes are paired (that is, before the first division) **crossing-over** can occur at points along their length (see section 1.5). An exchange of DNA segments can occur between either of the two chromatids from one replicated chromosome and either of the two chromatids from the other by a special enzyme system which breaks two chromatids in corresponding positions, and rejoins them at the break point to each other (Fig. 3.9). In this way chromosomes carrying new combinations of alleles can be generated. Exchanges between the two identical chromatids belonging to the same replicated chromosome have no genetic effect, and are normally suppressed.

Since gametes all contain one copy of each item of genetic information, the original cell of the parent must possess two versions, a pair, of each chromosome, these becoming separated at the first meiotic division. These two copies are called **homologous** chromosomes, because although they carry the same set of genes as each other, they may possess different versions (alleles) of any one gene. Cells with pairs of each chromosome are called **diploid** cells, while cells which contain only one copy of each chromosome, like the gametes, are described as **haploid** cells; and when haploid gametes fuse to produce a zygote this contains a pair of every chromosome and is diploid again. Sexually reproducing organisms all possess a haploid and a diploid phase in their life-cycle, although these may vary in relative importance. In mammals, the gametes (sperm and egg) are the only haploid cells, while in many fungi the zygote is the only diploid cell. Fig. 3.6 illustrates various possible life-cycles (see sections 2.1–2.4). Species in which the diploid phase is predominant are called **diploid organisms**, and those in which the haploid phase is predominant are called **haploid organisms**.

The existence of a diploid phase and the process of meiosis in a sexually-reproducing organism complicates the pattern of inheritance. This will be illustrated by describing the results of some breeding experiments; it was this type of experiment that established the genetic basis of the process of sexual reproduction.

The fungus *Aspergillus nidulans* has a life-cycle like that shown in Fig. 3.6c. The predominant phase, a filamentous colony (see section 2.3) resembling the patches of grey or green mould that form on bread, is haploid. The gametes arise by mitosis from this colony, and the zygote produced when two of them fuse is the only diploid cell. The products from meiotic cell division of the zygote are spores ('ascospores') which germinate to produce further filamentous colonies.

Normal (or, in genetic terminology, **wild-type**) colonies of *A. nidulans* are green, but mutation can lead to strains with yellow colonies. When a yellow strain crosses with a wild-type (green) strain, and the spores that are produced from the zygote by meiosis are germinated, it is found that each spore gives rise either to a green colony or to a yellow one, and that these two types of spores and colonies are present in approximately equal numbers. This shows that both gametes contribute information to the zygote. In addition, each of the progeny resembles one or other of the parental strains in colour. No new colour (for example yellow-green) is produced which would imply mixing or blending of the two types of information during meiosis. Each product of meiosis has received from the zygote either the information for a green colony, or the information for a yellow one.

These two alternative pieces of information are the alleles of the gene specifying colony colour, where the word 'gene' is now used to indicate a piece of genetic information which it is convenient to regard as a unit of heredity. The reappearance in the progeny of characters from the parents in unaltered form is called **segregation** of the characters concerned. By extension, the process by which the products of meiosis receive one or other of two alleles is called segregation of the alleles. Mixing of the two types of information, to produce a new piece of genetic information with a phenotypic effect corresponding to a blend of the effects of the two alleles, does not occur, and no mechanism is known which could bring this about.

Simple breeding experiments with diploid organisms

The following breeding experiment involves a more familiar sort of organism, that is one where the diploid phase is predominant, the garden pea (*Pisum sativum*). The pioneer of genetic analysis, Gregor Mendel, had several strains of pea which differed from each other in a number of characters, and which were **true-breeding**: when pollen from a plant was used to fertilise the same plant (self-fertilisation) this only gave rise to progeny similar to the parent. It could be assumed that plants of these true-breeding strains possessed genetic information of only one type for each of the characters analysed. The pea plant is diploid: only the gametes, and a few other cells associated with them, are haploid. The gametes, pollen and egg cells, are produced by meiosis from diploid tissue in the male and female sex organs of the plant. During self-fertilisation or cross-fertilisation the gametes fuse in pairs, one from each type of sex organ, and the pea seeds develop in the pod by a set of mitotic divisions from the zygotes.

Two of the true-breeding strains Mendel used differed in that one produced round seed and the other wrinkled seed. When these strains were cross-fertilised, so that pollen from a plant of the strain grown from round seeds was used to fertilise a plant of the strain grown from wrinkled seeds, or vice versa, it was found that all the seeds produced were round, whichever strain had provided the pollen. These seeds, and the plants grown from them, are called the F_1 **generation**. They still carried the information for wrinkled seeds, however, because when these F_1 plants were grown and self-fertilised, the seeds then produced (the F_2 **generation**) consisted of round and wrinkled types in an approximate ratio of 3 round: 1 wrinkled. The two alleles for seed shape are called 'round' and 'wrinkled', using inverted commas to indicate that the phenotypic effects of the alleles, and not their genotypic natures, are being used as their names.

Each member of the F_1 generation will have received a 'round' allele from one parent and a 'wrinkled' allele from the other. Since they are round seeds, the expression of the 'wrinkled' allele must be suppressed in the presence of the 'round' allele. The 'round' allele is said to be **dominant** to the 'wrinkled', and 'wrinkled' **recessive** to 'round'. When a diploid individual carries two identical alleles of a gene, it is said to be **homozygous** for that gene (or a **homozygote**). If the two alleles differ, it is said to be **heterozygous** for the gene (or a **heterozygote**). In the example of Fig. 3.7, the F_1 seeds are heterozygous for the 'round' and 'wrinkled' alleles.

As was demonstrated in the *Aspergillus* experiment described above, half the products of meiosis from a heterozygous diploid cell receive one of the two alleles carried by that cell, and half receive the other allele. In the case of the peas, these products of meiosis form the gametes which then fuse in random (male–female) pairs during self-fertilisation. Fig. 3.7 shows the genotypes of the four kinds of progeny which are expected to be produced in equal numbers in the F_2 generation. Letters have been used to represent the alleles: *R* for 'round seeds' and *r* for 'wrinkled seeds' (a capital letter conventionally denotes a dominant allele, and a lower-case letter a recessive allele). Of the four classes of progeny in the F_2 generation shown in Fig. 3.7, the seeds homozygous for the 'round' allele will be phenotypically round. Since 'round' is dominant, both the heterozygotes will also be round, and only the seeds homozygous for the recessive 'wrinkled' allele will be wrinkled. These comprise one-quarter of the expected progeny, and this accounts for the 3:1 round:wrinkled ratio that Mendel found.

In many cases in higher organisms, the molecular basis of the dominance relationships of alleles is unknown. However, mutant alleles of a gene coding for a specific enzyme are often recessive to the wild-type allele. Diploid cells which carry one wild-type allele, and one mutant allele producing no functional enzyme, will be able to function normally as long as the single wild-type allele produces enough enzyme. If it does, the heterozygous diploid individual will appear normal, and the wild-type allele be dominant.

Sometimes, pairs of alleles of a gene show no dominance. For example, a gene in *Antirrhinum* (snapdragon) is known which when homozygous for one particular allele leads to the production of red flowers, and when homozygous for another allele produces white flowers. Plants heterozygous for these two alleles produce pink flowers. The white colour is due to lack of red pigment, and the production of red pigment depends on an enzyme specified by the allele for red flowers: the pink colour results from the inability of plants with a single 'red' allele to produce enough enzyme to synthesise enough pigment to cause a full red colour.

The next breeding experiment shows the consequences of meiosis in a diploid organism that is heterozygous for two different genes carried on different chromosomes. Two of the four products of any one meiosis will carry one of the alleles of the first gene, and the other two products will carry the other allele of that gene. However, the choice of daughter cell to which each member of any one chromosome pair moves at the first division of meiosis is random (see section 1.5). If the two genes concerned are on different chromosomes, therefore, the

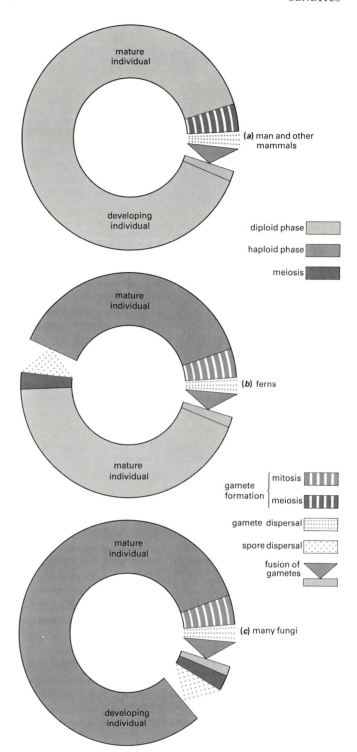

Fig. 3.6. Diagram illustrating the relative importance of the haploid and diploid phases in three types of life-cycle. (a) Man, other animals, and higher plants. The haploid phase is either restricted to the immediate products of meiosis (the gametes), as in man and other animals, or consists of a very few cell generations, as in higher plants. (b) Ferns. These lower plants have two distinct types of individual: the haploid type, which is a small inconspicuous heart-shaped block of cells; and the diploid, which is the familiar fern plant. (c) Like that of many fungi. The diploid phase is highly restricted, so that the zygote undergoes meiosis as soon as it is formed. Some organisms have life-cycles intermediate between these three.

two alleles of the second gene should be distributed randomly among the four meiotic products with respect to the distribution of the alleles of the first gene.

Mendel analysed the consequences of an organism being heterozygous for two different genes by studying the inheritance of both seed shape and seed colour in peas. When a true-breeding strain with round yellow seeds was crossed with a true-breeding strain with wrinkled green seeds, the F_1 all had round yellow seeds. The allele for 'yellow seeds' is therefore dominant to 'green seeds', as well as 'round' being dominant to 'wrinkled'. Self-fertilisation of these F_1 plants produced an F_2 generation with seeds in the approximate ratios: round yellow, 9: round green, 3: wrinkled yellow, 3: wrinkled green, 1. Some of these progeny are like the parental strains, but phenotypes in non-parental (**recombinant**) combinations are also found. Y denotes the allele for yellow and y the allele for green seeds; R represents the allele for round and r for wrinkled as before.

The F_1 plants are heterozygous for both these genes, and half the gametes produced by them are expected to carry r and half R. If Y and y have segregated randomly with respect to R and r, four classes of gametes should be equally frequent (Fig. 3.8a). The combinational (checkerboard) diagram of Fig. 3.8b shows what is expected from a fusion of each possible pair of these types of gamete. Assuming that each kind of fusion is equally likely to occur, the ratios of the different phenotypes expected give the $9:3:3:1$ ratios found. The segregation ratios for each character separately is still $3:1$, as found in the single-character cross, and moreover within each category for one character the ratio for the other character is also $3:1$. This situation is called **independent segregation** of the two characters.

In a diploid individual, one member of each pair of homologous chromosomes is derived from one parent, and the other member from the other parent. When gametes are produced from that individual, each gamete can receive its single version of any chromosome from either of these two sets. In organisms with more than a few chromosomes this can lead to a formidable number of different possible gametes from a single parent. A member of a species with 20 pairs of chromosomes will be able, just by the independent segregation of chromosomes, to generate more than one million different types of gamete, provided that at least one gene on each of the chromosomes is heterozygous.

Linkage of genes

When the two parental strains used in a breeding experiment differ in two genes which are on the same chromosome, it might be expected that any given combination of alleles of these two genes would remain intact through meiosis, since they are physically connected. The gametes produced could then only carry the combinations of alleles already present on the parental chromosomes (the 'parental' combinations in Fig. 3.8a, for example).

A final breeding experiment with peas will show that the situation is actually more complicated. A third character difference, the presence or absence of tendrils, is used; the allele for presence of tendrils (T) is dominant to that for absence (t). The F_1 generation from a cross between two true-breeding strains, one strain with round seeds and tendrils and another strain with wrinkled seeds and no tendrils, all have round seeds and produce tendrils when grown to plants. In this experiment, these F_1 are then crossed to a strain homozygous for the recessive alleles of both genes (rt/rt) (Fig. 3.9a). All the gametes from this double recessive homozygote will carry the alleles for wrinkled seeds and no tendrils (rt), while the F_1, heterozygous for both genes (RT/rt), would be expected to produce four types of gametes if the two genes were on different chromosomes. Fig. 3.9b shows these four types, as well as the genotype of the zygotes they form with the rt gamete and the phenotype of the progeny which then develop.

Each of the types of gamete from the F_1 individuals leads to a distinct phenotype in the progeny of this cross. The frequencies of these phenotypes directly measure the frequencies of the respective types of gamete produced by the F_1 generation, assuming that all the zygotes are equally viable, and this is thus called a **test-cross**. Fig. 3.9c shows the results of a typical cross like this.

Most of the gametes produced by the F_1 plants indeed contain the same arrangement of genes as did the original parents (classes A and D), but 16 gametes were recombinant (classes B and C). The two genes are thus not on two different chromosomes, as then equal numbers of parental and recombinant types would be formed; the genes are in fact on the same chromosome, and the small number of recombinants arise from crossing-over between the members of that chromosome pair when it forms before the first meiotic division in the F_1 generation.

As shown in Fig. 3.9d, crossing-over is the exchange of segments of DNA between two chromatids, one from each of the two homologous chromosomes present, when they pair closely in their replicated state before the first division of meiosis (see section 1.5). In order to produce recombinant gametes, such an exchange must occur in the region of the chromosome between the two genes which are heterozygous in the F_1, and the frequency of recombinant gametes then is a measure of the physical distance separating the two genes on the chromosome. Crossing-over elsewhere will lead to the production of gametes resembling those of the parents at these genes, and is thus not detectable in this way.

The **recombinant fraction** (or **r.f.**) for a pair of genes is the number of recombinant types produced in such a test-cross, expressed as a percentage of the total number of progeny. Two genes on different chromosomes have an r.f. value of 50%, and genes which have an r.f. value of less than 50% are said to be **linked**.

Sometimes a group of genes can be identified, any pair of which can be shown to be linked. Values measured for the

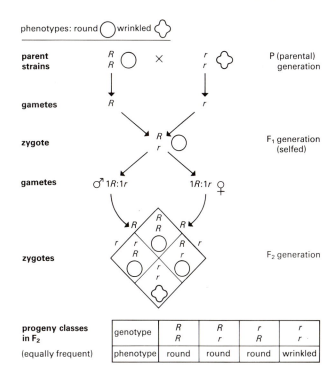

Fig. 3.7. Explanation, in terms of gene symbols, of the results of crossing two true-breeding strains of pea differing in seed shape, and of selfing the progeny obtained.

various recombinant fractions for these genes are found to be approximately additive, as long as the individual r.f. values are not near 50%, and the genes can then be arranged in a linear order. The arrangements of genes derived in this way are called **linkage maps**, corresponding to the relative positions of the genes on the chromosome.

The r.f. values thus obtained, measuring the frequency of crossing-over between pairs of genes, represent the physical distance between the genes, and are called 'map distances'. They do not however necessarily correspond accurately to the relative numbers of base-pairs of DNA separating the genes. A cross-over in any interval may be accompanied by one or more other cross-overs in the same interval, and some of the multiple cross-overs restore the parental combination of alleles of the two genes. This is more likely to occur when genes are widely separated, and can be avoided by building up the chromosome maps using only fairly closely linked genes, or by applying a mathematical correction. By reducing the frequency of recombinants, multiple cross-overs reduce the apparent map distance between well-separated genes. Two genes on the same chromosome may be so far apart, and crossing-over between them so frequent, that alleles of these two genes are no more likely to be included in the same gamete than they would if they were on different chromosomes, and so the r.f. value for such pairs of genes will be 50%; however, the map distance between them, measured as the sum of the map distances between all the intervening genes, will exceed this value.

Secondly, crossing-over does not occur with equal probability at all points on the chromosome, and in many cases is known to be to some degree localised. The location and frequency of crossing-over is controlled in many organisms by a variety of mechanisms. Its potential for generating variability, in the form of new combinations of alleles of genes on the same chromosome, is therefore itself variable, and can most significantly be affected by the genotype of the individual.

Multiple alleles and gene interactions

There are some important features of genes not illustrated in the breeding experiments so far described. For example, more than two alleles of a gene may be known, although of course a diploid individual can only carry two of these alleles at one time. In general, the number of mutant alleles detected will depend on the physiological effects of changes in the protein that is the gene product, and of course on the sensitivity of the method used to measure the phenotype.

Three alleles are known of the single gene which determines the ABO system of blood groups in man. This gene specifies some of the antigenic carbohydrate molecules present on the surface of red blood cells. The allele (I^A) specifies a molecule called 'A antigen', another (I^B) specifies 'B antigen', and the third (I^O) produces neither 'A' nor 'B' antigens. The presence and type of the antigens can be detected directly by blood tests using antibodies. I^A and I^B are both dominant to I^O because I^AI^O and I^BI^O heterozygotes possess, respectively, antigens 'A' and 'B'. I^A and I^B are said to be **codominant** alleles, because I^AI^B heterozygotes possess both 'A' and 'B' antigens.

Character differences can of course be due to a number of different alleles of a single gene, and where two different recessive mutant alleles are alleles of the same gene the heterozygote carrying one of each mutant allele will also be phenotypically mutant. A particular mutant phenotype may however be caused instead by two copies of a recessive allele at one of two (or more) different genes, and then a double heterozygote carrying one copy of each of the different mutant alleles will be phenotypically wild-type. The occurrence of wild-type doubly heterozygous diploids in these circumstances is called **complementation**, and the two genes are said to be **complementary**. Tests to detect complementation vary since the diploid stage is obtained in different ways in different organisms, but they are a very powerful technique for determining whether the mutations carried by two similar but unrelated mutant strains are present in the same or different genes.

Because the products (or, more generally, the effects) of two genes may interact at the physiological level, allelic differences at one gene may affect the expression of another gene. As a consequence, relationships between genotype and phenotype may seem more complex. For example, it is possible for mutation in one gene to alter the phenotype in such a way that the expression of another gene is masked. Several genes are known in the fruit fly *Drosophila melanogaster* in which mutation leads to alteration of the wild-type red eye colour. However, strains homozygous for a mutant allele of another gene do not develop eyes at all: in such individuals, this phenotype is not affected by which alleles of the eye-colour

(a)

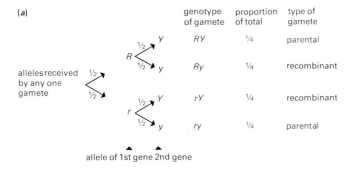

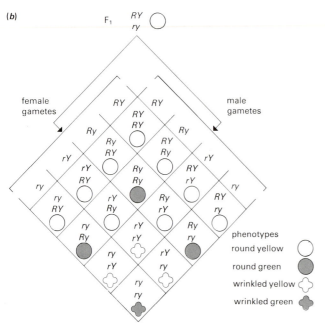

Fig. 3.8. Two factors segregating independently in the pea. (a) Choice diagram showing the four types of gamete which can arise, and the proportion of the total gametes formed that each would be expected to be. (b) Checkerboard diagram showing the types of progeny expected, and their proportions when gametes fuse at random.

gene they carry. The eyeless mutation is said to be **epistatic** to the eye-colour mutation. In addition, dominance relationships between alleles of one gene can be modified by allelic differences at another, and the degree of expression of a mutant phenotype, that is, how extreme the departure from normal is, may be affected by the alleles of other genes present.

Sometimes the genes which modify the effect of a gene under study may not in fact themselves be identified. This is often the case when strains isolated from different wild populations are compared, since such strains often differ from each other in a large number of genes. Unanalysed but consistent differences in genotype between strains are called differences in **genetic background**, a somewhat evasive but useful concept. Both dominance relationships and the degree of severity of mutant phenotypes may vary in different genetic backgrounds.

Characters showing continuous variation

The hereditary variation described so far is of the type called **discontinuous variation**: it has been possible to classify individuals into distinct classes, such as round or wrinkled

peas, or green or yellow *Aspergillus* colonies. Some apparently hereditary variation is of another type, however, in that no clear categories of distinct phenotypes can be discerned. An example is height in humans: the classification of a large number of people chosen at random into separate classes on the basis of their heights requires that arbitrary class limits be set. There is a continuous distribution of the phenotypes, but this type of variation, called **continuous variation**, can in fact be due to the action of genes similar to those already described.

It might be that the range of values of the continuously varying character, such as height, is due to only a few different possible genotypes, but that so much variation is introduced by environmental factors, which are not of genetic origin, that the distinction between the different classes of phenotype is blurred. In the case of height in humans such environmental factors might include diet or exercise. Alternatively, there might be so many different genotypes affecting height present in the population that they are impossible to identify solely from the phenotypes. This might occur if there are a large number of genes which have an additive effect on height (Fig. 3.10).

So long as it is possible to measure the continuously varying character, and to assign a numerical value to each individual, two useful statistics can be calculated to describe how a character varies in a population: the **mean** and the **variance**. The mean is the average value measured for the character in the population, while the variance, which equals the mean of the squares of the deviation of individual values from the mean of the population, increases as the spread of values within the population becomes larger. The variance of the population, the mathematical measure of the variation of this character within the population, can be assumed, in the simplest possible theory, to be equal to the sums of two individual variances due, respectively, to environmental and genetic differences. In more complex models allowance is made for the interaction of genotype and environment, and the genetic variance itself is further subdivided.

The following simple example illustrates how breeding schemes can be combined with statistical analysis to reveal whether that part of the continuous variation that has a genetic basis conforms to the framework of behaviour of individual genes illustrated earlier, that is, whether the genes involved behave in a Mendelian fashion. This requires the effects of genetic and environmental variation to be separated. It is necessary to start with two differing strains which breed as near to true as possible, and these can be produced in self-fertile organisms by repeated self-fertilisation of individuals from a population. In successive generations the resulting lines will become more and more nearly homozygous for all their genes, until they become **pure lines**, and are thus analogous to the lines Mendel used which were true-breeding for individual characters. Variation in these pure lines in the mean value of variance of the character under analysis can be assumed to be due purely to environmental factors.

(*a*) **breeding experiment**

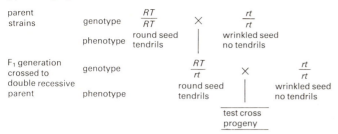

parent strains	genotype	$\dfrac{RT}{RT}$	$\times$	$\dfrac{rt}{rt}$
	phenotype	round seed tendrils		wrinkled seed no tendrils

F_1 generation crossed to double recessive parent	genotype	$\dfrac{RT}{rt}$	$\times$	$\dfrac{rt}{rt}$
	phenotype	round seed tendrils	test cross progeny	wrinkled seed no tendrils

(*b*) **possible types of test-cross progeny**

phenotype	class of progeny	gamete from F_1	gamete from recessive homozygote	genotype of zygote
round seed tendrils	A	RT	rt	$\dfrac{RT}{rt}$
round seed no tendrils	B	Rt	rt	$\dfrac{Rt}{rt}$
wrinkled seed tendrils	C	rT	rt	$\dfrac{rT}{rt}$
wrinkled seed no tendrils	D	rt	rt	$\dfrac{rt}{rt}$

(*c*) **typical test-cross progeny from the breeding experiment**

class of progeny	phenotype	number found	
A	round seed tendrils	516	calculation of recombinant fraction using data at left:
B	round seed no tendrils	9	recombinant fraction (r.f.)
C	wrinkled seed tendrils	7	$= \dfrac{\text{number of recombinant progeny}}{\text{total number of progeny}} \times 100\%$
D	wrinkled seed no tendrils	492	$= \dfrac{(\text{number in B}) + (\text{number in C})}{1024} \times 100\%$
		1024	$= \dfrac{9+7}{1024} \times 100\% = 1.56\%$

Fig. 3.9. Measuring recombinant frequency in a test cross. (a) The F_1 from crossing two true-breeding strains which differ in two characteristics is crossed to a true-breeding strain with the appropriate double-recessive phenotype. (b) Possible genotypes of members of the test-cross progeny. (c) Some typical data. (d) Crossing-over between the markers during meiosis in a double heterozygote generates recombinant gametes. This is illustrated diagrammatically for the pea chromosome which carries the two linked genes: one for seed shape and the other for presence or absence of tendrils. At the

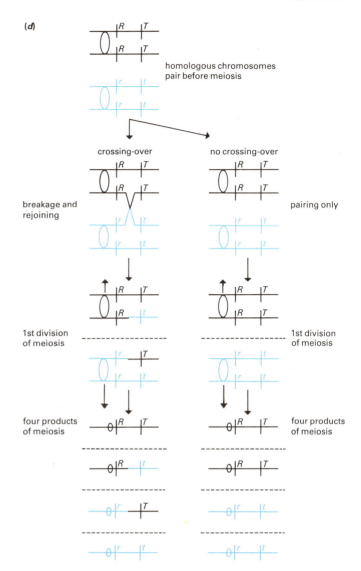

(*d*)

homologous chromosomes pair before meiosis

crossing-over　　　　no crossing-over

breakage and rejoining　　　　pairing only

1st division of meiosis　　　　1st division of meiosis

four products of meiosis　　　　four products of meiosis

start of meiosis in an F_1 plant, the two homologous chromosomes pair. If crossing-over occurs in the region of the chromosome between the two markers (left column), then the products of meiosis are two recombinant gametes, and two parental ones. If no crossing-over occurs between the two markers (right column), then the four products of meiosis are all parental gametes. The other pea chromosomes are not shown.

When two such pure lines are crossed, the progeny (the F_1 generation) should be a group of individuals which do not differ from each other genetically, because each is heterozygous for nearly all the genes affecting the character to be measured quantitatively. Nearly all the variation in this generation too is expected to be caused by environmental factors.

Self-fertilisation of the F_1 individuals then produces an F_2 generation, and if statistical tests show this to have significantly more variation than did the F_1 generation, then genes affecting the character can be concluded to be segregating in the F_2. Assuming that the growth conditions in the experiment have been kept the same for each generation, the contribution to the variance of environmental factors can be assumed to be approximately constant in each generation, and the increase in variance in the F_2 can be assumed to be a result of the genetic variation shown by this generation. The estimates obtained in this and other ways can be used to calculate the **heritability** of the characteristic in this situation, that is, the proportion of its variance in the mixed population that is due to the genetic factors.

Following the same genetic logic that was used to map the relative locations of genes where individual allelic differences led to discontinuous variation, it is sometimes possible to use complex breeding schemes and statistical techniques to identify the regions of chromosome maps where genes which have a major effect on a continuously varying character are located. The effects of allelic substitutions at the genes concerned are assumed to be additive, although the magnitudes of the phenotypic effects of different alleles differ between genes. Those genes where variation has the most effect are, of course, the easiest to analyse.

Artificial selection

Characters which show continuous variation often respond to **artificial selection**, when selected members of a population are used as parents for the next generation, and this process repeated for many generations, instead of allowing random cross-fertilisation. If the parents in each generation are chosen because they possess a higher value for the character in question than do others in the same generation, then under this breeding regimen the mean value of the character increases in successive generations, at least initially. A similar process can reduce the mean value of the character by choosing as parents individuals with a lower value of the character. At the same time as the mean responds to selection (in whichever direction), the genetic variance tends to decrease as selection proceeds.

Consider the effects of artificial selection for increased seed weight in a plant, starting with a variable population (that is, not a pure line or an inbred strain). If at least some of the variation in seed weight between individuals in the starting population is due to genetic factors, then the plants chosen as the parents of the next generation because of the high weight of their seeds will probably possess more alleles for high seed weight than do unselected plants. Such alleles will thus be more frequent in the next generation. As this process continues, however, more and more individuals will become homozygous for the relevant genes, and increasingly each gene will be represented only by its 'high-seed-weight' allele. The genetic variance therefore declines as selection proceeds, and as a consequence the response to selection also decreases and eventually ceases. However, if the selection regimen is maintained, providing a continued **selection pressure**, a further slow increase in seed weight may occur dependent upon the occurrence of new genetic variation in subsequent generations. The ability to produce new variation is called the **genetic variability** of a population: the new genotypes affecting a continuous character could be generated by mutation or by recombination.

The results of breeding experiments in particular species confirm most of the features of this analysis. As expected, selection for increased seed weight in pure lines of beans has little effect, because a population that possesses no genetic variation cannot respond to selection; and characters which respond quickly to selection often have a substantially reduced response after a certain amount of selection has occurred.

Regimens of artificial selection imposed by plant and animal breeders have often produced dramatic improvements in crops and livestock. However, at the same time as selection is carried out to improve the agronomic value of a strain, deleterious characters like sterility are often also selected for unwittingly.

For example, the congenital diseases associated with certain breeds of pedigree dogs have almost certainly arisen as an unintended consequence of selection for the biologically arbitrary characteristics of the breed.

Genetic variation is essential if selection, artificial or natural, is to have an effect. The extinction of agronomically obsolete species and strains, as a result of current farming practices, is a matter of concern because of the knowledge of agricultural breeders that such strains are an irreplaceable future source of genetic variation.

Genetic variation in populations

A population of individuals of a species is defined as a freely interbreeding group, and there is a certain degree of genetic variation in all natural populations. Some examples have already been given: the variation of blood group and of height in the human species are both evident in natural populations. The extent of genetic variation in a population, and the mechanisms by which it is maintained and yet changes over time, are part of the study of the genetic structure of populations.

A biochemical technique called gel electrophoresis can be used to detect the different structural forms of a protein, and Mendelian breeding experiments can readily determine whether these forms are due to different alleles of the gene specifying the protein. These alleles arise by mutations of the kind which lead to an amino-acid substitution in the protein, but where the substitution concerned does not impair the enzymic or other function of the protein. In terms of the phenotype of the whole organism, these variants would be classified as wild-type alleles. Sampling of natural populations has revealed that a surprisingly large number of such alleles is present for most of the genes studied over a wide range of species. A gene is said to be **polymorphic** in a population if more than one allele of it is present, ignoring those alleles so rare that their presence could be due solely to recurrent mutation. More generally, **genetic polymorphism** is used to describe the situation where two or more discontinuous forms of a phenotypic feature under genetic control are present in the population. Enzyme polymorphisms are clearly a case of this where the phenotypic feature is due to a single gene product. The MN blood group system in humans is another example: the phenotypic feature is the response to blood tests, and Fig. 3.11 shows the distribution of the different alleles. At a much higher level of phenotypic complexity, the sexual system in species where individuals are of one sex or the other is also a polymorphism: here the phenotypic feature is the totality of sexual characteristics, and the genetic specification of the two forms, male and female, is also complex.

The **allele frequency** or **gene frequency** of an allele of a certain gene is the proportion of that allele among all the different versions of the gene in the population. It is a variable central to many of the arguments of **population genetics**,

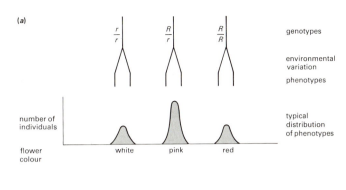

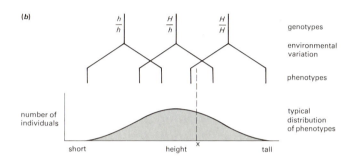

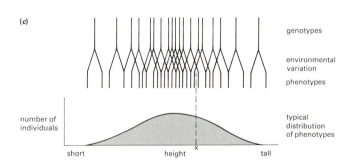

which attempts to relate changes in gene frequency within a population over time to the effects of selection and the genetic system of the species, often considering only one or a few genes at a time.

One of the principal simplifications used in these analyses is the **Hardy–Weinberg Law**, which relates gene frequencies to the proportions of the different diploid genotypes. It is a demonstration that segregation of the alleles of a gene that behave in the way shown by Mendel does not by itself lead to a change of allele frequencies for that gene between one generation of the population and the next. Moreover, a state of equilibrium can be reached, where successive generations each have the same proportions of individuals of the different genotypes. The major conditions that must be met for this 'Hardy–Weinberg' equilibrium are those of **random mating** (that is, that the individuals in any pairing are chosen effectively at random from the population) and the **absence of selection** (that is, that the zygotes of all the different genotypes are equally viable). If two alleles (A and a) of a gene have frequencies p and q, respectively, so that $p + q = 1$, then that numerical ratio of the frequency of the genotypes $AA : Aa : aa$ in the population that is stable is $p^2 : 2pq : q^2$. A simple argument, not in itself a rigorous proof of the law, shows that these ratios are correct. When gametes are formed by one generation of the population, each gamete produced will receive one allele of the gene. If we consider all the gametes produced by the population as a whole (the 'gamete pool') the proportion of gametes carrying allele A will be p and that of gametes carrying allele a will be q, since these are the proportions of the alleles carried by the parental population. Random mating implies that the gametes fuse in randomly chosen pairs. A diagram like that shown in Fig. 3.12 gives the proportion of genotypes and phenotypes in the next generation, which equals the proportions in the previous generation if these were in the equilibrium ratio $AA : Aa : aa$ of $p^2 : 2pq : q^2$.

Artificial selection leads to changes in the frequencies of alleles of genes relevant to the character selected. Natural selection also causes changes in allele frequencies because some genotypes produce organisms with more success in reproducing and in handing on their genes to the next generation. As a consequence the alleles carried by these 'selected' or reproductively more successful genotypes become more frequent (see section 11.1). The quantitative measure of reproductive success is called **fitness** by geneticists, and it is genotypes of greater fitness that natural selection makes more frequent. The looser meaning of fitness, namely aptness or suitability for a role, is normally expressed by **adaptation**, so that an organism may be described as being adapted to its environment.

There has been much debate on the question of how natural selection can maintain polymorphism. One of the possible forms of a genetic polymorphism might be expected to be fitter than the other forms, and thus to come to replace the others over time, but in fact many mechanisms have been shown to be able to maintain polymorphism as a stable state. The mechan-

Fig. 3.10. Genetic explanations of continuous variation. (a) Underlying variation. Variation caused by non-genetic factors can produce a spread of phenotypes within each category. (In this case the categories are due to the segregation of two alleles of an imaginary gene for flower colour in a plant, where red shows no dominance over white.) Nonetheless, the genotype of each individual can be deduced unambiguously from its phenotype. (b) When greater environmental variation is imposed on a similar genetic situation (this time involving genes affecting height), the distinction between categories is blurred. The genotype of an individual height x, for example, would be uncertain without further tests. (c) When variation in many genes of additive effect can alter the phenotype, the range of phenotypes is again continuous – despite the fact that environmental variation is no greater than in (a) – because several different genotypes can lead to any given height.

ism thought to be the most common is **heterozygote advantage**, whereby individuals heterozygous for two alleles of a gene are of higher fitness than either of the two homozygotes. Selection therefore acts to keep both alleles in the population. Alternatively, where the polymorphism produces two distinct phenotypic forms, it is sometimes found that either of the forms is at a selective advantage only when it is not the predominant form in the population. **Frequency-dependent selection** of

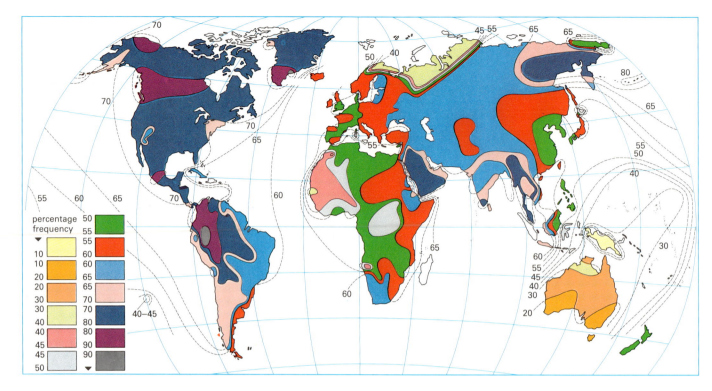

Fig. 3.11. The variation in allele frequency in indigenous human populations polymorphic for the gene specifying MN system blood group. The data on which this contour map is based (contours connect locations with the same frequency of the M allele) were obtained by testing the blood groups of members of samples, using antisera to identify MN blood types.

this kind can also maintain polymorphisms. Similarly, one of the forms may be at a selective advantage at one stage of the life-cycle, or season of the year, but at a disadvantage at another. It is often, however, difficult to assess whether these mechanisms are or are not operating in a particular case of polymorphism in a natural population.

Some biologists believe that selection plays no part in maintaining enzyme polymorphisms such as those detected by gel electrophoresis, and that these alleles are **selectively neutral**, that is, they do not significantly affect the fitness of the organism. The frequency of such neutral alleles would vary at random, by **genetic drift**. Random changes in gene frequency can also be analysed theoretically, and they are of more importance in small populations than in large ones (see section 7.5).

The genetic structure of a population depends also on the breeding system adopted. Where sexual reproduction is employed the degree of relatedness of the partners in a mating is significant, and if mates are in general more closely related to each other than they would be if chosen at random from the population, inbreeding is said to occur. Inbreeding can result from a restricted population size, but it can also be due to departures from random mating. The most extreme cases of non-random mating are self-fertilisation (in species where this is possible), and then the mating of individuals with both, or one, of their parents in common. The pure lines of beans described above are highly inbred. Some degree of inbreeding can result when individuals of like genotype mate together

more often than their frequency in the population would justify under random mating.

One result of inbreeding is that genes, including deleterious recessive alleles, become increasingly homozygous. For this reason, inbred lines of species that are not naturally inbreeding often show a decline in fertility and vigour compared with natural populations. However, hybrids between two different inbred lines are often more fertile and vigorous than either of the parental lines, the phenomenon of **hybrid vigour**. Remarkable increases in yield have been obtained by using, in place of the individual cultivated varieties of maize (corn, *Zea mays*), strains which are hybrids between different cultivated varieties.

The degree of inbreeding (or of its reverse, outbreeding) that occurs in a natural population is affected by the mating system of the species concerned. For example, among potentially self-fertile (hermaphrodite) plants and animals, many species possess reproductive structures designed to prevent self-fertilisation and hence to promote outbreeding, which increases and maintains genetic diversity. However, other species seem to be adapted to a certain amount of inbreeding, as in these cases self-fertilisation is allowed or even encouraged.

The availability of genetic variation on which selection acts is clearly an important feature of the response to natural selection. All the features of the genetics of organisms described above, as well as several others, affect this responsiveness to changing conditions. The use of sexual or asexual

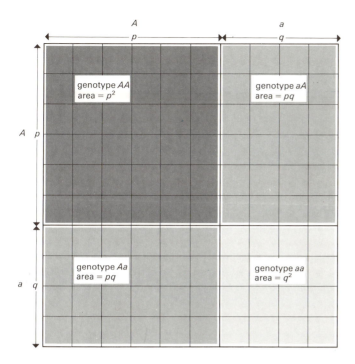

Fig. 3.12. Diagram illustrating the proportions of the different genotypes for a gene with two alleles, A and a, in a population in Hardy–Weinberg equilibrium. If the allele frequency of A is p, and that of a is q, when the sides of the square are divided in the ratio p : q, the areas of the sections of the square produced (expressed as a proportion of the area of the whole square) represent the proportions of the individuals in the population with the relevant genotypes. The diagram is to scale, with p = 0.6 (that is, six of 10 alleles of this gene in the population are A) and q = 0.4. Of the 100 grid squares, 36 are in the AA section, 24 in each of the Aa sections – making 48 Aa in all – and 16 are aa.

reproduction by a population is especially important. In the diploid stage of the life-cycle, dominance can mask the effects of recessive mutant alleles until chance mating leads to the production of a homozygote and the alleles becoming subject to selection. Recombination can generate diversity, whether it is mediated by independent segregation of chromosomes (and thus more likely with organisms with a large number of pairs of chromosomes) or by crossing-over between genes (more likely where there is a low degree of linkage between the genes). Departures from random mating can also have important effects on the manner in which natural selection acts. Sexual reproduction can also lead to the bringing together, in one individual and its descendants, advantageous alleles of different genes which happen to arise in separate lineages, for example by mutation, and many types of organism use within their life-cycle both sexual reproduction to generate diversity of the sort acted on by natural selection, and asexual reproduction to ensure rapid propagation of successful genotypes. Selection acts on phenotypes, and for the study of inheritance the connection between genotype and phenotype is important in each case.

Further reading.

Sheppard, P.M. *Natural selection and heredity.* (4th edn) London: Hutchinson, 1975.
Strickberger, M.W. *Genetics.* (2nd edn) New York: Macmillan, 1976.
Suzuki, D.T., Griffiths, A.J.F. and Lewontin, R.C. *An introduction to genetic analysis.* (2nd edn) San Francisco: W.H. Freeman, 1981.
Szekely, M. *From DNA to protein: The transfer of genetic information.* New York: Macmillan, 1980.
Watson, J.D. *Molecular biology of the gene.* (3rd edn) Menlo Park: Benjamin, 1976.

4 Behaviour and Sociobiology

Niko Tinbergen argued that animal behaviourists, or **ethologists**, commonly ask four types of question about patterns of behaviour. These questions concern causation, development, adaptive function and evolutionary history: for example, humans walk by moving particular sets of muscles in response to environmental stimuli (**causation**); humans learn to walk after a period of crawling and then using supports to practise walking upright (**development**); humans walk because natural selection favoured that mode of locomotion in the particular habitats in which we evolved (**adaptive function**); and if we possessed information about our ancestors we might find a transition from brachiation, using arms to swing from branch to branch, as practised by modern gibbons, through knuckle-walking, as found in present-day gorillas, to upright walking (**evolutionary history**).

Causation

Causal interpretations of behaviour are usually based on simple models, either expressed neurophysiologically or in terms of processes chosen as analogues, and the models become increasingly complex as more sophisticated behavioural processes are analysed. Among the lower levels of behavioural organisation are simple reflexes, such as the well-known knee-jerk reflex. The brain has no direct involvement in simple reflexes and there is usually no feedback interaction between successive responses. Behavioural sequences often involve the use of particular patterns of behaviour, which Lorenz called **fixed action patterns**: these are the stereotyped and heritable responses typical of each species, which are centrally programmed and not dependent on feedback of any sort. Although the existence of the first three criteria for all fixed action patterns is debatable, they are centrally programmed so that neural mechanisms controlling the behaviour are permanently present ('hard-wired') in the brain. Egg retrieval by the greylag goose is an example. A bird sitting on a nest stretches its neck to retrieve a lost egg. The response does not involve coordinated feedback during the sequence since, if the bird loses the egg during retrieval, it will finish the movement even though its bill is only retrieving empty space. Such central programming of fixed sequences is common among invertebrates and the lower vertebrates, and is used for many simple behavioural patterns among the higher vertebrates.

There is a gradation of behaviour sequences from rigidly stereotyped fixed action patterns through to direct **stimulus–response patterns** where sensory feedback occurs so that, if the environment changes, the response is adjusted accordingly. Most behaviour of the higher vertebrates is quite variable and involves feedback. Egg retrieval in the greylag goose can be achieved through a fixed action pattern, but nest-building among most birds requires the flexibility afforded by the ability to respond to changing stimuli.

The development of models of behaviour based simply on causation requires the animals' sensory abilities to be measured quantitatively. This raises experimental problems because, although a response to a stimulus means that the stimulus has been detected, lack of a response does not mean that the stimulus has not been detected: the animal may be ignoring the stimulus. Different animals vary in their sensory capacities, and those stimuli to which animals give attention are termed sign-stimuli or **releasers**. The sight of a hawk silhouette acts as a releaser for passerine birds, and red-bellied male sticklebacks act as releasers for other red-bellied male sticklebacks during the mating season. In the first case the response is escape, and in the second it is intrasexual aggression.

The filtering of stimuli, which results in a response being given only to particular releasers, is termed an **innate releasing mechanism**, and ensures that animals give attention only to the relevant stimuli in their environment. One classical mechanistic interpretation of innate releasing mechanisms suggests that sense organs receive all incoming information and pass it on faithfully to a higher filtering mechanism in the brain, which then integrates it with other relevant information.

This view can be erroneous. For example, frogs may show a prey-catching response towards small round moving objects such as flies, and detailed studies of the neurophysiology of this response show that the filtering and integration of relevant visual information starts at the rods and cones of the retina. In several other studies, using a variety of stimuli, filtering has been demonstrated at levels from the actual receptor of the stimulus right through to higher cortical areas of the brain. Although the idea of innate releasing mechanisms helps us to model reception of stimuli in the lower vertebrates and the invertebrates, for the high vertebrates at least we must recognise that cognitive processes, such as learning, are important in the selective perception of stimuli. In such cases the exact form of the perceived sign stimuli can become extremely complex.

Animals perform different behaviour patterns according to the environments in which they find themselves, but internal states or **drives**, such as hunger, influence whether or not a particular pattern of behaviour is performed. Drives are postulated to be the intangible motivational forces behind the expression of behaviour patterns, causing an animal to be more or less likely to perform a particular behaviour in response to a specific stimulus. Lorenz devised a psycho-hydraulic model to describe drives within organisms, and this is shown in Fig. 4.1. Consider hunger as the drive. A high level of water in the upper reservoir represents high motivation (extreme hunger). In such a situation the valve will open and release water which causes the behaviour (eating). Whether or not the valve opens also depends on the weight attached to the valve, which represents the strength of stimulus (amount or quality of food). The water flowing through the valve enters the lower reservoir and escapes through tubes in ascending order, the number of these depending on the quantity of water released into the lower reservoir. This means that behaviour 1 is seen first, followed by behaviour 2 and so on. The model has certain attractive features: for example, it describes fluctuating levels of responsiveness. Once an animal has eaten (water released from the system) it will wait for food deprivation, resulting in hunger (the upper reservoir to fill), before eating again. If the animal has not eaten sufficiently then the head of water in the upper reservoir remains high and the animal will not have to wait so long for the reservoir to fill to such a level where water is lost through the valve again. The temporal organisation of patterns of behaviour is also described by the model: with low levels of motivation, only earlier parts of the behavioural repertoire are seen (fluid is only lost from the lower tubes of the lower reservoir). Hence, if a cat is not sufficiently hungry it might catch a prey item without eating it; motivation must be sufficiently high for the prey to be captured, killed and eaten.

The psycho-hydraulic model and many like it are analogues, and we are forced to use them because we do not fully understand the neural mechanisms behind motivation and drives. The value of the models is therefore limited. Motivational 'forces' are hypothetical: we do not know of suitable energy sources within the central nervous system, analogous to the water pressure in Lorenz's model, nor are physiological 'drive centres' known. In addition, drives are not dependent solely upon deprivation, but hormones and endogenous rhythms (biological clocks) interact to cause the expression of sets of behavioural patterns. For example, bouts of feeding are often determined by intrinsic feeding rhythms rather than physiological deficit. The feeding of blowflies is one such well-understood behavioural repertoire and is explicable in terms of reflexes and negative feedback in populations of neurons. In such a system we do not need to postulate the existence of drives.

Animals rarely find themselves in a position where a single motivational system governs their behaviour. The behaviour of a bird feeding in a flock will be influenced by the need for food, the need to be wary of predators, and intraspecific interactions resulting from sexual, aggressive and defensive drives. The tendency for any particular pattern of behaviour to be performed will be some function of both the size of the drive and the intensity of the stimulus relevant to that drive. Within this framework, ethologists have attempted to determine how different motivations interact, and thus how animals switch from one behavioural repertoire to another. If an animal is both hungry and thirsty, traditional theory predicts that it should switch rapidly between eating and drinking, but in fact long bouts of feeding are observed interspersed with long bouts of drinking. The site where this process is determined physiologically is not known, but it is hypothesised that the thresholds which exist for turning any particular behaviour on and off are different, and hence rapid switching between behaviours is not seen.

When two or more kinds of motivation are present in roughly equal intensity, and only one can be expressed physically at any moment, the result is a conflict. Such conflicts between competing motivations are often resolved by animals

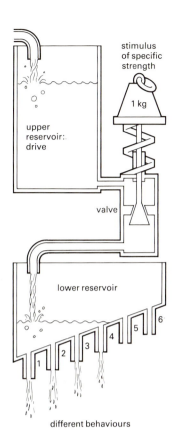

different behaviours

Fig. 4.1. Lorenz's psycho-hydraulic model of drives.

performing displays that contain components of responses appropriate to both motivations. For example, in contests between rival male birds, threat displays often contain actions normally associated with aggression and fear. In other cases of conflict between drives, strange and apparently irrelevant behaviour patterns occur. These have been termed **displacement activities**. It has been proposed that, in such cases, the resolution of motivational conflicts occurs with removal of the inhibition on some other behaviour pattern, which is then performed out of context. Alternatively, it may sometimes be the case that other relevant yet minor stimuli dictate which displacement activity is seen.

The role of hormones in carrying out certain aspects of behaviour, such as reproductive behaviour, is reasonably well understood. Hormones exert three types of direct effect on the behaviour of animals: a driving effect by stimulating the central nervous system, a peripheral modulating effect by altering physiology or anatomy, and a signalling effect by changing the state of one animal so as to influence that of another. Any one hormone produces effects of several kinds, while the effects of a variety of hormones acting together are necessary to produce the majority of behavioural repertoires.

'Biological clocks' of various sorts are found in all eukaryotes and they influence most patterns of behaviour. They measure time both directly and in response to environmental cues. All biological clocks are controlled endogenously and run freely on their own rhythm in the absence of any external synchronising stimulus. Many behavioural rhythms can, however, be related to obvious environmental cycles such as circadian (24 hour), lunar or annual cycles, and certain cues, *Zeitgebern*, are used to entrain the behavioural rhythms, the phases of which are shifted slightly each cycle to fit changing environments. For example, rats and cockroaches use dusk or sunset as daily markers to set their internal circadian rhythms, and artificial laboratory environments can be used to take the animals quite out of phase with nature. Sources of short-term rhythms can occasionally be identified within small groups of neurons, or even in single oscillator neurons, but the physiological basis for longer-term rhythms is more complex. For example, in birds the pineal gland is necessary for the normal functioning of circadian activity cycles. We do not yet have a reasonable understanding of any one of the circadian rhythms found in the animal kingdom.

Migration is a common phenomenon and many birds that breed in temperate latitudes often show particular patterns of migration throughout the year. Migration and effective navigation have obvious direct functional advantages in ensuring that such birds move speedily between favourable habitats. Here again, control of the rhythms is little understood, although hormones have certainly been recognised as mediating the behaviour. The navigational aids used depend on the species studied and on the animals' circumstances and experience; they include the sun, stars, landmarks, and magnetic fields, used singly or in combination.

Development

Some patterns of behaviour are known to be under close genetic control, as can be demonstrated by breeding experiments. For example, a strain of honeybees is called 'hygienic' because when one of the larvae dies, the workers uncap the cell containing the larva and remove the corpse. Other strains are 'unhygienic' and leave the rotting corpse. Hybrids between hygienic and unhygienic strains are phenotypically unhygienic, but test crosses (see section 3.2) reveal the presence of two loci (chromosomal sites), one of which controls uncapping the cells and the other removing the corpse (Table 4.1). Some of the offspring from the backcrosses will, therefore, only remove a corpse if the cell has previously been uncapped, and others will uncap cells but then will not remove the dead larvae. Among higher animals such strong genetic influences can rarely be demonstrated. Even behaviour once recognised as innate is now believed to result from a complex interaction between predispositions controlled by many genes and environmental influences during an animal's development.

Development of behaviour requires the previous development of sensory and motor mechanisms. Many animals require long periods after birth before their sets of behavioural responses are sufficiently complete and integrated for them to leave the natal environment or parental care. During this time environmental stimuli often play a large part in the development of behaviour patterns. For example, cats require visual experience during the first few weeks of life for their sight to

Table 4.1. *The difference in behaviour between the hygienic and non-hygienic strains of honeybee is due to a difference in genes at two chromosome loci. One locus (alleles U or u) controls the uncapping of cells and the other locus (alleles R or r) controls the removal of dead larvae. Hygienic bees have two copies of the recessive allele of each locus (uurr); non-hygienic strains are UURR. When the two strains are crossed, all the progeny (F_1 generation) are non-hygienic (UuRr). When these F_1 hybrids are backcrossed with the pure hygienic strain (uurr), four different genotypes are produced in equal frequencies.*

F_1 hybrid ♀ UuRr Gametes from ♀	ur	UR	uR	Ur
Hygienic strain ♀ gametes ur	uurr*	UuRr†	uuRr‡	Uurr§

* uncaps and removes larvae
† non-hygienic
‡ uncaps cells but does not remove dead larvae
§ removes dead larvae, but only if cells are previously uncapped

develop properly and to function normally. This allows a 'plasticity' of development which might be adaptive, since a hunting cat requires accurate binocular vision and perception of depth; any slight misalignment of the two eyes could be catastrophic if vision was fixed into the central nervous system from birth.

The importance of environmental stimuli in the development of coordination between sensory input and motor response varies from species to species. Some human sensory-motor integration is totally dependent upon learning, while much of that in the salamander is fixed from birth. Development of bird-song is a well-studied topic in sensory-motor integration. Some bird species have a song that is totally uninfluenced by the environment during their development, whereas other species have songs that depend totally on the songs that they heard while young. The chaffinch lies between the two extremes, and the development of its song has been used to show how experience and genetic predisposition interact during development. A chaffinch must hear a song during a sensitive period early in life if it is to develop a complete song, rather than just a simple sub-song, but the song which the young chaffinch hears must be a chaffinch-like song otherwise it will not be learned.

Imprinting is a particularly impressive type of active learning which occurs during development. A well-known example is **filial imprinting** of newborn young onto their parents. Shortly after hatching, birds such as ducklings and chicks come to recognise and follow only their mother, or, in experimental conditions, some substitute for the mother. Simultaneously, the mother learns the characteristics of her young and becomes so selective in her parental behaviour that she may attack and even kill young of other broods. Meanwhile, the young also learn the characteristics of their siblings

*Fig. 4.2. The typical body postures assumed by (a) subordinate and (b) dominant rhesus monkeys (*Macaca mulatta*).*

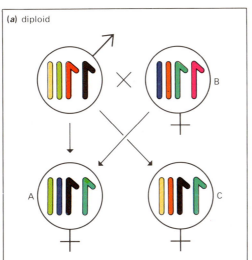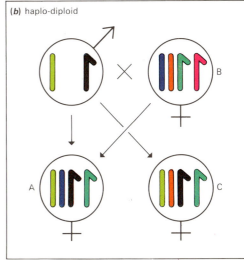

Fig. 4.3. In a normal diploid species (left), female A has half her genes in common with her mother, B, and also half in common with her sister, C. In a haplo-diploid species (right), female A' has half her genes in common with her mother, B', but three quarters in common with her sister, C', through complete acquisition of all of the father's genes by both sisters. This predisposes haplo-diploid species to the evolution of female based sociality.

(brothers and sisters). This process of familiarisation, together with filial imprinting, can leave a long-term effect on the choice of mate, since the birds prefer not to mate with their immediate kin. They do, however, prefer a mate looking rather like the individuals to which they were exposed when young, as can be strikingly demonstrated when birds are reared with members of a different species. **Sexual imprinting**, as this is called, is found to occur after siblings have moulted into their adult plumage but before they have dispersed. It has been proposed that a single learning process sets a standard for what immediate kin look like, and that the birds subsequently prefer to mate with an individual who looks slightly different, thus avoiding the detrimental effects of inbreeding. Imprinting on the odour of siblings has been experimentally demonstrated among social insects, which are then able to recognise aliens in their colony and to defend it effectively against them.

Adaptive function

The diversity in nature is, in large part, a consequence of natural selection acting in different ways on a variety of independently evolving lineages. Variation in behaviour as well as in morphology can be profitably analysed from an evolutionary standpoint, but the causes of behavioural dif-

ferences among animals are little understood: in most cases we do not know the extent to which genetic, rather than environmental, differences provide the basis for behavioural adaptation. As a consequence, it is convenient for behavioural ecologists and sociobiologists who are interested in the function of behaviour to define adaptation by its effects rather than by its causes.

Adaptation can be recognised when a difference between alternative behaviours leads to a difference in reproductive success between the individuals exhibiting these different behaviours. The behaviour causing its bearer to have higher reproductive success (a higher **fitness** for that environment) is said to be more **adaptive** than the other. Adaptation is, therefore, a comparative concept, and viewed in this way adaptations need not have direct genetic causes. The presence of mechanisms such as learning or cultural transmission, which can modify behaviour in an adaptive fashion within the lifespan of an individual, indicates that organisms can be even more closely fitted to their environments than if adaptation could only be produced by genetic change. Nevertheless, the actual ability to learn, or the ability to learn particular things with particular ease, may well be genetically based and be the product of natural selection; patterns of behaviour that are particularly successful, including the ability to respond ap-

Table 4.2. *Clutch size (number of eggs laid) and the average number of young fledged from such clutches is shown for one study of the swift carried out between 1958 and 1961. Swifts lay two or three eggs per clutch depending on their maturity, and the clutches of four eggs were produced by egg-transfer experiments. Group selectionists had argued that birds, such as swifts, reduced the number of eggs they laid so that they reared fewer young than they could if they had had more eggs, and consequently the food resources of the species would not be depleted. The evidence in fact indicates that individual swifts raise the maximum number of young by laying only two or three eggs, as laying four eggs greatly reduces the chances of any chick surviving to fledging. (Data from D. Lack, Population studies of birds. Oxford: Oxford University Press, 1966)*

Clutch size	Per cent lost	Average number raised per brood
2	3	1.94
3	15	2.55
4	58	1.68

propriately to environmental change, will be favoured by natural selection. Individual organisms result from the propagation of genes from previous generations, and there is no connotation of any genetic change or behaviour directed towards a specific goal.

Misunderstandings about the process of evolution through the mechanism of natural selection led many early ethologists to erroneous conclusions about the adaptive significance of social behaviour. Natural selection acts on individuals and through their differential mortality and reproductive success results in changes of gene frequencies in populations (see sections 3.2 and 11.1). A tradition in ethology has been the belief that animals can behave for the benefit of the group or the species as a whole, rather than just in their own selfish and individual interests. The theoretical foundation of such beliefs was made explicit in the early 1960s, when it was argued that animals behave so as to restrict their population density and rate of reproduction, so that the maximum yield sustainable over many generations (measured as units of productivity) is maintained from the available food supplies. It was argued that several social phenomena were manifestations of animals cooperating to restrain population sizes. For example, many behaviours were thought to be epideictic (meant for display) so as to allow members of a population to assess their own numbers, and dominance hierarchies were believed to be a mechanism evolved by the species to prevent unrestricted reproduction by entrusting reproductive decisions to a few dominant animals. Much of social behaviour seemed to be explained by this unifying theory.

Criticism of these ideas came from two quarters. First, evolutionary biologists pointed out that although group selection is an evolutionary force, it provides very weak selection compared to individual selection. Biologically unacceptable models of population structure, that assume extreme cohesion within groups and frequent extinction of whole groups, have to be envisaged for group selection to outweigh the importance of individual selection. Mutant selfish individuals which exploit the altruistic tendency of others will be selectively favoured within the group by individual selection even though this opposes the interests of the group as a whole. The second attack on group selection was not concerned with mechanisms but with the evidence for the phenomenon. Ecologists and field ethologists pointed out that, with few exceptions, animals seem to produce as many surviving young as possible each generation (Table 4.2). Social displays can in fact often be interpreted in terms of individual rather than group interests. For example, dominance hierarchies may result from interactions between pairs of animals, with the weaker individuals avoiding overt competition for food or mates: the dominant members of a group are expected to win in physical combat against subordinates (Fig. 4.2).

Although animals seem generally to have been selected to maximise their own reproductive success, there are many exceptions. These involve cases of **altruism**, in which an individual sacrifices some of its own potential reproductive success while acting to increase another's reproductive success. For example, there are many species of social Hymenoptera (wasps, bees and ants) where the majority of females develop into 'workers', and spend their time and energies rearing sisters rather than producing their own offspring. However, an individual helping a close relative may be favouring the spread of its own genes because the kin are particularly likely to share copies of the altruist's genes, as they are descended from a common ancestor. Among the Hymenoptera, 'haplo-diploid' inheritance results in a female's sisters being genetically more similar to her than are her own daughters (Fig. 4.3). Because males are haploid and females diploid in these species (see section 1.5), sisters contain identical genes from the male parent, while sharing one-half of their mother's genes; therefore on average two sisters share three-quarters of their genetic material. As mothers only pass on one-half of their genes to their daughters, it may well be in a female's genetic interests to be sterile, remain in the colony and rear her sisters, rather than to leave and produce her own offspring. This is an example of **kin selection**. The fact that males are haploid therefore predisposes the Hymenoptera to the evolution of sterile female castes, the workers. Even in groups without haplo-diploid inheritance, such as the vertebrates, there are well-documented cases of altruism which appear to be maintained by kin selection. For example, many birds and mammals give alarm calls which warn members of the same species of the presence of predators. Although such calls are often directed towards offspring, in many cases they are given in the absence of offspring but are then restricted to contexts in which other close relatives are present. Recent research on ground squirrels and prairie-dogs in particular provides clear evidence of how

Fig. 4.4. Living in groups.
(a) Young emperor penguins huddle together for warmth on the Antarctic ice.
(b) Wildebeeste aggregate in huge herds. Unlike the gazelles, calves are precocious and follow their mothers as soon as they can stand. The animals reduce predation by close birth synchrony which swamps the impact of local populations of predators.
(c) Thompson's gazelle graze in a tight-knit herd. One advantage of grouping is that each animal benefits from the enhanced ability of the group to detect predators. Animals feeding on their own have to check their surroundings for predators at regular intervals.

Fig. 4.5. (a) A cow elephant turns to defend her departing family unit. Groups of cows usually consist of a matriarch and her close relatives. (b) Adult musk-oxen shield a calf.

the alarm calls function to protect close relations in these groups.

Not all cases of altruistic behaviour will necessarily result from kin selection. Under certain circumstances **reciprocal altruism** may evolve; here one animal acts to its own detriment but benefiting another individual because the altruism is likely to be reciprocated at a later date. If the costs, measured in some unit of fitness, are less than the benefits then both participants gain in the long term. A clear example of reciprocal altruism is found in the olive baboon (*Papio anubis*). When a female comes into oestrus (the receptive stage of the sexual cycle), one particular mate becomes her consort. A pair of other males sometimes form a coalition so that one member of the pair engages the consort male in battle and, while they are fighting, the other member of the coalition escapes with the receptive female. Both members of the coalition gain from such behaviour because, on subsequent engagements with consorting pairs, they take turns to fight with the male and mate with the female. As long as the fights are not costly, such behaviour is clearly adaptive for lower-ranking males who might not be able to obtain a mate without the cooperative help.

Such a process is distinct from **mutualism** where there is no time delay between helping and being helped; mutualism does not involve altruistic behaviour and seems to be the reason why most animals form social groups in the first place.

Living in a group

Various advantages and disadvantages of living in groups (Fig. 4.4) have been proposed, and some have been tested experi-

Fig. 4.6. (a) Two mature red deer stags fight for the possession of a harem in the October rut. Fighting is dangerous and one in five stags show some sign of injury by the end of the mating season. (b) A red deer stag roars at a rival. The rate of roaring that stags can sustain is related to their fighting ability and is used by challenging stags to assess their rivals. (c) A lying hind sniffs the harem holder. During the rut, both sexes regularly check each other for olfactory cues.

mentally. The advantages include defence against predators, obtaining food, obtaining mates, learning from other members of the same species, and resisting harsh environments. Set against these are disadvantages which centre around increased ease of detection by predators, interference in feeding, and the spread of disease.

The chances of any individual being attacked by predators are reduced by group living. If groups are barely more conspicuous than are individuals, then living in a group of four can reduce the chances of predation by about three-quarters. In addition, the common phenomenon where groups close up when predators approach may well be the result of animals attempting to get into the centre of the group, thus reducing their own probability of being attacked because animals on the periphery are more likely to be picked off by predators:

this is the so-called 'selfish herd' principle. It is also likely that predators are less successful when attacking groups than when they are preying on lone individuals. Experiments with sticklebacks feeding on water-fleas (*Daphnia*) demonstrate a confusion effect: the sticklebacks find it more difficult to focus on just one *Daphnia* when several are continuously passing through the field of vision. It has been suggested that the stotting (bouncing) behaviour of various cervids (deer) when they are disturbed serves a similar function. Members of groups can, of course, cooperate to their mutual benefit in active defence against predators while single animals may not survive an attack. Cooperative group defence (Fig. 4.5) can be either passive or active: for example, elands array themselves in a protective formation around their calves to protect the young from attacks by hyenas, while many species of birds actively mob owls, hawks and other potential predators. Finally, many eyes are better than a single pair and it can be demonstrated that members of larger flocks detect predators at longer distances and, as a consequence, predators are less likely to make even a single kill.

Group living is also associated with certain feeding advantages. The sight of members of the same species feeding often attracts others, as is repeatedly demonstrated by the use of decoys by duck-hunters. Carnivores will join together for hunting larger prey: a single lion will have difficulty overcoming a healthy wildebeest even after a successful ambush, but a pride of lions makes short work of the job which provides food for them all. However, group hunting need not always be cooperative. Each member of the group may be attempting to capture the prey, and even cutting off potential escape routes may be an individual rather than a collective group strategy. Making it easier to feed may also explain some examples of group living; individual sawfly larvae for instance, cannot eat through the waxy coating of pine needles, whereas a group effort allows the nutritious interior to be reached.

Other advantages to individuals of grouping include enhanced access to mates, for example in species which hold 'leks', where large congregations of displaying males attract receptive females. In addition, among species in which the young are born comparatively well developed, parental care and the opportunity for cultural transmission may together select for the young remaining initially in the same locality as their parents. Finally, animals tend to congregate in areas containing limited resources such as nest sites, food clumps or suitable sites for hibernation. In any particular case of grouping, several of the above advantages may apply, but they will be set against clear disadvantages.

Above some optimal group size, factors that restrain the advantages of grouping become important. Large groups, such as the massive migrations of herbivores through the Serengeti, become the focus of attention for predators, and once groups are sufficiently large to provide predators with a continuous food supply then individuals may well profit by leaving the groups. Also, interference in feeding becomes more important as animals become associated into larger groups. The size and density of food patches sets the limits beyond which subordinates are forced to leave the group as a consequence of continual interference in their feeding. Finally, disease is, of course, more likely to be picked up by animals that associate with others. At the moment, constraints on group living set by the vectors of diseases is a little-understood and poorly researched topic.

Breeding systems

When animals live in groups, individuals have access to more than one potential mate. In general, one sex becomes a limiting resource for the other, and selection occurs for adaptive sexual behaviour in the choice of mate and competition among members of one sex for mating access to members of the opposite sex. Commonly, females do not profit from mating with more than a single male, whereas males can provide sufficient sperm in a single mating for the female's needs and can mate on several occasions over a short time period. As a consequence, males compete for mating access to females and often defend groups of females from the approaches of other males. This is a common situation among mammals and results in mate-defence **polygyny**: females group for protection against predators and successful males defend groups of females. As species become more polygynous (that is, as the number of females per male in breeding groups or harems gets larger) so, if there is a 50:50 sex ratio in the population as a whole, there are more single males outside the breeding groups and an increasing premium on the intrasexual competitive ability of the males. The conflicts among males (Fig. 4.6) can lead to differences in their morphology, compared to that of females; dimorphism in size increases with harem size so that males are relatively larger than females in more polygynous species, and weapons such as canine teeth in primates or antlers in deer are also relatively enlarged. Among monogamous mammals the males and females are invariably about the same size.

Male mammals cannot lactate, and females suckle the young; this situation facilitates the evolution of polygyny. Among birds the situation is different, as males and females are equally capable of looking after the nestlings. As a consequence, it is to the female's advantage to elicit help from her mate in rearing the young, and if she can do this she will probably raise more young than will another female whose mate is putting his energies into courting other females. This leads to monogamy being far more common in birds than it is in mammals, and indeed the whole system for choice of mates differs. Among mammals, the males defend groups of females (mate-defence polygyny), while birds instead defend the resources of their habitat. Among temperate bird species, the males partition the available habitat into territories and females choose some combination of mate and territory. The resources can be distributed patchily through the available territory, and the lark bunting (*Calamospiza melanocorys*) provides an example where this is often the case. The main resource defended by males is shade for nest sites and many males in populations of this species defend territories containing just one mate and help to feed the young. However, females are often better off mating with a male who has more than one well-shaded nest site in his territory, even though he will only feed the young of his primary mate. The alternative for the female would be to mate with a male who has no sufficiently shaded sites in his territory; even though the monogamous male would help to feed the young, they would be more likely to die from exposure to the sun.

Most fishes do not show parental care, but among those that do the male tends to guard the eggs when fertilisation is external and the female guards when fertilisation is internal.

With external fertilisation, the female first lays the eggs and has a chance to escape while the male is fertilising them, assuming that one parent can raise the young alone. With internal fertilisation, the male can be long gone by the time the female lays her eggs. Parental guarding of the eggs is far more common in freshwater than in marine habitats, perhaps because open oceans are more homogeneous environments than are pools and rivers, and in these freshwater habitats parental care may be necessary to prevent eggs drifting into inhospitable places.

Different types of breeding system have important consequences for the structure of populations, and a knowledge of population structure is a necessary prerequisite for constructing realistic models of evolutionary change. Unless the rate of dispersal of individuals throughout the population is known, we have no idea of the effective size of the population and therefore are unable to model processes such as speciation or the relative effectiveness of group selection compared with individual selection. Behavioural studies on marked animals observed over long periods of time reveal that animals return very faithfully to particular breeding sites, although there are often differences in dispersal between the sexes.

Dispersal

Most of the suitable data are from birds and mammals, and clear differences between the two groups are immediately obvious. Dispersal can be divided into **natal dispersal** which is movement from the site of birth to the site of first breeding, and **breeding dispersal**, which is movement between successive breeding sites. Breeding dispersal is almost invariably less extensive than is natal dispersal. Once an animal has bred successfully in a particular group or in a particular locality it is loath to move. Natal dispersal is more common, but it is usually more restricted in one sex than the other. Among mammals, the females usually stay in their natal group or area for their whole life, while males move to a nearby group or territory when they reach maturity. Such movement may be voluntary, or enforced by parents or other members of the group. The opposite pattern of sex differences occurs in birds where males typically move very short distances, if at all, to breed for the first time, whereas females move greater distances.

If natal dispersal is analysed as a strategy for avoidance of inbreeding, then the differences between birds and mammals begin to make sense. Birds that were raised in a particular area will return to breed there, other things being equal; it is a familiar locality and is known to provide a suitable breeding habitat. Males generally set up territories before the females choose their mates (and territories), and females who move some distance away are more likely to avoid inbreeding. Among mammals the situation is different, as females tend to live and breed within the group in which they were born, and males defend groups of females; males thus move and search for suitable mates. Dominant male baboons are known to move between groups of females, choosing the group containing most females on heat at any given time.

There seems little doubt that avoidance of inbreeding is an important consideration (see pages 114–17). Data from zoo animals show that when captive groups are given no opportunity but to inbreed, the offspring are likely to die. In one field study of the great tit (*Parus major*), occasional matings between siblings (when the males had moved too far and the females too short a distance during natal dispersal) produced offspring with an extremely high nestling mortality.

Resolution of contests

As group living, choosing and competing for mates, parental investment and dispersal all clearly demonstrate, there are repeated conflicts of interest between members of the same species. How are these resolved? When group sizes get too large, which individuals leave? When males fight over mates, what rules govern their behaviour in contests? Which sex looks after the young and why? Which sex disperses in order to avoid inbreeding? Early analyses of contests used theories of group selection to explain why contests do not escalate until one or both animals receive fatal injuries: it would be bad for the species if that happened. An approach to such questions along the lines of individual selection considers the different strategies that animals might adopt, compares the outcomes of encounters between pairs of animals in terms of changes in fitness, and concludes that the animal with the higher payoff from a contest has a better strategy. More specifically, **evolutionarily stable strategies** are defined: these are unbeatable strategies which, when followed by the population as a whole, are immune to invasion by any particular mutant strategy.

A simple example considers a hypothetical contest between individuals of one species, some of which exhibit a strategy we shall call 'hawk' while others play 'dove'. 'Hawks' fight until they win or are injured, whereas 'doves' play a waiting game and if they are attacked they withdraw. Costs and benefits are measured in units of fitness, that is, units of future reproductive success. Injury costs 100 units, victory provides a benefit of 60 units, and penalties incurred for long contests are 10 units. When a 'hawk' meets a 'dove', the 'dove' runs away which costs it nothing (payoff zero) and the 'hawk' wins the contest (payoff 60 units). When two 'doves' meet they both waste time settling the contest although one eventually wins (giving an average payoff of $(60/2) - 10 = 20$ units). When two 'hawks' meet, one gets injured while the other wins (average payoff $(60 - 100)/2 = -20$ units). Given these different payoffs, 'hawks' can successfully become established in a population of 'doves' while 'doves' can also become established in a population of 'hawks'. Neither pure strategy, 'hawk' or 'dove', is evolutionarily stable and the population will come to contain a mixture of animals, some playing 'hawk' and some 'dove'. Now consider a 'bully' which starts off by being

Fig. 4.7. Like red deer stags, male howler monkeys deter intruders by repeated vocalisations. In this case, though, the females howl as well. The call is produced by blowing air across the top of an enlarged cup-like hyoid bone.

aggressive but retreats if attacked. Such a 'bully' will be able to become established in a population of 'hawks' since it is never injured, and it will also become established in a population of 'doves' since the 'dove' always runs away. Given a pure population of 'bullies', 'hawks' will be successful since 'hawks' win against 'bullies' and the 'hawks' do not get injured in such contests. A contest between two 'bullies' ends in one running away and so time is not wasted and the average payoff is 30 units. Obviously, the bullying strategy is added to the already behaviourally polymorphic population. Some ingenuity can be used to design strategies that are evolutionarily stable for the whole population, so that the population is resistant to any mutant strategies if all members play this single stable strategy, but it is clear from this simple example that the payoff from any given strategy depends on the behaviour of other animals in the population.

Contests such as the above are symmetric. This is often not the case. Asymmetry in fighting ability is common and can be assessed through, for example, relative size; the weaker individuals usually withdraw before injury is inflicted. Under some circumstances, it is conceivable that asymmetries uncorrelated with the fighting abilities of the contestants may be used to settle contests. If for example two animals were competing for a resource and one, termed the 'owner', had previously had access to the resource, it can be shown that, with the right costs and benefits being included, such uncorrelated asymmetries can be used to settle contests: the rule 'don't fight an owner but do fight if you are the owner' is an evolutionarily stable strategy. Experiments where, by continued replacement, two butterflies have been persuaded that each is the owner of a territory have led to escalated contests of an intensity never observed previously!

Evolutionarily stable strategies are defined in terms of a set of imagined strategies. It may always be that some other as yet unthought of strategy would win the day, and successful application of the analytical technique depends on an intimate knowledge of the possible behaviours of the participants.

Evolutionary history

Behaviour does not fossilise and so, unlike morphologists, ethologists cannot trace the evolution of behaviour using the fossil record. However, evolutionary trees based on morphological evidence can be used to trace a behavioural phylogeny, the history of the behavioural pattern through the evolutionary development of the species. As far back as 1951, Niko Tinbergen wrote 'the fact that the development of morphology is so far in advance of ethology renders it possible to use comparison for the purpose of evolutionary study without a detailed knowledge of behavioural homologies. Once morphology has succeeded in giving us a picture of the phylogenetic relationships within a group, we may take the picture for granted, and compare the behaviour of the species concerned'.

The method used has been termed **outgroup comparison**. For example, consider a hypothetical genus containing some arboreal and some terrestrial species. We can ask whether arboreality or terrestriality is primitive to the family that contains that genus. To answer that question, we would first examine the characteristics of other genera in the family. Those other genera would comprise the outgroup, and if they all contained only arboreal species the simplest hypothesis would be that arboreality is primitive to the family. However, if some genera in the family contained arboreal species while others contained terrestrial species, we could not decide which trait is primitive to the family and which is derived. The method does, of course, depend on having an outline phylogeny of the group that is based on characters other than those being studied.

Parasitism among the cowbirds provides an example of outgroup comparison. Some cowbirds are parasitic while others are not. However, since none of the close relatives of cowbirds is parasitic, we conclude that parasitism is a relatively recently acquired type of behaviour.

The evolutionary history of many patterns of behaviour which do not appear to serve specific functions have attracted considerable interest. For example, social signals which form part of courtship or appeasement displays constitute **derived**

activities, since they originated in some other form of behaviour and have become adopted as fixed action patterns for use in a new context. Sir Julian Huxley termed the evolutionary process for the derivation of these behaviour patterns **'ritualisation'**, when describing the remarkable courtship display of the great-crested grebe; in courtship these birds use behavioural patterns that seem to be derived from nest-building activities.

Balloon flies of the genus *Empis* provide an example where behavioural phylogeny involving a derived activity can be traced using contemporary species. In one species, the male can be observed presenting a silken ball to the female during courtship (Fig. 4.8). Intermediate stages in the development of the pattern of behaviour allow us to trace its origins. Females have a voracious appetite and are likely to attack males during courtship, and some species are known where the males present an insect prey to the female for her to consume while he mates. The intermediate stage has also been found, where the male wraps the prey in silk thus allowing him more time to mate without danger. The final stage in the sequence appears to be the presentation of an empty ball. In other instances, the evolutionary history of displays seems lost to us since related behaviour patterns are not even observed in closely allied species.

Part of courtship behaviour is often associated with preventing an animal from mating with a different species. When two species come to occupy the same geographical range after having evolved into different species while being geographically separated, there may be strong selection to accentuate the distinguishing components of courtship or mate-attracting behaviour. For example, species of North-American fireflies living in the same habitat use subtle differences in patterns of light flashes to attract mates. Presumably, these differences arose through selection to prevent wasted effort in unsatisfactory mating attempts with other species.

Conclusion

Ethologists, then, are typically concerned with four types of question about patterns of behaviour: their causation, their development, their function and their evolutionary history. The answers to these questions are not independent of each other; for example, the evolutionary route from a mode of locomotion typical of one species to that typical of another will be constrained by the necessity for all the required intermediate stages to be able to survive and reproduce. Not only does the study of each type of question draw on information from other areas of ethology, but also on information from other areas of biology and the physical sciences. For example, in order to tackle functional problems, we must be sure that there are appropriate models of population structure and population genetics: invoking the idea of group selection to account for the evolution of alarm calls in mammals is contrary to the outcome of population genetic models that examine how

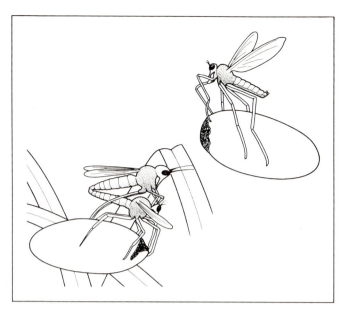

Fig. 4.8. The male of one species of Empis *presents an empty silk balloon to a female during courtship. This behaviour appears to serve no specific function. Examination of other* Empis *species suggests how this behaviour might have been adaptive and become ritualised in the ancestors of this* Empis *species. The behaviour pattern is now vital for the mating success of a male.*

such a behaviour can evolve in species with mammalian population structures. Similarly, causal questions are often usefully answered in terms of mechanical models developed by engineers: the study of flight is an example. The practising ethologist is increasingly required to maintain a broad perspective on behavioural science while being able to draw on expertise from colleagues working in other disciplines.

Further reading

Hinde, R.A. *Animal behaviour: A synthesis of ethology and comparative psychology.* New York: McGraw Hill, 1970.

Krebs, J.R. and Davies, N.B. *An introduction to behavioural ecology.* Oxford: Blackwell, 1981.

Manning, A. *An introduction to animal behaviour.* London: Edward Arnold, 1979.

Tinbergen, N. *The study of instinct.* Oxford: Clarendon, 1951.

Wilson, E.O. *Sociobiology, the new synthesis.* Cambridge, Mass.: Harvard University Press, 1975.

5 Ecology

Ecology is that branch of the biology of whole organisms that investigates the effects of the external environment on the behaviour, physiology, life-history pattern, productivity, distribution and abundance of living organisms. The external variables concerned may be physical (for example, climate, rock type or soil type), other members of the same species, or members of other interacting species such as food species, parasites, predators or competitors.

Traditional subdivisions of ecology reflect the variety of aspects of the biology of whole organisms that may be affected by the external environment, and the wide range of external variables that can influence organisms: **autecology** is the study of the reactions of the individual organism, usually in terms of behavioural, physiological or growth responses, and therefore subdivides into disciplines such as physiological ecology (environmental physiology), behavioural ecology (see Chapter 4), and so on; **population ecology** (see section 5.2) is concerned with populations of a single species and the processes changing population size, range and gene-pool, and its subdivisions include evolutionary ecology, production ecology, ecological genetics and a range of applied studies on the exploitation and control of populations; and **community ecology** (or synecology or systems ecology) (see sections 5.3 and 5.4) investigates associations and interactions between different species in space and time, including the fluxes of matter and energy, the patterns generated in diversity of species, and the constancy, stability and maturity of an ecosystem. Each of these branches of ecology has developed its own principles, and each interrelates with a characteristic series of other biological disciplines.

5.1 THE ORGANISM AND ITS NICHE

All organisms have specific ranges of tolerance of various environmental variables. They can survive only in certain types of soil or sediment, in certain light intensities, temperature regimens, conditions of salinity, ranges of humidity, and so on; biological variables include, for heterotrophic species, the availability of preformed food materials from the environment. In addition the value of any one variable at any moment may influence the ability to tolerate the others, such that, for example, the maximum range of temperature can be tolerated only when other environmental factors are optimal, and if one or more of these factors is away from its optimum then the range of temperature which can be withstood may be much reduced. Often young stages, reproductive stages and (in the case of arthropods) moulting stages are particularly sensitive and have reduced tolerances.

If each physical or biological variable is given an axis set at right angles to all the other relevant axes (possible only in the imagination!), and the range of values an organism can tolerate is marked on each axis, then the result is an n-dimensional hypervolume within which that organism can survive. This is one way of arriving at a concept of an organism's **fundamental niche**; each type of organism inhabits its own hypervolume, and the hypervolumes of different species overlap with others to differing degrees.

This imaginary space portrays where an organism is able to live at various stages of its life-history, but not necessarily where it does live. Historical and geographical factors may combine to prevent organisms from gaining access to certain suitable environments; if introduced by human activity to such areas new species may thrive even though absent originally, as has happened with the European starling in North America, ragwort in New Zealand, and the Chinese mitten-crab in Northwest Europe. Of more general importance, however, is the observation that organisms are usually denied occupancy of the peripheral zones of their fundamental niche hypervolumes by interactions with other species. A region on the periphery of one organism's niche is normally the centre of the niche of another organism, and organisms are nearly always more successful in the centre of their range, whether geographical or climatic, than they are towards the margins. Organisms thus usually live well within their physiological tolerance ranges as a result of competition with other species where their niches overlap, and the **realised niche** is a small hypervolume near the centre of the fundamental niche.

Organisms are therefore assumed normally to be capable of surviving the physical conditions and climate found in the centre of their ranges, and they then have only four particular necessities, three acting in the short term and the other in the longer term. In order to remain alive, organisms need sufficient food-energy and materials, they need to escape becoming the food of others and they need to occupy the appropriate amount of physical space; in the longer term organisms need to produce as many surviving offspring as possible. All other biological attributes of organisms serve merely to permit these four necessities to be achieved. Food and space share several common features and can be considered together under the general term **resources**.

Some of the resources required by organisms are present in excess of their requirements, such as oxygen for the respiration of terrestrial organisms, and water for aquatic species; but other resources are available in quantities or at rates that may be insufficient to meet the requirements of all the potential users, for example light, water and nutrients for terrestrial photosynthesisers, and fixed organic compounds for heterotrophs. Wherever or whenever the demand for resources exceeds their supply in regions where the niches of different species overlap, competition for these resources may occur. In the short term this may result in decreased growth and reproduction of individuals, or even their death; over evolutionary time this competition leads to one of three outcomes. An organism may be forced to become a **specialist** on that small section of the shared spectrum of resources for which it is the superior competitor, and to use that part with increasing efficiency (Fig. 5.1). This is likely to occur where potentially specialist resources are available throughout the year, that is, in

Fig 5.1. The ancestral toothed 'beak' of Archaeopteryx, *a generalist feeder, and a series of specialised, toothless beaks of modern birds.*

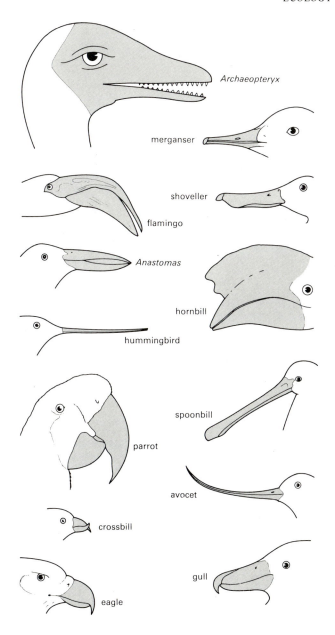

relatively low latitudes: it would be difficult to survive, for example, as a specialist feeder on blackberries in Britain when that fruit is available only for a small fraction of the year, although dormancy during the non-blackberry season, living off stored food taken in during the brief season of plenty, would be a possibility. The second evolutionary response would be to widen the spectrum of resources able to be used so as to include items not utilised by the superior competitor: by maintaining as catholic a set of requirements as possible, the chance is maximised that, if one particular resource proves to be insufficient, another resource can be obtained. Such **generalist** species (Fig. 5.1) can be described as having large niches, the precise volume of which will depend on which competitors are present. Local absence of a particular competitor frequently results in the range of generalist species expanding into the vacant resource space. Tropical intertidal crabs in mangrove and mud-flat zones show this particularly well: *Metaplax*, for example, often excludes *Macrophthalmus* from the upper part of the lower shore, but in regions from which *Metaplax* is absent, as in tropical Australia, *Macrophthalmus* occupies both the upper and lower zones of the lower shore. The third possible long-term outcome is that the inferior competitor becomes extinct locally as a result of competitive exclusion.

Theory predicts that species with identical niches cannot coexist indefinitely, and it is important to know how different two or more competing types of organism have to become in order to prevent competitive exclusion of one by another. The answer to this is only known in general terms: each species must be able to exploit exclusively some refuge, within the spectrum of shared resources, that is sufficient to satisfy its requirements for the resource in question. Studies on closely related species which do overlap in a part of their distributions, however, have provided some individual empirical answers.

The more similar two organisms are, the more their requirements would be expected to be the same, and the more areas they would be expected to compete in. It is usual to find, with very similar animal species, that where they occur alone their requirements are most similar, but where they occur together they are most different from each other. When similar species live sympatrically (in the same geographical area), they are observed to differ more from each other in such features as preferred microhabitat and diet, and often in the size of all or part of the organism (a phenomenon termed **character displacement**), and the competition between the species is thereby diminished. Size differences in these cases are normally in the ratio of 1 : 1.3 in respect of linear dimensions (a mass ratio of 1 : 2), and the same ratio of sizes is seen in a wide variety of coexisting organisms exploiting similar resources, such as species of water-fleas, snails, lizards, birds and mice. It would appear that this difference in length (of beak, head, feeding appendage, and so on) of 1.3-fold is the minimum necessary to permit organisms to avoid competitive exclusion. If we continue with the analogy of the niche as a hypervolume, then

the niches of the coexisting organisms, without necessarily changing their hypervolume, slide apart a given distance along one (or more) axes, and reduce the overlap.

5.2 POPULATIONS OF ORGANISMS

Population size

Individual organisms rarely exist in isolation from other members of their own species, and from the human viewpoint it is often the number of some organism per unit area, be it food organism or pest, that is the point of greatest ecological interest. The factors responsible for the differing densities of different types of organism, the marked fluctuations in numbers of some species while others remain fairly constant from year to year, the amount of mortality that a given population can withstand, and the methods of human control of the numbers of a pest species, are demographic considerations and lie within the realm of population dynamics.

A **population** is an interbreeding group of organisms of the same species to which, ideally, no new members are recruited except through birth or some other form of multiplication, and from which no members depart except through death. This may be true of a few populations living on small islands, but generally organisms are mobile or can be transported at some stage of their life-history; immigration to and emigration from local centres of abundance are thus common, and few populations are in fact self-contained. In practice, therefore, most population studies have investigated population density, in numbers per unit area, rather than total population size, on the assumption that the study site is typical of the population as a whole. The smaller the study area, and the larger and more heterogeneous the population, the less likely this assumption is to be correct.

The change in population size per unit time is given by

$$\text{change in size} = B + I - D - E$$

where B is the number being added by reproduction and multiplication, I is the number immigrating, D is the number dying from all causes, and E is the number emigrating (one region's emigrants will, of course, be other regions' immigrants). If the population approaches an ideal one, I and E can be ignored. Since B and D are in part functions of the population size, N, it is more convenient to replace them by the per capita **birth rate**, b, and **death rate**, d. The rate of population change with time will then be

$$\text{rate of change in size} = bN - dN = (b - d)N$$

The term $(b - d)$ will be characteristic of the population concerned, and is known as r, the intrinsic rate of increase, expressed perhaps as some percentage per year. The intrinsic rate of increase is that which is possible if there are no constraints on the birth rate and if the death rate results from old age alone. As Malthus, Darwin and others realised in the eighteenth and nineteenth centuries, population increase under these ideal circumstances would be exponential (Fig. 5.2a). Exponential increase is rarely seen in nature, however, and therefore something must check the growth.

One simple assumption that can be made is that these constraints on population growth cause the death rate to increase linearly with the size of the population, and the birth rate to decrease linearly with the size of the population. Therefore

$$b = b_0 - k_b N \quad \text{and} \quad d = d_0 + k_d N$$

where k_b and k_d are positive constants and b_0 and d_0 are the birth and death rates extrapolated to zero population size. The population will cease to increase when the birth rate equals the death rate, that is, when

$$b_0 - k_b N = d_0 + k_d N$$

which will occur at a value of the population size of

$$N = (b_0 - d_0)/(k_b + k_d)$$

This stable value of the population size N is denoted by K, the **carrying capacity** of the habitat for that particular population, and growth up to K will no longer be exponential but will be along a sigmoid curve called the logistic curve (Fig. 5.2b). The growth rate is initially gradual (the lag phase), then rapid (the exponential phase), and then slow again until the stationary phase is reached. In fact, the assumptions of this simple logistic equation are rarely if ever met, but when brought closer to reality by the addition of extra terms it forms the basis of most mathematical models of population growth.

Factors affecting birth rates and death rates

There are several processes which can depress the birth rate and increase the death rate with increasing population size, thereby setting a value for the carrying capacity of the habitat.

Changes in the birth rate

Organisms have rates of division or budding, and numbers of spores, seeds or eggs, that are variable within certain limits; each species has a characteristic range and an average value. The average, which can vary from the production of one propagule every few years to the production of thousands of millions per year, is subject to variation only over evolutionary time, but the precise numbers produced within this genetically determined range are subject to a more short-term control.

In most organisms, as the **physical conditions** depart from their optimal values there is a concomitant decrease in the numbers both of vegetatively and of sexually produced progeny, in some cases down to zero. The survival of the relatively few propagules produced under adverse climatic conditions may also be comparatively poor.

The other main factor capable of altering the birth rate is **parental vigour**, the fitness of the potential parents. Individuals suffering from a shortage of essential resources or from heavy parasitic infection produce fewer progeny than do healthy individuals. In animals the shortage of resources need not be absolute: food may be present, for example, but a hierarchical social system may result in subordinate individuals experiencing scarcity. In 'higher' animals with social systems, the evolution of territoriality may also have repercussions on the total numbers of young produced, by influencing the size of the breeding population. Several species of bird take up and defend territories during the breeding season, and the territory of one individual is adjacent to that of the next. Although the size of these territories is by no means constant, a given breeding site (presumably selected because it is in some way a particularly favourable area) can only accommodate a finite number of territories; and hence individuals which fail to establish a territory are forced to suspend breeding for that season, or else to emigrate to a less favourable site in which the chances of successful reproduction are lower.

Fig. 5.2. (a) The pattern of increase in numbers shown by exponentially increasing populations. (b) The pattern of increase in numbers shown when birth and death rates are related linearly to population size (birth rate negatively and death rate positively): the logistic curve.

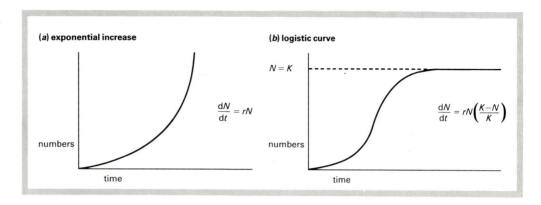

Changes in the death rate

Changes in the death rate are generally more important agents of potential population control than are changes in the birth rate, although often the same environmental factors are involved. These include climatic variables, competition for resources including the special case of socially induced mortality, and consumption by other species.

With the exception of general catastrophes such as hurricanes, **physical factors** are a more potent cause of mortality in marginal parts of a range than they are centrally. This is particularly well shown by the reaction of British marine organisms to the severe winter weather of 1962–63. Britain is the northern limit of the range of several species, and these experienced severe mortality; many were too torpid in the cold to prevent themselves from being stranded by the tide, being taken by predators or falling off rocks, and others asphyxiated because the cilia on their gills beat more slowly in the cold water. Britain is also in the southern extreme of the range of other, Arctic, species, and for these the severe winter posed no problem. Factors other than low temperature, such as lack of or excess water, or altered salinity, are able to check population increase in a comparable fashion.

The second agent of mortality is **competition** for resources. Sharing a need for the same resource is a necessary but not a sufficient prerequisite for competition: competition will only occur if the quantity of the shared resource is insufficient to satisfy the requirements of all the consumers of that resource. Several different types of competition are distinguished: it may occur between members of the same species, when it is called **intraspecific competition**, or it may occur between different species, when it is known as **interspecific competition**. Also among the forms of competition are scrambles and contests. In a **scramble** for resources each individual stands the same chance of obtaining a given share of the limiting resource, and differences in the sizes of the shares obtained are largely due to the operation of random factors. In a **contest** for some arbitrary resource (that is, one not supplied in precise quantity by the environment), such as social status, different levels of which carry different rights of access to the real resources at stake, a number of animals compete for positions in a hierarchy, success resulting in disproportionate quantities of food, space and/or matings so long as the high status can be maintained. Finally, competition can either be relatively direct **exploitation**, as when a competitor finds and uses part of the resource for itself and removes it from the common pool, or it can be by **interference**, when a given species discourages others from using a vacant resource by, for example, chemical conditioning

of the environment, attacking others, or altering the nature of the habitat to the detriment of potential competitors. An organism may thus safeguard and store supplies of some resource before this has declined to levels which might induce competition by exploitation: it has been suggested, for instance, that the rotting of fruit is a microbial interference strategy for discouraging consumption by animals of that resource.

The final agent of mortality is **predation**, which generally includes all natural enemies: some consumers kill the organisms which they eat, such as lions consuming zebras, whereas others only browse parts that can be regenerated, such as cows consuming grass. Predators react to differing abundances of their prey organisms in one or more of three ways. First, they may catch and consume more prey per unit time when more prey is available, in many cases switching from one species to another depending on their relative abundances. There is of course an upper limit to the amount consumed by an individual predator, although when faced with abundant food predators may become selective in which parts they consume. Secondly, predators can aggregate in areas containing more than average amounts of prey. Thirdly, an abundance of prey will permit predators to breed more successfully, leading to larger numbers of predators in the next generation regardless of the numbers of prey then available; this is a delayed or **intergeneration** effect.

The roles of different factors in limiting population size

There has been copious argument on which of these several factors affecting birth and death rates are generally most important in limiting the size of populations, and several authors have sought to explain population dynamics largely in terms of just one factor: climatic factors by Andrewartha and Birch, resource availability by Nicholson, and social interactions by Wynne-Edwards. There is however a distinction between processes affecting marginal zones of populations and those acting centrally, and between factors initiating change and those tending to resist it.

Of central importance is how often populations are near the carrying capacity of their habitat. A population is most likely to achieve and keep close to the carrying capacity if that value of the carrying capacity does not fluctuate much, which is generally the case when environmental change is minimal and density-dependent mortality (mortality proportional to the population density) simply removes the surplus individuals. Populations in relatively constant (such as tropical) climates and those near the centre of their ranges are most likely to come close to this state, and in these cases competition between

Fig. 5.3. Examples of organisms subject to different forms of selection: (a) K-selection: elephant; (b) S-selection: saguaro cactus; (c) r-selection: poppies on a roadside verge.

individuals is likely to be a potent density-dependent factor causing the population to follow small changes in the carrying capacity. Alternatively, where the climate changes and alters the carrying capacity faster than a population can respond, it is unlikely that the population density will actually be at the carrying capacity for more than a small proportion of the time.

Climatic fluctuations are generally likely to act as major factors perturbing population size, either by causing mortality directly or by altering the quantity or quality of the resources, and climatic effects normally occur independently of population size or density. Climatically induced increases in the death rate will periodically lead to this being greater than the birth rate; population size then falls until the conditions improve, and peripheral populations may well become extinct from these causes. Under these circumstances, mortality due to competition will be induced by the climatic effects, not as a factor regulating a population to a certain carrying capacity but rather causing the reduction in numbers as the carrying capacity drops rapidly. The direct cause of some of the mortality may thus, for example, be competition for food, but the ultimate cause is climatic deterioration reducing the food supply. Populations most subjected to or susceptible to variations in their physical environment are therefore likely to fluctuate most in numbers, and those least affected by the climate are likely to be regulated by density-dependent factors such as competition. It seems likely that species which have substituted 'conventional' goals for actual resources as the objects for competition, as in contests to determine social hierarchy, are likely to fluctuate least since the social system provides a buffer against the fluctuation in actual resources.

Competition is a process central to much evolutionary and ecological dogma, but has been clearly demonstrated on remarkably few occasions. This is often because mobile species may respond to competition for a resource not by death (which

is easy to measure) but by emigrating or by subsisting on resources diverted from elsewhere. In order to demonstrate that competition is occurring, it is usually necessary to remove experimentally a potential competitor and see if the species under study responds by increasing in density, biomass or productivity. This removal is not always easy to achieve, and because the species under study might be decreasing anyway for other reasons it may not necessarily react to the absence of the competitor by increasing in density.

Because competition is so important in biological theory, two actual demonstrations of its action will be described here. On rocky shores in North-west Europe, two barnacles typically occupy distinct zones at the top of the beach, *Chthamalus stellatus* above *Balanus balanoides*. If, however, *Balanus* is removed from its zone, *Chthamalus* can survive successfully there. Indeed young *Chthamalus* do settle in this zone, but *Balanus* grow faster and cover, undercut and crush the young *Chthamalus*; the result is that the latter cannot persist in mixed populations containing high proportions of *Balanus*. This is an example of interspecific scramble exploitation competition for space; the same phenomenon occurs intraspecifically within populations of *B. balanoides*. *Chthamalus* has a refuge higher up the beach because it has a greater resistance to desiccation than has *Balanus*.

The second example is of intraspecific contest competition. Red grouse compete for a surrogate resource, territory, and those birds which fail to secure a territory are aggressively ejected to the periphery of the territorial area by other birds defending their own territories. These non-territory-holders do not breed unless territory-holders die (including as a result of being shot), in which case the outcasts can move back in, take their place, and breed successfully. If they cannot obtain a territory in this way, the chances of survival of non-territory-holders are very poor: predators, for example, take seven times

more non-territory-holders than they do territorial birds. The onset of this differential mortality coincides with the ejection from the breeding grounds of the non-territory-holders, and although predation, disease and adverse climatic effects are directly responsible for the deaths of these outcast birds it is the pattern of social behaviour resulting in their forcible expulsion from territories that is the ultimate cause of the mortality.

The role played by predators in controlling populations of prey species is controversial, and most clear cases of control by predation appear to refer to situations perturbed or deliberately manipulated by human activity. Under natural conditions, the numbers of vertebrate predators certainly seem to reflect the availability of their animal or plant prey, rather than the number of predators determining the population size of the prey species. Because of the intergeneration response of predator numbers, however, predation is capable of accelerating the decline of an already decreasing population, as seen for example in the grazing down of phytoplankton blooms (see section 6.3), but it rarely appears to initiate any decline. The severity of predation by invertebrates has been less intensively studied and no generalisations are yet possible. In many contexts the more general statement can be made that the quantity of a consumable resource may govern the level of consumers, but rarely will the consumers control the amount of their consumed resource.

The factors determining the total extent of a population are not necessarily the same as those which affect its density. Many populations are far from the ideal assumed above, and there is often much movement of individuals from one subpopulation to another. The whole population is often a large group, stretching across heterogeneous terrain and containing much genetic heterogeneity (partly as a result of the patchiness of the habitat); decreases in the size of one unit of the population as a result of local conditions are likely to be balanced by increases

elsewhere. In an abundant and widely spread population, such independent unconnected changes will tend to cancel each other out, and although local population densities can fluctuate markedly the overall numbers may remain fairly constant. The causes of occasional population eruptions, as has recently occurred with the collared dove (*Streptopelia decaocto*) in Europe, are largely unknown.

Habitat stability and instability

A final axiom is that species are adapted to the kinds of environment in which they live. Thus, the life-histories of species living in habitats in which achievement of the carrying capacity is usual differ from those of species in unpredictably fluctuating areas.

If a population is generally at the carrying capacity, the death rate will equal the birth rate and so few offspring or propagules can be expected to survive; and, since competition for resources is in these areas the most important source of mortality, only those individuals most able to survive in this highly competitive regime are likely to establish themselves. Reproduction costs energy and materials, and hence is often only attempted after a relatively long pre-reproductive life during which the individual establishes its own position in the system. Progeny cushioned from external competition for resources by food reserves, parental care, and so on are most likely to succeed, but since parental investment in each of such progeny is large, few can be produced per unit time, and in order to maximise the number of descendants the reproductive life of individuals will have to be relatively long. In reasonably stable habitats, therefore, these pressures, leading to a large investment in each offspring, long life and so on, are known as **K-selection**, after the carrying capacity to which they relate;

135

a

b

Fig. 5.4. Colonization of a newly created clearing in a Ghanaian forest: (a) shortly after creation; (b) nine months later.

Fig. 5.5. Bare ground left by the retreat of a glacier in the Ruwenzori Mountains, Uganda.

larger vertebrates (Fig. 5.3), oak trees, and tree-ferns are examples. A similar set of characteristics of the lifestyle is correlated with stressful habitats in which resources are scarce not because of the high demand but because of adverse physical conditions: this is called **S-selection**, and examples are desert plants (Fig. 5.3) and deep-sea animals.

Where the environment fluctuates, however, and suitable areas for occupation appear unpredictably in time and space and do not persist for long, an alternative strategy is required, relying on an ability for fast dispersal and rapid utilisation of abundant resources available only in the short term. Competitive mortality is insignificant, and energy can be devoted to the production of very many small propagules easily transported by air or water. If an organism produced 10 offspring with the same characteristics as itself each year for 10 years, the total number of descendants, if all survived, would be nearly 26 thousand million: exactly the same number as if that organism had lived for only one year but had produced 11 offspring again all with the same characteristics as itself; and if it lived for

only one year but produced 12 young, then after 10 years its potential descendants would number nearly 62000 million. Thus, in order to maximise the intrinsic rate of population increase (r), organisms should breed as soon as possible, producing many offspring and investing all their available energy to this end, and need only live short lives. This strategy is the result of **r-selection**: it typifies opportunist organisms, such as 'weeds' (Fig. 5.3).

K-selection, S-selection and r-selection are descriptions of extreme situations, and most organisms show a combination of these features. Even in a single habitat, some populations will be relatively r-selected (for example bacteria, algae and protozoa) while others will be comparatively K-selected (for example large consumers such as tigers and elephants); fungi producing thousands of millions of spores may grow on trees producing only tens of fruits, and teleosts (bony fish) spawning millions of eggs coexist with elasmobranchs (cartilaginous fish) producing one or two eggs only.

5.3 COMMUNITIES AND ECOSYSTEMS

Characteristics of ecological communities

Because r-selected organisms are small, short-lived and rapidly growing, they have little biomass (quantity of living tissue present per unit area at any given time), but a high productivity (amount of new organic material created per unit area per unit time), especially when the productivity is expressed per unit of their existing biomass. Conversely, K-selected species, which generally are larger and grow more slowly, will tend towards a large biomass but a low productivity per unit of that biomass, that is, they maintain large biomasses per unit of their production. This applies to the individual organisms, but in addition, because K-selected species are characteristic of biologically rich and highly competitive systems in which competition for resources will favour an increasing efficiency in the utilisation of the resources, whole systems dominated by K-strategists will tend towards a large total biomass of organisms supported by each unit of photosynthetic production. On the other hand, systems dominated by r-selected

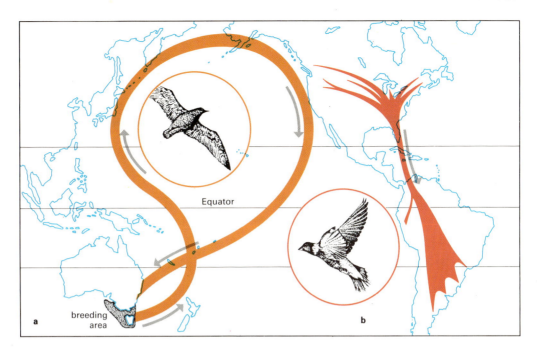

Fig. 5.6. Paths taken by two long-distance migrants. (a) The largely overland seasonal migration of the songbird Dolichonyx oryzivorus. (b) The trans-Pacific circuit of the Tasmanian mutton bird (Puffinus tenuirostris).

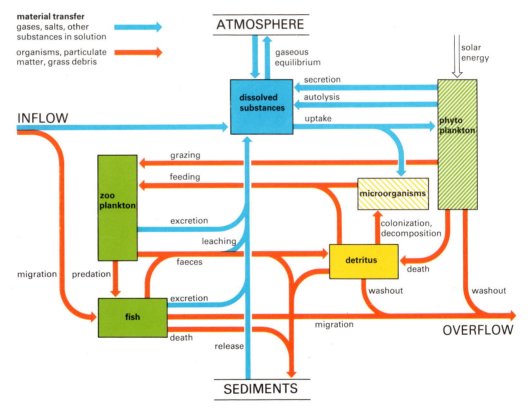

Fig. 5.7. A diagrammatic representation of the complex inter-relations of the major trophic compartments in an ecosystem: the pelagic zone of the sea.

organisms will have little total biomass of organisms supported by each unit of photosynthetic production. The ratio of annual production to average annual biomass is therefore a useful measure of the efficiency of utilisation of resources within ecological systems, and can be used to predict a wide variety of characteristics of the system and of its member species. This ratio cannot of course be used to indicate the actual magnitude of either the productivity or the biomass separately; the same value of the ratio can be obtained from an oligotrophic lake with a low productivity and from a coral reef with a high productivity.

The systems formed by coexisting populations of different species are **ecosystems** (large, more or less self-contained systems such as large lakes, peat-bogs or rain-forests) and **communities** (spatial subsystems within ecosystems, for example the organisms inhabiting the body of water in a lake, or the soil of a forest). Neither of these concepts is any more realistic than is that of the ideal population: one ecological system grades into others, and passage of energy or materials across the boundaries of different systems is inevitable. In practice, therefore, community ecologists study the structure and dynamics of associations of species within certain areas of study, rather than in any notional closed systems.

Zonation and succession

The properties characteristic of different communities and ecosystems show both **zonation** in space (latitudinally and altitudinally) and **succession** in time. Some authors have regarded zonation and succession to be reflections of the same underlying processes, different zones being the spatial expression of stages in a hypothetical successional sequence, although it is not yet known whether this is always the case.

When the physical environment destroys or perturbs an existing system or creates a new colonisable habitat, a sequence or succession of dominant organisms then appears (see Fig. 5.4). The perturbations may vary in scale from the crash of a rain-forest tree creating a clearing, to the oscillations of glacial ice alternately advancing to destroy pre-existing systems and retreating to expose new ground for colonisation (Fig. 5.5). Newly available space is likely to be occupied first by the propagules of opportunist, pioneer, r-selected species, and for some time a system with few species and little community biomass will persist. Eventually, larger species that are dispersed more slowly enter and establish themselves, increasing at the expense of the competitively weak opportunists as resources become more completely exploited and less freely available. Hence, over time, some species are replaced by others and the total number of species also increases; all these changes are in the direction of increasing efficiency of utilisation of resources. Thus when a ploughed field is abandoned it passes through various stages from being covered with annual weeds to a longer-lived herbaceous ground cover, then scrub, through to woodland, and animal consumers become part of the system once a suitable food-base is established.

This succession is broken if a system is further perturbed, and the extent to which any perturbed site passes along this kind of succession depends on the prevailing climate and the frequency of disturbance. In a climate that favours plant growth, and with infrequent perturbations, a high efficiency of utilisation of the environmental resources is achieved. Thus if currently Arctic regions were to experience a tropical climate, they would pass in time through stages equivalent to the existing zones of coniferous woodland, temperate forest, and rain-forest or grassland depending on the amount of rainfall.

Efficiency and specialisation

The tropical systems have been regarded as the potential, and sometimes actual, end-points of a succession, and the selective pressure for high efficiency has produced systems in which resources do not remain unused for long. Most of the total pool of nutrients at any one time is present in living tissue, and nutrients are cycled rapidly through the living components. Coral reefs, for example, support a high production of green algae, but this is not visible because the algal production is grazed down by herbivores as fast as it is produced (see section 7.4). One of the reasons why tropical systems are the most efficient is the relatively constant climate of low latitudes. Efficiency of utilisation of resources is usually correlated with specialisation of each species on one particular resource due to competition for resources that are available throughout the year, as is particularly the case in the stable tropics. Since more specialists than generalists can coexist on a given spectrum of resources, the diversity of species is often high in the tropics, and because of the maximal input of solar energy, productivity is also high and limited only by the availability of nutrients.

The very high species diversity of, for example, rain-forest trees (see section 8.11), under the relatively constant tropical climate, is not immediately expected, however. One or a few types of tree would be expected to be competitively superior to the others, with the competitively dominant species eliminating the weaker species over the long period of time for which rain-forest has existed. But rain-forest is not such a monoculture; some process must oppose this competitive exclusion, and this process is probably perturbations in the forest environment such as the crash of dead trees, or damage by hurricanes.

Specialisation is a reaction to a shortage of resources, and high efficiency is a consequence of circumstances unfavourable to the individual. It would in fact appear advantageous for individuals to counteract the trend of ecosystems to become more efficient, by moving down the successional ladder to less efficient systems in higher latitudes in which the quantities of food per consumer are larger. Many species are indeed migratory, spending that part of their lives in which the demand for resources is highest (such as when raising young) in habitats with more easily obtainable resources: many geese, terns, swallows and a host of other birds in the northern hemisphere move into higher latitudes to breed (Fig. 5.6); fish move into shallow food-rich bays and estuaries; and terrestrial insects often have aquatic young. Seasonally available foods cannot be used efficiently by species resident throughout the year because of the suddenness of the appearance of this resource compared to the time-lag in increasing population sizes by reproduction, and provided that the problems of timing can be overcome migrant species can use the excess. This gradient of increasing relative availability of resources usually coincides with a gradient of decreasing pressure from predators. During the Arctic, boreal or temperate winter, however, when no resources at all are available, migrants must move back into lower latitudes where food is now more abundant than further north.

This exploitation of resources in systems in which the resources are used inefficiently has been compared by Margalef to the creation and exploitation of colonies by some human systems. One human society can exploit the resources of an 'underdeveloped' colony, thereby maintaining its own efficiency high and keeping that of the colony low in the process. In a similar fashion, the plankton of aquatic ecosystems exports

Fig. 5.8. The fungus Termitomyces *on a termite nest mound.*

Fig. 5.9. The polypore Piptoporus betulinus *on the trunk of a birch tree.*

food to the benthos (see section 6.3), and each unit of photosynthetic production in the planktonic community supports relatively little plankton biomass, whereas the benthic community has a larger biomass than its own productivity could maintain.

Food-chains

The patterns of passage of energy and materials through a system are characteristic of the particular type of system and, although generally modelled by simple linear chains, trophic (feeding) interactions are usually complex webs (Fig. 5.7). Solar energy is fixed by photosynthetic organisms, and this energy is then dissipated as heat by the primary producers themselves during their own respiration, and by other organisms which consume their living or dead tissues. The more familiar chain of herbage to herbivore to carnivore (such as grass to deer to wolf) does not in fact carry most of the energy because of the abundance of indigestible and/or non-nutritive structural tissues in plants; there is also a decomposer food-chain, based on dead tissues and faecal material, of bacteria and fungi to microfauna to consumer, and perhaps an average of 90% of the fixed energy flows along this pathway (see section 5.4).

Only part of the energy taken in by an organism is devoted to bodily growth, and only this part will be available to its predators: most is dissipated in respiration. The loss of energy in this way at each stage in a food-chain, between consumed and consumer, has been estimated to be 90% on land and rather less in the sea. This means that in a food-chain of A to B to C to D to E, if the energy content of A is 100 units, only 0.01 units will be represented by E: food-chains are thus finite and can have few links.

The sun may provide an effectively limitless supply of energy, but the building blocks which this energy is used to assemble into organic compounds may be strictly limited. Low quantities of elements such as nitrogen, phosphorus and various trace metals may limit production. Ecosystems contain a finite pool of these nutrients (although some bacteria and blue-green algae can fix atmospheric nitrogen), and once a given atom has been incorporated into tissues it is removed from the pool of available nutrients until it is released again from its organic form. Bacteria, blue-green algae and photosynthetic eukaryotes all have high demands for nutrients, and although some bacteria, protozoa and algae can use soluble organic nutrients, most photosynthesisers can only take in nutrients that are in the soluble inorganic form. This vital conversion from a particulate organic state back to the dissolved inorganic form, (**remineralisation**: for example the degradation of nitrogen-containing proteins to ammonia or nitrates) is carried out mainly by the metabolism of heterotrophic protists, fungi and animals, and their processes of excretion recycle the nutrients. Soluble organic compounds, leached from or released by photosynthetic organisms, pass along the decomposer trophic pathway, being released as they travel. Some particulate and dissolved organic materials, humic substances for instance, are very resistant to decay and have very long half-lives; others may become incorporated into sediments before remineralisation and there form coal or oil, substances usually very low in nutritional value and which are avoided by most consuming species.

5.4 FUNGAL ECOLOGY

Decomposition of organic matter

The primary producers in ecosystems are mainly green plants using the energy of light in photosynthesis. Photosynthetic bacteria and chemosynthetic bacteria, using the energy of

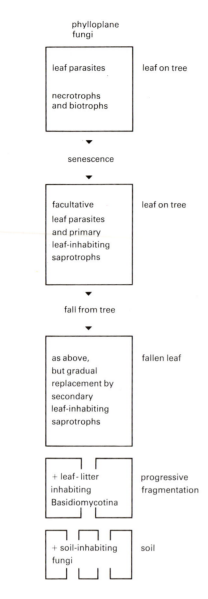

phylloplane
fungi

| leaf parasites | leaf on tree |
| necrotrophs and biotrophs | |

↓

senescence

↓

| facultative leaf parasites and primary leaf-inhabiting saprotrophs | leaf on tree |

↓

fall from tree

↓

| as above, but gradual replacement by secondary leaf-inhabiting saprotrophs | fallen leaf |

| + leaf-litter inhabiting Basidiomycotina | progressive fragmentation |

| + soil-inhabiting fungi | soil |

Fig. 5.10. General outline of the fungal succession on tree leaves.

reduced chemical compounds, are relatively minor producers. The net production of organic matter by terrestrial and aquatic green plants is of the order of 70000 million tonnes of carbon transformed yearly from atmospheric carbon dioxide into plant tissues. Carbon is the major component of living organisms, constituting approximately 50% of the dry mass of organic matter. The supply of carbon as carbon dioxide from the atmosphere is, however, not infinite, and the carbon of organic matter must eventually be recycled through decomposition by micro-organisms, particularly bacteria and fungi, which return the carbon as carbon dioxide to the environment. If decomposition were to cease while photosynthesis continued at the present rate, life would stagnate for lack of carbon dioxide in less than 20 years.

The primary production of an ecosystem may be used in two main ways by heterotrophic organisms. It may be eaten alive by herbivores (primary consumers) which may in turn be eaten by carnivores (secondary consumers) in a grazing food-chain (see page 139); alternatively the primary producers, the primary consumers and the secondary consumers may die,

their bodies decompose, and their carbon enter the **detritus food-chain**. Maybe 90% of the total primary production flows through this decomposer food-chain, and it is this part of the overall carbon cycle, and the role of fungi in particular, that is considered here.

Decomposition of cellulose

About one-third of all the organic matter produced by photosynthesis is in the form of cellulose. Cellulose is an integral part of plant cell walls and is discarded when plant parts are shed. In mature wood tissues 40 to 60% of the dry mass is cellulose; cereal straw contains about 40% cellulose. Thus it is the major carbohydrate available to heterotrophic organisms, and the degradation of cellulose is required for the maintenance of the carbon balance.

Fungi are the major decomposers of cellulose. In the decomposition of tough woody tissues, the hyphal filament has the advantage over single cells such as yeasts and bacteria. Hyphae grow by extension from their tips (see pages 67–9); just behind the growing tip the wall becomes rigid, and the many rearward branches anchor the growing fungal web (the mycelium) in the material in which it is growing. This allows the tip to exert considerable forward mechanical pressure. Together with the production of extracellular cellulases, which soften and dissolve the cellulose, this mechanical pressure enables fungal hyphae to penetrate and permeate completely even the hardest woody tissues. Bacteria can only cause breakdown by enzymic erosion at their surface of contact with the cellulose, producing small pits rather than extensively branched tunnels. The secretion of the cellulase enzyme to cause breakdown of the food material outside the cell, followed by absorption of the resultant soluble carbohydrates, means that all these organisms are saprotrophs.

Bacteria are of more importance than fungi in three particular environments: in very moist or wet conditions, where the bacterial cells can spread in moisture films; in environments such as the rumen of herbivores where the cellulose is greatly fragmented, which increases the surface area of contact; and under anaerobic or near-anaerobic conditions where most fungi cannot thrive.

The ability to grow on cellulose is by no means general even in the fungi, and vigorous cellulose decomposers are in fact in the minority. In the Mastigomycotina and Zygomycotina the ability to degrade cellulose is rare, but cellulolytic ability is common in Ascomycotina and Deuteromycotina. The best-known cellulolytic genera from these subdivisions are *Chaetomium*, common on straw, and *Trichoderma*, common in soils. The ability to use cellulose reaches its peak in the Basidiomycotina with the agarics, polypores and puffballs and their relatives, such as *Agaricus*, *Coriolus* and *Lycoperdon*, together with very many other genera.

The other organisms which produce cellulase include a large number of bacteria, but relatively few other types, although

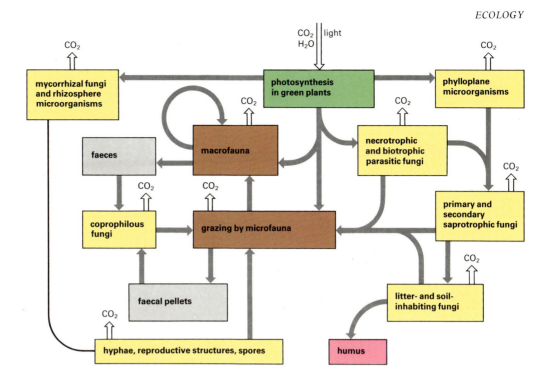

Fig. 5.11. Flow diagram illustrating the carbon cycle.

these include insects, molluscs, and a few crustaceans and protozoans. Many herbivores such as cows contain cellulose-digesting bacteria or flagellate protozoans in their guts; the micro-organisms are in turn digested by their hosts, which thus absorb their carbon in a preconverted form. The best-known animal capable of producing its own cellulase is the snail *Helix pomatia*, but although it is a voracious herbivore it rarely feeds on bulk cellulose such as wood. Among arthropods, the silverfish (*Ctenolepisma lineata*) and the larvae of the death-watch beetle (*Xestobium rufovillosum*) have been shown to produce cellulase in their intestines. This is also possibly true for the earthworm (*Lumbricus terrestris*). The extent to which these and other animals use cellulose may be low in terms of the overall rate of its decomposition, but much more important is the physical breakdown of the material which occurs on passage through their guts; faecal pellets are usually a much more favourable habitat for fungi and bacteria than are the original food materials. Some of the 'lower' termites rely upon intestinal micro-organisms to digest the cellulose in the wood they eat, while the 'higher' termites, which grow agaric fungi (for example, *Termitomyces*) in combs in their mounds (Fig. 5.8), actually acquire an essential component of the cellulase enzyme complex by feeding on the fungus.

Decomposition of lignin

Perennial woody plants are the dominant vegetation over much of the earth, and wood contains 20 to 30% lignin as well as 40 to 60% cellulose. Lignin is a complex hydrophobic polymer cementing together the cellulose microfibrils in the plant cell walls, and increasing the mechanical strength of the wood. In doing so it appears to act as a physical barrier preventing the cellulase enzyme from reaching sufficient bonds in the cellulose to permit any large-scale hydrolysis. For this reason, and because of its high carbon content, the degradation of lignin is also necessary in the carbon cycle. It appears that only fungi which cause white rot of wood, and some litter-decomposing

Basidiomycotina, have the capacity to degrade lignin, and thus to decompose wood completely to carbon dioxide and water. Other fungi attack but only partially degrade wood, giving substances which are ultimately incorporated into the stable components of the soil humus as 'humic acid'.

In terrestrial environments, two major types of wood decay can be recognised: these are white and brown rots. In **white rots**, the wall polysaccharides, such as cellulose, hemicelluloses and pectin, are attacked more or less simultaneously with the lignin, and the wood becomes markedly paler and more fibrous as the pigmented lignin is removed. **Brown rots**, however, use principally the wall polysaccharides, leaving a residue of unchanged or relatively unchanged lignin, and with decay the wood thus becomes darker. In both these types of rot the hyphae branch extensively in the cell cavities of the wood. The walls also are penetrated mechanically through pits or, by coupling mechanical penetration with enzymic erosion, by bore-holes somewhat wider than the hyphae. In white rots there is a progressive thinning of the walls outwards from the cell cavity as all the wall components are used, with decomposition occurring uniformly in the region of attack. In brown rots, however, there is no thinning of the wall and while the secreted enzymes diffuse away from the hyphae and act at some distance on the entire wall they remove the structural fibrils of the cellulose to leave the amorphous lignin to maintain the general shape. There is thus little apparent damage in brown-rotted wood until the cell wall collapses completely. The Aphyllophorales, the bracket polypores, are a group of fungi almost entirely confined to wood; a good example is *Coriolus versicolor*, one of the commonest British polypores, which is found as a saprotroph on a great variety of hardwoods (Fig. 5.9).

Soil microfauna

In any ecosystem animals play their part in the recycling of carbon. Herbivores and carnivores have already been mentioned in the grazing food-chain. In woodland ecosystems, the microfauna, such as mites, springtails and millipedes, consume much of the annual litter fall, and earthworms are important under grassland. However, more than 60%, and often over 90%, of the dry mass which is eaten by the microfauna is returned as faecal pellets, and this includes most of the cellulose. The microfauna are thus eating large amounts of leaf and other litter from which they extract little of nutritional value, excreting most of the litter unchanged chemically but greatly fragmented. The rate of decomposition of the litter is greatly increased when the material is converted to faecal pellets, which are then readily decomposed by soil and dung fungi and by bacteria.

Fungal hyphae and reproductive structures form a rich source of carbohydrate, lipid and protein for animals, and are readily grazed (**mycophagy**). As only a fraction of the litter eaten by microfauna is actually consumed, the microfauna must rely on the litter becoming colonised by fungi to gain access to the remaining nutrients. The fungi degrade the cellulose, lignin and other polymers, converting these to fungal biomass to be digested by the microfauna.

For such detritus-feeders, fungi may also fulfil other nutritional requirements. They are rich in choline, B vitamins, and ergosterol, the commonest fungal sterol which can easily be converted to cholesterol. Fungi growing in substances such as wood also concentrate important mineral elements like phosphorus and nitrogen. A wood-inhabiting insect would have to consume 13 grams of wood to obtain as much nitrogen as it could from 1 gram of the fungal hyphae growing on the walls of its burrows. An additional benefit of mycophagy is the acquisition of a set of fungal enzymes which extend the digestive capacities of the consumer, contributing for example to the digestion of cellulose, hemi-celluloses, pectin and chitin in arthropods feeding on wood and litter.

Fungi on leaves and leaf litter

Aerial and terrestrial environments

Tree leaves, and indeed any plant surface, trap an immense variety of airborne spores. Some of these germinate immediately and grow on the leaf surface, the **phylloplane**, and dense populations of yeasts and yeast-like fungi (such as *Sporobolomyces roseus*), a few filamentous fungi (such as *Aureobasidium* and *Cladosporium*), together with a multitude of bacteria, can be found. These grow as saprotrophs, causing no harm to the plant and deriving their nutrition from simple substances such as sugars, amino-acids and inorganic ions exuded from or diffusing out of the leaf. Similarly the microbial population in the soil immediately adjacent to a root, the **rhizosphere**, is influenced by root exudates. The phylloplane inhabitants persist until after leaf-fall, and members of some genera, such as *Aureobasidium* and *Cladosporium*, then colonise the decomposing leaves as primary saprotrophs.

Spores of parasitic or pathogenic fungi also germinate on the surface of living leaves, but then penetrate the tissues of the leaves. Some, the **biotrophs** such as the rusts and mildews, derive their nutrients directly and only from living cells and cause minimal tissue damage, at least initially. Material fixed as sucrose during photosynthesis by the host plant is diverted to the fungus and converted to trehalose, mannitol or glycogen which the host cannot use. Mycorrhizal fungi (fungi that live symbiotically with plant roots) are nourished similarly, but the host is more than compensated by the fact that the fungus vastly improves the uptake of mineral nutrients, especially phosphate, into the roots. Other fungi, the **necrotrophs** such as those causing leaf spots, kill cells in advance of penetration and then derive their nutrients from the dead tissue. Both groups of leaf-invading fungi may be restricted to discrete lesions, or may spread through the leaves.

With leaf senescence any parasites restricted to discrete lesions may spread if they are facultative parasites (obligate parasites can only grow on living tissue). Spores of other fungi, the primary saprotrophs, if they have not already germinated and made limited growth in the phylloplane, will then germinate and rapidly colonise the leaves. The majority of these are Ascomycotina, mostly in their asexual states, including *Cladosporium* species, *Aureobasidium pullulans*, *Epicoccum purpurescens* and *Alternaria alternata*. These commonly colonise many types of leaf, whether from trees or herbs, or monocotyledons or dicotyledons. Most of these fungi use simple carbon compounds, such as sugars and starch, but some can use cellulose, if only slowly. After leaf-fall, and in the higher humidities at the litter surface, these produce spores profusely but eventually, usually by the summer after leaf-fall with leaves such as beech and oak, they are replaced by a wide range of secondary leaf-inhabiting saprotrophs, again mainly Ascomycotina in their asexual states. (**Primary** saprotrophs colonise intact dead leaves; **secondary** saprotrophs colonise leaves that have been partially decomposed by the action of primary saprotrophs.) Once the leaves are incorporated well into the litter, they are permeated by the mycelia of the litter-inhabiting Basidiomycotina (agarics or toadstools), which use still undegraded leaf polymers such as cellulose and lignin. These fungi are the major decomposers in terms of dry mass used. The leaves become progressively fragmented by the activities of the fungi and microfauna in the litter, and their remains, together with the remains of the previous colonisers, eventually become incorporated into the mineral layers of the soil to be colonised by true soil fungi (rather than litter fungi) such as *Mortierella*, *Penicillium* and *Trichoderma*.

Thus on every leaf a fungal succession develops which is depicted in outline in Fig. 5.10. It is important to appreciate that this is a series of overlapping rather than discrete events, and that it can be interrupted at any time by changing the physical or chemical environment of the leaves.

Aquatic environments

If leaves of deciduous trees, such as alder, oak or sycamore, already colonised by the small group of common primary saprotrophs, fall into shallow, fast-flowing freshwater streams, these fungi are rapidly replaced by a number of asexual aquatic fungi, the aquatic hyphomycetes; in stagnant waters containing less oxygen, other groups of fungi occur and bacterial degradation becomes more important. The aquatic hyphomycetes are a very striking group, producing asexual dispersal spores of a wide variety of shapes, but most are four-armed. The modes of development of these four-armed spores vary, suggesting an independent but convergent evolution from a number of different stocks. The special shape of the spore must therefore have some biological value, and fungi of other aquatic habitats, such as the marine wood-inhabiting Ascomycotina, produce similar spores. It is possible that these four-armed spores attach more readily on impact on submerged leaf surfaces than do spores of a more normal form. A number of these aquatic asexual fungi have a sexual state as terrestrial Ascomycotina or Basidiomycotina, with normal wind-dispersed sexual spores. This amphibious life-cycle allows these fungi to use as widespread and abundant a substrate as deciduous tree leaves in both aquatic and terrestrial habitats.

Leaves form the most substantial element in the annual addition of organic matter to well-aerated freshwater systems, and fungi play a key role not only in the decomposition process, but also as intermediates in the food-chain. Many streams have a low primary productivity, especially if they run through woodlands and are partially shaded. They are, however, often well supplied with organic matter in the form of dead leaves and twigs from adjacent terrestrial vegetation. A stream in a wooded valley receives at least 1 kilogram of leaves per metre of its length each year, and animal communities thrive due to this added organic material. As in terrestrial ecosystems, however, only a small fraction of the energy and organic compounds in these leaves can be directly exploited by the microfauna of the stream, such as crustaceans or insect larvae, which rely on the aquatic hyphomycetes to enable them to gain access to the remainder. The fungi degrade the cellulose and other polymers in the leaves, and the fungal carbohydrates, fats and proteins are then digested when the microfauna consume invaded leaves. The protein content of leaves colonised by fungi in streams may be more than double that of uncolonised leaves, and many members of the detritus-feeding fauna of streams actively prefer partly decomposed leaves to sterile or freshly fallen ones; the fungal mycelium represents a form of nourishment much more concentrated than the original leaf.

Decomposition of tree leaves begins from the moment they unfold and continues through their whole life, senescence and death. It is thus not a process confined entirely to the litter layer of the woodland floor. The fungi involved may initially vary with the type of leaf, but the physical factors of the environment into which the leaves fall then determine the remainder of the sequence of fungal colonisers.

The role of fungi in the carbon cycle is shown in Fig. 5.11. The rate of return of the organic carbon to atmospheric carbon dioxide depends upon its chemical complexity when fixed, that is, whether it is a simple sugar, such as sucrose, or a complex polymer, such as cellulose or lignin.

Further reading

Barnes, R.S.K. and Hughes, R.N. *An introduction to marine ecology*. Oxford: Blackwell Scientific, 1982.
Campbell, R. *Microbial ecology*. Oxford: Blackwell Scientific, 1977.
Grime, J.P. *Plant strategies and vegetation processes*. Chichester: Wiley, 1979.
Harper, J.L. *Population biology of plants*. London: Academic Press, 1977.
Hudson, H.J. *Fungal saprophytism*. (2nd edn) London: Edward Arnold, 1980.
Moss, R., Watson, A. and Ollason, J. *Animal population dynamics*. London: Chapman and Hall, 1982.
Pianka, E.R. *Evolutionary ecology*. New York: Harper and Row, 1974.
Ricklefs, R.E. *Ecology*. London: Nelson, 1973.
Whittaker, R.H. *Communities and ecosystems*. (2nd edn) New York: Macmillan, 1975.

Part Two
Environments

In the second part of this book the various types of environment are considered with respect to the ways in which they affect the plants and animals that live in them.

In some of these environments the existence of living organisms is carried on against harsh physical opposition; in others physical factors are not necessarily limiting and competition between organisms may be more obvious.

Elucidating the patterns of energy flow between organisms takes painstaking effort, and in some environments species are disappearing before there is a chance to recognise and name them, let alone to establish their interactions with other organisms. This is so particularly for some of the world's great rain-forests.

In the chapters which follow, marine environments are dealt with first. The world's oceans comprise a far larger habitable volume than terrestrial environments and biological productivity, energy flow and nutrient cycles have been particularly well studied for the sea.

Many terrestrial organisms must have had their ancestries in the sea, and indeed both physiological constitution, described in the first part of this book, and the fossil record described in the final part, testify to this. Some of the problems of the design of land plants and especially land animals are due directly to the increased effects of gravity on land, when the supportive medium of water is no longer available. Relative lack of water in terrestrial environments also dictates that land-living organisms conserve water, and a wide range of biological strategies is found.

Environmental diversity, then, can profitably be considered in the light of the adaptations of organisms and the chronological evidence of long-term climatic change over geological time. The theme of the interdependence of biological disciplines has been developed throughout this volume, and develops naturally because organisms themselves do not operate as isolated physiological systems, do not interact with one another in the absence of physical constraints, and are adapted to the particular environments in which they live. Scientific progress in biology is made largely by isolating organisms or parts of them in such a way that particular aspects of their organisation can be studied without a multitude of complicating factors. It is, however, these complicating factors with which organisms must cope in the natural world, and a consideration of organisms in their environment encourages the constant revision and refinement of ideas about the strategies they adopt in order to survive.

*Afroalpine vegetation at about 3900 m in the Ruwenzori Mountains, Western Uganda. In the foreground are patches of overnight snow. Large rosette plants (*Dendrosenecio adnivalis *and* Lobelia wollastonii*) and smaller shrubs (*Helichrysum*) are the dominant vegetation.*

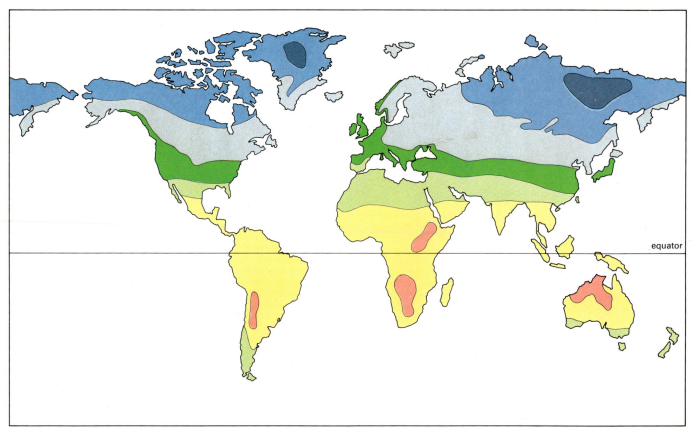

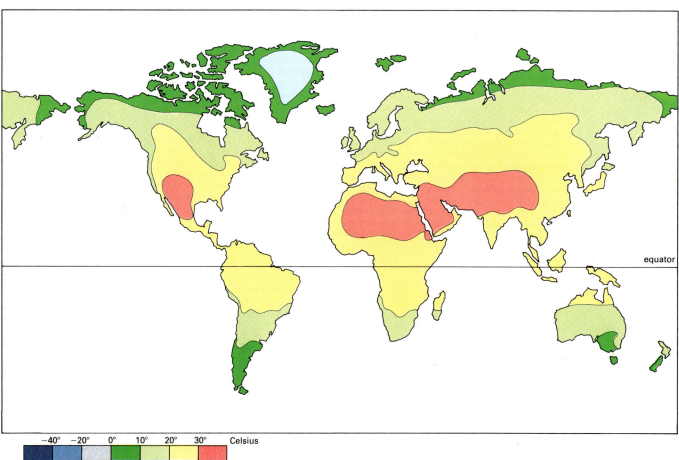

−40° −20° 0° 10° 20° 30° Celsius

Temperatures throughout the world in January (top map) and July (lower map).

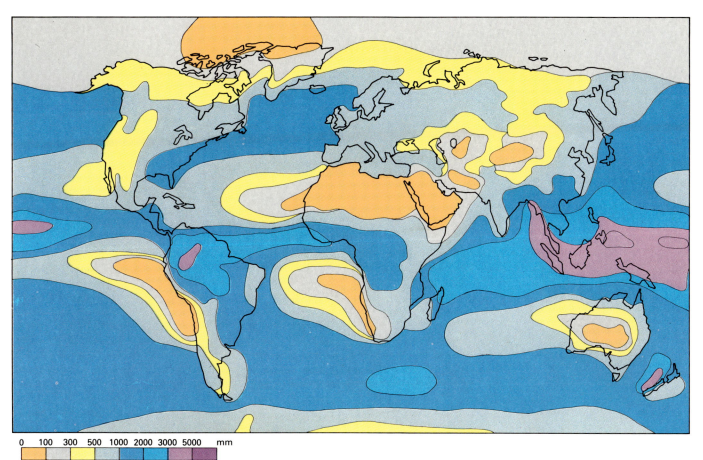

0 100 300 500 1000 2000 3000 5000 mm

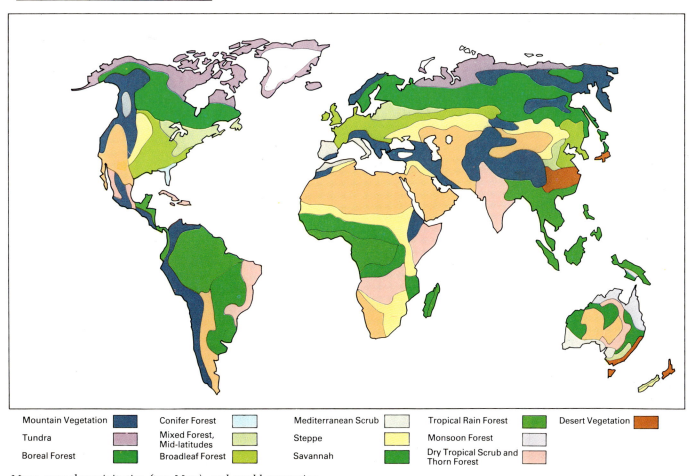

	Mountain Vegetation		Conifer Forest		Mediterranean Scrub		Tropical Rain Forest		Desert Vegetation
	Tundra		Mixed Forest, Mid-latitudes		Steppe		Monsoon Forest		
	Boreal Forest		Broadleaf Forest		Savannah		Dry Tropical Scrub and Thorn Forest		

Mean annual precipitation (top Map), *and world vegetation (lower map).*

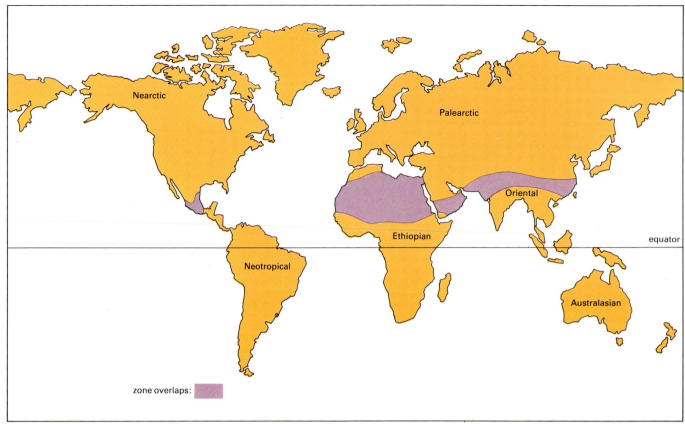

Nearctic

Palearctic

Oriental

Ethiopian

equator

Neotropical

Australasian

zone overlaps:

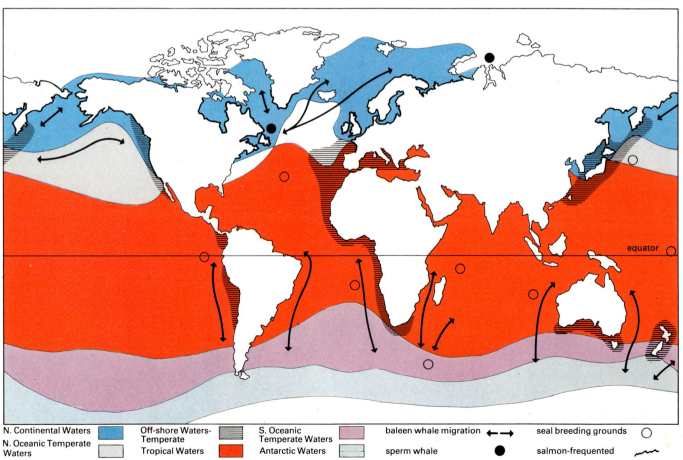

equator

N. Continental Waters		Off-shore Waters-Temperate		S. Oceanic Temperate Waters		baleen whale migration		seal breeding grounds	
N. Oceanic Temperate Waters		Tropical Waters		Antarctic Waters		sperm whale		salmon-frequented	

Distribution of fauna. The main zoogeographical land areas (top map) showing transitional zones between different animal *assemblages, and types of marine fauna (lower map).*

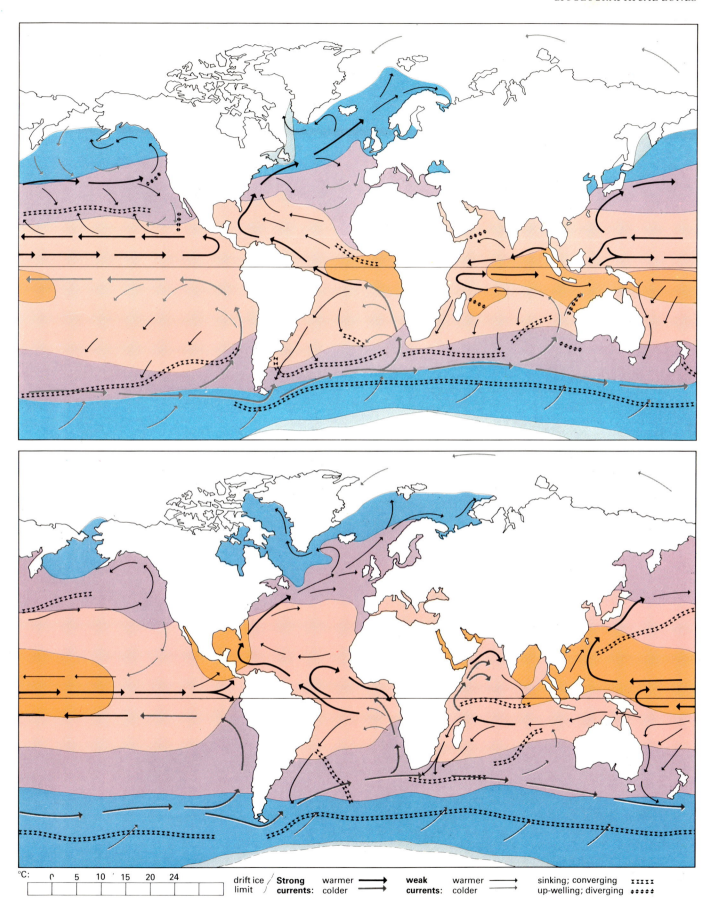

°C: 0   5   10   15   20   24

drift ice / **Strong**   warmer ⟶   **weak**   warmer ⟶   sinking; converging ⅹⅹⅹⅹⅹ
limit / **currents:** colder ⟶   **currents:** colder ⟶   up-welling; diverging ✦✦✦✦✦

Surface temperatures and general circulation in January (top map) and July (lower map).

6 Marine Environments

6.1 THE OCEANS

The oceans occupy 71% of the earth's surface area, yet even this figure underestimates the relative importance of the sea as a habitat for living organisms. The ocean is inhabited throughout its depth down to the maximum of just over 11 000 metres; its average depth is about 3800 metres. In contrast, although some insects and various spores are swept high above the surface of the land, and some species of bird fly or migrate well above tree-top height, the vertical zone inhabited by life on land is very small, perhaps an average of between 10 and 15 metres from the lower limit of the soil to the top of the tallest vegetation. The volume of the marine environment able to support life can be calculated as 1400 million cubic kilometres, while that of the aerial environment is only 2 million cubic kilometres: the seas provide 99.9% of the inhabited space of our planet.

The ocean basins

The oceans of the world form one large interconnecting system, and in a sense there is really only one huge world ocean. From the ocean floor rise a number of masses of low-density rock forming the continental blocks and floating on the underlying layers of the earth's crust and mantle (see section 12.2). These blocks are not equivalent to the continents as we know them, for only parts of these blocks of rock project above the water surface, and several blocks can be pressed together to form a single land mass. Both the oceans and the continents are dynamic in that they have changed size, shape and position over time by the processes of plate tectonics (sea-floor spreading producing new crustal rocks, and subduction removing these back down into the mantle), processes which are fundamental to our understanding of the nature of the ocean basins (see section 12.2). The position of sea-level through time has also altered with changes in the amount of water locked up as ice in glaciers and polar ice-caps.

If the abyssal plains, which form the floor of 42% of the ocean at a depth of some 4000 to 5000 metres below current sea-level, are taken as a reference level, the continental blocks can be envisaged as steeply sided lumps rising to 4400 to 6000 metres above this plain, with an average height of 5300 metres (Fig. 6.1). The folded areas of continental rocks buckled by the movements of the plates soar to 13 300 metres above the abyssal plain, although land more than 6000 metres above the plains (1500 metres above present sea-level) occupies a miniscule percentage of the earth's surface.

The slopes of the sides of the continental blocks, dropping from the margins of the continental shelves, may originally have been very steep, with slopes exceeding 20%, but in many areas this has been much modified by the deposition of sediments. Moving continents have leading edges and trailing edges, and along the trailing edges sediments have been discharged from rivers onto the continental margin for many hundreds of millions of years, and waves have eroded the coastline producing equivalent material. These sediments have accumulated in the ocean and now soften greatly the angle between the continental blocks and the abyssal plain. Two zones can be distinguished: the relatively steep **continental slope** marking the uppermost part of the continental mass, with relatively little accumulation of sediment (slopes of about 7%), and the more extensive **continental rise** occupying the basal angle, with great quantities of deposited material reducing the gradient to about 1.5%. Continental slopes may extend over horizontal distances of up to 100 kilometres and the continental rises may extend for up to 600 kilometres, so that together they account for almost 16% of the surface area of the sea-bed. Major rivers are responsible for the transport of much of the material lost by the land to the sea, and their valleys may continue beneath the sea as 'submarine canyons' cut into the continental slopes and continuing down part of the rises, thereby continually adding material to the rises. Currents in the deep sea may then redistribute these sediments over large areas.

Not all the surface of the continental blocks is above present sea-level. The upper angle between the continental surface and the sides of the blocks is often clear-cut, and occurs on average at a depth of 130 metres below present sea-level. The margins of the continental surfaces, except where leading edges of continents lie immediately adjacent to trenches, are therefore below sea-level. Gently sloping plains, the **continental shelves**, with average gradients of only 0.2%, thus usually occur near coastlines, and may extend offshore for distances of more than 1000 kilometres. They account for 5% of the ocean's area. Because their slope is so shallow and because so much of the earth's water is bound up in the polar ice-caps and glaciers, small alterations in the ocean–ice balance can change the size of shelf seas dramatically. For example, a fall of 100 metres from the present sea-level would convert most of the continental shelves into land. The continental shelves are so flat because they have been produced from dry land by erosion and flooding by the sea, and they have been subsequently covered by a level blanket of sediments, largely sands and muds, derived from the land both by marine and by other forms of erosion.

The ocean floor

Thus far the sides of the bowl containing the world ocean have been considered, and the three essential parts of the bottom of the bowl have also already been mentioned: abyssal plains, mid-oceanic ridges and trenches.

The **abyssal plains**, at depths of 4000 to 5000 metres, lie under some 42% of the ocean, and consist of extremely flat and featureless expanses of fine sediment, most of which is marine rather than terrestrial in origin. Three components predominate in the sediment (Fig. 6.2). In both equatorial and polar regions, siliceous sediments formed from the hard shells or

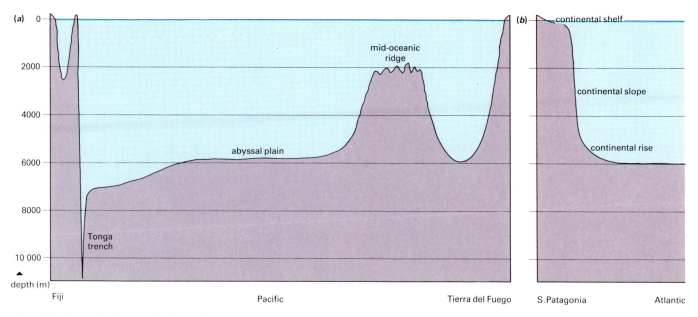

Fig. 6.1. (above) The morphology of ocean basins. (a) A semi-diagrammatic section of the South Pacific Ocean from Fiji to the southern tip of South America, showing the Tonga Trench and the mid-oceanic ridge. (b) The continental shelf, slope and rise on the Atlantic coast of the tip of South America.

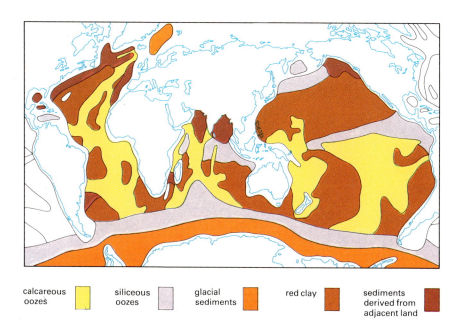

Fig. 6.2. The sediments on the floors of the world's oceans.

calcareous oozes siliceous oozes glacial sediments red clay sediments derived from adjacent land

cases of minute planktonic single-celled organisms (diatoms and radiolarians) cover wide areas and account for 14% of the world's abyssal plains. Other planktonic protists, such as foraminiferans and coccolithophores, produce calcareous shells called tests, and even larger areas of the ocean bed, totalling 48% of the abyssal plains, are covered by calcareous oozes derived from these. Calcite and aragonite, the two forms of calcium carbonate laid down by organisms, dissolve, however, below certain depths called their 'carbonate compensation depths'. Surface sea water is always supersaturated with calcium carbonate, which organisms can easily use to construct hard parts, but at depths the sea is not saturated with calcium carbonate. Aragonite dissolves in relatively shallow waters, but most calcareous organisms make their shells from calcite, and in the Atlantic Ocean, for example, calcite dissolves only below 4500 metres. Hence, calcareous oozes characterise the shallower areas of the abyssal plain, and those areas in which

the rate of sedimentation of the calcite exceeds the rate of its dissolution. The floor of the remaining 38% of the abyssal plains is made of fine red clays derived from a wide range of non-biological sources, and which are red because they are oxidised. This inert type of substratum typifies the deepest regions and those underlying areas of small planktonic productivity.

The **mid-oceanic ridges** are formed along the lines through which new materials are being inserted in the oceanic crust, and as a result of subsequent spreading of the sea-floor extend on either sides of these lines for distances of up to 2000 kilometres. Commonly the peaks of the ridges are some 2500 metres below sea-level, but several islands (notably Iceland, the Galapagos, and the various mid-Atlantic islands) represent emergent portions of these ridges rising up to 4000 metres above the sea-bed. Although the ridges occupy 36% of the area under the ocean, they are relatively little known from a

151

biological point of view, largely as a result of the difficulty of sampling their rugged topography. Island chains may be formed by a combination of sea-floor spreading and volcanic activity, where intermittent volcanic action at one 'hot-spot' in the earth's crust produces a sequence of volcanic cones rising above the moving sea-bed.

The converse of an area of insertion of new oceanic crust is an **oceanic trench**. Such trenches are, however, much less extensive than the ridges, comprising less than 2% of the area under the ocean. Trenches are deep chasms which descend from the abyssal plain down to a maximum known depth of just over 11000 metres below sea-level. Although they are narrow, several being only 15 to 20 kilometres across, they may be very long and characteristically occur adjacent to coastlines and along some island arcs. Those trenches running along the western coast of South America essentially form one single trench system almost 8000 kilometres in length.

Therefore, each ocean basin can be likened to a huge water-filled bowl, 4000 to 5000 metres deep, with a flaring lip extending over the continental margins. The resemblance is broken only by the deep gashes in the floor of the bowl (the trenches) and by the ridges issuing towards the surface which subdivide each bowl into two or more semi-isolated compartments. The whole bowl is covered with a layer of sediment, the nature and thickness of which varies according to local topography, history and the nature of its source.

Sea water

Sea water is a 3.5% solution by mass of a large number of different salts; it is customary, however, to express its concentration, its *salinity*, in parts per thousand, indicated by $^0/_{00}$. The salinity of sea water is thus $35^0/_{00}$. Over 75 elements have been detected in the sea, but just two, the sodium and chloride ions, account for 85.7% by mass of the dissolved substances, and 99.4% of the dissolved materials are contributed by only six ions: chloride (55.1%), sodium (30.6%), sulphate (7.7%), magnesium (3.7%), calcium (1.2%) and potassium (1.1%). The remaining constituents, although present only in trace amounts, do include those important nutrient salts required by the primary producers of the oceans. Nitrogen in the form of nitrate and ammonia, for example, only occurs with an average concentration of 0.5 parts per million parts of sea water, and phosphorus as inorganic phosphate is ten-fold less abundant still. In addition to these inorganic components, sea water also contains an average of just over 1 part per million of dissolved organic compounds, and suspended in the sea are various particulate organic materials, both living and dead.

What is the origin of the salts in the sea? River water does contain dissolved salts, although their concentration only averages $0.1^0/_{00}$, and many of the salts in the sea have been derived from the weathering of rocks on the land masses and their subsequent transport to the ocean via groundwater and rivers. Yet sea water is very different in composition from river

water concentrated the necessary 320 times. After correcting for the addition to rivers of salts recycled from the sea through the atmosphere, the dissolved ionic components that the average river brings to the sea are mainly bicarbonate (48.9% by mass of dissolved material), calcium (12.5%), silicate (11%), sulphate (8.5%) and magnesium (3%). The difference in the relative amounts of some constituents between river water and sea water can be explained on the basis that they are precipitated from sea water, and become incorporated eventually into marine sediments, such as siliceous and calcareous oozes accumulating in certain areas of the sea-bed. Erosion of terrestrial rocks, however, could have supplied only a small portion of the total quantities of some other elements, such as chlorine, sulphur and bromine, present in the ocean. These elements have probably been derived from volcanic activity, as indeed has the water itself.

Below a depth of 1000 metres in the sea, salinity varies little, so most of the water in the oceans has a salinity of between $34.5^0/_{00}$ and $35^0/_{00}$. Near the surface, however, a higher rate of loss through evaporation over gain through precipitation leads to increased salinities, so that the surface salinities of tropical oceans commonly exceed $36.5^0/_{00}$. Conversely, surface waters may be diluted by the discharge of rivers or, in high latitudes, by the melting of ice during the summer; there is freshwater hundreds of miles out into the Atlantic Ocean off the mouths of the Amazon and the Zaire rivers. Such effects, however, are most marked in the shallow coastal waters.

The second feature of major importance which must be considered is the temperature of sea water at different places. Salinity and temperature are the two factors determining the density of sea water, and upon its density many features depend. Apart from geothermal sources of heat, which are only important locally, sea water is heated by radiation from the sun. It is the surface of the sea which receives this heat, and therefore becomes less dense, and the hot surface layers tend to remain floating above the cooler water below. This is the opposite principle to that on which a domestic kettle depends, where the heating element is below the body of water and convection causes mixing of the hot and cold waters. Winds blowing over the surface of the sea cause some mixing of the surface layers, but the effects of winds rarely penetrate below 200 metres depth. The result is the formation of a layer of warm water floating at the surface, and sharply demarcated from the vastly greater volume of water below by a zone of rapidly decreasing temperature and increasing density called the **thermocline** (Fig. 6.3).

Where the input of solar radiation is large throughout the year, the thermocline is permanent and is situated relatively deep in the water. The quantity of solar radiation received declines with increasing latitude, as does the magnitude of the permanent thermocline. A relatively shallow seasonal thermocline is superimposed on the permanent one during the summer months, building up in spring, lasting over the summer, and waning again in the autumn until destroyed by wind-induced

Fig. 6.3. Characteristic temperature profiles at different latitudes in the open ocean. (Note that the occurrence of cold, low-salinity water near the surface in polar regions disturbs the otherwise vertical profiles there.)

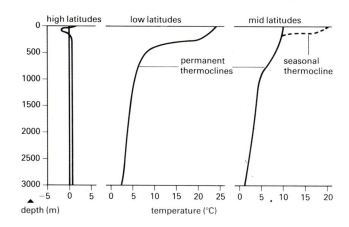

mixing in winter. In polar latitudes, no thermocline is present at any time. Below about 1000 metres, therefore, the temperature of the sea is almost constant regardless of latitude, being from 1 to 5 °C and reaching about 1 °C at extreme depth. Surface waters, however, may vary from an average maximum of 30 °C in areas such as the Red Sea to −1.3 °C around Antarctica. At any one point on the globe, daily temperature variation of the sea water is very small, normally only fractions of a degree except in shallow coastal water, and regardless of the much larger fluctuation in the temperature of the air.

Many freshwater lakes are also subject to the formation of thermoclines (see section 9.2). In these, the bottom water frequently becomes deoxygenated, since oxygen can only diffuse into water from the surface downwards, and the presence of the thermocline indicates that no mixing is occurring to speed up diffusion. Deoxygenation does not occur in the sea, however, except in a few partially land-locked coastal waters, and oxygen is present from the surface to the deepest regions of the ocean at 4 to 6 parts per million by mass. Moreover, because less oxygen can be dissolved in warm water than in cold water, there may even be less oxygen in the surface waters than there is at depth. A layer of minimum concentration of oxygen does in fact occur at a particular depth somewhere between 400 and 1000 metres, being located at that depth at which oxygen is extracted at a maximal rate in relation to the rate of its replenishment by downward diffusion, but even here the water is usually far from being free of oxygen.

Other gases are also dissolved in sea water, but their dissolved proportions are very different from those in the atmosphere because of their different solubilities. Carbon dioxide, for example, comprises only 0.03% by volume of the atmosphere but more than 74% by volume of the gases in sea water: there is always more than sufficient carbon dioxide for photosynthesis. Most of the carbon dioxide is present as the bicarbonate ion, which buffers sea water against changes in pH. Sea water is slightly alkaline, with a pH of 8.1 to 8.3.

Ocean currents

The reason why the depths of the sea are well oxygenated, whereas the equivalent regions of many lakes are not, relates to the large-scale currents generated by changes in the density of sea water. Polar ice-sheets cool the sea water in contact with them, and increase its density. The formation of sea-ice from the water also increases the salinity of the remaining water and therefore its density. The denser water sinks and flows down the continental slopes, of necessity towards the lower latitudes, being replaced meanwhile by more water from the surface, which is cooled in turn. The increase in density is relatively minor (surface water in the tropics has a density of between 1.025 and 1.026 grams per cubic centimetre, whereas the water descending the Antarctic slope has a density of 1.028), but this difference is sufficient to keep the mass of cold water close to the sea-bed. In the Atlantic Ocean, cold dense water flowing

northwards from Antarctica can be traced up to 30 °N of the equator, and volumes of some 20000 cubic metres flow northwards in the Atlantic each second. Having originated from the cold surface waters of polar regions, the descending water is rich in oxygen, and this bottom current from the Antarctic thereby introduces some 160 litres of oxygen per second into the deep Atlantic waters.

Most marine organisms live in the surface waters of the ocean, and of more immediate impact to them are patterns of water movement other than those driven by density gradients. Surface waters are moved by wind belts of the earth in patterns dictated by local topography and by the **Coriolis force** resulting from the earth's rotation. Winds blow over the surface waters, impart energy to them and set them in motion. Since the earth rotates about an axis through the poles, the waters are flowing over a solid surface which is moving at different speeds at different latitudes: a point on the earth near either pole travels in unit time through the same angle, but a much shorter actual distance, than does a point on the equator. Water moving into the lower latitudes, from pole to equator, will thus tend to lag behind the rotating solid surface beneath it, and will deviate towards the equator, while water moving into higher latitudes, from equator to pole, will be moving faster than the underlying surface of the earth and will deviate towards the poles. Currents in the northern hemisphere thus deviate to the right, and those in the southern hemisphere deviate to the left, of their original directions of travel. (This deflection is of course only by reference to the earth's surface, and viewed as motion through space the currents travel through straight courses.) In this way, large rotating bodies of water are established in the surface levels of the ocean, moving in a clockwise direction in the northern hemisphere and in an anticlockwise direction in the southern hemisphere (Fig. 6.4).

Because surface water just to the north of the equator tends to deviate increasingly northwards, and that to the south increasingly southwards, as a result of the earth's rotation, a trough along the equator would tend to form but is filled by water **upwelling** from below the surface. Such upwelling occurs wherever surface water masses move apart from each other. Conversely, wherever water masses converge, surface water **downwells**. In a similar manner, where persistent winds blow water away from a coastline, water upwells to make good the loss at the coast, sometimes from as deep as 600 metres, and when water is blown onto the coastline it downwells. The trade winds, coupled with the Coriolis deflection, therefore cause upwelling along the western coasts of the continents and downwelling along the eastern coasts. The downwelling of

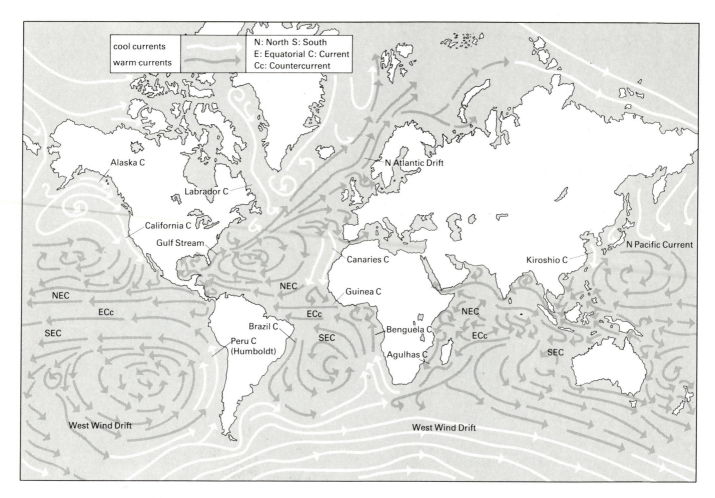

Fig. 6.4. (above) The surface currents of the world's oceans.

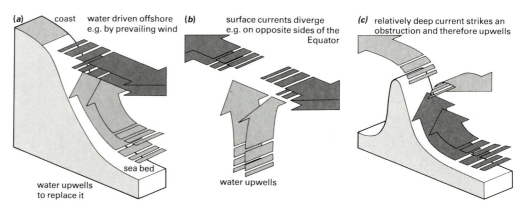

Fig. 6.5. Mechanisms of upwelling, consequent on (a) the movement of water away from a coastline, (b) surface currents diverging, and (c) a current striking an underwater ridge.

water around Antarctica necessitates compensatory upwelling, and such are the volumes involved that water upwells even from depths below 2000 metres. The significance of upwelling is that it is the only major mechanism whereby water from relatively deep in the ocean can be mixed with and injected into the surface layers (Fig. 6.5).

The last environmental factor which needs to be introduced here is the extent to which the oceans are illuminated by sunlight. Much incident light is scattered at the surface of the sea, and most of that which does penetrate is quickly absorbed. The intensity of light falls ten-fold for every 85 metres of depth in the clearest open-ocean water, and falls at a much faster rate near the coast. Thus, sufficient light to permit photosynthesis is a feature only of the surface layer of the sea, down to 250 metres

at most and usually much less than this. Except for light produced by organisms themselves, the ocean is effectively lightless below 1250 metres. The surface layer in which photosynthesis is possible is termed the **photic zone**, the remainder being **aphotic**. The presence of suspended sediment, of organisms, and so on, will reduce the extent of penetration of light. The short wavelengths (blue light) penetrate further down than do longer wavelengths, and marine photosynthesisers are adapted to use these short-wavelength energy sources.

6.2 MARINE ORGANISMS

Types of habitat

Life almost certainly originated in the sea, and was confined to it for many hundreds of millions of years; the oceans still provide the habitat for the greatest variety of phyla, classes and orders of organisms. The early diversifications of protists (single-celled organisms) and metazoans (multi-celled animals) occurred in the sea and produced, by a series of adaptive radiations, many of the subsequent radically different structural types. A few of these were able later to invade the land, either by penetrating estuaries, coastal swamps and rivers into freshwater and ultimately onto dry land, or by direct movement up the shore; and only the groups which gave rise to the vascular plants, to the fungi, to arachnids, insects and myriapods, and to the tetrapod vertebrates succeeded well on land. Members of most of these essentially terrestrial groups have subsequently reinvaded the marine environment, but almost invariably have managed to establish themselves only in the transitional intertidal zone and adjacent coastal regions.

The oceans comprise, and always have comprised, one single interconnecting system, with large-scale currents moving water and organisms from one region to another. The terrestrial environment, however, is fragmented into a series of separate continents and islands, and individual continents are further subdivided by mountain ranges, deserts and other natural barriers to the disperal of land organisms. Differentiation into species largely results from the isolation by geographical barriers of members of what was once an interbreeding unit, and the extent to which a given group of organisms is rich in species is often a function of the existence and frequency of origin of geographical barriers to gene flow (see Chapter 11). Accordingly, although few groups have managed to invade the land, those which have done so have speciated extensively. In contrast, major groups which have remained in the sea have produced relatively fewer species, and the sea contains only a small proportion of known species and genera.

Further evidence for this relation between numbers of species in the sea and the extent of fragmentation of marine environments derives from two sources. Marine organisms can be divided into **pelagic** species, which live in the water column, and **benthic** species, which live on the sea-bed. The two categories do overlap somewhat (some fish, for example, bury themselves into the bottom sediment at times but otherwise swim in the water, and several invertebrates are benthic as adults but are pelagic when juvenile), but the distinction is very useful and widely applicable. The ocean-floor approximates to the terrestrial condition to a much greater degree than does the pelagic realm: ridges and areas of unsuitable sediment can form geographical barriers to movement of species which do not have pelagic larvae, and the deep trenches are effectively isolated from each other. This is believed to explain why 98% of all marine species are benthic.

Secondly, many benthic species are confined to the shallow water surrounding continents and islands, and these coastal waters may be separated by tracts of ocean which the shallow-water species cannot cross. The number of major land masses has varied through geological time, and therefore so has the extent to which coastal habitats have been isolated from each other. The number of different fossil families of coastal benthic invertebrates during each period of time shows a rough correlation with the number of continents in existence then: when many continents were present, the global diversity of benthic families was high, and vice versa. This implies both that diversification occurred when barriers to dispersal arose, and also that when continents collided and faunas could mix competition between members of different groups resulted in a loss of diversity.

The diversity of a group of animals, in terms of the numbers of species, genera or families in it, is only one measure of the 'success' of that group. Other possible indices of success, for example the numbers or biomass of individuals, or the length of time for which the body plan characterising that group has persisted, do not correlate well with the numbers of species surviving at any one time. Many marine groups date back to the Precambrian and have therefore persisted for at least 1000 million years; and many pelagic species are represented by more living individuals than are the whole of the terrestrial vertebrates put together (although of course the extent of the habitat available to a pelagic species is much greater than is that which can be occupied by any terrestrial species).

Characteristics of pelagic organisms

Pelagic organisms range in size and taxonomic position from bacteria to blue whales, but they all fall fairly naturally into two categories differentiated by their ability to swim against natural water movements. The **plankton** are those usually small organisms simply suspended in the water, and the **nekton** are those larger organisms capable of sufficiently powerful locomotion to be independent of currents. Many members of the plankton possess no locomotory powers at all, but although some can swim they cannot by definition make headway against a current.

The tissues of an organism are more dense than sea water; therefore, unless some particular mechanism has been evolved for reducing their specific gravity, all organisms will naturally sink. This problem is most acute for planktonic organisms, which could be removed from their most favourable position in the water column, and they have responded in different ways. Many, especially the smallest, rely on turbulence induced by winds and currents to maintain them at the appropriate level, which is usually near the surface. Other, larger, species are able to swim upwards at a rate that can offset or if necessary exceed their speed of sinking. Finally, groups may have evolved buoyancy devices of a wide variety of different types, such as oil droplets, gas vacuoles or chambers, or have substituted relatively heavy internal ions such as calcium and sulphate by lighter ones like ammonium and chloride. In most species, the buoyancy devices minimise but do not overcome

*Fig. 6.6. Two pleustonic coelenterates: (a) the Portuguese man-o'-war (*Physalia); (b) the by-the-wind-sailor (*Velella). *Both are shown stranded.*

the problem of sinking, but some nektonic species of fish, and cephalopods such as *Nautilus* and cuttlefish, have become independent of the tendency to sink by the possession of a controllable gas-based float which can be adjusted to maintain neutral buoyancy at the required depth.

Several members of the plankton, particularly in warm surface waters in the tropics, bear a series of needle-like or feather-like projections on their body surface. These certainly increase their surface area markedly for a minimal increase in weight or volume, and may increase the frictional resistance to sinking. It is perhaps more likely, however, that the main function of these projections is to increase the overall size of the organism for a minimal increase in mass, so that the number of species of predator capable of capturing or engulfing them is decreased: it is easier, and safer, to ingest a sphere than it is to ingest a needle of equivalent volume.

A few pelagic species have developed positive buoyancy and float at the air–water interface. The larger species have a gas-filled float projecting into the air, with the remainder of the body dangling down into the water. These form the **pleuston** and include the well-known Portuguese man-o'-war (*Physalia*) and by-the-wind-sailor (*Velella*) with their hanging tentacles (Fig. 6.6). The smaller species are usually associated only with the underside of the surface of the water film, and are collectively termed the **neuston**. Both types are moved across the sea's surface by wind action rather than by currents.

Excluding the pleuston, however, and in spite of the other adaptations mentioned above, most pelagic species are heavier than sea water and there is a continual slow downwards rain of those organisms which cannot swim upwards sufficiently fast. Other losses from the populations result from predation, and planktonic species must be able to build up their numbers sufficiently rapidly to make good the losses from both these causes.

Throughout the living world there is a correlation between size and potential rate of population increase. Large organisms must devote much energy to growth in order to achieve their size, energy which could theoretically have been put into

reproduction, and larger organisms have therefore to live longer lives in order to produce sufficient progeny. Small organisms, however, devote relatively little energy to growth and a large amount to multiplication, often having generation times to be measured in days or hours. The plankton consists of small creatures which can multiply sufficiently fast to make good the losses caused by gravity and by consumers.

The photosynthetic primary producers on land are macroscopic plants, herbs, shrubs and trees, characterised by a large total biomass of which only small parts are available to herbivores. In the sea, however, the dominant photosynthetic organisms are small single-celled algae, few of which are larger than half a millimetre in diameter, and which can thus be engulfed whole by consumers. Terrestrial plants need supporting tissues to maintain the position of their leaves in the atmosphere and to permit them to grow upwards towards the light in competition with other photosynthesisers. The photosynthetic algae of the sea, the **phytoplankton**, have no need for these supporting tissues as suspension in the surface waters is the only means of remaining near the light. The lack of coarse supporting structures also renders them more ingestible and digestible.

Terrestrial plants also require extensive root systems of a large surface area in order to take up sufficient nutrients. The small size of the phytoplankton directly gives them a sufficiently large surface area in relation to their volume for maximal uptake of ions with no special structural adaptations. Even the tendency to sink may be a positive advantage to the phytoplankton in that this takes them to new volumes of water from which the nutrients have not been extracted, and being small also removes the possibility of mechanical damage occurring as a result of turbulence.

Although there is a degree of exchange of faunas between different depths, organisms from the same level in the sea do tend to share certain features. Species living very close to the surface are often coloured in shades of blue. In part this may afford some protection from ultraviolet radiation, but it will also serve as camouflage, rendering the pleuston and neuston

Fig. 6.7. *Members of the nekton* (a) *a manta ray (*Manta birostris*); (b) a butterfly-fish (*Chaetodon semilarvatus*); (c) Weddell seals (*Leptonychotes weddelli*).*

difficult to see both from below and from above (birds such as skimmers feed on organisms living at the surface). The colour of pelagic animals, and its distribution over the body, can often be interpreted in terms of camouflage. In the most highly illuminated regions of the surface waters, the plankton are often transparent and the nekton counter-shaded; at depth, where only blue light penetrates, both plankton and nekton are black, brown, violet or brilliant red, as in blue light all these colours will appear as black as the background. At even greater depths, where no light at all reaches, pigment of any type is frequently lacking.

Pelagic species inhabiting the twilight zone from 250 to 1000 metres, most notably various fish and cephalopods, have small light-emitting organs, **photophores**, which contain bacteria that can be stimulated to emit light of several wavelengths; less frequently the bacteria emit light continuously, but in such cases a curtain of opaque tissue can be drawn down to 'switch off' the organ. By emitting light of the appropriate intensity and wavelength, the photophores can camouflage their bearers by matching the background light. Luminous organs have other uses, however, such as permitting recognition of members of the opposite sex, as searchlights and lures aiding capture of prey, and as an escape mechanism in the form of a luminous discharge which confuses predators while the prey disappears lightless.

The production of light and its use as camouflage implies that other organisms present are capable of detecting light. Fish from the surface down to 1000 metres possess large eyes, with the pupil diameter being correlated with depth. Below that depth, sunlight is completely absent and light from living organisms decreases; eyes if present at all are rudimentary. Food is scarce and pelagic organisms are present at very low density: there is for example on average one fish to every 1000 cubic metres. Life below this depth therefore poses severe problems to a pelagic animal, not least in finding a mate and sufficient food. One solution to the problem of finding a member of the opposite sex at the right time is for individuals of the two sexes to join together permanently when they do

happen to meet. In a number of angler fish, the small males spend a brief free-living phase after maturing from larvae, and then seek and attach themselves to a female of their species. The males then degenerate to a small testes-containing appendage of the much larger female, being fed by the female's blood stream via a placenta-like organ.

Capture of food by deep-sea predators is maximised by a set of equally bizarre adaptations. Many of the fish have hugely distensible stomachs, and enormous mouths which can gape widely, so that fish twice as long as themselves can be swallowed as prey and accommodated in the gut. Nevertheless, long periods may be spent without encountering any prey, and hence demands for maintenance energy must be kept very low. The bodies of the deep-sea pelagic fish, many of which are very small, are watery, limp and gelatinous, with poorly developed bones and muscles; energy-requiring tissues and activities have been sacrificed in order to survive on only the rare meal. Capture of items of prey may thus pose problems: several predator species have retained sufficient muscular power only

*Fig. 6.8. The Greenland right whale (*Balaena mysticetus*), showing the baleen plates in its partly open mouth.*

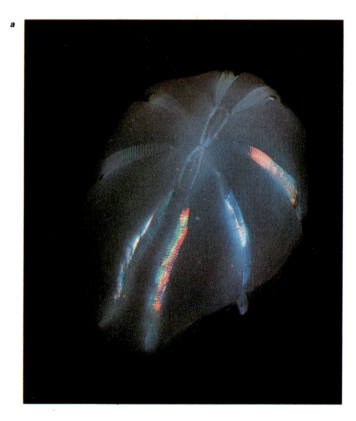

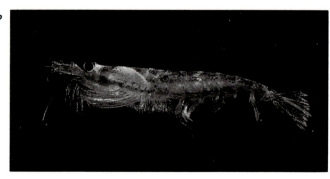

*Fig. 6.9. Two members of the zooplankton: (a) a ctenophore; (b) Antarctic krill (*Euphausia superba*).*

to lunge over a short distance, and hence the prey must be induced to come to them. Where the potential prey possess eyes, a luminous lure mounted in front of the mouth can be used to attract the prey almost into the mouth, which when opened to its full extent creates an inrush of water helping to draw the victim in. Escape is then prevented by long backward-directed teeth. If the prey is too large to be swallowed whole, it may even be digested a bit at a time. Eyeless prey are probably encountered by chance, and their presence detected by sensory barbels, tentacles, or by the pressure changes which their movements induce in the water.

The nekton and the plankton, including the abundant bacteria which comprise the **bacterioplankton**, form an ecological system complete in itself, with the phytoplankton as the primary producers synthesising organic matter, incorporating some into their tissues and those of their descendants, and releasing the remainder as dissolved organic compounds. The organic matter of the phytoplankton is then directly consumed by animals of the **zooplankton** (see Fig. 6.9) and nekton or, in the case of the dissolved organic substances, is taken up by bacteria. Excretion from animals recycles the required nutrients.

Most of the herbivorous zooplankton capture the phytoplankton by filtration through a mesh of one form or another. Several, including the tunicates (Fig. 6.11), use sheets of mucus of very fine mesh size which can retain algae of only a few micrometres diameter. Others, for example the crustaceans, possess setae (bristles) on their limbs which form a sieving lattice-work; the setae are coarse and catch only the larger species of algae. A third category of herbivore uses cilia to convey food particles relatively indiscriminately, and then sort edible from inedible material before ingestion. The food-catching mechanisms serve to take up food materials other than phytoplankton: bacteria in some cases, and particles of organic detritus in others. A number of phytoplankton cells, in some cases aided by sheets of mucilage, can pass living through the guts of herbivores and, unless trapped in a heavy faecal pellet, can resume their activities after being voided. Others, however, although not consumed, are damaged mechanically while being sieved out of suspension, and die without being eaten.

Many planktonic animals are carnivores, seizing their prey individually, or entangling or otherwise subduing it with tentacles bearing stinging-cells (see front cover) or adhesive

Fig. 6.10. Many phyla are represented in the benthos: (a), (b), (c) echinoderms (a – starfish; b – sea cucumber; c – sea-urchin); (d) a coelenterate (sea-anemone); (e) an arthropod – an isopod crustacean; (f) a vertebrate (moray eel).

Fig. 6.11. Two suspension-feeding benthic animals and their feeding apparatus: (a) a colonial sea-squirt (with an internal filtration system); (b) a solitary fan-worm with an external crown of tentacles.

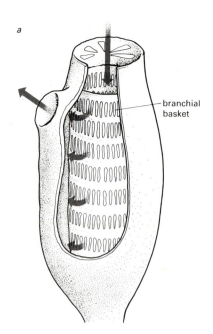

branchial basket

structures, as in the coelenterates (such as jelly-fish and sea-anemones), and their relatives the ctenophores or comb-jellies. These and the herbivorous species are then the prey of the nekton (Fig. 6.7). The largest nektonic species, the basking and whale sharks and the baleen whales, have sieves on or near their mouths through which a stream of water is passed (Fig. 6.8), and the dominant zooplankton species, usually crustaceans, are filtered out. Most of the other members of the nekton capture food particles individually, either zooplankton or other nektonic species. Several of the predators actively chase their prey through the water, and the squids and fish which do this have dispensed with the buoyancy mechanisms of their ancestors in order to be able to change depth rapidly, although this has meant that they have to swim continuously in order not to sink. The food-catching devices of these consumers at the top of the food-chain are relatively limited: jaws bearing teeth in the case of the vertebrates, and tentacles bearing hooks or suckers in the cephalopod molluscs.

Migrations of plankton and nekton

The plankton moves around together with the mass of water it inhabits, and thus reaching fresh supplies of food can prove difficult. Some members of the phytoplankton reach the nutrients in new volumes of water by sinking; others are mobile on a small scale and use flagella to set up currents for bringing new nutrients. The animal plankton (the zooplankton, Fig. 6.9) has solved the same problem by an elaborate series of behavioural reactions, collectively termed **vertical migration**.

During the daylight hours many planktonic animals are found relatively deep in the surface layers of the sea, but at dusk they swim towards the surface, disperse somewhat during the night, and then reassemble near the surface at dawn prior to migrating back down to their daytime depths. For the smaller zooplankton the vertical distances covered twice daily are of the order of 100 to 400 metres, while larger species may migrate through depths of 600 to 1000 metres. The triggering and timing mechanisms for these movements are changes in the intensity of the light reaching the zooplankton, with the animals following a particular light intensity as they move

through the water column throughout each 24 hours, and dispersing when it is completely dark at night. This particular pattern of migration, although widespread, is by no means universal, and varies considerably from species to species, area to area, and from day to day. In addition, some species may at some times undertake reversed migrations, accumulating near the surface during the day, and in deeper water at night. Migrations are rarely shown by non-feeding individuals, and are seasonal in areas characterised by seasonal food supplies.

The functional significance of these patterns of behaviour concerns the maintenance of the supplies of food and nutrients required by the zooplankton. Since currents at different depths in the ocean vary in their speeds and directions, zooplankton can use a pair of vertical migrations to cover large horizontal distances for little energetic cost. When the food and nutrients in a particular volume of water are exhausted, vertical migrations therefore allow new supplies to be reached relatively easily.

Vertical migrations of the zooplankton also have several wider consequences. Movement between different layers of water varying in their speeds and directions can cause populations of individual species to become mixed and spread over wide areas, facilitating gene flow and hindering speciation. Secondly, predators will follow their migrating prey species, and since predators of the photic zone use eyes to locate their prey it is advantageous for the prey species to time their movements so as to remain as far as is possible in areas of low light intensity. Predators of deeper regions in the ocean, however, can migrate upwards to meet potential food species as these move down to greater depths. These aggregations of larger mobile predators, especially fish, can be detected on the tracers from echo-sounders, and are known as the 'deep scattering layers'. It is also possible that consumers that migrate vertically in this way may gain more energy from their food. In the warmer surface waters, levels of activity are relatively high and so more food items can be caught, but the requirements for energy will also be relatively high and more of the food is used to fuel the high metabolic rate. By moving to the lower, cooler, depths to digest captured food under conditions resulting in a lower metabolic rate, more energy

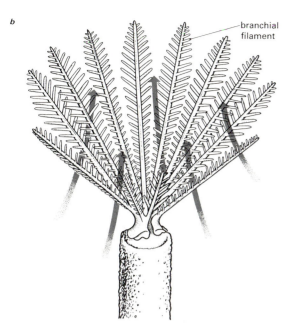

branchial filament

from the food is available for growth and reproduction. Finally, if areas depleted of stocks of food are vacated by predators, the prey species are given an opportunity to recover, and the areas are once more suitable for colonisation when the consumers migrate into them again. Thus vertical migration of consumers in response to changing levels of food stocks can give rise to a horizontal patchwork of areas of different types, from those dominated by consumers to those with high concentrations of producers.

Powerful locomotion is one of the dominant factors in the lives of the nekton. A number of whales migrate from the poles to the equator and back again seasonally, and several species of fish may cross oceans during their lives. Invariably they use currents to aid them in their directional movements, choosing the depth at which they swim in order to take advantage of transport by different currents. Even fish of continental shelves, like the plaice, use currents in this manner. In the North Sea, for example, tidal currents flow in opposite directions on alternate states of the tide, and so, if swimming northwards, plaice rest on the bottom during southwards tidal streaming and then move up into mid-water when tidal currents flow northwards.

Directional movements of this kind are often associated with movement to and from breeding grounds. On the breeding grounds fish spawn, and the eggs and the larvae into which they develop often drift passively in the surface waters as members of the plankton until a 'nursery area' is reached. Since most animals consume different foods at different stages in their lives, correlated with the size of the individual, juveniles of a particular species may not be able to feed on the same items as do the adult, and hence a rich and productive nursery area is needed. This area is the one in which younger versions of the adult can grow rapidly after metamorphosis from their larval form. There is in general an advantage in growing as rapidly as possible, as many predators can capture small prey but relatively few can take large prey. From the nursery, the young fish slowly move towards the adult population as they grow. The migratory circuit of these species can therefore be portrayed as a triangle involving spawning site, nursery area and adult habitat. The movements of other

nekton besides fish also approximate to this pattern, although in the case of the whales, which give birth to their young at a late stage in their development, there is no larval stage or metamorphosis.

Despite their mobility, the majority of nektonic species do not undertake such long-distance migrations, although most species of commercial importance do. They more often use their powers of swimming to stay in the same place in spite of the movement of currents. This behaviour is particularly associated with species living near the sea-bed that maintain territories, home ranges or other systems of ownership or familiarity with defined areas. This state is very close to a benthic or semi-benthic life.

Benthic organisms

The variety of organisms living on the sea-bed, the benthos, is essentially similar to that of the plankton and nekton, but there are in addition several novel types. These include the only true marine plants, in the rooted angiosperms of salt-marshes, mangrove-swamps and sea-grass meadows, and the macroscopic sea-weeds (kelps, wracks, coralline algae, and so on) which are attached to, but not rooted in, the substratum. The sea-weeds, which are multicellular relatives of the planktonic photosynthetic single-celled algae, are most common on rocky outcrops, but other photosynthetic algae occur in the interstices between sand and mud particles, and some species form mats on the surface of the sediment. All these primary producers are confined to that part of the sea-bed to which sufficient light for photosynthesis can penetrate, which in practice is only down to depths of some 30 metres, and hence are considered in detail in chapter 7 on coastal habitats.

Since sea-weeds are attached to the substratum and are bathed by a body of sea water continually renewed by tides and currents, they escape the size limitation imposed on the planktonic algae, and some grow to more than 50 metres long. The animals on the sea-bed can also be much larger than can the majority of those of the water column; for example, typical pelagic crustaceans are copepods of lengths in millimetres, but benthic crustaceans include large lobsters and crabs.

Fig. 6.12. *Three planktonic larvae of species whose adults form part of the benthos. (a) Nauplius larvae of a barnacle; (b) the anemone-like* Cerianthus; *(c) pagurid zoea larva.*

The organisms of the vast majority of the ocean floor are at depths where no photosynthesis can occur and, whether bacteria, protists or animals, are consumers, not producers. They must therefore rely ultimately on food produced in the pelagic or coastal systems. Some bacteria, however, are chemosynthetic, and can for example use elemental sulphur as an energy source for the fixation of carbon dioxide; abundant bacteria and very high bacterial productivity are associated with volcanic vents along the mid-oceanic ridges. Such areas are the exception, however, and other forms of bacterial chemosynthesis use compounds produced by the decay of pre-existing organic matter, originally fixed by photosynthesis. Hence, the benthos is generally fuelled only by a rain of organic debris and faecal material from above, and the nature of benthic organisms revolves around the capture and utilisation of this sedimenting or sedimented material, and on the need to avoid being consumed as the food of others.

Benthic life may originally have been conducted only at the sediment–water interface, with some animals then evolving the ability to burrow into the sediment and thereby escape the attention of predators. Benthic protists (the **microfauna**) can of course move within sediments without special locomotory adaptations. Multicellular animals less than 0.5 millimetres long, the **meiofauna** (see section 7.3), can also move through sediments without displacing the grains by swimming or crawling in the interstitial spaces, while the larger **macrofauna** must actively displace material and burrow.

Burrowing, in a large animal, necessitates the possession of a skeleton, which in the earliest burrowers was a hydrostatic (fluid-filled) body cavity (see pages 73-6). Burrowing may also be facilitated by having the body cavity divided into a series of compartments which can act independently. The first successful burrower constructed on such a basis would have been an annelid-like worm. The invasion of sediments resulted in problems of obtaining sufficient oxygen, and the evolution by the segmented annelids of blood pigments capable of binding oxygen may then have resulted. Such a burrowing worm was the first large member of the **infauna**, the assemblage of animals living beneath the surface, animals up to then having been **epifaunal**, living on the surface. Circumstantial support for the idea that pressure from predators provided the impetus for the macrofauna to invade the sediments comes from the observation that in the deep sea, where predators are relatively scarce, several groups otherwise infaunal in habitat have returned to an epifaunal existence.

Potential food materials for benthic organisms are suspended in the water or have sedimented out of it on to the sea-bed. Certainly at depth, and probably more generally, these food precursors are converted into assimilable food by bacteria, and the primary consumers of the benthos in fact feed on the bacteria and bacterial metabolic products; similar detritus food-chains on land involve fungi (see section 5.4). Only in shallow waters is living plankton directly available to benthic organisms.

On land and in the pelagic system animals must move about in order to seek new supplies of food; water currents move past the static sea-bed, however, and hence animals that filter material from suspension or that collect particles as these settle can be immobile (**sessile**), relying on the movement of their environment relative to them to supply them with food. Members of many groups of benthic animals have adopted a sessile filter-feeding or suspension-feeding existence, and often then form colonies by budding asexually to produce many genetically identical units called **polyps**. Colony formation is particularly marked among filter-feeders because of the mechanics of filtration: many small filters work more effectively than one large one. In some cases not only are the animals sessile, but the act of filtration is also entirely passive, a filtering screen growing oriented appropriately across the water current. Most suspension-feeders however create their own local feeding currents in the water by the beating of cilia or appendages (Fig. 6.11).

Sessile species are especially characteristic of hard substrata such as outcrops of rock. Rock provides a suitable attachment site, and rocky substrata remain as bare rock precisely because the velocity of the current flowing over them is high. Hence, supplies of suspended food are likely to be plentiful and there is no danger of an immobile animal being buried by sedimenting silt. Nevertheless, the sessile habit can also be adopted on fine sediments if an organism can anchor itself in the sand or mud and be raised well above the surface of the sediment by a stalk. Stalked sea-squirts, sea-lilies and sea-pens all show similar adaptations in this direction.

Being sessile and epifaunal places an organism apparently at the mercy of predators, and so it is not surprising to find that chemical and morphological deterrents to being consumed are widespread. The living tissues may be encased in jelly, calcium carbonate or leathery armour; tissues may grow over a rubbery or brittle fibrous matrix, or contain high concentrations of chemicals such as sulphuric acid; or tissues may be easily regenerated. For growing colonies, a further hazard is competition for space with other colonies of the same or a different species. Here, defence against encroaching organisms often involves a larger element of aggression, including chemical warfare and special structures which can kill the tissues of other colonies with which they come into contact.

Benthic suspension-feeders need not be colonial or sessile or epifaunal. An alternative strategy is to live protected beneath

b

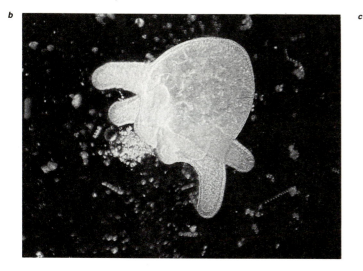

c

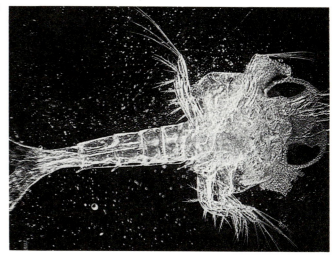

the surface of the sediment in a temporary or permanent burrow, and either to extend a retractable filtration apparatus up into the overlying water, or actually to draw a current of water down through the burrow. Such burrowing species are invariably non-colonial and, although largely sedentary, they are capable of movement within the burrow. The burrows provide considerable protection from predators. The decapod crustaceans (shrimps, prawns and crabs) which live under the sediment have thinner and less heavily calcified exoskeletons than do related species living on the surface, attesting to the protection afforded by burrowing.

Suspension-feeders are most characteristic of areas of the sea-bed underlying shallow and/or productive seas, regions in which the water contains relatively large quantities of suspended organic matter. Other areas of the sea-bed are dominated by deposit-feeders, organisms that consume the organic matter associated with the sediment that has gradually accumulated. These creatures may be infaunal or epifaunal, but very few are colonial. Most are mobile and move over or through the sediment, either selectively ingesting organic particles or consuming the sea-bed indiscriminately, digesting from it the bacteria and other living micro-organisms and meiofauna. The massive or cumbersome protective armour of the sessile suspension-feeders would not be practical for a mobile organism, and instead an infaunal existence appears to be favoured in areas with heavy predation pressure. Epifaunal deposit-feeders do, however, include the relatively well-protected gastropod molluscs.

The demarcation between sessile suspension-feeders and mobile deposit-feeders is of course blurred, as the adaptations of representatives of both types can also be almost identical, and several species can feed in both modes. Some bivalve molluscs live within the sediment, drawing down a current of water through long siphons and filtering off material suspended in it. If the water is drawn from the water column directly, then the bivalve is defined as a suspension-feeder; if instead the water is drawn from the sediment–water interface, the surface deposits being resuspended, the species is a deposit-feeder, 'vacuum-cleaning' the surface of the sediment. Apart from the degree of flexibility of the siphons, the adaptations of the two types of bivalve are the same.

Although organisms possess adaptations which can be interpreted as serving to minimise predation, they are nevertheless frequently consumed by predators, and benthic species

are no exception. Large colonial and sessile suspension-feeders are often attacked by much smaller predatory species: these creep over the surface of the colony sucking out individual polyps where these protrude through the colonial jelly or armour. This relationship would appear to have given rise to several cases of permanent association: various pycnogonids (sea-spiders), for example, dwell on their sessile prey. The individual burrowing suspension-feeders or deposit-feeders are mainly consumed by organisms at least as large as themselves, the predators burrowing through the sediments in search of prey, while many species of fish feed at the sediment–water interface: they may only be able to consume those feeding structures projecting above the surface, although some can disturb the surface sediments and capture the displaced organisms whole.

Many benthic organisms are sessile or sedentary and, since few can swim effectively, dispersal may be difficult. The rapidly growing young might also be expected to compete for food with the adults. One or both of these problems may be alleviated by having a pelagic larval phase, and indeed many benthic animals have planktonic larvae which bear no resemblance to the adult form (Fig. 6.12). In broad terms, planktonic larvae can be divided into lecithotrophic and planktotrophic types. Lecithotrophic ('yolk-feeding') larvae are provided with food reserves and serve for dispersal only. Planktotrophic larvae feed on the plankton and may remain in the photic zone for over a year, although most remain planktonic only for a few days or weeks. In either event, after a certain period of time the larvae descend back to the sea-bed and swim close to the bottom until a suitable settlement site is found. They then complete their metamorphosis into a juvenile version of the adult form. If a suitable site is not found, metamorphosis can be postponed for a little while, although in most cases they must settle sooner or later in an unfavourable area if a favourable one has not been encountered.

A number of giant larvae have been discovered in plankton samples, and these may represent planktotrophic larvae which have managed to postpone metamorphosis for a long time and have continued growing. Some show the beginnings of the development of sex organs, and this may illustrate the way in which various planktonic groups have evolved from benthic ancestors by the acquisition of sexual maturity by juvenile forms (neoteny).

Benthic species which lack a planktonic larval stage mostly

show direct development, the eggs hatching into miniature adults. Often more eggs are laid than will eventually hatch, and the first few young to hatch consume the remaining infertile eggs. In a few species, a larva resembling pelagic types is produced but spends its short larval life within the sediment, sometimes even within the burrow system of the parent. The only two large categories of benthic species that lack pelagic larvae are those in the highest latitudes from which food is absent for much of the year, and deep-sea species for which the distance between the habitat of the adults and the photic zone where pelagic larvae would feed is too great. Both these types of benthic organism live in an environment in which the supply of food is insufficient to permit anything other than infrequent and sparse egg production, and correspondingly the organisms live to great ages, sometimes in excess of 100 years, in order to produce sufficient progeny.

6.3 THE PELAGIC ECOSYSTEM

Productivity of the plankton

The primary productivity of the seas in fixing carbon dioxide into organic compounds is dependent mainly on photosynthesis by the pelagic phytoplankton. Hence the factors determining the global pattern of this production, and its local or seasonal magnitude, are of prime importance in marine biology. Ultimately, the distribution of phytoplanktonic productivity is a direct consequence of the pattern of solar radiation received by the earth in the forms of light and heat, and of the predictability of this influx, but the limiting factors can be considered under four interacting headings: light, the depth to which wind-induced mixing takes places, the supply of nutrients, and the effect of grazing by the herbivorous zooplankton.

The requirement for light

The basic chemical reaction of photosynthesis is the reduction of carbon dioxide, the required hydrogen being obtained from water in algal photosynthesis, or from other inorganic compounds in bacterial photosynthesis. Light is used by algae as the energy source to remove hydrogen from water molecules, leaving oxygen which is evolved as a gas. Light however only penetrates the sea for a short distance, and its intensity decreases logarithmically with depth, the shorter blue wavelengths penetrating furthest. The dominant chlorophyll of the phytoplankton can absorb light of a wavelength of 670 to 695 nanometres, but wavelengths as short as 400 nanometres are absorbed by a large number of other 'accessory' pigments,

such as xanthins and carotenes (see section 2.2).

In spite of this adaptation to the most deeply penetrating wavelengths, there is nevertheless always a relatively shallow depth at which the light intensity is reduced to the point where the amount of carbon which an alga can fix during photosynthesis only just balances that which must be dissipated in metabolism. The light intensity just permitting this balance is known as the **compensation light intensity**, and the depth at which it occurs, which will vary with the light intensity at the surface, the clarity of the water, and so on, is called the **compensation depth**. The compensation depth will clearly change on a regular diurnal cycle, and may well change seasonally too, so it is usual to express it as an average over a 24-hour period. Below the compensation depth, which usually lies no deeper than 250 metres, an alga can survive only by drawing on its accumulated reserves, while above this depth photosynthetic production can exceed respiratory breakdown and allow algal growth and multiplication.

Where light intensities at the surface are very high, photosynthesis may in fact be impaired there by the excess radiation, both directly by the harmful effects of ultraviolet radiation, and also by a light-stimulated increase in respiration and from an overflow of light energy into oxidative biochemical pathways. Hence, in bright light, production may be relatively low at the surface, increase to its maximum just below the surface, and decline rapidly with depth thereafter. In less intense light, the photosynthetic maximum is at the surface, and dense blooms of algae that form there may, by self-shading, be an important factor contributing to the lack of light below the surface.

Mixing by winds

The surface layers of the sea are mixed by the action of winds. If the compensation depth is relatively near the surface, phytoplankton may be carried below this depth by the turbulence and while below it will be unable to photosynthesise. Provided that the algae are able to fix sufficient carbon while they are above the compensation depth to balance these losses, net production will continue, but when light intensities are low this may not be the case.

It is possible to predict whether or not turbulence will result in the phytoplankton spending too much time below the compensation depth. If the depth to which mixing takes place, which may be down to 200 metres, is less than some calculated **critical depth**, photosynthetic production will more than offset respiratory needs, but if the range of depths over which the algae are carried by mixing extends down to below this critical depth, net production will not be possible until the wind intensity abates or the light intensity increases.

Supplies of nutrients

Photosynthesis requires supplies of carbon dioxide and water, and these are present to excess in the sea, but it also requires quantities of nutrient elements such as nitrogen and phosphorus. These nutrients are extracted from the water into proteins and protein derivatives in living tissues in the photic zone, and then pass up the food-web eventually to become part of all living and dead tissues throughout the ocean. However, where there is no mixing of the photic and aphotic water masses, as indicated by the presence of a thermocline (see section 6.1), the water in the photic zone may become depleted without the possibility of replenishment from the vast pool at greater depth. To a considerable extent, nutrient elements cycle within the photic zone, but the inevitable descending rain of dead tissues, and the transport of material to the depths in the form of living organisms, will result over time in nutrient impoverishment of the surface layers if there is no compensatory upward movement of material. Concentrations of nitrogen and phosphorus in tropical oceans may be several tens of times more abundant below the thermocline than above it.

A permanent thermocline is thus indicative of permanent nutrient scarcity, but when the thermocline is seasonal nutrients may be abundant in the colder and relatively lightless months of winter when the water column becomes mixed, but may be reduced in concentration during the summer period, producing an annual cycle of nutrient concentration. As the phytoplankton populations build up in spring with increasing light intensities, nutrient concentrations in the surface layers decline from their winter high, and reach a minimum when the abundance of the phytoplankton is greatest and most of the available nutrients are in the tissues of the algae and of the organisms that have consumed them or their products. Thereafter, nutrient concentrations remain low until the thermocline breaks down on the approach of winter.

Algal photosynthesis therefore reduces the environmental pool of nutrients, but it is not clear whether the magnitude of the nutrient pool limits planktonic production. The correlation between global productivity and mean surface nutrient concentrations is good, and laboratory studies have demonstrated a reduction in the productivity of single algal species when the nutrient concentrations in their growth media are reduced. Artificial nutrient enrichment of semi-enclosed water masses, such as occurs in marine bays receiving sewage discharges, often also leads to enhanced algal productivity. These correlations do not however necessarily indicate causality, and it is not always easy to extend the findings of laboratory experiments on single species under controlled conditions to the natural environment, in which whole communities are subjected to many continuously varying parameters. Equally, a small nutrient pool does not necessarily indicate potentially low productivity, as the algae will in fact be limited instead by the total quantity of a nutrient available over a given period of time, and hence the rates of nutrient input are as important or

more important than are the concentrations of nutrients present at any moment. The herbivorous zooplankton excrete 2 to 10% of their bodily nitrogen and 5 to 25% of their phosphorus each day under normal circumstances, and higher percentages when their algal food is abundant, and these nutrients can be rapidly taken up by the algae. Phosphorus atoms may be recycled in this way once every one and a half days.

Organic nutrients may be just as important for algal growth as are inorganic nutrients such as nitrogen and phosphorus, and may vary in concentration in just the same way. Representatives of most photosynthetic algal types, and especially the dinoflagellates, cannot synthesise all the organic compounds that they require, and must obtain certain organic substances, often specific vitamins, from the surrounding water. All algae leak organic compounds into their environment, and hence a species requiring, say, vitamin B_{12} can only grow well when the quantities of vitamin B_{12} released by other species have achieved a certain level.

Declining concentrations of nutrients are observed in nature to be associated not just with reduced productivity of individual species, as in the laboratory system, but also with a change in the species composition of the phytoplankton as a whole in favour of species capable of taking up nutrients efficiently from the progressively lower external concentrations. Indeed, throughout the seas, the species typical of areas in which food is scarce relative to the number of possible consumers are highly efficient at finding, consuming and using these food resources and cycling them through the food-web. The species characterising areas or times of nutrient scarcity are inherently less productive, so low nutrient levels, primarily low concentrations of nitrate, may limit total planktonic productivity by selecting for less productive types of algae.

Differences in nutrient concentrations in space, often over distances only of millimetres, are just as important as are differences over time. An alga can take up nutrients only from the thin film of water immediately surrounding it, and local concentrations of both organic and inorganic nutrients, as well as various physical variables, form shifting kaleidoscopes over time. It is probably this spatial and temporal heterogeneity which permits so many different species of phytoplankton to coexist: conditions are never uniform over a sufficiently large area and for a sufficiently long time to permit any single species to gain enough of a selective advantage to displace the other species by competition.

Consumption by herbivores

The fourth and final potential limit on phytoplankton production is the consumption of the algae by herbivores. If phytoplanktonic tissues are consumed faster than they are produced, overall algal productivity will decline, but it is uncertain whether or not this is common. It is possible to estimate the algal biomass which should be present after a given time, assuming the initial biomass, light intensities, multiplication rates, and so on. The difference between this calculated figure and that actually present can be taken as the amount consumed by herbivores. Estimates made in this way vary widely, but in some areas it appears that more than 99% of the algal production is consumed by herbivores.

Pelagic food-webs

By consuming phytoplankton and digesting their tissues, herbivores release back into the environment a high percentage of the nutrients incorporated by the algae. Other nutrients fixed by the algae leak out into the water in the form of dissolved organic compounds, and these are absorbed by bacteria. Knowledge of the productivity of pelagic bacteria is scanty, but some estimates indicate that it may rival that of the phytoplankton. Bacteria also act as a sink for inorganic nutrients, but the smaller zooplankton (as well as some larger species, particularly those using mucus-net filters) can capture and digest bacteria and release their incorporated nutrients for potential uptake by algae. Evidence from the benthos (and there is no reason to think that the plankton behave differently) indicates that, although most of the phosphorus is released as dissolved inorganic phosphate, the form required by the algae, animal consumers release some of their nitrogen in dissolved organic forms which require further cycling before being converted to inorganic nitrogen available for algal uptake. This may explain why nitrogen rather than phosphorus is most often considered to act as the limiting nutrient for phytoplankton productivity.

Another pathway for nutrient flow is the detritus food-chain based on dead tissues, the bacterial and other agents of their decay, and the microscopic consumers of these decomposers (compare section 5.4). Estimates of the importance of this detritus pathway in the pelagic system range widely, but have been put at up to 90% of the total flow of energy to consuming species.

The production of living algal tissue by photosynthesis is the basis of all pelagic food-webs, and for many years it was assumed that herbivores simply then consumed the living phytoplankton and were in turn consumed by carnivores. Undoubtedly this type of food-chain does occur, but the food-chain based on soluble organic compounds leaked by the plankton, and the detritus food-chain based on dead tissues, are also very important parts of the system. Nevertheless, throughout these various types of pathway, it is phytoplanktonic photosynthesis that fuels the pelagic system in all but immediately coastal regions. The productivity of the consumers generally mimics that of the algae, but the efficiency with which food-energy passes through the food-web varies with the relative abundance of food. In areas of high algal productivity, plenty does not necessarily mean efficiency, and the production of the herbivores may only be some 5% of that of the phytoplankton, whereas where algal productivity is relatively low the production of herbivores may exceed 25% of that of the phytoplankton. The ratios of the productivity of consumer and consumed are approximately 20% for herbivores–algae and 10 to 15% for carnivores–herbivores and carnivores–carnivores. These ratios are much higher than those typical of the land, largely because marine algae are much more digestible than are terrestrial plants. The seas, therefore, support a much greater secondary production per unit of primary production than does the land and, although marine primary production is much less in total than that of the land, its secondary production is greater.

Exceptions to the close relationship between marine primary and secondary productivity are found during intense growths or blooms ('red-tides') of certain dinoflagellates, which release organic substances toxic to many animals, and also in the most productive regions under special conditions when night-time respiration of the algae and decomposition of the tissues of dead phytoplankton create a lack of oxygen in the water. When water upwells from the oxygen-minimum layer off the south-western coast of southern Africa, for example, mass mortality can occur in the plankton and the water may contain considerable quantities of hydrogen sulphide.

Global patterns of planktonic productivity

The open oceanic waters of the tropics receive high levels of light and heat radiation throughout the year. Photosynthesis can therefore occur to some depth in the water column, but a pronounced thermocline is permanently present, resulting in low nutrient concentrations in surface waters. The constant environmental conditions and persistent shortage of nutrients produce a low but stable level of phytoplankton productivity, and the predictable algal food resources permit the herbivores to achieve their maximal levels for the habitat (the 'carrying capacity') and to consume a high percentage of algal production. For purposes of comparison, a value of unity is allotted here to the productivity of the tropical oceans.

On progression from the tropics towards open oceans in the higher latitudes, the seasonal nature of the input of light and heat becomes progressively more marked. Winters are characterised by low light intensities, a shallow critical depth higher in the water column than the maximum depth of mixing, and a non-stratified water column. Productivities are then limited by the lack of light and by turbulence carrying algae to below the critical depth. Herbivores may overwinter as non-feeding stages. These conditions improve in spring or summer, and while nutrients are plentiful in the surface waters the phytoplankton can fix quantities of carbon well in excess of their respiratory requirements. In the highest latitudes this period when both light and nutrient supply are favourable is very brief, but during these three months or so productivity can be so high that the total production per unit area of sea surface achieved during the whole year is some two and a half to three times that achieved in tropical waters. In intermediate, tem-

Fig. 6.13. Average daily phytoplankton productivity in the world's oceans.

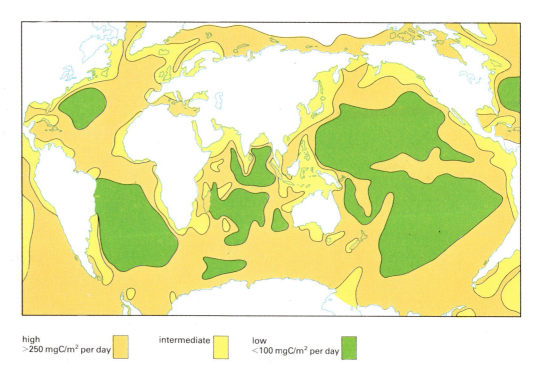

high
>250 mgC/m² per day

intermediate

low
<100 mgC/m² per day

perate, latitudes, however, a thermocline develops in summer, rendering the pool of nutrients potentially exhaustible. Production builds up in spring while the thermocline is being established, and is limited thereafter by lack of nutrients and/or grazing by herbivores, until the return of low light intensities in winter conditions.

In some regions, such as the North Pacific Ocean, the seasonal resumption of production in spring appears to be sufficiently predictable for some of the dominant consumers to reproduce in advance of the phytoplankton bloom, using food reserves accumulated before winter, and therefore to be at a numerical advantage when the food supply increases and to graze down algal production as fast as this appears. Algal biomass in the North Pacific therefore remains relatively constant during the productive season. In the North Atlantic, in contrast, the herbivores do not reproduce until the algae have begun to multiply, and hence the numbers of herbivores do not reach a peak until some six weeks after the peak of algal biomass. Nutrient shortage due to the summer thermocline may halt the initial increase in population of the phytoplankton, but thereafter pressure from herbivores becomes intense, and causes the algal populations to crash. If the thermocline breaks down before the combination of light and turbulence become once again unfavourable for net photosynthesis, a second minor increase in the algal population can occur in the autumn.

A second important gradient, besides the latitudinal one in open oceanic waters, is that from the open ocean to the coast. Coastal waters are almost invariably rich in nutrients: they are often shallow, and hence the whole water column can be mixed by turbulence so that loss of nutrients to deep waters does not occur, and they may also receive an input of both inorganic and organic nutrients from rivers and drainage of groundwater. The result is productivities in coastal waters of about three times those of the adjacent oceanic areas. Various well-defined coastal zones are also subject to upwelling of nutrient-rich water from relatively deep in the sea (see section 6.1), as indeed are some oceanic areas, and when this upwelling occurs it supplies effectively limitless quantities of nutrients. Productivity in such areas averages eight times that of the open ocean.

Throughout the world ocean, therefore, phytoplankton productivity is greatest along shallow tropical coasts subject to upwelling, in high latitudes, and in shallow waters and upwelling zones in general, and it is least in the vast tropical oceans (Fig. 6.13). Nevertheless, the size of these last is so large that they contribute 80% of the total world phytoplankton production.

Although these broad differences between marine regions are apparent, individual stretches of ocean are far from uniform in their productivity. In any one region or water mass there may be a patchy distribution of phytoplankton, with areas of high algal biomass interspersed with those supporting less than one-twentieth that concentration of phytoplankton. Even relatively dense algal patches vary internally over distances of metres or tens of centimetres. These spatial variations result from the effects of the grazing zooplankton, from microturbulence and small-scale circulation patterns, from local variations in nutrient concentrations or water clarity, and from several other physical and biological causes. The comparative productivities suggested above are therefore gross averages over large expanses of sea.

The actual organisms responsible for the productivity also vary both seasonally and spatially. Diatoms are characteristic of water masses of high nutrient status and are therefore predominant in coastal regions, in high latitudes, and in upwelling zones; dinoflagellates and many very small planktonic flagellates, on the other hand, are more typical of tropical oceans.

167

Production by the nekton: fisheries

The annual production of the nekton is of particular interest as it is this which is exploited by fisheries. The sea provides less than 1% of the total food intake of the human species and, although sophisticated technology is increasingly being employed, exploitation of marine productivity is still at the hunter–gatherer level of cultural development. Further, marine organisms are caught at an energetic loss in many cases, in that the energy content of the fuel used to make the catch considerably exceeds that of the fish as food, and the catch is in any case then used very inefficiently. More than one-third of the world's fish harvest is converted into meal or oil for use as food for domestic animals or as agricultural fertiliser: the human species gets the benefit only after terrestrial food-chains have dissipated most of the energy.

This is not to imply that the marine harvest is unimportant; rather, its importance lies only in certain well-defined areas. For example, one-third of Peru's export earnings in 1967–1970 was obtained from the sale of meal derived from the anchoveta. In poor sections of society and relatively poor nations, fish are an extremely important source of protein, and may provide more than three-quarters of the protein intake. Secondly, in the affluent world, there is a large consumption of luxury marine products such as oysters, prawns, lobsters, crabs, salmon and tuna. Suggestions are made at intervals that by increasing the harvest from the sea, part of the world's food problem could be solved.

The current yield (fresh weight) of the harvest from the sea is 60 million tonnes, of which fish comprise 87%. The herring-like fish, for use largely as meal, are the most important (23% of the weight of fish landed), followed by gadoid species (cod, haddock and so on) (19%); flatfish now form less than 2% of the catch, and this value is exceeded by the catches of squid and benthic crustaceans.

Although the total annual catch from the sea has been constant for the last ten or more years, the effort required to harvest this amount of fish has been steadily increasing. This is a symptom of **overfishing**, a malady that now affects most existing fisheries.

Low yields can be sustained indefinitely with the expenditure of only a little effort, and yields can be increased if more effort is applied. If, however, the effort applied to capture fish is too high, and too great a fraction of the standing stock of a species of fish is consistently removed over many years, the ability of that fish population to maintain its numbers with this additional mortality will be impaired, the stock will decline, and catches will decrease. Somewhere between these two extremes will be the maximum catch that can be sustained indefinitely for the least relative effort of capture.

The value of a catch is made up of two independent factors. A yield of, say, 100 kilograms could be achieved by catching 100 fish each of 1 kilogram, or else 1 fish of 100 kilograms, and both the numbers of fish in a population and their average size

can be affected by fishing. A number of species of fish continue to grow throughout their life, and can increase in size several-fold after reaching reproductive maturity. If these are caught when the fish are relatively small, all the benefit that would have been gained if the fish had grown for longer is lost. Catching such species when they are too small will decrease the yield, and is called 'growth overfishing'. Other species of fish do not grow much after reaching reproductive maturity, and by catching too many immature fish the numbers in future generations decrease; this is described as 'recruitment overfishing'.

For the types of fish currently being harvested, provisional estimates of the world's maximum sustainable yield are in the order of 100 million tonnes fresh weight per year, a figure not greatly in excess of the current catch. Since most currently exploited stocks are already overfished, increased future yields can only be achieved by turning to as yet unexploited stocks or areas, while permitting the recovery of those which have been hardest hit. Potential additional annual yields have been estimated at 10 million tonnes of squid and possibly up to 100 million tonnes of krill, much of this 'released' by the destruction of one of the natural consumers of krill, the large baleen whales.

We are still however in ignorance of most aspects of the ecology and biology of the sea's consuming species, and certainly many large species of the nekton remain to be described scientifically.

6.4 THE BENTHIC ECOSYSTEM

Productivity of the benthos

Benthic photosynthesis, whether by plants, algae or bacteria, is possible only in the shallowest of coastal waters, which occupy in total only 0.1% of the area of the oceans; there is no primary generation of food materials on the deep sea-bed apart from the few centres of chemosynthesis. Except where shallow water rich in plankton is in contact with the bottom, the benthos is entirely dependent on the rain of dead material falling from the pelagic system. This input comprises faecal pellets, cast exoskeletons and other items of low nutritive value, and by the time it reaches most areas of the ocean-floor it has slowly passed through several thousands of metres of water column, providing ample opportunity for bacteria or animals to remove what digestible material was present originally. Perhaps only 1 to 3% of the surface productivity ever reaches below 2000 metres depth, and accordingly the deep-water benthos is sparse and unproductive.

The productivity of the benthic consumer species must thus also be low unless these can capture living plankton. This is possible over the shallower parts of the continental shelves, where large biomasses of suspension-feeders can exist, and secondary productivity here may be 5000 times that possible in the deep sea. Even so, production on the continental shelf rarely exceeds 5% of that of the water column above, although, as in the pelagic system, the animal benthos plays a vital role in regenerating nutrients into a form which can be used by the phytoplankton.

Our knowledge of benthic productivity is in fact very limited, the best estimates deriving from scanty information on biomass multiplied by guesses of likely growth and turnover rates. Over all but the shallow continental shelves, biomass is lower than 10 grams living mass per square metre, and most of the ocean-floor supports less than 0.1 grams per square metre. Values on the continental shelf may attain 500 grams per square metre, and occasionally twice this as on the rich Antarctic shelf, although even in these regions productivities are very much lower than those in the water column. Growth rates also appear to be very slow in the deep sea: a small bivalve mollusc, for example, of a size which might be achieved in less than one year in shallow water, takes 50 years to become mature at depth, and probably lives to over 100 years; and bacterial growth rates are 100 times slower than those of bacteria kept at the same temperature at the surface.

The guts of the larger consumers of the ocean floor do not possess enzymes capable of breaking down the materials of which the rain of pelagic debris is composed, and they are thus dependent on bacteria which contain enzymes that can perform this task. The bacteria may be consumed directly with the ooze, or else only after passage through a food chain of protists and/or the meiofauna. Even in the shallows, where benthic algae are present, organic matter itself comprises only a small fraction of the sediment ingested by debris-feeders, and these animals can in any case digest relatively little of the organic matter that is present. Benthic polychaete worms, crustaceans and molluscs from intertidal sands and muds may be able to assimilate less than 10% of the organic content of their sedimentary habitat, although pure cultures of diatoms or bacteria can be assimilated with up to 70% efficiency. The efficiency with which the abyssal consumers can digest the alga-less oozes in which they live is presumably much less than this 10%, and through much of the ocean-floor the total organic content of the oozes is less than 0.25%. Sediment-ingestors must therefore eat their way through large amounts of the sea-bed in order to extract sufficient food.

There are approximately one million bacteria per gram of sediment through most of the ocean-bottom, but their productivity is very low, maybe only 3% of the pelagic algal productivity of the tropical open oceans. The processes occurring in the ocean as a whole can only be inferred from the relatively few studies which have been conducted in shallow water. These indicate that many of the bacterial colonies on the surface of the sediment particles are not actively growing and, as only a small percentage of the surface of any particle is covered by bacteria, even in the most organic of habitats, space is not the limiting factor. Rather it appears that shortage of nutrients limits bacterial productivity in the sediment.

The deep waters of the oceans are relatively rich in nutrients, but the abyssal and shelf sediments are fine-grained and hence are of low permeability. Once the nutrients in the immediate interstitial water have been taken up, their replenishment by diffusion through the benthic oozes from the overlying water is extremely slow. Bacteria have a high demand for nitrogen and phosphorus and, because the debris sinking from the pelagic system is poor in or completely devoid of these nutrients, they can only be obtained from the interstitial water. The current view is thus that many bacterial colonies are not dividing because they have exhausted the nutrients in their immediate vicinity. The turbulence caused by the movement of the meiofauna through the interstitial spaces may help to keep the bacteria supplied with nutrients, but local nutrient supplies can only otherwise be remobilised by animals ingesting the sediment, digesting the bacteria, and excreting the inorganic nutrients back into the water. In either case, bacterial productivity is regulated by the activity of the consumers and not by the supply of debris to the sediment. In the deepest areas of the ocean, however, it may well be that the supply of organic carbon is so low that it is this which limits growth, and organic material never appears to accumulate in the deep sea as it does in some shallow benthic habitats.

The productivity of benthic bacteria is thus, for whatever reason, very low, but because of its ultimate dependence on phytoplanktonic production the relative spatial pattern of benthic productivity generally mirrors that of the pelagic zone (see section 6.3) (Fig. 6.14). Nevertheless, areas of unexpectedly high production and biomass do occur in regions receiving imported debris from adjacent coastal zones, and in those surrounding regions of chemosynthesis. Deep water lying immediately offshore, for example, can receive wood and other vegetable debris brought in from rivers or mangrove-swamps; one such area between Timor and Maluku, in Indonesia, and 7000 metres deep, supports a biomass of organisms some 70 times that normally to be found at that depth. Biomasses of 500 times the background level are associated with the chemosynthetic sulphur-bacteria supported by the flux of reduced sulphur compounds issuing from volcanic vents on the Galapagos ridge. The leaves of some coastal sea-grasses can also be transported well away from land and be deposited on the ocean floor: sea-grass material was seen in almost every one of the series of over 5000 photographs taken of the sea-bed at an average depth of 4000 metres.

Diversity of sea-bed communities

The roles of competition between species, and predation, in determining the nature of marine communities have been studied with particular reference to the benthos since, among the marine ecosystems, the sea-bed is essentially a two-dimensional habitat. It has thus proved easier to study some biological interactions there than in the more accessible water column, although investigations involving the enclosure of large masses of water in plastic cylinders are beginning to yield results. Studies on food and feeding relationships have attempted to explain why different areas of the sea-bed support different numbers of benthic species, for some areas are dominated by one or a few species, whereas other regions, like the deep sea, although poor in total numbers of individual organisms per unit area, have a fauna in which many species coexist.

One approach to highly diverse environments, deriving from deep-sea work, suggests that when animal populations exist in a stable environment they can attain their maximal level, the carrying capacity of their habitat (see Chapter 5). The intense competition (usually for food) which results is proposed to yield over evolutionary time a set of specialist species which avoid interspecific competition by becoming increasingly specialised on, for example, different food items. A larger number of specialist species can coexist in a habitat than could generalists, as these would compete with each other where their diets overlapped. Hence, provided a habitat and its resources have remained constant for a sufficiently long period of time, the result is supposed to be a diverse assemblage of species each limited by the quantity of that resource to which it has become specialised.

An alternative view, derived from work both in shallow and in deep-sea waters, stresses that if a habitat has remained constant for a long period of time a single superior species would be expected to have ousted all the other species by competition, resulting in a monoculture of this dominant type rather than a diverse assemblage of specialists. Such **competitive exclusion** could in this viewpoint only be prevented by maintaining all the potential competing species below the carrying capacity of the habitat, so that competition does not occur. On this second basis, diverse communities on stable areas of the sea-bed indicate not intense competition for food resulting in specialisation, but control of population densities in some way, such as by predators, maintaining high diversity.

There are other factors besides predation that have been suggested as keeping populations below the level at which they will compete, or at least that could serve to check the increase of competitively dominant species. Sediment, even in the deep sea, is mobile and can be eroded from some areas together with the organisms it contains, and it is also deposited elsewhere, smothering the existing fauna. In shallow areas, storms may disturb the sea-bed, while the activities of organisms eating the ooze may result in indiscriminate mortality of smaller organisms which, although not necessarily digested, are nevertheless killed.

These two approaches to diversity are not in fact completely mutually exclusive, and both the approach stressing competition and that emphasising predation probably contain elements of truth. They highlight the important question of whether benthic species are limited in their abundance by lack of food, or by predators and other agents of mortality. Organic detritus is present to excess, at least in some areas, and the animal consumers may in fact not be limited by the total quantity of organic matter in the sediment but by the rate at which bacteria can convert this food-precursor into usable food; thus there is a possibility that consumers are limited by bacterial productivity. Mechanisms using predation or disturbance to avoid competitive exclusion are likely to apply to the maintenance of high levels of local diversity, while the avoidance of competition by specialisation takes a long-term view of the generation of diversity.

Most of the relevant work on the importance of competitors and predators has been carried out in shallow waters, and the results have then been applied more generally. The actual evidence for competition between species within the marine benthos is still rather circumstantial, although interactions between species are well documented, and there is evidence for competition for space among intertidal species on rocky shores (see pages 182–5). In part this uncertainty reflects a lack of precise information on what detritus-feeders really digest from the material they take in. Systems in which a number of species divide the total available resource between them seem explicable only if they have evolved in order to reduce competition between the species. Many benthic species, for example, are known to prefer or to be restricted to sediments of specific particle size or liquidity, and species also divide up the depth gradient within a given sediment so that some live near the surface and others at depth. A comparable phenomenon occurs in the intertidal zone where different species occur at different levels on the shore, and sometimes if one species is absent from a certain geographical region others are observed to have expanded their vertical ranges into the vacant zone and occupy regions of the beach which they would not occupy in the presence of the missing species. In a limited number of cases, two species are known to be more dissimilar to each other when they occur together than when they are occuring apart (see section 5.1), and the divergence when they coexist can again be interpreted as a mechanism for the avoidance of the competition which would otherwise occur. Finally, artificially increased densities of individual species have been shown to cause complete elimination of their food species. In all these cases competition, either now or in the evolutionary past, is inferred, but of course past competition cannot actually be demonstrated.

Other cases of competition are perhaps more accurately described as indiscriminate interference. Species which move actively through the sediment can disrupt the more permanent burrow-systems of sedentary species, for example, and conversely the massed tubes of infaunal species can restrict the freedom of movement of burrowers. Many of the sedentary tube-dwelling or burrow-dwelling species are suspension-feeders and they can destroy, if not actually consume, the larvae of other (and indeed of their own) species as these endeavour to settle on the substratum. Delicate larvae may be wrapped up in sheets of mucus by the filtration apparatus of the suspension-feeders and be unable to escape on being

Fig. 6.14. The biomass (wet weight) of benthic organisms in the world's oceans.

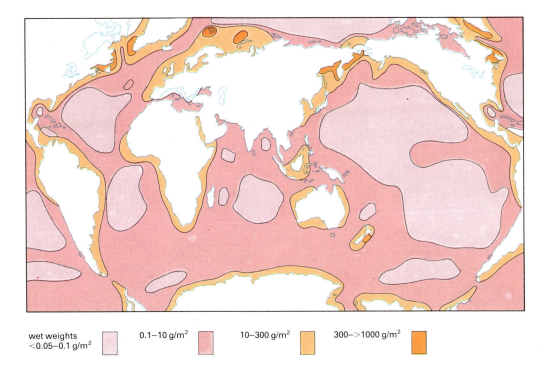

wet weights
<0.05–0.1 g/m² ▢ 0.1–10 g/m² ▢ 10–300 g/m² ▢ 300–>1000 g/m² ▢

deposited on the sediment surface in the pseudofaecal pellet (the bundle of material retained by the filter, but then rejected and not ingested). Some species are also known to release organic substances into the interstitial water which render it unattractive or distasteful to other species. These and other examples of the activities of some species may result in the exclusion from certain areas of species that are susceptible to these kinds of disturbance, and thus they can be classed as competition for space, but they do not necessarily indicate that other kinds of competition would subsequently have occurred.

The evidence for control of benthic species by their predators is equally incomplete. Many predators can only crop those portions of their infaunal prey which project above the surface of the sediment, such as the suspension-feeding structures of tube worms, the siphons of bivalve molluscs, or the tails of lugworms when these back up out of their burrows to defaecate on the surface; the individuals affected are able to regenerate the lost portions. Epifaunal species are in the minority over much of the ocean-floor, but members of these can be consumed in their entirety and in such cases predators have been shown to maintain high local diversities of their prey species by concentrating on the competitively superior prey. Artificial removal of the predators can therefore result in a significant increase in the population of the preferred prey, as seen in Nova Scotia when sea-urchin densities increased dramatically after overfishing of their lobster predator. However, the ranges or microhabitats of epifaunal predators and their prey rarely coincide exactly, and this sets a maximum on the pressure to which any predator can subject a particular prey species.

The deep-sea fauna has a high diversity and, from what is known of the abyssal species, it does not show the characteristics of heavily predated populations. Deep-sea faunas have, for example, low reproductive rates, a high frequency of old individuals in their populations, and no obvious adap-

tations against predators. Indeed, the density per unit area of abyssal organisms is so low that predators are scarce or absent from these regions.

Almost nothing of the deep-sea benthos, however, is known. The lowering of remote-controlled cameras to the continental slopes, mid-oceanic ridges and the abyssal plain has disclosed a wealth of species, including some types of organisms which have never been captured by standard methods of coring and trawling. Several entirely new groups of protists and animals have recently been discovered, including the 1-metre long vestimentiferans, and the large protistan xeno-phyophorians and komokiaceans, whose scientific names perhaps adequately express their unusualness!

Further reading

Barnes, R.S.K. and Hughes, R.N. *Introduction to marine ecology.* Oxford: Blackwell Scientific, 1982.

Cushing, D.H. *Marine ecology and fisheries.* Cambridge: Cambridge University Press, 1975.

Cushing, D.H. and Walsh, J.J. (Editors) *The ecology of the seas.* Oxford: Blackwell Scientific, 1976.

Gray, J.S. *The ecology of marine sediments.* Cambridge: Cambridge University Press, 1981.

Hardy, A.C. *The open sea. Part I. The world of plankton.* (2nd edn) London: Collins, 1970.

Marshall, N.B. *Developments in deep-sea biology.* Poole: Blandford, 1979.

Parsons, T.R., Takahashi, M. and Hargrave, B. *Biological oceanographic processes.* (2nd edn) Oxford: Pergamon, 1977.

Seibold, E. and Berger, W.H. *The sea floor.* Berlin: Springer-Verlag, 1982.

Steele, J.H. *The structure of marine ecosystems.* Cambridge, Mass.: Harvard University Press, 1974.

Vermeij, G.J. *Biogeography and adaptation: patterns of marine life.* Cambridge, Mass.: Harvard University Press, 1978.

7 Coastal Environments

7.1 CHARACTERISTICS OF COASTAL HABITATS

The term 'coast' is taken here to include four types of habitat. First, there are those terrestrial systems that have either been created by the erosional powers of the sea, for example cliffs, or have been constructed by the action of wind and waves, such as sand dunes and shingle formations. Although maritime in many of their detailed features, these systems approximate the remainder of the land which is considered in Chapter 8, and are only considered briefly here. Second are intertidal zones, which will be considered in the greatest detail. Thirdly, whole ecological systems that only occur coastally are dealt with, such as estuaries and lagoons, even though these are composed of a variety of the habitats covered separately elsewhere in this section. Fourthly, and at the marine extreme of the coastal zone, are the shallow coastal seas overlying the continental shelf. These coastal seas share many features with the open ocean, treated in Chapter 6. The final part deals with the terrestrial organisms of small islands, particularly of those islands found at some distance from any other land mass.

Changes over time

One of the most characteristic features of the coastal interface between land and sea is that it is in a state of flux. This may occur with a regular diurnal (daily) or semi-diurnal (twice-daily) rhythm, with the rise and fall of the tide, but the coast also changes on a longer time basis.

Waves batter the land, particularly during storms, and rapidly erode soft cliffs and imperceptibly but insidiously erode rocky headlands. The pressure generated by waves can be up to 26 000 kg/m² (2 tons/ft²). One million cubic metres of the soft cliffs of the Holderness region of England are lost to the sea each year, and the land there has retreated at 1 to 6 metres per year for at least the last 1000 years. The sediments eroded join those on the continental shelf, and some find their way back to the fringe of the land again. Although waves which plunge vertically downwards, and therefore have a much larger backwash (force of movement away from the shore) than swash (force of movement towards the land), are destructive, those with a large swash are constructive and can move sediments up an incline. Sand and shingle can be moved onshore to form beaches and spits. Coastal water, by virtue of its vigorous motion, maintains silt particles in suspension, but in quiet backwaters this silt can settle out of suspension to form mud-flats, and these can grow by steady addition of new material (accretion) at rates of up to 20 centimetres per year if aided by the vegetation in the intertidal zone. New land can be formed by this process, and indeed where facilitated by mangroves the extension of muddy semi-terrestrial areas can occur at the rate of 125 metres per year. Often, however, land formed in this manner is only temporary, as phases of accretion can be interspersed with those of erosion. Nevertheless, more land is currently being gained in the world than is being lost by erosion.

Increasingly, human activities are encouraging reclamation of areas of intertidal sediment and even expanses of coastal water, and the main problem affecting coastal marine habitats is probably not pollution but their total destruction by reclamation. On a modest scale, land has been reclaimed from the coastal sea for well over 2000 years, but in the last 50 years the building of large barrages has made possible the reclamation of whole bays and estuaries of more than 4000 square kilometres in area, in order to build housing, industrial and power-generating complexes, reservoirs, and ports for both sea and air traffic, and to create agricultural land.

On a longer time scale, the glacial cycles have a pronounced effect on coastlines. Sea water is periodically locked up in polar ice-caps and glaciers and then released again to the sea, causing alterations in the sea-level. At the moment we are in an interglacial phase, and the melting of the ice at the end of the last glaciation some 12 000 years ago (see section 15.1) inundated low-lying land to form shallow coastal seas, such as the southern North Sea, and drowned river valleys to produce estuaries. During glacial periods, sea-level was 100 metres or more below its present level, and the area of the land was greatly increased at the expense of the sea, particularly of shelf seas where the offshore shelf is gently sloping. If all the existing ice-caps were to melt, the sea would rise by about a further hundred metres, and cover much existing land. Hence, in many areas, the present-day coastline is not where it was 15 000 years ago, and a similar time into the future will find the coastline once more in a very different location.

Compared to further inland, the more terrestrial parts of the coastal zone are relatively barren and unproductive. Salt spray makes the habitats severe for most plants, while the ground is often unsuitable, consisting of dry nutrient-poor sand, barren shingle, crumbling unconsolidated cliffs, or hard rock on which plants can only gain a roothold in crevices and on ledges. Compared to the deep oceans, however, coastal seas are rich in nutrients and highly productive; here the photosynthesis of the phytoplankton can be supplemented by that of benthic algae and aquatic or semi-aquatic flowering plants, together with all the litter and detritus that results from their decay. The photosynthetic productivity of the seas around the coasts is usually between 35 and 75 times that of the open ocean, and coastal benthic production per unit area exceeds that in the water column by a factor of ten. The coastal regions of the sea may therefore be likened to food factories, with the benthic photosynthesis from 0.1% of the ocean's surface area contributing about 10% of the total marine photosynthetic production; 20% of phytoplanktonic photosynthesis is also located in coastal seas, so that more than 25% of total marine productivity is coastal.

Marine pollution

Although trans-oceanic voyagers have consistently reported the occurrence of polluting substances on the surface of the sea in mid-ocean, the seas as a whole are still relatively free from pollution. It is the coastal zones, and especially land-locked arms of the sea (bays, harbours and estuaries), that are most severely affected, and even the large inland Baltic and Mediterranean Seas are now giving ample cause for concern. There are a great variety of offending substances, but the main categories of pollutants are oil and its derivatives, organic compounds including sewage that cause oxygen levels to be depleted, and various chemicals that are harmful when concentrated.

A number of incidents, for example oil-spills (Fig. 7.1), are accidental discharges, and could be avoided by the application of more care or better control. Other types of discharge are deliberate and planned; some of the substances thereby released to the sea are relatively innocuous at the concentrations at which they are discharged, but can be accumulated in the tissues of species not susceptible to them and then have a marked effect on some of the top predators, which receive doses of the chemical concentrated maybe more than a million times. Organochlorines and heavy metals such as cadmium and mercury, are particularly noteworthy in this respect, not least because human deaths have resulted from consuming marine organisms which have accumulated massive concentrations of these; radioactive isotopes, such as isotopes of caesium, strontium and iodine, also become similarly concentrated.

The third type of discharge is those deliberate discharges, for example of organic matter, which are a serious problem if not adequately dispersed. Semi-enclosed bodies of water have slow rates of flushing, that is, it may take days to replace all the water in the system. Pollutants naturally accumulate if they are discharged into such areas faster than they can be flushed out. Heterotrophic bacteria can break down the organic matter, but in so doing they remove oxygen from their environment. The sewage produced each day by one million people, together with such other material as finds its way into the average sewer, requires about 300 tonnes of oxygen for its complete breakdown, equivalent to the oxygen content of 30 million cubic metres of coastal sea water. This daily rate of oxygen removal will often be in excess of the supply, and hence estuaries into which raw sewage is dumped are often anoxic. If, however, this same quantity of sewage is oxidised in filter beds before being discharged, in an attempt to maintain the quality of the water, there will still be an input of 9000 kilograms of inorganic nitrogen and 2000 kilograms of inorganic phosphorus, which can stimulate algal productivity and cause widespread eutrophication and depletion of oxygen (see section 9.2). The appropriate siting of outfalls so that they discharge into fast-flowing currents and/or at peak flow periods can successfully reduce the pollution of coastal waters.

7.2 COASTAL HABITATS ON LAND

The land is affected wherever it meets the sea. This may only be manifest in a few salt-scorched branches or the presence of a few maritime species in otherwise typically terrestrial vegetation; alternatively the area may be very evidently coastal, as in sea-cliffs, sand dunes or shingle formations. Cliffs, dunes and shingle all occur inland as well, and certain species may be found wherever these types of habitat occur, but several species are characteristic of these habitats on the coast.

Dunes (Fig. 7.2) are formed by wind-blown sand. Where the intertidal zone is an extensive beach of clean sand, the surface of which dries out at low tide, winds of over 16 kilometres per hour can move the surface sand grains, and when the winds blow off the sea they will carry the sand up the beach. Salt-tolerant plants growing along the drift-line or strand-line, where nutrient levels are relatively high due to the decomposition of stranded debris, provide a wind-break. If the wind velocity drops below the threshold of 16 kilometres per hour, small embryo dunes can develop in the lee of the drift-line, or on top of these plants. Some species, especially various grasses, can grow as fast or faster than the accreting sand, and these plants both stabilise the embryo dune with their root systems and further impede the wind causing more sand to accumulate. Marram grass (*Ammophila*) is an excellent dune-builder on both these counts, and can capture and fix large quantities of wind-blown sand.

Provided that the sand removed from the beach is replaced by the action of waves, dunes can continue to increase in height. Since wind speed near the ground increases with height from the ground, a balance point is eventually reached at which the rate of removal of sand from between the plants comes to equal the rate at which it is supplied. The highest coastal dune, on Moreton Island, Australia, attains 275 metres in height, although most are very much smaller. Alternatively, the sand supply may be cut off by the development of further embryo dunes to seaward, and in this fashion a series of parallel dune ridges can form, with the dunes increasing in age from sea to land.

When the supply of sand to an individual dune ceases, the grasses which typify the growing phase of the dune die out and are replaced by an increasingly terrestrial series of mosses, lichens and flowering plants. Young dunes are well drained, poor in nutrients and often slightly calcareous as a result of fragments of shells in the sand. As a vegetation cover develops, so the amount of humus in the soil increases, enabling the retention of water, while rain (which is slightly acid) progressively leaches the calcium carbonate from the sand. In the temperate zone, it takes some three centuries for the surface 10 centimetres of dune sand to lose their content of calcium carbonate, which is initially present at 5% by mass, but older dunes are frequently acid and may support an acid-heath type of vegetation.

Although generally stabilised by vegetation, dunes or parts

Fig. 7.1. Oiled mute swan on the Moray Firth, Scotland.

of dunes may become mobile if the wind can erode sand from their windward faces. This often occurs as a result of the enlargement of an initial bare area, created by burrowing animals or human feet, followed by undermining of the adjacent and hitherto stable regions. Sand eroded from the side of the dune facing the wind is deposited on the side sheltered from the wind, and as the process continues the whole dune can move landwards at a speed of 5 to 7 metres per year. As mobile dune fields can encroach on human activities, dunes are often stabilised by planting trees, especially pines.

Except in the troughs between parallel dune ridges ('slacks'), which can contain standing water, dunes are dry habitats because sand is highly porous. The plants characteristically have adaptations to resist loss of water. The leaves of marram, for example, are tightly rolled to shield the stomata

Fig. 7.2. Embryo (a), frontal (b), and mature (c) sand dunes.

Fig. 7.3. A colony of gannets on the Bass Rock.

from being in the wind; and, in the temperate zone, a number of plants flower and set seed very early in the year before the summer heat evaporates the small store of water gained during the winter. Apart from the specific dune-builders, however, most of the plants on dunes, and the vast majority of the animals, are those generally associated inland with dry sandy habitats or calcareous grasslands.

In regions experiencing high winds, large waves, large tidal ranges and frequent storms, **shingle** can replace sand as the material deposited by waves. This occurs where the adjacent shallow shelf sea has received an input of pebbles scraped from the land by glaciers. Intertidal shingle is devoid of life because the action of waves rotates the pebbles against each other, grinding any organism so unfortunate as to have sheltered between them. Higher up the shore, the strand-line can contribute organic material to the stony matrix, and thereby both stabilise and enrich it, and even further from the sea airborne silt can fill some of the interstices. These additions to the shingle also help to reduce its high permeability and to retain sufficient moisture for plants to be able to establish themselves. The resultant vegetation cover is, however, patchy and somewhat scruffy.

Many plant species found on or near dunes can also occur on shingle and on sea-cliffs, and a high percentage of these have adapted to the scarcity of freshwater by becoming succulent, that is, by storing water in their tissues. Leaves, stems and roots may all be relatively fleshy, and several species have thus been taken into cultivation for human consumption. Cabbages and their allies, radish, beet, lettuce, carrots and asparagus all occur as wild forms on coastal rock, shingle or sand.

Cliffs are perhaps most noteworthy for their provision of breeding sites for sea-birds (Fig. 7.3), as they once probably did for the pterosaurs (see section 14.2). The main reason for this is the relative freedom from interference and from terrestrial predators that is obtained at such sites. Many sea-birds will also nest on the flat tops of isolated islands; only when such sites are scarce, or are disturbed by human activity and the accompanying rats, feral cats and so on, are cliffs exclusively chosen for breeding sites. The main species concerned are gulls, auks and their ecological equivalents, and very few construct any form of nest, the egg normally being laid onto the bare rock. The individuals of these species, particularly the auks, prefer to breed under very crowded conditions, rather than seeking more room on vacant ledges, and a given stretch of cliff may be crowded with birds while other apparently suitable sites nearby are ignored. If, however, a few individuals colonise these empty ledges, many others may quickly join them and nest close by. This may relate to group defence against predatory or egg-stealing birds (see section 4.1), for should a gull seek to steal a guillemot's egg, it would be faced by a battery of beaks on the crowded ledges, but by only one beak should the guillemot be nesting singly.

7.3 INTERTIDAL HABITATS

Salt-marshes and mangrove-swamps

Throughout the world, the upper parts of shores of soft sediment support salt-marshes or mangrove-swamps. These two assemblages of amphibious plants and algae are parallel communities, with salt-marshes occurring in the cooler and drier parts of the world and mangrove replacing them in the hot and wet tropics (Fig. 7.4). Very few regions possess both types of vegetation, south-eastern Australia and the Gulf states of the USA being the only instances, but in dry areas within the tropical mangrove belt a form of salt-marsh may occur over the highest parts of the intertidal zone. Although these habitats are the geographical equivalents of each other, there is a marked difference in the growth-forms of plants in each: salt-marshes are dominated by grasses, small herbs and low bushes, while mangroves include a large number of trees attaining heights of 30 metres.

Both systems form in a manner essentially similar to that described in section 7.2 for sand dunes, but with water instead of wind providing the motive power for transport of the deposited material. Some of the silt held in suspension in coastal water can sediment out in sheltered spots during periods of slack tide, and if it settles at high tidal levels will not often be disturbed by scour or removed on the ebbing tide. The

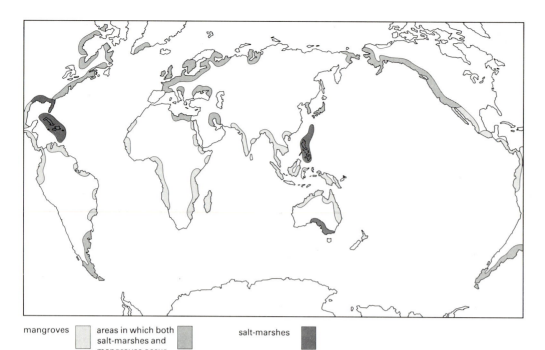

Fig. 7.4. (left) The distribution of salt-marshes and mangrove-swamps around the fringes of the world's oceans.

Fig. 7.5. (right) Salt-marshes. (a) The salt-marsh grass Spartina. (b) A salt-marsh on the Suffolk coast showing sea lavender.

silt that settles out sticks to mucilage produced by benthic algae and to other silt particles, and slowly raises the level of the shore. Seeds, fruits and fragments of coastal plants are also left behind by the tide, and some of these will germinate or take root. As a sparse vegetation cover develops, the water is further stilled, permitting more silt to settle out, and the plants themselves help to trap sediment. The increased rate of deposition of silt raises the level of the shore still more and decreases the time during which it is covered by tidal water. Plant species less tolerant of submergence can then become established, and some of these will outcompete the pioneer colonists. Once established, several of the species can spread vegetatively, forming a sward of grass in the salt-marsh (Fig. 7.5), and several types of mangrove tree can produce seedlings viviparously (attached to the tree) which drop into the mud around the parent, take root, and form a forest in the mangrove-swamp (Fig. 7.6). When the height of the shore approaches the level of the highest tides, the supply of waterborne silt decreases, but organic debris may continue to raise the shore level more slowly. Meanwhile, further pioneer colonists will be establishing themselves to seaward.

Silt and plant fragments are mainly deposited where the water is flowing most sluggishly, and as the vegetation cover spreads out from these nuclei so the flow of the tide is progressively confined to the original zones of highest water velocity. These form the main creeks, and eventually the flooding tide enters a marsh or swamp through a limited number of main trunk routes, and thence along their branching tributaries, before spilling over into the marsh or swamp as a whole. The ebbing tide follows the reverse pattern, lengthening the minor creeks by eroding their tips as it does so, until an intricate network of minor creeks is created (Fig. 7.5). Apart from these creeks, the whole of the shore from the high-water mark of spring tides down to mean tide level can eventually become clothed in vegetation, although some varieties of salt-marsh, including those of North-west Europe, only extend down to the high-water neap-tide mark. During this process of growth of the marsh or swamp, any given spot may therefore pass in time through a succession of different plant com-

munities as the level of the shore slowly rises, while at any one moment an equivalent series of zones in space can occur from low to high shore levels.

The dominant flowering plants of salt-marshes or mangrove-swamps are an assemblage of unrelated species that have convergently adapted to this life in unconsolidated and often anaerobic marine sediments periodically covered by salt water. The term 'mangrove' covers species from 20 plant families in 12 orders. Few of the plant species that grow in these conditions have a requirement for salt, and most plants therefore need special mechanisms to adapt to or to remove the unwanted salts that they cannot but take up through their roots: salt may be excreted by special glands in the leaves, it may be sequestered into inactive tissues, or high internal salt concentrations may be withstood by the plant storing water too and becoming

a

succulent. Indeed, in the absence of salt many plants of salt-marshes or mangrove-swamps grow more vigorously, and they are restricted to these salty habitats only because the salt serves to keep out potential competitors. Several salt-marsh plants, for example, are competitively weak and light-demanding species which can only survive in the absence of competition from stronger species; some also occur in other habitats that are free from competition, such as the tops of mountains.

Marine muds have very low permeabilities, and the breakdown by bacteria of plant debris incorporated into the sediments soon exhausts any free oxygen in the interstitial water. Various types of anaerobic bacteria can obtain their required oxygen from dissolved nitrate and, when this is exhausted, from sulphate. Hence, below the immediate surface layer which is in contact with the atmosphere or with tidal water, marsh and swamp muds are anoxic and contain poisonous sulphides. Roots which serve only to anchor plants can have an inert layer in contact with the sulphurous soil, but fine roots are also needed to take up water and nutrients. In mangroves, these are only in the thin aerobic surface layer, and some species have special aerial structures, pneumatophores and 'knees', that serve as chimneys allowing air to diffuse in

Fig. 7.6. A mangrove, Rhizophora. *(a) The trees grow out of the brackish water. (b) Stilt roots and lenticels. (c) Viviparous seedlings hang from the branches.*

and ventilate the tissues of roots below the surface. Because of the anoxic sediment, mangroves do not have any deeply penetrating roots, and to support a large tree the roots are very extensive in the horizontal plane. Some mangroves have cable roots extending like the feet of a hat-stand only a fraction of a metre below the surface, while *Rhizophora* possesses a whole series of aerial props on which the trunk balances (Fig. 7.6).

Although the vascular plant species are most apparent, both salt-marshes and mangrove-swamps support microscopic and macroscopic algae on the mud surface between the plants and growing on the plants themselves. These algae are derived from marine types. Most of the animal inhabitants of these systems probably rely for food mainly on the living algae rather than on the coarser tissues of the larger flowering plants. The living plants are grazed only by a few insects and, in mangrove-swamps, by leaf-eating monkeys. Therefore there is a large amount of litter produced when the foliage dies back annually in temperate regions, or as the leaves fall throughout the year in the tropics. Some of this litter is incorporated into the sediments, but the flooding tide floats the remainder from the surface of the marsh or swamp. In many mangrove-swamps and in relatively open salt-marshes, particularly where the tidal range is small and the prevailing winds blow off the land, the tides export this litter and detritus to the sea. Storms may also remove large mats of vegetation, and even in normal weather conditions half of the net production of the system may be exported. The coastal sea nearby is enriched with this fixed organic matter. In more closed systems, and in those subject to large tidal ranges, material from the surface of the marsh may be deposited as a broad strand-line along the boundary between the marsh and dry land, and several of these marshes may on balance be importers of detritus, more debris from the adjacent sea settling out and being trapped on the marsh than is carried away by the ebb tide.

Whatever the fate of the plant debris, these swards and forests high up the shore are highly productive, perhaps mainly as a result of the abundant nutrients. The pool of nutrients around the roots of most land plants is finite, but nitrate and phosphate are brought in to salt-marshes and mangrove-swamps by every covering tide, so that production of fixed organic matter can continue indefinitely. Even so, all the nutrients provided by the sea may be used, because if a marsh surface is fertilised artificially with additional nitrogen then productivity increases still further.

For part of each day the marshes and swamps may effectively be dry land, while for the other part they are sea; and the tops of mangrove trees always project above the water, while their roots are permanently in marine mud. Accordingly, the faunas in these habitats are a mixture of marine and terrestrial animal species: land mammals may venture on to a marsh to feed during low tide, and fish may swim into a swamp at high tide for the same purpose. Clearly, the aerial parts of the plants will carry a fauna that is basically terrestrial in nature, although a few hardy marine winkles do climb right up mangrove trees, as do various crabs at low tide, and one marine bivalve mollusc may even be found living on mangrove leaves. Several birds roost on marshes and swamps at high tide while waiting for the tide to fall and uncover their intertidal feeding grounds, or else use the branches of the trees as a convenient coastal nesting site. Equally, marine species which live on rocky shores (epifaunal species) are able to colonise the trunks and prop-roots of the mangroves.

In general, marine species characteristic of soft sediments dominate the creek systems, areas of standing water, and the sediment surface at relatively low tide levels. In salt-marshes, the sediment surface is the interface between the marine and terrestrial spheres, and is colonised equally by species from both habitats. Several of the terrestrial arthropods avoid being drowned by the incoming tide by retreating below the surface into air-filled burrows or crevices in the mud in advance of submergence, following an innate behavioural rhythm, while others fly to higher ground. The degree of liquidity of the surface of the sediment in part determines the dominant element in the fauna. The softer muds are inhabited mainly by marine species, although the softest unconsolidated muds, such as are associated with rapidly growing *Spartina* (rice-grass or cord-grass) marshes, may possess an impoverished fauna, and animals in these marshes are confined to the creeks and their margins.

Neither mangrove nor salt-marsh plant species can withstand the longer periods of submergence found below mean tide level, and over the lower parts of the shore they may be replaced by algae and/or by sea-grasses.

Sea-grass meadows

Sea-grasses are the only thoroughly marine vascular plants, and the members of the six families of monocotyledons that comprise this ecological grouping occur in all latitudes. Some species extend up into the lower parts of the intertidal zone, but most show their maximum development from the low-water mark down to a depth of 15 to 30 metres, dependent on the clarity of the water, with a few records of their occurrence down to 60 metres and in one instance to 90 metres. Although sea-grasses can inhabit open sandy coasts, they are characteristic of enclosed and sheltered bays, lagoons, reefs and the lee of offshore barrier islands. Many have the strap-shaped, grass-like leaves that give them their common name, although none is a true grass and a variety of leaf shapes are borne by the various genera. These leaves arise in bunches from an underground stem or rhizome, and in the smaller species up to 15000 shoots, with several leaves per shoot, can occur per square metre of sea-bed.

The living leaves of sea-grasses are consumed by turtles, dugongs, manatees, some fish, and by sea-urchins. The guts of these animals contain colonies of micro-organisms equivalent to those possessed by ruminants, and they are therefore able to digest cellulose (see section 5.4). Few other animals are capable of digesting the living leaves, although many consume the abundant small algae which live attached to the surface of the leaves. Most of the leaf material therefore ends up as litter and detritus, and sea-grass leaves have been recorded down to 8000 metres in the deep sea. Large floating rafts of sea-grass leaves have been observed off Florida after storms have ripped them from the sediment.

If the leaves of sea-grasses and of salt-marsh and mangrove species are cast off the plant naturally, most of the nutrients they contain are withdrawn into the remainder of the plant before the leaf is shed. Most of the remaining nutrients are leached out very rapidly into the surrounding water, and after some 2 to 4 weeks all the leachable sugars have also been lost. Bacteria then begin to colonise the leaf surface, and after 7 to 10 weeks a rich microbiota of bacteria, protists and meiofauna is associated with the eroding surface. In the tropics, sea-grass leaves may lose from 10% to 20% of their initial mass each week, but decomposition takes place at only one-eighth to one-tenth this rate in temperate latitudes, and in the deep sea leaves may last for years. After some 15 weeks, the debris will be much richer in nitrogen, as a result of the growth of microbial organisms, than when the leaf was shed, and will thus be a much richer food source for detritus-feeders. One analysis showed that each gram dry mass of aged sea-grass detritus contained 10^9 to 10^{10} bacteria, 5×10^7 to 10^8 flagellate protists and 10^4 to 10^5 ciliate protists. Another analysis showed that each millilitre of interstitial water from mats of decaying *Spartina* debris contained more than 10^7 bacteria and 10^5 heterotrophic flagellate protists and ciliate protists, together with more than 10^5 photosynthetic flagellate algae and 10^5 diatoms. Thus even if the plant leaves provide substances which are only digested with difficulty, the primary herbivores are much more utilisable as food.

Because sea-grasses are more thoroughly aquatic than are other coastal plants, their productivity will enter marine food-webs to a much greater extent than will that of salt-marsh or mangrove-swamps. With the associated benthic algae, the productivity of which may account for half the total, sea-grass meadows can support an abundant fauna and are used as nursery areas by numerous nektonic prawns and fish (see section 6.3).

Sands and mud-flats

Not all shores composed of soft sediment support sea-grasses, salt-marsh or mangrove-swamp. Exposed sandy beaches are often devoid of vascular plants except along the strand-line and so are sheltered muddy shores below high-water neap or mid-tide level. Photosynthetic organisms may however be abundant in the form of benthic flagellates and diatoms, and on mud-flats there may be macroscopic green algae and a wide variety of surface mat-forming green and blue-green algae. These may be responsible for as much photosynthetic activity per square metre as there is in the richest of zones of upwelling offshore

(see section 6.3); in general, the more sheltered shores have greater photosynthetic production.

In contrast to the coastal habitats considered earlier, however, flat stretches of sand and mud are dominated by animals, and the greatest number and diversity of animals are found on muddy-sand beaches where there is a moderate exposure to wave action and water movement.

Exposed sandy shores are pounded by surf which temporarily suspends the upper centimetre or more of the sand. Buried organisms must be able to dig themselves in very rapidly to avoid being suspended too and washed away. The action of waves also prevents any lightweight material, most particularly organic matter, from settling out, and such beaches receive very little food for opportunist scavengers. The only food available may be that maintained in the water column, and hence the dominant animals are the suspension-feeders.

At the other extreme, highly sheltered shores are formed of fine silts and retain much organic matter. Even gentle water-flow over their surfaces will suspend some of the silts, clogging the filtration structures of suspension-feeders. The fine particle size of the muds and the abundant organic debris combine to produce anoxic conditions only a few millimetres below the surface. Few species can withstand these conditions, but the abundant food allows those that can to achieve large biomasses and high productivity. The small gastropod *Hydrobia*, for example, can achieve densities in excess of 100000 individuals per square metre in such areas. Detritus-feeding gastropod molluscs, annelid worms, amphipod crustaceans and, in the tropics, crabs are the dominant animals. Most feed by ingesting the surface millimetre or two of sediment (although some preliminary sorting into edible and non-edible material may take place), and digest out some items from among the inorganic content. The detritus-feeders are probably fairly catholic in their diets and will accept different items dependent on their availability and nutritional value. The polychaete worm *Nereis*, for example, will consume sediment and digest out, among other items, the meiofauna; it will take carrion, pieces of green alga, and living materials smaller than itself; and it can filter living and dead particles from suspension by use of a plug of cotton-wool-like mucus secreted across the neck of its burrow. Like other burrowers, *Nereis* must maintain a current of water through the tube in which it lives to bring in oxygen for respiration and for combating the reducing power of the surrounding sediment.

Shores intermediate in shelter between the two extremes described above provide a supply of sedimentary organic matter without excessive quantities of silt, and hence both suspension-feeders and deposit-feeders can live there. While wave-disturbed sands are mobile, and fine silts can be semi-liquid, muddy sand is firm and stable permitting the construction of permanent burrow-systems by species living in the substratum (infaunal species). Species diversity may therefore be high: a variety of tube-dwelling polychaete worms extend their filtration fans into the water at high tide, bivalve molluscs, prawns and other crustaceans, and further poly-chaete worms live below the surface while drawing down a current of water to filter, and gastropod molluscs, echino-derms, crabs and annelid worms feed on materials associated with the sediment itself. There is also a variety of predators, including molluscs and types of worm.

Fish come close to all these shores at high tide to feed, and may consume more invertebrates than do the wading birds more obvious to the human observer. Flatfish, including large numbers of juveniles, are characteristic high-tide predators, either seizing such parts of living animals as project above the sediment surface or else engulfing mouthfuls of sediment and sieving out the smaller organisms. Large flocks of wading birds are equally characteristic, probing the exposed sediment at low tide or following the tide as it ebbs and flows. Those species that follow the tide take both small organisms disturbed by the flooding water and also organisms that are following the ebb-tide down to their low-tide depth. The bird species that pick over or probe into the sediment select items from different depths in the sediment depending on the length of their bills (Fig. 7.7). Those with long bills (oyster-catchers, ibises, godwits, curlews and some of the larger sandpipers) can catch the deeper-burrowing bivalves and polychaete worms. The tips of their bills are both touch-sensitive and flexible, so that the end part can open and pick up their prey while the base remains unopened. Rather than probe randomly, the birds watch for signs of activity in or near the burrow openings (Fig. 7.8), and then strike when the chance of successful capture is high. Several species of duck also frequent soft-sediment shores, and pick or filter small organisms from the wet surface.

The sand microenvironment

Sand, wherever it occurs in terrestrial or aquatic habitats, is a protective environment which insulates against heat and cold as effectively as does as a solid, but it has some of the properties of a fluid. Animals can burrow through it, or swim if they are small enough to pass between the grains. These minute **interstitial** organisms depend on the presence of water held in the sand by capillary attraction. Even in hot deserts, such as the Namib desert of south-western Africa, the sand retains traces of water which are sufficient to sustain living algae at a depth of a few centimetres from the sun-scorched surface. The tortuous and narrow nature of the water channels has, however, a serious disadvantage, in that the diffusion of oxygen and nutrients is restricted. Below a certain depth in marine sand, for example, only specialised bacteria can survive.

Another serious problem for the interstitial fauna in marine and some freshwater environments is the danger of being washed out of the sand by water currents. Many species prudently burrow down into the sand before each high tide, following an innate rhythm of behaviour which is displayed even by the unicellular flagellate protozoa and diatom algae. Another adaptation is the behavioural response of most

interstitial organisms to contact with a solid surface: they cling tightly to the sand grains by means of specialised bristles, cilia or adhesive glands. This is called thigmotaxis. Indeed, some cannot be dislodged even by vigorous shaking of the sand in a jar of water.

The interstitial fauna is difficult to observe in this natural state, and the thigmotactic behaviour makes the organisms hard to extract. In one method, used by Uhlig, the sand is placed in a deep vessel and cooled at the top with frozen sea water. Many of the organisms flee downwards from the cold into a small volume of water placed below, which is free of sand grains. They may then be captured and studied. Such methods reveal a fauna rich in quantity and sometimes in variety, particularly from sands rich in organic material, such as those found in sheltered bays and estuaries. The microfauna may also be an important component even of apparently clean sand. Fenchel examined sand at a depth of 10 metres from the coast of Denmark, and found that the microfauna represented only 2% of the total mass of living material, which was composed mostly of large clams. Mass for mass, however, small organisms are metabolically more active than large ones, and Fenchel calcu-lated that the inconspicuous microfauna of this sand was responsible for one-third of the total oxygen consumption.

Because of the difficulties of observation the interstitial fauna was scarcely studied until the 1920s. Now many hundreds of characteristic interstitial species are known, and new ones continue to be described at a high rate. The interstitial spaces are small and most of the multicellular organisms found there are the smallest species of their group. All the major invertebrate types are represented as miniatures: the tiny mollusc *Caecum glabrum* is only 2 millimetres long, and the sea-cucumber *Leptosynapta minuta* is as small. On the other hand, the interstitial protozoa are often giants for their group, such as the ciliate *Helicoprorodon* which is 4 millimetres long.

Animals from quite different groups have come to resemble each other in this environment. The majority are to some degree worm-like or flattened, and in comparison to related non-interstitial organisms these little vermiform creatures are often simplified. For example, there are hydroid coelenterates with very few tentacles, and there is a tendency for organs which are normally found in pairs, such as testes, to be single. The cells composing these miniature organisms are not any smaller; rather, there are fewer cells per organ and, related to this, fewer eggs are produced. These simple organisms have sometimes been regarded as primitive ancestors of non-interstitial forms and this is reflected in names such as Archiannelida. It is more likely that they have become secondarily simplified as an adaptation to interstitial life, by loss of complex structures. A controversial case is that of the ciliated protozoans. Most ciliates, including the familiar *Paramecium*, have large nuclei which contain more DNA than do those of other organisms, and which are highly polyploid (they contain many copies of the genomic DNA, see section 1.5). Some interstitial members of this group have nuclei of the ordinary type, small and diploid,

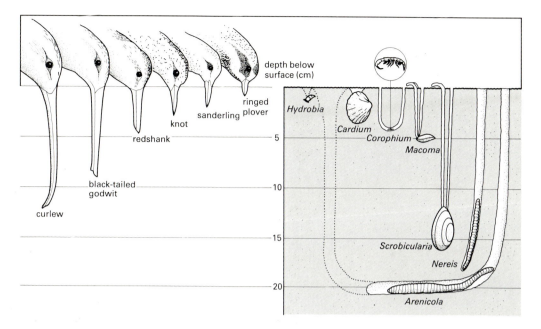

Fig. 7.7. The lengths of the bills of various wading birds in relation to the positions within the sediment of their infaunal prey items.

and it is not known whether these are 'living relics' or have become secondarily simplified.

Because of its insulating properties, and the low rate of diffusion of dissolved substances, sand can sustain large gradients of temperature, light, oxygen and nutrients. This means that a small quantity of sand can contain many quite different microenvironments lying at different depths. This phenomenon leads to a pronounced vertical zonation of the microfauna and microflora. Fenchel has worked on the shore and sea-bed of the Baltic coast of Denmark, in areas particularly suitable for study because they have little or no tide. By inserting three tubes vertically into the sand, and pulling out a column of contents (a 'core'), it was possible to find the distribution of many types of organism with depth. Below a certain depth, which varied with the season and the weather, the colour of the sand darkened because of the presence of sulphides, oxygen became scarce and the sulphide ion (HS^{-1}) was abundant. Mainly because of the latter, a wire pushed progressively down into the sand recorded a negative electrical potential which increased to approximately 0.5 volts relative to

Fig. 7.8. (left) Surface burrow marks. The star-shaped mark is made by Scrobicularia. Lugworm (Arenicola) casts can also be seen.

Fig. 7.9. (below) Vertical distribution of interstitial fauna and electric potential in a sandy beach in Denmark.

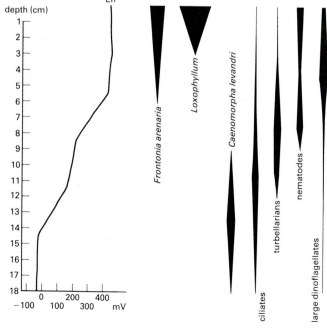

Fig. 7.10. A rocky shore at Tresco, Isles of Scilly, showing zonation of algae.

the surface (Fig. 7.9). Fenchel pointed out the importance of the steepest part of the voltage against depth curve: it marks the upper boundary of the store of reduced organic compounds resulting from decomposition in the sand. Many bacteria use these compounds, and in turn are a source of food for the interstitial fauna. If the boundary rises to the surface of the sand, coloured patches of sulphur-bacteria develop, with a characteristic fauna of ciliates and nematodes. The sulphur-bacteria carry out photosynthesis in a way different from ordinary green plants, using hydrogen sulphide instead of water as a source of reducing power, and unlike green plants, therefore, they do not give off oxygen. These bacteria probably resemble those present in the oxygen-free waters of the earth before plants or animals appeared: they are the real relics of the interstitial world.

Rocky shores and kelp forests

Where waves or currents are particularly strong, or where coastal cliffs descend to well below the low-water mark, the intertidal zone is rocky. This type of habitat may continue out sublittorally (below the low-tide mark). Water movement is so vigorous that sediments are maintained in suspension and may indeed aid the water in eroding away the land. The extent to which the rocks in the intertidal zone are dissected by erosion into boulders or large stones depends on many factors, including the type of rock, its angle of dip, the frequency of bedding or fracture planes, the magnitude of the platform cut by wave action, if one is present, and the pattern of erosion by frost and other atmospheric processes. Hence rocky shores range from whole beaches of boulders to vertical rock-faces continuous with the cliff above. Since fissures, caves the underside of boulders and other relatively sheltered microhabitats provide sites for a wider range of organisms than would a sheer, smooth rock face, a richer diversity of organisms is found on highly dissected rocky shores. The other major factor influencing the species diversity of organisms on these shores is the relative degree of exposure to waves. As seen for

beaches of soft sediment, shores of intermediate exposure often support the most diverse faunas and floras.

One of the most striking features of the distribution of organisms on rocky shores is the phenomenon of **zonation**: the majority of species each occupy only part of the vertical range between the high-water and low-water marks. This can sometimes give the impression that the whole shore is divided into distinct zones, each characterised by one or a few species (Fig. 7.10). Where the fauna and flora are richer, though, it is found that the zones inhabited by individual species do overlap. The zonation patterns of the larger or more abundant organisms do not automatically indicate the pattern with which every species is zoned. Three general zones of dominant species have however been recognised as occurring throughout the world.

At the highest tidal levels, wetted only by splash from breaking waves or by the largest of spring tides, is the real transitional region between land and sea, inhabited, particularly in crevices, by a few terrestrial species tolerant of salt and occasional submergence, and by the marine forms most resistant to desiccation. Small winkles are particularly characteristic, as are various encrusting lichens and blue-green algae. This **supralittoral fringe** is most extensively developed on shores subject to the heaviest wave action, because here splash and spray may be thrown well above the high-water level of the sea.

The second zone, the **littoral zone**, extends from the lower limit of the supralittoral fringe, often marked by the first appearance of barnacles, down to that part of the shore uncovered only by spring tides or, on exposed coasts, uncovered only when the lowest of spring tides occurs in calm weather. Characteristically, and especially under exposed conditions, the whole of this zone is dominated by acorn barnacles, but it is subject to much local variation. In several regions, various species successfully compete for space with the barnacles over the lower parts of the zone. Mussels, limpets, polychaete worms inhabiting calcareous tubes, and in the tropics colonial soft corals are frequently codominant or

Fig. 7.11. Rocky habitats. (a) A rock pool at Thurlestone. The inhabitants include limpets and sea-anemones. (b) The wall of a sea-cave at Signy Island, Australia, inhabited by a variety of animals including sponges and starfish.

183

Fig. 7.12. Algae on the lower shore at Tresco, Isles of Scilly. The flat fronds and stalk of an individual of Laminaria digitata *can be seen.*

dominant. In northern temperate latitudes, fucoid sea-weeds (wracks) may cover all but the upper portion of the zone in all but the most exposed localities. In Britain, for example, a classic succession of four fucoids, channelled wrack (*Pelvetia canaliculata*), spiral wrack (*Fucus spiralis*), bladder wrack (*F. vesiculosus*) and saw wrack (*F. serratus*), occurs down moderately exposed shores, but this zonation of sea-weeds is only found in parts of North-west Europe.

The third zone is transitional between the intertidal region and the permanently submerged **sublittoral zone**, and its rich fauna contains many species only briefly exposed to the air by the lowest of tides. Bare areas of rock are typically encrusted by coralline red algae generally called Lithothamnion. In temperate latitudes and in regions of upwelling water (see section 6.1) large brown algae, the kelps, are dominant, and these may be only the upper members of large sublittoral kelp forests. In warmer latitudes, the zone may be dominated by large ascidians (sea-squirts), and in all regions small red algae form a turf-like understorey.

The patterns of zonation of individual species, both the dominant species as well as the myriad of associated types, appear to be determined by two types of factor. Any rocky shore contains two gradients, one of increasing physical harshness on progression up the shore (fluctuations in temperature and salinity increase, for example, and the problems of desiccation become more intense), and a second gradient of increasing biological harshness down the shore (with competition for food and/or space, and pressure from predators, increasing towards the sublittoral regions). The upper limit to the distribution of a rocky-shore species seems to be determined by the first gradient, while the lower limit is set by the second. In other words, species that are competitively weak or sensitive to predators can inhabit an area relatively free of these biological pressures by adapting to the more physically and climatically rigorous regions further up the shore, but there is a limit to the extent to which the anatomy and physiology of a marine species can be adapted to a life spent in air rather than in sea water. Therefore, the marine fauna and

flora become progressively more impoverished higher up the shore, but are augmented by the relatively few terrestrial species that can withstand periodic submergence in the sea.

Highly exposed rocky shores may be dominated by only a few species because of the severe nature of this environment, and the most sheltered of shores may be clothed in a lush tangle of large wracks or other vegetation to the exclusion of all else. The majority of rocky beaches with an intermediate degree of exposure provide a wide diversity of types of habitat capable of supporting a wealth of species (Fig. 7.11). Various organisms provide habitats for smaller species: the holdfasts of kelps give shelter to small polychaete worms, nemertine worms, and gastropod and bivalve molluscs, while several small animals inhabit empty barnacle shells. The undersides of boulders are not accessible to large predators, and encrusting sea-squirts, bryozoans (sea-mats), sponges and hydroids together with sedentary polychaete worms, crustaceans, sea-urchins and star-fish are safe there from predation by fish; there are, however, predators such as nudibranchs (sea-slugs) and pycnogonids (sea-spiders) which are often smaller than their prey species and which can occupy confined spaces too. Rock pools (Fig 7.11) permit organisms which require to be covered permanently by sea water to occur higher up the shore than otherwise allowed by the range of the tide. Rock pools, and many other microhabitats within a rocky shore, support a fauna of grazing and suspension-feeding animals that is richer than most other intertidal zones, excepting only coral reefs and some areas of muddy sand.

The actions of waves and currents may maintain clean rock surfaces below the intertidal zone, and in areas rich in nutrients these are dominated by the kelps down to the greatest depths at which photosynthesis is possible. Kelps are large brown algae such as *Laminaria* and have an attachment structure called a holdfast, a tough stalk, and one or more flat blades or fronds which grow continuously from their bases (Fig. 7.12). The largest species can attain lengths in excess of 50 metres, with the floating frond being borne up by the moving water, or in some species by gas-filled bladders. The kelp forests are one of the most productive ecosystems of the world, with the giant kelps, for example, being able to grow at a rate of 25 centimetres a day; the kelps also release copious quantities of dissolved organic compounds into the water. Vast beds of these algae can fringe the coast, yet they are consumed by relatively few animals, namely certain sea-urchins, and some sea-hares (opisthobranch molluscs). The sea-urchins graze the early stages of the life-cycle of the kelps, and can even climb up the fronds and bear them down with their weight, thereby making them available to other individuals on the rock surface. The Californian sea-hare can eat half a metre of stalk per day, apparently rather noisily, but the majority of kelp-forest production enters the food-web in the form of detritus, joining the large pool of plant and algal debris from the other types of coastal habitat.

Coral reefs

Coral reefs are productive, diverse in species and beautiful, the peak of the marine ecosystem. The corals which dominate these reefs are often colonial and are coelenterates, relatives of the sea-anemones. They deposit an external and protective cup-like structure made of calcium carbonate, called a calyx, from which they extend to feed, mostly at night and when covered by water, and into which they can withdraw to minimise the risks of predation and desiccation (Fig. 7.13). The calcium carbonate accumulated over many years by corals and by other organisms with the same encrusting ability (coralline algae, molluscs, and so on) become cemented by chemical, algal or microbial action and forms extensive reefs along coasts and around islands. Coral reefs occur scattered over an area of 190 million square kilometres of the globe, wherever there is a suitable substratum within the lighted waters of the tropics beyond the influence of continental sediments and away from the zones of upwelling of cool water in the eastern parts of the oceans' basins.

The formation of modern reefs has been closely determined by the rise in sea-level that has occured during the last 12 000 years. Although species of coral are found in most latitudes and at most depths, reefs are produced only in shallow warm waters: their maximum development occurs in depths of less than 10 metres and at temperatures of 25 to 29 °C. As the sea-level has risen, so some coralline organisms have been able to grow and keep pace with it, remaining in surface waters on top of a biologically created ridge or platform of calcium carbonate. The boundary between each layer of the reef marks a zone which was once its surface. Corals can do no more than keep pace with rising water levels, since they cannot survive the desiccation resulting from prolonged exposure to air, but not all reefs have in fact managed to keep pace. When a combination of actual rising sea-levels and local sea-bed subsidence is too great for the upward growth rate to compensate, then the reef dies, and dead reefs eventually lie some distance below the surface. Where, however, the corals have been able to grow

upwards with the rising water, reefs now exist as **fringing reefs** (where corals have colonised the shallow seas created by drowning of coastal land), as **offshore barrier reefs** (where a coastal reef is now separated from the modern coastline by a sea or lagoon overlying inundated land), and as **atolls** (in which a central lagoon marks the position of the submerged island around which the reef originally grew) (Figs 7.14 and 7.15).

Two features of reefs seem paradoxical: their productivity is enormous, yet many are situated in the middle of the tropical oceans which are poor in food and nutrients (see section 6.3), and secondly they appear to be dominated by consumers. It is comparatively easy to find the producers required to support the feeding animals, as although many of the photosynthesisers are not obvious or are not green they are nevertheless abundant. Several algae are encrusted with calcium carbonate as a protection against herbivores and/or the powers of the waves. Others, filamentous green algae growing on and among the reef limestone, are grazed down by herbivores so rapidly that their biomass on the surface of the reefs is very small, yet their productivity is high. A third category of algae, the **zooxanthellae**, are symbionts found within the cells of most of the reef coelenterates including the corals, as well as in some molluscs (such as the giant clam) and sea-squirts (see section 10.2). Zooxanthellae are the non-motile form of species of dinoflagellate, and can occur in coral tissues at a density of 30 000 individuals per cubic millimetre.

The reasons why these islands of biological activity can have a photosynthetic productivity 3000 times that attained in the surrounding water are more complex. Nitrogen is generally regarded as the limiting nutrient in the open oceans, and films of blue-green algae, capable of fixing gaseous atmospheric nitrogen, occur on reefs. Much of the fixed nitrogen is released into the surrounding water, from which it can be withdrawn by other photosynthetic algae, and herbivores grazing on the blue-green algae also release this nitrogen to the environment via their excretion. A second, and very important, means of achieving the high productivity involves the efficient cycling of those nutrients incorporated into reef tissues over many previous years, and this cycling is both internal and external.

Internal cycling of nutrients concerns the symbiotic zoo-xanthellae and their role in the nutrition of their hosts, the soft and the stony corals. Corals are anatomically carnivorous, with batteries of stinging cells on their tentacles, similar to sea-anemones, but at least some soft corals have never been observed to catch any items of food, and for others the supply of plankton may be insufficient to meet their minimum requirements. Corals are also known to consume detrital materials and to take up dissolved organic compounds from the water; some are even suspension-feeders, capturing planktonic bacteria on threads of mucus. In the majority of species of coral, however, the zooxanthellae are likely to be important nutritionally, although the animal host cannot digest its algal symbionts; indeed, if the host is starved or otherwise disturbed, the zooxanthellae develop into their motile form and leave.

Fig. 7.13. Corals. (a) Goniopora, *showing extended polyps. (b) A soft coral from the Maldives. (c) The soft coral* Dendronephthya *from the Sudanese Red Sea. (d) A mushroom coral,* Fungia.

The zooxanthellae are algae photosynthesising in the normal manner, but the carbon dioxide required comes both from the respiration of the coral and from the environment, ammonia as a source of nitrogen is the excretory product of the coral, and other nutrients are obtained as available in the water or from the metabolic processes of the host. The algae also benefit from living inside the protective environment of the tissues of a host. On the other hand, each coral stimulates its zooxanthellae to release soluble organic products of photosynthesis, and renders the algal cell walls leaky to facilitate the rapid diffusion out of these substances. This organic material then becomes incorporated into the tissues of the coral, and the circuit is completed when the breakdown products of the corals'

metabolism diffuse back to the algae. Plankton can be removed as food by the corals from the surrounding water, and the zooxanthellae can take nitrogen and phosphorus from the same source, but within the coral–algae association there is an internal cycling of nutrients, greatly reducing the rates of loss of these scarce commodities to the environment, and increasing productivity.

External cycling of nutrients through the food-web also appears to be highly efficient in the coral system. The size of the animal populations is close to, if not actually at, the maximum carrying capacity of their habitat (see section 5.2), and so food for each herbivore is scarce even though in absolute terms algal productivity may be very large. There is thus a large selective

Fig. 7.14. A lionfish (Pterios volitans) on a coral reef in the Egyptian Red Sea.

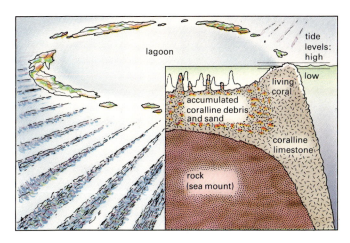

Fig. 7.15. A diagrammatic section through a coral atoll. At the surface, coral islands surround a lagoon.

advantage for efficiency in finding, capture and utilisation of food: for example, nutrients are taken up very rapidly by the algae, and filamentous green algae are rapidly consumed by the abundant herbivores. This again minimises the opportunities for loss of nutrients from the reef system. A very high proportion of the environmental pool of nutrients is maintained within living tissues, a marked parallel with the peak of terrestrial ecosystems, the tropical rain-forests. Nevertheless, opportunities to enlarge the accumulated pool of nutrients result in more vigorous growth, as shown by the corals in closest proximity to the surrounding ocean.

The role of the symbiotic zooxanthellae is not restricted to nutritional aspects of their host's biology. In the stony corals, they may also permit the rapid rate of deposition of calcium carbonate that is essential in maintaining the living reef organisms in warm surface waters. Corals lay down calcium carbonate many times faster in the light or when zooxanthellae are present, than in the dark or when zooxanthellae have been removed. Calcium ions and bicarbonate ions are in equilibrium with carbon dioxide and precipitated calcium carbonate, and this positive effect of light and algae suggests that the photosynthesis of the zooxanthellae provides a sink for carbon dioxide, forcing the reaction towards precipitation of calcium carbonate. Changes in the rate of precipitation under conditions of darkness, however, indicate that other mechanisms are also involved.

The deposition of limestone by corals and other reef organisms is of immense importance to the seas now, as it has been at various times in the past: several ranges of hills are fossil reefs. The protection of their calcareous exoskeletons, together with the stinging cells on their tentacles, provide corals with a defence against potential predators. Few species appear to prey on stony corals, although rapid rises in the level of one predator, the crown-of-thorns star-fish, have recently occurred.

The sediment between the coral heads and that flooring the lagoons of coral atolls derives largely from the calcium carbonate deposited by reef organisms. Some fish bite off pieces of coral and grind the material in their guts in order to gain access to the small proportion of living tissue; other animals, such as sponges, polychaete worms and bivalves, bore into the coral, much as comparable species excavate burrows in limestone or chalk. Both types reduce the coralline rock to fine coral sand, as do waves pulverising coral heads, coralline algae and mollusc shells. In coral lagoons, this sand is often colonised by sea-grasses and by dependent communities of deposit-feeders and their predators.

7.4 AQUATIC SYSTEMS

Estuaries

Estuaries are amalgams of various intertidal habitats, commonly with mud-flats backed by salt-marsh or mangrove-swamp, rocky headlands if the estuary cuts through hills or hard rocks, perhaps sandy beaches near the mouth, and sea-grass meadows at lower tidal levels (Fig. 7.16). The special characteristic of estuaries is that they are the regions in which freshwater discharged by rivers mixes with coastal sea water. Along many coastlines, they are also the areas experiencing the greatest shelter from wave action, and so particles of organic detritus may accumulate, as well as silts, and estuaries invariably contain abundant food for deposit-feeders.

Most modern estuaries occupy drowned river valleys, although several coastal inlets which have the physiographic form of estuaries, and many biological features in common with them, do not show the diagnostic gradient of salinity between freshwater at the head of the inlet and sea water at the mouth. Where the drowning of low-lying coastal land has not intercepted a major river system, the estuary is in fact only a partially land-locked arm of the sea containing undiluted sea water. The close similarities in the faunas and floras of these systems and of true estuaries suggests that the main factor determining the nature of the organisms present is not the particular salinity, but the type of food-rich habitats found in highly sheltered regions.

The salinity of estuaries can be even greater than that of the

Fig. 7.16. The Thames estuary on the Essex coast showing the river, flats and salt-marshes.

adjacent sea: in the dry season of some subtropical areas, the rate of loss of water from the surface of the estuary through evaporation can exceed the rate of input of water by rivers and rain, and hence the salinity increases with time while these conditions persist. Conversely, some tropical rivers, for example the Amazon and Zaire, discharge so much freshwater that the flaring mouth of the river, which one might assume to be the estuary, only contains freshwater, and the zone of mixing occurs out at sea.

Apart from a few freshwater organisms which can penetrate estuaries to a small extent, the aquatic inhabitants of estuaries are essentially similar to marine types and many do occur in the sea as well. These organisms are faced with the physiological problem of life in an environment of non-optimal and/or varying salinity. The solution may lie in appropriate patterns of behaviour, such as movement within the estuary to maintain the animal in an environment of relatively constant and favourable salinity. Less mobile species must endure fluctuations, and especially reductions, in external salinity, and accordingly have evolved the ability to regulate their salt balance so as to maintain their cellular fluids within acceptable levels of concentration (see section 2.4). This **homeostasis** may be carried out at the cellular level or by specific organ systems, but the problems remain the same: water from a dilute external environment tends to enter the tissues along an osmotic gradient, while particular ions will tend to diffuse out of the tissues down their own concentration gradients. These ionic problems are aggravated by the necessity to pump out the excess water, as scarce ions will then be lost as well. Some **osmoconforming** species are relatively tolerant and let the concentration of their body fluids equilibrate passively with the environment, while their individual cells regulate osmotically and ionically, often aided by the ability to adjust the intracellular levels of osmotically active non-essential amino-acids. Other species have reduced surface permeabilities, localising the problem, and centres of active uptake of ions from the environment, sometimes coupled with an ability to discharge the excess body fluids after ions have been re-

absorbed; the cells of these **osmoregulatory** species are bathed by fluids more constant in their concentration as a result of the regulatory processes performed by the whole body.

At any given point within estuaries the salinity can change rapidly, for example with the tidal flow in and out of sea water, with changes in the volume of river flow, and with changes in the mixing patterns of the freshwater and salty waters. Organisms living in the estuarine environment therefore have to adapt not only to a salinity different from that of the sea, but also a salinity that fluctuates.

Lagoons

Organisms inhabiting coastal lagoons are exposed to a salinity that is much more constant over time than is that to which estuarine creatures are exposed. Lagoons chiefly differ from estuaries in the interrelated characteristics of the width of their communication with the adjacent sea (the mouths of estuaries are broad, those of lagoons are narrow) and the volume of freshwater flowing through (lagoons typically receive a relatively minor flow in from rivers). Although, therefore, lagoons often have salinities differing from that of sea water, they are relatively stable in any one geographical region and vary only with seasonal changes in the ratio of evaporation to precipitation. Fluctuating salinity is hence less prevalent, as indeed is variation in the water level because the relatively narrow connection between the lagoon and the adjacent sea dampens the tidal oscillations of the parent water mass.

Although similar to estuaries in a number of respects, lagoons form in a different manner. Characteristically, coastal lagoons are elongated areas of very shallow coastal sea semi-isolated behind sand barriers which have developed as spits or offshore sand-bars. If the tidal range is small and the input of freshwater minor, the sand barrier may become complete and the lagoon evolve eventually into a coastal freshwater lake. Alternatively, if the tidal range is large, it may be sufficiently powerful to maintain gaps in the barrier, and the region comes to resemble a wadden, a shallow marine bay semi-enclosed by a

Fig. 7.17. A line of washed-up pebbles, shells and sea-weeds forms the strandline on this flat sandy beach.

chain of offshore barrier islands, such as the Waddenzee of the Netherlands, Germany and Denmark. Lagoons are common in the tropics and in higher latitudes; their distribution is complementary to that of coral reefs, in that lagoons require mobile sediment for their formation, whereas mobile sediment smothers the sessile corals.

Somewhat atypical lagoons form in areas, such as in Britain, where the input of energy from the waves is high. Here shingle can be moved onshore and seal the mouths of small drowned river valleys. Such lagoons are normally aligned perpendicularly to the coastline, while other lagoons generally run parallel to the coast.

The faunas and floras of lagoons are also closely comparable to those of estuaries; both environments comprise a similar set of types of habitat. In any given region, the faunas may differ at the specific level, though not at the generic level, and pairs of sibling species are found in the two systems. It is by no means clear why this is so. In some cases it would appear that the estuarine sibling is more vigorous and competitively superior, and small, relatively ephemeral lagoons may provide a refuge for species which are sensitive to interspecific competition in the more rigorous and fluctuating environment outside the barrier.

Shelf seas

Coastal shelf seas are shallow and, as light can penetrate to the sea-bed in areas less than 30 metres or so deep, benthic photosynthesis can occur over much of their area. The shallowness of the seas also permits the wind to keep the whole water column mixed, so that nutrients sedimenting out of the photic zone (in the form of dead phytoplanktonic algae or the faecal pellets of the herbivores), and those released into the water by the animals of the sea-bed, can be reinjected into surface waters. Further, some shelf seas receive water which has upwelled from deep zones offshore, and such water is also particularly rich in nutrients (see section 6.3). In addition, since the resident consumers in several coastal habitats, including salt-marshes, mangrove-swamps, sea-grass meadows and kelp-forests, do not use the primary photosynthetic production efficiently, normal tidal and current movements, as well as storms, may remove plant matter from these systems and carry it out to the sea nearby. On average, river water also contains twice the concentration of nutrients per unit volume than does sea water, and groundwater, which also discharges on the coast, probably contains even higher concentrations. Coastal shelf seas therefore receive an input of inorganic nutrients and dissolved organic materials leached from the soil over the 100 million square kilometres of the land, together with the particulate detritus from the semi-aquatic and submerged fringing stands of coastal plants.

For all these reasons, coastal seas contain high concentrations of those substances that encourage both primary and secondary production. Many fish of commercial importance use the shallowest shelf regions, which are most favourably positioned to receive the inputs of nutrients listed above, as nursery grounds for their rapidly growing young; and most coastal benthic species produce planktonic larvae, many of which exploit the rich coastal populations of phytoplankton. Coastally nesting sea-birds fish in these waters, as do schools of dolphins and porpoises, and the shelf seas make an overwhelming contribution to human fisheries.

Objects stranded on beaches after storms, most frequently in a high-level drift-line, often provide the only indication of the nature of life seaward of the intertidal zone (Fig. 7.17). In Britain, common objects of the drift-line are the bivalved shells of horse-mussels (*Modiolus*) and, locally, oysters; the egg-cases and shells of the edible whelk; the dried fronds of the bryozoan horn wrack, formed of thousands of small rectangular boxes each originally containing a filter-feeding polyp and created by the repeated asexual division of a single founding individual; pieces of a variety of sponges; large hydrozoan colonies; and the occasional star-fish. All these come from a community, called the *Modiolus* community, that is dominated by suspension-feeders, although it contains representatives of all feeding types: the whelk, for example, is a scavenger, and the star-fish is a predator. This community carpets the sea-bottom in shallow water where suitable substrata, mainly mollusc shells, are found. Beneath the surface of the sediment occurs an equally rich shelf fauna of bivalves, polychaete worms, amphipod crustaceans and echinoderms, to consider only the larger forms, but fewer of these are cast on to shores. Those with hard parts, however, may eventually become part of the terrestrial environment when their surrounding sediment is compressed into sedimentary rock and raised above sea-level: such organisms from the bottom of shelf seas are among the most commonly preserved fossils.

Fig. 7.18. *The marsupials, isolated on the island of Australia, have radiated to fill a variety of ecological niches. (a) The koala* (Phascolarctos), *which is arboreal and feeds only on* Eucalyptus. *(b) The ground-dwelling, herbivorous red-necked wallaby* (Thylogale thetis).*(c) The brush-tailed possum* (Trichosurus vulpecula), *a smaller arboreal form. (d) The wombat* (Vombatus ursinus) *which lives in burrows.*

7.5 REMOTE ISLANDS

Islands vary enormously in their size and distance away from the nearest large land mass. The smallest of islands may carry no terrestrial organisms at all, while the largest may show no essential biological differences from any other land mass. Islands which lie within a few hundred metres of a larger block of land may be identical to a similarly sized piece of that land, while those isolated in the middle of an ocean may show a whole set of peculiar and characteristic features. Relatively remote islands and their terrestrial faunas will be examined here.

The vast majority of terrestrial organisms disperse over land or through the air, and there is only a slight chance that any will accidentally reach a small island well away from the mainland. For this reason, such islands possess relatively few species. Those species which do reach remote islands and become successfully established are also likely to have small popu-

lations, because of the small size of the island and because the populations have been founded by very few original colonists. These considerations have profound genetic and evolutionary consequences (see section 11.1). The few founding individuals will carry only a small sample of the gene pool of the parent stock, and so from the moment of successful establishment the ancestral and descendant populations differ genetically. Thereafter, through the process of random genetic drift to which small populations are susceptible, the island gene pool is likely to become even smaller, and more divergent from that of the parental stock. Many founding populations are therefore genetically ill-equipped to cope with their new environment, and speedily become extinct, but the few species which do persist are soon sufficiently different from the ancestral stock to become separate species, **endemic** to (only found on) the island colonised.

Birds and insects, being capable of flight, are among the more likely animal colonists of distant islands. Flocks or

Fig. 7.19. The giant Hood Island tortoise from the Galapagos Islands.

swarms blown off course by stormy weather may make landfall on an archipelago of islands, and processes of genetic diversification may result in each island containing its own endemic species of that group of birds or insects.

Since remote islands are colonised successfully by only few species, any founding population will inhabit an environment in which there is little or no competition with other species (**interspecific competition**). As the population size increases, however, competition with members of the same species (**intraspecific competiton**) may become intense because small islands possess limited food resources, and all the available habitat will soon be occupied, with emigration effectively impossible. An ecological category which will be markedly under-represented is that of predators, because the random arrival of colonising predators will seldom coincide with a sufficiently large pre-existing population of prey to support them. In the absence of emigration, of competition with other species, and of predation, animal populations may soon attain the maximum levels that their small habitat can carry, and are normally then limited by the amount of food available.

The intense intraspecific competition but no interspecific competition that occurs on remote islands appears in a number of cases to have brought about the radiation of island faunas and floras into a variety of adaptive forms. When the food resources being exploited by a particular species become relatively scarce, even though other potential foods are abundant but unexploited, there will be a selective pressure in favour of a widening of the diet. If only some members of a population become able to take the new food, and especially if these are relatively isolated geographically from the remainder of the population, divergence into two species may eventually result. The new species may remain in a separate valley, or on a different island, or can extend its geographical distribution back into the parental range. A single type of organism may thereby give rise to a whole range of species each exploiting a different food or other environmental resource.

Classic examples of such radiations from a single stock in the absence of other potential competitors are various insect groups in Hawaii (see Fig. 11.4), the Galapagos finches, marsupials in Australia (Fig. 7.18), and lemurs in Madagascar. In the latter two cases, the original colonisation was probably effected overland when the island, as it exists today, was part of a larger land mass; but the subsequent isolation of Australia and Madagascar has prevented access by potentially superior competitors which evolved subsequently on other land masses. The fate of these sets of endemic island species after the arrival of superior competitors is demonstrated by the fauna of edentate and subungulate animals which evolved on the island South America during the Tertiary era (see section 14.3). Reconnection of South America to North America permitted the entry of mammal groups originating outside the island, and many of the endemic South American species became extinct. The continued survival of the very ancient reptile the tuatara on islands off New Zealand may owe much to the failure of other groups to reach the islands.

The intense intraspecific competition experienced by species endemic to islands may be the cause of the gigantism and longevity displayed, for example, by the giant tortoises of the Galapagos (Fig. 7.19), Aldabra and elsewhere. The reproductive strategy most likely to contribute the largest number of genes to future generations, under conditions of high mortality due to competition, is to produce at any one time a small number of large offspring, each of which can be given a large amount of food reserves or parental care to provide it with an initial competitive advantage, or to protect it from competitive interactions, until it can 'hold its own'. This requires the parental organism to survive long enough to produce a requisite minimum total of offspring. If growth is continuous throughout life, adults will achieve large overall sizes, often of competitive advantage, both in behavioural contexts and in the quantity of food reserves that can be carried.

In birds, large size may make flight energetically expensive, and flight under these circumstances may even be disadvantageous since being airborne increases the chance of being blown away from the small island that is inhabited. Flight is often an important means of avoiding predators, but predators are likely to be scarce or absent on islands, and thus there are no disadvantages attendant on flightlessness. Many islands contain or contained species of large flightless birds, such as the dodo and Galapagos cormorant, but the advent of the human species as a predator rapidly led to the extinction of the dodo which could not use flight to escape.

Further reading

Barnes, R.S.K. *Estuarine biology* (2nd edn). London: Edward Arnold, 1984.

Barnes, R.S.K. (Editor) *The coastline.* London: Wiley, 1977.

Barnes, R.S.K. *Coastal lagoons.* Cambridge: Cambridge University Press, 1980.

Barnes, R.S.K. and Hughes, R.N. *Introduction to marine ecology.* Oxford: Blackwell Scientific, 1982.

Brafield, A.E. *Life in sandy shores.* London: Edward Arnold, 1978.

Phillips, R.C. and McRoy, C.P. (Editors) *Handbook of seagrass biology.* New York: Garland, 1980.

Ranwell, D.S. *Ecology of salt marshes and sand dunes.* London: Chapman and Hall, 1972.

Schäfer, W. *Ecology and palaeoecology of marine environments.* Edinburgh: Oliver and Boyd, 1972.

Stephenson, T.A. and Stephenson, A. *Life between the tidemarks on rocky shores.* San Francisco: Freeman, 1972.

8 Terrestrial Environments

8.1 SOILS

Soil is the material on that part of the surface of the earth not covered by the sea in which plants may grow. It ranges in depth from a few millimetres to many metres, and may be entirely absent, as on the ice of the polar regions. It is composed of mineral material, which has usually been weathered, often to produce new substances such as clays; additions from the atmosphere, such as water; some organic matter; and living organisms.

Soils can be understood by considering four factors which influence their formation, their present distribution and their characteristics. These factors are the parent materials of the soil, the climate during its formation and at present, the vegetation during its formation and at present, and the topography of the site. These four categories are not however totally separate, for example the climate will affect the vegetation, but they are useful divisions.

The parent material, the original substance from which soils have been formed, is often extremely important. For example, sandstones give rise to sandy soils, and limestones often give rise to shallow soils with little mineral matter (besides limestone fragments) and large amounts of organic matter. Sometimes it is not obvious what the parent material might be; this is true when loess (wind-blown particles) or glacial till is deposited over surfaces, or when thin geological strata have completely weathered to give soils which now overlie different strata.

The composition of soil depends both on the mineral composition of the parent material and on the results of weathering. Weathering is the process by which substances are dissolved, chemically changed or physically disturbed. Some materials such as quartz (a form of silicon dioxide) are very resistant to weathering, while others are less resistant and may be altered to form clays. Some are easily altered and removed, for example the calcium carbonate of limestone which dissolves in water containing carbon dioxide.

Climate affects the formation of soil directly through the effects of rainfall, evaporation and temperature on weathering and leaching. Leaching is the result of the movement of water down through the soil removing dissolved substances and particles in suspension. The balance between rainfall and evaporation is crucial: if evaporation is greater than rainfall the predominant effect will be to create horizons (horizontal layers) in the soil in which certain compounds such as calcium carbonate are concentrated.

The climatic history is also important, particularly with respect to the world climatic changes that occurred in the Pleistocene. During this epoch the ice-caps extended from the poles, although very variably (approximately to London and Hamburg in Europe, and to just south of Chicago in the USA), tropical regions became drier, so that the extent of land capable of carrying tropical rain-forest was much reduced, tree-lines and snow-lines were lower on mountains, and sea-levels became lower all over the globe. These changes in climate are important for at least four reasons. First, many areas in cool temperate regions had their soils removed completely by glacial action. Secondly, the glaciers produced a mass of material of various sorts, such as clays, sand and rock-flour (finely divided rock material) which were distributed over the surface of the land and subsequently became the parent materials for the formation of new soils. Thirdly, in certain areas such as Australia drier climates resulted in hardening of laterite layers (layers of iron and aluminium oxides in soils), a process which was irreversible. Finally, subsequent rises in sea-level created extensive new waterlogged areas, as in the Netherlands and Florida.

Vegetation affects soil because it provides organic matter. This organic matter can be of various forms; it may be a distinct upper layer which may be **peat** (usually waterlogged) or **mor humus** (not waterlogged and usually of low pH and without earthworms), or it may be mixed with mineral matter to form **mull humus** (the pH is usually moderate to high and earthworms are usually present). Organic matter affects many of the physical and chemical parameters characterising the soil, including soil pH (the degree of acidity or alkalinity), the cation exchange capacity (the ability to hold cations such as the important nutrients potassium, calcium and magnesium), the drainage of soils and the degree of aeration.

There are many specific effects of plants on soils. For example, some plants commonly produce litter that does not decompose rapidly. This leads to an accumulation of organic matter, the formation of organic acids, and an increased cation exchange capacity, which in turn allows the build-up of hydrogen ions, thus lowering the pH. The organic acids cause leaching of cations and further falls in pH resulting in nutrient-poor soils, a process called podzolisation that is not easy to reverse. In the north temperate zone, soils under pine trees are commonly podzolised.

Topography is important mainly through its effects on drainage. Soils in the bottoms of gullies and in hollows are better supplied with water than are those on ridges and slopes. The movement of water down a slope is often coupled with the movement of important nutrients and fine particles, so that vegetation in hollows is often better supplied with nutrients and may be composed of species different from those on ridges. The soils which form in an area as a result of differences in topography are called a **catena**.

The important characteristics of a soil that can influence the vegetation are its drainage and aeration, its fertility, and the living organisms in it. Soil drainage and aeration are affected by many things, but particularly by topography and by the mineral and organic compositions of the soil. In well-drained soils plants may experience water shortage; in poorly drained soils waterlogging may lead to low oxygen concentrations leading to root death. Soil fertility can really only be established for particular species or groups of species and then only by growing plants in soils or making observations of vegetation. There are, however, important and commonly

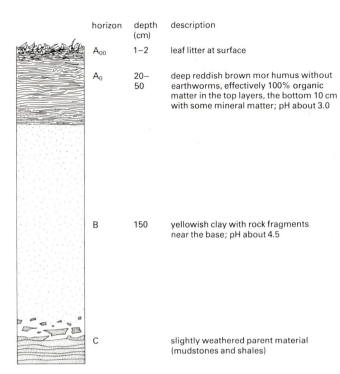

Fig. 8.1. Diagram showing layers in a montane forest soil from Jamaica.

measured characteristics of soils which are related to fertility. These include the soil pH, the cation exchange capacity (the ability to bind important nutrients such as ammonium, calcium, magnesium and potassium), and the amounts of extractable nitrate and phosphate. Many plant species have particular nutrient requirements for vigorous growth which cannot be met by certain soils of low fertility; this results in differences in the vegetation on soils of differing fertility. Living organisms within the soil affect soil fertility through mediating decomposition and through mycorrhizal associations, while other organisms may be pests or cause plant diseases.

There are many classifications of soils. One of the most widely used is the USDA (United States Department of Agriculture) 7th approximation, which is a hierarchical classification with orders, suborders, groups, subgroups, families and series. There are ten orders and many thousands of series.

Soils are classified by studying exposures in boreholes, pits or road cuttings, using depth and colour, and for more detailed classification a variety of tests is carried out in laboratories. Many soils are composed of three horizons, an upper (A) horizon which contains organic matter, a lower (B) horizon which is friable mineral matter, and the unaltered soil parent material (C). Fig. 8.1 shows a description of a soil from montane forest at an altitude of 1500 metres in Jamaica which exhibits three horizons very clearly.

Soils are very diverse because of differences in their formation, but this diversity is not necessarily reflected in the vegetation growing upon them. Many broad vegetation types do, however, have a characteristic range of soils. The following examples of soils under the different vegetation types are based on typical specific cases.

Boreal forest soils have at their surface a layer of partially decomposed conifer needles, which may be 10 centimetres deep and is acid (pH 5); then comes a bleached grey or white sandy horizon 45 centimetres in depth; below this is a horizon 35 centimetres in depth where organic material and iron oxides have been deposited; and below this is the little-altered parent material. This is a spodosol or **podzol**.

Temperate forest soils are very variable. Many are brown earths with 50 to 70 centimetres of mixed mineral and organic matter, coloured brown, of pH 5.5 to 7 and lying above a paler mineral horizon. Some temperate forest soils are podzolised and resemble the less extreme podzols beneath some boreal forests.

North American prairie soils have at their surface a layer of mixed mineral and organic matter 50 to 70 centimetres deep, dark brown in colour with a pH of 6 to 7, below which is a mineral layer which may be several metres in depth and in which, in those parts of the prairie with lower rainfall, a zone of accumulation of white calcium carbonate may be present. These are molisols or **chernozems**.

Arid zone soils are little leached, often sandy or stony, and often have soluble salts at or near the surface, such as sodium chloride in the soils around the Dead Sea and calcium carbonate (caliche) in many desert soils in the USA.

Montane soils are often on slopes and, if so, are thin, with solid rock less than 50 centimetres below the surface, and may not have a well-developed structure; such soils are classified as **entisols**.

Tropical rain-forest soils are very diverse. The commonest are deep soils derived from parent materials which weathered to form clays, which have themselves undergone further weathering to leave free iron oxide and aluminium oxide; in some instances these oxides harden irreversibly, when exposed at the surface, to form rock-hard **laterite**. Some rain-forest soils are equally old but developed over sands which have been weathered for long periods (some millions of years) so that all that remains is a deep layer of white quartz, tens of metres deep, covered by a layer about 20 centimetres thick of sand mixed with decomposing humus, from which the vegetation obtains most of its nutrients. Some rain-forest soils are derived from limestone, and consist of small pockets of clays held in depressions in the limestone, with the whole being overlain by 2 to 5 centimetres of decomposing organic matter; limestone rocks are frequently apparent at the surface.

8.2 POLAR REGIONS

The two polar regions of the earth resemble each other only in their high latitudes and their coldness. The high Arctic is a frozen ocean, while the Antarctic continent is a land mass mostly lying between 3000 and 4000 metres above sea-level, so that it is exceedingly cold and is almost entirely covered by ice; this ice is up to 3000 metres thick in places (Fig. 8.2).

The climates of the polar regions are extreme. During the winter the sun is below the horizon for months on end, and inflows of air from lower latitudes are the only source of heat.

Fig. 8.2. The Antarctic continent is mostly covered by ice; only in a few places do rocky mountain ranges break through, but they have no plant cover.

Even during the summer, the sun is low in the sky and provides little heat, although slopes facing the sun can have relatively warm microclimates. Flowering plants grow in such sites at latitudes above 80 °N in Greenland, where there are 60 frost-free days in summer and a mean July temperature of 6 °C.

Although the Antarctic Peninsula extends north to 65°S, there are only two species of flowering plant on the whole continent (Fig. 8.3); Spitzbergen, in contrast, lying between 76 and 81 °N, has 160 species. There are also mosses, lichens and terrestrial algae in the Antarctic, but nowhere do these form anything approaching a continuous vegetation cover (Fig. 8.4). In the absence of vegetation to provide food for herbivores, the animals living in these regions are mostly dependent, directly or indirectly, on the sea for their food, and the poles are able to support high populations of seals and, in the Antarctic, whales and penguins.

The Antarctic is almost devoid of terrestrial animals, with only a few species of mites and some midges but the Arctic contains the polar bear (Thalarctos maritimus), a large mammal with a circumpolar distribution, and numerous insects, although admittedly most of the latter are in evidence only during the brief summer. Flies (Diptera) form the bulk of the insect fauna, with mosquitoes and black flies (Simulium) so prominent that they can make life almost unbearable for people. Butterflies are also common, and even relatives of the earthworm (Enchytraeidae) can be found burrowing in the snow. The wealth of insect life attracts birds which enter the Arctic in the summer in order to breed, but these are really creatures of the tundra rather than of the Arctic ice.

Seals have not entirely divorced themselves from the land, for they must come ashore each year to breed. Five species of seal occur in the Arctic and their ranges overlap. The breeding grounds, or rookeries, vary in size; hundreds of thousands of harp seals (Pagophilus groenlandicus) gather together in one spot on the ice floes, while at the other extreme females of the ringed seal (Pusa hispida) give birth alone in burrows hollowed out of drifted snow. The walrus (Odobenus rosmarus) is a huge relation of the seals that is distinguished by its bulk (up to 1500 kilograms in males), and by its protruberant canine teeth or tusks. The walrus is not an oceanic animal as are many of the seals, but remains within shallow coastal waters.

Seals are prominent in Antarctica too; there are four species, not counting the huge elephant seal (Mirounga leonina) which normally breeds north of the Antarctic Circle. Most of the Antarctic seals are much more marine than are their Arctic cousins and come ashore only onto floating ice. The largest species is the leopard seal (Hydrurga leptonyx), so called not for a spotted coat but for its predatory habits; its favourite prey is penguin.

Penguins are the most typical Antarctic animals, although some species occur in southern Africa and in South America and one, Spheniscus mendiculus, lives as far north as the

TERRESTRIAL ENVIRONMENTS

Fig. 8.3. Deschampsia antarctica *is one of only two flowering plant species that grow on the Antarctic continent. Here an isolated plant grows among moss on one of the South Orkney Islands.*

Fig. 8.4. *Over much of the Antarctic, soils are poorly developed. Here a brightly coloured lichen,* Xanthoria candelaria, *covers bare rock, while mosses grow on the loose gravelly soil.*

Galapagos Islands on the equator. Altogether four of the 18 species of penguin live on Antarctica, but only the emperor penguin (*Aptenodytes forsteri*; Fig. 8.5) is entirely confined to this continent. It is the only bird to breed in midwinter when there is permanent darkness. Penguins have a layer of blubber to keep them warm, and this is adequate in the comparatively warm sea-water where temperatures can never fall below about −1.8°C. The temperature on land, however, can be as much as 80 degrees lower, and in order to survive penguins often huddle together so that only a small part of each bird's surface is exposed. The birds take it in turns to be on the colder, outside ranks.

8.3 TUNDRA

Vast areas of northern Asia and northern Canada are covered with low treeless vegetation known as tundra. Throughout this area the summers are too short, the winters too cold and dry, and the soil too unstable, to support tree growth. Most of the Asian tundra lies north of the Arctic Circle, but around Hudson Bay in northern Canada tundra extends down to 55 °N. Tundra vegetation is absent from the southern hemisphere; the corresponding latitudes on the Antarctic continent are high plateaux covered by ice. The sub-Antarctic islands such as Kerguelen carry a low treeless vegetation of tundra type.

Within the tundra zone, daylength varies enormously through the year; north of the Arctic Circle daylight lasts for 24 hours for part of the year and there is perpetual night or twilight in winter. Along with this variation in incoming solar radiation goes great variation in temperature. Summers may be warm but winters are very cold; the tundra zone is often defined as having no month with a mean temperature above 10°C. The extent of temperature variation through the year depends on the region, and oceanic sites are less extreme than continental ones. Annual precipitation is low, falling mostly in

Fig. 8.5. *Emperor Penguins breed on the Antarctic ice cap during the winter. The chicks are well grown by the summer.*

A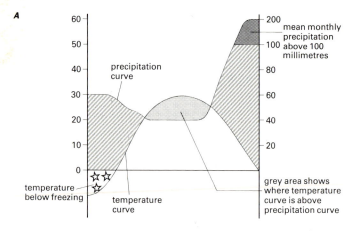

B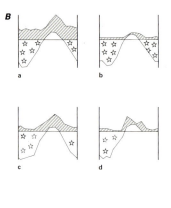

Fig. 8.6. The Klimadiagrams in this chapter are based on those of Walter, Harnickell and Mueller-Dombois (1975). The horizontal axis shows the 12 months of the year: from January to December in the northern hemisphere and from July to June in the southern hemisphere, so that the warm season is always central. The left-hand vertical axis shows mean monthly temperature, and is marked every 10°C. The right-hand vertical axis gives mean monthly precipitation and is marked every 10 millimetres up to 100, and every 100 millimetres thereafter. A generalised diagram (A) serves as a key. In the individual captions, alt = altitude (m); a.p. = annual precipitation (mm); m.a.t. = mean annual temperature (°C).

(B) Tundra climates		alt.	a.p.	m.a.t.
a Frobisher Bay, Baffin Is.	63°00′N, 67°00′W	21	342	−9.0
b Thule, Greenland	76°00′N, 68°00′W	37	64	−11.1
c Dikson, USSR	73°40′N, 80°05′E	13	166	−12.7
d Medvezhi Is., USSR	71°00′N, 161°00′E	13	110	−12.1

summer, but evaporation is also low and if the ground is not frozen scarcity of water does not limit plant growth, except in some very dry polar deserts and semi-deserts of the high Arctic where annual precipitation is less than 200 millimetres. Over much of the tundra the annual mean temperature is below 0 °C, so that the ground is permanently frozen (permafrost), often to great depths; only the surface layers thaw during summer.

The annual freezing and thawing of the soil causes it to swell and shrink. This leads to a gradual churning of the soil (frost-heaving, cryoturbation) and to its sorting into patterns outlined by the larger stones; these patterns tend to be polygonal on flat ground and linear on slopes (Fig. 8.7). Frost-heaving can also damage plant roots.

In the tundra, plant growth may vary greatly from one site to another because of local environmental variations. The winter snow is redistributed by the wind, accumulating in some places and being cleared from others. Sites of accumulation are insulated from extreme cold, but growth cannot start in the spring until the snow has melted. The aspect of each site is also important because of the low angle of the sun's rays; south-facing slopes are considerably warmer than level sites or north-facing slopes.

Tundra vegetation

The growing season in the tundra is too short for most plants to complete their life-cycles within it, although a few, such as some species of gentian (*Gentiana*) and *Koenigia islandica*, are annuals and manage to survive. The vast majority of tundra plants, however, are perennial with their buds for the next season's growth surviving the winter at or just below the surface of the soil, producing a low vegetation of herbs and dwarf shrubs. Dwarf birch (*Betula nana*) and species of dwarf willow (*Salix*) predominate in better-drained sites, and sedges, such as species of *Eriophorum* and *Carex*, in less well-drained

places. The driest sites often carry almost pure stands of lichens, and in boggy hollows mosses are often the only plants.

The shortness of the growing season also poses problems for perennials. Seed production may be impossible within a single year, and many species form flower buds in the late summer, opening them in the following year as soon as the snow melts. Many have relatively large and showy flowers which are pollinated by the scarce insects; the size and showiness of the flowers (Fig. 8.8) is often said to be needed to attract the insects. It has been shown that the dish-shaped flower of the Arctic poppy (*Ranunculus glacialis*) functions as a solar collector, focusing the sun's rays on the centre of the flower to form a hot spot attractive to insects. Most tundra plants have small wind-dispersed seeds, but some, particularly in the more southerly parts of the tundra, have berries which are eaten by mammals or birds which disperse the seeds.

Although the growing season is short (50 to 100 days), growth can be rapid during this period because water is plentiful and there is continuous daylight. Annual primary production in Arctic tundras typically reaches totals of 100 to 300 grams per square metre, while the most northerly tundras, the polar semi-deserts, produce 10 to 50 grams per square metre each year. In the low average temperatures decomposition is slow, and there is usually some accumulation of peat.

The low productivity of tundra means that it is very susceptible to disturbance, as damage is not repaired quickly. At present little use is made of the tundra other than by the indigenous peoples, who exist at extremely low densities. Recently it has been found that many tundra regions contain valuable resources such as oil, gas, and minerals, and the exploitation of these has significantly disturbed some areas (Fig. 8.9).

Fig. 8.7. This striking aerial view shows the polygonal patterns developed in the tundra by seasonal freezing and thawing of the surface soil layers.

Animals of the tundra

The short growing season and the consequent low plant production result in a low biomass of animals. The most common large herbivore in the tundra is the barren-ground caribou (*Rangifer tarandus groenlandicus*; Fig. 8.10), which lives in the far north of Canada and makes long-distance migrations. The herds winter in the south on the edge of the timber-line, but migrate northwards in the spring to calve and feed on the rich summer pasture. Migration is essential for many tundra species, because conditions are so severe during the far northern winter that few animals could survive. The Eurasian equivalent of the caribou, the reindeer (*Rangifer tarandus fennicus*), also migrates south each winter and this seasonal pattern persists even in the domesticated reindeer. A favoured food of reindeer is lichen, which grows where no other plant can survive, and it is important that reindeer should not remain in one spot for too long for lichens are slow-growing and take years to recover from heavy grazing. Reindeer are true deer but are unusual in being the only species in which the female carries antlers.

The other large herbivore of the tundra is the musk-ox (*Ovibos moschatus*; Fig. 4.6) which is one of the 'goat-like' antelopes showing closer affinities to sheep and goats than to oxen. Unlike caribou or reindeer, the musk-ox does not migrate but braves the winter within the Arctic Circle, protected by its thick underwool and heavy top coat. It does show seasonal movements, however, and feeds on any available vegetable matter: grasses, sedges and willow in summer, and mosses and lichens in winter.

The dominant small herbivore of the tundra is the lemming (Fig. 8.10), of which there are several species. The population dynamics of lemmings are typical of any small mammal living in a demanding environment: mass dispersions, constituting the famous migrations, follow the periodic build-up of numbers. Lemmings do not deliberately drown themselves, but many perish in attempting to swim across water barriers. There are normally north–south seasonal migrations each year independent of these mass movements. Arctic hares (*Lepus timidus*), which are the other herbivores occurring in the far north, forage throughout the winter.

The lemmings and hares support several predators, the numbers of which rise and fall in phase with those of the herbivores. The stoat (*Mustela erminea*; Fig. 8.10) occurs throughout the polar regions and is one of the chief predators of lemmings; another predator is the Arctic fox (*Alopex lagopus*). Both these turn white for camouflage in winter. The most common large predator is the wolf (*Canis lupus*), which has a huge range with numerous subspecies throughout the whole tundra. Its principal prey is caribou, and it follows these deer in their migrations. Wolves also attack musk-oxen if a solitary weak animal is found, but the musk-oxen's habit of forming a defensive circle when threatened means that this species generally cannot be killed by wolves (Fig. 4.5). The

wolf's success depends on its social habits, for a single animal would not be able to hunt such large mammals.

The tundra is an important breeding area for waterfowl, particularly geese and swans, during the brief Arctic summer when the long days provide plenty of time for feeding. Few birds can find enough to eat during the winter, but the power of flight makes it easy for them to migrate south. Some hardy species, however, remain in the Arctic all year round; these include the ptarmigan (*Lagopus mutus*) and willow grouse (*L. lagopus*; Fig. 8.10), both of which turn white in winter. These birds are preyed upon by the huge white snowy owl (*Nyctea scandiaca*), which is unusual for an owl in being active during the day, and by the gyr falcon (*Falco rusticolus*); this is the most northerly bird of prey, and tends to be whiter in the far north than at lower latitudes.

8.4 TAIGA

The taiga, also known as boreal forest, covers a vast area of the northern hemisphere. It extends from north-eastern Europe across Russia to the Pacific Ocean, and right across North America from Alaska to Newfoundland. At its northern margin it merges into the treeless tundra, the trees becoming smaller and more restricted to favourable sites as one goes further north. At its southern margin the taiga grades into deciduous forest or grassland through a broad transition zone of mixed forest or parkland.

Much of the taiga lies north of the Arctic Circle, and its climate is similar to that of the tundra but with warmer

Fig. 8.8. Many tundra flowering plants have large and conspicuous flowers. Four examples from Greenland are shown here. (a) Cassiope tetragona. (b) Saxifraga oppositifolia. (c) Veronica fruticans. (d) Papaver radicatum.

Fig. 8.9. (above) Tundra vegetation is fragile and very susceptible to disturbance. The seismic survey lines made for oil prospecting can persist for years. (a) A fresh trail. (b) An older trail site; compaction and darkening of the surface have led to selective thawing and erosion of the vegetation.

Fig. 8.10. Some typical examples of the tundra fauna. (a) The stoat in its winter pelage. (b) Barren ground caribou, which make extensive migrations to and from the summer grazing lands in the far north. (c) The collared lemming lives in high latitudes and is the only lemming that turns white in winter. Numbers fluctuate greatly over a 3–4-year cycle. (d) A black phase of the grey wolf, the principal mammalian predator of the Arctic. (e) A young grizzly bear. The bear's diet varies throughout the year from entirely carnivorous to entirely herbivorous. (f) A male willow grouse in Canada. Mass movements in winter to areas well south of the normal range are common and may be due to high densities in the north.

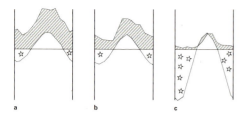

Fig. 8.11. Taiga climates

			alt.	a.p.	m.a.t.
a	Fort William, Canada	48°20′N, 89°10′W	700	195	2.7
b	Yarensk, USSR	61°10′N, 49°08′E	509	81	0.0
c	Oimyakon, USSR	63°25′N, 143°10′E	131	800	−15.3

summers. The winter cold may be just as great as in the tundra, and in fact the 'cold pole' of the northern hemisphere lies within the taiga of eastern Siberia. Even here, with a mean January temperature of −50 to −60°C, July temperatures reach a mean of 20 °C, and the growing season is about 150 days long. Much of the taiga has a mean annual temperature below zero, and permafrost is widespread. Although frost-heaving is less obvious than in the tundra, it may tilt trees from the vertical and produce 'drunken forest'. Annual rainfall is generally low, ranging from 150 millimetres in the most continental part to 600–700 millimetres in the most oceanic areas; most rain falls in the summer. During the winter months there is a substantial blanket of snow, beneath which animals and plants can survive.

The soils of the taiga are podzols (see section 8.1) with strong leaching of humus and clays to leave an upper soil layer of bleached sand overlying a pan of redeposited iron and humus. The tree roots are mostly confined to the upper soil layers, and to the superficial layer of undecomposed humus where they form abundant mycorrhizae (see pp. 277–80).

Vegetation of the taiga

The taiga is dominated throughout by coniferous trees (Fig. 8.12), which are evergreen except for the larches (*Larix*). In northern Europe, the common species are the Norway spruce (*Picea abies*) and the Scots pine (*Pinus sylvestris*). Further east, Siberian larch (*L. russica*) appears at about 39 °E and Siberian fir (*Abies sibirica*) at about 42 °E; in the same region Siberian pine (*Pinus sibirica*) joins the Scots pine, and Siberian spruce (*Picea obovata*) replaces Norway spruce. The Dahurian larch (*Larix gmelinii*) dominates the taiga in the extreme continental climatic region east of the Yenesei River. In North America the forest is much more varied. White spruce (*Picea glauca*) and jack pine (*Pinus banksiana*) extend from coast to coast; balsam fir (*Abies balsamea*) is common in the east. Black spruce (*Picea mariana*) is common in boggy areas, and near the northern limits of the taiga; tamarack (*Larix laricina*) occurs in the more continental regions.

The undergrowth of the true taiga is strikingly similar in Eurasia and America, and there are some species that are common to both continents. Shrublets in the heather family (Ericaceae), such as species of *Vaccinium* (Fig. 8.13) and *Arctostaphylos*, are very widespread, and various attractive flowering herbs such as twinflower (*Linnaea borealis*), the wintergreen (*Moneses uniflora*) and the creeping orchid (*Goodyera repens*) occur throughout the taiga. Mosses are often very abundant and luxuriant on the forest floor. In the driest taiga, however, lichens may be the only ground vegetation.

The coniferous forests are the climax vegetation of this climatic zone. If they are cleared by man, or killed by forest fires, a succession begins, leading to the climax state (see section 5.4). The early colonisers are small broad-leaved trees, species of birch (*Betula*) and poplar (*Populus*). Both have small windborne seeds which require light for germination, and their saplings then grow rapidly. The winged seeds of the pines also arrive early; those of the jack pine are held in the cones which remain on the tree until they are singed by fires, when they open and release the seeds. Pines grow more slowly than the birches and poplars, but live longer and eventually outgrow them. Spruce can regenerate in partial shade, but attains dominance only after a long time, perhaps hundreds of years. The increasing frequency of forest fires caused by human activities has led to the increase of pine at the expense of spruce in parts of northern Europe. This birch–pine–spruce succession is similar in Eurasia and North America.

During the winter most of the herbs die down to underground parts, and the small shrubs are covered by snow which insulates them from extremes of cold. The trees, other than the larches, retain their foliage throughout the winter. In the autumn the leaves enter a dormant state in which photosynthesis ceases and respiration falls to an extremely low level. In this state the leaves can endure the very low winter temperatures. In spring, the rising temperatures and increasing daylength stimulate a reactivation of photosynthesis and respiration. Primary production in the taiga is generally 500 to 1000 grams per square metre per year, and more than half of this is wood. Seed production varies greatly from year to year, which is of great importance to seed-eating birds and mammals.

Animals of the taiga

The taiga is a harsh environment for animals in winter and many avoid its rigours by hibernation or migration. Others, generally large vertebrates well adapted to the cold, remain active throughout the long dark winter. Invertebrate life is obvious only during the short summer, the winter usually being spent as resting stages, either eggs or pupae, or sometimes as hibernating larvae.

Some of the plant-eating animals exploit the conifers, feeding on the bark or cones. Examples include the squirrels and the tree porcupine of North America (*Erethizon dorsatum*), a species with a range extending south almost to the tropics in suitable forests. These northern forests also have flying squirrels, with the Siberian flying squirrel (*Pteromys volans*) in Eurasia and the northern flying squirrel (*Glaucomys sabrinus*) in North America. The largest herbivore in the northern forests, and at up to 500 kilograms the largest deer in the world,

Fig. 8.12. Two aspects of the taiga in Finland. (a) Old pine forest with young spruce trees growing up – a late stage in the successional development of the northern coniferous forest.

(b) Dry pine forest with a ground flora made up almost entirely of lichens.

is the moose (*Alces alces*, Fig. 8.14), known in Eurasia as the elk (not to be confused with the North American wapiti (*Cervus canadensis*), which Americans call elk). Although the moose lives amongst the conifers, it does not feed on them but rather eats the broad-leaved undergrowth. It also feeds on water plants, often wading out to considerable depths to get at them. During the winter it has difficulty in finding enough food, but makes use of its weight to trample down the snow to expose the branches of bushes.

Small herbivores may pass the winter in hibernation. An example is the woodchuck (*Marmota monax*) of North America; this is a marmot, a type of ground squirrel, and it spends up to eight months in the year hibernating in its burrow sometimes as much as 150 centimetres below the surface. Some rodents do remain active throughout the winter, feeding on the vegetation under the thick blanket of snow which acts as an insulating layer as well as providing cover from predators. The wood lemming (*Myopus schisticolor*) of the Eurasian boreal forests is a small (10 centimetres long) vole-like rodent which feeds extensively on moss under the fallen trunks of trees. The related voles are represented by the heather vole (*Phenacomys intermedius*) in North America and the root vole (*Microtus oeconomus*) in northern Europe and Siberia. Shrews keep the

rodents company under the snow and also remain active throughout the winter. Shrews in the genus *Sorex* are present in the Eurasian boreal forest, and the dominant shrew in the North American coniferous forests is the pygmy shrew (*Microsorex hoyi*). Because of their small size and high metabolic rate, shrews need to feed frequently and have numerous short rest periods. They feed on insects and other invertebrates, depending largely on insect larvae during the winter.

Mammalian carnivores include a number of interesting mustelids. The smallest are the weasels (*Mustela*), that are found throughout the boreal forests of the world. They are small enough to live under the snow with the voles and shrews on which they feed. The larger stoat or ermine (*Mustela erminea*) has an extensive range throughout the whole of the northern temperate and Arctic regions, and is common in the taiga. It is a catholic feeder and is big enough to take hares where these occur. Both the weasel and the stoat turn white in winter in the colder parts of their range.

The martens (*Martes*) are the most typical predators of the pine forests in both the Eurasian and American regions of the Holarctic (the Palaearctic and Nearctic; respectively). They are closely related to the stoats and weasels and include the pine marten of Europe and western Siberia, the sable of Siberia and

201

*Fig. 8.13. The forest floor of the taiga bears a vegetation of dwarf shrubs, herbs and many mosses. Illustrated here are one shrub (*a – Vaccinium uliginosum*), two herbs (*b – Ledum palustre *and* c – Pyrola grandiflora*), and one moss (*d – Ptilium crista-castrensis*).*

eastern Asia, the American marten, and the fisher of North America which, despite its name, is predominantly a terrestrial carnivore.

The largest of the boreal mustelids and one of the largest in the world is the wolverine (*Gulo gulo*), which shows certain similarities with its African relative the ratel or honey badger (*Mellivora capensis*), not least in its willingness to dispute ownership of carcases killed by larger predators. It is a ferocious animal and with its loose skin and powerful jaws can twist around and inflict serious damage on any animal that grabs it. Wolverines are essentially scavengers, but also hunt their own prey, mainly birds, and raid nests for eggs.

Large predators include bears and the lynx, although these are by no means confined to the boreal forests. Brown bears (*Ursus arctos*) are rare, and the common bear of the North American coniferous forest is the black bear (*U. americanus*). This is a smaller species, rarely weighing more than 135

kilograms, and feeding mostly on berries, roots and other vegetable matter. The lynx (*Felis lynx*), on the other hand, is exclusively carnivorous, taking birds, hares and rodents. It has a wide distribution over North America and Eurasia.

Birds of prey in the taiga are the nocturnal owls and the diurnal (active by day) hawks and eagles. Owls feed largely on rodents, which like the owls are active at night. Broad rounded wings give the owls excellent manoeuvrability, and the structure of their feathers permits silent flight so that owls are able to approach their prey unnoticed. Owls also have extremely good night-sight with a wide sweep of binocular vision. The hawks and eagles have to feed on birds above the treetops, or upon squirrels and sometimes martens which they snatch from the upper branches. A typical example is the goshawk (*Accipiter gentilis*) which can manoeuvre agilely as it chases birds between the trees; it occurs throughout Eurasia and North America.

Several species of birds are specially adapted for feeding on the conifers. Birds which feed on the growing conifer needles include members of the grouse family, of which the largest is the Eurasian capercaillie (*Tetrao urogallus*), with the cock birds able to reach a mass of 8 kilograms. As with most grouse, the male displays on lekking grounds during the breeding season. It shares its range with the smaller black grouse (*Lyrurus tetrix*), with which it occasionally hybridises. The black grouse is less of a specialist, however, and occurs in other habitats such as moorland and rocky hills, where it feeds largely on heather. In North America the forest grouse are represented by the spruce grouse (*Canachites canadensis*) and the western blue grouse (*Dendragapus obscurus*).

A group of finches, the crossbills, have evolved specifically to deal with pine cones. The nutritious seeds of the pines are protected by tough scales, and most birds have to wait until the cones open before they can get at the seeds. The mandibles of the crossbill overlap at their tips thus enabling them to exert sufficient pressure to cut through the scales. The common crossbill (*Loxia curvirostra*) occurs in both America and Eurasia and feeds largely on spruce, the Palaearctic crossbill (*L. pityopsittacus*) is slightly larger and has a much heavier bill because it feeds on the thick-scaled pine cones, and a third species, the two-barred crossbill (*L. leucoptera*), found in all northern forest, has a delicate bill for it feeds mainly on the thin-scaled larch cones. The pine grosbeak (*Pinicola enucleator*), also Holarctic in distribution, is very similar in appearance, but is larger and its heavy bill does not cross over: it feeds on cones by battering them open to obtain the seeds. The nutcracker (*Nucifraga caryocatactes*) is a member of the crow family with similar habits to the grosbeak.

Reptiles and amphibians do not feature in the fauna of boreal forests due to the long winter and dry climate, but there are a few insects that have adapted to the unpromising diets available in the pine woods. The resinous exudations from the trees, besides being unpalatable, tend to trap small animals, and some of the best preserved fossils are of insects that were similarly embedded long ago. Insects which specialise on conifers include the sawflies, a group of hymenopterans the caterpillar-like larvae of which feed on pine needles and can cause serious damage in plantations before pupating in the soil. Another hymenopteran pest is the wood wasp, whose larvae bore into the heartwood of trees and pupate within their burrows. Wood-boring beetles include weevils; both adults and weevil larvae bore, the adult making the initial penetration through the bark and then excavating side burrows for the larvae. Sometimes weevils penetrate the wood itself, but other insects are confined to the bark.

The scarcity of insects leads to a similar scarcity of insectivorous birds, except in the brief summer, but the woodpeckers exploit the larvae of wood-boring insects. Most typical are the red-capped black woodpecker (*Dryocopus martius*) of Europe and Asia, and the three-toed woodpecker (*Picoides tridactylus*) which occurs also in North America.

*Fig 8.14. A moose (*Alces alces*) with antlers in velvet. This, the largest of deer, feeds extensively on aquatic vegetation during the summer.*

8.5 TEMPERATE GRASSLANDS

In the centres of the great continents the climate is too extreme to permit the survival of forests, and the natural vegetation is open grassland. This vegetation type (**steppe**) occurs in eastern Europe, and extends eastwards through Russia to Mongolia. Similar vegetation (**prairie**) occupies the centre of North America, another (**pampa**) is found in Argentina, and similar grassland occurs in the South Island of New Zealand. Some of the Australian grasslands resemble temperate grasslands in structure, but their climate is never as extreme and most are subtropical (see section 8.10).

The climate of the grasslands is extreme. Rain falls throughout the year, but there is a peak in the spring and early summer. Annual totals lie between 200 and 750 millimetres. In the winter, snow often lies 20 to 30 centimetres deep, and temperatures are very low with two to three months in which the mean is below 0 °C; in the summer, the warmest months have mean temperatures of 20 to 24 °C. The Siberian steppes have the most extreme climate; the pampas are considerably warmer, with no month having a mean below zero. The main growing season is early summer.

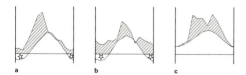

Fig. 8.15. Temperate grassland climates

		alt.	a.p.	m.a.t.
a	Rapid City, S. Dakota, USA 44°00'N, 103°00'W	965	432	7.8
b	Poltava, USSR 49°35'N, 34°35'E	160	451	6.9
c	Santa Rosa, Argentina 36°40'S, 64°30'W	189	569	15.3

Perennial grasses form the bulk of the vegetation of these temperate grasslands. Associated with the grasses are many broad-leaved perennials of which the smaller species mostly flower early in the season before the grasses have attained maximum height, while the larger species flower later, sometimes after the grasses have finished flowering and have died down. Most of the perennials have large underground parts.

The Eurasian steppes

These grasslands extend from eastern Europe right across the USSR almost to the Pacific. They lie between the forests in the north and the deserts to the south. The main grasses of the northern steppes are species of *Helictotrichon*, *Bromus* and *Agrostis*; in the warmer southern steppes these tend to be replaced by *Stipa*, with *Koeleria* and *Festuca*. The earliest flowers of the steppes are species of *Pulsatilla*, *Adonis* and *Anemone*, together with bulbous plants such as *Hyacinthus*, *Tulipa* and *Gagea*. These all flower very early, soon after the melting of the snow and before the grasses have begun to grow. A little later, species of *Paeonia*, *Myosotis*, *Iris* and *Lathyrus* flower, followed in late May and June by the grasses. Finally, large perennial herbs, such as *Veratrum*, *Delphinium* and *Carduus*, flower when the grasses have shed their seeds. Steppe grasslands are very rich in species, and although grasses dominate the vegetation they do not make up the bulk of a species list. A study in the Streletsk steppe found 180 species in 12 square kilometres and of these only 20 were grasses.

The species of *Stipa* have long bristles called awns attached to their seeds; these awns are twisted, and the spiral winds and unwinds in response to changes in humidity. These twisting movements move the seed around and can help its sharp point to enter cracks in the ground, so that the seed is buried and protected from the heat of fires and from seed-eating birds and mammals. Other steppe plants are tumbleweeds, in which the inflorescence breaks away entirely from the plant and is rolled across the grassland by the wind, shedding its seeds as it goes.

The soils of the Eurasian steppes are called **chernozems** (see section 8.1). They are very dark in colour in their upper layers, and become paler below. The parent material is fine wind-blown dust (loess), which is extremely uniform over large areas. The dark, humus-rich layer can be as much as 50 centimetres deep, and the soil stained by humus extends down to 150 centimetres or more before the pale unaltered loess is reached. The pale layers contain dark patches which are infilled burrows of ground squirrels; these animals are or were extremely abundant and contributed enormously to soil

circulation by their burrowing. Nowadays vast areas of steppe have been turned over to the cultivation of wheat, and only relics of the original steppe vegetation of European Russia remain in reserves. Further east, more extensive areas still exist.

The sparseness and poor quality of the vegetation makes the steppe an inhospitable region for animals, yet many species flourish. The large mammalian herbivores have to move long distances to seek adequate grazing and most of them live in herds. Przewalski's horse (*Equus przewalskii*; Fig. 8.16), probably now extinct in the wild, was a dominant herbivore of the steppe. It is a possible ancestor of the domestic horse, which was first domesticated in the Eurasian steppe 6000 years ago. Further west Przewalski's horse was replaced by the now extinct tarpan (*E. gmelini*). The other once-common equid on the Eurasian steppe is the wild ass (*E. hemionus*). More horse-like than the African asses, which are the donkey-ancestors of donkeys, the wild ass still maintains a tenuous hold on its native habitats. Further to the south-west, in and around northern Iran, is another race, the onager, which was domesticated in antiquity until the stronger and more tractable horse appeared.

Nowadays, the most common large mammal is the saiga antelope (*Saiga tatarica*). This curious-looking beast with its enlarged nose was once hunted nearly to extinction, but rigorous protection since the 1930s, coupled with the saiga's remarkable reproductive powers, led to its recovery so that now a carefully controlled crop can be harvested every year. The bactrian, or two-humped camel (*Camelus bactrianus*) is a rare species of the Mongolian steppe, although there is some doubt that it is a truly wild species rather than a feral animal descended from domesticated forms.

Colonial rodents are, or were, very common and account for much of the consumption of steppe grasses. The commonest species is the suslik (*Citellus citellus*), a ground squirrel that digs long burrows more than 1 metre below the surface where it hibernates during the winter. The related bobac marmot (*Marmota bobak*) is about four times the size of a suslik and makes correspondingly larger burrows, which may extend over hundreds of square metres, forming virtual 'towns' with several entrances on mounds of excavated soil like miniature volcanoes.

Mammalian carnivores are represented by the wolf (*Canis lupus*), now greatly reduced in range, the fox (*Vulpes vulpes*), and, wherever there is sufficient cover, by various species of mustelid such as the badger (*Meles meles*) and steppe polecat (*Mustela eversmanni*).

Bird life is rather poor, with only a few resident species. Conspicuous among these are the bustards, a group of ground-living birds that rarely take to the air and then only in a ponderous and uncertain fashion. The demoiselle crane (*Anthropoides virgo*) and the common crane (*Megalornis grus*) are other gregarious birds of the steppe. Sand grouse are also common in the more desert regions, and are also gregarious.

Fig. 8.16. Herbivores of the grasslands. (a) The pronghorn is the only surviving member of a largely extinct group of ungulates, the Antilocapridae. (b) The American bison was, with the pronghorn, the dominant species of the North American grasslands until its numbers were greatly reduced in the last century. (c) Przewalski's horse is the only surviving species of wild horse. Although it may now be extinct in the wild, adequate numbers are held in captivity. (d) The capybara is a rodent but has the habits of an ungulate. It grazes at night but spends much of the day in or near water.

Many of the birds of the steppe are nomadic, particularly the insectivorous species that rely on finding the shifting and suddenly appearing populations of grasshoppers. Larks, such as the common skylark (*Alauda arvensis*), and pipits (*Anthus*) are also widespread in grasslands.

Birds of prey are typical of the steppe, with large eagles such as the imperial eagle (*Aquila heliaca*) and steppe or tawny eagle (*A. rapax*). The limiting factor for the birds of prey seems to be nesting sites, for there are few trees or cliffs, and some, even large eagles, nest on the ground.

Steppe is not favourable to amphibians and the few species found there are burrowers. Reptiles are not much more numerous, and include only those that can survive the long winter in hibernation. The season is too short to allow eggs to develop and most species are ovoviviparous, that is, they produce eggs which hatch within the mother's body, and the young are born live.

The prairies of North America

The grasslands of North America occupy the centre of the continent from southern Saskatchewan to Oklahoma. Rainfall declines from east to west, and winter cold increases from south to north. The eastern prairies, with higher rainfall and deeper soils, bear tallgrass prairie in which the bluestem grasses (*Andropogon scoparius* and *A. gerardi*) are dominant. Broad-leaved herbs are abundant, as in the Eurasian steppes; as many as 70 species may be in flower at the same time. *Andropogon* is a tropical genus and these prairie grasses do not flower until late in the summer, in contrast to the Eurasian steppes where most of the grass species belong to temperate genera and flower earlier. Further west the taller grass species are joined by shorter species such as blue grama (*Bouteloa gracilis*) and buffalo grass (*Buchloë dactyloides*), forming the mixed prairie. Further west still, the tall species disappear and the short species become dominant.

Much of the prairie has now been ploughed at one time or another and few areas persist unchanged. Grazing has also

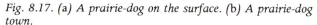

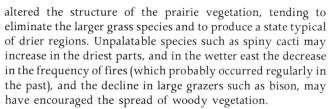

Fig. 8.17. (a) A prairie-dog on the surface. (b) A prairie-dog town.

altered the structure of the prairie vegetation, tending to eliminate the larger grass species and to produce a state typical of drier regions. Unpalatable species such as spiny cacti may increase in the driest parts, and in the wetter east the decrease in the frequency of fires (which probably occurred regularly in the past), and the decline in large grazers such as bison, may have encouraged the spread of woody vegetation.

Two species of large mammal once dominated the prairies: the American bison (*Bison bison*; Fig. 8.16), and the pronghorn antelope (*Antilocapra americana*). The latter is not a true antelope, but is the sole living representative of the Antilocapridae, a group separate from both deer and bovids. Both these species suffered disastrous declines in the last century. In the case of the bison this was mainly the result of a deliberate policy to deprive the American Indians of their food supply during the wars that accompanied the expansion of settlers onto the prairies. The bison is a huge animal, with bulls weighing nearly a tonne. It is thought that they were instrumental in extending the grasslands through their habit of breaking down trees by rubbing against them, and with the virtual disappearance of the bison trees have regenerated in areas not affected by agriculture. The resulting woodlands have been colonised by mule deer (*Odocoileus hemionus*), which often spread out into the surrounding grasslands.

Ground squirrels and marmots are common in North America, where they fill a similar ecological niche to that occupied by their cousins on the Eurasian steppes. One group of marmots, called prairie-dogs because of their dog-like bark, dig elaborate tunnels under the grasslands. The black-tailed prairie dog (*Cynomys ludovicianus*) has such a widespread system of interlinked tunnels that, as with the bobac marmot in Eurasia, the whole complex has been called a 'town' (Fig. 8.17). Such a community of prairie-dogs is usually split into subgroups, or wards, and further into family units, called coteries, each consisting of a single male and several females with their young. Another widespread group of burrowing rodents allied to squirrels is the pocket gophers. Their name comes from the large cheek pouches which are used to store food, mainly roots and tubers which they then take underground into shallow burrows. Pocket gophers also have an elaborate system of excavations, with burrows near the surface for feeding and deeper chambers in which the animals sleep and rear young.

The rodent fauna of the prairies forms the staple food of a wide variety of predators. The range of the wolf does not spread out into the prairie, but a small relative, the coyote (*Canis latrans*) takes its place there. The coyote is a resourceful and successful carnivore that will support itself by scavenging if its rodent food becomes scarce, as for example in winter when many of the ground squirrels hibernate. Other mammalian predators include the American badger (*Taxidea taxus*), which specialises in digging out gophers, the spotted skunk (*Spilogale putorius*), and the bobcat (*Felis rufa*), which has a wide distribution in many habitats.

There are various ground-dwelling plant-eating birds of the grouse family. The sage grouse (*Centrocercus urophasianus*) in the west is replaced in the east by two species of prairie chicken (*Tympanuchus cupido* and *T. pallidicinctus*). All three are lekking species in which the males strut and boom on territorial grounds in front of receptive females. Wildfowl too are plentiful on the North American grasslands. Most are migratory, but whereas the geese and swans are birds of passage, the ducks are there to breed.

Birds of prey are present in similar abundance as on the Eurasian steppe, although different species may fill similar ecological niches. Thus the tawny eagle (*Aquila rapax*) is replaced by the golden eagle (*A. chrysaetos*), and the black-shouldered kite (*Elanus caeruleus*) by the white-tailed kite (*E. leucurus*). Many of these raptors are migratory because of the shortage of food in the long cold winter. Many birds of prey, especially the buzzards, scavenge on the carcases of the large mammals of the plains, although this source of food has declined with the reduction of the large herds. The turkey vulture (*Cathartes aura*; Fig. 8.18), breeds out on the prairie because it is small enough to be able to use gullies as nesting sites. Several species of owls hunt the grasslands, including the snowy owl (*Nyctea scandiaca*), which winters here and breeds in the Arctic. The burrowing owl is a resident living in the abandoned burrows of prairie-dogs.

Frogs and toads occur in the temporary and permanent ponds, called sloughs, found in the wetter prairies, and reptiles are well represented by tortoises, terrapins, lizards and snakes, particularly where the soil is sandy and burrowing is easy.

a

b

Fig. 8.18. Grassland birds of prey. (a) Turkey vulture. The vultures of America belong to a different family from that of the Old World vultures. This species extends as far north as southern Canada. (b) The caracaras are aberrant falcons, often with the habits of a vulture. This is Forster's caracara from the Falkland Islands.

Fig. 8.19. The open grassland of the Argentine pampa. Most of the grasses are flowering.

Fig. 8.20. The giant anteater from South America is one of the largest animals to feed exclusively on insects. It breaks open the nests of ants and termites with its powerful front claws.

The pampas of Argentina

This grassland area lies between 32 and 38 °S and is thus nearer the equator than are the other grassland areas discussed here. It is warmer, and also moister (500 to 1000 millimetres of rain per year), but the increased warmth leads to greater evaporation and thus the pampas are about as arid as the steppes and prairies, and bear only grasses (Fig. 8.19). Most of the pampas have been very much modified by human activity, with the native grasses being replaced by introduced species which provide better grazing for the introduced cattle. The composition of remnant areas suggests that the main grasses in the moister parts were species of *Stipa* and *Bothriochloa*, and that other tussock-forming species of *Stipa* dominated the dry south-west. Further south the climate becomes colder and drier, as the westerly winds lose most of their water as they cross the barrier of the Andes. Close to the mountains, with a rainfall of 400 to 600 millimetres per year, steppe grassland with *Stipa* and *Festuca* is found, but further east much of Patagonia is covered by a very dry steppe or semi-desert in which various plants with a cushion form of growth occur.

Large mammals are not a feature of the pampa probably because the bovids, the group of mammals particularly adapted to a grazing life and including oxen, bison, sheep and antelopes, are absent from South America. Nor are there any indigenous horses, and there is only one member of the deer family, the pampa deer (*Ozotoceras bezoarticus*). This niche for large herbivorous mammals is filled by a group of rodents which is very characteristic of the South American continent. This group is the Hystricomorpha, and contains such familiar animals as the guinea-pig and porcupine. The hystricomorph rodents of South America constitute a distinct sub-group, the Caviomorpha, which resembles the marsupials of Australia in that it has evolved in isolation for millions of years and so has radiated into a great variety of distinctive species. One of these, the capybara (*Hydrochoerus hydrochaeris*; Fig. 8.16), is the largest rodent in the world, and although a grazer is also semi-aquatic and lies in the swamp forests (see section 9.3). The most common herbivore of the grass pampas is the mara (*Dolichotis patagonum*), which is an agile hare-like creature but with the long legs of an antelope. Another caviomorph rodent of the pampas is the plains viscacha (*Lagostomus maximus*), which shows a close ecological similarity to the marmots of North America and Europe. Like these it excavates an elaborate system of burrows making up a large colony complete with large mounds of excavated earth. The plains viscacha has long hind legs like a kangaroo, but it lacks the kangaroo's long tail.

The cuis or wild guinea-pig (*Cavia pamparum*) is one of many cavies found in grassland. It is not necessarily ancestral to the common guinea-pig, which was domesticated by the Incas so long ago that the ancestral form is unknown. Cavies do not burrow but shelter within tufts of grass, unlike other caviomorph rodents that have adopted almost a mole-like existence. The tuco-tucos (*Ctenomys*) construct long shallow tunnels, although they do not live wholly underground, and their closest ecological equivalent is the North American gopher, which they closely resemble apart from the lack of cheek pouches. Like marsupials in Australia, the South American caviomorph rodents have suffered from the arrival of alien rodents introduced by man. Because of their slow reproductive rate, the indigenous rodents cannot compete successfully with the more prolific introduced species.

The complexity of the plant-eaters is matched by that of the insectivorous and carnivorous mammals. Many of these belong to an order of mammals, the Edentata, of which only one species, *Dasypus novemcinctus*, the nine-banded armadillo, extends its range beyond South America. The armadillos are well represented on the pampas and all burrow in the soil, although they come to the surface at night to feed. The most notable feature of the armadillo is its body plates, which give it the appearance of a reptile. Another group of edentates are the anteaters, which differ from the armadillos in having soft furry hides. The giant anteater (*Myrmecophaga tridactyla*) has powerful claws on its front feet; these are used in fighting and for breaking open termite mounds, as termites are its preferred diet (Fig. 8.20).

Carnivores on the pampas are the pampa fox (*Dusicyon gymnocercus*), which is more like a jackal or coyote than like a British fox, and the curious long-legged maned wolf (*Chry-*

socyon brachyurus) which has a long erectile mane on the back of its neck. Smaller carnivores include several species of skunk and the didelphid opossums which differ from most of the Australian marsupials in lacking a pouch.

The largest birds on the pampas are the two species of rhea (*Rhea americana* and *Pterocnemia pennata*), members of the ratites, a group of large flightless birds represented elsewhere by the ostrich of Africa, the cassowaries and emus of Australasia, and the kiwi of New Zealand (Fig. 8.21). Except for the kiwi, these birds are similar to each other and most are swift runners across the grasslands. Much smaller, partridge-like birds, which scuttle across the South American grasslands, are the tinamous; they are not related to game birds but form a primitive group of their own, close to the ratites although tinamous are not flightless. Another curious group is the screamers, which despite their appearance (they do not have goose-like bills or webbed feet) are related to the geese and swans; their habits are like those of a terrestrial goose, for they are primarily grazers on the open plains.

New Zealand grasslands

These are found in the south-east of the South Island, where, as in Patagonia, the prevailing westerly winds have lost much of their rain in crossing a mountain barrier. Tussock grasses in the genera *Festuca* and *Poa* are the main vegetation; at higher altitudes larger tussocks of species of *Danthonia* replace them.

There are no indigenous mammals in New Zealand, and their place on the grasslands was taken by the now extinct moas, giant birds up to 3.5 metres in height and completely flightless, having no vestige of wings. They were probably exterminated through overhunting when the Maoris arrived some 700 years ago. The original fauna of the grasslands also included songbirds and insects, and these remain along with the introduced sheep and cattle which now dominate the scene.

Fig. 8.21. Three large flightless birds (ratites) from different continents. Each fills a similar niche as a grazer on open plains. (a) The emu from Australia. (b) A male ostrich from Africa; this is the only ratite with a marked difference in the appearance of the sexes. (c) The rhea from South America.

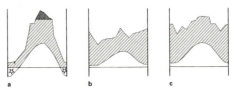

Fig. 8.22. Cool temperate forest climates

		alt.	a.p.	m.a.t.
a	Antung, China	40°10′N, 124°18′E	5	1007	6.6
b	Bruxelles, Belgium	50°51′N, 4°21′E	108	835	9.7
c	Roanoke, Va, USA	37°19′N, 79°55′W	358	1056	13.7

8.6 TEMPERATE FORESTS

South of the taiga, in the moister parts of the continents, lies a zone of forests made up largely of deciduous trees. Such forests were found in eastern North America, eastern Asia, and western Europe, but everywhere they have been extensively cleared by man to provide land for cultivation and pasture. In the southern hemisphere rather similar forests occur in similar climatic zones. It is possible to distinguish three main types of temperate forests: **cool temperate**, **warm temperate**, and **oceanic temperate**. These divisions are not as clearly reflected in the fauna as in the flora, and certain of the distinctions that do apply may be due as much to geographical separation as to climatic differences.

Production in deciduous temperate forests is restricted to the leafy period; the smaller herbs probably contribute an insignificant amount to the total. On an annual basis, cool temperate forests produce between 1000 and 1500 grams per square metre per year, and much of this is stored as wood. Less is known of the productivity of the warm and oceanic temperate forests, but, since they have a longer growing season, their annual productions are probably higher.

Cool temperate forests

The cool temperate forests are made up largely of deciduous trees, sometimes with a few evergreen conifers. Summers are relatively cool and winters mild; although frosts and snow occur in four to five months of the year, the mean monthly minima are usually above −5°C and at least 120 consecutive days have a mean temperature above 10 °C. Rain is moderate in amount (500 to 1500 millimetres per year) and evenly distributed through the year, or with a summer maximum. In eastern Asia and eastern North America these forests are relatively rich in species, but in western Europe they are much poorer. The reasons for this are historical: during the glaciations the flora of the first two areas was able to retreat southwards and then to reinvade in warmer periods, while in western Europe the Alps, Pyrenees and the Mediterranean Sea formed a barrier to southward movement, and some species became extinct (see section 15.3).

The cool temperate forests have a layered structure. The uppermost layer is formed by the larger tree species which attain 20 to 50 metres in height; sometimes there is a second tree layer 7 to 10 metres tall. Beneath these is a layer of shrubs which reach 3 to 4 metres, and below this is a layer of herbs which flower and make most of their vegetative growth in the spring before the canopy trees produce their leaves. There may be a layer of moss and lichen on the ground, but this is often sparse or absent because of the carpet of dead leaves that covers the forest floor every autumn.

The dominant species in these forests vary from continent to continent, but the same genera occur in all three: *Quercus* (oaks), *Tilia* (lime, basswood), *Ulmus* (elm), *Fagus* (beech), and *Acer* (maples). In western Europe, human influence on the forests has been so pervasive that it is sometimes difficult to be sure of the natural distributions of the various dominant trees of the forest; undisturbed sites are often on steep slopes, very dry sites or very wet ones, and none of these is likely to carry the typical forest. It appears, however, that beech (*Fagus sylvatica*) is the natural dominant in the better-drained sites where winters are relatively warm and summers relatively moist. Beechwoods are often so dense and vigorous that few other plants can survive (Fig. 8.23).

In regions with colder winters, and particularly in places with clay soils which tend to be waterlogged for part of the year, the pedunculate oak (*Quercus robur*) is the most successful species. Its close relative, the sessile oak (*Q. petraea*), is usually found on better-drained sites, and extends into the oceanic western fringes of Europe where *Q. robur* is rare and beech absent. Oakwoods have generally been heavily modified by man. In some places an understorey of shrubs and small trees of hazel (*Corylus avellana*), field maple (*Acer campestre*), hornbeam (*Carpinus betulus*) and small-leaved lime (*Tilia cordata*) has been encouraged by thinning of the oaks, and is cut regularly. This system, coppice-with-standards, provides small wood for fuel and building, on a short rotation of seven to 14 years, and large timber, also for building, on a larger rotation of perhaps 100 to 200 years. In other areas the oaks themselves are coppiced, mainly for charcoal, and in a third system the oaks are encouraged to form a more or less pure stand which is harvested on a 100 to 200-year rotation (Fig. 8.25). The herb layer of the oakforest is much more varied than that of the beechwoods; most of the plants flower in the spring before the trees come into leaf. At this time, species such as bluebell (*Hyacinthoides non-scripta*; Fig. 8.24), dog-violet (*Viola riviniana*), wood anemone (*Anemone nemorosa*; Fig. 8.24) and early purple orchid (*Orchis mascula*) form a most attractive community.

In eastern Asia, in Korea and the regions along the borders of China and the USSR, there are deciduous temperate forests. Here the climate is more extreme than that in western Europe, with 2 to 3 months in which the mean temperature is below 0 °C, and one or more summer months with a mean above 20 °C. There are some evergreen conifers such as Korean Pine (*Pinus koraiensis*), but also many deciduous trees including oaks (such as *Quercus mongolica*), limes (*Tilia*), birches, maples and walnuts. There is an understorey of smaller trees and shrubs, and mosses and ferns predominate on the forest floor.

Fig. 8.23. The beech woodlands of southern England, here with an understorey of holly (Ilex aquifolium), may be in part artificial. Some certainly owe their preservation to their former use as royal hunting parks.

Fig. 8.24. (a) Woodland ground flora, predominantly wood anemone (Anemone nemorosa) and Hepatica triloba. (b) A carpet of bluebells (Hyacinthoides) in a beech wood.

a

b

Fig. 8.25. Trees in an oakwood: (a) grown as coppice, with a mature crop of poles; (b) standards above hazel; (c) left to right, regenerative felling of hundred-year-old trees, well-established seedlings before a second thinning and strong straight saplings after a final cut.

The north-eastern USA also carries much deciduous forest; here again the main trees are of the same genera as in Europe, with species such as American beech (*Fagus grandifolia*), American lime (*Tilia americana*), ash (*Fraxinus americana*) and sugar maple (*Acer saccharum*). Eastern white pine (*Pinus strobus*) is the commonest conifer. Just as in the European forests, there is a rich and attractive spring ground flora including species of *Trillium*, *Uvularia*, *Dicentra* and *Hepatica*. Many of these forests were very heavily cut, and are only now regenerating following the widespread abandonment of agriculture in this region.

Warm temperate forests

The best development of forests of this type, in which, although the winters are distinctly cooler than the summers, frost is never prolonged, occur in eastern Asia, and the eastern USA. Less rich forests are found in southern Europe, there are isolated fragments in the Caucasus area, and a most unusual but distinctive type occurs on the Canary Islands.

The northern plain of China formerly carried warm temperate forest, but this has been virtually eliminated by centuries of cultivation and clearance. The northern parts of the area have two to three cold months which may have frosts and snow, but to the south these become rare. Rain is most abundant in the summer, and 1000 to 1500 millimetres annually is normal. The forests in the north are largely of deciduous species. Several species of oak are common, associated with eastern species of ash, lime, walnut and elm. Smaller trees, such as maples (*Acer davidii*) and birch (*Betula fruticosa*), form a lower layer. Shrubs include many species which are familiar in gardens in Europe, such as *Cotoneaster multiflora*, *Rosa bella*, *Lonicera nitida* and *Rhododendron mucronulatum*.

In China south of the Ch'iang Chang (Yangtze Kiang) river the climate becomes milder and frosts are rare, although the winters are cool. Rain is plentiful, between 1000 and 2000 millimetres falling each year, mostly in the summer months since the area lies within the area of influence of the monsoon. These forests are extremely rich in species; reports speak of 50 species of maple (*Acer*), 30 species of whitebeam (*Sorbus*), 10 species of hornbeam (*Carpinus*) and ash (*Fraxinus*), together with several species of lime (*Tilia*), elm (*Ulmus*), and birch

(*Betula*). All of these are familiar trees of Europe and North America, but here they are joined by other genera such as the cork-trees (*Phellodendron*), foxglove-tree (*Paulownia*) and *Magnolia*. These are all deciduous, but there are also evergreen representatives of more tropical groups such as *Lithocarpus* (a kind of oak), *Castanopsis* (related to the sweet chestnut, *Castanea*), and *Cinnamomum* (*C. camphora*, the camphor tree). This very mixed forest, with evergreen and deciduous components, extends also into southern Japan, which has a moist oceanic climate. These forests of southern China are rich in species because there is no barrier to north–south migration, so that the climatic changes of the Pleistocene did not cause widespread extinctions.

Rather similar warm temperate forests are found in the south-eastern USA; the richest are found in the southern Appalachians, where a considerable range in altitude and a very diverse topography combine to produce a wide range of habitats. In at least some areas these forests have never been cleared and some now lie within National Parks. The richest are the forests of moist slopes, often north-facing. The rainfall here is high, with 1500 to 2000 millimetres per year, and frosts occur during three to four months of each year. Twenty-five to 30 species of tree make up the upper layers of the forest, including lime and basswood (*Tilia*), horse chestnut (*Aesculus*), maple, silverbell (*Halesia*), tulip tree (*Liriodendron*), beech, sweet chestnut (*Castanea*), wild cherry (*Prunus*), and birch. Hemlock (*Tsuga canadensis*) is a common conifer in some places. Smaller trees and shrubs include juneberry (*Amelanchier*), *Rhododendron* and *Magnolia*. There is a rich ground flora of spring-flowering genera including *Trillium*, *Erythronium*, *Dicentra* and *Dentaria*.

West of the Mississippi, in the Ozark Uplands, the forests are of oak and hickory (*Carya*). Understorey trees and shrubs include dogwood (*Cornus florida*), ironwood (*Ostrya virginiana*), and juneberry. These brief remarks cannot really do justice to the extremely varied warm temperate forests of the southern USA, nor to the warm temperate forests of the south-east dominated by pines (*Pinus palustris* and *P. taeda*).

The deciduous forests of southern Europe have generally been very much damaged and modified by human activity. Trees with useful fruits, such as olive (*Olea europaea*), sweet chestnut (*Castanea sativa*) and walnut (*Juglans regia*), tend to be

Fig. 8.26. Warm temperate forest climates		alt.	a.p.	m.a.t.
a	Kuling, China	20°35′N, 116°02′E	1070	1914	11.5
b	Melbourne, Australia	37°40′S, 145°00′E	38	649	14.7
c	Batumi, USSR	41°30′N, 41°30′E	3	2404	14.3

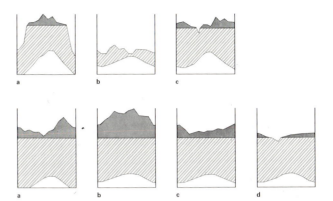

preserved, while the less useful species are cleared. Thus the composition of the forests has been modified over the centuries. Other species in these southern European woods are various oaks, horse chestnut, Montpellier maple (*Acer monspessulanum*) and Turkish hazel (*Corylus colurna*).

An isolated and peculiar area of warm temperate forest is found on the eastern shore of the Black Sea, in Georgia, USSR. The trees are mainly deciduous and include genera such as *Zelkova* and *Pterocarya*, together with endemic species of hornbeam (*Carpinus caucasica*) and beech (*Fagus orientalis*). Many of the smaller trees and shrubs are evergreen; several species of *Rhododendron* and the laurel (*Prunus laurocerasus*) occur here. The climate is warm temperate and wet, with up to 4000 millimetres of rain each year.

Finally among the warm temperate forests are the laurel forests of the Canary Islands. These are best developed on the moister western islands such as La Palma and Tenerife, and are made up of broad-leaved evergreen species such as *Persea indica*, *Ocotea foetens* and *Laurus azorica*. These forests have now been extensively cleared but relics remain. A moderate rainfall is concentrated in the winter months and is reinforced at other seasons by frequent fogs. Some of the genera have their closest relatives in the New World and it has been suggested that these forests are relics of a type which was formerly widespread.

Oceanic temperate forests

Forests of this type occur in western North America, western Chile, and the South Island of New Zealand. In all three areas steep mountains face the sea, and when moist winds from the west strike these mountains heavy rains result. In all three areas the evenly distributed annual rainfall is above 4000 millimetres and may reach 8000 millimetres in New Zealand.

The forests on the western coast of North America extend from northern California to Alaska. In northern California the dominant tree is (or was) the coast redwood (*Sequoia sempervirens*), some individuals of which reach 100 metres in height. Further north, a more mixed forest with western hemlock (*Tsuga heterophylla*), western red cedar (*Thuja plicata*) and Douglas fir (*Pseudotsuga menziesii*) replaces the redwoods. These forests are of enormous stature and the trees grow close together, so the standing crop is huge. The trees may reach 70 to 80 metres, although many of the largest have been removed for timber. The undergrowth is mainly of mosses and ferns which form a dense carpet over the forest floor. Further north still, the climate becomes cooler, although frosts are rare and seasonal

Fig. 8.27. Oceanic temperate forest climates.
(*Mulrany supports blanket bog.*)

			alt.	a.p.	m.a.t.
a	Yakutat, Alaska, USA	59°50′N, 139°44′W	2	3408	4.1
b	Milford Sound, N. Zealand	44°54′S, 167°47′E	6	6337	9.9
c	Puerto Aisen, Chile	45°10′S, 73°00′W	10	3018	8.9
d	Mulrany, Eire	53°54′N, 9°47′W	30	1743	10.0

fluctuations are small. The dominant tree here is the Sitka spruce (*Picea sitchensis*).

The oceanic temperate forests of the southern hemisphere resemble each other in many ways; the forests of Chile are much more like those of New Zealand than they are like those of western North America. Both the forests in the southern hemisphere have abundant southern beech (*Nothofagus*) and podocarps (*Podocarpus*). The forests of Chile extend from about 40 °S to about 55 °S, between the Andes and the sea. In the extreme north of this narrow strip, where there is marked summer drought, are forests of *Nothofagus obliqua*, a deciduous species. A little further south the rain becomes evenly distributed throughout the year, and here the beech species is the evergreen *Nothofagus dombeyi*, associated with several unusual conifers such as *Fitzroya patagonica* (alerce), *Austrocedrus chiliensis*, *Saxegothaea conspicua*, *Araucaria araucana* (monkey-puzzle), and species of *Podocarpus*. Further south the dominant trees are again deciduous, including *Nothofagus betuloides* and *N. procera*. These forests have an understorey of evergreen shrubs including familiar garden plants such as *Desfontainea spinosa* and *Pernettya mucronata*, and are extremely rich in mosses, liverworts and ferns.

The New Zealand forests of this zone (Fig. 8.29) are best developed on the west coast of the South Island, and here, as in southern Chile, the forests are evergreen, with many conifers. Among the flowering plants, *Metrosideros robusta* (rata) and species of *Leptospermum*, *Laurelia*, *Corynocarpus* and many others are common. The conifers include species of *Podocarpus* (such as totara (*P. totara*) and kahikatea (*P. dacrydioides*)), *Dacrydium cupressinum* (rimu) and *Phyllocladus trichomanoides* (tanekaha). The forests are dense, and the tree-trunks are often covered with climbing plants such as *Freycinetia banksii*, a member of the pandanus (screw-pine) family. Many ferns, liverworts and mosses grow abundantly both on the ground and as epiphytes (plants growing on other plants). In the southern part of the island species of *Nothofagus* become more common. The flora of the New Zealand forests is being severely damaged by introduced deer.

The moorlands of North-west Europe

The western margins of continents in both the northern and southern hemispheres thus carry oceanic temperate forests. In northern Europe, however, such vegetation is absent although the same conditions prevail. Rainfall is not as high as in some of the other areas, amounting to only 400 to 1000 millimetres per year, but is evenly distributed, and evaporation is low because of heavy cloud cover and low temperatures. At low altitudes, frost and snow both occur but do not generally persist for long, and no month has a mean temperature below 0 °C. These areas in Ireland, Scotland, England, Denmark and parts of northern Germany and southern Sweden all carry areas of vegetation known as heath and composed of low shrubs, many of them belonging to the heather family (Ericaceae) (Fig. 8.30). In many areas, however, heathland has been reclaimed for agriculture.

The heathland community is dominated in many areas by a single species, *Calluna vulgaris*, called heather or ling. In the drier and more southern heaths, bell heather (*Erica cinerea*), St Dabeoc's heath (*Daboecia cantabrica*) and Cornish heath (*Erica vagans*) dominate the more oceanic areas; further inland, leguminous shrubs such as *Ulex* (gorse), and *Sarothamnus* and *Genista* (both types of broom) are often common. These heaths generally occur on very poor and shallow sandy podzols (see section 8.1), but in the most oceanic regions of Ireland and western Britain vast areas are covered by peat (blanket bog), which carries a wet form of heath in which sedges are common along with many mosses and the heather *Erica tetralix* (see section 9.3).

The origin of these heaths has been much discussed. It seems that many have carried trees in the past, but that these cannot recolonise the heaths because of grazing or burning. Sheep graze many western heaths and prevent tree regeneration by eating seedlings. Much of the heathland of northern Britain is managed for shooting of grouse (*Lagopus scoticus*), involving the regular burning of the heather at intervals of 10 to 15 years to provide a patchwork of young heather in which the grouse can feed, and long heather for nesting. This regular burning also prevents recolonisation by trees. Evidence from archaeological sites and from pollen analysis shows that the disappearance of trees from heathland sites often coincides with the appearance of pollen of weeds and of crops (see Chapter 15); much of the original clearance probably occurred in the Bronze Age or Iron Age.

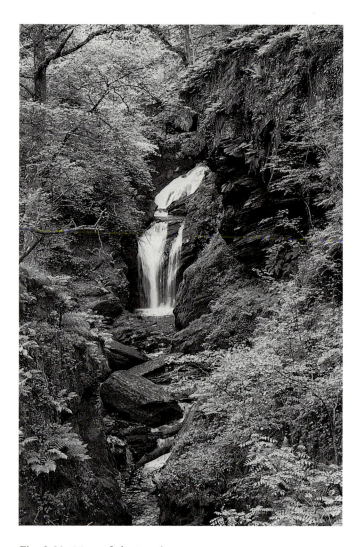

Fig. 8.28. Most of the North-west European oceanic temperate forest zone is occupied by heathland, but here and there, as in this moist, fern- and moss-rich rocky woodland in North Wales, rather stunted and probably relict forests are found, mostly in sites too unpromising to have been cleared for agriculture.

Animals of temperate forests

The large herbivorous mammals of the cool forests are principally deer. The largest of all, the moose (*Alces alces*), extends its range southwards from the coniferous forests, but more typical deer are the commonest inhabitants. The red deer (*Cervus elaphus*; Fig. 4.7) is the only species occurring throughout the Holarctic region (provided one accepts that the North American wapiti is a race of *C. elaphus*, and not a separate species *C. canadensis*). Red deer are often found in open country, but this is only because their original forest home has been destroyed by man. These grassland deer are noticeably smaller than are the forest types because of the poorer nutrition available in the grassland. In the far eastern forests the red deer is replaced by the closely related sika deer (*C. nippon*). Other forest deer include the white-tailed deer (*Odocoileus virginianus*) and the mule deer (*O. hemionus*) in North America, and the roe deer (*Capreolus capreolus*) in Eurasia.

The forest tarpan (*Equus ferus sylvaticus*) was a wild horse

Fig. 8.29. This forest of southern beech (Nothofagus) in the North Island of New Zealand shows the richness in ferns and other epiphytes that is found in even greater degree in the wetter forests of the South Island.

Fig. 8.30. A heath in southern Sweden on shallow soils over granite. Heather (Calluna) is frequent on soils of medium depth; juniper (Juniperus) is common. In the background pine and birch are invading, probably on deeper soils.

Fig. 8.31. Some examples of the fauna of temperate woodlands. (a) The lesser (or red) panda. This is a species of uncertain relationships although it is usually classed with the procyonids (the racoon family). (b) Grass snake. This is a non-poisonous species that is often found in water, where it preys upon frogs and fish. (c) Bank voles are abundant in deciduous woodlands throughout most of Europe and as far east as Lake Baikal. They occasionally cause damage to timber plantations. (d) Dormouse. There are several species of dormouse, which are named for their long sleep during hibernation.

which became extinct in the last century. The European bison (*Bison bonasus*) also became extinct in the wild, but survived in captivity and has now been reintroduced into the Białowieza Forest in eastern Poland. It is a true forest-dweller and a taller, longer-legged animal than the American bison of the prairies. A smaller herbivore is the beaver (*Castor fiber*), which occurs in both North America and Eurasia although it is rare and declining in Europe. The beaver is famous for its dam-building, and although not all beavers make dams they all construct lodges in which to pass the winter months (see Fig. 9.7).

The wild boar (*Sus scrofa*) occurs widely throughout the Eurasian north temperate regions and its distribution extends into tropical regions. It does not occur in North America and it has no ecological equivalent in the temperate forests there. Among the woodland carnivores are a number of mustelid species, of which the badger (*Meles meles*) is the most widespread in Eurasia. The American badger (*Taxidea taxus*) is a different animal although it has much the same habits; neither species is confined to woodland. Skunks are also typical inhabitants of temperate forests in North America. The red fox is a common woodland carnivore on both sides of the Atlantic, and other small carnivores include the wild cat (*Felis sylvestris*) in Eurasia and the raccoon (*Procyon lotor*) in North America. The red panda (*Ailurus fulgens*; Fig. 8.31) is an inhabitant of bamboo forests in Nepal and West Burma as well as southern China, but the giant panda (*Ailuropoda melanoleuca*) is found only in southern China and is a specialist herbivore on bamboo. The larger carnivores include bears, the American black bear (*Ursus americanus*) in North America and the Asiatic black bear (*Selenarctos thibetanus*) in eastern Asia and Japan.

Bird life is abundant in the cool northern forests, and includes many of the songbirds found in suburban gardens such as the bullfinch (*Pyrrhula pyrrhula*) and hawfinch (*Coccothraustes coccothraustes*). The crow family is represented by the jay (*Garrulus glandarius*), magpie (*Pica pica*) and jackdaw (*Corvus monedula*). The widespread management over several centuries of European woodlands has had a profound effect on the bird populations. Many of the European woodlands have been so broken up into small patches that grassland hawks have taken to hunting over them, such as the kestrel (*Falco tinnunculus*), which hovers while hunting for prospective prey, a technique easily adapted to forest glades. Apart from the great many owls, few birds of prey are actually confined to the forests.

The New Zealand forests have a wealth of specialised birds. New Zealand has no native land mammals, apart from bats, because of its long isolation and great distance from any other land. Consequently there were no mammalian ground predators before the advent of human beings and many of the native birds have lost the power of flight. The most unusual is the kiwi (*Apteryx*), usually classed with the ratites but more likely to have evolved independently. Kiwis have a much better sense of smell than any other bird, and use this in searching for the worms on which they feed: their eyesight is correspondingly poorly developed. The feathers of kiwis are hair-like, and their wings vestigial. The female lays a single huge egg which weighs one-fifth to one-quarter of her body weight.

Some 45 species of bird became extinct in New Zealand after the arrival of the Maoris less than 1000 years ago. Many of these extinct birds dwelt in the forests covering most of the islands. The takahe (*Notornis mantelli*) is a large flightless rail once believed to be extinct, but which was rediscovered in 1948 in a valley in South Island. There are several species of parrot in New Zealand, including the kea (*Nestor notabilis*), normally a vegetarian but the only parrot to eat meat, although it does not take living prey. It ventures out into the grassland, and has become a nuisance to sheep farmers from its habit of opening up sores on the backs of sheep. The kea shares its range with the kakapo (*Strigops habroptilus*), a very rare forest parrot that has almost lost the power of flight, although it can glide from tree to ground.

Reptiles are well represented in the temperate forests of the world, with some large snakes (pythons) in the warmer Australian regions. Elsewhere snakes are smaller and generally non-poisonous, and include the widespread grass snake (*Natrix*

c

d

natrix) and the equally harmless and ecologically similar common garter snake (*Thamnophis sirtalis*). Both these snakes take readily to water and prey upon frogs and small fish, as well as upon mice and other terrestrial animals. Numerous lizards occur on the forest floor and in the trees. The tuatara (*Sphenodon punctatus*) of New Zealand is the sole surviving representative of an order of reptiles, the Rhynchocephalia, that became extinct some 100 million years ago. It owes its survival to the long isolation of New Zealand, and is now found only on small islands off North Island. It has a well-developed light-sensitive area on top of the head, called a 'third eye' although it does not focus light nor is it apparent on the surface.

Amphibians are not typical of temperate forests in general, although toads occur, and in the warmer forests tree-frogs may be found. Frogs and newts abound in streams or ponds.

Insect life is rich, although temperate forests cannot compete with the rain-forests in the abundance of butterflies and moths. The total numbers of butterfly and moth larvae, however, is high, and hawkmoths with their plump colourful caterpillars are numerous. Many of the leaves show worm-like swellings marking the tunnels of leaf-miners, the caterpillars of very small moths. Some emerge from the interior of the leaf before pupating and continue to feed on the surface, while others form blotch mines rather than tunnels and pupate within the leaf. Some leaf-miners, forming blotches rather than tunnels, are the larvae of flies (Diptera).

Many of the forest trees have galls (see Fig. 10.7), which are mostly caused by insects, particularly the solitary wasps. Usually the wasp lays its eggs in the leaf and the plant tissues respond by swelling around the point of entry. The galls provide food and shelter for many other insects, and sometimes the original wasp is parasitised by a chalcid wasp which lays its egg on the developing larva. The chalcid larva may even be parasitised itself by a further invader, an ichneumon fly, in an example of hyperparasitism. The trees do not seem to suffer unduly from the presence of galls although there must be some loss of photosynthetic capability. The sum total of the depredations due to insects through the course of a growing season, however, can sometimes be a significant proportion of the primary production of the forest.

8.7 THE MEDITERRANEAN ZONES

Closer to the equator than the oceanic temperate forest zone are areas with a very distinctive climate, in which the winters are cool and moist and the summers are hot and dry. The total rain for the year is usually between 300 and 800 millimetres, and four summer months are usually almost completely dry; during these months mean temperatures reach 20 to 25 °C. The mean temperature of the coldest months is about 10 °C, and frosts are occasional and do not last long. Growth is thus best in spring and autumn.

Climates of this type are widespread around the shores of the Mediterranean Sea, which gives its name to the zone of climate and vegetation, and also occur in southern California, the central latitudes of Chile, the Cape of Good Hope in South Africa, and south-western Australia. The vegetation of all these areas is extremely similar in physiognomy (overall appearance), although the main species and even families are quite different in the various areas. It is possible that all once carried evergreen woodland or shrubland, and clearance for cultivation, grazing, and burning have substantially altered the type of vegetation; these changes are continuing.

Mediterranean vegetation

Much of the original vegetation around the Mediterranean was probably evergreen woodland dominated by holm or evergreen oak (*Quercus ilex*). Below the trees grew evergreen shrubs such as box (*Buxus sempervirens*), *Viburnum tinus* and species of *Phillyrea*. Plants on the forest floor included butcher's broom (*Ruscus aculeatus*) and *Asparagus acutifolius*. In the western Mediterranean, on siliceous soils, the cork oak (*Quercus suber*) may replace *Q. ilex*, and in the drier parts the small Kermes oak (*Q. coccifera*) may be the most abundant woody species. The soils of the *Quercus ilex* woodland, on limestone, consist of a humus layer over a clay-rich red underlying soil; the whole is called a **terra-rossa** (see section 8.1).

Regular cutting, and intermittent burning, leads to the replacement of the holm oak woodland by a community of

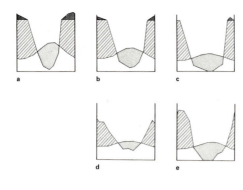

Fig. 8.32. Mediterranean climates.		alt.	a.p.	m.a.t.
a Zante, Greece	37°47′N, 20°54′E	2	1115	18.5
b Perth, Australia	31°57′S, 115°52′E	60	883	17.9
c Valparaiso, Chile	33°02′S, 71°40′W	41	490	14.3
d Danger Point, South Africa	34°40′S, 19°17′E	28	544	16.0
e Santa Barbara, Calif., USA	34°25′N, 119°40′W	37	471	15.6

and to the south into various types of temperate forest.

The winter rainfall area of South Africa is also small, yet it is astoundingly rich in species. Two thousand species are known from the 20 square kilometres of the Jonkershoek Nature Reserve. Within the small area there is a great diversity of habitats, with an altitudinal range of nearly 1000 metres and rainfall averages between 300 and 1800 millimetres per year. Certain genera have speciated to a remarkable extent: there are about 600 species of *Erica* (heather), 100 species of *Protea*, 115 species of *Muraltia* (Polygalaceae) and 120 species of *Restio* (Restionaceae). This Cape flora is a very isolated one, and virtually none of the species is found elsewhere. There are many geophytes (plants with the perennial organs or buds buried in the soil), which tend to flower when the shrubby vegetation has been removed by fires. There are few trees, but there is a well-developed sclerophyllous scrub, known locally as **fynbos**, in which members of the Proteaceae are common; this burns regularly. The Cape flora is threatened by over-frequent fires, by settlement, and by the spread of introduced species of trees and shrubs.

The winter rainfall areas of Australia lie in the south-west corner of the country, and also to a lesser extent in southern Australia around Adelaide. Their vegetation is similar in appearance to that of the other winter-rainfall areas of the world, but it contains more woody plants. Members of the genus *Eucalyptus* (gums) are common here, and plants characteristic of this habitat are the grass-trees (*Kingia*, *Xanthorrhoea*, from the family Xanthorrhoeaceae), and many species of the families Epacridaceae and Stylidiaceae. Members of the Proteaceae are also very abundant, with genera such as *Banksia*, *Hakea* and *Grevillea*. Within the south-west Australian winter rainfall zone it is possible to distinguish at least three vegetation zones, following the rainfall which declines on moving northwards. In the wettest and most south-westerly regions, with an annual rainfall of 1200 to 1500 millimetres, forests of karri (*Eucalyptus diversicolor*) are the climax vegetation. The trees reach 60 to 70 metres in height, but many of the best stands have been felled for timber. In somewhat drier regions, with 700 to 1200 millimetres of rain a year and a pronounced summer drought, jarrah (*Eucalyptus marginata*) is the main tree. Areas with still lower rainfall cannot support continuous woodland, although various shrubby species of *Eucalyptus* occur. In such areas, particularly on sandy soils very poor in nutrients, a heath-type vegetation very rich in species occurs, dominated by members of the Proteaceae. These heaths are burned at irregular intervals, and many of the species in them do not flower or reproduce by seed unless this happens. The seeds of *Banksia* species are held in woody capsules which do not open until they have been burned, and the species of *Xanthorrhoea* only flower after fires. These features suggest that fire has been a natural feature of these heaths for a very long time.

much shorter trees and shrubs known as **maquis** (Fig. 8.33); *Quercus coccifera* is often common, as are species of *Phillyrea*. More frequent cutting with burning and grazing produces a much more open vegetation dominated by hummocks of low-growing shrubs, such as small forms of *Quercus coccifera*, *Juniperus oxycedrus* or, in the east, *Sarcopoterium spinosum*. This vegetation is locally called **garrigue**. Aromatic shrublets such as rock-rose (*Cistus*), lavender (*Lavandula*), thyme (*Thymus*) and rosemary (*Rosmarinus*) are often very common. In the gaps between the shrubs a rich flora of annual species appears in late winter and spring, as well as many bulbous and tuberous plants such as orchids, crocuses and irises (Fig. 8.34) which flower in the spring and die down during the summer. Extremes of land use lead to the loss of most shrubs; species of asphodel (*Asphodelus*), a bulbous plant which is not grazed by animals, then come to be the most prominent constituents of the vegetation.

The trees and shrubs are mostly evergreen, and tend to have small hard leaves which are very resistant to water loss in the heat of summer. Such plants are known as sclerophylls. Many also contain large amounts of aromatic oils, which may help to make them less palatable to browsing animals, but also makes them inflammable.

Just as in the Mediterranean lands, the original vegetation in the zone of Mediterranean vegetation in southern California was open oak woodland in the moister parts; *Quercus agrifolia* and *Q. engelmannii* are common species. The equivalent of maquis in California is the **chaparral**. Species of *Quercus* occur here also; they are joined by species of *Ceanothus*, *Arctostaphylos*, and many others, forming a low scrub which, like the maquis, is highly inflammable. Fires, often started by lightning, are a feature of this habitat, and many of the plants are able to sprout from the base when all their above-ground parts have been destroyed by fire.

The winter rainfall area of Chile is small because it occupies a narrow coastal strip between the Andes and the sea, between about 30 and 37 °S. Little remains of the original flora, but there are relict fragments of sclerophyllous woodlands in which important species are *Quillaja saponaria* (Rosaceae), *Peumus boldus* (Monimiaceae) and *Lithraea caustica* (Anacardiaceae). There are also many sclerophyllous shrubs. To the north this vegetation zone grades into the extremely dry coastal deserts,

Fig. 8.33. *Mediterranean vegetation in Crete. In the foreground clumps of spiny shrubs form 'garrigue', with plants of* Asphodelus *suggesting heavy grazing. In the background is an area of taller 'maquis', of* Quercus *and* Olea.

Fig. 8.34. *Some of the perennial bulb-, tuber- or corm-bearing plants characteristic of the spring flora of the Mediterranean lands: (a) the sawfly orchid (*Ophrys tenthredinifera*), (b) the wild gladiolus (*Gladiolus segetum*), (c)* Iris xiphoides.

*Fig. 8.35. Animals of the Mediterranean region. (a) The eyed lizard (*Lacerta lepida*) preys upon small rodents and other reptiles. (b) The ladder snake (*Elaphe scalaris*) can move very quickly and preys upon rodents and birds as well as lizards and insects. It is not venomous. (c) The mouflon is the wild*

*sheep of Europe although its present distribution may have been influenced by man. (d) An oil or blister beetle (*Meloe*). Oil beetles are related to* Cantharis, *the 'Spanish fly' and have a complicated life-history with the larvae parasitic on bees.*

Animals of the Mediterranean zones

In all the Mediterranean zones of the world the populations of large mammals have been severely reduced by human activity. North Africa once possessed a wide variety of big game species, as well as such Palaearctic types as the Barbary stag (*Cervus elaphus barbarus*, a race of the red deer) and the wild boar (*Sus scrofa*), and the Atlas Mountains still contain the Barbary ape (*Macaca sylvanus*), a type of macaque typical of Asia and not closely related to the African monkeys south of the Sahara. Large herbivores that probably owe their present distribution to human influence include the fallow deer (*Dama dama*), and the wild sheep or mouflon (*Ovis musimon*) which was originally present on Corsica and Sardinia. A smaller herbivore that certainly owes its present wide distribution to human introductions is the common rabbit (*Oryctolagus cuniculus*). Predators used to include the lion, and possibly a few leopards still remain in North Africa, but the commonest present-day predators are small.

The Mediterranean has a rich bird fauna with lapwings (*Vanellus vanellus*), curlews (*Numenius arquata*) and cattle

egrets (*Bubucus ibis*) among the coastal birds. Bustards roam the grasslands, with the great bustard (*Otis tarda*) in Europe and the Houbara bustard (*Chlamydotis undulata*) in Africa. The red-legged partridge (*Alectoris rufa*) and the rock partridge (*A. graeca*) live in rocky scrub country in the western and eastern Mediterranean, respectively. Birds of prey include some large eagles, such as the Imperial eagle (*Aquila heliaca*) and the golden eagle (*A. chrysaetos*), as well as many smaller hawks and falcons.

There are many species of tortoise (*Testudo*), lizards and snakes in the Mediterranean region (Fig. 8.35), including the whip snake (*Coluber gemonensis*), one of the fastest and more aggressive snakes in Europe although it feeds mainly on rodents and lizards and is not dangerous to man.

The fauna of the southern extremity of Africa shows close parallels to that of the Mediterranean, although of course there are no resident Palaearctic species. Many of the large animals are no longer present, but in the recent past there were distinct subspecies of bontebok (*Damaliscus dorcas*), mountain zebra (*Equus zebra*), eland (*Taurotragus oryx*), elephant (*Loxodonta africana*) and lion (*Panthera leo*). Only one full species, however, is now extinct, the blaauwbok (*Hippotragus leoco-phaeus*), which was a relative of the roan and sable antelopes. The Barbary ape is replaced by an ecologically similar primate, the chacma baboon (*Papio ursinus*), and the rabbit by the hyrax (*Procavia capensis*) or more closely by the springhaas (*Pedetes capensis*), a kangaroo-like hystricomorph rodent. Carnivores include the Cape grey mongoose (*Herpestes pulverulentus*) and the Egyptian mongoose (*H. ichneumon*). There are several species of meerkat (*Suricata*), a type of mongoose named for its association with water and cat-like body.

Bird life is very rich, with numerous nectar-eating birds exploiting the wealth of flowering plants, including the sunbirds, and the sugarbirds (*Promerops*), a group peculiar to the Cape region where they are closely associated with *Protea* bushes. Migrants from the north are present, including the white stork and the European swallow (*Hirundo rustica*). The greater flamingo (*Phoenicopterus ruber*) occurs at the Cape, as does the jackass penguin (*Spheniscus demersus*) which is named after its braying call. Gulls and terns are abundant, often either the same species as, or near relatives of, those found in the Mediterranean, emphasising the close similarity between the two regions.

8.8 ARID ENVIRONMENTS

The arid parts of the world mostly lie in the subtropical zone between 15 and 40° north and south of the equator. In Africa there are the Namib and Kalahari Deserts in the south, and the Sahara in the north is essentially continuous with the Arabian, Iranian and Thar Deserts of Asia. North of the Himalayas lie the cold deserts of Central Asia, the Takla Makan and the Gobi. Much of central Australia has a low and irregular rainfall and is considered to be desert or semi-desert. In America, there are deserts in Mexico and the southern parts of the USA, and perhaps the driest of all is the coastal Atacama Desert of Peru and Chile.

The weather of the subtropical arid zones is dominated by high pressure, giving sparse and irregular rain, clear skies, high temperatures, strong winds, and intense evaporation. Rain is not only small in amount but also irregularly distributed in time and space: the central parts of deserts can receive rain at any time. The equatorial margins of the arid belt receive the extreme edge of the monsoon rains during the hot summer, and the deserts grade into savannas at their equatorial margins. The polar margins of the arid belt receive some winter rains, and grade into Mediterranean vegetation. At these margins, therefore, it is extremely difficult to demarcate desert and semi-desert from savanna and maquis. Economically, desert has been defined as a type of land where no cultivation is possible; specialised dry-land crops can be grown in semi-desert regions. Botanically, desert has been defined as a region in which perennial plants, if present at all, are confined to watercourses and other places where water accumulates, while in semi-

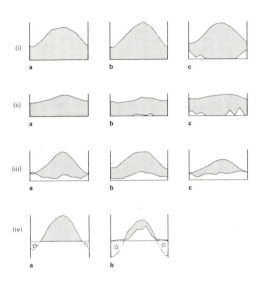

Fig. 8.36. Arid zone climates.

(i) subtropical hot deserts, virtually no rain		alt.	a.p.	m.a.t.
a Luxor, Egypt	25°41′N, 32°8′E	78	1	24.2
b In Salah, Algeria	27°10′N, 2°32′E	279	15	25.1
c Dharan, Saudi Arabia		150	54	26.9

(ii) subtropical coastal deserts, cold water offshore, frequent mists				
a Antofagasta, Chile	23°50′S, 70°30′W	94	4	17.2
b Swakopmund, Namibia	22°37′S, 14°30′E	10	15	15.3
c Cape Juby, Morocco	27°55′N, 12°55′W	8	51	18.8

(iii) warm temperate and cool temperate deserts, irregular rainfall				
a Las Vegas, Nevada, USA	36°10′N, 115°05′W	571	112	18.1
b Charlotte Waters, Australia	25°56′S, 134°54′E	211	134	21.6
c Puerto Madryn, Argentina	42°48′S, 65°04′W	12	155	13.6

(iv) temperate deserts of the Central Asian Plateau, great winter cold				
a Charchan, China	38°04′N, 85°16′E	966	9	10.6
b Dalandzadgad, Mongolia	43°37′N, 104°17′E	1466	119	3.9

deserts specialised perennial plants can survive in most sites.

Deserts are always thought of as being hot. This is so during the day, but during the night the lack of vegetation and of cloud allows rapid outward flow of radiation, and the temperature falls quickly to give daily ranges as great as 30 °C. Furthermore, since most arid zones are some way from the equator, there is considerable seasonal temperature variation, and frosts may occur during winter nights. Certain coastal deserts such as the Namib and the Atacama have a peculiar climate in which an almost total lack of rain is mitigated by frequent fogs caused by cold water offshore. These fogs deposit heavy dews on the ground, and where they contact rocks or other obstructions enough water may be deposited to run off and moisten pockets of soil.

Fig. 8.37. Heavy storms in desert areas lead to the flowering of small, ephemeral plants as here in the Atacama Desert in South America. The amount of rain has not been sufficient to wet the parched, cracked ground but the seeds have been enabled to germinate.

Vegetation of arid zones

The vegetation of arid zones is limited by lack of water: no other factor is as significant. The plants which grow in these environments fall into two main classes, the **ephemerals**, which avoid periods of water shortage by surviving as seeds, and **perennials**, which endure water shortage in various ways. Of the perennials, some store water in specialised tissues, others tap deep-lying water resources, and yet others have underground bulbs and produce aerial parts only when conditions are favourable.

The ephemerals germinate after heavy storms and grow rapidly, completing their life-cycles in as little as two weeks (Fig. 8.37). They tend to be extremely adaptable, remaining very small and producing only a few flowers in unfavourable conditions, but growing much larger if more water is available. Many have seed dormancy mechanisms which permit germination only when large amounts of rain have fallen, and which also produce heterogeneous populations of seeds so that not all germinate simultaneously, a clear adaptation to rains of uncertain timing and quantity. For example, a dwarf composite, *Asteriscus pygmaeus*, which occurs in the deserts of the Middle East, bears fruits enclosed by bracts which open and release a few fruits each time they are wetted. After being released the seeds in the fruit will not germinate until enough rain has fallen to wash out a water-soluble inhibitor. In the desert regions of western Australia and the southern USA the winter rains and the summer rains produce different species of ephemeral plants; experiments suggest that seeds of different species have different temperature requirements for germination, and that this feature determines the different composition of the ephemeral flora at different seasons.

Many of the ephemeral plants have large and conspicuous flowers, perhaps an adaptation to attract the sparse insect population. Apart from this, however, and their unusual seed biology, they do not have any very obvious features which could be considered adaptive. Rather, their whole life-cycle can be considered as an evasive adaptation, avoiding the harsh conditions of the arid zones and making all their growth during the short and unpredictable wet spells.

Perennial plants of arid zones show many adaptations to their water-starved environment. Some, such as geophytes with bulbs or corms underground, effectively evade periods of water shortage. It appears that these do not produce aerial parts every year, but only after heavy rain. While the surface soil of arid regions can be extremely dry, there is usually some water below the surface, sufficient to saturate the soil air and thus to make the rate of water loss from a buried corm or bulb extremely slow. Only after heavy rain, though, will enough water penetrate to allow formation of roots and the production of aerial parts, although a few species may produce flowers when there has been no rain, using either water stored in the bulb or underground water sources.

The most familiar perennial plants of arid zones are the succulents, plants with greatly swollen stems or leaves which act as water reservoirs. Coupled with this is a reduction in surface area, a greatly thickened cuticle, and often a covering of spines which may discourage herbivores from feeding on the succulent plant body. Different plant groups dominate the succulent floras of different continents (Fig. 8.38). In America the family Cactaceae is very abundant and characterises the arid lands. There are over 2000 species of cacti, and of these only one species, *Rhipsalis baccifera*, occurs naturally outside America. In Africa species of *Euphorbia* occupy arid sites, their growth forms often closely resembling those of the cacti. In southern Africa the mesembryanthemums (family Aizoaceae) are abundant and extremely diverse; most of the 2300 species are not found elsewhere. The eleven species of the peculiar succulent family Didiereaceae occur only in Madagascar.

The root system of many succulents is extensive and shallow, and water from small showers can thus be absorbed quickly. During long droughts the parts of the root system furthest from the plant body die, but new absorbing roots are formed within a few days of rain. The water absorbed is stored in the swollen plant body in large thin-walled cells. Cacti lack any continuous woody cylinder in the stem; even in the large

Fig. 8.38. Various drought-enduring plants. (a) Aloe *sp. The leaves are thick and fleshy with spiny margins. (b)* Idria columnaris, *an unusual member of the cucumber family from South Africa. It has no leaves and is covered in branched spines. (c)* Aeonium *sp. The thick leaves are arranged in a tight rosette and have a greyish waxy covering which reflects much of the light falling on the plant. (d)* Mamillaria vivipara, *a cactus from North America. Note the spine-tipped tubercles and the large flowers.*

columnar species the cylinder is made up of cross-connected ribs which give a good deal of elasticity to the structure. The ribbed or tubercled surface of many cacti allows shrinking and swelling, like the bellows of a camera, with changing water content.

Water loss from cacti is slow because the surface-area-to-volume ratio is very low: very few have leaves, and some are almost spherical, giving the lowest possible value of this ratio. Old plants can lose up to 25 % of their fresh weight and still survive; seedlings can lose rather more, but do so more quickly than adults. The cuticle is very thick, so that water loss is effectively restricted to the stomata, which are deeply sunken and in some species are covered by the woolly spines. Many cacti and other succulents have a whitish waxy or woolly layer on their plant body or leaves which reflects much of the incident light, reducing the temperature at the surface of the plant and thus the rate of water loss (Fig. 8.39). Lastly, cacti and many other succulent plants show an unusual method of carbon dioxide fixation (see section 2.2) called crassulacean acid metabolism. During the night the stomata open, and gas

Fig. 8.39. (below) Oreocereus neocelsianus, *a cactus from the high-altitude deserts of Bolivia. The covering of hairs probably reflects much incident light, thus reducing heating during the day, and may also act as an insulating blanket at night.*

exchange is possible with little loss of water. Carbon dioxide is fixed into organic acids in a process which does not need light. During the day, the carbon dioxide fixed in the dark is released inside the plant and is used for the formation of carbohydrates by light-dependent photosynthesis, but the stomata can remain closed during the day since no carbon dioxide needs be taken up then, contributing greatly to water conservation.

Many succulents, cacti included, have large and showy flowers. The production of these is usually related to rain, with extensive flowering following a shower. The large flowers of cacti are mostly pollinated by insects, but a few are pollinated by birds, and some (including those of *Carnegia gigantea*, the saguaro) are pollinated by bats. The succulent *Euphorbia* species of Africa have much less obvious flowers, which are attractive to wasps. Most succulents produce abundant seeds which germinate when moisture conditions are favourable, but a reasonably long moist period is needed for successful establishment of the seedlings. This sensitivity of the young stages limits most succulents to places rather moister than the limits of tolerance of the adult plant.

A third group of perennial drought-enduring plants show few obvious adaptations to their harsh environment. Examples are the tamarisk (*Tamarix*) of North African and Middle Eastern deserts, the creosote bush (*Larrea*) and mesquite (*Prosopis*) of southern North America, and species of *Eucalyptus* and *Acacia* in Australia. These are mostly small trees, usually with very small leaves with thick cuticles. Some survive by tapping deep-lying water reserves, with roots sometimes reaching depths of 50 metres. Leafy species often lose their leaves during dry spells, and may even shed branches if the drought is severe.

Perennial water-storing plants of dry environments are clearly potential food for herbivores. Some are covered in spines, and cacti for instance are often formidably armed. Some animals habitually feed on such plants though, and to them such armament provides little deterrent. Camels in Africa are undeterred by the thorns of *Acacia*, and the pack rat of the southern USA moves easily over cactus and uses pieces of them to build nests. Other species of desert plant are poisonous or distasteful. All the African species of *Euphorbia* contain a copious irritant latex which spurts out when the plant is cut or broken, but baboons can and do eat succulent *Euphorbias*. Finally, some plants mimic their surroundings and are very difficult to see. Various mesembryanthemums have rounded or angular white leaves resembling quartz pebbles, and normally only grow among these kinds of stone. Members of the genus *Lithops* (Aizoaceae) have only two leaves, which are buried in the soil with only their tips exposed, and these tips are rounded and coloured like pebbles.

Animals of arid zones

The shortage of water is the most important factor limiting the spread of animals into the deserts. The large daily fluctuation in temperature is also significant, and the problems posed by extreme heat are made more severe by the need to economise in the use of water. Some animals found in the desert are freed from the restrictions imposed by water through their extreme mobility, for example sand grouse (*Pterocles*) which fly long distances to water-holes in a short time, but other creatures have to conserve their water resources. Every animal loses water and must take in at least as much water as is lost in order to maintain its water balance. Sources of drinking water are rare in the desert, and for the most part desert animals must rely on water present in their food, and produced by oxidation of the food (metabolic water).

Animals can reduce the amount of water they need by conserving what is already in the body. Water is lost in the urine, and significant amounts are also lost in the faeces and through evaporation from the lungs and other moist body surfaces. Most terrestrial animals have waterproof skins but mammals may lose water through the skin in sweat. Sweating is primarily a means of keeping cool, but is grossly extravagant of water and desert mammals sweat to reduce their temperature only in extreme conditions.

Size is an important factor controlling the ability of an animal to survive in deserts. Animals that are sufficiently small to hide under a stone or to burrow into the sand can avoid the problems of coping with heat by becoming nocturnal, and most desert species are smaller than their near relatives in wetter regions. Another advantage of small size is that water which condenses on rocks or between sand grains during the cold night provides an excellent drinking supply. A single dew drop can supply the day's needs for a small insect or spider. A disadvantage of small size is that the surface area of the body is larger relative to the volume, so that evaporative water loss is correspondingly high, and for this reason few insects or arachnids move out of cover during the heat of the day. Carnivores rely on the body fluids of their prey for their water supply, but in order to avoid excessive water loss they have to hide away by day. This is no problem for the invertebrate predators, but mammals adapt only by becoming small: the kitten-sized fennec fox (*Fennecus zerda*) and the tiny sand cat (*Felis margarita*) are both very much smaller than average for their groups.

Deserts that are completely devoid of growing vegetation support no large mammals. Such deserts are not entirely lifeless, however, for small burrowing insects and other invertebrates can subsist on seeds and vegetable debris blown there from more fertile regions. Some of this plant material may have been produced a long time ago, for decomposition is slow in hot waterless deserts due to the scarcity of bacteria.

Despite the rigorous conditions, all the types of animal that have managed to colonise the land have penetrated the desert, including snails and amphibians. Snails solve the problem of prolonged waterless periods by a form of dormancy called aestivation. The opening of the shell is plugged by an impermeable cover, and the snail can remain in a state of suspended animation for years if necessary.

Large mammals, which cannot burrow or hide under stones, have to endure rather than avoid the climatic rigours of the desert and have evolved a number of ways of reducing the effects of heat. One adaptation is to be light in colour, and to reflect rather than absorb the sun's rays. Another is to develop a dense curly coat, as has the camel, since a woolly covering keeps heat out as well as in, although it is essential for air to circulate to the skin if sweating is to be effective. Desert mammals also depart from the normal mammalian practice of maintaining a constant body temperature. Instead of trying to keep down the body temperature deep inside the body, which would involve the expenditure of water and energy, desert mammals allow their temperatures to rise to what would normally be fever height, and temperatures as high as 46 °C have been measured in Grant's gazelle (*Gazella granti*). The overheated body then cools down during the cold desert night, and indeed the temperature may fall unusually low by dawn, as low as 34 °C in the camel. This is an advantage since the heat of the first few hours of daylight is absorbed in warming up the body, and an excessive build-up of heat does not begin until well into the day. Naturally, there are limits beyond which the body temperature cannot go, but this flexibility is important in permitting survival.

Another strategy of the large desert mammals is to tolerate loss of body water to a point which would be fatal for non-adapted animals. The camel can lose up to 30% of its body weight as water without harm, whereas human beings die after having lost only 12 to 13% of their body weight. An equally important adaptation is the ability to replenish this water loss at one drink. Desert animals can drink prodigious volumes in a short time and camels have been known to imbibe over 100 litres in a few minutes. A very dehydrated person, on the other hand, cannot drink enough water to rehydrate at one session, because the human stomach is not sufficiently big and because a too rapid dilution of the body fluids causes death from water intoxication. The tolerance of water loss is of obvious advantage in the desert, as animals do not have to remain near a water-hole but can obtain food from grazing sparse and far-flung pastures. Desert-adapted mammals have the further ability to feed normally when extremely dehydrated; it is a common experience in people that appetite is lost even under conditions of moderate thirst.

One problem in allowing the body to desiccate is that the blood becomes more viscous and cannot circulate about the body adequately. Death from heat stroke occurs when the blood is no longer able to transport the metabolic heat from inside the body to the skin. The desert mammal avoids this problem by withdrawing water only from the tissues, leaving the blood at its normal dilution.

Water conservation is also practised, of course, with the production of concentrated urine and dry faeces, but however efficient these adaptations may be some water is lost every day and the animal has eventually to take in water to keep in balance. Behavioural adaptations may ensure a sufficient supply of water. It has been calculated that a Grant's gazelle in the semi-arid region of northern Kenya needs about 3 litres of water each day, of which 0.5 litres is produced by oxidation of food materials. The deficit cannot be made up by drinking because that much free water is not normally available in the desert, and the gazelle copes by using the water that condenses from the atmosphere onto vegetation during the cold nights. The gazelle's main food plant, *Disperma*, contains only some 3% by weight of water by day and its leaves are so dry that they crumble to the touch, but after eight hours' exposure to the damp night air their water content has risen to 40%. Hence it is essential that the gazelle should graze at night when the water in the food and the dew ensure that it receives an adequate water supply.

Birds show few adaptations to desert life, presumably because they are generally only visitors which can quickly return to more congenial habitats such as oases. Sand grouse can nest in the desert because of the ability of the male to carry water in its breast feathers, which are deliberately soaked by the bird while drinking. The water is essential for cooling the eggs and supplying the needs of the nestlings.

Reptiles are by nature suited to a desert environment because their thick dry skins prevent much water loss, and their lethargic way of life does not require them to undertake energetic water-consuming activities. Their low metabolic rate and the generally small size of modern reptiles enables them to hide away in small crevices during particularly harsh periods. The most notable adaptation of reptiles in deserts is to the difficult terrain over which they must move. Some lizards have elongated scales fringing the toes, which act in a way similar to snow-shoes, while others have webbed toes to give support on shifting sand (Fig. 8.40). Snakes move easily through sand in a fashion akin to swimming, although the side-winder (*Crotalus cerastes*) has a novel sideways movement, and many lizards wriggle through the desert like snakes with the contours of their head and body modified accordingly. The eyes of desert reptiles may be protected by transparent eyelids which are permanently fused together.

Amphibians have a more difficult problem because their skin is not watertight and because they need water in which to breed. The toads, the most terrestrial member of the class, are successful in deserts and survive by burying themselves in the sand to avoid the heat, and by physiological adaptations to water shortage. They have an extremely brief tadpole stage and can breed in the temporary puddles that form after the infrequent showers.

Fig. 8.40. Some desert lizards. (a) The horned lizard (Phrynosoma cornutum) from south-western USA and northern Mexico. (b) The gila monster (Heloderma suspectum) occurs in the same regions as the horned lizard. It is the only poisonous lizard but its venom is not normally lethal to people.

(c) Agama blandfordi. The agamids are a large family of mainly arid land lizards found in Africa, Asia and Australia. (d) Phrynocephalus arabicus, another agamid, uses the lateral fold of skin to heap sand on its body while burrowing. It has fringed toes, which help it to run over the sand.

8.9 MOUNTAINS AND HIGH-ALTITUDE ENVIRONMENTS

Mountain vegetation

Temperature falls with increasing altitude at a fairly constant rate of 0.5 to 1.0 °C for every 100 metres. Thus vegetation growing on mountains is exposed to lower temperatures than is that in lowland sites at the same latitude, and mountains tend to be surrounded by zones of vegetation closely related to altitude. These zones tend to be lower on isolated mountains than on larger mountain masses. On ascending a mountain in the temperate forest zone, one passes first through deciduous forest of broad-leaved trees, then through evergreen coniferous forest, and finally through a tundra-like zone of dwarf shrubs and herbs, before the permanently frozen and more or less lifeless highest zones are reached (see Fig. 8.41). This of course parallels the zonation observed on travelling towards the pole in the northern hemisphere.

The environmental changes that occur with increase in altitude do not however exactly parallel the changes that occur on moving towards the pole from the temperate or tropical zones. First, daylength is the same at the top of a mountain as at its base. This means that the tundra-like environment of a mountain top in the temperate zone, such as the Alps, is very different from that of the tundra of northern Finland where there is continuous daylight for part of the summer and continuous night for part of the winter. It also leads to peculiar climates on the top of tropical mountains. The clear air of high mountains, and the smaller amount of atmosphere that has to be crossed by incoming and outgoing radiation, can lead to very rapid temperature changes and to very bright sunshine when the sky is clear. The precipitation on mountains is usually greater than that on the lowlands in which they stand, because air displaced upwards by passing over mountains expands, cools and loses some of its water-carrying ability, and the excess moisture falls as rain. Before falling as rain the moisture condenses to form clouds, and when these envelop a mountain their minute water droplets are trapped by the vegetation, so that the rainfall measured by a standard rain-gauge may not give a true picture of the amount of available precipitation. Finally, mountains are often more windy than the lowlands in which they stand.

a

b

c

d

e

f

Fig. 8.41. Vegetation zones on the Ruwenzori Mountains, Uganda. (a) Lower montane rain-forest at about 1550 metres, seen across an old clearing. (b) Lake Mahoma, 2960 metres, surrounded by cloud forest with ericaceous trees, and trees of Rapanea *and* Podocarpus. *(c) Cloud forest at about 3000 metres, showing the abundant lichens (Usnea) on the trees, and the fern-rich ground flora. (d) Giant heath forest at about 3300 metres; the tree trunks and the ground are densely overgrown by mosses and liverworts. (e) Dendrosenecio woodland with* D. adnivalis *and* Lobelia wollastonii, *near Lake Bujuku at about 4000 metres. (f) Helichrysum ('everlasting flower') scrub near Lake Bujuku at about 4000 metres.*

Fig. 8.42. Giant rosette plants from the high mountains of Africa and South America. (a) Lobelia wollastonii *from Ruwenzori, at about 3300 metres. (b)* Puya *from the Andes of Ecuador, at about 3100 metres. Both produce a tall spike of flowers, and in both the rosette dies after flowering.*

As a general rule, though, the vegetation of mountains in high latitudes has very close similarities with that of low altitudes in higher latitudes. Thus many of the plants of the high alpine zone of Scottish mountains are found at low levels in the Arctic or Norway. However, few of these plant species extend very far south: some reach the Alps and the Pyrenees, but virtually none extends further south into the mountains of tropical Africa. The main reason for this is ease or difficulty of dispersal. Few mountain chains extend very far in a north–south direction, and the alpine belts of most mountains are isolated biogeographical islands in the lowland vegetation; migration between different mountain chains is difficult and unlikely to occur except at long intervals.

On mountains in the temperate zone, the succession of vegetational zones encountered on ascending a mountain will generally be deciduous forest, coniferous forest, and tundra-like alpine vegetation. At the northern edge of the zone, the species concerned will usually be those of the taiga and the Arctic tundra, and further south different but similar species often replace these. Thus in the Alps the bases of the north-facing slopes bear mixed oak (*Quercus*) forest; above this is beech (*Fagus sylvatica*) forest, then spruce (*Picea abies*) forest which extends to the tree-line. Above this lie alpine meadows and the high alpine vegetation rich in mosses, lichens and cushion-plants. The southern slopes of the Alps have Mediterranean vegetation at their bases; this is succeeded by beech forest which extends to the tree-line, above which there are the same alpine meadows and high-alpine vegetation as are found on the northern slopes. In some places in the central Alps there is a zone of dwarf woodland with *Pinus montana*, which forms the tree-line.

The limit of tree growth on mountains, the tree-line, is produced by a number of factors. Chief among these is the fall in temperature, which means that the growing season becomes shorter at higher altitudes. A deciduous tree requires a certain minimum time in which to produce new leaves, grow, reproduce, and mature its new growth. Young unmatured growth is liable to be damaged by frost, and on mountains where there is much sun this frost damage can be compounded by drying: if the foliage of an evergreen tree is heated by the sun outside the growing season, when the soil and often the trunk are frozen, water is lost which can only be replaced with difficulty if at all. The foliage can thus easily be damaged by 'frost-drought'. Very small differences in microclimate can make considerable differences in the length of the growing season, and the exact position of the tree-line varies with aspect, slope and other factors.

Further south, there are more potential vegetation zones on mountains because these span a greater range of environments. The eastern Himalayas, for instance, extend from tropical forest up to alpine tundra and beyond. The foothills bear tropical or subtropical rain-forest in which mainly evergreen broad-leaved trees and shrubs predominate, including species of *Rhododendron*. Above this is a mountain forest, mainly of

conifers, but with some deciduous broad-leaved trees. This extends to the tree-line, above which may be found shrubby rhododendrons and willows. Above this zone lie alpine meadows, and finally the high alpine vegetation which may reach to 5000 metres.

The vegetation and climate of tropical mountains are both peculiar. There is little seasonal variation except perhaps in rainfall and the greatest climatic variations are between day and night. During the day the temperature may be quite high, but as soon as the sun sets, the thin clear air allows rapid loss of heat by radiation and temperatures fall quickly to give a frost on most mornings in the alpine belt. The climate has been described as 'winter every night and summer every day'. The daily frosts make the soil surface very unstable, but some mosses and lichens can survive loose on the surface as 'solifluction floaters'.

The general zonation of vegetation on tropical mountains (Fig. 8.41) begins from lowland rain-forest. This grades into upland rain-forest, where there are fewer lianes, fewer buttressed trees, and more epiphytes. Upland rain-forest gradually diminishes in stature with increasing height and is finally replaced by a dwarf woodland in which the trees are small and crooked, usually with small thick leaves, and heavily overgrown with mosses and lichens. This 'elfin woodland' extends to the tree-line. Above is a zone of shrubby growth, sometimes with large sparsely branched rosette plants which may reach five to eight metres in height. Above this the vegetation becomes very open, often very dry, and low-growing. The large rosette plants (Fig. 8.42) are one of the most striking features of tropical mountain vegetation. In tropical Africa the genera *Dendrosenecio* and *Lobelia* are most prominent, in South America *Espeletia* includes species with a growth-form identical to that of *Dendrosenecio*, and there are parallels with *Lobelia* in *Puya* (family Bromeliaceae) and in *Lupinus* (Leguminosae). On the mountains of Hawaii there are species of *Argyroxiphium* (Compositae) which resemble *Puya* and *Lobelia* in growth habit. Only South-east Asia seems to lack plants of this growth form, and although *Anaphalis* (Compositae) is sometimes stated to include similar species these are well-branched and shrubby and lack the huge rosettes and large leaves.

Observations on the mountains of East Africa have suggested that this growth-form is an adaptation to the diurnal climate. During the night the leaves of the rosette fold inwards over the central bud and protect it from freezing. In the giant *Lobelia* species, a pool of liquid secreted by the plant accumulates around the central bud, retained by the overlapping leaf bases. This liquid may have a layer of ice on it by the morning, but the bottom of the pool remains above freezing point, as does the bud. In addition, the stems of the giant rosette plants are also protected from freezing by an insulating layer formed either from the dead leaves which remain attached to the stem (as in *Dendrosenecio johnstonii cottonii*), or by thick corky bark (as in *D. johnstonii barbatipes*).

The grasses associated with this vegetation, both in Africa

a

b

and in South America, form dense tussocks. It has been suggested that this growth-form also has an insulating function; the dense mass of old stem and leaf bases restricts the flow of air and heat and prevents the growing base of the tussock from freezing at night.

In South America this vegetation is known as **paramo** and occurs at high altitudes where rain is plentiful. Where rain is scarce, as further south in the Andes, a high-altitude semi-desert known as **puna** is found, consisting mainly of short tussock-forming grasses in the genera *Festuca* and *Calamagrostis*.

Animals of mountainous regions

Mountains are not evenly distributed over the globe and their fauna tends to reflect that of the surrounding country. There are however also some relict species, left behind after climatic changes or other factors have isolated a mountain from neighbouring peaks. There is also a tendency for mountain species to be **endemic** to a small region, that is to occur nowhere else. The Usambara Mountains in Tanzania, for example, are extremely rich in endemic species with 85% of the millipedes, 70% of the chameleons, 25% of the snakes and 5% of the birds that occur there being found nowhere else.

The tops of the highest mountains have much in common with polar regions, but one great difference is the amount of

oxygen available, and the animals that colonise high mountains have to adapt to the reduced oxygen levels as well as to the cold. The vicuña (*Vicugna vicugna*; Fig. 8.43), which lives at altitudes between 4000 and 5500 metres in the high Andes, has three times as many red blood cells per unit volume of blood as has a human being. Individual animals can respond to increased altitude by manufacturing more red blood cells, and this phenomenon, which also occurs in mountaineers moving from low to high altitudes, is probably the most important factor in acclimatisation to low levels of oxygen. Mammals, including many ungulates, often make seasonal movements up and down mountains to exploit the rich summer grazing near the tops, and their red blood cell counts probably vary with their migrations.

Ultraviolet light is stronger on the mountains, because less has been filtered out by the atmosphere than at sea-level. This may explain the tendency for mountain species to have a high proportion of melanic (dark-pigmented) individuals, as the black pigment absorbs ultraviolet light and reduces damage to the body tissues. Black leopards, black servals and black golden cats are frequently reported, but of course they also lose their camouflage and this may be why the black genes have not spread throughout the population.

A further factor important in the ecology of animals living at high altitudes is the high wind velocity. Animals can tolerate much lower temperatures in still air than they can in even

Fig. 8.43. The vicuña, a relative of the camels, lives in the puna of the High Andes.

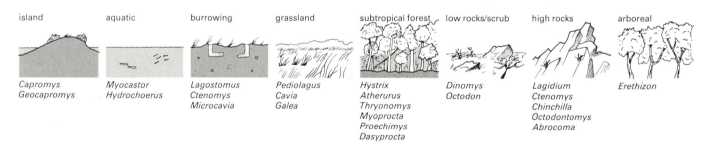

island	aquatic	burrowing	grassland	subtropical forest	low rocks/scrub	high rocks	arboreal
Capromys Geocapromys	Myocastor Hydrochoerus	Lagostomus Ctenomys Microcavia	Pediolagus Cavia Galea	Hystrix Atherurus Thryonomys Myoprocta Proechimys Dasyprocta	Dinomys Octodon	Lagidium Ctenomys Chinchilla Octodontomys Abrocoma	Erethizon

Fig. 8.44. The habitats of some hystricomorph rodents.

moderate winds, as wind rapidly dissipates body heat.

The largest herbivore in the Himalayas is the yak (*Bos grunniens*), which shows numerous adaptations to its cold environment. The surface area, and therefore heat loss, are reduced by the development of a barrel-shaped body with short legs. The tail is not visible among the long shaggy hairs that grow from its root, and similar hairs cover the whole body. Underneath this matted coat is a second coat of thick fur. The yak has been domesticated for at least 3000 years, but the domesticated form differs from its wild ancestor only in being

smaller with shorter, thinner horns, and often a piebald coat. Wild yaks are now rather rare and restricted to northern and north-eastern Tibet above 4500 metres, but previously their range extended over the whole of Tibet and into neighbouring regions of China, Nepal and India.

Three races of the red deer still exist in the Himalayas. The hangul or Kashmir stag (*Cervus elaphus hanglu*) lives on the forested slopes above the Vale of Kashmir, but only a few hundred individuals remain. Another, which may well be extinct, is the shou (*C. e. walleri*), which occurs higher up the

a

Fig. 8.45. Two large vultures. (a) The condor occurs among the mountains of South America, spending much of the day on the wing searching for carrion. (b) The lammergeier or bearded vulture has a large range throughout Africa, Southern Europe and Central Asia.

b

mountains on the Bhutan–Nepal border. There is a third race (*C. e. macneilli*) surviving in Tibet and western China. A smaller deer, the antlerless musk deer (*Moschus moschiferus*), occurs lower down in the forest at around 3500 metres. The males have long projecting canine teeth, which are used as a substitute for antlers in fighting, and an abdominal musk-secreting gland for which they have been much hunted by man.

Two antelopes occur on the high plateau of Tibet. One is a gazelle (*Procapra picticaudata*), which occurs above the timberline up to 5500 metres, and the other is the Tibetan antelope or chiru (*Pantholops hodgsoni*), which ranges between 3500 and 5500 metres. Both have longer and thicker hair than have their relatives in warmer regions. The Himalayan tahr (*Hemitragus jemlahicus*) is a sort of goat with a broad altitudinal range, but it does not often go above the timber-line and is found through most of the Himalayas. More typical goats are the markhor (*Capra falconeri*), with several races, and the Himalayan ibex (*C. sibirica*), which has the longest and finest horns of any ibex. Several members of the goat-antelopes occur in the Himalayas including the goral (*Nemorhaedus goral*) and the serow (*Capricornis sumatraensis*), both of which occur elsewhere in Asia in mountainous regions.

The North American mountain ungulates include the Rocky Mountain goat (*Oreamnos americanus*), which is a goat-antelope and not a true goat, and is one of the few naturally white mammals. Another large ungulate is the bighorn sheep (*Ovis canadensis*).

South America lacks sheep, goats or antelopes, and their place in the Andes is taken by two species of cameloids, the vicuña and the guanaco, and by the caviomorph rodents. The vicuña (Fig. 8.43) lives on the flat and rolling country of the puna and feeds on the sparse, desert-adapted vegetation. The feet of the vicuña are padded and splayed like those of the camel, and unlike the sharp hooves of the bovids, and consequently they do not destroy the habitat through trampling of the vegetation as occurs elsewhere at high animal densities. The vicuña was originally very numerous, but was then hunted to near-extinction for its coat, the wool of which is the finest in the world with each strand about one-quarter the diameter of a human hair. With rigid protection, numbers have recovered and the vicuña should now be out of danger. The other cameloid, the guanaco (*Lama guanicoe*), is probably the ancestor of the domesticated alpaca and llama. It is larger than the vicuña and occurs lower down the slopes.

The Andean rodents include the mountain viscacha (*Lagidium*) and chinchilla (*Chinchilla*) which with the plains viscacha (*Lagostomus*) make up the family Chinchillidae. Mountain viscachas have a range of some 4700 kilometres, from the altiplano of Peru (10 °S) to the Andean foothills of Patagonia (52 °S), and their normal altitudinal distribution is from 4000 to 5000 metres. They look like a long-tailed rabbit, weigh from 900 to 2000 grams depending on the species, and have thick fur. They live on rocky outcrops, and nest underneath boulders or on ledges on the crags. Unlike the plains viscacha, they are active by day and their ecology is similar to that of the rock hyrax of Africa. The chinchillas are similar to the mountain viscachas in appearance and habitat, but live in arid or semi-arid regions.

Many other caviomorphs live in the Andes (Fig. 8.44). On the lower slopes these include the pacarana (*Dinomys branickii*), a handsome nocturnal animal with two rows of white spots along each brown flank, and the degu (*Octodon degus*), which looks like a long-tailed guinea-pig and which shares the same rocky scrubland habitat. Caviomorphs from the high rocks, besides the mountain viscachas and chinchillas, include tuco-tucos (*Ctenomys*), chozchoz (*Octodontomys*) and chinchilla rats (*Abrocoma*).

Mountain predators include the common leopard (*Panthera pardus*) in Africa and Asia, the snow leopard (*P. uncia*) in Asia and the puma (*Felis concolor*) in both the Rocky Mountains and the Andes. There are also numerous smaller cats. Bears are represented by the Himalayan black bear (*Selenarctos thibetanus*), which reaches as high as the tree-line of the Himalayas, and the spectacled bear (*Tremarctos ornatus*) which is the only bear in South America and is almost a vegetarian. Foxes are also common on mountains; the Andean fox (*Dusicyon culpaeus*) is the only serious predator of the caviomorph rodents, and even takes young vicuña.

Outside South America the ecological niches of the caviomorph rodents are filled by other rodents and by pikas, which are short-eared lagomorphs (relatives of the rabbits and hares) with two centres of distribution, one in Asia and the other in North America. Some pikas live on the grassland plains, but there are also mountain species with a coat of fur on the sole of each foot which helps them to move over the snowy slopes. Marmots and chipmunks also occur on Eurasian mountains, with the various species showing a distinct zonation on the slopes, the smaller species being present towards the summits.

Birds are found at all levels on the mountains, often in a bewildering variety on the forested lower slopes, and again there is usually a very precise altitudinal zonation of the species. Sunbirds are common at high altitudes in Africa, as are their ecological equivalents in South America, the hummingbirds. High-altitude birds in Eurasia include the accentor family (of which the hedge sparrow (*Prunella modularis*) is a lowland example), the alpine chough (*Pyrrhocorax graculus*) and the wall-creeper (*Tichodroma muraria*). The latter, a relative of the nuthatch, has especially long claws which help it to scale vertical rock faces. Birds of prey include the golden eagle, but the vultures are the raptors of really high altitudes (Fig. 8.45). The Andean condor (*Vultur gryphus*), has a wingspan of over 3 metres and is still widespread; its equally huge relative, the Californian condor (*Gymnogyps californianus*), is in great danger of extinction. The equivalent bird in Eurasia and Africa, the lammergeier or bearded vulture (*Gypaëtus barbatus*), is found at all levels, but in the Himalayas it remains within the range of 1200 to 4000 metres. The largest Himalayan bird is the Himalayan griffon vulture (*Gyps himalayensis*) which occurs at lower altitudes, usually 600 to 2500 metres, although it often ranges up to 4500 metres or higher.

Reptiles, amphibians and invertebrates abound in the lower forested reaches of the mountains and some can survive at high altitudes, even above the snow-line. There is little plant production at these heights, for often there is no soil even if the temperature is adequate, and the animals rely on windborne debris. The many detritus-feeders include the group of flightless insects called springtails, and these in turn constitute the food of numerous small predators such as mites, centipedes and flies. The layer of snow provides an insulating blanket, much as it does on the polar tundra, and protects these animals from the extreme sub-zero temperatures.

8.10 TROPICAL SEASONAL VEGETATION

A belt of very strongly seasonal climate lies between approximately 10° and 25° north and south of the equator, and is called the monsoon zone. Here rain falls during the summer, when the sun is overhead and temperatures are highest. At the equatorial edge of the zone, annual rainfall may be as high as 1800 millimetres; towards the poles, where this zone grades into semi-desert, about 500 millimetres is normal. This rain falls in a wet season, which lasts seven to eight months in the most equatorial regions, declining to three months or less at the

Fig. 8.46. *Monsoon vegetation climates*

		alt.	a.p.	m.a.t.
a	Darwin, Australia	12°20′S, 130°50′E	32	1538	28.1
b	Parana, Brazil	12°30′S, 47°40′W	260	1580	22.8
c	Kaduna, Nigeria	10°30′N, 7°21′E	644	1297	24.9
d	Lusaka, Zambia	15°28′S, 28°16′E	1278	835	20.6
e	Ahmadabad, India	23°00′N, 72°40′E	49	741	27.9

Fig. 8.47. *Types of African savanna. (a) Guinea savanna in northern Ghana, at the end of the dry season. The grass has been burned and has not yet sprouted; the trees and shrubs, however, are producing new leaves in anticipation of the rains. (b) Dry savanna in the north of Kenya. Shrubs and scattered trees of* Acacia *and* Commiphora *stand in a largely annual grassland in which a flowering* Stipagrostis *is prominent. The overall appearance is reminiscent of Sudan savanna. (c) Open* Themeda–Hyparrhenia *grassland with scattered* Capparis *bush clumps and a few* Euphorbia candelabrum *trees in western Uganda. Here there are two dry and two wet seasons each year as the area lies on the Equator and this type of savanna is developed in such conditions.*

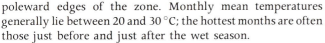

poleward edges of the zone. Monthly mean temperatures generally lie between 20 and 30 °C; the hottest months are often those just before and just after the wet season.

The naturalness of the present vegetation of this climatic zone, and the role of fire, have been the subjects of much argument. At present the predominant vegetation in this zone is grassland with a variable tree cover. The trees are generally small by tropical standards, and are often twisted and much-branched. As a general rule, the higher the rainfall, the more grass is produced during the wet season and the more fuel is available for fires in the subsequent dry season. At present much of the vegetation of this zone in Africa is burned every year, and while there are some definite records of fires started

by lightning, there can be little doubt that the frequency of burning must have increased greatly since man discovered how to make fire.

The African woodlands and grasslands

The term **savanna** has long been applied to the vegetation of the monsoon zone at least in West Africa, and there are three distinct types, the Guinea, Sudan and Sahel savannas (Fig. 8.47). These form more or less parallel belts which run east to west from Chad to Senegal, and are clearly related to the contour lines of equal rainfall.

Guinea savanna is the wettest of the three types. It receives

Fig. 8.48. *A grass fire in African savanna. The flames are, here, too low to damage the trees seriously; only the grass layer is consumed.*

1000 to 1500 millimetres of rain each year in a rainy season six to eight months long. The vegetation is tall grassland, with many small trees, mostly broad-leaved. The grasses generally belong to the tribe Andropogoneae, with species of *Hyparrhenia* and *Andropogon* being very common. Common trees include *Daniellia oliveri*, *Isoberlinia doka* and *Parkia clappertoniana*. At the end of the wet season the grasses stand 3 to 4 metres high and the larger trees may be 10 to 15 metres high.

Fires occur annually throughout most of this zone (Fig. 8.48), and can be very hot and violent if they occur late in the dry season, with flames leaping 10 to 15 metres into the air and damaging the crowns of the trees. There is strong controversy about the role of fire in maintaining the savanna vegetation. Experiments have shown that if fire is excluded, or if burning is carried out early in the dry season so that fires are not violent, then the tree cover increases and eventually species typical of forest appear. On the other hand, if fires are lit late in the dry season each year, trees decline because some mature trees are killed and no seedlings can regenerate.

Savanna trees can resist fires mainly because they have thick bark which insulates the living cambium from the heat of the fires. Forest species usually have thinner bark and are more easily killed by fire. Some savanna trees also have seedlings which are morphologically adapted to resist fires. These adaptations, which are quite widespread, suggest that fire may have been a feature of these environments for a very long time.

Fig. 8.49. *An olive baboon, one of the few species of monkey to be found in the open grasslands.*

Fig. 8.50. Browsing niches. The black rhinoceros (a) feeds on bushes near the ground but the gerenuk (b), by rearing on to its hind legs, can reach foliage higher up. The giraffe (c) can feed higher up than any other browser, although very often it does not do so but browses small bushes, as here.

Fig. 8.51. (below) Black-backed jackals scavenging a wildebeest killed by a lion. These small canids also hunt young antelope, rodents, birds and other small prey.

The Guinea savanna has a rich community of large mammals, but they are not present in large numbers. The ungulates are essentially West African species, such as bushbuck, buffalo and bushpig and show as a common feature a west–east gradation from light to dark coloured races; there are no zebras or other equids, and rhinos are probably now extinct here. Primates are represented by the olive baboon (*Papio anubis*; Fig. 8.49), and by the patas monkey (*Erythrocebus patas*) which is the only primate adapted for an exclusively grassland life. The marked seasonal changes in the Guinea savanna influence the breeding patterns of birds, and seasonal migrations within the zone or between other parts of Africa are common.

To the north of the Guinea savanna lies the **Sudan savanna**. This zone has a rainfall of 650 to 1000 millimetres each year, and the rainy season is five to six months long. Over most of West Africa this zone is very heavily settled and cultivated, and little of the original vegetation remains. The grasses are a mixture of annual and perennial species, and there are both broad-leaved trees and species of *Acacia* with finely divided leaves. Two trees typical of this zone are the baobab (*Adansonia digitata*) and the branching palm (*Hyphaene thebaica*).

To the north of the Sudan savanna is the **Sahel savanna**. This has a rainfall of 250 to 650 millimetres each year, and although the wet season lasts for three to four months rain tends to be unreliable in quantity and in timing. Most of the grasses are low-growing annuals, and the woody plants are mostly shrubs or small trees, with various species of *Acacia* common. This zone has been much damaged by overgrazing by large herds of domestic animals. Formerly these herds were limited by the small number of dry-season water sources, and some also avoided the rigours of the dry season by moving southwards, but such movements are now unpopular with governments which find migratory peoples difficult to administer and to tax. The provision of extra water sources and the lessening of migrations have increased pressures on the dry-season grazing grounds. Fires are rare in the Sahelian grasslands, as there is not usually enough fuel.

The animals of the Sudan savanna, and particularly of the Sahel, show desert adaptations. They include the red-fronted gazelle (*Gazella rufifrons*), the dama gazelle (*Gazella dama*) which is the largest of all gazelles, and the magnificent scimitar-horned oryx (*Oryx dammah*). Weavers are perhaps the most numerous birds, but the largest is the ostrich. The carnivores of these grasslands include the leopard (*Panthera pardus*) and lion (*P. leo*), although the latter is not common and is rarely found in the Sahel, where the cheetah (*Acinonyx jubatus*) is the more typical predator.

There is an equivalent stretch of grassland, the **bushveldt**, across southern Africa from Angola in the west to Mozambique in the east. It too is a transition zone, between the miombo woodlands in the north and the desert or semi-desert to the south. Large mammals are abundant, where they have not been eliminated by man, and all the large predators are present, including the spotted hyena (*Crocuta crocuta*) and the wild dog

(*Lycaon pictus*). Birds are equally obvious with several species of hornbill, numerous starlings, weavers, bee-eaters, shrikes, eagles and hawks. Many species are identical to those that occur in the northern grasslands although they are absent from the intervening country. The white rhinoceros (*Ceratotherium simum*) similarly has a race in South Africa and a race 3000 kilometres to the north.

The three savanna types so easily recognised in West Africa extend eastwards into Sudan, before the highlands of Ethiopia disrupt the zonation. To the south, in East Africa, there are also open grasslands and savannas of various kinds, which are anomalous in that the region lies on the equator and tends to have two wet seasons and two dry seasons each year. Further west, the rainfall is much higher and the climax vegetation is tropical rain forest, but in East Africa the rainfall over large areas is both low and unreliable, especially because either or both of the two wet seasons may fail. The vegetation of the region is complex. The best-known areas are the open plains grasslands developed on volcanic ash deposited comparatively recently, and which cover large parts of many of the National Parks such as Nairobi, Amboseli, Masai Mara and Serengeti. Here *Themeda triandra* is often the commonest grass, and there are often scattered *Acacia* trees.

The grasslands of western Kenya and northern Tanzania are characterised by great herds of ungulates, the most spectacular of which is the wildebeest or brindled gnu (*Connochaetus taurinus*; Fig. 4.4). During the rains, the wildebeest are found on the eastern treeless plains, where they calve and mate. There are no rivers or permanent water here, so at the start of the dry season the animals move, first west and then north, to well-watered woodlands. Zebra also migrate along a similar route. Gazelles too are prominent inhabitants of the East African grasslands, and the two species more or less confined to the area are Grant's gazelle (*Gazella granti*) and the smaller Thomson's gazelle (*G. thomsoni*); hartebeest are also common. Buffalo (*Syncerus caffer*) occur wherever there is sufficient water for them to wallow. They are of a big, black, huge-horned race, occurring in herds of sometimes several hundred animals. Warthog are universally distributed, and it is rare not to find elephants in grassland, if only seasonally.

Browsers also occur in the East African grasslands, for there is usually some bush cover (see Fig. 8.50). The commonest browser is the impala (*Aepyceros melampus*), the females of which form large herds 50 to 100 strong and usually tended by the local territorial male. Impala are remarkable leapers, as are eland (*Taurotragus oryx*), which are also browsers and the largest of all antelopes, with the males standing about 2 metres tall at the shoulder and weighing up to 750 kilograms. Giraffes (*Giraffa camelopardalis*) are represented by the Masai race with irregular blotches on the skin. The gerenuk (*Litocranius walleri*) is a long-legged, long-necked gazelle that stands like a goat on its hind legs to eat leaves that would be out of the reach of an ordinary antelope of similar weight. A browser at lower levels is the black rhinoceros (*Diceros bicornis*), with a prehensile

upper lip which can grasp leaves almost as effectively as can human fingers.

Further west, in Uganda, the grasslands are dominated by heavier animals, such as elephant, hippo and buffalo, with waterbuck (*Kobus defassa*), kob (*Adenota kob*) and topi (*Damaliscus korrigum*) also present. The number of species is less than further east but the region as a whole supports the highest biomass of wild animals found anywhere on earth.

The predators on the plains are dominated by the lion, which occurs in its highest abundance here. Leopards are found wherever there is a little cover, but the cheetah (*Acinonyx jubatus*) is the predator best adapted to live on the plains; only cheetah can run faster than their prey, although they cannot maintain full speed for long. The wild dog is also a grassland specialist, but curiously it is becoming rare. This is partly due to its being killed by people (including conservationists), and to disease, but there is also an unexplained imbalance between the sexes, with many more males than females being found. The spotted hyena (*Crocuta crocuta*) can be an active predator as well as a scavenger, although all predators, except generally the cheetahs, will scavenge whenever possible. Specialist carnivores include the jackals (Fig. 8.51), of which three species occur, and the vultures. Among the vultures, only the huge Nubian vulture (*Torgos tracheliotus*) is able to break into thick-skinned carcasses, and the smaller species have to wait until it or the mammalian scavengers have opened the skin.

Bird life in the East African grasslands is abundant and headed by the ostrich (*Struthio camelus*; Fig. 8.21). Each male ostrich has a senior hen plus a number of secondary females, all of which lay in the same nest, but the eggs of the dominant hen are in the centre and are the most likely to hatch. Birds of prey are numerous; the largest is one of the largest eagles in the world, the martial eagle (*Polemaetus bellicosus*), which takes small or young antelope as well as guinea-fowl and hyrax. The most curious bird of prey is the secretary bird (*Sagittarius serpentarius*), named from its head plumes, which look like pens stuck behind its 'ears'; it feeds on snakes, lizards, rodents and large insects.

Reptilian life is also abundant on the plains, with many species of venomous snakes as well as the huge pythons. Crocodiles (*Crocodylus niloticus*) are usually found in rivers or large pools.

Nearer the coast, in the Tsavo National Park in eastern Kenya, the rainfall is lower, the soils largely derived from ancient rocks, and the vegetation is a low woodland or shrubland, with some grass beneath during the wet season. Many of the trees are thorny and have only a brief leafy period during the year. As in many of East Africa's National Parks, vegetation change here can be rapid as populations of large mammals, particularly elephant, increase and selectively damage the woody plants. This **thornbush** used to be dominated by elephant (until the slaughter by ivory poachers in the mid-1970s) and also contained probably the largest

concentration of black rhinoceros in Africa. The region has changed over the past 30 years through the actions of elephants and of fire into more open grassland, to the advantage of grazing animals such as zebra, fringed-eared oryx (*Oryx beisa*) and warthog (*Phacochoerus aethiopicus*).

South of the equator in Tanzania, northern Mozambique, Zambia, southern Zaire, Angola and parts of Malawi and Zimbabwe, is the southern counterpart of the Guinea savanna. This is the **miombo** woodland. Trees, mainly species of *Brachystegia*, form an open canopy at about 15 metres high, and grass grows beneath them. During the dry season this grass is burned. The miombo system covers a vast area, and has been very little studied. It is difficult to clear and cultivate and produces little of economic value apart from some timber and honey. Much of the miombo woodland occupies gently undulating country and the vegetation varies with the topography: typical miombo occupies the middle slopes and level ground, while the valleys are occupied by open grasslands because seasonal waterlogging prevents the establishment of trees. The hilltops often bear rock outcrops with a more varied woody vegetation, because runoff from the rocks and the weathering of fresh minerals provide better soil conditions than elsewhere. This kind of regular sequence of topographically related vegetation types, called a **catena**, was first recognised here, and such sequences are widespread in the tropics and elsewhere.

The miombo woodland is arguably the most important wildlife reserve in the world. The density of large mammals is not high, but the area is huge and unbroken, and the total number of animals supported is very large. The region is similar to the Guinea savanna in faunal composition, although richer in species, and often the actual species present are different. Thus, the bubal hartebeest in the north is replaced by Lichtenstein's hartebeest (*Alcelaphus lichtensteini*), the kob by the very similar puku (*Adenota vardoni*), and the Nile lechwe (*Kobus megaceros*) by the red lechwe (*K. leche*). Many of the species common to both regions also occur in the intervening country. The miombo is the real home of the wildebeest, for the whole region is populated by them and the wildebeest in the Serengeti are in fact occupying only a narrow northern extension of the species' range. It also contains large numbers of buffalo and elephants and the magnificent giant sable (*Hippotragus niger variani*) which has massive horns.

Bird life is abundant, with most types represented. The nests of weaver birds festoon the trees, but hornbills, secretary birds, and birds of prey are all prominent. The beautiful southern carmine bee-eater (*Merops nubicoides*) is an avian example of a southern species with a northern equivalent, which in this case is the carmine bee-eater (*M. nubicus*). The miombo also shelters numerous migrants from northern tropical regions as well as from Europe.

Fig. 8.52. (left) Cerrado in Brazil. The grass is dry and may soon be burned; however, the trees are producing new leaves which would be badly damaged by a fire. Notice the striking similarity between the woody vegetation in this picture and in the Guinea savanna (Fig. 8.47a).

Fig. 8.53. (right) Caatinga in Bahia State, Brazil. A tall cactus (Cereus sp.) dominates the picture; the other plants are mostly also leafless and spiny, and there is little or no grass.

South American woodlands and wooded grasslands

Vegetation equivalent to the savannas of tropical Africa is found both north and south of the equator in South America. To the north, there are wide areas of grassland, called llanos in Venezuela and Colombia. South of the forests of the Amazon Basin, there is the vast and featureless expanse of the Matto Grosso, covered largely with a vegetation which bears a striking resemblance to some African Guinea savannas. In the north-east of Brazil there is a dry area which bears a thorny vegetation known as caatinga, and to the south of the Matto Grosso there is an extensive area of seasonally wet grassland and woodland called the Gran Chaco. There is considerable argument about the naturalness of all these areas of dry savanna-like vegetation; as in Africa, the argument turns on whether fire is or is not a natural feature.

The **llanos** of Venezuela and Colombia occupy the flood plains of rivers but are only partially submerged during the wet season. There is often a very hard layer in the soil which is said to prevent the growth of trees by restricting their root development, and much of the llanos are covered with grasses; species of *Trachypogon*, *Paspalum* and *Axonopus* are common. Small trees such as *Curatella* (Dilleniaceae) and *Bowdichia* (Leguminosae) are scattered in the grassland. These flower and make much of their growth during the dry season, and they must root through cracks in the hard layers of soil and use water stored below it.

To the south and, less extensively, to the north of the great forest of the Amazon Basin is a series of different vegetation types, differing in the height and density of trees and in the relative importance of grass. Nearest the forest there is a type of dry forest with rather few grasses, known as **cerradao**. Rather drier or less favourable sites adjoining this are known as **cerrado** or **campo cerrado** (Fig. 8.52). The tree species in the two are similar, but in the cerradao they are taller, reaching 10 to 15 metres, and species characteristic of the true forests may also be present. The cerrado is composed of trees which are low and twisted, usually 4 to 8 metres tall, with an undergrowth of grass in which species of *Tristachya*, *Paspalum* and *Aristida* are prominent. The trees include species of *Qualea*, *Salvertia* (both Vochysiaceae), *Caryocar* (Caryocaraceae), *Curatella* (Dilleniaceae) and *Dimorphandra* (Leguminosae). Most have thick, rather leathery leaves, some have very hairy ones, and a few have much-divided leaves. The bark of the trees is thick and often furrowed, and resistant to fire. In general appearance this vegetation is remarkably similar to the Guinea savanna of West Africa, but no species and few genera are common to the two areas.

In the same area as the cerradao and cerrado are found open grass plains, seasonally waterlogged; these are locally called **campo limpo**. These may be studded with termite mounds, which bear trees and shrubs growing in the better-drained environment that they provide; such sites are known as **pantanal**. These various types of savanna are distributed relative to local topography in a catenary pattern like that seen in the miombo of Africa.

To the south of the Matto Grosso with its various savanna types lies another area of relatively open vegetation with a very seasonal climate, the **Gran Chaco**. Here much of the ground is flooded in the wet season, and the vegetation is a mosaic of woodland on the higher ground and grassland on the lower, seasonally flooded portions (see section 9.3).

The **caatinga** (Fig. 8.53) occupies the very dry portion of north-eastern Brazil, and is a dry woodland in which grasses are not important. Cacti, some very large and including species of *Cereus*, *Pilocereus* and *Opuntia*, are prominent on the sandy soil, together with deciduous thorny trees such as *Caesalpinia*, *Quebrachia* and *Zizyphus*.

The fauna of the South American savannas is similar in type to that described for the pampas (see section 8.5).

Asian and Australian woodlands and grasslands

Very large areas of peninsular India, as well as parts of Burma, Thailand and Kampuchea, are covered by vegetation comparable in appearance to the Guinea savanna and the cerrado, and which occurs under similar climatic conditions. These regions have summer rain, with the amount varying considerably from place to place, but most of the regions carrying this type of vegetation have a dry season lasting from five to seven months and an annual rainfall of between 600 and 1600 millimetres. Mean daily temperatures throughout the year lie between 20 and 30 °C.

The drier areas of monsoon vegetation in peninsular India are open woodland with grass beneath the trees and shrubs. The main trees in the drier areas are *Prosopis*, species of *Acacia*, *Anogeissus* and *Pterocarpus*. The grasses beneath them include *Dichanthium*, *Cenchrus* and *Themeda*. In wetter areas two species of tree, sal (*Shorea robusta*) and teak (*Tectona grandis*), with various associates such as *Terminalia*, *Dalbergia* and *Pterocarpus*, form the main tree cover. In the drier areas these woodlands are deciduous, but the wetter ones have a mixture of evergreen and deciduous species.

All these open woodland formations of peninsular India have been heavily used for grazing, and cleared for cultivation, for centuries; during this time there has also been burning and collection of firewood. All these uses have influenced and altered the vegetation.

The animals of the oriental grasslands have adapted well to the vegetational changes caused by human activity, although only remnants of the once-extensive herds remain. Typical antelopes of the plains include the large nilgai (*Boselaphus tragocamelus*), blackbuck (*Antilope cervicapra*) and the chousingha (*Tetracerus quadricornis*), the only four-antlered antelope in the world. Immigrants from nearby arid regions include the chinkara or Bennett's gazelle (*Gazella bennetti*) and the striped hyena (*Hyaena hyaena*). The large predators have mostly disappeared, although the wolf (*Canis lupus pallipes*) survives in a few isolated regions and the Asiatic lion (*Panthera leo persica*) maintains a precarious hold in the Gir forest of North-West India. The Asiatic cheetah (*Acinonyx jubatus venatus*) is probably extinct, and has certainly gone from the grasslands.

The peninsula of Indo-China also has a strongly seasonal climate, and here also there are seasonally dry woodlands with a grass understorey which is regularly burned. Many of the species from peninsular India also occur here, but there are in addition species of *Dipterocarpus* and some pines including *Pinus kesiya*. Further south, in the Indonesian archipelago, there are regions with a seasonally dry climate where similar species are found, but towards the south some Australian elements including species of *Eucalyptus* appear.

The tropical woodlands and grasslands of Australia fall into two main groups. First, there are the northernmost areas of the Cape York Peninsula and Arnhem Land, which bear a vegetation similar in appearance to tropical wooded savannas in other parts of the world. Then there are the subtropical grasslands of eastern Australia, in which *Acacia* species, rather than *Eucalyptus*, are often the most common trees.

The most widespread open woodland type of the north is that dominated by *Eucalyptus miniata* (woollybutt) and *E. tetrodonta* (stringybark). These trees can reach 25 metres, but are usually shorter. Their popular names refer to their fibrous barks, which are fire-resistant; dry-season fires are common in these northern monsoon areas. The grass layer beneath the trees contains mainly perennial genera such as *Sehima*, *Themeda* and *Heteropogon*, but annual *Sorghum* species are also abundant.

The eastern grasslands enjoy a less tropical climate than do those mentioned above; temperatures are lower, and rain may occur both in summer and in winter, but is liable to fail at either or both these seasons. The most widespread trees in this zone are brigalow (*Acacia harpophylla*) and mulga (*A. aneura*). These differ from the African species of *Acacia* in lacking spines, and in bearing broad leaves which are in fact expanded petioles.

In south-western Queensland there are open grasslands with species of Mitchell grass (*Astrebla*) and Flinders grass (*Iseilema*). The climate of these is more arid than in the other types mentioned; annual rainfall lies between 300 and 500 millimetres, and most of it falls in summer. Even more arid grasslands bear distinctive hummocks of species of *Triodia* and *Plechtrachne*.

Fig. 8.54. *The kangaroo of Australia occupies the grazing niche filled by ungulates on grasslands in other parts of the world.*

The mammals of the Australian grasslands are marsupials; large numbers of placental mammals have appeared only in the last two centuries. The only indigenous non-marsupial mammals are bats and a distinct group of rodents including some endemic water rats. Neither birds nor reptiles are unique. There are no newts or salamanders, and of the tail-less amphibians only a few tree-frogs, plus the common frog which may have been introduced by man. The freshwater fish fauna is equally impoverished, despite the presence of a distinctive lungfish. Altogether the fauna of Australasia is poor, although it is of great zoological interest.

The niche for large mammalian herbivores is occupied by the macropods, that is the kangaroos (Fig. 8.54) and wallabies, which form one of the few marsupial groups with a distinctly different appearance from the analogous type of placental mammals. There are three species of kangaroo, the red and two greys, and three species of the slightly smaller wallaroos; all these animals are placed in the genus *Macropus*. Wallabies differ from kangaroos and wallaroos only in their still smaller size; many of the smaller wallabies are similar to hares in their ecology, size and habits, resting by day in a 'form' scraped in the grass.

The quokka (*Setonix brachyurus*) is a water-loving macropod, and with its short hind legs and spindly tail does not look much like a kangaroo. It is, however, a convenient experimental animal, and much of the work on the digestive and reproductive systems of macropods has been carried out using the quokka.

The smallest members of the kangaroo family are the rat kangaroos, many of which excavate large communal warrens as do rabbits, but unlike rabbits they are also arboreal with prehensile tails. Rat kangaroos hop like the larger kangaroos, and although they cannot move particularly quickly they are able to avoid predators by making sudden changes in direction. Another group of grazing marsupials is the wombats (Fig. 7.18),

which show convergence with the woodchucks of North America and have a rodent-like dentition.

The introduced placental herbivore the rabbit (*Oryctolagus cuniculus*) is ideally suited to the dry grassland of Australia and became a serious competitor of sheep, causing severe financial losses to sheep farmers. The lethal disease myxomatosis was deliberately introduced in 1950, and although not all the rabbits died the resistant survivors have remained at relatively low numbers, possibly because of sporadic outbreaks of new strains of the disease.

The most significant carnivore of the plains is the dingo (*Canis dingo*). This is not a marsupial but is a placental dog and was brought to Australia, as a domestic animal by the aborigines within the last few thousand years, subsequently escaping and spreading over the whole island. The native carnivore, the thylacine or marsupial wolf (*Thylacinus cynocephalus*), was displaced and, if not extinct, is now found only in Tasmania where the dingo has not established itself. A smaller native carnivore, the insectivorous rabbit-eared bandicoot (*Thylacomys*), has also suffered a drastic reduction in both its numbers and range.

The emu (*Dromaius novaehollandiae*; Fig. 8.21) is the largest grassland bird of Australasia and is very similar to, though larger than, the rhea of South America. Its diet includes grass, fruits, leaves and insects. Other typical birds are parrots (Fig. 8.55), including the impressive galah or rose-breasted cockatoo (*Kakatoe roseicapilla*) and its close relative the little corella (*K. sanguinea*), which are both widely regarded as agricultural pests. The most familiar parakeet is the budgerigar (*Melopsittacus undulatus*), which is green in its natural form. It is an opportunistic breeder, nesting only in times of good rainfall, and like many such species experiences huge and rapid fluctuations in its numbers. The zebra finch (*Poephila guttata*) also has similar habits, nesting within a few days of rain.

The mallee fowl (*Leipoa ocellata*) is one of the megapodes, a group of birds which incubate their eggs in warm sand or decomposing vegetation. During the six-month breeding period the male is in constant attendance at the nest, opening up the mound daily and testing the temperature with its tongue. On hatching, the chicks are extremely precocious, burrowing to the surface unaided and then scuttling off at once into the nearby scrub. They are able to fly within a day or so.

Birds of prey on the plains include the wedge-tailed eagle (*Aquila audax*), which has a wing span of over 2 metres. It takes young kangaroos as well as emu chicks and other birds. The ubiquitous kite (*Milvus migrans*) is the same species as that found in Europe and Africa, and an opportunistic scavenger from human rubbish dumps. Another common bird of prey is the brown falcon (*Falco berigora*), often found in completely treeless regions where it has to roost on the ground.

The Australian reptiles are not all unique to that continent, but are nevertheless interesting. Grassland species include several large monitor lizards, all of which are scavengers, with the biggest, the giant goanna (*Varanus giganteus*), reaching 240

centimetres in length. The frilled lizard (*Chlamydosaurus kingi*) has a frill of skin, supported by cartilaginous rods, around its head.

Marsupials in Australian forests have filled most of the ecological niches occupied elsewhere by placental mammals. The most familiar forest marsupial is the koala bear (*Phascolarctos cinereus*; Fig. 7.18). The Australian opossums, called the phalangers, belong to a different family from the American forms; they are mostly arboreal, and some are gliders. Some wallabies live in forests, and even the grey kangaroo rests in the forests during the day. Numerous carnivorous marsupials hunt on the forest floor or in the branches, including the Tasmanian wolf (*Thylacinus cynocephalus*), the more common Tasmanian devil (*Sarcophilus harrisi*), and the banded anteater (*Myrmecobius fasciatus*) which closely resembles the South American anteater.

Australian forests support the lyre birds (*Menura*), which derive their name from the lyre-shaped tail feathers used in display. The nest, which is tended only by the female, is a cavity inside a huge dome of sticks and vegetation. The well-known kookaburra or laughing jackass (*Dacelo novaeguineae*) is a woodland kingfisher of western Australia.

8.11 TROPICAL RAIN-FOREST

Tropical rain-forest is found throughout the tropics, wherever there is sufficient rain. Regions with an annual rainfall of 2000 to 3000 millimetres, reasonably evenly distributed through the year, carry true **evergreen tropical rain-forest.** Such climates are found in much of tropical South-East Asia, the basin of the Zaire (Congo) River, much of the Amazon Basin but particularly the north-west, and the eastern coast of Madagascar. Many other parts of the tropics, such as the coastal regions of West Africa, parts of North-East Australia, the western coasts of India and Burma, and parts of the eastern coast of Brazil, have annual rainfalls that may equal or exceed those of the ever-wet tropics, but which are interrupted by a dry season. Thus Singapore, with an annual rainfall of 2400 millimetres and monthly totals ranging between 170 and 250 millimetres, has a typical evergreen tropical rain-forest climate. Freetown in Sierra Leone, however, with an annual rainfall of 3400 millimetres and monthly totals between 5 and 360 millimetres, has a dry period lasting three to four months each year, and the climate favours **tropical seasonal forest;** if the dry season were a little longer and the rainfall lower, it would carry vegetation akin to Guinea savanna (see section 8.10). Temperatures in tropical rain-forests are very even and high. Frosts are unknown, and mean monthly temperatures usually lie between 24 and 28 °C; daily fluctuations are greater than any seasonal variations. Unlike other vegetation types (see sections 8.2 to

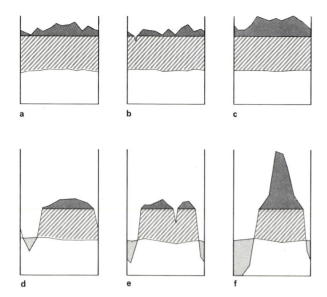

Fig. 8.56. *Tropical rain-forest climates, ever-wet climate of evergreen tropical rain-forest*

		alt.	a.p.	m.a.t.
a Iquitos, Peru	3°45'S, 73°10'W	106	2623	24.8
b Djolu, Zaire	0°45'N, 22°05'E	400	2052	24.3
c Bogor, Java, Indonesia	6°36'S, 106°46'E	240	4119	25.0

more seasonal climates, tropical seasonal forest often partly deciduous

d Manaus, Brazil	3°00'S, 60°00'W	45	1771	27.2
e Kumasi, Ghana	6°41'N, 1°38'W	287	1481	25.5
f Freetown, Sierra Leone	8°30'N, 13°10'W	11	3510	26.8

8.10), the tropical rain-forest has been treated as a whole, rather than region by region, because the structure and floristic composition is so complex that it is not possible to characterise particular areas of rain-forest by species or groups of species.

Forest structure

Throughout its extensive range, tropical rain-forest has a distinctive structure, more complex than that of any other vegetation type. The tree crowns are often described as being arranged in three separate layers, and while some tree crowns often occupy intermediate positions, layering (**stratification**) of the tree crowns provides a convenient framework for description of the complex canopies of a tropical rain-forest (Fig. 8.57). The uppermost layer is normally discontinuous, and is made up of the crowns of the largest trees (**emergents**) which project above the general canopy (Fig. 8.58). Below these emergents is a second layer of large trees, usually like the emergents in having rounded or spreading crowns. Together with the emergents, these form a continuous canopy. A third tree layer is often made up of smaller trees with vertically elongated crowns, which grow to maturity, flower and fruit below the main canopy. Young individuals of canopy species, must of course also pass through this layer before attaining maturity.

Below the trees there is often a lower layer of woody plants, made up of juveniles of upper-storey species, a few shrubs, and small single-stemmed woody plants which are best called miniature trees. Sometimes these are joined by large herbs in families such as Zingiberaceae, Marantaceae and Strelitziaceae. The herbs of the forest floor form a sparse and discontinuous layer close to the ground. Mosses are usually absent from the deeply shaded and litter-strewn ground, although they may be abundant on the bases of tree trunks.

This complex stratified structure of the tropical rain-forest produces within itself a great variety of habitats. The canopy intercepts light and rainfall, modifying the environment of the layers below it. Temperatures at canopy level may show considerable daily fluctuation, while at the forest floor temperatures fluctuate much less because incoming radiation is blocked by the canopy during the day, and outflow of radiation is similarly checked during the night. Heat exchange by mixing of air is also slowed because the speed of windflow declines at least 100-fold between the canopy and the forest floor. Humidity is always very high near the forest floor; while above the canopy it is much more variable. Thus the forest floor is always damp, even though some of the rain that falls on the canopy evaporates from there and never reaches the ground.

Unlike most temperate forests, where canopies made up of 20 species are rare, the tropical rain-forest is normally made up of a large number of species. A single hectare (100 metres by 100 metres) of forest may contain 50 to 150 tree species, although not all will be canopy species. If all vascular plants are included, species richness becomes even greater, and 190 species have been recorded from one plot of 25 metres by 25 metres in West African rain-forest; undoubtedly even richer areas could be found in South-east Asia. Such forests are the most diverse vegetation types in the world.

The possible reasons for this diversity are still much discussed. First, the tropical rain-forest is an ancient type of vegetation. Although relatively untouched by climatic fluctuation, it contracted greatly in the dry periods which occurred in the tropics during the glaciations of higher latitudes. Contraction into a few refuges could have led to some extinctions, but also to genetic isolation, which would have encouraged speciation. Secondly, the structure of the forest vegetation produces many different habitats, as do ridges and valleys which give minor local variations of soil and water conditions; both of these types of factor are equally present in temperate forests, however. Thirdly, it has been suggested that since species in tropical rain-forests tend to occur as isolated individuals, self-pollination may be relatively common and lead to speciation by genetic drift (see section 11.1). However, recent work has shown that many forest species are self-incompatible so that, like other hypotheses, this cannot fully explain the diversity of tropical rain-forest.

Forest plants

Within the forest it is possible to distinguish groups of plants that share a similar growth-form and make similar demands on their environments. These groups have been called **synusiae**. Some have already been mentioned: the canopy trees, the understorey trees, the shrubs and miniature trees, and the ground herbs. In addition there are the lianes, the epiphytes (see Fig. 8.61), the stranglers, and the parasites and saprophytes (see section 10.1).

Fig. 8.57. Diagram of stratification in a mixed rain-forest in Nigeria, showing all trees of 4.6 metres and above in height.

Fig. 8.58. Lowland tropical rain-forest has a complex structure. This example, from the eastern foothills of the Andes in Ecuador, at about 450 metres, is typical. Many different types of tree can be seen, including palms. On the ridge in the middle distance, several trees stand clear of the main canopy and show the long, smooth, almost untapered trunks characteristic of canopy species. One leafless tree can be seen, as can three flowering individuals, probably all of the same species.

Trees and shrubs

The emergent trees of the tropical rain-forest are often extremely large. They are not, however, the tallest trees in the world nor the most massive (*Eucalyptus regnans* in the subtropical forests of South-east Australia, and *Sequoiadendron giganteum* of the western USA, hold these records). Nor are they the oldest; probably few reach one-quarter of the 8000 years attained by bristlecone pines (*Pinus longaeva*) (see section 15.1). The tallest emergent tree measured was a specimen of *Koompassia excelsa* at 83 metres and at least four other South-east Asian tree species have been reliably measured as exceeding 60 metres. In Africa and South America such heights are decidedly rare. These large forest trees have trunks which are almost cylindrical; a specimen of *Balanocarpus heimii* measured in Malaysia had a girth of 8.25 metres at 1 metre above the ground, and 6.9 metres at a height of 26 metres where it first branched.

The bases of the trunks of many rain-forest trees bear flange-like outgrowths known as buttresses (Fig. 8.59). Many species have these, but not all, which makes their function difficult to understand. The most plausible suggestions are that they help to hold the trunk upright against the wind, and that they spread the weight of the tree over a larger area. Buttresses tend to be more common in forests on swampy sites. Other, mainly small, tree species have stilt roots (Fig. 8.59) which probably serve the same function.

The leaves of the trees, when compared to those of a temperate forest, are remarkably uniform in size and shape. The majority are ovate, with a gently tapering base, a pointed tip, and a smooth surface. It is generally agreed that the long-pointed tip, which is often best developed on understorey leaves and on the seedling leaves of canopy species, may help the leaf surface to dry quickly. Leaves in the understorey are long-lived, and older leaves acquire a coating of algae, lichens and bryophytes (**epiphylls**), which shade the leaf. These epiphyllous organisms grow best on wet leaves, so a leaf that drains quickly is more likely to remain free of them.

The production of leaves by the trees of tropical rain-forest is not continuous, but tends to occur at long intervals, with each shoot then making several often brightly coloured leaves at once. This production of new leaves in flushes (Fig. 8.60) has been interpreted as a mechanism for evasion of leaf predators; in the tropical environment leaf-eating insects are always active, so that if young leaves were produced continually they could well all be eaten. In the absence of a regular supply of new young vegetation, herbivorous insects remain at a low level, and when large quantities of new leaves are occasionally produced most of the leaves mature and become less palatable before the predator populations can increase.

Many forest trees only flower at long intervals too, but then many individuals of one species may flower simultaneously over wide areas. The factors which stimulate simultaneous flowering have been little studied; in some shrubs, heavy rain, or the drop in temperature which usually accompanies it, appears to be the stimulant, although drought may initiate flower formation in other species.

Some of the shrubs and understorey trees bear their flowers and fruits on the main stem or on the larger branches, a condition known as **cauliflory**. The reasons that have been advanced for this include better visibility of the flowers to pollinating insects, and of the fruits to fruit-eating birds and mammals which disperse the seeds, and the ability to produce a large fruit with large seeds when the ultimate branches would be too slender to carry this.

Herbs of the forest floor

Herbs do not make a continuous ground cover in the tropical rain-forest, but tend to occur in scattered patches, often of one species. Rather few families have abundant members in the understorey, but members of the Zingiberaceae, Commelinaceae, Rubiaceae and Acanthaceae are common. Grasses are rare, and those which do occur usually have broad leaves quite unlike those of open-country grasses. The almost windless forest floor makes wind-pollination difficult, and at least some of the forest grasses and sedges (Cyperaceae) are pollinated by insects or other animals. Most of the ground herbs spread largely vegetatively, and flowering is often rare and irregular.

Lianes

Many species of plants in the tropical rain-forest are not mechanically and nutritionally self-supporting, but depend on other plants for their support (the lianes and the epiphytes) and occasionally also for their nutrition (the parasites).

The **lianes** are woody climbers which attain their greatest abundance and diversity in the tropics. Most begin life as small shrubs, but later long branches armed with tendrils or hooks attach themselves to the understorey and the liane eventually extends to the canopy. Once there, the liane may produce a large crown extending across several supporting trees. As much as 40% of the canopy may be made up of liane leaves; since these compete with the tree leaves, and make felling difficult, cutting of these climbers is an important operation in tropical forestry.

The structure of liane stems is often peculiar. The wood, instead of being deposited as a continuous cylinder, is often produced in isolated blocks, or in a lobed or flanged arrangement (see section 2.2), and within the wood the vessels are extremely large. The stem of a liane requires little mechanical strength as it does not have to support the crown, but only the weight of the stem itself; on the other hand it requires flexibility, and this is given by its rope-like structure. The large vessels allow sufficient water to be drawn up into the large crown through a stem of relatively small diameter; the tension in the water columns in the stem is considerable and air can often be heard hissing into the cut vessels of a partially severed liane.

a

b

Fig. 8.59. (a) Many rain-forest trees have large buttresses at the base of the trunk. This is Acrocarpus, *from South India. (b) A few trees in rain-forest, such as this one,* Musanga cecropioides *from West Africa, have stilt roots at the base of the trunk.* Musanga *is a fast-growing tree of secondary forest.*

Fig. 8.60. (below) Young leaves in tropical rain-forest in Malaya. Leaf expansion takes place very fast, so that the leaves droop because strengthening tissue is still being produced. The red colour is due to anthocyanins, and may indicate the presence of unpalatable compounds in the young leaves.

Stranglers

The group of plants called **stranglers** is found only within the tropical rain-forest, and most are species of fig (*Ficus*). After a period of slow growth and establishment as epiphytes in the canopy layer, they send out roots which descend the trunk of the host tree and enter the soil. Growth then becomes very rapid, the crown of the strangler increases in size and competes with the canopy of the host, while the roots multiply and fuse together until they completely surround the trunk of the host. Finally the host tree dies and decays, and the strangler is left as a tree crown supported by a hollow trunk.

Epiphytes

Epiphytes are plants which grow on the surface of others. They obtain only support from their hosts, and are not parasitic. Their habitat, although always severely restricted in the availability of water and nutrients, is very varied; the small outer branches of the crown of a canopy tree and the base of its trunk represent the extremes. Large horizontal branches provide the habitat of the greatest number of epiphytes.

Orchids are the commonest epiphytes, and probably half the 18 000 known species of orchid are epiphytic. Most of the 2000 species of the New World family Bromeliaceae grow only as epiphytes (Fig. 8.61). Ferns are also commonly epiphytic.

Fig. 8.61. Tillandsia, a bromeliad, from Florida. Bromeliads are common epiphytes in the American tropics. They grow attached to the thinner tree branches and have few roots; much of their water requirements are met from rain which collects in the centre of the rosette.

Most epiphytes are to a certain degree xeromorphic, that is, they are adapted to prevent loss of water by evaporation; they have small and/or thick and leathery leaves and some possess swollen water-storing organs. The roots of epiphytic orchids are covered with a layer of dead cells, the velamen, the walls of which are pierced by holes. When wetted, these cells fill with water very quickly and retain it until it is absorbed by the underlying living cells, and the velamen functions therefore like a sponge. Many epiphytic bromeliads have a rosette form of growth, with the rosette standing upright and the leaves forming a cup in which water accumulates. The plant is capable of absorbing water from this tank; the roots are small and serve only to attach the plant to its support.

Parasites

Parasites are uncommon in tropical rain-forest. Hemiparasites in the family Loranthaceae (mistletoes) are often frequent; these have green leaves but depend on their host for water and inorganic materials. There are also a few root parasites, including *Rafflesia arnoldii*, which is reputed to have the largest flower of any living plant.

Saprophytes

Saprophytic fungi are abundant in tropical rain-forest, although their fruit bodies are not often seen; less common are the saprophytic flowering plants. These are generally very small, delicate, white or brownish, and are dependent on decaying material for their nutrition. Species of *Burmannia* (Burmanniaceae), *Thismia* (Thismiaceae), *Leiphaimos* (Gentianaceae) and various genera of Orchidaceae are the commonest, and generally contain mycorrhizal fungus in their roots to aid in the absorption of soluble compounds from the litter.

Regional variations

There are, some general regional trends in the rain-forest vegetation. The forests of South-East Asia, for example, are the richest in the world: the Malay Peninsula has about 7900 species of flowering plants in 130000 square kilometres, compared to the British Isles with 1430 species in 311000 square kilometres. Within the South-east Asian rain-forests, one family (the Dipterocarpaceae) is predominant, with several large genera, such as *Shorea* which contains 180 species. South America has the largest area of continuous rain-forest in the world, covering much of the Amazon Basin. Here no family is dominant, although members of Leguminosae and Moraceae are prominent. Perhaps the most characteristic family of this region is the Bromeliaceae, most of whose members are rather small epiphytes. The forest of the Amazon Basin has a number of local variants, including the seasonally flooded **várzea**. The rain-forests of Africa are poorer in species than are either of those already mentioned. This may be the result of very severe shrinkage of the forests during the dry periods of the Pleistocene; it is possible that there may have been only three or four refuge areas into which the forests retreated.

Local variations

Rain-forest varies along two main local gradients, of altitude and of rainfall. In all the main areas of tropical rain-forest there are mountains, and on ascending these several different zones of vegetation are passed through. As a general rule, increase in altitude brings increasing rainfall, and the precipitation from rain is increased by the deposition onto leaves of mist droplets during the frequent spells when the forest is covered by cloud. With increasing altitude, the trees become smaller and epiphytes more abundant, especially mosses, liverworts and lichens, so that these upland forests are characterised by great masses of mosses covering the branches (Fig. 8.41) and trailing wisps of lichen. There are also changes in floristic composition, with some species disappearing and being replaced by others with increasing altitude.

The main change that occurs down a gradient of changing rainfall is that the number of deciduous trees increases with

Fig. 8.62. Rain-forest cleared for cattle ranching in Brazil: livestock graze amid the skeletons of old forest trees. Such pastures often lose productivity after only a few years, prompting more destruction of forest.

decreasing rainfall until, at the boundaries of the forest, almost all the trees lose their leaves during the dry season. There is no sharp boundary between evergreen and deciduous forest, but rather a gradual increase in the proportion of deciduous species. It has also become clear in recent years that the largest trees are not found in the wettest forests, but tend to be found in forests with a distinct dry season, and that the average size of trees in the wettest forests is lower. This is possibly due to a reduced supply of nutrients to plants in the wettest forests due to leaching.

Productivity of rain-forest

The estimation of primary productivity in the tropical rain-forest is not easy but an annual figure of 2000 grams per square metre may be reasonable. Thus, the tropical rain-forest is one of the most productive communities in the world. The diversity of the forest also means that it contains many useful plants. Timber species are of course abundant. Many spice plants, such as pepper (*Piper nigrum*), nutmeg (*Myristica fragrans*), vanilla (*Vanilla planifolia*) and cardamom (*Elletaria cardamomum*), also originate in forests. Bamboos and rattans (climbing palms) produce material for use in local buildings and for making furniture for export. Drugs such as quinine from *Cinchona*,

emetine from *Cephaelis ipecacuanha*, and strophanthin from *Strophanthus* are all forest products, as are many gums, resins, dyes and essential oils.

Unfortunately the tropical rain-forests have an uncertain future (Fig. 8.62). Harvesting for timber is rapid in many places and even more serious is exploitation for pulpwood for making paper. Timber exploitation uses only some of the trees, and so a residue is left from which regeneration can occur, but pulpwood mills take all the trees. A greater threat still is posed by cultivators who move in after the timber has been harvested, clear and burn the residual forest, and plant crops. Most of the nutrients in tropical forests are in the vegetation, and so when it is cleared and burned there are rapid losses through leaching and runoff. Because of this, crop yields fall quickly and new areas of forest must be cleared and cultivated. This practice of shifting cultivation has been going on for thousands of years, and when human populations are low it poses little threat because in any one place there is a very long interval between successive cultivations. With increasing population long periods for regeneration of the forest can no longer be afforded, however, and larger areas of forest must be used. Some ecologists have put the life expectancy of tropical rain-forest as a type of vegetation at less than 20 years.

Fig. 8.63. *Lemurs are the most primitive group of primates, the order which includes the monkeys and apes. They are confined to Madagascar. The diurnal ruffed lemur is one of the largest lemurs with a combined body and tail length of about 120 centimetres.*

Fig. 8.64. *The cotton top marmoset of South America is a primate with a diet of insects, small mammals and fruit.*

Animals of tropical rain-forest

Although the tropical rain-forest is among the most productive ecosystems in the world, the animal biomass is generally low. Many of the animals are adapted to arboreal life, and consequently tend to be small; large mammals are rare and live in small groups. The largest terrestrial mammal, the elephant, is, however, found in the rain forest as well as in seasonal forests and scrubland, and some other large ungulates live in the rain-forests, including the okapi (*Okapia johnstoni*) from eastern Zaire. The okapi is the only living relative of the giraffe, but little is known about it due to its solitary habits and the inaccessibility of its habitat.

Pigs occur in the rain-forest and two are present in Africa: the bush pig or red river hog (*Potamochoerus porcus*), which is a bright rufous red, and the giant forest hog (*Hylochoerus meinertzhageni*), which is a true forest-dweller, although its preferred habitat is the forest edge. Three wild pigs live in the rain-forests of Asia: the common wild boar (*Sus scrofa*) also occurs in other habitats, but the bearded pig (*Sus barbatus*) is confined to the rain-forests and in terms of biomass is the most

important mammal there. The third Asian species is the babirussa (*Babirussa babyrussa*), which lives in the forest of Sulawesi and adjacent islands and has upward growing tusks. The pig family is represented in the South American rain-forests by the two species of peccary; only the white-tailed peccary (*Tayassu pecari*) is a true tropical forest species.

The rare pygmy hippopotamus (*Choeropsis liberiensis*) from West Africa is a true forest-dweller, and is much more terrestrial and less a social animal than its larger cousin. The chevrotains are a curious group of forest animals, forming the family Tragulidae. They have characteristics of deer, antelope and pigs and probably resemble the primitive ancestors of these groups. The African representative is the water chevrotain (*Hyemoschus aquaticus*), which in diet and general behaviour closely resembles a pig. There are three species of chevrotain (*Tragulus*), in Asia; these are smaller than the water chevrotain and are commonly known as mouse deer.

Many bovids occur in the rain-forests, with a great variety of duikers (*Cephalophus*) and other small antelopes in Africa, including Bate's pygmy antelope (*Neotragus batesi*), and the tiny royal antelope (*N. pygmaeus*) standing only 25 centimetres

Fig. 8.65. Predators of South American rain-forests. (a) A jaguar from Brazil. This large cat is the South American equivalent of the leopard. (b) The harpy eagle hunts for monkeys in the forest canopies.

high at the shoulder and with a mass of only 3 to 4 kilograms. The bushbuck (*Tragelaphus scriptus*) is a medium-sized antelope of the African rain-forest, although it also occurs elsewhere, and a related species is the bongo (*Boocercus euryceros*), an unusually large forest antelope weighing up to 225 kilograms. Antelopes are not a feature of Asian forests and their place is taken by deer, cattle and other forms including tapirs and rhinoceroses. The largest member of the cattle family is the gaur (*Bos gaurus*), a wild forest ox with a range extending from India to Malaysia; the banteng (*B. javanicus*), ancestor of the Bali cattle, now occurs mainly in Java. The kouprey (*Bos sauveli*) is a rare cattle species discovered only in 1937. The Asian water buffalo (*Bubalus bubalis*) prefers marshes, swamp and flooded grasslands to forests, although it usually lies up in the forest during the day. The remaining related forest oxen include the anoa (*Bubalus depressicornis*) from Sulawesi, the smallest of all cattle, and the slightly larger tamarau (*Bubalus mindorensis*), from the Philippines. It is typical for island races to be smaller than their relatives on the mainland, and similar dwarfing is found in many other groups (see section 7.5).

Forest deer of tropical Asia include the sambar (*Cervus unicolor*), which resembles a large red deer, the swamp deer or barasinghas (*C. duvauceli*), which prefers the wetter forests, and the axis deer or chital (*C. axis*), widespread throughout India and Sri Lanka.

There are three species of rhinoceros in Asia, and two in Africa, but only the Asian rhinos occur predominantly in forests. The largest, the great Indian rhinoceros (*Rhinoceros unicornis*), is also the commonest, but even so numbers only around 1000 animals. There are a few hundred Sumatran rhinoceros (*Dicerorhinus sumatrensis*), but the Javan rhinoceros (*Rhinoceros sondaicus*) is highly endangered, with only about 20 animals left in one reserve in Java. Both these rare species are small, which again is typical of island forms. Tapirs are distant relatives of the rhinos, and there are four closely related species in Asia and South America. The Asian species, the Malayan tapir (*Tapirus indicus*), bears a striking black-and-white pattern which contrasts markedly with the dull brown of the South American species. Two of the three South American species, the Brazilian tapir (*Tapirus terrestris*) and Baird's tapir (*T. bairdi*), are forest-dwellers.

The most familiar group associated with tropical forests is probably the primates, including the monkeys and apes. The lower primates (prosimians), which are mainly confined to forests, include the lorises of Asia and the pottos of Africa. These are slow moving and stalk roosting birds and other small prey at night. The closely related galagos, or bushbabies, of Africa are quite different in their habits, and move more quickly by bounding along on their hind legs like miniature kangaroos. The Asian equivalent of the bushbaby is the tarsier. The lemurs are a group of lower primates confined to Madagascar where, in the absence of the monkeys, they have evolved into a variety of forms occupying the niches occupied elsewhere by monkeys (Fig. 8.63). One family, the mouse or dwarf lemurs, is similar to the lorises and galagos, but most lemurs belong to the family Lemuridae, which includes both tree-dwelling and ground-living forms. The very rare and grotesque aye-aye (*Daubentonia madagascariensis*) is placed in a family of its own. The South American primates, all of which are forest species, are completely different in origin from those in the Old World (see section 14.4); and there are no prosimians, but their place is taken by the marmosets and tamarins, which are similar in size and habits (see Fig. 8.64). Unlike most primates, marmosets and tamarins have claws rather than nails on their digits.

Most Old World monkeys (Cercopithecidae) and all New World monkeys (Cebidae) live in the rain-forests. The New World monkeys are particularly adapted to life in the trees as they have prehensile tails. The Old World monkeys however include a larger number of genera, of which typical forest forms are the leaf-eating colobus monkeys (*Colobus*) of Africa and the leaf monkeys and langurs of Asia. The other important group of monkeys in the Asiatic forests is the macaques (*Macaca*), which include the well-known rhesus monkey (*M. mulatta*). All macaques have short tails and *M. negra*, the 'black ape' of Sulawesi, and its relatives, have very short, stumpy tails.

The anthropoid apes (family Pongidae) are found in the rain-forests of Africa and Asia (see section 14.4). The African apes comprise the gorilla (*Gorilla gorilla*; Fig. 14.15), and the two

Fig. 8.66. *The sparkling violetear, a humming bird from Peru. Humming birds, which are confined to the New World, sip nectar with their long tongues while hovering in front of flowers.*

species of chimpanzee. The common chimpanzee (*Pan troglodytes*) has a wider distribution than has the gorilla, and occurs throughout the rain-forest and into more open country both to the west and east. The pygmy chimpanzee or bonobo (*P. paniscus*) is more lightly built, with proportionately longer limbs and a dark, rather than white, face. The Asian rain-forest apes comprise the gibbons (*Hylobates*) and the orang utan (*Pongo pygmaeus*; Fig. 14.15). These apes are far more arboreal than are their African relatives, and the gibbons in particular have very long arms for swinging from branch to branch (brachiation). Unlike other apes, the gibbons are monogamous, with each pair holding a territory which is maintained by means of a loud hooting song. The distribution of gibbons extends from Assam through Indo-China and Malaysia to the Indonesian islands. Orangs no longer occur on the Asian mainland but are confined to the forests of Sumatra and Borneo.

Smaller mammals of the rain-forest include the tree shrews of South-east Asia, which have been variously placed with primates and with insectivores, but are probably a separate order. They are rather squirrel-like in their habits, except that they consume large numbers of insects. True squirrels are abundant in the Asian and African rain-forests. Some have taken to the air, and glide from tree to tree using sheets of skin stretched between the limbs, this gliding habit has evolved at least twice in the squirrels. A quite different flying mammal is

Fig. 8.67. Ecological equivalents. The great Indian hornbill of tropical Asia (a) and the toco toucan (b) of South America. Both feed on the fruits of forest trees.

the colugo (*Galeopithecus volans*) which is placed in an order of its own, the Dermoptera. Australian forests have the marsupial equivalents of flying squirrels in the flying phalangers. Squirrels do not occur in the South American forests, but perhaps their niche is filled by marmosets. Australian and New Guinea rain-forests also lack squirrels, and here the substitutes are probably the agile tree-kangaroos.

An arboreal group confined to the South American rain-forests is the sloths. Sloths are probably more closely adapted to living in trees than is any other mammal, and spend almost all their lives hanging upside down among the branches.

In South America the small mammals of the forest floor include various opossums and caviomorph rodents such as the paca (*Caniculus paca*) and the agouti (*Dasyprocta*). In African forests there are the elephant shrews. The tenrecs of Madagascar are an endemic group of insectivore that shows convergent evolution with other kinds of insectivore: there are tenrecs resembling hedgehogs and tenrecs resembling shrews. Asian forests are also rich in insectivores, including the moon rats, which are relatives of the hedgehog. The Australasian forests include among their small mammals two species of echidna or spiny anteater which lay eggs.

There are some large mammalian predators of the rain-forest floor, such as the tiger (*Panthera tigris*) in Asia, the jaguar (*P. onca*; Fig. 8.65) in South America, and the leopard (*P. pardus*) in Africa and Asia. The various species of bears in Asia are mainly insectivorous or herbivorous, except for the Himalayan black bear (*Selenarctos thibetanus*), which also occurs in the forests of Indo-China. Numerous species of viverrids, such as genets (*Genetta*), occur in the rain-forests of the Old World, their place in South America is taken by a group related to raccoons (procyonids), including the kinkajou (*Potos flavus*) and coati-mundi (*Nasua*). Small to medium-sized cats are numerous in all rain-forests except of course in Australia, where their place is taken by the marsupial tiger cat (*Dasyurus maculatus*), which preys mainly on birds in treetops.

Birds are plentiful in the rain-forests, and are particularly numerous and diverse in South America. The hummingbirds (Fig. 8.66), toucans and woodcreepers are unusual forest birds confined to the New World. The oil bird (*Steatornis caripensis*)

is a relative of the nightjars and nests in dark caves; it is the only bird known to possess an ultrasonic navigating ability similar to that of bats. The hoatzin (*Opisthocomus hoazin*) is the only living bird to possess claws on the wing, although only the fledgling does so; these claws are similar to those found in the first known bird, the extinct *Archaeopteryx* (see pp. 345–7).

Africa has a number of endemic groups of forest birds including the colourful chicken-sized turacos. Hornbills take the place here of toucans (Fig. 8.67) and sunbirds that of the hummingbirds. The game birds are represented by guinea-fowls and the Congo peacock (*Afropavo congensis*). Asian rain-forests share many types of bird with the African rain-forest, including hornbills and sunbirds, but they are particularly rich in pheasants including the jungle fowl (*Gallus gallus*) from which our domesticated chickens are descended. The original home of the peacock (*Pavo cristatus*) is the forest of India and Sri Lanka, where it is rather a retiring bird and rarely seen.

Australasian rain-forest birds show many affinities with the Asian communities, but groups peculiar to the region are the birds of paradise from New Guinea and the related bower birds, the males of which construct decorated ' bowers' to attract the females. The cassowaries (*Casuarius*) are unusually large forest birds, standing 150 centimetres high and weighing up to 50 kilograms; they are ratites, related to emus, rheas and ostriches, but differ in their colourful wattles and bony helmets. Parrots are abundant and the cockatoos, lories and pygmy parrots that occur are not found elsewhere. The pigeon family, although not endemic, is well represented, and includes the largest pigeon in the world, the 90-centimetre-long crowned pigeon, which lives on the forest floor rather than in the trees.

*Fig. 8.68. Invertebrates of the tropical rain-forests.
(a), (b), (c) Three butterflies from central and southern
America: Agraulis vanillae; Morphopeleides insularis;
Amauris niavius. Such bright irridescent colours are typical of
tropical butterflies. (d) A nest of the African termite
Cubitermes on a tree trunk. The overlapping brackets direct
rainwater streaming down the trunk away from the nest. (e) A
pill millipede (Oniscomorpha). Many tropical millipedes are
very long but some, like this specimen, are short and can roll*

*up into a ball. (f) A 'bird-eating' spider from Amazonia.
Although there are records of such spiders killing small birds,
most feed on grasshoppers and other insects. (g) Taphronota
calliparea, a large grasshopper from Uganda. (h) Driver ants
occur throughout the tropics and are known as safari ants in
Africa. They are nomadic and when on the move the workers,
guarded by the large soldiers, proceed in a column. Periodically,
they fan out and destroy any living creature unable to run or
fly away.*

Reptiles and amphibians are well represented in the tropical rain-forests. Some have taken to gliding between trees; these include the flying lizards (*Draco*) of Malaysia and Indonesia, which support their flying surfaces with folding spokes formed from extensions of the ribs. The other flying lizard is a gecko (*Ptychozoon kuhli*), also from South-east Asia, which uses flaps of skin more as a parachute than as a wing. There is even a flying frog, with expanded webbing between the toes of its feet, and a flattened tree snake (*Chrysopelea ornata*), which

launches itself into the air from trees. Chameleons are typical lizards of the rain-forests, and have independently swivelling eyes and long, sticky tongues which they flick out to catch insect prey at long range. Most chameleons are African, but there is one species in India and another in southern Europe.

Numerous frogs live in the rain-forests. Many are tree-frogs with suction pads on their digits for clinging to the surfaces of leaves. Some lay their eggs in temporary pools of rainwater in the trees, and others make foam nests in which the tadpoles

hatch before being washed out onto the forest floor when heavy rain causes the nest to disintegrate. Some South American frogs lay their eggs on the back of the male, who carries the developing tadpoles; and some ground-living frogs have no tadpole stage at all but hatch out in the damp litter as miniature adults. Rain-forest frogs often have poisonous mucus, presumably as a deterrent to predators. The most unusual amphibians are the caecilians, which are legless and look like colourful earthworms. They burrow in the soft earth of the forest floor and probably feed on earthworms and other small invertebrates.

There is an immense variety of invertebrates in the rain-forests (Fig. 8.68). These are often very large, with centipedes and millipedes 30 centimetres long and beetles the size of mice. There are many butterflies, often with impressive wing spans, and some of the spiders are huge, the largest being the hairy bird-eating spiders which can have a leg-span of 25 centimetres. Snails are not common in rain-forests because of the lack of calcium in the soil, but in West Africa giant snails (*Achatina*) occur, growing up to 15 centimetres in length.

Further reading

Attenborough, D. *Life on earth*. London: Readers Digest Association, 1980.

Bliss, L.C., Heal, O.W. and Moore, J.J. *Tundra ecosystems: A comparative analysis*. IBP vol. 25. Cambridge: Cambridge University Press, 1981.

Coupland, R.T. (Editor) *Grassland ecosystems of the world: Analysis of grasslands and their uses*. IBP vol. 18. Cambridge: Cambridge University Press, 1979.

Holdgate, M.W. (Editor) *Antarctic ecology*. 2 vols. Academic Press, 1970.

Larsen, J.A. *The boreal ecosystem*. Academic Press, 1980.

Matthews, L.H. *The life of mammals*. 2 vols. London: Weidenfeld & Nicolson, 1971.

Richards, P.W. *The tropical rain forest*. Cambridge: Cambridge University Press, 1952.

Simpson, G.G. *Splendid isolation. The curious history of South American mammals*. New Haven: Yale University Press, 1980.

Stonehouse, B. and Gilmore, D. (Editors) *The biology of marsupials*. London: Macmillan, 1977.

Walter, H. *Vegetation of the earth and ecological systems of the geo-biosphere*. Berlin: Springer-Verlag, 1979.

Walter, H., Harnickell, E. and Mueller-Dombois, D. *Climate-diagram maps of the individual continents and the ecological climatic regions of the Earth*. Berlin: Springer-Verlag, 1975.

9 Freshwater and Wetland Environments

Freshwater covers less than 1% of the earth's surface, but because of the tremendous diversity of this kind of habitat, its interest to the biologist is disproportionately great. The term freshwater is applied to any type of water which is neither saline nor brackish (partially salty), and so refers not only to natural rivers and lakes, but also to those which have been much changed by engineering activities or pollution (see Fig. 9.1). The highly polluted lower reaches of the Rhine are freshwater to a biologist, just as much as are the alpine streams which form the ultimate tributaries of this river.

Wetlands also include a wide variety of environments, some of which have rather little in common with one another. The term provides however a useful way of describing all those habitats which are in some way intermediate between permanent open water and dry land. Wetlands are treated more fully below (section 9.3) but it will be helpful to describe the main types here, before dealing with rivers and lakes. The key factors determining the type of wetland are the height of the water column or water table, and the extent to which this changes over the year. Some areas have a more or less permanent cover of water, but one sufficiently shallow to permit the extensive growth of higher plants above the water surface. This applies, for instance, to many marshes covered by reed or bulrush, but sometimes also to forest, such as some of the swamp-cypress forests of the south-eastern USA. Another type of wetland is one which is submerged completely for part of the year, but which largely or completely dries out for the remainder. Examples of this include the deep-water rice fields of Bangladesh and Burma, and extensive tracts of forest alongside the Amazon. A third type of wetland is one in which there is little open water present, but where the water table remains very close to the surface throughout the year. The mires (bogs) of temperate regions, dominated by *Sphagnum*, provide an obvious example.

One other type of environment is dealt with in this chapter although it is neither freshwater nor wetland. This is the inland saline lake, and in spite of their great differences in water chemistry, inland saline lakes are usually studied along with freshwater lakes rather than with the open sea. Although their flora and fauna are very restricted, some of the organisms present are of much interest for research, and several may also prove to be of economic importance.

9.1 STREAMS AND RIVERS

Streams and rivers are of great importance for many plants and animals, including the human species. Many types of wetland vegetation depend on seasonal flooding by major rivers such as the Amazon, Brahmaputra and Nile. The dispersal of many animals, and to a lesser extent of plants, has often taken place via rivers. Some of the largest engineering schemes ever undertaken dam or change the flow of major rivers: almost always these have resulted in profound ecological changes,

Fig. 9.1. A polluted ditch showing domestic refuse.

many of them unexpected and often unwanted. Many more such schemes are planned, so the study of plants and animals in rivers is becoming increasingly important if biologists are to inform planners of just what are the likely effects of future dams and river diversions.

The organisms of flowing waters are easiest to understand by considering first those in small streams, and then looking at the types of changes that take place on passing downstream.

In the areas that feed rivers (their **catchments**) there is often a tremendous variety among the small streams present. Springs bringing water from deep strata of rock, and seepages draining old mines, often have a similar flow, temperature, and chemistry throughout the year. In the tropics the vegetation of these springs may also remain little changed throughout the

Fig. 9.2. The trout zone of an upland stream showing boulders and relatively clear, fast-flowing water.

Fig. 9.3. Dense growths of weed can often choke rivers. A common example is the water-buttercup (Ranunculus) seen here in the La Truyère river in France.

Fig. 9.4. Two freshwater invertebrate larvae: (a) a mayfly, Ecdyonurus dispar; (b) a stonefly, Dinocras cephalotes.

Fig. 9.5. One of the largest freshwater invertebrates, the crayfish (Astacus fluviatilis).

year, but in temperate regions changes take place as a result of the seasonal cycle in light, as with the water-cress beds (*Rorippa*) of calcareous springs. In well-illuminated situations the aquatic vegetation may be very dense, although sometimes there are only a few species of plant and animal present. A complete contrast to springs rising from deep substrata are streams draining the surface of the land, and these may be subject to great fluctuations in flow, temperature, and chemistry throughout the year. Aquatic flowering plants are usually absent from such streams, and the flora is restricted to algae and a few lichens and bryophytes (liverworts and mosses). Some of these plants are restricted to parts of the stream where water flows permanently. Areas of the stream-bed which become submerged as a result of a rise in water-level in spring are usually colonised by species of algae that can spread easily and grow relatively fast. Lichens and some mosses, on the other hand, are very tolerant of intermittent wetting, but may be absent if the stream is markedly scoured by ice when this

breaks up in spring. The moss *Cinclidotus fontinaloides* is conspicuous in many large streams of Europe and Asia, where the rocks are subject to periodic submergence; in limestone regions the almost black colour of dried plants of this species provides a striking visual contrast with the rocks.

Zonation

In order to describe the changes taking place in passing downstream from a small stream to a large river, the system is classified into different zones, usually named after the characteristic fish present, as these vary in a diagnostic way with the type of stream or river. A well-known classification is that of Huet; this recognizes four zones, the upper two with fish of the salmon family and the lower two with 'coarse' (non-salmonid) fish.

The **trout zone** has streams with steep gradients and rapid currents. The stream-bed is usually of rock, boulders or pebbles, and the water is shallow, well aerated and cool (Fig. 9.2). The characteristic fish is the brown trout (*Salmo trutta*).

In the **grayling zone**, the streams are large but with a gradient less steep than that of the trout zone; pools up to 2 metres deep alternate with shallow sections where the current is quite rapid. The stream-bed consists of finer material than in the trout zone, often of washed gravel. The water in summer is often lower in oxygen than is that in the trout zone, but it is still sufficiently aerated for salmonid fish like the grayling (*Thymallus thymallus*).

Further down the river, where the gradient is moderate and rapids alternate with extensive stretches of quiet waters, is the **barbel zone**. The barbel (*Barbus barbus*) is the characteristic 'coarse' fish, but trout may still be present in rapid stretches.

The **bream zone** includes the lower stretches of rivers, and also canals and ditches. The current is slight, summer temperatures are high and oxygen levels can fall quite low. The water is turbid and often over 2 metres deep.

The recognition of these zones is rather arbitrary, but they do give a framework for describing the changes that occur on passing from an upland stream to a lowland river. A complication arises because not all the species of fish are found in every river. The grayling is, for instance, absent from some British rivers, and the minnow (*Phoxinus phoxinus*) is then a

a

b

Fig. 9.6. Two freshwater amphibians: (a) the European fire salamander, Salamandra salamandra; *(b) the leopard frog,* Rana pipiens, *from the USA.*

more characteristic species of this zone. Chub (*Leuciscus cephalus*) is more common than barbel in British rivers and is therefore a better characteristic fish for the barbel zone in Britain. In the tropics the classification based on fish breaks down completely, because salmonid fish are absent. Salmon, trout, grayling and their relatives all require a plentiful supply of oxygen in the water and survive well in temperate regions, but because of the high temperatures in the tropics much less oxygen is dissolved in the water and the salmonids are absent.

It is not only the fish fauna which changes on passing downstream; there are marked changes in the rest of the fauna and in the flora. The species compositions of many invertebrate groups change on passing downstream, and this is particularly obvious for the flat-worms, non-biting mites, mayflies and stoneflies. All these animals move over much shorter distances than do fish, and so the presence or absence of a particular species reflects conditions on only a small area of river-bed.

Submerged flowering plants become increasingly abundant on passing downstream, as the current becomes less rapid, and bryophytes become less common. Just where the changes become significant depends on the extent to which the river is subject to great variations in flow. Many flowering plants are susceptible to damage by floods, particularly if these take place in late summer when plant growth is at its maximum. Only one family of flowering plants, the Podostemaceae, has adapted successfully to withstand torrential currents, but it is restricted to the tropics. In temperate regions, species of water-buttercup (such as *Ranunculus fluitans*) are often the first flowering plants to appear in the main river (Fig. 9.3). These are followed further downstream by species of pondweed (*Potamogeton*), water-starwort (*Callitriche*) and, especially in warmer climates, *Vallisneria*. When the waters become very deep, however, attached plants can no longer survive in the main channel of the river, because of the lack of light. The almost cosmopolitan species *Potamogeton pectinatus* is often the last flowering plant to survive in lowland rivers carrying heavy loads of suspended material in the water. This species stores sufficient food each autumn in rhizomes buried in the silt of the river-bed so that the fresh shoots can grow for some weeks each spring, before they get near enough to the surface of the river to receive sufficient light to begin photosynthesis.

Invertebrates

The availability of suitable food is usually the most important factor determining the abundance of the various types of invertebrate in different stretches of streams and rivers. As with any other type of environment, the invertebrates may be herbivores, detritivores or carnivores, but the particular orders and species present change on passing downstream. Among the carnivores, for example, stoneflies (Fig. 9.4) are most common in the trout and grayling zones, while dragonflies become increasingly abundant in the barbel and bream zones. Many more animals than plants are found only in flowing waters, because many animals, like the caddisflies, are detritivores, collecting and feeding on particles passing downstream. These particles need not necessarily be fragments of organisms which have lived in the river: animals which are abundant in late summer and autumn feed mainly on leaves and other vegetable debris washed in from the surrounding catchment area (see section 5.5). It has been argued that detritivores are much more important than herbivores in rivers, because there is much more vegetable matter washed into the water than is available from the plants actually growing there. Further, many of the large living aquatic plants appear to provide poor grazing for animals, at least in temperate waters. Few animals, for instance, graze the common alga *Cladophora*, which can form huge masses in many lowland rivers. The films of unicellular algae, however, are grazed very effectively by many species of mollusc, damsel fly and beetle. These are probably responsible for removing the thick films of diatoms and other small algae which develop each spring on the bed of most temperate streams and shallow rivers. These films seldom become as thick again during the summer, almost certainly due to grazing by the invertebrates.

The largest invertebrates in many streams and rivers are crabs or crayfish (Fig. 9.5), though the two seldom occur together in the same stretch of water; crabs are confined to warmer climates, but crayfish can occur in most regions. These animals are both typically omnivorous, eating plant or animal material, living or dead, according to availability. In many rivers crayfish are apparently responsible for the removal of many of the dead leaves present, but their activities are often overlooked because they move mostly at night.

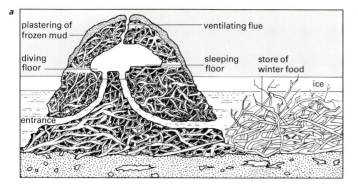

a
plastering of
frozen mud
diving
floor
ventilating flue
sleeping
floor
store of
winter food
ice
entrance

*Fig. 9.7. (a) Diagrammatic section through a beaver lodge.
(b) A beaver lodge and dam in the Rocky Mountains, USA.*

Vertebrates

Besides the fish, many types of vertebrate are associated in some way with running water. Some both live and feed entirely in the water, but many are much less strictly confined to the water than are the fish. A number of amphibians are entirely aquatic, such as the giant salamander of small mountain streams in the Far East; this carnivore can grow to 80 centimetres or more in length, and so presumably has a considerable impact on the stretch of stream where it is living.

Three groups of reptiles are associated with flowing waters, the crocodiles, the freshwater turtles and some snakes. Crocodiles, caiman and alligators occur throughout most of the warmer parts of the world and at least in the past were often present in large numbers. Their numbers have often been severely reduced by human activity, and this has almost certainly had a considerable ecological impact on the rivers involved. The effects may be complex, however, as shown by studies in the Amazon. The exploitation of hides of caiman (mainly *Melanosuchus niger*) for large-scale commercial purposes started in about 1940. Fifteen years later, the commercial statistics for the port of Manaus alone listed 5 million hides and within this period the animal had become almost extinct. The diet of the caiman is almost entirely fish, so it was an unpleasant surprise to local fishermen to find that far from their hauls increasing in the absence of the caiman, there was a marked decrease. The explanation of this is that the caiman used to feed on enormous shoals of migratory fish which passed through the bays where the caiman lived. Digestion of these fish led to the release of nutrients into water otherwise very poor in nutrients, which led to increased algae in the water, which in turn provided food for the populations of those fish exploited by the fishermen. Freshwater snakes are also carnivores, different species feeding variously on crayfish, frogs, toads and small fish; in contrast the freshwater turtles are mostly omnivorous, though some of them, such as the snapping turtles (*Chelydra*), consume quite large amounts of fish.

Many birds and mammals are also associated with streams and rivers. Most of the birds are also found on lakes, but some mammals are particularly characteristic of rivers, or have a marked effect when they are present. Some species of dolphin are confined to rivers such as the Amazon and some of the large rivers of India. Rodents are probably the most important group of river mammals, as there is a whole range of species, many of which can undermine river banks by their burrowing

activities. This may alter the flow in channels and the beaver (*Castor fiber*) can change the nature of a stream entirely by building dams (Fig. 9.7). Hynes has described the effects that these animals have had in recent years in Canada. Because trapping has been reduced, beavers are reoccupying areas from which they had been long absent, and which had become sufficiently dry for colonisation by forest. Extensive flooding caused by the beavers' dams has led to large areas of dead trees, the roots of which have been drowned.

Downstream and upstream movement

If nets of different mesh sizes are suspended in a stream or river, they usually trap not only debris, but also many live organisms. Many of these organisms typically live or grow on the bed of the stream. Microscopic algae can be swept up into the main body of water, and at least some species can continue to grow as they drift downstream. Much of the suspension of normally bottom-living forms is no doubt simply a mechanical effect, but studies have shown that some algae are more likely to be swept into the moving water by day than at night. The opposite seems to be true for many invertebrates and the extent of this drift of invertebrates increases at night, particularly just after sunset, while light exerts an inhibiting effect and reduces the chances that animals such as the freshwater shrimp (*Gammarus pulex*) will be swept up by the current. Presumably such drifting animals either find a new site to settle, or are eaten by predators such as beetles or the carnivorous species of net-spinning caddisfly.

When an upland stream is in flood after very heavy rains, there is a possibility that downstream drift may increase to such an extent that whole populations may be removed to areas in which they cannot live. No doubt this is an important factor restricting the growth of many species in the trout zone. On the other hand, in times of drought the stream may become so dry that aquatic animals will perish unless they have some special method of survival. Some plants and animals have resistant stages which can resume growth when the water starts flowing again, and a number of animals survive by burying in the pebbles in the stream-bed, to depths of 50 centimetres or more, where some water is always retained.

The upstream movement of fish is well known, especially that of migratory salmon returning to their spawning grounds. Upstream movement of invertebrates is much harder to observe, but certainly often occurs. The rapid spread of the

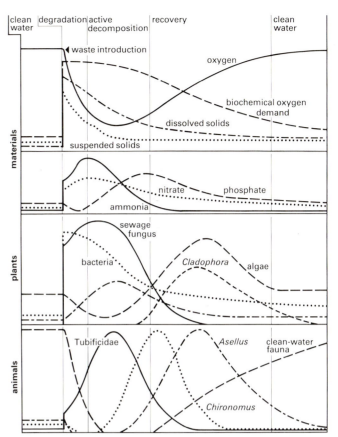

Fig. 9.8. *The effects of organic waste pollution on the chemical and biological characteristics of a river. Gradual recovery occurs downstream until the water is clean.*

little snail *Potamopyrgus jenkinsi* throughout north-western Europe in recent decades must often have involved upstream migration, and even large species of snail can move against a current. Large aggregations of *Campeloma decisium* have been found at the downstream ends of rapids in streams in Michigan, and it is believed that this snail has been attempting to move upstream, but cannot pass the barrier of swifter water of the rapids. Crustaceans can also readily travel upstream, the most striking example being the mitten-crab (*Eriocheir sinensis*). This breeds in brackish water, but it regularly travels 750 kilometres up the Ch'iang Chang (Yangtze Kiang) River and has been found as far as 1400 kilometres from the sea. The same species has been introduced to Europe and been found at sites 1000 kilometres upstream on the Danube.

Changes due to engineering schemes

The types of plants and animals in a river, and the events taking place on passing downstream, have become profoundly changed in many regions by human activities, and often it is difficult even to guess what the undisturbed river was like. In many areas forests have been removed, so that streams receive high light intensities throughout the year; in some parts of Britain, however, the situation is currently being reversed with extensive planting of coniferous forest. These changes affect the growth of aquatic plants and the relative success of grazers and detritivores, but few quantitative studies of these effects have so far been made.

Many rivers have been dammed for hydroelectric purposes, to supply water for drinking and industrial needs, or to regulate the flow. Flow regulation may have profound effects on downstream plants and animals. The removal of flooding can lead to large increases in plant growths, particularly those of floating species which would otherwise tend to be washed away. This has occurred, for instance, in the Tuolumne River, California, with the development of luxuriant growths of water-hyacinth (*Eichhornia crassipes*). The completion of the Volta Dam on the lower Volta in Ghana had many effects downstream, some beneficial and some harmful, judged by human standards. There was a rapid development of extensive stands of submerged plants (*Potamogeton octandrus, Vallisneria aethiopica*). A gastropod mollusc (*Neritina*) which fed on *Vallisneria* increased, as did the fish *Tilapia*. However clam fisheries decreased in the lowermost parts of the river, because tidal influences had encroached upstream.

Many examples are known of rivers where the construction of a dam has had a marked influence on fish populations and their behaviour. The dam may of course be a direct barrier to migration, unless a fish-ladder or other special provision is made. The effects may however be more subtle, such as cooler temperatures in spring, and warmer ones in autumn, in the rivers of temperate regions. Where the water which is allowed past the dam is drawn from deep in the reservoir, it may be severely reduced in its oxygen content. If there is insufficient

flow in the river downstream of the dam, gravel may not be sufficiently cleaned of silt to provide a suitable spawning ground for trout.

Sewage pollution

The effects of sewage on rivers are often particularly marked. Heavy pollution by organic wastes from silage or a sewage-works can lead to conspicuous growths of a 'sewage-fungus' community. This may take the form of a white or pale brown slime over the surface of the substratum, or it may be a fluffy, fungoid growth, with long streamers. This community is in fact dominated by a bacterium, *Sphaerotilus natans*, but several fungi, other bacteria, many protozoa and sometimes a few algae are present as well. Although not strictly part of the sewage-fungus community, tubificid worms are usually very abundant in waters heavily polluted by organic materials, sometimes reaching densities of more than a million animals per square metre. Different species of these worms are successively eliminated as conditions become more severe, and in very severe conditions usually only *Limnodrilus hoffmeisteri* and/or *Tubifex tubifex* remain. These animals can be very conspicuous not only because of their numbers, but also because they possess the red pigment haemoglobin, which permits them to make use of what little oxygen there is in such highly polluted water.

If a river which has received a major input of organic materials then flows for some distance without further pollution, the organic materials are gradually removed, and the amount of dissolved oxygen increases as there is less bacterial action. At the same time successive changes occur in the types of plants and animals present (Fig. 9.8). Sewage-fungus disappears, to be replaced by algae or higher plants. Tubificid worms decrease in abundance, to be replaced first by larvae of the midge *Chironomus riparius* ('blood worm') and then by a zone where the isopod crustacean *Asellus aquaticus* is abundant, with leeches, molluscs and the alder fly *Sialis lutaria*. Where recovery is almost complete, then relatively sensitive organisms like the freshwater shrimp (*Gammarus pulex*) appear again.

Nutrient enrichment and weed management

The levels of nitrate, phosphate and other mineral ions which are nutrients for plants, tend to increase naturally in rivers on passing downstream, but this effect is much increased by sewage effluents, and also by fertilisers washed from agricultural and forestry land. Because of the increased mineral nutrients, many shallow lowland rivers become choked with an overgrowth of plants each summer. These aquatic weeds can be a serious nuisance, hindering the flow of the river, making fishing almost impossible due to lines becoming entangled, and they may even cause the death of many fish. Killing of fish can happen for two rather different reasons and it is not always obvious which is responsible in a particular instance. One cause can be the massive growths of plants respiring intensely at night or when the plants are starting to decay, leading to very low levels of dissolved oxygen, which kills the fish. The other possible cause is almost the exact opposite, as the intense photosynthetic activity that takes place by day can use up so much carbon dioxide that the water becomes very alkaline; this in turn makes any ammonia present from sewage effluents highly toxic, and kills the fish.

Weed management has long been important in many lowland rivers. In the past this was concerned mostly with plants, such as bur-reed (*Sparganium erectum*), which grow above the water level at the side of the river, but control is more and more having to be extended to submerged species. Cutting has sometimes been carried out on both the emergent and the submerged species, but is expensive, and not much help if the fragments of weed are simply left to float downstream. The controlled use of herbicides is now becoming popular with some water-management bodies, but is not yet accepted by all; the aim is to kill small areas of pondweeds and other submerged plants, but only to introduce sufficient herbicide into the water to have a local effect. More permanent solutions are to shade the sides of small rivers by planting trees such as alders, as has been widely carried out in the Netherlands and North Germany, and more logically to reduce the levels of nutrients entering the water.

Toxic pollution

In addition to pollution by organic materials and by increased mineral nutrients, pollution can occur from a wide variety of potentially toxic materials. These include heavy metals such as copper, zinc, mercury and lead from industrial or mining processes, cyanides, acids and alkalis, and organic compounds such as organochlorine pesticides and herbicides. Different species vary in their vulnerability to specific pollutants, so it is hard to give a general picture of the effects of such toxic materials. The metal zinc provides one example, and has been the subject of considerable research. If a previously unpolluted river becomes contaminated by dissolved zinc, then sensitive species such as the alga *Cladophora* and molluscs may vanish, and with increasing concentrations of zinc more and more species will be eliminated. Nevertheless, waters which have been exposed to zinc for many years usually have obvious growths of algae or other plants. Most of the species present under such conditions have acquired resistance to the zinc; this is a permanent genetic change, because the organisms retain resistance if they are grown for a while in the absence of the metal and are then re-exposed to it. The plants that can survive in the drainage waters from old mines often grow so densely, due to the lack of competition from other species, that it is hard for the casual observer to realize that the waters are polluted. Nevertheless these waters are still highly toxic to sensitive species. An increase in the amount of growth, but a decrease in the number of species, is a widespread response to many types of pollution.

Zinc may be used to illustrate another aspect of pollution which causes difficulty for water management. The toxicity of zinc to many different organisms, including algae, invertebrates and fish, is profoundly affected by other features of the water, such as the kinds of dissolved calcium or magnesium salts (the hardness of the water). It is therefore impossible to state that one particular level of zinc (or of any other metal) is toxic, while all waters containing less than this are safe. Fixed limits for pollutants are easy to monitor, but a more empirical approach, judging pollutants by the effects they can cause at any particular site, may be more appropriate. For instance, most, if not all, fish can tolerate much more zinc if the water is very hard than if it is soft, while copper is generally a lot less toxic if much dissolved organic matter is present.

Acid mine drainage

Drainage waters from some mines are highly acidic because sulphide minerals have become oxidised to sulphuric acid. Where a stream receives much acid drainage water, then the effects on plants and animals may be profound, sometimes virtually eliminating all the species. In 1972 there were about 16 000 kilometres of streams seriously affected by surface mining operations in the USA alone, mostly in the east of the country, and mainly in the Appalachian mountains. The issue

Fig. 9.9. Acid mine drainage is a major problem in old coal-mining areas such as this one in West Virginia, USA. Few plants and animals can tolerate the iron oxide in the water which gives it the brown-orange colour seen here.

has subsequently acquired considerable political significance because of the rapid expansion of mining activities in states just to the east of the Rockies. Mining operators in these states are put at a disadvantage because they are subject to strict pollution regulations, whereas no such pressure has yet been put on mine operators in the Appalachians because streams have already been polluted there for many decades, often by abandoned mines for which no one is responsible. An understanding of this needs a knowledge of the chemistry and biology of these waters.

When coal containing the mineral pyrites (iron sulphide), or various other sulphide-rich minerals, is exposed to the oxidising action of air and water, a series of reactions take place which eventually form sulphuric acid. The process may start by purely chemical means, but if conditions are already somewhat acid two bacteria, *Thiobacillus thiooxidans* and *T. ferrooxidans*, are usually present and play an important role in bringing about the conversion of sulphate to sulphuric acid. The resulting highly acid mine water dissolves metals such as iron, copper and zinc, adding to the pollution problems. This is partly because of the direct toxicity of the metals at the high concentrations that often occur, but even more because the iron soon comes out of solution again, forming vast orange or deep brown precipitates which smother all life on the stream-bed. Such precipitation occurs when highly acidic waters meet less acid waters, permitting the pH to rise above 3.0.

In spite of the severe conditions, a number of organisms can live at even the lowest pH values (highest acidity). Most of these are microscopic and morphologically simple forms. Besides the bacteria, the alga *Euglena mutabilis* is particularly widespread, but a number of other algae and protozoa are usually also present, and by the time the pH has risen to 3.0 often also rotifers and at least one beetle. Paradoxically the effects on the organisms often appear more severe as the water becomes less acidic further from the mine; this is because of the iron-rich precipitate which prevents photosynthesis by plants and which clogs the respiratory surfaces of invertebrates. The particular problem with acid mine drainages is that once they

have started, they are very hard to stop. Attempts to pump bactericidal materials into disused mines have had little success and the only solution is to seal the mine sufficiently so that air is excluded from any exposed surfaces where oxidation could take place.

Thermal pollution

Electricity-generating stations require large amounts of cooling water, which is returned to the river (or sea) at a higher temperature than that at which it was removed. Such waste heat can bring about many changes in the plants and animals living downstream, though the ecological effects are in general less severe than were originally predicted. Species intolerant of warm conditions may disappear, while other species not normally found in unheated water may now thrive. Respiration and growth rates may be changed, altering the feeding rates of animals. An indirect effect of thermal pollution is to promote bacterial action, which reduces the level of oxygen dissolved in the water, particularly when the water has already become polluted by organic materials. Recently efforts have been made to use waste heat for biological purposes, such as growing carp and eels.

9.2 LAKES, RESERVOIRS AND PONDS

There is a great variety of physical and chemical types of lake, but three factors always play major roles in determining the plants and animals that live in them. Any one lake can be considered in relation to its particular combination of these three factors.

Depth influences events in a lake in all sorts of ways, but one of the most obvious is the extent to which rooted flowering plants can develop. Very shallow lakes often have an extensive cover of plants with floating leaves, like water-lilies, or with stems and leaves that emerge from the water surface, like the club-rush (*Eleocharis*). In contrast, the rooted flowering plants in very deep lakes are mostly restricted to the edge, although a few species can grow at the bottom to depths of 15 metres or more, providing that the water is sufficiently clear for light to penetrate to that depth.

The **temperature** of the lake, and mixing of waters from different depths, are also important. The water throughout some lakes is always mixed by vertical currents resulting from wind action, but in many lakes the water separates into upper and lower zones at certain seasons, with hardly any mixing between the two zones. This **stratification** happens during late spring in most deep lakes of temperate regions, when the heat of the sun causes an upper zone of warm water to form, floating on a lower cool zone, with a narrow transition zone between the two known as the thermocline (see also section 6.1). In autumn the stratification is destroyed and the water is again mixed from top to bottom.

Lastly, lakes can be divided into three classes according to the level and type of **nutrients** present. An **oligotrophic** lake is very low in the mineral nutrients that plants need, while a **eutrophic** lake is rich in these nutrients; a **dystrophic** lake has soft water (containing little calcium or magnesium) with much peaty material, and usually has a relatively low level of nutrients. These types are of course the extremes, and all intermediate types of lake are found.

Windermere

One lake will now be considered in detail to see how these factors apply. Windermere, in the English Lake District (Fig. 9.10), has been the subject of intensive research for over 50 years, and is well known to many tourists, but many other lakes are quite similar. Windermere is the largest natural lake in England, although it is only 17 kilometres long and at its widest is 1 kilometre across. It was formed by glacial action during the Ice Age and so is relatively deep, reaching a maximum of 67 metres. The depth varies, because the lake level changes with the amount of water from inflow streams, but the range in most years is little more than 50 centimetres. This is, however, enough to have a marked effect on some plants and animals at the edge.

Most of the plant life in the lake consists of small algae suspended in the water, the phytoplankton. Submerged plants do grow but only round the edge, and because of the depth of the lake they are much less important than the phytoplankton. The phytoplankton are present throughout the year, but a period of very slow growth in winter is followed by increasingly rapid growth in spring. Diatoms such as *Asterionella* are particularly abundant at this season. The spring burst of phytoplankton occurs for a variety of reasons: light intensity and daylength are increasing, nutrients have accumulated in the water during the winter, and grazing by small animals, the zooplankton, is only moderate because lake temperatures are low.

The lake stratifies in May and during summer almost all the sun's energy is trapped in the upper zone. Green and blue-green algae are particularly important in the plankton at this time of year. The blue-green algae sometimes form a thin scum at the surface of the water near the edge of the lake, but the nutrient levels in the lake are not high enough for the algae to produce dense scums offensive to the tourists. Windermere is intermediate in nutrient content between an oligotrophic and eutrophic lake. The next stage in the cycle of changes takes place in early autumn when the upper and lower zones become mixed again. Such conditions are unfavourable to the blue-green algae, but several of the diatom species continue to grow well at this time of year.

The plankton algae grow at very different speeds at different times of year, but in midsummer some single-celled species have a generation time of only a few days. It is clear that Windermere would become choked with algae by the end of the summer if their numbers were not controlled. This control results from grazing by small animals, the zooplankton, by attack by fungal parasites known as chytrids (see Fig. 2.11) and, in the case of the blue-green algae, by attack by bacteria. It is surprisingly difficult to quantify for a particular species of alga just how important is a particular form of control, but grazing is overall the most important factor. The herbivores involved include rotifers and cladocerans (water-fleas; Fig. 9.11). These, in turn, may be eaten by small carnivores, such as fish larvae. The algae are thus the first link in many different food-chains or food-webs.

Human activities have had a profound effect on the fish population of Windermere, as on many lakes in Europe and North America. Windermere has relatively few native species, presumably because other species potentially capable of living there have had no opportunity to reach the lake since the time of the last glaciation. Species that are native include both members of the salmon and trout family, the Salmonidae, and coarse fish, members of other families. The native Salmonidae are the arctic char (*Salvelinus alpinus*), the brown trout (*Salmo trutta*) and the salmon (*Salmo salar*), although this last merely passes through the lake on its way to inflow streams to spawn. The trout also spawn in inflow streams, but the young fish return to the lake, usually within two years. In contrast, the char breeds in the lake, burying its eggs in gravel in deep water. Among the coarse fish, eels (*Anguilla anguilla*) and sticklebacks (*Gasterosteus aculeatus*) are native, but pike (*Esox lucius*), perch (*Perca fluviatilis*), minnows (*Phoxinus phoxinus*) and bullheads (*Cottus gobio*) have been introduced. In addition to introducing new species of fish, man also has a continuing effect on the numbers of fish in different size classes. This is true especially of the pike, since larger animals have been removed selectively by netting since 1944, with the aim of favouring the trout and char.

The plants and animals in the water column make up the bulk of the living material in the lake. Nevertheless many species are restricted to the edges or the bottom, and some of these are of considerable importance in the ecology of the lake.

Fig. 9.10. Windermere, an oligotrophic lake in the English Lake District.

Much of the shoreline is rocky, and a fringe of emergent plants such as the common reed (*Phragmites australis*) is restricted to sheltered areas with fine sediments. Beneath the water, to a depth of about 4 metres, other rooted plants may grow. Most of the submerged plants form flowers, but these are nearly always inconspicuous.

The majority of the bottom-living invertebrates live in shallow water; these include various snails, limpets, flatworms, leeches, mites, insect nymphs and larvae, and freshwater shrimps. Below 10 metres the fauna shows many differences, consisting mainly of oligochaete worms, pea mussels (*Pisidium*), chironomid (midge) larvae and the larvae of the phantom fly (*Chaoborus*).

Arctic, temperate and tropical lakes

Many other lakes in the lowland parts of the far west of Europe resemble Windermere in that the surface of the water rarely freezes in winter: about once in every 10 years in this particular case. Most lakes in northern Europe, America and Asia, however, not only freeze but also have a cover of snow for some months. This reduces or eliminates the penetration of light into the water, making winter particularly unfavourable for algal growth. As a consequence, the period of rapid spring growth of the phytoplankton comes later than in Windermere. Under more extreme conditions, as in northern Canada and the USSR, the period of ice cover is so long that it has a much greater effect on the plants and animals. This is especially obvious if the lake is shallow, since much, if not all, of the oxygen present in the water may be used up by respiration before the cover of snow and ice melts in spring. As a consequence many of these lakes have no native fish. Introduced fish can only survive in such a lake if enough ice is regularly broken to permit adequate oxygen to enter naturally, or if air is deliberately pumped into the water.

Many small tropical lakes show hardly any tendency to stratify, but there are two other types of lake in the tropics which have no real parallel in temperate regions. The large

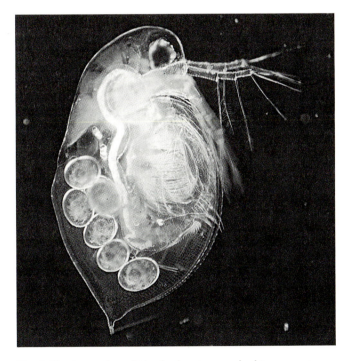

Fig. 9.11. A member of the freshwater zooplankton: a water-flea, Daphnia. *Embryonated eggs can be seen through the transparent shell.*

lakes of the Rift Valley in Africa are stratified permanently into an upper warm zone and a lower cold one ; hardly any mixing occurs across the thermocline. This means that when plants and animals in the upper part of the lake die their bodies drop below the thermocline and the materials that these contain remain permanently in the lower part of the lake. The lake sediments are thus continually accumulating valuable plant nutrients. If it ever proves economic to break down the thermocline of any of these lakes, a tremendous increase in

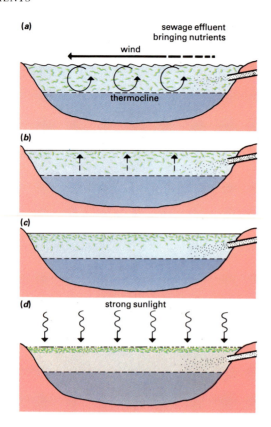

Fig. 9.12. Development of algal blooms in a nutrient-rich lake. (a) Wind activity mixes the water in the upper part of the lake. (b) During calm weather, filaments start to float to the surface. (c) A longer calm period leads to accumulation of filaments at the top of the lake. (d) Dense masses of filaments rapidly become unhealthy, particularly under intense solar irradiation, leading to filament breakdown, foul smells and a generally unpleasant appearance to the water (e).

nutrients may be expected in the upper part of the lake, leading to increased algae and hence increased stocks of fish. Obviously there are many environmental aspects that would need to be considered before such a scheme were undertaken.

Another type of tropical lake is almost the exact opposite. The water stratifies, becomes mixed and then restratifies many times during the year. The stratification occurs by day when there is no wind and much heat energy is entering the lake; at night there is a wind, which causes mixing, and also the surface waters cool by convection and radiation. The best examples occur in the mountains of Ethiopia and in the Andes, where there is a high rate of nightly heat loss at the high altitudes, and this sequence of changes may happen every day over a period of some months. These types of lake are often very productive, with their fish forming an important source of food for the local human population.

Eutrophication

Most lakes have a relatively short existence on a geological time-scale. They tend to accumulate sediments and become shallower, and communities of higher plants gradually encroach from the shore. It is possible to follow the changes which have taken place by studying the chemistry of successive layers of sediments, and their plant and animal remains. This has been done in great detail in, for instance, the English Lake District, Lake Työtjärvi in Finland, several lakes of the Canadian Shield, and Lake Biwa in Japan. As a result it has become clear that in many, if not most, lakes a sequence of changes has occurred associated with increasing levels of the nutrients which influence algal growth. Algal crops have increased and the species composition of the plants and animals has changed: the lakes have become more eutrophic. The most important exception to this general trend is at the very early

stages in the life of the lake, when there may be relatively high levels of nutrients as a result of glaciation or whatever other form of disturbance led to the origin of the lake. Such lakes first show a gradual decrease in the levels of nutrients present, and then the process reverses and they start becoming more eutrophic again as the sediments increase in amount and more organic matter is accumulated by photosynthesis or from debris washed in by the inflow streams.

Many lakes have shown much greater changes in their nutrient levels during the past century compared to previous slow natural changes. Such eutrophication has resulted from the increasing influence of human activity on the water chemistry, particularly with the increased levels of phosphate from detergents and fertilisers. Microscopic algae such as *Microcystis* may become so abundant that they colour the water, especially when they are concentrated at the surface. These 'blooms' may appear rapidly because the cells of the blue-green algae involved contain tiny cylinders of gas, which make them buoyant. Sometimes, in still weather, the appearance of a lake may change virtually overnight. Water-blooms are unpopular not just because people find their appearance offensive and swimming is made unpleasant, but also because some of the species involved can be highly toxic to animals (including man) if water containing the alga is drunk. Even if the water does not become toxic, it is of little use as a water supply, as it has an unpleasant taste and odour and often contains a lot of dissolved polysaccharide material which may form a precipitate. In many parts of the world manufacturers of soft drinks have had at some time to throw away stocks of lemonade because such a precipitate has formed when the water was acidified.

The formation of dense algal populations in turn affects other organisms. Large submerged plants tend to disappear, because the algae absorb the light before it can reach the

Fig. 9.13. *Massed flamingos (*Phoeniconaras minor*) on Lake Nakuru in Kenya.*

submerged leaves. This has occurred, for instance, in the Norfolk Broads area of eastern England, where conditions began to deteriorate markedly during the 1960s. Whereas all the broads had at one time obvious underwater growths of higher plants, 11 of 28 broads surveyed in 1972 and 1973 were almost or completely devoid of them. Large submerged plants provide food or homes for many animals, and in Loch Leven, Scotland, a large flock of mute swans (*Cygnus olor*) has virtually disappeared as the result of the loss of pondweeds and other submerged plants. Typical changes which have occurred among the animal populations of many lakes as a result of eutrophication have been the replacement of crustaceans in the bottom fauna by chironomid larvae, oligochaete and tubificid worms and, in temperate regions, of salmonid fish by coarse fish.

Eutrophication results from a continued supply of nutrients at high levels, so it is possible to reverse the process by reducing the level of nutrients reaching a lake. This is, however, not always easy to do if the lake is shallow and is enriched in nutrients from many places, as occurs with lakes in lowland agricultural areas. There are a number of well-known success stories, but the sums of money involved have sometimes been very large. In the case of Lake Washington in north-eastern USA, nuisance problems due to nutrients from sewage, which had become increasingly serious during the 1950s and early 1960s, were diminished by diverting almost all the sewage to the sea at Puget Sound, and improving the quality of

the effluent. By the time the project had been completed in 1968, the cost was 125 million dollars, but some of the problems have only been transferred from the lake to Puget Sound. Another possible method is to remove much of the phosphate from sewage effluents before these are released to a lake. This is an expensive process which has to be carried out continuously, and is usually only undertaken when the lake is an essential source of drinking water.

Reservoirs

Reservoirs are artificial lakes where the quality of the water is particularly important because it is used for drinking or industrial purposes. In many ways they resemble normal lakes, but because of the way they are managed, many have certain features in common. Reservoirs may be on-stem or off-stem, that is, they may be formed by damming a stretch of river or by pumping water some distance from a river or underground source. On-stem reservoirs obviously require a suitable river valley and are usually found in upland areas, whereas off-stem reservoirs are usually found in lowland areas. The reservoirs around London and adjacent to many other large cities in North-west Europe are of the off-stem type.

On-stem reservoirs are often quite similar to the lakes which occur naturally in a particular region, although nuisance growths of plants are sometimes evident during the early years because of the release of nutrients during decay of terrestrial

a

b

Fig. 9.14. Two British pond insects: (a) a waterboatman, Notonecta; *(b) a saucer bug,* Naucorus.

vegetation which has been submerged. Some of the large man-made lakes of the tropics, such as Lake Kariba, Zimbabwe, have had particularly serious problems at the beginning, with dense growths of water-hyacinth and the fern *Salvinia*. Unless the terrestrial vegetation is removed effectively before the dam is closed, there is little that can be done about such weed growths other than to wait until most of the nutrients are transferred to the bottom mud. Spraying the floating plants with herbicides causes as many problems as it cures. Another problem with on-stem reservoirs, particularly small ones, is the appearance of a zone with little plant cover when the water level is drawn down at periods of peak demand. Not only is this unsightly, but erosion by waves may then be a problem due to the lack of cover. Although the vegetation of many areas in the world has become well adapted to an annual cycle of flooding and drought, relatively few species of temperate regions can tolerate such conditions. Such species successful in northern Europe are short-lived annuals growing on recently exposed moist soil (not on gravel or rock), the seeds of which can survive for long periods when submerged.

Off-stem reservoirs are usually excavated near densely populated regions where land is expensive, so frequently their sides are vertical and there is no fringe of submerged plants. Because these reservoirs are in lowland areas, they are much more likely to have water rich in nutrients and be prone to algal nuisance problems. The development of blooms of blue-green algae has often been prevented by the spreading of copper sulphate over the surface of the water, but this is both expensive and potentially toxic, and so is not an ideal solution. A much better approach, which was first introduced on several of the London reservoirs but which has now been adopted in many countries, is to keep the water in the reservoir mixed throughout the year, preventing a thermocline forming in summer. Algal growth is reduced because the cells are in the dark for much longer, and the gas-vacuolate blue-green algae, which are the particular nuisance, are put at a particular disadvantage.

Saline lakes

These occur in semi-desert regions, where evaporation is greater than the rainfall. Saline lakes tend to receive the drainage of large areas, so they often contain high levels of nutrients such as phosphate as well as having a high sodium content. They also tend to undergo marked seasonal changes in the level of the water and in the salinity. A number of shallow, alkaline, slightly saline lakes in the tropics form dense populations of the alga *Spirulina*. The huge flamingo populations of some of the Rift Valley lakes in Kenya (Fig. 9.13) not only depend on the *Spirulina* and their associated zooplankton for their food, but the pink colour of the flamingo feathers is derived from carotenoids formed by the alga. *Spirulina* from slightly saline lakes has also provided a source of human food in at least two countries, Mexico at the time of the Aztecs and Chad at the present-day. Large farms have now been built in Mexico, Thailand and Taiwan to grow this alga under more controlled conditions, and it is sold as a very expensive health-food.

With increasing salinity the flora and fauna become more restricted and large very saline lakes like the Dead Sea contain only a few, highly specialised species. Three organisms which are almost always present in very saline lakes have been the subject of much research. These are the bacterium *Halobacterium*, the single-celled wall-less green alga *Dunaliella* and the brine shrimp *Artemia*. In shallow saline lakes the *Halobacterium* sometimes forms dense populations and colours the water a deep crimson. Such growths are often very obvious when flying over coastal and sometimes also inland regions of semi-deserts such as Baja California and the Gulf coast of Saudi Arabia.

Ponds

Ponds differ from lakes not so much because they are often artificial, but because they are small. Because of this they tend to undergo rapid changes unless a deliberate attempt is made to prevent this. Obviously, the smaller the pond, the more such management is important. The ponds of most suburban gardens would soon become choked with algae and higher plants if the

Fig. 9.15. Blackwaters in Amazonia. (a) A blackwater oval lake in palm forest within the Amazonian rain-forest.

(b) Water-weed grows on sand and grasses at the edge of the Rio Negro.

growths were not regularly thinned. Chance can play an important role in the sequence of events which takes place when a pond is freshly built, especially if little effort is made to stock the pond right from the start with a wide range of plants and animals. Many of the common flowering plants in ponds reproduce easily from small pieces of shoot or underground parts; if such a piece is introduced, by accident or design, the plant may grow so rapidly that it chokes the site for some years. Species which arrive later have to compete with a species which already fills the pond.

Some of the plants and animals which are especially typical of ponds and small pools are those which live on or at the surface of the water. Such organisms can only thrive where the water is sheltered from wind disturbance. This applies to the duckweeds *Lemna* and *Wolffia*, and to a variety of insects (Fig. 9.14) including several water-bugs (Hemiptera), beetles (Coleoptera) and pond-skaters (Gerridae). These last have legs with pads at the end which actually support the animal on the surface of the water. Another feature of small ponds is the speed with which the temperature or the amount of oxygen dissolved in the water may change. Apparently minor events like accidental pollution by fertiliser or weed-killer can cause marked changes which might never be detected in a larger body of water. All the fish suitable for stocking small ponds, such as the goldfish (*Carassius auratus*), must be able to tolerate a wide range of temperatures and of oxygen levels.

9.3 WETLANDS

A simple classification of the types of wetland in the world has already been given in the introduction to this chapter. A few general comments are needed before returning to describe these types in more detail. The mires of north temperate regions have been the subject of intensive study over many years and it is possible to give a clear overall impression of their various types and the factors which give rise to them. In contrast, many of the wetland communities of the subtropics and tropics are among the least well researched of all types of vegetation. These wetland communities are usually difficult to penetrate and often differ greatly from season to season, making mapping and

ecological survey tiresome. Disease is still a problem which cannot be ignored: bilharzia (schistosomiasis), for instance, causes difficulties for wetland research in extensive areas of Africa and parts of Asia. Unfortunately, wetland areas frequently seem to be the subject of grandiose schemes by planners even though little, if any, investigation of the biological and ecological impacts of such developments have been made. For instance, the Jonglei Canal scheme to drain large areas of the Sudd region of southern Sudan, characterised by floating masses of living plant material, was at an advanced stage of planning before ecologists were sent to survey the likely impact of the canal.

Wetlands with open water

The dominant life-forms of those wetlands which are submerged by freshwater for all or part of the year may be forest or reed-like vegetation with species of grass, sedge or bulrush. The best-developed wetland forests are those of the Amazon basin, although these mostly grow on areas flooded for only part of the year. One of the most specialised of these types of forest is the igapó forest which grows alongside the tributaries on the north side of the basin. These are the **blackwater** tributaries, bringing in water which is dark brown due to its content of humic acids, has a low pH, and is very poor in nutrients (Fig. 9.15). The forest is flooded when the river is high, but much of the area is dry for the rest of the year. The fauna too is aquatic for part of the year, with fish migrating from the main river to the forest, and then back again when the water recedes; terrestrial animals expand their ranges into the forest when this dries, and retreat with the next floods. The levels of the mineral nutrients in the waters and surrounding soils are so low that many types of plant are either present only in very low numbers or are absent altogether. Phytoplankton crops are very sparse even in the open water of the main river, and there are no floating meadows of water-hyacinth or similar species, which are widespread elsewhere in the Amazon Basin. The leaves of the trees which form the igapó forest are attacked by very few animals and, when they fall into the water, break down only very slowly under bacterial and fungal attack. It is not surprising therefore that animal populations are also low in

Fig. 9.16. A stilted house in riverine forest is surrounded by the flood waters of the River Amazon.

these blackwater rivers and the adjacent igapó forest. Some of the animals there have adapted to specialised diets, such as fish like the tambaqui (*Colosoma bidens*) which depends heavily on flowers and fruit fallen from the forest trees into the water. Despite being tall forest, the ecology of this community results from the very low levels of plant nutrients in the environment just as does a typical oligotrophic lake in mountainous areas like the high Alps.

Quite different communities occur in the floodlands of the middle and lower Amazon (Fig. 9.16). Here both the water itself and the sediments which it deposits are much richer in nutrients and both the flora and fauna are very varied consisting of many species. These floodlands, or **várzea**, contain a complex mosaic of environments, the composition of which is most apparent when the water is low. There are numerous permanent channels, lakes and islands covered with forest in the more elevated parts. The islands are formed from sediment brought down by the river, so their highest points just about correspond to high-water level. Particularly in the more upstream parts of the Amazon (the Solimoes river), where the distinction between várzea vegetation and the normal forest becomes less distinct, some of the trees which are submerged for part of the year do just the opposite of what most species of tree do: they lose all their leaves at the time of high water and only start to grow them again as the waters recede. This unusual behaviour happens because the waterlogged silt in which the tree grows lacks oxygen and the whole meta-

bolism of the tree slows down greatly at this season.

Floating grasses, sedges and other plants form a fringe round the forest on each of the islands; when the river is at its highest, they form extensive meadows sometimes covering open water of 4 centimetres or more in depth. The roots of these plants hang freely in the water from every node and contain perhaps the richest and most diverse fauna of all the communities in the Amazon and its wetlands. As the water recedes, the roots tend to clog up with silt and eventually much of the meadow comes to rest on wet mud rather than open water.

Large areas of south-eastern USA were at one time wetland and, although their extent is now much reduced due to drainage, good examples of these forests still exist. The best known is in the Everglades (Fig. 9.17), where there are pockets of freshwater mangrove and other types of wetland forest as well as extensive meadows dominated by sedge (*Cladium*). Perhaps the best preserved, however, is further north, just over the Georgia border. This is the Okefenokee swamp (Fig. 9.18), which consists of an intricate mixture of swamp-cypress forest, communities developing over peat, meadows of aquatic herbs and perennials, channels and small lakes. Although it does not contain as many species of plant and animal as does the várzea of the Amazon, the swamp is one of the most species-rich of all wetlands outside the tropics. There are many turtles, including for example the snapping turtle, which is carnivorous, and the box turtle which is predominantly herbivorous. Snakes are also abundant, while alligators, which were hunted

*Fig. 9.17. (above) Views of the Everglades, Florida: (a) swamp cypress (*Taxodium*); (b) water-lily (*Nymphaea*); (c) great white heron (*Egretta alba*); (d) alligator (*Alligator*).*

intensely for their skins at the turn of the century, have now been allowed to increase again and are quite frequently encountered.

Brief mention will be made of two other wetlands which lie at approximately the same latitude as the Okefenokee swamp (31°N), but which have entirely different types of vegetation. These are the marshes of southern Iraq (30–32°N) and the deep-water ricefields of South-east Asia (mostly about 20–24°N).

The Iraqi marshes depend almost entirely on the waters of the Euphrates and the Tigris, since the surrounding region is semi-desert. At times of peak flood, which occurs in spring when melted snow from the mountains reaches the area, about 35 000 square kilometres are covered by water, but only about one-quarter of this area is permanently flooded. Apart from small areas of open water, the permanently flooded area is

*Fig. 9.18. (right) Pitcher plants (*Sarracenia*) in the Okefenokee Swamp. Such insectivorous plants are particularly conspicuous in the swamps of the south-eastern USA.*

269

stable climate

climatic variation

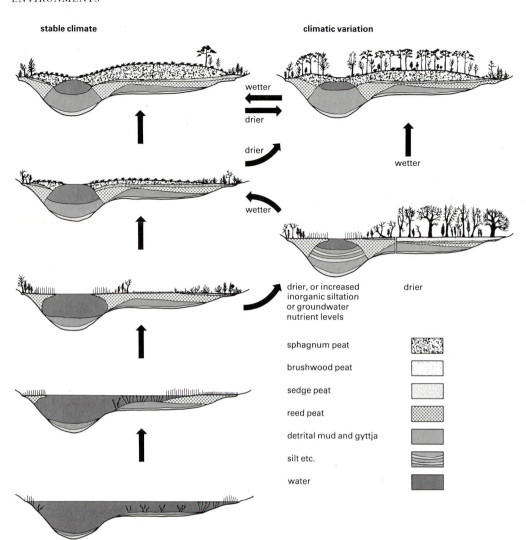

wetter

drier

drier

wetter

wetter

drier, or increased
inorganic siltation
or groundwater
nutrient levels

drier

sphagnum peat

brushwood peat

sedge peat

reed peat

detrital mud and gyttja

silt etc.

water

*Fig. 9.19. Development of
fens and bogs. A sequence
from open water to domed
bog in a small lake basin is
shown in the central column.
To either side are climate-
dependent variations.*

covered almost entirely by stands of either of only two species. These are the common reed (*Phragmites australis*) and the bulrush (*Typha angustata*). Although the marsh flora also includes many small aquatic herbs, most of these are confined to channels or lakes. In contrast to the Okefenokee swamp, the waters are highly calcareous (hard) and snails and snail shells are conspicuous everywhere. Bilharzia, which depends on a snail to spread the disease, is said to be widespread, although definite data are lacking. Fish are abundant in the numerous channels through which the water eventually finds its way back to the main rivers; their species composition has however almost certainly changed markedly within the last 20 years due to the deliberate (and probably unfortunate) introduction of catfish. Wild pigs can sometimes have a destructive effect on the marsh vegetation, but humans are by far the most important overall destructive factor. Reeds are cut extensively as fodder for buffalo and for a local paper industry. Although the human population of the marshes is relatively low, the area lies close to one of the oldest areas of civilization, and it is difficult to speculate as to the original state of these wetlands.

In the deep-water rice fields of Bangladesh, human activity has destroyed the natural vegetation altogether. Large areas of southern Bangladesh are submerged by the flood waters of the Ganges and the Brahmaputra from July to October. Most of this flooded land is planted with rice (*Oryza sativa*), though some

open water remains and jute (*Corchonil*) is also important. In contrast to most rice elsewhere, which is grown in paddy fields, the rice here is a remarkable plant able to grow with the rising water level. Many strains exist, some of which can keep up with a peak water height of 4 metres. In spite of the fact that the land is dry for the rest of the year and that only a single species of plant is grown over much of the area, there is a diverse aquatic flora and fauna. It is not always clear just how each species persists through the dry season, though dormancy in pockets of undisturbed mud, survival in village ponds, and re-inoculation from the main river channels are all possibilities.

Mires

A **mire** is an area of land that is more or less permanently waterlogged but contains no open water. This applies, for instance, to much of the Okefenokee swamp. Nevertheless mires in the northern hemisphere reach their greatest extent at much higher latitudes, increasingly forming the natural vegetation of any region the nearer one approaches the Arctic Circle. Vernacular English is rich in words for this type of wetland, including fen, bog, marsh, swamp, carr, moor and moss, but the same word may represent quite different types of vegetation in different regions. Ecologists use the word **fen** for a mire that develops under the influence of groundwater, and

Fig. 9.20. Tufts of the cottongrass Eriophorum angustifolium.

bog for a mire that receives water only from direct rainfall. Fens and bogs are also known as minerotrophic and ombrotrophic mires, respectively, since the mineral nutrients needed for plant growth are also brought in with their particular water supply in each case. Waterlogging reduces the amount of oxygen available for the micro-organisms which normally break down plant and animal remains. As a result, many mires accumulate peat, the partially decomposed remains of the plants which once grew on the surface of the mire.

Fens can develop in two different types of environment: as a zone around the edge of open water, or on slopes under the influence of slowly flowing water. Fen vegetation developing round a pool or lake provides a clear example of the hydrosere, the process of ecological succession by which areas of open water develop into mires as plant remains accumulate. There is first a phase of deep-water swamp around the open water, usually with tall grasses such as the common reed, or with species of bulrush. If the angle of the slope at the edge of the pool is slight, the peat deposited by this community gradually fills the water until the surface of the peat approaches that of the water. Other species then invade the community, giving rise to typical fen vegetation. Just which the species are depends on how rich the fen is in nutrients. The tussock sedge (*Carex elata*) is common in nutrient-rich fens over much of Europe, whereas cottongrass (*Eriophorum*) is common in nutrient-poor fens. If the angle of the slope at the edge of the pool is steep, however, the pioneer community which develops into the pool may be rather different: although in direct lateral contact with the main body of the fen, the vegetation spreads further and further over the surface of the water, forming a floating raft of vegetation or schwingmoor. One of the most widespread types is found over deep hollows containing nutrient-poor water. Under these conditions the raft consists largely of the moss *Sphagnum* bound together with rhizomes of cottongrass or similar species. As peat accumulates, the surface of the schwingmoor becomes drier and trees can invade; if they grow to too large a size before the peat has become thick, then they may sink through the peat and drown.

Fens formed under the influence of flowing water such as springs also differ in their flora according to whether the water is nutrient-rich or nutrient-poor. Calcareous fens are usually distinguished by having an especially varied flora and fauna.

Sedges are the dominant plants, as they are in most other types of fen, but there are many smaller herbs, often including orchids such as the marsh helleborine (*Epipactis palustris*). At the other extreme are fens formed under the influence of soft water very poor in nutrients. Here many of the species are the same as those of bogs.

Although the lush vegetation of most fens makes them appear natural, human activity has often played a major role in determining their composition. Many areas have been subject to a regular programme of cutting reeds for thatch, and this still occurs in parts of England, Ireland and Poland. This prevents colonisation by shrubs and trees. Grazing by the larger herbivores, such as elks (*Alces alces*) in central and eastern Europe, may also keep tall fen in a relatively open condition. A more drastic regime of mowing or grazing converts the fen to fen-meadow.

Bogs develop in several different ways, although they all depend entirely on rain for water and nutrients (Fig. 9.19). The two main types of bog in north-western Europe, raised bogs and blanket bogs, will serve as examples. Species of bog moss (*Sphagnum*) constitute the bulk of the vegetation in both cases. These mosses thrive in nutrient-poor conditions where the pH of the water is low; in fact they actually make their surroundings more acid as they grow. Raised bogs sometimes develop over fens as the peat continues to accumulate, rising above the level at which it is influenced by nutrients from the groundwater. Such bogs are restricted to cool, wet climates where the surface remains permanently waterlogged as the raised dome of peat starts to form. The *Sphagnum* plays a key role in keeping the surface moist, because both the living plants and their dead remains act as an enormous sponge, keeping the dome charged with water.

Blanket bogs occur mainly in upland regions where the balance between rainfall and evaporation is such that sloping ground is in a permanently wet condition. Under the high rainfall of Ireland they can even occur on slopes of 25° or over limestone, which is porous and alkaline. Large areas of blanket bog elsewhere have become degraded because of grazing, burning and probably also because they are sensitive to industrial fumes. The resulting vegetation often consists largely of cottongrass (*Eriophorum*; Fig. 9.20), or, if burnt regularly, heather (ling, *Calluna vulgaris*).

Further reading

Etherington, J.R. *Wetland ecology*. SIB, no. 154. London: Edward Arnold, 1983.

Kabish, K. *Ponds and pools*. Hemmerling: Croom Helm, 1983.

Mason, C.F. *Biology of freshwater pollution*. London and New York: Longman, 1981.

Moss, B. *Ecology of freshwaters*. Oxford: Blackwell, 1980.

Sterling, T. *The Amazon*. Amsterdam: Time-Life Books, 1973.

Whitton, B.A. *Rivers, lakes & marshes*. London, Sydney, Auckland and Toronto: Hodder and Stoughton, 1979.

10 Living Organisms as Environments

The vast array of living organisms that exist on the earth occupy three general habitats. These are the aquatic and the terrestrial environments (see Chapters 6–9), and the less obvious but equally extensive habitat that is provided by other living organisms.

The body surfaces, natural cavities, and internal tissues and cells of free-living organisms provide a diverse range of environments. During the course of evolution many species have invaded these habitats, and some have even become partially or entirely dependent on the host organism. Simply in terms of numbers, living in association with another organism may be the norm rather than the exception. It has been calculated, for example, that in the human body only about one-tenth of the cells are human; the rest are bacteria or other micro-organisms colonising the skin, the gut and various natural openings.

Lifestyles based on another living organism have many remarkable and intricate adaptations, but the very intricacy of the relationships is often an obstacle to their experimental analysis. In many cases we have only a superficial knowledge of the interactions between the two partners. To a large extent, therefore, classification on the basis of types of interaction still relies on subjective and imprecise criteria, such as the relative benefit or harm of the association, whether it is transitory or permanent, and whether it is essential or optional to one or both partners.

The relationships between living organisms described in this chapter are examples of symbioses. **Symbiosis** simply means 'living together', but implicit in the scientific use of the term is some intimacy of physical and physiological contact between the partners, and a degree of specificity and permanence in the relationship, with in addition one or both partners being dependent on the other for some or all of their metabolic needs. 'Symbiosis' in its original sense made no assumptions regarding the relative benefit or harm of the association to either partner, but it has often been used exclusively to describe associations presumed to be mutually beneficial, such as lichens. Most biologists today favour a return to the original usage, with symbiosis subdivided into **parasitism**, where the relationship is detrimental, or potentially so, to one partner, and **mutualism**, where it is of apparent benefit to both. These categories of symbiosis are not absolute; depending on other factors, such as shifts in environmental conditions, mutualism may become parasitism and *vice versa*.

Relationships in which the host simply provides shelter, support or transport for the other organism, with little or no morphological integration between the partners, and no exchange of metabolites, are common in the animal and plant kingdoms. These associations may however possess several of the characteristics typical of other, more highly integrated relationships. For example, epiphytic orchids growing on the branches of tropical forest trees show a high degree of specificity to one or a few tree species and, similarly, insect–plant interactions involved in pollination are highly specific as well as mutually beneficial. Neither example, however, is normally considered as a form of symbiosis between organisms.

A further consideration in classifying associations is the degree of dependence of one partner on the other. Some parasites, for example, are opportunistic species capable of colonising another organism when available, but retaining the ability to compete with free-living species in the absence of a suitable host; such species are **facultative** parasites. In contrast other, **obligate**, parasites have completely lost their capacity for an independent existence, and are therefore entirely dependent on the host for their survival. Again, these categories are not absolute, and there is a continuous series of associations exhibiting varying degrees of dependency. Finally, the relative position of the colonising organism on the host may be used in describing relationships. Thus, **ectoparasites** attach externally to the host, while **endoparasites** colonise internal organs and tissues.

10.1 PLANTS AS HOSTS

Plants as habitats for symbionts

Autotrophic green plants, by virtue of the process of photosynthesis, are the primary producers in all ecosystems and as plants form the base of every trophic pyramid, they represent the major part of the biomass in the ecosystem (see section 5.3). All heterotrophic organisms, such as animals and the majority of micro-organisms, are ultimately dependent upon green plants for their energy and materials for growth. Most of the available energy trapped by autotrophic plants passes directly to decomposers, or is consumed by herbivores, but organisms capable of colonising living plant tissues gain direct access to organic nutrients at the sites of their production. Heterotrophic plant parasites are thus primary consumers able to short-circuit the usual food-chain.

In morphology green plants range from minute unicellular algae to giant forest trees such as the redwoods, the largest living organisms on earth. There is a correspondingly large variety of habitats available for symbiotic species living in intimate association with plants (Figs. 10–7). Useful comparisons can however be drawn between the parasitism of microscopic fungi on planktonic algae and associations between parasites and terrestrial plants, because all plants have certain features in common as hosts for other organisms. The photosynthetic reactions, for example, and the soluble sugars they produce, appear to be similar in most cases, and organisms living in association with plants are therefore likely to be tapping the same types of primary nutrients. While the central photosynthetic pathways are similar, however, the secondary metabolism of plants is extraordinarily diverse. The chemical environment encountered by an invading organism will therefore vary widely depending upon the species of host plant.

Fig. 10.1. Southern corn leaf blight, a disease of maize. The necrotic lesions are caused by T-toxin, produced by the necrotrophic fungus Helminthosporium maydis.

Several other generalisations are possible, particularly when comparing green plants with animals as hosts. Usually, the pH of plant tissues is rather low, and this acidity may pose problems for organisms such as bacteria which grow better at the neutral or alkaline pH typical of animal tissues. The ratio of carbon to nitrogen is also less favourable, with nitrogenous compounds often being in short supply in plant tissues, and this has been suggested as one of the reasons why fungi are generally more abundant as plant parasites than are bacteria. In addition, plant parasites have to grow at the fluctuating and often low temperatures of the plant body, and must cope with physiological extremes not experienced by the colonists of warm-blooded animal hosts.

Anatomically, the major feature of plants is the rigid cell wall (see section 1.2). This structure, composed largely of cellulose microfibrils but often impregnated with other complex polymers such as suberin (in corky material) or lignin (in woody material), represents a substantial barrier to colonising organisms. As well as presenting a physical obstacle, the preponderance of cell-wall material in the adult plant inevitably means that the major part of the energy and nutrients stored in the plant is in the form of polymeric compounds, many of which are highly resistant to enzymic degradation. This is particularly so in perennial, secondarily thickened, plants such as trees and shrubs. Organisms capable of exploiting woody tissues as nutrient substrates must possess specialised enzymes, such as cellulases and ligninases (see section 5.4). Comparatively few parasites seem to use the food reserves locked up in the heartwood of trees, the notable exceptions being a few genera of higher fungi which break down the internal trunk tissues causing the diseases known as heart rots. Animals such as termites which consume dead wood rely upon large populations of symbiotic micro-organisms within their digestive tracts to enable them to use the cellulose as a food source. The major part of woody tissues is dead, and thus species living on this substrate may have more in common

Table 10.1 *Associations between green plants and heterotrophic organisms*

Autotrophic plant partner	Heterotrophic partner	Type of relationship	Nutritional type of the heterotroph	Examples
ALGA	INVERTEBRATE Protozoa Porifera Coelenterata Turbellaria Mollusca	Mutualistic	Biotrophic	Green hydra, corals
ALGA or BLUE-GREEN ALGA	FUNGUS	Mutualistic	Biotrophic	Lichens
HIGHER PLANT	MICRO-ORGANISM: FUNGUS	Parasitic on the plant	Necrotrophic	Many pathogens (soft rot, damping-off fungi)
			Biotrophic	Rusts, powdery and downy mildews
		Mutualistic	Biotrophic	Ectotrophic and endotrophic mycorrhiza
	BACTERIUM	Parasitic on the plant	Necrotrophic	Many pathogens (*Erwinia*)
			Biotrophic	*Agrobacterium*
		Mutualistic	Biotrophic	Legume and other root nodules
	MYCOPLASMA	Parasitic on the plant	Biotrophic	Aster yellows, citrus stubborn
	VIRUS	Parasitic on the plant	—	Tobacco mosaic and many others
	VIROID	Parasitic on the plant		Potato spindle tuber
	HIGHER PLANT (some partly or wholly autotrophic)	Parasitic on the autotrophic plant partner	Biotrophic	True and dwarf mistletoes, witchweed, dodder
	ANIMALS: PROTOZOA	Parasitic on the plant	—	*Phytomonas* (infection of palm, coconut, coffee)
	NEMATODA	Parasitic on the plant	—	Root-knot and cyst nematodes
	MOLLUSCA	Predation	—	Slugs and snails
	ARTHROPODA Several classes, including mites, millipedes and centipedes, but mainly INSECTA Major orders involved: Hemiptera	Predation	—	Leafhoppers, bugs and aphids
	Lepidoptera			Butterflies and moths
	Coleoptera			Beetles
	Hymenoptera			Bees, wasps and ants
	Diptera			Flies

with saprophytes than with parasites attacking living cells.

When considering terrestrial plants as hosts, a useful distinction can be drawn between the aerial organs exposed to atmospheric conditions, and the subterranean root system. There are important differences between these two zones as habitats for other organisms. Roots develop in a physically and biologically buffered environment, the soil, where fluctuations in temperature, moisture and other factors are less extreme than occur on the exposed aerial surfaces of plants. Leaves, for example, during the course of a single day, may experience frost followed by bright sunshine, or rain followed by a desiccating wind. Organisms that colonise the leaf surface (the **phylloplane**) must be able to tolerate these extremes. While many foliar (leaf) parasites have to survive for a brief period on the surface of the leaf prior to penetrating the tissues, a few species such as certain bacteria, yeasts and filamentous fungi form resident populations on the phylloplane, and the activity

of such micro-organisms is probably intermittent rather than continuous. In contrast, the growing zone of roots (the **rhizosphere**) is colonised by an active community of micro-organisms and nematode worms, subsisting on sloughed-off cells and root exudates rich in soluble nutrients.

Both the aerial and subterranean surfaces of multicellular green plants are covered by a protective epidermis, or in secondarily thickened parts by bark or other impermeable layers which prevent entry by most organisms. Aerial organs such as leaves and stems are usually further protected by a waxy and water-repellent cuticle which efficiently sheds water droplets together with any spores, eggs or microbial cells these might contain. Other protective structures also have roles in defence of the plant. The outer layers are, however, breached at numerous points by natural openings such as stomata and lenticels (see section 2.2), through which potential colonists may enter. Furthermore, the indeterminate growth habit of

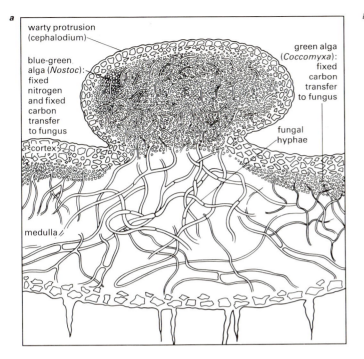

Fig. 10.2. (a) Vertical section through the thallus of the lichen Peltigera aphthosa, *a three-membered symbiosis between a fungus and two algae. (b) Lichens colonising an exposed rock face in the coastal splash zone. The species present illustrate the three main growth forms of lichens, with a tufted (fruticose)* Ramalina *species, the leaf-like (foliose)* Xanthoria parietina, *and, at bottom right, a crustose type,* Lecanora atra, *in which the lichen appears to be an integral part of the rock.*

plants, whereby some organs and tissues senesce, die and are shed, while others are being formed, means that opportunities exist for parasites to gain a foothold. There are numerous examples of microbial parasites using senescing plant parts, such as the remains of flowers, as a food-base from which to attack adjacent living tissues. In root systems, too, breaches in the defences of the plant may appear at sites of lateral root formation, where the cortex and epidermis are ruptured by the emerging root.

The final important consideration regarding plants as habitats for other organisms is the life-history of the host species. Annual plants complete their entire life-cycle from seed to seed within a single growing season, and symbionts living with such hosts must therefore possess survival strategies to ensure that they can carry over between seasons. Perennial plants continue to grow from several to many years, and in the case of trees may remain alive for many centuries; once established on such a host an associating organism may itself remain active for many years.

The range of associations

Symbiotic relationships between green plants and other organisms are too varied and complex to fit neatly into a single classification system. The central unifying theme, however, is the transfer of nutrients between the partners. The autotrophic plant loses a proportion of its photosynthate to the heterotrophic symbiont, but may itself benefit in return in **mutualistic** symbioses, by receiving fixed nitrogen or an enhanced supply of other mineral ions. In **parasitic** symbioses the host plant sacrifices both organic carbon compounds and other nutrients, but gains nothing in return.

The main associations between autotrophic green plants and heterotrophic organisms are listed in Table 10.1. A convenient but rather arbitrary distinction can be drawn between associations where the plant is the microscopic partner, and those where the plant is a macroscopic host. The former category consists of **associations** involving unicellular green or blue-green algae, **where** the photosynthetic cells appear to have been captured by the heterotrophic partner; examples include the endosymbiotic algae of various invertebrate animals, including corals (see section 7.4), and the combination of an alga and a fungus known as a lichen. The category in which the plant is the macroscopic host contains a wide variety of associations between a plant host and a heterotrophic colonist.

Associations involving unicellular algae

Approximately 150 genera of invertebrates harbour unicellular algal symbionts within their own cells and tissues. One of the best-known examples is the green hydra *Chlorohydra viridissima*. In this coelenterate each gastrodermal cell lining the gut cavity contains 12 to 25 cells of the green alga *Chlorella*. When kept in the light under conditions where other food sources, such as brine shrimps, are limiting, green hydra grow more quickly than 'albino' hydra which have been freed of the algal partner. Experiments using radioactive isotopes have shown that carbon fixed by the algae during photosynthesis is subsequently released to the animal cells in the form of the sugar maltose. Algal cells isolated from green hydra differ from similar free-living *Chlorella* in that the algae from the hydra leak large amounts of sugar into the external medium. This suggests that a substantial proportion of the photosynthate produced by the algae is lost to the animal partner. Studies on similar relationships between algae and sea-anemones have shown that extracts from the animal host may in fact stimulate algal photosynthesis, as well as inducing leakage of photosynthetic products. Thus the animal partner may be able to alter the metabolism of the endosymbiotic algae with maximum benefit to itself. It has been suggested that the animal cells remove waste algal products, or simply provide a sheltered habitat for the alga, but experimental verification of this is lacking.

A similar type of nutritional relationship occurs in lichens, although in this case the heterotrophic partner is a fungus (Fig. 10.2). Lichens are a very large group of almost 20000 species,

275

well known for their ability to survive in extreme habitats such as exposed rock faces. In the sub-Arctic tundra zones, lichens represent a significant proportion of the total vegetation, and may in fact be the main producers in these regions. Although the gross morphology of lichens varies, from a prostrate crust-like thallus (a plant body not differentiated into root and shoot) to a highly-branched erect structure superficially resembling a moss, their internal anatomy is usually similar. The major part of the thallus comprises interwoven hyphae of the fungus, with the algal cells either confined to a thin layer just below the surface or scattered more uniformly among the hyphae. Contact between the two partners is intimate, with the fungal hyphae closely enveloping the algal cells and in some species actually penetrating the algal cell wall (Fig. 10.2). This suggests that nutritional exchange can take place between the auto-trophic and heterotrophic partners, and by feeding radioact-ively labelled carbon dioxide to lichens in the light it has been shown that carbon fixed by the algae can be detected in fungal hyphae. In some species the proportion of fixed carbon transferred to the fungus may be as high as 40% within a few hours. The actual compound transferred depends upon the nature of the algal partner. Green algae leak a sugar alcohol which is subsequently taken up by the fungus and converted into typical fungal carbohydrates, and when the photo-synthetic cell is a blue-green alga the carbohydrate transferred is glucose. In both cases the fungus benefits by gaining some of the carbon and energy fixed in algal photosynthesis.

An even more complex nutritional relationship is found in the lichen *Peltigera aphthosa* (Fig. 10.2). The thallus of this species contains a layer of the green alga *Coccomyxa*, while wart-like protuberances on the surface of the thallus contain colonies of the blue-green alga *Nostoc*. In addition to the usual transfer of carbon from the algae to the fungus, the *Nostoc* cells fix atmospheric nitrogen, which may also be exported. The fungus in this partnership receives both organic carbon and reduced nitrogen compounds produced by its two associates.

Traditionally, lichens have been regarded as classic ex-amples of mutualistic symbiosis. Although the advantages for the fungus can be experimentally verified, the benefits of the relationship for the alga are less obvious. The fungus may provide a protective environment for the alga, aiding the retention of water or uptake of essential mineral ions, but some authors have argued that the fungus parasitises its algal symbiont. Irrespective of the nutritional benefit or harm to each member of the symbiosis, lichens are a highly successful partnership; they are capable of colonising habitats too severe for most other organisms, including the separate partners that constitute the lichen, which therefore both benefit by an extension of their ecological range.

Associations between higher plants and bacteria and fungi

Among the associations between bacteria and fungi and higher plants are found the whole spectrum of symbioses, ranging from transitory parasitic infections that damage or kill the host, to long-term stable mutualistic relationships of apparent benefit to both partners. Fungi, in particular, are notorious as the causal agents of many destructive plant diseases, including rusts, powdery mildews, downy mildews and potato blight (Fig. 10.3). The recent epidemic of Dutch elm disease which has severely reduced elm populations both in North America and in Europe is caused by a fungus, *Ceratocystis ulmi*, which is spread by bark beetles and infects the sapwood of the tree. Certain bacteria and fungi which infect plant roots, however, form mutualistic associations which are of great value to agriculture and forestry.

Symbiotic fungi and bacteria can be divided into two nutritional groups, the **necrotrophs** and **biotrophs**. The former derive their energy and nutrients from dead host tissues, while the latter are dependent on living cells for their energy. Both of these groups should be distinguished from **saprotrophs** which grow on dead organic remains such as plant litter rather than on a living host. All mutualistic relationships involve biotrophy. Biotrophy and necrotrophy are not absolute categories, and a parasite may pass through both biotrophic and necrotrophic phases, initially forming a balanced relationship with host cells, but subsequently killing them and surviving on the dead tissues. These nutritional classes are useful, however, as they reflect differences in host–parasite physiology, and in the ecological behaviour of each group.

Typical necrotrophs are opportunist parasites invading wounds or senescent or seedling tissues, and rapidly killing cells through the production of large amounts of hydrolytic en-zymes or toxic metabolites (see Fig. 10.3). For instance, the soft-rot bacterium *Erwinia carotovora* infects plant storage tissues, giving rise to spreading, slimy lesions in which host cells are separated and quickly die. Bacterial and fungal soft-rot pathogens are important causes of the spoilage of fruit and vegetables that can occur after harvest. In contrast, biotrophs form more benign and extended relationships, altering the physiology of the host and, in particular, the pattern of translocation, so that simple soluble nutrients are diverted from their usual sinks in storage tissues or at meristems and instead accumulate at the sites of infection. Usually biotrophs have a restricted host range, occurring on only one or a few closely related species and, although several have been grown success-fully in pure culture away from any host, ecologically they are obligate symbionts. The degree of specialisation onto a par-ticular host, coupled with the type of nutrition, suggest that biotrophy is an advanced form of symbiosis, although it is possible to argue the alternative case, that necrotrophs may have evolved from biotrophs through a progressive ability to use polymerised substrates and to survive away from the hosts's living cells.

Biotrophy is more common among fungi than bacteria, but the few bacterial biotrophs that are known exemplify some of the most highly integrated and specialised relationships between micro-organisms and plants. Two examples are the closely related genera *Agrobacterium* and *Rhizobium*.

Agrobacterium tumefaciens infects a very wide range of plants, giving rise to tumours known as crown galls (see Fig. 10.3). The pathogen gains entry to plant tissues via wounds, where it binds to the surface of exposed cells and secretes cellulose microfibrils that secure it to the host cell wall. It then transfers into the host cell, by an unknown mechanism, part of an extrachromosomal genetic element, called a plasmid. This fragment of bacterial DNA is integrated into the host genome, where it is transcribed and translated, coding for the production by the plant of unusual amino-acids which only the bacterium can use as a food source. In addition, host cells containing the plasmid are transformed, so that they divide continuously, forming a tumour or gall, even in the subsequent absence of the bacterium. *Agrobacterium* is currently the focus of intense study by biologists, mainly because it is a naturally occurring 'genetic engineer', but also because crown-gall tumours bear similarities to certain forms of animal cancer.

The root-nodule bacterium *Rhizobium* also induces morphological changes in its hosts, which are members of the family Leguminosae, but in this case the relationship is mutualistic, with the plant providing carbon compounds and the bacterium providing nitrogen fixed from the atmosphere. The bacteria multiply in the vicinity of host roots, causing curling or branching of root hairs. Following attachment to a root hair, the bacteria enter and form an infection thread which grows down into the cortex of the root. Host cells in this region then begin to divide to form a young nodule, and *Rhizobium* cells are released from the infection thread into these host cells, where they become enclosed within a membrane derived from the plant cell plasma membrane. The bacteria then enlarge and differentiate into spherical or branched nitrogen-fixing cells, known as bacteroids. The mature root nodule (Fig. 10.4) is a highly organised structure, with a meristematic region, and vascular tissues supplying water, mineral ions and sugars to a core of cells containing bacteroids.

The nodule is a fully integrated and finely balanced mutualistic system, with the biochemical environment within the nodule promoting efficient nitrogen fixation by the bacteroids. For example, the enzyme responsible for fixation of nitrogen, nitrogenase, is rapidly inactivated by oxygen; oxygen, essential to cellular metabolism in aerobic tissues, is thus inhibitory to biological nitrogen fixation. Root nodules contain the pigment leghaemoglobin, which binds oxygen in a fashion similar to animal myoglobin, and this provides protection for the nitrogenase enzyme system; abundant mitochondria in the plant cells respire and remove free oxygen, and the leghaemoglobin facilitates the diffusion of oxygen while buffering its actual concentration near the bacteroids at a low level. The leghaemoglobin molecule may in fact be a joint product of the two biological partners, with the bacteria producing the haem portion that binds the oxygen and the plant producing the colourless apoprotein to which the haem group is attached. Thus in the legume root-nodule symbiosis there is intimate biochemical as well as morphological integration.

A number of other nitrogen-fixing bacterial or blue-green algal associations with plants have been identified, including nodulated root systems in shrubs and trees: alder (*Alnus*), for example, has as a microbial symbiont, an actinomycete from the genus *Frankia*. Certain other bacteria capable of fixing nitrogen form loose associations with roots, either in the rhizosphere or inside root tissues. For example, species of *Azospirillum* colonise cereal roots, especially in tropical or subtropical soils. Invasion by this bacterium does not induce any morphological changes in host roots, and there is debate as to whether the nitrogen that is fixed significantly benefits the plant. Viewed overall, however, associations between green plants and nitrogen-fixing prokaryotes contribute a substantial proportion of the reduced nitrogen that enters terrestrial ecosystems.

The filamentous growth habit of fungi (see section 2.3) is uniquely suited to the penetration and colonisation of plant tissues. Biotrophic fungi induce translocation of substances into infected regions, with corresponding short-falls in the amounts of photosynthate available for plant development, and it might seem unlikely that any of these fungi should actually benefit the host. Of particular interest therefore are the associations between certain fungi and plant roots, known as **mycorrhiza**, which were first described by the German botanist Frank in 1885, who noted that the young feeding roots of forest trees were often infected by fungi which had no apparent pathogenic effects on the host. Mycorrhiza are divided into two major groups, **ectomycorrhiza**, in which the fungi form an external sheath entirely enclosing the root, and **endomycorrhiza**, where the fungal hyphae penetrate within root tissues and form structures inside cortical cells (Fig. 10.5). Ectomycorrhiza occur in forest trees common in temperate and subtropical regions, including pines, beeches, oaks and eucalyptus, while endomycorrhiza are found in shrubs of the heather family and in orchids. A specialized type of endomycorrhiza, known as a vesicular-arbuscular mycorrhiza, is common and widespread among both wild and cultivated herbaceous plants. The frequency and range of occurrence of the association has prompted the comment that for most plants the mycorrhiza are more important than the roots.

Comparisons of the growth rates of uninfected plants and plants inoculated with mycorrhizal fungi have shown that the infected plants are more vigorous, especially when the soil is deficient in essential mineral nutrients such as phosphorus. Attempts to introduce exotic tree species for forestry have in some cases failed due to the absence of the necessary fungal

a

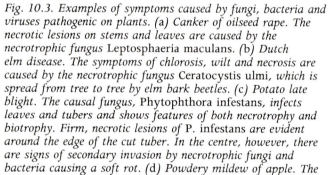

b

Fig. 10.3. Examples of symptoms caused by fungi, bacteria and viruses pathogenic on plants. (a) Canker of oilseed rape. The necrotic lesions on stems and leaves are caused by the necrotrophic fungus Leptosphaeria maculans. *(b) Dutch elm disease. The symptoms of chlorosis, wilt and necrosis are caused by the necrotrophic fungus* Ceratocystis ulmi, *which is spread from tree to tree by elm bark beetles. (c) Potato late blight. The causal fungus,* Phytophthora infestans, *infects leaves and tubers and shows features of both necrotrophy and biotrophy. Firm, necrotic lesions of* P. infestans *are evident around the edge of the cut tuber. In the centre, however, there are signs of secondary invasion by necrotrophic fungi and bacteria causing a soft rot. (d) Powdery mildew of apple. The*

superficial white mycelium and spores of the biotrophic fungus Podosphaera leucotricha *are visible on the surfaces of the infected leaves. (e) Crown gall on sunflower. The cause of crown gall is the bacterium* Agrobacterium tumefaciens, *a pathogen capable of infecting a wide range of dicotyledonous plants. A unique feature of crown gall is the irreversible transformation of the tissues of the host to a tumerous state. This transformation is effected by a DNA plasmid which passes from the cells of the bacterium to the cells of the plant. (f) The mosaic of chlorotic patches on the infected leaves of* Abutilon *is caused by a virus spread from plant to plant by a species of whitefly.*

partner in soil. These findings, coupled with the very limited ability of mycorrhizal fungi to use the polymeric nutrient substrates exploited by free-living species, suggests that mycorrhiza are truly mutualistic relationships.

Most of the information concerning the physiology of mycorrhizal associations has been gained using ectomycorrhiza, where the fungal partner can be dissected away from host tissues. In this way, in isotopic feeding experiments where radioactive carbon is supplied to the host plant and radioactive mineral ions, such as phosphate, are supplied to the fungus, the final proportions of each isotope in the two partners can be calculated. Quite large amounts of the carbon fixed by the plant have been shown to be transferred to the fungus, while the uptake of phosphate ions into the plant root from the soil is enhanced by the presence of the fungus. Several factors may account for the more efficient scavenging for mineral ions by infected roots. First, mycorrhizal roots are more highly branched than equivalent uninfected roots, and thus have a greater surface area available for uptake, especially if the external mycelium in the soil is able to translocate ions to the sheathing hyphae. Secondly, mycorrhizal roots survive longer than uninfected roots, and therefore remain functional for a longer period. Finally, the uptake of mineral ions per unit area of root surface may be stimulated.

Vesicular-arbuscular mycorrhiza are more difficult to

analyse, in part due to the morphology of the association, but also because the fungi concerned, species of *Glomus* and *Endogone*, have not yet been cultured apart from the host. Nevertheless there is convincing evidence that the mineral nutrition of the host is again improved by infection. In legume roots, vesicular-arbuscular mycorrhiza often occur in conjunction with bacterial nodules, so that a complex triangular exchange of nutrients may take place.

Not all mycorrhizal relationships have the nutritional basis described above. Many orchid seeds contain insufficient food reserves to complete the process of germination and establishment of the seedling; these species depend upon infection by a fungus to obtain exogenous nutrients for growth. In this instance, the usual nutrient flow seems to be reversed: fungal carbohydrates, obtained saprotrophically from the soil, are leaked to the plant. Orchids exhibit varying degrees of dependence upon their mycorrhizal fungi, and some species of orchid entirely lack chlorophyll and therefore rely on an external supply of carbon throughout the life of the plant. An even more intriguing relationship occurs in the chlorophyll-lacking dicotyledon *Monotropa hypopitys*, commonly known as yellow bird's-nest. This species was originally believed to be parasitic on the roots of certain trees, especially pine and beech, but more recent work has shown that the plant and its tree host both share a common mycorrhizal fungus. The fungus may

c

d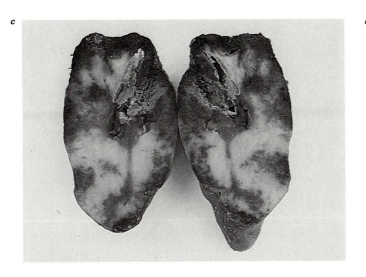

e

f

Fig. 10.4. (below and right) (a) Typical nodules formed by the nitrogen-fixing bacterium Rhizobium *on the roots of a legume, broad bean. (b) Lucerne (*Medicago sativa*) plants inoculated (left) or uninoculated (right) with* Rhizobium. *The uninoculated plants are chlorotic and deficient in nitrogen and have made poor growth compared with the treated plants.*

b

a

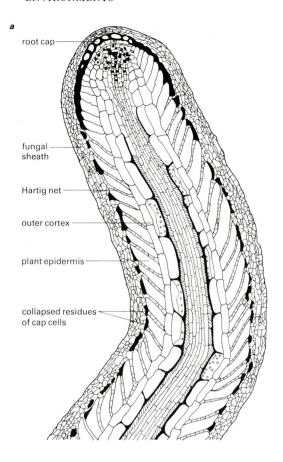

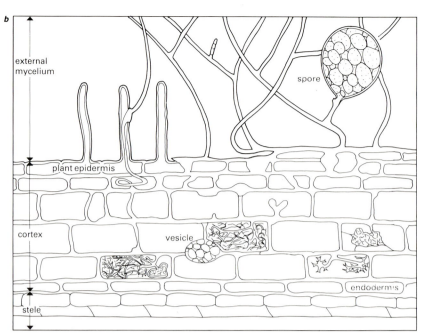

Fig. 10.5. *Longitudinal sections through (a) an ectomycorrhizal root, showing a fungal sheath entirely enclosing the plant tissues, and (b) a vesicular–arbuscular mycorrhizal root, with the fungus forming highly branched arbuscules within plant cells.*

thus serve an intermediary role, obtaining soluble sugars from the tree roots and passing them on to *Monotropa*.

The various associations between fungi and plant roots therefore illustrate quite different patterns of exploitation. Mycorrhizal fungi may, in fact, have evolved from root parasites by gradual selection of less necrotrophic strains, so that the relationship became more prolonged and ultimately mutualistic, with the fungus losing any ability to compete with free-living saprotrophic species for polymeric substrates in the soil.

Associations between higher plants and viruses and viroids

Viruses are small particles composed of protein and nucleic acid, sometimes wrapped in a membrane (see pages 18–20), and are incapable of leading an independent existence; once inside a living cell, however, they subvert the host's metabolism so that it produces many copies of the virus. The special nature of viral parasitism means that these non-cellular agents are not strictly comparable with cellular parasites such as bacteria or fungi. The inability of viruses to exhibit any kind of biological activity outside a living cell has important consequences: in particular, the total dependence of most viruses on vectors, such as aphids and nematode worms with sucking mouthparts, to transmit them between hosts introduces another dimension into plant–virus relationships. There are many destructive viral diseases of plants, including tobacco mosaic, cocoa swollen shoot and potato leaf-roll.

Until recently, viruses were regarded as the smallest infectious agents, but another group, the viroids, has recently been discovered. Viroids consist simply of a small, naked

strand of RNA, approximately one-tenth of the size of the smallest known virus genome, and not protected by any bound protein. The RNA contains between 250 and 350 nucleotides (see section 1.1), but in spite of the extraordinarily limited genetic information present, insufficient to code for even a small protein, viroids are able to replicate in host cells and to cause characteristic symptoms of disease such as stunting and abnormal pigmentation. The entire nucleotide sequence of the viroid responsible for potato spindle tuber disease has recently been worked out, but the molecular basis of its replication and pathogenesis remain obscure.

Higher plant parasites of plants

Between 2000 and 3000 species of higher plants have evolved a parasitic mode of nutrition based on other green plants. Although they belong to a number of widely separated plant families, all the proven parasitic plants are angiosperms producing flowers and seeds. Their degree of dependence on the host plant varies considerably. Some, such as the European and American mistletoes, *Viscum album* (Fig. 10.6) and *Phoradendron flavescens*, have well-developed leaves containing chlorophyll, and are self-sufficient for organic carbon compounds. Others have leaves reduced to minute scales, little or no chlorophyll, and may depend on the host for energy, nutrients and water. However, some angiosperm parasites which were once believed to be entirely heterotrophic, such as certain species of dodder (*Cuscuta*), are now known to have at least a rudimentary photosynthetic capacity. Nevertheless, these parasites must still obtain a proportion of their carbohydrate from the host plant.

Parasitic angiosperms that depend on the host plant for some or all of their carbohydrate have effects on the pattern of host translocation similar to those caused by many biotrophic fungal

*Fig. 10.6. Mistletoes. (a) European mistletoe (*Viscum album*) growing on a poplar tree. (b) Pine branch infected with a dwarf mistletoe,* Arceuthobium.

infections. For instance, the dwarf mistletoe (*Arceuthobium campylopodium*) on species of fir (*Abies*) acts as a powerful sink preventing sucrose produced by photosynthesis in the leaves from being translocated to host tissues below the site of infection. In contrast, green mistletoes do not appear to affect the pattern of translocation in the host, and it has even been suggested that there might be a movement of photosynthate to the host, although experimental verification is lacking.

Parasitic higher plants are often regarded as curiosities, but a number cause economically important infestations of crops and plantation trees. The witchweeds (*Striga*) infect crops such as maize, sugarcane and rice, mainly in Africa and Asia, while the dwarf mistletoes (*Arceuthobium*) cause serious damage to conifers along the Pacific coast of North America.

Associations between plants and nematodes

Nematode worms probably outnumber all other multicellular animals on this planet. The majority are free-living, but some species are parasitic on animals or plants. Nematodes on plants are usually divided into ectoparasitic species which feed on the surface and external tissues of roots, and endoparasites which penetrate plant tissues and feed internally. Another distinction is made between migratory species which move freely within and between hosts, and sedentary species which remain attached to the original site of infection.

The most specialised plant–nematode relationships are found with endoparasitic sedentary species, such as the cyst nematodes. These penetrate the cortex of the root and feed on cells adjacent to the stele. Here the injection of nematode saliva induces the formation of a large and often multinucleate 'transfer cell' which aids the passage of nutrients to the parasite. The ability of the worm to extract nutrients from the host cells over a long period without killing the food source suggests that there is a close enzymatic match between the two

partners. In fact, cyst nematodes exhibit many of the characteristics of highly evolved plant parasites, such as a biotrophic mode of nutrition, a prolonged relationship between the two partners, and a restricted host range.

Nematodes parasitic on plants often interact with other agents to cause complex disease syndromes. Wounds caused by the feeding of nematodes provide sites for the entry of parasitic fungi, and some nematodes act as vectors of soil-borne viruses.

Associations between plants and arthropods

The co-evolution of plants and arthropods, in particular insects, has proceeded along three distinct paths. First, there are the diverse and remarkable mechanisms involved in the pollination of flowers by insects; secondly, there are the equally remarkable and sometimes bizarre adaptations associated with insectivory, whereby plants trap and digest insects as a supplementary source of nutrients; finally, there are the numerous instances where insects themselves exploit plants as food.

Perhaps surprisingly, only 9 of the 29 orders of insects use plants directly as a major source of food. This probably reflects the adverse environment encountered on the exposed surfaces of plants, coupled with the highly effective mechanisms that plants have evolved to limit attack by predators and pathogens.

The use of plants as food by insects is herbivory rather than parasitism, and usually involves grazing on leaves or other accessible tissues rather than the formation of an intimate and extended relationship with the host. As usual there is a whole spectrum of biological interactions, and at one extreme insect–plant relationships have much in common with the parasitism involving certain fungi and nematodes. Two examples are leaf-miners and the insects which induce plant galls.

The larvae of some insects feed inside plant leaves, where they excavate 'mines' within the epidermis or between the two

281

epidermal layers. These feeding chambers appear on leaves as translucent or discoloured areas, often in characteristic twisting patterns. Within the mine the larva gains a degree of physical protection from environmental extremes, and may feed selectively: for instance, leaf-miners on oak leaves tend to favour the spongy mesophyll cells, which contain lower levels of indigestible tannins than the palisade tissues (see pages 52–5). The miner may spend its entire life, prior to emergence of the adult insect, enclosed within this physically buffered environment, or it may emerge at a late stage in larval development to feed on the leaf surface.

The development of other insect larvae in plant tissues can lead to the formation of highly specialised and often spectacular plant galls (Fig. 10.7). The morphology of such galls is sufficiently characteristic to be diagnostic for the insect responsible. Certain wasp larvae, developing from eggs deposited in leaves, induce active cell division and cell enlargement in mature leaf cells; this reversion to the meristematic state is brought about by plant growth regulators produced by the larva. In particular, evidence now suggests that cytokinins (see pages 59–61) may be the stimulus involved in reprogramming host cells and thereby ensuring an adequate supply of nutrients throughout the period of larval development. The presence of the young larva is a prerequisite for maintenance of the gall, as once the larvae pupate or are removed the galls rapidly senesce. In many respects, the interaction between plants and gall-forming insects bears similarities to the deformities in growth and diversion of nutrients induced during infection by cyst nematodes.

Stages in the host–symbiont interaction

The morphology and lifestyles of the different types of organisms associating with plants are extremely varied. Nevertheless, they all share certain common features in their interaction with the host. For convenience, the main steps in host–symbiont interaction can be identified as location of the host, attachment and penetration, colonisation of host tissues, and reproduction and dispersal. In reality these are not separate stages, but are instead key points in the gradual establishment and subsequent perpetuation of a relationship with the host plant. The stages may overlap; for instance, dispersal between hosts often includes some strategy for locating a new host. Similarly, in ectoparasitic species attachment and penetration are synonymous with colonisation.

The specificity of the host–symbiont interaction may be determined at one or several of these steps, with the unsuccessful symbiont either failing to locate a host, or proving incapable of penetration, growth and/or reproduction within host tissues. The plant itself possesses a series of highly effective defence mechanisms for preventing or limiting invasion, and these must be considered in parallel with the parasite's weapons of attack.

Locating the host

Chance plays a large part in determining whether some parasites successfully establish contact with a new host. The likelihood is frequently increased, however, by a specific recognition mechanism based on a chemical signal produced by the host plant. Dormant cyst-nematode eggs in soil are stimulated by 'hatching factors' exuded from plant roots. Similarly, germination of seeds of the parasitic angiosperm witchweed (*Striga asiatica*) is induced by extremely low concentrations of a potent stimulant released from cotton roots. Motile bacteria and fungal zoospores are attracted to roots and, while most of their movement responses are towards general compounds such as amino-acids, some may be host-specific.

Resistant resting bodies of fungi, known as sclerotia, which may lie dormant in soil for long periods, are also triggered to recommence growth by exudates from host roots. Sulphur-containing flavour compounds released by onion roots are broken down by soil bacteria, and the products specifically activate sclerotia of the onion white-rot fungus *Sclerotium cepivorum*. Experiments have shown that only cultivated onions and closely related wild species produce the specific chemical signals capable of inducing germination of these fungal survival structures. Other volatile sulphur-containing compounds produced by cabbages and allied plants may attract insect pests, such as cabbage root fly. Many of the insects which feed on plants locate their preferred host species by recognising secondary metabolites characteristic of that plant. When these insects are vectors of other agents, such as viruses, the host range of the latter may also be determined by this highly specific feeding behaviour.

All these recognition mechanisms aid the re-establishment of the association at each generation; an alternative strategy is the linked transmission of the two partners from one generation to the next. Continual vegetative propagation of plants ensures the transmission of parasites such as viruses and mycoplasmas (a form of small wall-less bacteria), so that eventually the entire crop may be affected. Many lichens produce vegetative propagules known as soredia, in which an algal cell is enveloped by fungal hyphae, thereby ensuring that both partners are dispersed together. Some viruses are transmitted through both seed and pollen, although the percentage of seed that is infected is usually small. In the case of pollen, both the fertilised seed and the mother plant may become infected via this route.

Attachment and penetration

Once the host has been located, the symbiont must attach to and penetrate host tissues in order to establish nutritional contact. Some of the most intricate and ingenious examples of adaptations to parasitism concern structures designed to aid penetration.

The aerial surfaces of plants can be smooth, waxy and

Fig. 10.7. An apple gall formed on an oak twig in response to the gall wasp Biorhiza pallida.

slippery, so that adhesion poses a problem. The fruits and seeds of parasitic plants often possess special adhesive tissues; the berries of mistletoe, for example, contain viscous sticky material that firmly attaches the mistletoe seeds to tree branches. These tissues are such an effective glue that they have been used, mixed with water, as bird-lime for trapping songbirds.

Attachment on a much smaller scale takes place between molecules in the outer envelope of bacteria and certain proteins located in plant cell walls. Such molecular binding may be highly specific, as in the interaction between different strains of *Rhizobium* and legume roots.

Following attachment, the penetrative phase of the association is initiated. Many fungi, bacteria and viruses parasitic on plants bypass the external structural barriers of the plant by exploiting natural openings (such as nectaries, stomata or lenticels), wounds or the feeding sites of vector organisms. In the latter instance the vector not only disperses the parasite between hosts, but also provides a breach through which the parasite can enter, often into a specific organ or tissue. Thus virus particles are injected into plant phloem elements via the stylets of aphids probing for sap, while spores of the Dutch elm fungus enter xylem tissues through feeding scars inflicted by the bark beetle that is the vector.

Other parasites possess structures that enable them to penetrate the external layers of plants directly. Insects and nematodes have penetrating feeding organs, such as aphid stylets, but the best examples concern the infection structures formed by parasitic fungi and angiosperms. Following germination on the surface of the host, many fungi develop a spherical or swollen attachment structure, known as an appressorium, and subsequently force an entry by producing a thin penetration peg which breaches the cuticle and epidermal cell wall of the host by a combination of physical pressure and enzymatic digestion. Parasitic angiosperms form highly specialised organs known as haustoria which initially serve an adhesive function, but then penetrate host tissues to establish an elaborate internal system which connects with the host vascular bundles. Biotrophic fungi may also form finger-like, club-shaped or highly branched structures which penetrate individual plant cell walls and invaginate the plasma membrane, thereby establishing intimate physiological contact between the partners. These haustoria may provide an increased surface area for the uptake of nutrients.

Colonisation of host tissues

The patterns of colonisation of plant tissues by symbiotic species are extremely diverse, ranging from localised penetration of a few cells around the entry site to widespread 'systemic' infections in which virtually every cell of the host plant is invaded. Many fungi and bacteria cause small, restricted lesions on leaves and stems, while viruses and viroids, due to their minute size, can pass between cells through plasmodesmata, and thereby colonise the whole plant body. The majority of symbionts, however, show some degree of tissue specificity; rather than growing indiscriminately throughout the host they instead favour certain organs and tissues. For instance, some fungi, bacteria and mycoplasmas migrate exclusively within vascular tissues, and cause serious wilt diseases by disrupting translocation or releasing toxins and enzymes into the transpiration stream. Symbionts that induce tumours, galls or other growth deformities in the host represent a special category; these organisms radically alter the morphology of host tissues and thereby create a novel physiological environment for their own growth.

Reproduction and dispersal

Unicellular or non-cellular agents, such as bacteria and viruses, reproduce continuously throughout their colonisation of the host. In contrast, many other parasites undergo an extended period of feeding and development on plant tissues prior to initiation of their reproductive phase. Cyst-nematode larvae, for example, first migrate within roots, leaving a trail of damaged tissue, but then settle down adjacent to phloem tissue where they extract nutrients, enlarge and moult several times before becoming sexually mature. With many fungi, too, quite extensive vegetative growth through host tissues may take place before active sporulation begins; reproduction may be triggered by the senescence and death of host cells, and the fungal spores are often highly resistant survival structures rather than propagules serving simply a dispersive function.

Organisms associating with plants have evolved a variety of solutions to the problem of dispersal between hosts. The first is to produce enormous numbers of propagules that saturate the surrounding environment and enhance the probability of random contact between a propagule and a potential host. Many parasitic fungi produce numerous wind-dispersed spores which blow short distances between plants within a crop, or which may be transported over much longer distances, and even over major physical barriers such as oceans and mountain ranges. The parasitic weed *Orobanche* produces around 100 000 seeds per plant, which are then dispersed by wind and water. Indeed, a common feature of parasitic species is the reduction or absence of all organs or structures except those concerned with nutrient uptake and those concerned with reproduction. Perhaps the most dramatic example of this trend is the bizarre parasitic angiosperm *Rafflesia*, which consists of a single enormous flower, almost a metre in diameter, attached to a thin, fungus-like, haustorial system branching within the host.

An alternative reproductive strategy is to produce comparatively few propagules, whether these are spores, eggs or seed, each of which is, however, capable of sustaining a period of independent growth fuelled by its relatively abundant stored reserves of nutrients. Flowers of dodder (*Cuscuta*) produce at the most only four seeds, but on germination each forms a seedling with an erect shoot system which spirals actively, thereby enhancing the chances of contacting a suitable host.

A further feature of the propagules of many parasites is their extreme longevity. Nematode cysts remain viable in soil for up to 30 years in the absence of a host, while soil-borne fungi often form resting spores which survive for similarly long periods. In fact, fungi are notable for producing a variety of types of spores and propagules designed to perform quite different roles. Lesions of rust fungi on cereals, for instance, generate abundant short-lived uredospores throughout the growing season, for rapid epidemic spread between host plants, but in autumn the same lesions switch to producing thick-walled resistant teleutospores, which ensure survival of the pathogen over the unfavourable winter period.

Finally, an important means of dispersal of parasites, particularly for those with little or no ability to grow away from the host, is to exploit an intermediary vector organism. Viruses are extremely dependent on this mode of transmission; indeed, certain viruses are not only transported from plant to plant by the vector, which is usually a plant-feeding insect, but also are able to reproduce within the vector. This is particularly interesting as the host range of the virus therefore overlaps both the animal and plant kingdoms. The vector insect thus remains continually infectious throughout its life, and, furthermore, in a few cases the eggs of the vector also carry infection, which means that subsequent generations continue to transmit the virus.

While viruses provide the classic examples of intimate parasite–vector relationships, many other groups of plant parasites also show a high degree of dependence on vectors.

Most mistletoes rely on birds to disperse their seeds, and in some instances the relationship may even be mutually obligate, with the bird feeding exclusively on mistletoe berries, and the excreted seeds sticking to the branches of potential tree hosts. The dwarf mistletoes (*Arceuthobium*) (see Fig. 10.6) have, however, developed an explosive form of seed discharge which has freed them from dispersal by birds. As the fruits mature, pressure mounts within the internal tissues until a basal fracture zone ruptures, shooting the bullet-shaped seeds with remarkable velocity for a distance of up to 15 metres. These parasites are thus able to spread slowly but inexorably through conifer plantations under their own motive power.

Today the ultimate vector is undoubtedly the human species. Intercontinental travel allows new and unprecedented opportunities for parasites to be inadvertently transported to distant geographical regions, and there are numerous instances of damaging pests and pathogens being introduced into previously disease-free countries on imported plant stock, produce or other contaminated materials.

Plant defence

Plants are subject to attack and infection by a remarkable variety of symbiotic species, and have evolved a diverse array of mechanisms designed to frustrate the potential colonists. It has been suggested that since plants are sedentary, and cannot therefore take evasive action, they have been forced to deploy a significant fraction of their metabolic budget on various forms of defence. These can be divided into preformed or **passive** defence mechanisms and inducible or **active** systems that only come into operation once the plant is under attack.

Passive plant defence comprises physical and chemical barriers that prevent entry of a pathogen, or render tissues unpalatable or toxic to the invader. The external surfaces of plants, in addition to being covered by an epidermis and a waxy cuticle, often carry spiky hairs known as trichomes, which either prevent feeding by insects or may even puncture and kill insect larvae. Other trichomes are sticky, and glandular, and effectively trap and immobilise insects.

If the physical barriers of the plant are breached, then preformed chemicals may inhibit or kill the intruder, and plant tissues contain a diverse array of toxic or potentially toxic chemicals, such as resins, tannins, glycosides and alkaloids, many of which are highly effective deterrents to insects which feed on plants. The success of the Colorado beetle on potato, for example, seems to be correlated with its high tolerance to potato alkaloids that normally repel potential pests. Other possible chemical defences, while not directly toxic to the parasite, may inhibit some essential step in the establishment of a parasitic relationship. For example, glycoproteins in plant cell walls may inactivate cell-wall-degrading enzymes produced by bacteria and fungi.

Active plant defence mechanisms are comparable to the immune system of vertebrate animals, although the cellular and

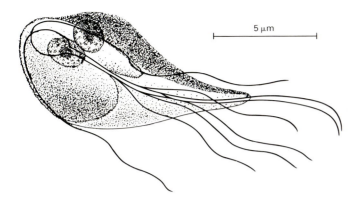

Fig. 10.8. Giardia lamblia (Flagellata), endoparasitic in association with the intestinal epithelium of man.

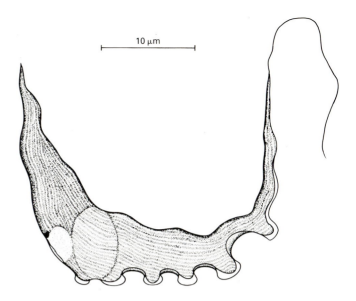

Fig. 10.9. Trypanosoma grayi (Flagellata), endoparasitic in the blood of African crocodiles (Crocodilus niloticus).

molecular bases are fundamentally different. Both, however, are triggered in reaction to invasion, implying that the host has some means of recognising the presence of a foreign organism. The most dramatic example of an inducible plant defence reaction is the hypersensitive response, in which the first cell or group of cells penetrated by a parasite undergoes rapid necrosis and dies. The parasite itself subsequently ceases to grow, and is therefore restricted to one or a few cells around the entry site. Several theories have been put forward to explain the basis of hypersensitive resistance; these include the death of the host cell interfering with nutrient flow to biotrophic parasites, accumulation of antibiotic compounds, and chemical changes in host cell walls.

It has been repeatedly shown that resistance responses to incompatible bacteria and fungi involve the synthesis of antimicrobial compounds, known as phytoalexins. In some cases the concentration of a particular phytoalexin accumulating following attack is sufficient to account for the cessation of growth of the parasite. Substantial strides have been made in recent years towards elucidating the molecular basis of host–parasite specificity, and in the systems that are best characterised it seems that invasion by the incompatible fungus activates resistance genes specifying synthesis of a phytoalexin. The phytoalexin theory is unlikely, however, to provide an explanation for inducible resistance to all parasitic species. Rather, synthesis of antimicrobial compounds represents one of many obstacles, both structural and biochemical, that the potential colonist must somehow clear or circumvent. The parasite must possess a variety of mechanisms, including molecular disguise to avoid recognition, so as to evade, suppress or destroy the defensive response of the host, if it is to colonise the plant successfully.

10.2 PARASITISM IN ANIMAL HOSTS

Introduction

Among the organisms that depend on other living animals for their habitats are parasitic representatives from many distinct groups. The term parasite is and has been defined in many ways, reflecting the interests of parasitologists at the time, but included in all definitions of a parasite is that its development cannot be completed unless some time is spent on or in the body of a living organism, known as the **host**. Hosts, in contrast,

never have any need for parasites, which not infrequently cause disease and even death. Parasites that live on the outer surfaces of hosts are called **ectoparasites**, while those that develop inside the bodies of hosts are known as **endoparasites**; both these types include **microparasites** (viruses, mycoplasmas, bacteria, fungi and protozoans) and **macroparasites** (such as worms and arthropods).

Living in close association with a host organism differs in certain respects from life in other habitats. Species capable of living as parasites inside other organisms are freed from competition with free-living animals, although they must be able to evade or counteract the defence mechanisms of the host. The parasite then has access to a large supply of soluble and thus easily utilised nutrients, whereas free-living heterotrophic organisms have to compete for prey or organic substances often in short supply or in a chemically resistant form. In addition, the host may provide a favourable environment for growth: bacteria, protozoans (Fig. 10.8) and other organisms inhabiting the digestive tract are continually supplied with food that has been partially broken down and softened by the host, and colonisation of a warm-blooded host, for example, ensures a stable temperature and no wide fluctuations in other physiological conditions.

Some parasites, for example the roundworm *Ascaris lumbricoides* (Fig. 10.10), are said to have a **direct** life-cycle because they require only one host to complete their development, and transmission occurs between hosts of the same species (which, in this case, is the human species). Other parasites, for example the blood fluke *Schistosoma mansoni* (Fig. 10.11), are said to have an **indirect** life-cycle because more than one species of host is required; the host in which sexual reproduction of the parasite occurs is usually called the **definitive** or **final host**, while the other species of hosts, in which some development of the parasite or its asexual reproduction occur, are known as **intermediate hosts**. In some cases, the intermediate host serves as a vector (Fig. 10.12). Such definitions break down, however, when the parasite is like the flagellate *Trypanosoma brucei* which is not thought to reproduce sexually at all, but does have more than one host.

Fig. 10.10. The direct life-cycle of Ascaris lumbricoides *(Nematoda) in the human species.*

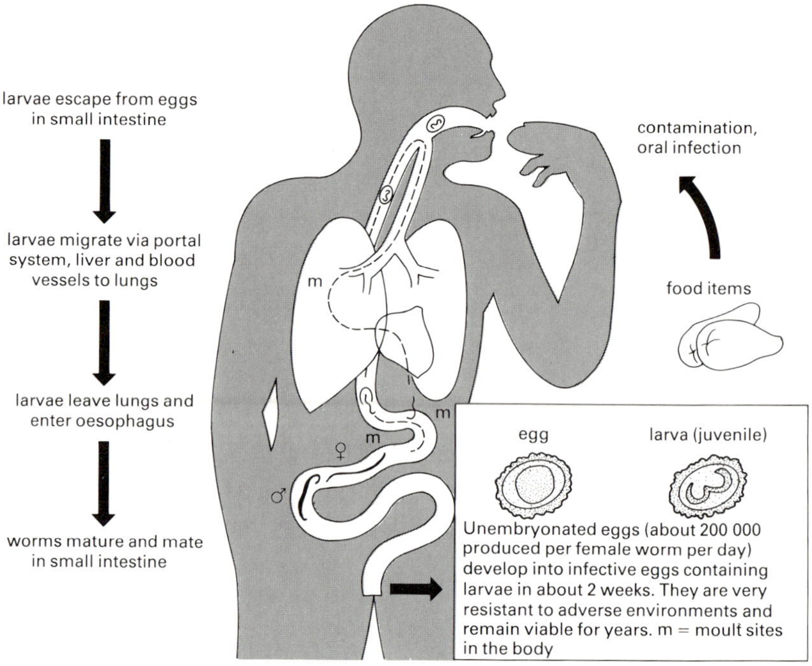

Fig. 10.11. (below) The indirect life-cycle of Schistosoma mansoni *(Digenea) in the human species (definitive host) and the freshwater snail* Biomphalaria glabrata *(intermediate host).*

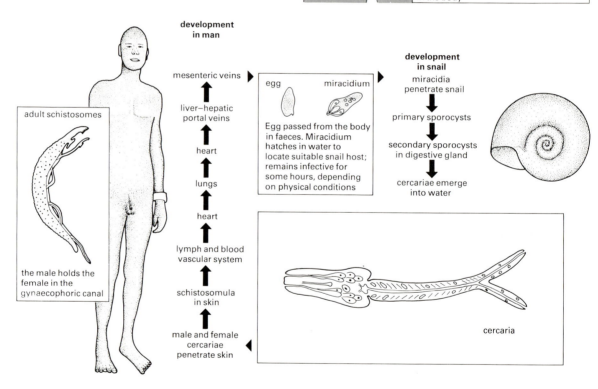

Hosts and parasites must always be considered together if parasitism or host–parasite relationships are to be understood; the subject is important not only because of the intriguing questions that it poses about natural science, but also because the health and quality of life of hundreds of millions of people are adversely affected by parasitic disease (see Table 10.3). Host–parasite relationships may usefully be considered from an ecological point of view; ecology deals with the relationships between an organism (in this case the parasite) and its environment, both at the individual level (the microenvironment within the host) and at the population level (the macroenvironment including the environment of the host or hosts).

Features of host–parasite relationships

A number of general features typify many animal host–parasite relationships.

Hosts are nearly always much larger than are their parasites, and nearly always have much longer life-spans and generation times.

Hosts and parasites possess different genetic material and belong to different species. This excludes the mammalian foetus from being defined as a parasite during its growth in the maternal uterus, and excludes examples, for example in deep-sea angler fish, where males become degenerate and permanently attached to the larger free-living female. The dif-

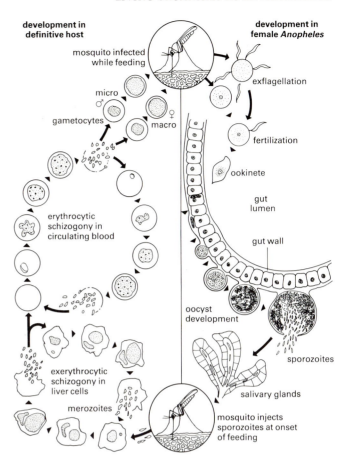

ference between the genomes of parasite and host means that parasites of vertebrate hosts must survive for a time in hosts that have the capacity to detect and react against material that is non-self. Adult *Schistosoma mansoni* are known to be able to continue to live and reproduce in the blood vessels of rhesus monkeys in which the immune system has recognised and responded to the invader.

Since the habitat for a parasite is another living organism, this has the capacity to evolve and change over a number of generations. Populations of parasites must themselves evolve, and adapt to these variations in the host population, and equally the appearance of a new and more aggressive variant of the parasite is likely to be followed by selection for a more resistant host.

Parasites usually occupy precise sites (microhabitats) on or in their hosts, and these may change as the parasite grows and develops during the course of the infection. Larval stages of the nematode worm *Angiostrongylus cantonensis* living in laboratory rats are first found dispersed in the general arterial circulation; after moulting they occupy tissue in the central nervous system, and finally the worms migrate to the pulmonary arteries where they live as adults.

Parasites usually have a much higher reproductive potential than do their hosts. A female *Ascaris lumbricoides* may produce and release as many as 200 000 eggs per day, and 73 million eggs in total during an average life-span of a year. A young girl, who may serve as the host for the *Ascaris*, perhaps carried 350 000 immature human eggs in her ovaries at birth, but it is likely that between puberty and menopause only about 375 of these will mature, and probably fewer than ten will give rise to children even in the absence of methods of birth control. Their high reproductive potential distinguishes parasites from predators, which generally have a lower reproductive potential than do their prey.

Parasites frequently possess special structures which enable them to maintain their positions on or inside their hosts (see Fig. 10.13 for examples). Specialisation to the parasitic way of life is usually accompanied by the parasite gradually losing many of the characteristics essential for survival as a free-living species. Many intricate mechanisms have thus arisen to facilitate the spread or transmission of parasites between hosts and their establishment in new hosts.

Different host–parasite relationships last for different periods of time, varying from a few days in the case of influenza virus to several years as has been observed with *Ancylostoma duodenale* (hookworm) in human hosts.

Parasites have the potential to initiate the development of disease and even to kill the host. This property is known as pathogenicity, and the term virulence may be used for a quantitative measure of pathogenicity. Although generally parasites stimulate the defence reactions of the immune response of both invertebrate and vertebrate hosts, the outcome is not always protection for the host. Hypersensitivity and immune damage to the tissues are major contributors to the

Fig. 10.12. The indirect life-cycle of the human malarial parasite Plasmodium vivax, *in which the intermediate host (a female anopheline mosquito) serves as the vector.*

nature and extent of many parasitic diseases.

Different host–parasite relationships show varying degrees of specificity. A relationship has high specificity when a parasite is believed to live only in one species of host, for example the nematode *Enterobius vermicularis* in the human species, and low specificity when several species of host may be infected, for example *Schistosoma japonicum* in cattle, dogs, goats, buffalos, pigs, rats and human beings.

The more a species of parasite is studied, the greater the chances of the discovery of various strains of that parasite. For example, the use of chloroquine for the treatment of malaria caused by *Plasmodium falciparum* may be worthless if the patients are infected with a chloroquine-resistant strain of the parasite. Variations between populations of host may be equally important, and the innate protection of many West Africans against death from malaria caused by *P. falciparum* is due to the high frequency of sickle-cell anaemia in the human population of the region.

Finally, a population of parasites established on or in a host does not under natural conditions live in ecological isolation. Parasites of the alimentary tract form part of a living community that includes the vast numbers of microbial cells that form the normal flora of the gut, and parasites inhabiting a sterile site, like blood flukes in the blood vessels, are not totally isolated from events related to the activities of organisms located elsewhere in the body.

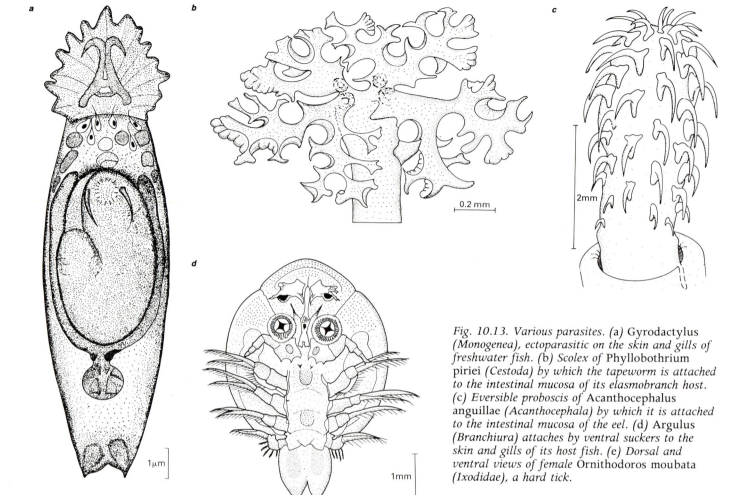

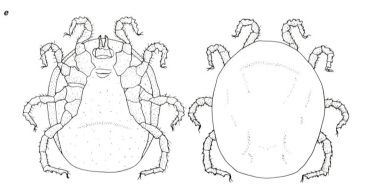

Fig. 10.13. Various parasites. (a) Gyrodactylus (Monogenea), ectoparasitic on the skin and gills of freshwater fish. (b) Scolex of Phyllobothrium piriei (Cestoda) by which the tapeworm is attached to the intestinal mucosa of its elasmobranch host. (c) Eversible proboscis of Acanthocephalus anguillae (Acanthocephala) by which it is attached to the intestinal mucosa of the eel. (d) Argulus (Branchiura) attaches by ventral suckers to the skin and gills of its host fish. (e) Dorsal and ventral views of female Ornithodoros moubata (Ixodidae), a hard tick.

Aspects of host–parasite population biology

The study of populations provides more information about the distribution, abundance and evolution of species than do detailed qualitative descriptions of the activities of organisms within their environments. This approach is developing rapidly in parasitology, and has been used to investigate the transmission or spread of parasites between hosts, the prevalence of parasites within populations of hosts, the incidence rates of parasitic infections, and the intensity of infection and distribution of parasites among hosts.

The **prevalence** of a parasitic infection is a measure of the number of hosts in a population that harbour the infection at a particular point in time. In practice, however, the collection of the data required to determine the prevalence may take longer than would strictly fit the description of a point in time. Infections with macroparasites are usually characterised by a prevalence that remains relatively constant over time (Fig. 10.14); this property is probably related to the longer generation times of macroparasites (compared to microparasites), their longer life-spans within the host, and their tendency to elicit allergic rather than protective responses from the host's immune system. In contrast, the prevalence of microparasitic infections tends to show a fluctuating pattern over time (Fig. 10.14). Outbreaks of influenza, measles, rabies and cholera, which are caused by microparasites, are described as epidemics, a term little used in the case of infections with blood flukes or hookworms. The erratic prevalence of microparasites depends mainly on their short generation times, short life-spans and the development of protective immunity in hosts that survive the disease. The **incidence** rate, which is the number of new cases of an infection developing in a population over a period of time, is particularly useful when investigating microparasites.

Information about the **intensity** of an infection (the number of parasites per host) is useful in understanding how macroparasites are transmitted and the extent of the morbidity they cause in a population. Macroparasites are generally found to be non-randomly distributed between their hosts so that, for a given population of hosts, while many individuals harbour none or a few parasites, a few have very many (Fig. 10.15). There are many practical consequences that arise as a result of this overdispersed frequency distribution. Some individuals are, apparently, more susceptible to infection than others, and individuals with high parasite burdens may serve as foci for infection for others. Heavily infected individuals will presumably suffer greater morbidity than will lightly infected hosts, and identification of the vulnerable hosts will be important in control of the parasite.

Overdispersion poses an intriguing problem for the parasitologist, as its biological significance or selective advantage for the parasite or host (or both) is not known. Overdispersion also presents problems for health workers who, for example, usually depend on the microscopic detection of eggs in a stool sample for the diagnosis of an infection of *Ascaris lumbricoides*. Until recently, it was accepted that a higher egg count per unit mass of sample meant a larger number of *Ascaris* in the small intestine. The environmental resources in the small intestine, however, are sufficient to support an optimal population of worms, and if many male and female *Ascaris* are present, their output of eggs per gram of faeces per day may be less than that for a smaller population with ideal opportunities for feeding and mating. Additionally, reliance on egg counts provides no information about the numbers of immature or male *Ascaris* present in the host.

The combined use of quantitative information about factors affecting transmission, prevalence, incidence rates and in-

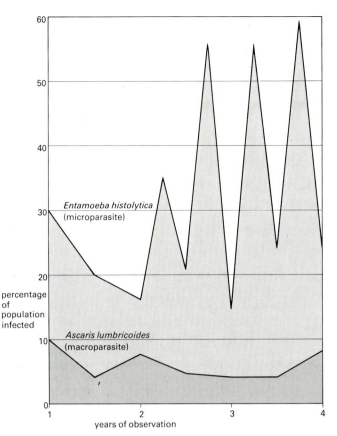

Fig. 10.14. Comparison of longitudinal prevalence of a microparasite and a macroparasite in the human species. The data do not apply to the same populations over the same years.

tensity of infection forms the theoretical basis for the planning of control strategies for parasites. For example, measures for controlling malaria that are based on mosquito population dynamics and are intended to reduce mosquito fecundity, survival and feeding activity, will be likely to reduce the incidence and spread of malaria.

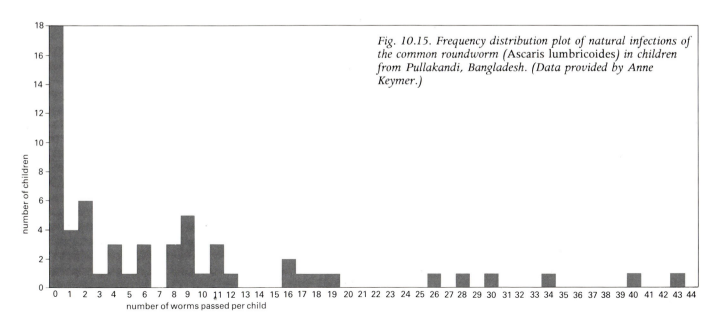

Fig. 10.15. Frequency distribution plot of natural infections of the common roundworm (Ascaris lumbricoides) in children from Pullakandi, Bangladesh. (Data provided by Anne Keymer.)

Table 10.2 *The diversity of parasites of animal hosts. Only examples of the parasitic members of each group have been given.*

I MICROPARASITES

A. *VIRUSES (endoparasitic; obligate intracellular parasites)*
Influenza virus, measles virus, rabies virus.

B. MONERA (bacteria: endoparasitic examples; prokaryotes)

1. Aphrogma bacteria (lack rigid cell walls: resistant to penicillin)
   Mycoplasma host-specific; endoparasitic in association with epithelium of mouth, respiratory and genital tracts of birds and mammals.

2. Fermenting bacteria (obligate anaerobes; cannot synthesize porphyrin)
   Bacteroides, Clostridium.

3. Spirochaeta (elongate, corkscrew-shaped cells).
   Treponema pallidum (syphilis), *Borrelia recurrentis* (relapsing fever).

4. Pseudomonads.
   †*Bdellovibrio* (parasitoids of other bacteria).

5. Aeroendospora (spore-forming; mostly Gram-positive cell walls)
   Bacillus, including *B. anthracis* (anthrax).

6. Micrococci (Gram-positive cell walls: require oxygen for growth).
   Staphylococcus.

7. Omnibacteria (large assemblage of forms requiring reduced organic compounds for growth)
   Neisseria, Rickettsia, Salmonella (typhoid fever), *Shigella, Yersinia pestis* (plague).

8. Actinobacteria (fungus-like in various respects)
   Mycobacterium tuberculosis, M. leprae (leprosy).

C. PROTOZOA (Eukaryotes)

1. Dinoflagellata (nearly all species are marine planktonic forms)
   Members of Blastodiniidae are endoparasitic in guts, eggs and body cavities of copepods, in guts of polychaetes and ectoparasitic on gills and skin of fish. Dinoflagellates are sometimes classified with euglenids as algae.

2. Rhizopoda (amoebae)
   Entamoeba endoparasitic in gut of invertebrates and vertebrates.

3. Zoomastigina (flagellates; many are endoparasitic species in invertebrates and vertebrates)
   Bodo, Giardia (Fig. 10.8), *Histomonas meleagridis, Leishmania* (cutaneous leishmaniasis and kala-azar), *Trypanosoma* (*Schizotrypanum*) *cruzi* (Chagas' disease), *Trichomonas, Trypanosoma brucei* group (sleeping sickness).

4. Ciliophora (ciliates)
   Balantidium endoparasitic in large intestine of mammals. Some species of ciliate are reported to be ectoparasitic on gills of crustaceans and others endoparasitic in guts of sea urchins. Communities of ciliates in the rumen and large intestine of herbivorous mammals contribute to digestion of complex materials from plants.

5. *Apicomplexa (Sporozoa: endoparasites, with many species living inside cells)
   Babesia, Eimeria, Gregarina, Haemoproteus, Isospora, Plasmodium (Fig. 10.12) (malaria), *Toxoplasma gondii.*

6. *Cnidosporidia (produce filaments and resistant spores; endoparasites mainly of insects and fish)
   Glugea, Myxobolus, Nosema.

D. FUNGI (various species have the potential for being biological control agents for insect pests)

1. Zygomycotina (reproduction by asexual conidia and by conjugation)
   Entomophthora coronata endoparasitic in aphids, *Empusa muscae* endoparasitic in houseflies and other dipterans.

2. Deuteromycotina (reproduction mainly by asexual processes)
   Candida albicans, Trichophyton (ring-worm)

II. MACROPARASITES (all eukaryotes)

A. ANIMALIA

1. Coelenterata (mainly marine and free-living; produce nematocysts)
   Hydrichthys boycei (hydroid) ectoparasitic on fish skin, †*Peachia quinquecapitata* (anemone) endoparasitic and then ectoparasitic on medusae of *Phialidium gregarium* (a hydrozoan coelenterate)

2. Ctenophora (comb-jellies: mainly marine and free-living)
   Gastrodes parasiticum: immature stages parasitic in mantle of tunicates.

3. *Mesozoa (minute worm-like animals with no organs except gonads: endoparasites of marine invertebrates)
   Dicyemids, in organs of cephalopods: *Dicyemenna eltanini.*
   Orthonectids: in tissues of flatworms, nemertines, annelids, molluscs and echinoderms.

4. Platyhelminthes (flatworms: large group of free-living, ectoparasitic and endoparasitic species)
   a. Turbellaria (most species are free-living and aquatic)
      Fecampia erythrocephala endoparasitic in crabs
   b. *Trematoda (flukes)
      Entobdella, Gyrodactylus (Fig. 10.13), ectoparasites on gills and skin of fish)
      Fasciola hepatica, Paragonimus westermani, Schistosoma (bilharzia, schistosomiasis) (Fig. 10.11) mainly endoparasites of vertebrates; Fig. 10.13
   c. *Cestoda (tapeworms: endoparasites in small intestine of vertebrates; Fig. 10.14)
      Diphyllobothrium latum, Hymenolepis, Taenia.

5. Nemertea (ribbon worms: mainly free living)
   Carcinonemertes ectoparasitic on gills of crabs, *Uchidana parasitica* endoparasitic in the mantle cavity of the bivalve *Mactra sulcataria.*

6. Rotifera (wheel animalcules: ciliated crown at anterior end; various species usually ectoparasites of freshwater invertebrates)
   Drilophaga bucephalus ectoparasitic on tubificid annelids, *Albertia vermicularis* endoparasitic in the gut of earthworms.

7. *Acanthocephala (possess a diagnostic eversible proboscis (Fig. 10.13): endoparasites in small intestine of vertebrates)
   Acanthocephalus, Moniliformis moniliformis, Neoechinorhynchus.

8. Nematoda (roundworms: moult; cylindrical in cross-section with a body-cavity; free-living, plant-parasitic and animal-parasitic species: endoparasites in animal hosts)
   Ancylostoma, Ascaris (Fig. 10.10), *Capillaria, Onchocerca volvulus* (river blindness)

9. *Nematomorpha (horsehair worms: endoparasitic as juvenile stages in tissues of arthropods; adults are free-living)
   Gordius, Paragordius.

10. Mollusca (large group; body comprises 'head-foot', mantle and visceral hump which often secretes a shell; nearly all species are free-living)
    a. Gastropoda (snails): Parasitica; at least 11 species are known as endoparasites of sea-cucumbers (holothurians)
    b. Bivalvia: larvae of family Unionidae, such as *Anodonta*, develop as ectoparasites in cysts on gills and skin of fish.

11. Sipuncula (unsegmented worms with tentacles around the mouth; generally regarded as free-living marine animals)
    Golfingia procera may be a parasite: it feeds by introducing its introvert into the body cavity of the polychaete *Aphrodite aculeata.*

12. Annelida (segmented worms with coelomic body cavity: most species free-living)
    a. *Myzostoma (ectoparasites and endoparasites of echinoderms)
       Asteriomyzostomum, Protomyzostomum and *Mesomyzostoma* endoparasites of starfish, brittle stars and sea-lilies respectively.
    b. Polychaeta (many species: mostly marine and free-living)
       †11 members of family Arabelidae endoparasitic in body-cavity of other polychaetes and spoon worms (echiuroids). *Ichthyotomus sanguinarius* is an ectoparasite sucking blood from fins of eels.

c. Oligochaeta (many species; mostly terrestrial, freshwater and free-living)
Members of family Branchiobdellidae (possibly related to leeches) ectoparasitic on gills of crayfish.
Schmardaella lutzi endoparasitic in urinogenital system of tree frogs.

d. Hirudinea (leeches: some blood-sucking species ectoparasites of vertebrates)
Hirudo, Theromyzon.

13. *Pentastoma (tongue worms, probably related to arthropods: blood-sucking endoparasites of carnivorous vertebrates, particularly reptiles)
Linguatula serrata, Porocephalus crotali.

14. Crustacea (mainly aquatic arthropods: 2 pairs of antennae)
a. †Isopoda (dorso-ventrally flattened)
Bopyrus ectoparasitic on gills of crustaceans, *Cymothoa* ectoparasitic on gills and skin of fish, *Pinnotherion vermiforme* endoparasitic in crabs.

b. Amphipoda (laterally flattened)
Cyamus boopis ectoparasitic on skin of whales.

c. Copepoda (lack compound eyes and carapace: many ectoparasitic species on marine hosts)
Numerous members of families Caligidae, Ergasilidae, Lernaeidae, Lernaeoceridae and Lernaeopodidae are ectoparasites, particularly on fins, gills and skin of fish. *Mytilicola intestinalis* endoparasitic in edible mussels, *Mytilus edulis*)

d. Branchiura (fish-lice ectoparasitic on skin of fish)
Argulus (Fig. 10.13), *Chonopeltis.*

e. †Cirripedia (barnacles; marine)
Rhizolepas annellidicola and *Anelasma squalicola* ectoparasitic on annelids and sharks respectively. Members of the families Sacculinidae and Peltogastridae endoparasitic in crabs.

15. Insecta (tracheate arthropods, 1 pair antennae, 3 pairs legs)
a. Dermaptera (earwigs: 16 species are considered to be ectoparasites of bats and rodents)
Hemimerus deceptus ectoparasitic on the rodent *Cricetomys gambiense.*

b. *Mallophaga (chewing lice: minute, wingless insects, ectoparasitic mainly on birds).

c. *Anoplura (sucking lice: exclusively blood-sucking ectoparasites of mammals).
Pediculus humanus, Phthirus pubis.

d. Hemiptera (bugs: many free-living species)
All members of family Polyctenidae are ectoparasites on tropical bats.
Members of family Acanthiidae (bed-bugs), e.g. *Cimex*, are ectoparasitic on birds and mammals.

e. Lepidoptera (butterflies and moths)
Bradypodicola hahneli spends its adult life as an ectoparasite in the fur of sloths (Edentata).

f. Diptera (two-winged flies, including black-flies, mosquitoes, sandflies and tse-tse flies)
Oestridae (warble-flies) and Gasterophilidae (bot-flies) endoparasitic as larvae in mammals
Hippoboscidae (louse-flies and keds; ectoparasitic on birds and mammals; suck blood)
Nycteribiidae (wingless: ectoparasitic on bats).
†Tachinidae (parasitoids; many species; endoparasitic as larvae in other insects and terrestrial arthropods)

g. *Siphonaptera (fleas; ectoparasitic as adults on birds and mammals; suck blood)
Ctenocephalides, Xenopsylla.

h. †Hymenoptera (numerous free-living and endoparasitic species, most with characteristic 'wasp waist': ichneumon flies, chalcid wasps and other species are parasitoids of many types of insects.)

i. Coleoptera (beetles: 71 out of an order of about 360000 described species are considered to be ectoparasites of mammals)
Leptinus testaceus ectoparasitic on rodents.

j. †Strepsiptera (minute insects; larvae and adult females endoparasitic throughout life, usually in hymenopteran hosts).

16. Acari (mites and ticks: arachnids with body composed of prosoma and opisthoma)
a. Mites (minute, numerous and often free-living; classified into 6 orders; some species are ectoparasitic)
Cryptostigmata, ectoparasites of birds and mammals: *Demodex folliculorum* on various mammals, *Sarcoptes scabie* causing scabies on human beings.

b. *Ixodoidea (ticks, Fig. 10.13; ectoparasitic, feeding on blood of amphibians, reptiles, birds and mammals)

17. Pisces (fishes: almost all species are free-living)
†Members of the family Trichomycteridae (catfish) are ectoparasitic in the gill chambers of other species of catfish in South America.

18. †Aves (birds: brood parasitism, in which a bird of one species delegates to a bird of another species the tasks of building the nest, incubating the eggs and raising the young)
Anatidae: one species (*Heteronetta atricapilla*) parasitises other ducks, swans, limpkins, gulls, coots, ibises and rails.
Cuculidae (includes cuckoos): *Cuculus canorus* (European cuckoo) parasitises about 125 species of bird (Fig. 10.16).
Indicatoridae (honey-guides): parasitise woodpeckers, barbets and other hole-nesting birds
Icteridae (cowbirds): *Molothrus ater* (brown-headed cowbird) parasitises at least 200 species of bird.
Ploceidae (whydahs): parasitise in particular weaver-finches and weaver-birds.

(schistosomiasis) — examples of diseases of the human species.
* All known members of the taxonomic group are parasitic species
† Includes species infecting hosts of the same phylum.

The diversity of parasites in animal hosts

Parasitic species are known from many of the major taxonomic groups (taxa) of animals, and probably parasitism evolved separately on many different occasions. A survey of this diversity of form of parasites in an equal diversity of animal hosts is presented in Table 10.2, and is illustrated for a minute sample of forms in the figures. The table provides little impression of the relative importance of the different groups of parasites, with viruses, which can be taken as the most highly evolved parasites, being given less space than the molluscs. In general, the greater the detail given in Table 10.2 about a specific parasite within a group, for example the sea-anemone *Peachia quinquecapitata*, the more difficult it is to find a genuine parasitic member of that group. Several phyla or major taxa comprise only parasitic species (marked with an asterisk in Table 10.2), and parasitic species in a given taxon not infrequently infect hosts of the same taxon (marked † in Table 10.2).

Species classed as **parasitoids** (the pseudomonal bacteria *Bdellovibrio*, the two-winged (dipteran) flies of the family Tachinidae, certain hymenopteran insects, and possibly nematomorphs, see Table 10.2) are those that eventually destroy their hosts. These organisms display several of the features of host–parasite relationships, including adaptations for transmission and infection, an extended relationship with the host, and some degree of host-specificity, and their hosts also possess immune mechanisms which may or may not overcome the parasitoid infection. However, the reproductive potentials of parasitoids and their host species are similar, and there is usually only one individual parasitoid per host.

Table 10.3 *Estimations of the prevalence of some protozoan and helminth infections of medical importance*

Parasitic infection	Number of cases
PROTOZOA	(World population is about 4200 million)
African trypanosomiasis (*Trypanosoma brucei* group)[a]	10000 new cases per year; 35 million at risk
American trypanosomiasis (*Trypanosoma cruzi*)[a]	10 million; 35 million at risk
Malaria (*Plasmodium falciparum, P. malariae, P. ovale* and *P. vivax*)[a,b]	160 million affected; 1163 million at risk
HELMINTHS	
Ascariasis (*Ascaris lumbricoides*)	800–1269 million
Hookworm disease (*Ancylostoma duodenale* and *Necator americanus*)	726–932 million
Filariasis (*Wuchereria bancrofti* and related species)[a,b]	250–383 million
Onchocerciasis (*Onchocerca volvulus*)[a,b]	20–40 million
Taeniasis (*Taenia saginata*)	38–77 million
Schistosomiasis (*Schistosoma haematobium, S. japonicum* and *S. mansoni*)[b]	200–271 million

[a] Requires an insect vector for development and transmission
[b] Associated directly or indirectly with water

Lack of information about the biology of various organisms has probably resulted in the exclusion of some species as ectoparasites from Table 10.2 and the inclusion of others. Marshall has recently defined ectoparasitic insects as those species that spend much of their adult lives in close association with the habitat created by the skin (and its outgrowths) of mammals and birds, or with the host's nest or roost, and that derive their food from their host. Thus only two orders, the lice and the fleas, are exclusively ectoparasitic. Other ectoparasitic species are to be found in the bugs and two-winged (dipteran) flies, and even in the beetles, earwigs, butterflies and moths. The only claim for ectoparasitic status for vampire bats is that they suck blood from living hosts; on this basis female mosquitoes could equally well have been included.

A considerable number of birds exist through brood parasitism (Fig. 10.16), and seem to exhibit several of the features of host–parasite relationships.

Transmission and infection

The number and variety of adaptations that ensure that host–parasite relationships continue are as extensive and diverse as the actual kinds of parasites found. Transmission encompasses the events from the departure of an organism from one host until contact is made with the next host in the cycle. Infection is considered to be the means by which the parasite then becomes established and physiologically committed to dependence on the next host. The role of the hosts is usually as important in transmission as that of the parasites, and often the parasitic stage involved is specialised for both transmission and infection, which cannot always be separated into two distinct phases.

The spread of parasites and their establishment in a proportion of susceptible hosts cannot occur unless there is some degree of spatial and temporal overlap in the distribution of the two populations. The processes involved are also affected by: the number of infective stages produced; the survival properties of these infective stages in the tissues of the present host, in the vector, and in the environment of the next host; the climatic conditions prevailing in the host's environment, which may have either direct effects both on the infective stages and on susceptible hosts, or indirect effects on populations of vectors; the role of predators and pathogens in destroying infective agents or in disturbing the populations of hosts and vectors; the behaviour of adult parasites, infective

stages and hosts (the behaviour of an infected intermediate host may be altered so as to increase its chances of contact with a predatory final host); and the nutrition of the infective stages, particularly as regards their endogenous reserves, and the nutrition of the hosts. Physicochemical conditions in the host are also important; for example, about 100 million cells of *Vibrio cholerae*, the bacterium which causes cholera, must be swallowed to establish an infection in the normal small intestine, but only about half this number when alkaline conditions exist; the physiological conditions, immunological state and previous immunological experience of the host are also relevant.

When the human species is the host, human behaviour and attitudes may have a variety of effects either on exposing populations or on protecting them from infection. Religious and tribal customs, cooking practices, relationships with animals, community structure and health awareness all play their part in human host–parasite relationships.

Host resistance and immunity

Parasitism involving animal hosts may be considered as a delicate physiological equilibrium between the activity of the parasite and the resistance of the host. Resistance can be classified according to whether it is non-specific or specific. An animal is born with certain capabilities to respond to infection, and these innate responses are generally non-specific, whereas specific responses develop as the animal ages and acquires immunological experience of particular foreign substances, intruders, or material generally termed 'non-self'. In mammalian hosts, protective factors may be transferred from mothers to offspring, both across the placenta during gestation and during lactation. In addition, some animal hosts, and particularly the human species, learn to respond to their environment so that some infections or their consequences are avoided.

In invertebrate hosts, resistance to endoparasitic infection depends mainly on the non-specific responses of individual mobile cells (amoebocytes and haemocytes), which take in by phagocytosis small particles like bacteria or which combine to encapsulate larger organisms like the developmental stages of parasitic worms and the larvae of insect parasitoids. There is little evidence in invertebrates for an immune memory, which characterises the specific responses of higher animals. In immunocompetent vertebrate hosts, foreign antigens or ma-

Fig. 10.16. A reed warbler patiently feeds the cuckoo chick which has displaced her own offspring from the nest.

terial that the body recognises as non-self stimulate the production of antibodies and the mobilisation of cells which together, in an ideal situation, neutralise or kill the invader. Two functionally distinct populations of small white blood cells called lymphocytes, in collaboration with larger white blood cells known as macrophages, are of fundamental importance in bringing about immune resistance in vertebrates. Some lymphocytes retain a memory of the foreign antigen, so that the protective reactions occur more rapidly and strongly when subsequent exposures occur.

In practice, however, many of the specific responses of vertebrates to the antigens of parasites lead not to protection but to hypersensitivity and immunopathology, which may be more damaging than the direct activities of the parasites. For example, schistosomiasis (bilharzia) frequently results in chronic liver damage as immunocompetent cells react, with little protective effect, against the eggs of *Schistosoma mansoni* as these become lodged in the liver.

Vertebrate hosts are also equipped with potent non-specific responses to infection, including protective factors secreted in sebum, mucus and tears, and various types of phagocytotic cell. Following exposure to viruses and other microparasites, some cells of higher vertebrates release a group of closely related proteins called interferons. Functionally, interferons appear to act upon other cells to reduce their susceptibility to microparasitic invasion. The properties of the skin, integument or cuticle of many animals form another effective barrier to infection. Genetic differences, which express themselves as variations between populations, may also convey powerful resistance to infection; perhaps the best known case is the virtual immunity of people with sickle-cell anaemia to death from *Plasmodium falciparum* malaria.

A vast array of parasitic organisms (see Table 10.2) is, however, quite able to survive and flourish in a living environment which contains so many protective responses. Parasites are variously able to stay one step ahead of antibody production, or to become disguised so that they appear as 'self' to the host, or to cause suppression of the immune system or occupy immunoprivileged sites within the host. Without the successful control of parasitic infections by the immune responses of the host, however, the host species, and therefore also its parasites, would perish.

Parasitic diseases of the human species

The capacity to initiate disease and the potential to cause death are axiomatic properties of a parasitic organism. Throughout its history, the human species has suffered from the ravages of parasitic disease, and this situation has scarcely changed when viewed globally (Table 10.3). In fact, most of the sufferers live in developing countries where many of them harbour more than one infection, and malaria, onchocerciasis (river blindness) and schistosomiasis (bilharzia) are of major public health importance. The general health impact of ascariasis (roundworm infestation), hookworm disease and other diseases caused by worms continues to be debated, but those individuals who harbour large burdens of parasitic worms are unquestionably disadvantaged.

Further reading

Agrios, G.N. *Plant pathology.* New York & London: Academic Press, 1978.

Baer, J.G. *Ecology of animal parasites.* Urbana: University of Illinois Press, 1952.

Burnet, M. and White, D.O. *Natural history of infectious disease.* (4th edn) Cambridge: Cambridge University Press, 1972.

Crompton, D.W.T. and Joyner, S.M. *Parasitic worms.* London: Taylor & Francis, 1980.

Darlington, A. *The pocket encyclopedia of plant galls.* Poole: Blandford Press, 1968.

Dickinson, C.H. and Lucas, J.A. *Plant pathology and plant pathogens.* (2nd edn) Oxford: Blackwell, 1982.

Dropkin, V.H. *Introduction to plant nematology.* New York: Wiley, 1980.

Edwards, P.J. and Wratten, S.D. *Ecology of insect–plant interactions.* SIB no. 121. London: Edward Arnold, 1980.

Gibbs, A. and Harrison, B. *Plant virology – the principles.* London: Edward Arnold, 1976.

Harley, J.L. and Smith, J.E. *Mycorrhizal symbiosis.* London: Academic Press, 1983.

Kuijt, J. *The biology of parasitic flowering plants.* Berkeley & Los Angeles: University of California Press, 1969.

Marshall, A.D. *The ecology of ectoparasitic insects.* London, New York & San Francisco: Academic Press, 1981.

Mims, C.A. *The pathogenesis of infectious disease.* London, New York & San Francisco: Academic Press, 1977.

Noble, E.R. and Noble, G.A. *Parasitology.* (4th edn) Philadelphia: Lea & Febiger, 1976.

Smith, D.C. *The lichen symbiosis.* Oxford: Oxford University Press, 1973.

Sprent, J.I. *The biology of nitrogen-fixing organisms.* London: McGraw-Hill, 1979.

Part Three
Evolution and the fossil record

There are two sides to biological evolution. The first is the idea that organisms gave rise, along with modification, to other organisms during the course of geological time. The fossil record, incomplete though it is, is made sense of if we accept this idea. The word **evolution** is often used as a shorthand description of what we think we know of the pattern of succession of organisms.

The second side to biological evolution is not separate from the first, but seeks to explain it. If we believe that the evidence for evolutionary succession is overwhelming, then it is natural to look for an explanation of the changing characteristics of organisms through time. Charles Darwin's own interest in animal breeding for domestic stock is a far cry from the vast amount of information derived from the study of genetics and molecular biology in this century.

The major problem in evolutionary biology is to establish the ways in which evolutionary change can occur. Must it, for example, always be by the gradual accumulation of small changes or can there be, on occasion, quite large changes in organisation leading to new, but viable, types of organism? Does change occur at a fairly steady rate or are there episodes of relative stasis punctuated by spurts of change?

In the following sections we consider both the possible mechanisms of evolutionary processes and the patterns which resulted from them. One of the most striking features uniting living organisms is the fact that they share most elements of the genetic code; that is, the way in which information about the constituents and timing of development is stored and transmitted by nucleic acids. Accordingly, it is necessary to consider the characteristics of the prebiotic environment in which the earliest life-forms evolved. The fossil record for this earliest period is very sparse and, by the time organisms were built of material which fossilised readily, there was already a considerable diversity of form. In the succeeding chapters documenting the major features of the fossil record, emphasis is placed on what we can establish about the physical nature of the environments in which plants and animals lived, and on how changes in the environment might have resulted in the favouring of innovations in the structure of organisms.

Finally, detailed consideration is given to the origins of the present-day flora and fauna which have a fossil record sufficiently complete to allow analysis of distributional changes with shifting climates through time.

Section through the ammonite Arietites *from the Lower Jurassic of Lyme Regis, Dorset. The walls and chamber partitions have been encrusted by several layers of iron-rich calcite.*

11 The Evolutionary Process

The most impressive feature of the living world is its diversity. The analytical approach of an academic biologist to this diversity conceals exactly the same astonishment as is shown by the amateur naturalist, and the answer to the question 'Why are there so many kinds of organism?' is usually sought in the theoretical framework of ecology and evolution.

Ecology is the study of the interrelationships of organisms with one another and with their environment. Inevitably most ecological studies are carried out on organisms at the present day. It is difficult enough to test ideas about why, for example, animals behave as they do, or why certain plants grow particularly well in certain climates, when in these cases we can potentially gather all the information we need. Applying the same quantitative methods to those organisms and environments which existed in the past is a far more difficult proposition.

In many ways the study of evolution may be regarded as the study of ecological relationships on a vastly extended time scale, one ranging over tens or hundreds of millions of years. There are several aspects to the study of evolution, and it is important to establish these. First, there is the search for the pattern of evolutionary relationships: the family tree of organisms traced through geological time, showing the serial development from earlier forms of the animals and plants we see alive today. Secondly, there is the study of the mechanism of evolutionary change. These two aspects cannot be separated from one another, but we are still learning how they are logically related.

Some biologists have argued that if we can reconstruct the pattern of evolution, the **phylogeny**, this will provide insight into the ways in which evolutionary change occurs. The opposite point of view is that knowledge of the processes of evolutionary change is essential before it is possible to find out the pattern of relationships between organisms.

Classifications

A related issue concerns the classification of organisms. At first sight it would seem reasonable that organisms which closely resemble one another should be grouped close together in a classification. If strong similarity between organisms does indeed reflect a close relationship in terms of common ancestry, then a classification based on their similarity should reflect precisely the evolutionary tree linking them in the past. It is widely appreciated, however, that similarity can be misleading. For example, the wings of bats and the wings of birds resemble one another: the inevitable physical constraints of aerodynamics ensure that this should be so. Yet bats and, for example, cows are classified together as mammals because the weight of other evidence suggests that these two sorts of animal are more closely related to one another than either is to the birds. Bats and cows both have hair, produce young which have been nourished via a placenta in the mother, and feed these young with milk from specialised glands. These and other

features, such as the structure of the middle ear, are shared by the two types of mammal, but are not possessed by the birds.

Of course, it is not necessary that a classification of organisms should precisely mirror the pattern of evolutionary relationships. Very often it is more important merely that a name can be unequivocally attached to a recognisable organism so that biologists can communicate this name to one another. This is important when, for example, some physiological measurements on an organism need to be repeated by another experimenter. Both need to be sure that they are considering the same organism. On these grounds a desirable characteristic of a classification is its stability. Often the evolutionary relationships are not really immediately relevant, for example in the case of pest control where correct identification allows the operator to look up the appropriate control measure.

Such a classification is, however, a nomenclature, a mere collection of names which do not mean much to the uninitiated. Information about the characteristics of the organisms is missing. Once some experience is gained a particular category name in the classification will evoke information about all the organisms included in that group. The group Aves, or birds, immediately calls to mind those adaptations which characterise birds in general. The statement: '*x* is a bird', will provide a good idea of the sort of features the creature possesses. We can convey more information by using a more restrictive category within Aves. For example, '*x* is a corvid' (a member of the crow family) will, once we are familiar with the classification, convey a more precise picture of the characters which *x* possesses.

The category **species** has a special and important role in classification: it is the most restrictive category generally used for communicating the characteristics of an organism. It was this category, of course, which was addressed by Charles Darwin in *The origin of species*, first published in 1859. The term 'species' is used for a collection of organisms which are capable, or which are presumed potentially to be capable, of interbreeding to produce offspring which are themselves fertile. Members of different species are either unable to mate successfully with each other, or do so only to produce sterile offspring. Members of a species tend to resemble one another more than they resemble members of any other species. There may be difficulties here when organisms have complex life-histories, with stages of very different appearance. For example, adult flies of different species may resemble one another more closely than the maggots resemble the adults of the same species. Again, where male and female are very different in appearance, there may be temporary difficulties of recognition: not for the organisms, but for the biologist studying them.

Darwinism and neo-Darwinism

So far the appearance of organisms has been taken to mean their morphological appearance, that is their visible structure, sometimes referred to as their phenotype. In this century the study of genetics has provided convincing reasons why individuals of a species should so closely resemble one another. These ideas were not available to Darwin, and hence the combination of the ideas of Darwin and his contemporaries with later work in genetics is often referred to as **neo-Darwinism**.

Darwin's work has two major aspects. First, he brought together evidence drawn from his own experience, and that of many others, in the various fields of natural history, comparative anatomy, geology, and the distribution of organisms, to suggest that the diversity of organisms through time could be most easily, economically and convincingly explained by assuming that species were not constant or unchanging entities. Secondly, Darwin drew on the large amount of information accumulated by the human species concerning plant and animal breeding to provide a possible mechanism for change occurring in groups of organisms over time, eventually leading to new species reproductively incompatible with their ancestors.

Darwin supposed that the variation between individuals of a population would often have a significant effect on their ability to survive in a given environment, mate and successfully rear offspring. Those individuals possessing characters which proved advantageous for survival and breeding would produce more young, which would themselves inherit the advantageous characteristics from their parents. In this way a gradual change would take place in a population as the new characteristics were propagated. This is Darwin's theory of **evolution by natural selection**, the 'natural' equivalent of selection of variant forms by an animal or plant breeder. Of course, since variant forms appeared in organisms more or less at random, disadvantageous variants would be likely to outnumber the advantageous ones.

The existence of differences between individual members of a species was crucial to Darwin's proposed mechanism of biological evolution, and the fact that such differences do obviously occur, in both man and other organisms, lent Darwin's arguments an immediate, intuitive appeal to many scientists and laymen.

Both Darwin's main lines of argument are based on extrapolation from what can be observed back to what may have occurred in the evolutionary past. He was able to call on existing geological evidence that the time-span over which life had existed on earth was vast. Observed geophysical phenomena, such as the deposition of sediment in river deltas, can be measured as occurring at a particular rate at the present day, and allow estimates of the time it must have taken for deposits of rock to accumulate over geological time (see section 12.1). These rocks contain fossils, and the conclusion was that biological evolution had taken place on a time-scale of hundreds of millions of years.

Correspondingly, the artificial selection of parents with extreme characteristics, for generation after generation, was known to establish true-breeding variant forms of plants or animals (see section 3.2). If a similar form of selection had occurred naturally in the geological past, then the transformation of life-forms to provide the diversity observable today and in the fossil record had a convincing explanation.

It has often been pointed out that the very element of Darwin's argument most obviously missing from *The origin of species* was the reason for **speciation** itself, the generation of new species not interbreeding with each other, as opposed to the change within any one species over time. In investigating the mechanisms and causes of speciation we are almost as handicapped as Darwin was, despite a vastly increased knowledge of genetics.

Evolutionary genetics

Modern genetics at the molecular level provides us both with an explanation for the similarities between parents and offspring, and with an explanation for the differences between them (see Chapter 3). These insights come from the fact that it is the genes of an organism that carry the coded information which determines its development. The genes are passed from parent to offspring with astonishing fidelity (see section 1.5), but the fidelity is not complete. The nucleic acids which carry the coded information are subject to damage and repair, and occasionally errors creep in. When the errors are non-lethal the organism may be well capable of surviving to breed, but will differ from its parents in its **genotype**, the precise nature of the coded message in its genes, and maybe in its **phenotype**, the characteristics of the organism due to the expression of its genes.

It is important to emphasise that the occurrence of these small changes in the genetic complement of an organism (in its genotype) are not of a directed nature, that is that they are not generated in direct response to an organism's needs in changing environmental circumstances. Natural selection acts on organisms, as some live, perhaps to reproduce, while others die, and it causes shifts in the frequencies of certain genes in the population. Natural selection can be viewed as editing the genetic composition of a population of organisms, because to a significant extent the survival and reproductive success of an organism depends upon the complement of genes it carries.

Natural selection as measured in the genetics of populations is thus a statistical phenomenon in which the genes of individuals compete with the corresponding, perhaps subtly different, genes of other individuals, due to the different effects of these genes on the viability of the whole organism.

Changes over time in the frequencies of genes in populations can have many causes, however, of which direct Darwinian natural selection on the basis of fitness is but one. Natural selection may, in any case, first have to act through the breeding system used, as some characters, such as the size of the tail of the male peacock, are selected for because they attract more mates, rather than because they increase directly the fitness of the offspring. New heritable variety can arise by mutation and by other events at the molecular level (see

Fig. 11.1. Industrial melanism in the peppered moth, Biston betularia. *The pale form, more conspicuous on sooty surfaces, was progressively replaced in the population by higher proportions of the dark form. The colour difference is due to a* single dominant mutation, and selection pressure of predation by birds led to gene pool changes. Now that atmospheric conditions are cleaner, the trend has reversed since dark moths are more conspicuous on lighter surfaces.

section 3.1). Gene frequencies can change randomly over time, by a process called genetic drift, which becomes increasingly important in very small groups of individuals. If such groups become geographically isolated from the main interbreeding population, then the new population can be significantly different from the parental stock. An extreme example of this would be the colonisation of an island by one pregnant female of a species, or by one seed of a self-fertile plant (see section 7.5).

Genetic changes need not be correlated with the observed rates of morphological change, which is of course all we can learn from the fossil record. Some mutations ('silent' or 'neutral' mutations) have no effect on the phenotype of the organism, because they occur in regions of DNA not coding for any protein nor controlling the rate of synthesis of proteins, or because they produce an insignificant change in protein structure. These kinds of mutation are believed to have accumulated at a constant rate over time throughout evolution. Equally, some changes in morphology are due to environmental effects alone, such as a progressively improving diet. A mutation in a regulatory gene controlling the expression of many genes coding for proteins, however, may allow a complete set of morphological changes to ensue.

The best evidence for the operation of simple natural selection comes from the study by population geneticists of polymorphic genes (genes of which more than one form, or **allele**, exist). For example, in certain areas of industrial pollution black (melanic) forms of moth have appeared, such as of the peppered moth (*Biston betularia*). Predators are less able to spot these dark forms than the original pale form (the **wild-type**) on soot-blackened tree-trunks, and thus the melanics make a greater contribution to the next generation of moths. The first specimen of the melanic form was recorded in 1848, and by 1895 98% of the moths of this species in Manchester, England, were black (Fig. 11.1). It is possible to predict the relative disadvantage of the non-melanic form in industrial areas by measurements of the observed changes in the gene frequencies in the population through succeeding generations; in the case of the peppered moth, this calculated disadvantage compared well with the observed lowered survival rates of the pale moths in towns, suggesting that the simple selection mechanism was sufficient to account for the spread of the morphological change throughout the population.

Evolution, however, is much more than the serial replacement of one form of a gene by another: completely new kinds of character have appeared, together with complicated mechanisms for the regulation of their expression. Nor need simple genetic changes be directly correlated with the evolutionary process of speciation, which requires the appearance of new, non-interbreeding populations. Biologists now distinguish those genetic changes spreading throughout a given population over many generations by natural selection from the genetic events which characterise the development of new species.

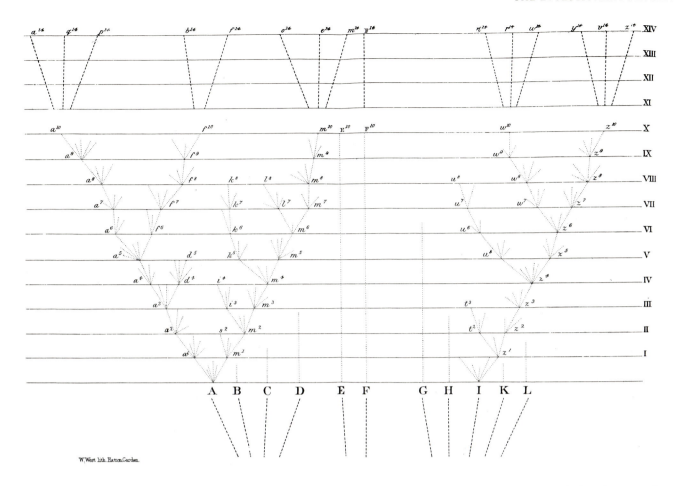

Fig. 11.2. Darwin's figure (from the first, 1859, edition of On the origin of species) *illustrating the production of varieties by descent with modification. The figure embodies the principles of radiation, selection and divergence over time.*

Mechanisms of speciation

In this century the prevailing interpretation of neo-Darwinism has been that the generation of new species is a **gradual** process occurring at a fluctuating, but predominantly low, rate. Such an interpretation would suggest that major gaps in our knowledge of fossil organisms are due largely to the difficulties of the process of fossilisation. In support of this it is clear that the fossil record is incomplete if one considers the numbers of organisms which must have existed throughout the vast span of geological time (see section 12.2).

More recently, however, it has been argued that gaps in the fossil record may often represent periods of relatively little change ('stasis'), which are **punctuated** by bursts of rapid evolutionary change. On this interpretation the fossil record, although still admittedly incomplete, gives a more or less accurate view of the tempo and mode of evolution. This more recent theory of 'punctuated equilibrium' has provoked renewed interest in the past ecological interactions of species and in the evolution of communities of organisms.

The difference between the gradualistic and punctuational models of evolution is perhaps best appreciated when the origins of major types of organism are considered. **Adaptive radiation** is the name given to the evolution of many different species all based on a single major theme and derived from a single ancestral type. Such a radiation might occur when a species acquires adaptations which enable it to enter a new environment. From this ancestral species many others evolve to take advantage of the new range of ecological possibilities. An example of such an occurrence is the invasion of land by fish able to breathe air. From one or more events of this kind arose the land vertebrates seen today and in the fossil record.

Under the gradualistic model, species radiating from the ancestral species change gradually through time. On the other hand, the punctuational model emphasises rapidly divergent speciation, followed by long periods of relatively little change. In the gradualistic model, morphological diversity builds up very slowly by gradual transformation of species; in the punctuational model morphological diversity is generated over a relatively much shorter period of time.

The study of genetics has been claimed to have contributed much less to resolving the punctuational/gradualistic argument than might have been expected. This is because small permanent changes in the genetic code of an organism (and in individuals of a population once the change has spread and become fixed) may have a very small phenotypic effect, perhaps even undetectable to the observer of morphology, or may in other cases be very large. Hence, merely using biochemical techniques to estimate the degree to which the genetic complement of two organisms differs may not tell us much about the extent of morphological difference to expect between them.

An ingenious way of examining the controversy has been to look at change in Pleistocene ('Ice Age') mammals of Europe.

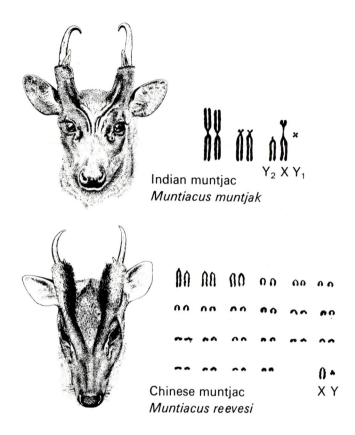

Indian muntjac
Muntiacus muntjak

Chinese muntjac
Muntiacus reevesi

Fig. 11.3. Muntjac chromosomes: cause or consequence of speciation? Muntiacus muntjak *and* M. reevesi *are closely related, yet their chromosome complements are very different.*

Here, it is claimed, rates of gradual change measured by direct observation of lineages in the well-preserved fossil record cannot nearly account for the observable differences between the numbers of species of mammals which evolved during the period. This very slow rate of morphological change is observed for human evolution just as it is for other mammals. On these grounds the rates of speciation can only be explained by a punctuational model: recognisably distinct species must have formed rapidly, punctuating the long periods of relative equilibrium during which change within the lineages seems to have occurred at a very low rate. In the punctuational model of evolution, speciation is viewed as occurring particularly during adaptive radiation, and involves very severe natural selection on the pronounced variability that is claimed to occur in small populations under new ecological conditions.

Speciation requires the development of mechanisms preventing breeding within the set of newly evolving species, and between each of these and their parental stock. One such mechanism might be chromosomal rearrangement, where large blocks of genetic material are moved to different positions in the genome. Differences may even arise in the number of chromosomes in the nucleus; this number is generally constant within a species. These chromosomal changes would prevent interbreeding by interfering with the pairing of homologous chromosomes at meiosis (see section 1.5).

A hypothesis for another kind of mechanism which might allow rapid speciation is based on the importance of regulatory genes. Regulatory genes control the operation of structural genes, which code for the sequence of amino-acids in proteins involved in the fabric and chemistry of the organism. A small change in a regulatory gene might, therefore, have a profound effect on the time or rate of production of many different proteins. The effect of this during development would be to produce an organism conceivably very different in appearance from the ancestral form.

Punctuational theory does no more than the more traditional ideas to explain the causes of speciation. Indeed, it makes use of the same proposed mechanisms, for example chromosome rearrangement. One of the problems of studying speciation is that in any case it is difficult to be sure what was the primary cause of divergence and which mechanisms may have acted only later on to maintain reproductive isolation. It may well be that speciation can be the outcome of several, or even many, different sorts of mechanism. For example, there may be mutations in the DNA of an organism which lead to a difference in amino-acid composition of a protein, or there may be local changes in the amount of DNA, or an increase in the number of copies of a particular stretch of DNA, as well as chromosome rearrangements such as inversion or translocation of parts of chromosomes within the genome.

The primary reproductive isolation of populations poses some unsolved problems also. Must such populations inhabit quite distinct territories with no overlap between them? Or can the populations overlap, or perhaps even occupy different parts of a common area, for example insects living on different food plants? The first model, of total separation, is referred to as **allopatric**, and the second as **sympatric**. An intermediate case, where populations overlap to a minor extent in a zone of hybridisation, is sometimes regarded as a separate case, and called the **parapatric** model.

Some of the difficulties in deciding between causes and effects of reproductive isolation could be resolved if we could study the process of speciation as it occurs. This possibility, however, is complicated by the time-scale involved and by the obvious fact that it is necessary to anticipate where, and in what existing species, the event is likely to occur. It remains true that there is no single case of speciation where we have all the information needed to make a decision about exactly how the event was caused and what have been its subsequent effects.

Because of the strong emphasis on geographical separation in the widely accepted allopatric model, island species have had a special importance, as indeed they had for Darwin when he considered the tortoises and birds of the Galapagos Islands (see section 7.5). The fruitfly *Drosophila* has provided a wealth of information in genetics partly because its short generation time makes breeding experiments possible, and it has also been studied intensively on the Hawaiian Islands (Fig. 11.4). Since the oldest of the main islands is about 6 million years old, and

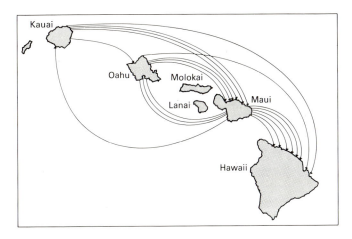

Fig. 11.4. Suggested minimum number of inter-island founder events amongst Hawaiian Drosophila *species.*

the others substantially younger, and since there are some 800 species of the drosophilid family on the Hawaiian archipelago, the adaptive radiation must have been relatively rapid. It has been suggested that the endemic species of the main island of Hawaii itself which is the youngest, must all be less than about 700 000 years old. Certainly, one of the most important observations to emerge from the 15 or so years of study in Hawaii has been the association of speciation with colonisation of new islands.

It has also been observed from laboratory breeding experiments that recently diverged species of fly quickly acquire so-called **post-mating** isolation mechanisms. The progeny of a cross between such species is either non-viable and dies as a pupa, or is infertile and can produce no further offspring. When species believed to have diverged longer ago are similarly examined they often exhibit **pre-mating** mechanisms which, for example by behavioural or genital incompatibility, prevent the occurrence of mating between species.

Another important conclusion from the study of Hawaiian drosophilids has been the recognition of the importance of **founder effects** in the evolution of the group: only a few flies, or perhaps even one pregnant female, were the initial founding colonisers of a new island.

Despite all the efforts, the study of the Hawaiian drosophilids has contributed little definitive evidence about the causes of speciation, although gene mutation and other changes in DNA at least accompany speciation. It is interesting that chromosomal rearrangements seem to have played a relatively small role as the primary cause of speciation, although these have been implicated in studies of lizards, rodents and grasshoppers.

Although islands have a very obvious geographical significance in studies of speciation, it should be borne in mind that speciation manifestly has occurred in other environments, and that perhaps different effects will predominate in these. Also it is an inevitable conclusion from the wealth of circumstantial evidence so far collected that different initial mechanisms may operate in different organisms in different circumstances. What we observe as the effect, speciation, is likely to have had different causes in different cases.

In recent years discoveries in molecular biology have led to a greater understanding of the complexities of organisation of the genome, leading to the proposal of new mechanisms of evolutionary divergence. For example, the concept of **molecular drive** makes use of the observation that parts of the DNA of an organism's genome may be subject to amplification, with the production of many copies of the original sequence of DNA. If mutation were to take place before amplification in such a section of DNA, the mutations would be present in all the subsequent copies. This is coupled with the evidence that some elements of DNA may 'convert' stretches of related DNA elsewhere in the genome into their own form, and this effect would accelerate the spread of the variant throughout an interbreeding population of organisms. Some of the regions of

DNA subject to these events might have an effect on the reproductive compatibility or on the embryonic development of the organisms carrying them. It is therefore possible to envisage a process whereby there is a constant pressure tending to promote genetic homogeneity within populations but genetic discontinuity between them. At the present this combination of mechanisms is highly speculative, but a theory of molecular drive might fit well with the punctuationalist view of evolution and provide a model very different from the longer-established gradualist model. What is important is not, of course, that the new or old theories necessarily be correct, but that they stimulate new experiments which test effectively the alternative hypotheses.

Further reading

Patterson, C. *Evolution*. London: Routledge & Kegan Paul and BM(NH), 1978.
Scientific American, 1978, **239** (3).
Stanley, S.M. *Macroevolution*. San Francisco: Freeman, 1979.
White, M.J.D. *Modes of speciation*. San Francisco: Freeman, 1978.

12 Palaeontology

12.1 STRATIGRAPHY, DATING AND FOSSILS

The rock sequence

Rocks can be divided into three classes according to their mode of origin. **Igneous** rocks are crystallised from molten material (magma), either at depth (such as granite and gabbro) or erupted from volcanoes (such as lava and volcanic ash). **Sedimentary** rocks are either derived from older rocks by weathering or erosion, subsequently transported by wind, water or glacial ice, and then deposited (such as sandstones and shales), or else are formed from the remains of living organisms (such as limestone and coal). **Metamorphic** rocks are recrystallised from older rocks by heat and/or pressure, usually at depth (such as schist, slate and marble).

It is rocks of sedimentary origin that form the basis of **stratigraphy**, the study of the sequence in which rocks have been laid down in successive **strata**, or layers, and with few exceptions fossils occur only in sedimentary rocks. Sediments originate primarily from erosion on the continents followed by transport and deposition either on land or in the sea. Most sedimentary rocks were deposited in shallow seas on the continental shelves. Chemical changes within the sediments, in particular promoted by the pressure of overlying deposits, result in loss of water, compaction and usually in the conversion of soft unconsolidated sediments into hard rock.

Sediments are usually laid down as flat, proportionately very thin, horizontal sheets. Clearly at any one time sediments of different types will be being deposited in different areas, and in most regions no sedimentation at all will be taking place. Subsequent earth movements may result in folding and faulting (fracture and displacement) of the original layers, while subsequent erosion may remove part or all of the rocks that were deposited in a particular area in a given period of time. At a later time the area may again be submerged beneath the sea, and a further series of sediments deposited. Many such cycles of deposition, deformation and erosion may follow, and still further complications are produced by the intrusion of molten igneous rocks, and by metamorphic processes (heat and pressure) (Fig. 12.1).

These complexities must be unravelled in order to work out the rock sequence, and the relative ages of the individual beds of rock. It is initially assumed that any bed of sedimentary rock must be older than the bed which overlies it and younger than the bed beneath (although in exceptional circumstances the sequence may have been completely overturned by earth movements). The relative ages of beds at a single locality can therefore be readily established. The next step is to correlate sedimentary rock units from one area to another, that is to establish which rock beds were deposited at the same time in the different localities. The dating method can be relative, giving only the order in which the rocks were formed and the geological events occurred, or absolute, establishing actual dates for the formation of the rocks in years before the present (BP). Relative dating methods include correlation using fossils, marker horizons, oxygen-isotope curves and palaeomagnetism; absolute methods include counting of annual structures, and measuring the extent to which radioactive isotopes have decayed.

Relative methods of dating

Correlation using fossils: biostratigraphy

The principal relative method of correlating sedimentary rocks from different areas is by means of their fossil content, and assumes that rocks deposited at the same time in different areas contain the same key species of fossils. Ideally, any fossil used for correlation should be geographically widely distributed, occur in a variety of rock types, be common and easy to recognise, and belong to a rapidly evolving lineage. The most useful are pelagic animals (from the middle depths and surface waters of the sea), such as the extinct ammonites and graptolites, but in practice a wide variety of animals and plants has been used.

The unit of time correlation is a zone, a sequence of rock units characterised by a particular fossil or assemblage of fossils. The appearance of a particular series of fossils in the fossil record may be due to the evolution of the group in that locality, but more commonly marks its immigration into the area from elsewhere. The rate of migration is assumed to be usually so rapid in relation to geological time that any possible inaccuracies in correlation due to slow migration can be safely ignored. Very few fossils had a worldwide distribution at any point in geological time, but nevertheless global correlations can be made with reasonable accuracy by using geographically overlapping occurrences of different species.

The correlation of non-marine sequences by fossils is less satisfactory, because throughout most of geological time terrestrial organisms were much less widely distributed than were marine organisms. Within continents, however, sequences have been correlated using non-marine organisms, especially vertebrates (such as the Cainozoic land-mammal ages of North America). Intercontinental correlations rely mainly on the occurrences of marine beds within the non-marine sequence, or on absolute dating techniques.

The Quaternary is too short to show considerable evolutionary change, and this therefore does not provide a sufficiently detailed basis for its subdivisions. However, changes in floral and faunal assemblages due to climatic changes, combined with patterns of immigration, evolution (in mammals) and extinction, allow correlation on a fine time-scale within restricted areas, such as North-west Europe.

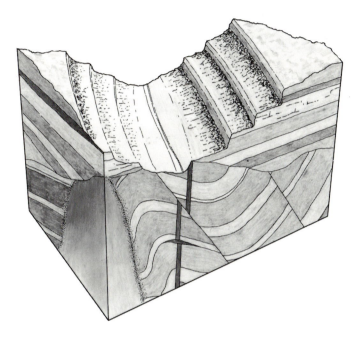

Fig. 12.1. Diagrammatic section showing sedimentary layers, their deformation and erosion, and the intrusion of molten rock.

Marker horizons

Volcanic eruptions can distribute ash over a wide area in a very short period of time, forming a thin band of rock, which serves as a time-marker **horizon**, in a variety of sedimentary rock sequences. Such beds are unfortunately rare. Other unusual beds such as glacial deposits, or evaporites of common salt or gypsum, may provide useful but more crude markers over limited areas.

Oxygen-isotope curves

At the bottom of the deep oceans, away from the continents, sedimentation has generally continued slowly and steadily for periods of millions of years. These sediments contain tests (shells) of single-celled Foraminifera. These tests are made of calcium carbonate, which contains the oxygen isotopes ^{18}O and ^{16}O. The ratio ^{18}O : ^{16}O is thought to reflect both the temperature of the sea water and the global ice volume, that is, how much of the world's water was locked up in ice-sheets at the time that the foraminifer was alive. Water that has evaporated from the sea and subsequently become incorporated into growing ice is richer in ^{16}O, leaving a higher concentration of ^{18}O in the oceans to be incorporated into the tests. The removal of ^{16}O into ice predominates in sediments from the Miocene onwards, after the formation of the Antarctic ice-cap, whereas ocean temperature is the factor monitored in the older sequences. Curves of oxygen-isotope variations show remarkably similar patterns for

many different areas of the world's oceans, and allow detailed correlations covering the period from the Cretaceous to the present day, and especially for the Quaternary.

Palaeomagnetism

Iron-containing minerals present in depositing fine-grained sediments and in cooling molten volcanic rocks become orientated in the direction of the earth's magnetic field, and the direction of the polarity becomes permanently recorded in the deposited sediments or cold rocks. A record of the polarity changes through geological time is thus preserved, and it is found that at irregular intervals of thousands or tens of thousands of years the earth's magnetic field has reversed its polarity. The patterns of palaeomagnetic epochs, especially in conjunction with absolute dating techniques, have been used to correlate sequences of lavas on land and on the deep-ocean floors with each other and with the deep-sea sediment sequences.

Absolute methods of dating

Annual structures

Some natural phenomena take place at rates which vary in a regular way throughout each year, and if a structural record is formed of these phenomena, this can form the basis of an absolute dating sequence. The first such method to be applied was that of counting layers of sediment in lake basins marginal to glaciers or ice-sheets. Here, fine-grained sediments are commonly deposited as very thin annual pairs, called **varves**: a thin, very fine-grained layer represents the winter, and a thicker, coarser layer results from deposits brought in with the summer melt-water. Patterns of variation in the thickness of the varves over periods of many years allow very precise correlations to be made between different localities within the same lake basin. Detailed chronologies for the last 12 000 years have thus been built up for the countries around the Baltic, and in North America.

Banded sediments deposited in lakes in temperate or warmer climates have also been interpreted as representing annual sedimentation, and hence give the period in years during which the sediments were deposited. Such evidence has provided estimates of the duration of the Quaternary interglacials, but it only yields a 'floating' chronology in that the duration of an event is accurately known, but not its absolute date in years BP.

Tree-ring dating, or **dendrochronology**, is in principle a similar method to that of varve dating, but is applicable over large areas of the world. In transverse section, wood exhibits a series of light and dark bands, each pair representing one year's growth. The relative thickness of these rings varies from year to year according to the rate of growth of the tree, which is affected by such factors as temperature and rainfall. By means

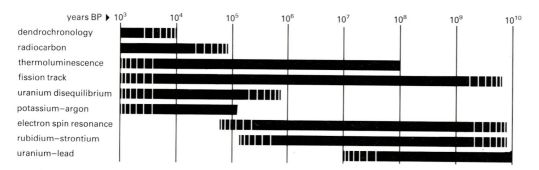

Fig. 12.2. Ranges of the principal methods of absolute dating.

of such variations in the width of the rings, timbers from archaeological sites or older buildings can be correlated with the older wood of living trees in the same area, and thus dated extremely accurately. Chronologies covering several thousands of years of postglacial (Holocene) time have been constructed by using such overlapping series of rings. Living bristle-cone pine trees up to 8200 years old, from the mountains of California, have proved of considerable value in the calibration of the radiocarbon dating method.

Although accurate to within one year there is little prospect of extending tree-ring dating much beyond about 10 000 years BP.

Radiometric dating

In atoms of a radioactive element the nuclei undergo spontaneous decay to a more stable form, with the emission of radiation and various energetic particles. The rate of radioactive decay is expressed by the **half-life**, that is, the time taken for half of the parent atoms to decay to the daughter atoms. Half-lives of radioactive isotopes vary from fractions of a second to thousands of millions of years. For example in carbon-14 (^{14}C), which has a half-life of 5730 ± 40 years, half of the ^{14}C atoms in a given sample will have decayed in 5730 years, half of the remainder in the next 5730 years, and so on; the level of radioactivity approaches closer and closer to zero but never completely disappears. Because radioactive decay involves only the nuclei of the atoms it is entirely independent of external factors such as temperature and pressure. The phenomenon thus provides potentially ideal clocks for absolute dating, if radioactive decay processes with half-lives appropriate to the desired time-range can be chosen. Most methods are based on the measurement of the ratio of daughter to parent isotope in a sample, or the ratio of the remaining parent isotope to a stable non-radioactive isotope.

The important assumption made is that the original proportions of these isotopes in the sample are known. The clock is set at zero when the rock is formed, and the parent isotope is incorporated into the crystal lattice of a mineral as an igneous rock cools from a molten state.

Whenever possible radiometric dates are cross-checked by applying more than one dating method to the sample. All radiometric methods are applicable on a global scale, and indeed many of them can be used also on extraterrestrial materials (moon rock and meteorites). The time ranges of the principal methods of absolute dating in current use are shown in Fig. 12.2.

Carbon-14 atoms are continuously produced in the earth's upper atmosphere by collision of neutrons (produced by cosmic rays) with nitrogen atoms. They are rapidly oxidised to carbon dioxide ($^{14}CO_2$), and probably become distributed throughout the atmosphere, oceans and all living organisms within a few years. The ^{14}C content of living organisms is, with rare exceptions, in equilibrium with that of the atmosphere, but after death the ^{14}C content of the bodies decreases steadily due to radioactive decay with a half-life of 5730 years. To determine the age of a sample containing carbon it is necessary to measure the proportion of the radioactive ^{14}C to stable isotopes of carbon, and to know the proportion of these isotopes in living organisms. The method assumes that the ^{14}C content of the atmosphere has remained constant for at least the past 50 000 years. However, radiocarbon assays of samples of wood from the long-lived bristle-cone pine, dated absolutely by dendrochronology, show deviations of as much as several hundred years when the age calculated by the radiocarbon methods is compared with the dendrochronological age. This phenomenon probably reflects periods of increased ^{14}C content in the atmosphere, resulting from a higher influx of cosmic rays. The more recent part of the radiocarbon time scale can thus be recalibrated by means of dendrochronology.

Potassium is a widespread element and contains a fixed natural percentage of the radioactive isotope potassium-40 (^{40}K); 11 % of this ^{40}K decays to argon-40 (^{40}Ar) and the half-life of the parent isotope is 13 000 million years. Very small amounts of the radioactive argon produced can be measured very precisely, so the method is applicable to a wide time-range. Silicate minerals and whole rocks of igneous origin are suitable, while certain sedimentary rocks can also be dated if they contain glauconite, because this mineral forms within the sediment and traps the parent potassium atoms soon after deposition. The main problem with the accuracy of this method is that dates can be too young due to loss of gaseous argon from the solid rocks.

Radioactive rubidium-87 (^{87}Rb) has a half-life of 4700 million years, decaying to strontium-87 (^{87}Sr). Ratios of these two isotopes can be measured in minerals containing rubidium, mainly micas and felspars, to give radiometric dates. These are commonly used to cross-check potassium–argon dates.

All naturally occurring uranium contains the radioactive isotopes ^{238}U and ^{235}U. ^{238}U decays in a series of steps with a half-life of 4510 million years to give ^{206}Pb (an isotope of lead), while the more radioactive ^{235}U has a half-life of 713 million years and decays in steps to give ^{207}Pb as its stable end-product. The measurement of the degree of decomposition of uranium isotopes is now very widely used as a dating method, since it has become possible to measure the very small amounts of uranium and lead in the common mineral zircon. Overestimates of age would result if lead were present in the original uranium-bearing mineral, but fortunately this can be detected by assay of the isotope ^{204}Pb which is not produced by radioactive decay. After correcting for any original lead, the ^{235}U/^{207}Pb and

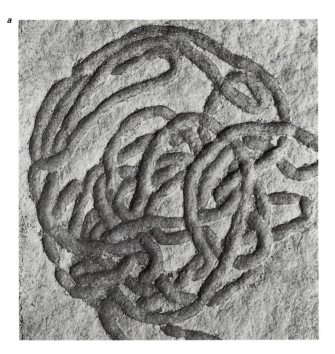

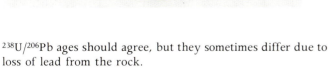

^{238}U/^{206}Pb ages should agree, but they sometimes differ due to loss of lead from the rock.

Fossilisation

A fossil is any trace of past life. This can include not just **body fossils**, which are the remains of organisms, such as bones or leaves, either in their original form or after some degree of chemical replacement, but also includes **trace fossils**, the burrows, tracks and other signs of the activities of creatures, and **chemical fossils**, organic compounds produced by ancient biochemical processes and surviving in rock to the present day. All these sorts of fossil are used by geologists as part of their description and classification of different strata of rock, but the

Fig. 12.3. Fossil specimens. (a) Trace fossil: worm cast of Lumbricaria *from the Middle Jurassic Lithographic Limestone of Solenhofen, Germany. (b) Ammonite with original shell preserved, from the Upper Cretaceous at Folkestone, Kent. (c) Permineralisation: well-preserved cutting tooth of the herbivorous dinosaur* Iguanadon *from the Lower Cretaceous of the Isle of Wight. The tooth is essentially unaltered, except perhaps for the deposition of secondary minerals in cavities left by the decomposition of the organic component of the original. (d) Internal and external moulds of the mineralised dorsal carapaces of trilobites (*Ellipsocephalus*) in a block of black mudstone from the Cambrian of Bohemia (Czechoslovakia).*

fossil record also contains a great deal of information on the course of the evolution of micro-organisms, animals and plants.

Many factors influence how much information about the original creature is preserved in the fossil. Soft tissues are generally rapidly degraded by being eaten by scavengers and by microbial decay, leaving the hard skeletons to form the fossil. Fossils of soft tissue, such as the frozen Siberian mammoths preserved in permafrost, are unlikely to survive for long on a geological time-scale, as those particular climatic conditions will eventually change. Where whole faunas of soft-bodied fossils do occur, it is due to an absence of microbial decay or scavenging, as would be found under anaerobic conditions and at low temperatures, such as after rapid burial in fine-grained sediment on a deep-ocean floor.

Relatively few body fossils are known from Precambrian rocks, the exception being the soft-bodied Ediacaran faunas (see section 13.2), which may have been preserved because of the absence of predators at that time. The large increase in fossil forms at the beginning of the Cambrian is due to the development of shells or mineralised skeletons by many groups of animals at this time, which greatly enhanced the chance of an animal's being preserved. Hard parts, though, are also attacked by boring organisms, and may be broken up by waves or currents so that only the strongest fragments survive. The tooth-shaped fossils made of calcium phosphate called cono-donts, from the Palaeozoic, have outlasted all the other parts of the body of the 'conodontophorid' animals from which they came, and the relationship of these creatures is obscure.

The remains of a creature must generally be buried in sediment to become a fossil, and must then survive the geological processes which occur as this sediment turns into rock, and any subsequent earth movements, changes in temperature or pressure, or erosion. Organisms actually living in sediment (the infauna) are much more likely to be preserved than are those living on the bottom of the sea (the epifauna) or those swimming or floating in the water (nektonic or pelagic organisms). Sudden burial by a rapid influx of sediment is needed to preserve the more delicate epifaunal organisms, which would otherwise break up before being completely buried.

Terrestrial animals and plants are only likely to be preserved if they live or grow in an environment such as a peat bog, or if their bodies are washed into lakes or rivers and thence buried or carried to the sea; in these latter cases, of course, the natural environment of the fossil may be difficult to deduce. Other-wise, formation of fossils of terrestrial organisms requires some relatively unusual circumstance, such as the creature being trapped in asphalt ('tar-pits'), as happened to many Pleistocene animals at Rancho La Brea, California, or the creature being carried into a cave by a predator and the bones being buried by fine-grained earth gradually accumulating on the cave floor.

As formation of sediment continues over time, the pressure drives water out of the lower layers, which become compacted, and this can sometimes change the shape of the fossil

dramatically. Chemical alteration of the components of the fossil, or replacement of one mineral by another, is very common, and can eventually result in the remains becoming rock. Calcareous skeletons of calcite or, particularly, aragonite (both forms of calcium carbonate) may gradually dissolve, and the cast can be filled with another mineral, or the original calcite may be replaced directly by, for example, silica or iron pyrites. Calcium phosphate and, especially, silica are the other important skeletal materials which may be preserved.

Plant tissues are frequently compressed and reduced to carbonised material, in which little of the internal structure of the plant remains. The best-known fossil floras, such as the Rhynie Chert from the Devonian of Scotland (see section 14.1), occur when the plants have become infiltrated at or soon after death by fluids containing minerals, such as silica in the case of the Rhynie Chert and the 'petrified forests' of the Triassic in Arizona.

Trace fossils are rarely found in association with body fossils. It is difficult to do more than allot individual trace fossils to a type of activity, such as walking, burrowing or feeding, and it is rare to be able to identify the animal responsible. However, the appearance of similar trace fossils over wide stretches of geological time shows that patterns of behaviour, such as the meandering movements of deposit-feeders, have not changed greatly.

Some of the complex organic chemicals characteristic of living organisms break down to very stable molecules, and sometimes form insoluble deposits called kerogen. Organic compounds found in Precambrian sediments include hydro-carbons, isoprenoids and porphyrins. Particular products of the breakdown of chlorophyll that are found in some early rocks have no other known natural origin, and their presence implies that photosynthetic organisms were present at the times when these rocks were formed.

12.2 CONTINENTAL DRIFT

Evidence for continental drift

Many features of the past and present distributions of animals and plants can be readily explained if continental areas now separated by deep oceans were joined at some time in the geological past. For example, the Upper Carboniferous rocks both of North America and of Europe have yielded virtually the same fossil floras and faunas, associated with coal swamps and an equatorial climate. The late Carboniferous and early Permian rocks of the southern continents (South America, Africa, India, Australasia and Antarctica), on the other hand, all show evidence of extensive glaciation, followed by rocks containing a cool-temperate fossil flora dominated by seed ferns, the *Glossopteris* flora.

Such palaeontological evidence, and the remarkably close match between the shapes of the Atlantic continental shelves of

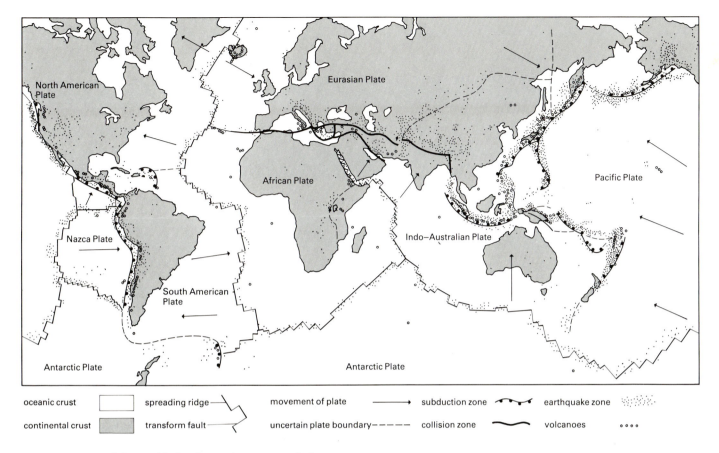

Fig. 12.4. Map of the world showing active zones and plate boundaries in the Earth's crust.

Africa and South America, led Wegener to propose his theory of continental drift in 1915. This suggested that a former single world-continent termed 'Pangaea' had broken up during the late Mesozoic, and that subsequently the continents slowly drifted apart to their present positions.

The theory of continental drift was not however generally accepted until the 1960s and 1970s, largely because geophysicists knew of no mechanism by which continents could be moved across the surface of the globe. Many biogeographers instead invoked hypothetical land bridges across the ocean basins to account for the patterns of distribution of past and present organisms.

Convincing evidence that the continents do indeed move has come first from palaeomagnetic studies on the continental rocks, and secondly from investigations of the deep ocean basins. Iron-bearing minerals in volcanic lavas behave like little compass needles, becoming orientated with the earth's magnetic field, and this direction is retained when the lava cools and becomes rock. Lavas of successive ages in a particular area therefore preserve a record of the apparent changes of the positions of the earth's magnetic poles through geological time. These 'polar wandering curves' are different for each continent, which confirms that the continents have actually moved relative to one another, and they can be used to reconstruct the positions of the continents at various times in the past. Secondly, and especially important, research on the geology of the deep ocean basins has resulted in the discovery of **sea-floor spreading**, whereby the floors of most of the world's oceans are increasing in extent.

The movement of the parts of the earth's crust is called **plate tectonics**.

Plate tectonics

The interior of the earth comprises three principal layers, the dense iron-rich core, the mantle made of silicate rocks which are semi-molten at depth, and the thin solid surface crust. There are two kinds of crust, a lower and denser oceanic crust which occurs over the entire surface of the globe, and an upper, lighter, continental crust found over only about 40% of the earth's surface. The rocks of the crust are of very different ages. Continental rocks include some of very great age (over 3000 million years old), while those of the ocean-floor are young, none being over 200 million years old, and half of the sea-bed is underlain by rocks of less than 75 million years old. Besides being young, the rocks of the ocean-floor are relatively thin, dense and rich in magnesium and poor in aluminium, in comparison with those of the continental masses.

The crusts and the top, solid part of the mantle, totalling about 70 to 100 kilometres in thickness, appear at the present day to consist of about 15 rigid plates, seven of which are very large (Fig. 12.4). These plates move over the semi-molten lower mantle. Active zones with extensive volcanic and earthquake activity are confined to the narrow interconnecting boundaries of contact of the plates. There are three main types of zone of contact, spreading contacts such as at mid-ocean ridges, converging contacts where crust is being consumed by being pushed down (**subduction**) into the mantle, and

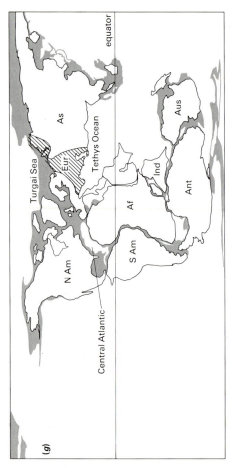

(a)

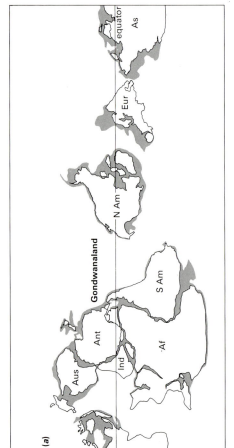

(b)

(c)

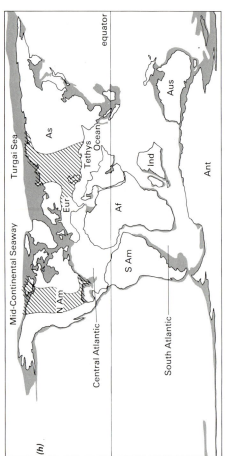

(g)

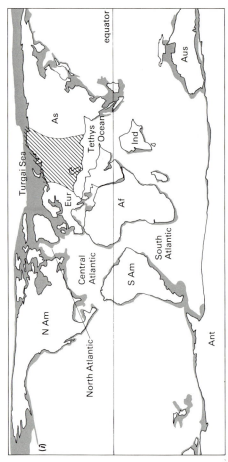

(h)

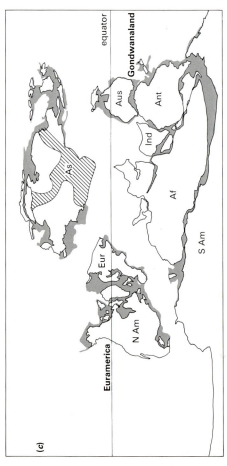

(i)

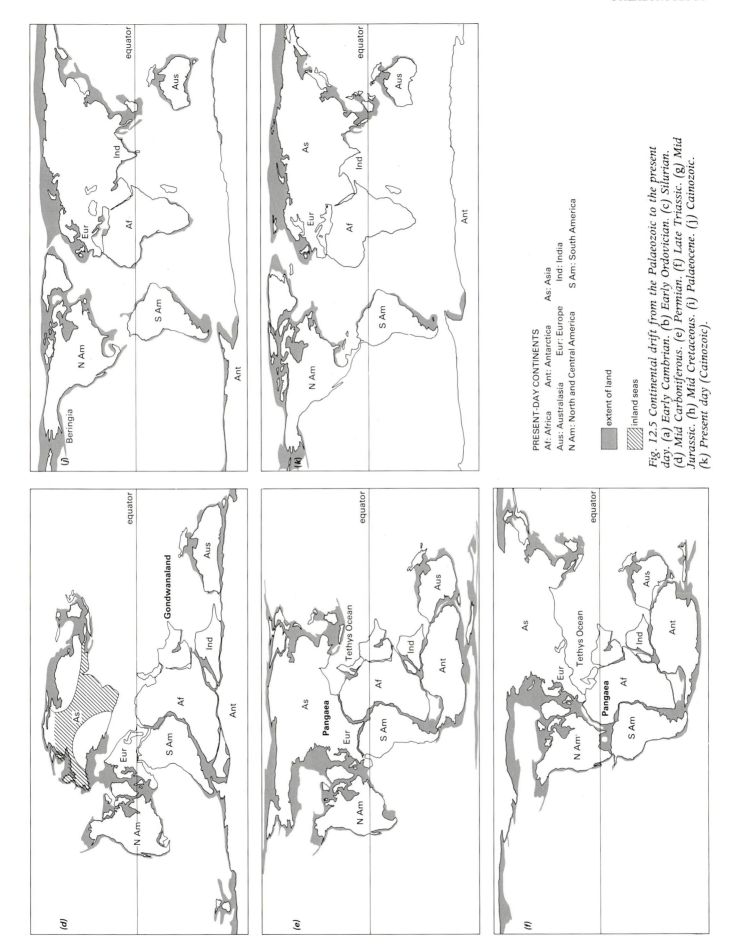

PRESENT-DAY CONTINENTS

Af: Africa   Ant: Antarctica   As: Asia
Aus: Australasia   Eur: Europe   Ind: India
N Am: North and Central America   S Am: South America

extent of land

inland seas

Fig. 12.5 Continental drift from the Palaeozoic to the present day. (a) Early Cambrian. (b) Early Ordovician. (c) Silurian. (d) Mid Carboniferous. (e) Permian. (f) Late Triassic. (g) Mid Jurassic. (h) Mid Cretaceous. (i) Palaeocene. (j) Cainozoic. (k) Present day (Cainozoic).

GEOLOGICAL TIMESCALE

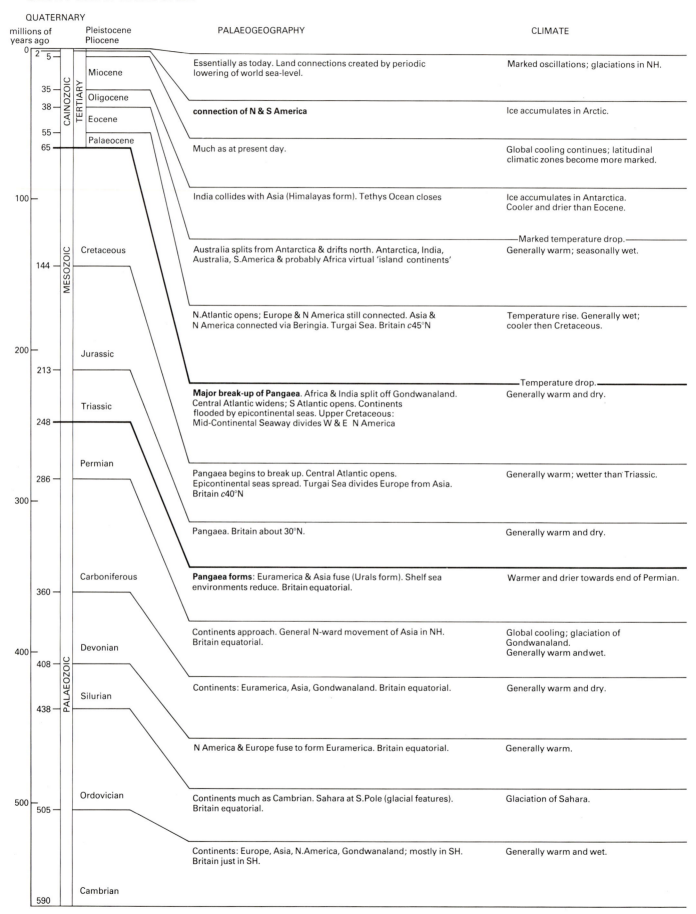

QUATERNARY

millions of years ago

Pleistocene
Pliocene

PALAEOGEOGRAPHY

CLIMATE

millions of years ago			PALAEOGEOGRAPHY	CLIMATE
0 2 5		Miocene	Essentially as today. Land connections created by periodic lowering of world sea-level.	Marked oscillations; glaciations in NH.
35		Oligocene		
38		Eocene	**connection of N & S America**	Ice accumulates in Arctic.
55		Palaeocene		
65			Much as at present day.	Global cooling continues; latitudinal climatic zones become more marked.
100		Cretaceous	India collides with Asia (Himalayas form). Tethys Ocean closes	Ice accumulates in Antarctica. Cooler and drier than Eocene.
				Marked temperature drop.
144			Australia splits from Antarctica & drifts north. Antarctica, India, Australia, S.America & probably Africa virtual 'island continents'	Generally warm; seasonally wet.
200		Jurassic	N.Atlantic opens; Europe & N America still connected. Asia & N America connected via Beringia. Turgai Sea. Britain c45°N	Temperature rise. Generally wet; cooler then Cretaceous.
213				Temperature drop.
		Triassic	**Major break-up of Pangaea.** Africa & India split off Gondwanaland. Central Atlantic widens; S Atlantic opens. Continents flooded by epicontinental seas. Upper Cretaceous: Mid-Continental Seaway divides W & E N America	Generally warm and dry.
248				
286		Permian	Pangaea begins to break up. Central Atlantic opens. Epicontinental seas spread. Turgai Sea divides Europe from Asia. Britain c40°N	Generally warm; wetter than Triassic.
300			Pangaea. Britain about 30°N.	Generally warm and dry.
360		Carboniferous	**Pangaea forms:** Euramerica & Asia fuse (Urals form). Shelf sea environments reduce. Britain equatorial.	Warmer and drier towards end of Permian.
400		Devonian	Continents approach. General N-ward movement of Asia in NH. Britain equatorial.	Global cooling; glaciation of Gondwanaland. Generally warm and wet.
408			Continents: Euramerica, Asia, Gondwanaland. Britain equatorial.	Generally warm and dry.
438		Silurian	N America & Europe fuse to form Euramerica. Britain equatorial.	Generally warm.
500 505		Ordovician	Continents much as Cambrian. Sahara at S.Pole (glacial features). Britain equatorial.	Glaciation of Sahara.
			Continents: Europe, Asia, N.America, Gondwanaland; mostly in SH. Britain just in SH.	Generally warm and wet.
590		Cambrian		

Vertical labels: CAINOZOIC / TERTIARY, MESOZOIC, PALAEOZOIC

FLORA	FAUNA
Vegetational zones shifting repeatedly with climatic changes.	**Rise of Man.** **Extinction of many large mammals.**
Modern flora.	**First hominids.** First elephants, voles.
Appearance and spread of grasses. Widespread increase of grassland at expense of forest.	**Maximum diversity of mammals. First apes.** First grazing ungulates: bovids, camels, horses. Large proboscideans in Eurasia and N.America. Marine life much as at present day.
Flora largely of modern aspect. ?Extinction of Antarctic terrestrial flora.	**First ape-like primates.** ?Extinction of Antarctic terrestrial fauna. Radiation of artiodactyls and rhinos. Fissipede carnivores replace creodonts.
Flora largely of modern aspect. Tropical floras in Europe, Spitzbergen, Greenland.	First whales, bats, artiodactyls, perissodactyls, proboscideans, sirenians. Radiation of rodents. Extinction of multituberculates & amblypods. Large marine foraminiferans abundant.
Flora largely of modern aspect. Marine diatoms abundant.	**Explosive radiation of mammals (mainly archaic). First edentates, rodents, lagomorphs, fissipede carnivores, S.American ungulates. First primates**: prosimians. Creodonts, condylarths and amblypods dominate northern faunas. Modern bivalves, gastropods; marked decline in brachiopods.
First flowering plants (angiosperms) in Lower Cretaceous; dominant in Late Cretaceous. Marine calcareous phytoplankton increase.	End of Cretaceous: **Major extinctions**: dinosaurs, pterosaurs, ichthyosaurs, plesiosaurs, ammonites. Upper Cretaceous: **First placental mammals. First marsupials.** First snakes. New dinosaur groups: hadrosaurs, ceratopsians. Marine ammonites & belemnites continue.
Flora similar to Triassic. Marine planktonic algae (dinoflagellates, coccolithophores) abundant.	**First bird**: *Archaeopteryx*. Pterosaurs. Radiation of dinosaurs - dominant land vertebrates. Marine ammonites, belemnites, brachiopods abundant; molluscs increasing. **Appearance and radiation of teleost fish.**
Horsetails, seed ferns, ferns, gymnosperms (*Ginkgo*, cycads, conifers)	**First mammals. First dinosaurs.** Extinction of mammal-like reptiles. Radiation of insects: Acme of ammonites; first scleractinid corals.
Seed ferns, ferns. *Glossopteris* flora in Gondwanaland.	**Major extinctions**: trilobites, many other invertebrates. Rise and spread of ammonites. Radiation of reptiles; abundant mammal-like reptiles. First insects with larvae.
Coal forests with giant club-mosses, horsetails, seed ferns. First conifers.	**First reptiles.** Radiation of amphibians, insects, sharks. Corals, brachiopods, molluscs, goniatites, nautiloids in sea.
Explosive radiation of land plants. *Psilophyton*, club-mosses, forms resembling ferns and horsetails. First seed-bearing plants. Green algae abundant.	Upper Devonian: **First land vertebrates**: amphibians. **First insects.** Maximum diversity of jawed and jawless fish. Lower Devonian: extinction of graptolites.
First land plants (vascular plants, e.g. *Cooksonia*). Green algae abundant.	Widespread coral reefs. Eurypterids at maximum. Radiation of armoured jawless fishes First jawed fish. Brachiopods abundant.
Blue-green algae, including stromatolite-building forms.	Maximum diversity of graptolites. Rugose & tabulate corals appear. Brachiopods abundant in shallow sea. Molluscs increasing: straight nautiloids abundant.
Blue-green algae.	**Sudden appearance of abundant fossils** because of evolution of shells & exoskeletons. Trilobites, brachiopods, molluscs, graptolites, echinoderms, archaeocyathids. **First vertebrates**: armoured jawless fish.

transform contacts where plates slide past each other.

New material is added along one or more margins of each plate by issuing from deeper layers of the earth's crust, for example by volcanic eruptions of lavas at the mid-ocean ridges, resulting in current rates of spreading of the sea-floor of 1 to 10 centimetres per year. If at such a spreading contact the two plates support continents which are moving away from each other, a rift is formed which gradually widens. When this occurs within one land mass, the rift will eventually become flooded by the sea. The Atlantic Ocean formed like this as the American and Afro-European plates moved in opposite directions, the Red Sea and the Gulf of California are examples of an earlier stage in the process, and the East African Rift Valley may be a rift at an even earlier stage into which the sea has not yet penetrated.

At the same time, at other margins of each plate, material of the crust is being reabsorbed by being subducted into the mantle, and remelted, beneath the ocean trenches. When the margins of one or more continental land masses reach such a boundary zone, the continental blocks, too light to be drawn down, continue to float on the lower layers and are therefore buckled to form a mountain chain along the length of the margin of the plates. The Himalayas have been produced where the Indian plate has collided with that of Eurasia, and the mountain chains of the western seaboard of the Americas (the Rockies and the Andes) are forming along the boundary between the American plates moving westwards and the plates of the eastern Pacific Ocean moving eastwards.

The mechanisms of creation and destruction of oceanic crust appear to be powered by heat energy from the radioactive decay of various unstable elements in the earth's interior, producing convection currents within the mantle, which eventually cause the changes in the position of land masses over time. The number and shape of the plates has also not remained constant, and so continental land masses have often been welded together and split apart throughout geological time.

The continental rocks have therefore survived to be old because they are light. Those underneath the oceans are young because they are being continually created along the central rifts of the mid-oceanic ridges, and are slowly moving away from their points of insertion, to be destroyed again at the trenches. The movement of the plates and the spreading of the sea-floor also explain the shapes of the ocean basins and the continental margins which enclose them.

Palaeogeography and continental drift

Palaeocontinental maps showing the configurations of the continental masses at various times in the geological past have been produced for all the Phanerozoic (the last 570 million years). Maps for the period from the Triassic to the present day have been reconstructed from data on sea-floor spreading, for all the modern ocean basins except the Pacific have originated

and expanded during this period of time. The maps for the Palaeozoic (Cambrian to Permian) have been produced from palaeomagnetic data and are thus more conjectural.

In each of the maps the continental land masses are defined by the margins of the present-day continental shelves. The present-day coastlines are also indicated to facilitate recognition of the continents, but it should be stressed that these had no reality in past geological periods. Shallow epicontinental (shelf) seas nowadays cover large areas of the continental masses, and in past geological periods similarly covered continental areas to a greater or lesser extent, but they cannot be reconstructed very accurately at present. Thus epicontinental seas have not been indicated on the maps, except where their existence was of major biogeographical importance because, for example, they completely separated areas within one continental mass for long periods of time.

During the Cambrian and Ordovician, four continental masses appear to have existed: North America, Europe, Asia, and Gondwanaland (which contained the southern continents of Africa, South America, India, Antarctica and Australasia) (Fig. 12.5a). These four continents were all situated close to the equator, or in the southern hemisphere. In the Ordovician, the area of North Africa which is now the Sahara Desert lay close to the South Pole and was extensively glaciated (Fig. 12.5b). In the Silurian, the North American and European continents collided along the line of the Appalachian, Caledonian and Scandinavian mountains to form Euramerica, which was situated equatorially (Fig. 12.5c). By the Carboniferous, the three continental masses were approaching one another, and South America may possibly have been in contact or nearly so with Europe (Fig. 12.5d). The palaeogeography of the time is illustrated by the distributions of fossil reptiles, largely confined to Euramerica, and the various distinct floral provinces of Euramerica, Gondwanaland, and two provinces in Asia separated by an epicontinental sea.

During the Permian all of the continental masses became united to form a single world-continent called Pangaea, surrounded by a single world-ocean (Fig. 12.5e). With few barriers to the migration of terrestrial organisms, a warmer global climate and a much less marked latitudinal zonation of the climate than now, the flora and the fauna of Pangaea appear to have been remarkably uniform. The extensive reduction in the area of the shelf sea may have been responsible for a major wave of extinction in marine invertebrates.

Pangaea persisted throughout the succeeding Triassic period and allowed such animals as the dinosaurs and early mammals to spread to all areas (Fig. 12.5f). In the Jurassic Pangaea began to break up with the opening of the Central Atlantic and the widespread invasion of the continents by epicontinental seas (Fig. 12.5g). This resulted in some fragmentation of the land areas and evolutionary divergence among land animals, in particular the dinosaurs.

During the Cretaceous, Africa and India parted company from Gondwanaland and drifted northwards. The Central

Atlantic widened further and the South Atlantic opened up. Epicontinental seas became very extensive, causing fragmentation of the land areas and increasing diversification of terrestrial organisms, especially the vertebrates. Although North America remained connected to Europe and Asia, the existence of two major epicontinental seas, the Mid-Continental Seaway and the Turgai Sea (Fig. 12.5*h*), effectively divided this northern continental mass, called Laurasia, into three portions: Europe and eastern North America, western North America, and Asia. This situation is strikingly reflected in the dinosaur faunas of the three areas, with for example advanced ceratopsian dinosaurs confined to western North America in the Upper Cretaceous.

In the early Cainozoic (Palaeocene) the Atlantic continued to widen, although North America and Europe still remained connected as shown by the strong similarity of their mammal faunas (Fig. 12.5*i*). South America and Australia remained connected via Antarctica, which may well explain why marsupials nowadays occur in these two continents and nowhere else.

By the Miocene the world map was not so different from that of today (Fig. 12.5*j*). India had earlier collided with Asia, perhaps in the Eocene, forming the Himalayas, but South America and Australia were 'island continents' and their peculiar mammal faunas radiated virtually isolated from the rest of the world. After a period of separation in the early Cainozoic there was some exchange of land mammals between Africa and Eurasia, but this exchange was only partial, indicating that there were barriers, such as shallow seas and later, in the Pleistocene, deserts, which prevented the free migration of most animals. The position of Antarctica over the South Pole, combined with global climatic cooling, resulted in extensive glaciation of the continent in the Oligocene and Miocene, and this was probably the cause of the extinction of virtually its entire terrestrial fauna and flora. Comparison of Miocene mammal faunas suggests some interchange occurred between Eurasia and North America across the region of the Bering Straits (Beringia), but in general the mammals of the two regions underwent separate radiations.

During the Pliocene, North and Central America were reunited with South America, resulting in a spectacular interchange of faunas, but immigration was predominantly from north to south.

In the Pleistocene, phases of extensive glaciation resulted in falls of sea-level of up to 100 metres or more. This connected chains of islands which are now separate again, and joined the British Isles to the European continent and Asia to North America across Beringia, allowing faunal and floral dispersal. Australasia, however, remained an isolated 'island continent' (Fig. 12.5*k*), as it is to the present day, with very many unique faunal and floral elements.

Further reading

Shipman, P. *The life history of a fossil: An introduction to taphonomy and palaeoecology.* Cambridge, Mass.: Harvard University Press, 1981.
The story of the earth. London: HMSO, 1977.
The age of the earth. London: HMSO, 1980.
Smith, A.G., Hurley, **A.M.** and Briden, **J.C.** *Phanerozoic palaeocontinental world maps.* Cambridge: Cambridge University Press, 1981.
Smith, D.G. (editor) *The Cambridge encyclopedia of earth sciences.* Cambridge: Cambridge University Press, 1982.

13 Early Events in Evolution

13.1 THE ORIGINS OF LIFE

The earth formed from lifeless dust and gases about 4600 million years ago. Recent studies of an extremely old geological formation in Australia (see section 13.2) make it probable that single-celled organisms, perhaps similar to blue-green algae, were already present about 3600 million years ago. Life must, therefore, have appeared on earth at some time during the first thousand million years of the existence of the planet.

Theories that living organisms originated elsewhere in the universe and were transported to the earth, accidentally or deliberately, have been put forward from time to time. These ideas are difficult to disprove, and it is hard even to assess their plausibility, but they have had little influence on thinking about the origins of life. In this section it is assumed that life evolved from non-living materials on the early earth.

It seems unlikely that fossils or other geological relics of pre-life or of the very earliest forms of life will be found. Theories of the origins of life therefore lean heavily both on inferences from our knowledge of contemporary biochemistry, and on laboratory reconstructions of the supposed chemistry of the primitive earth.

The abiotic synthesis of organic molecules

Recent work on the origin of life began with the ideas of Oparin in the 1920s. He proposed that the early atmosphere of the earth was strongly reducing, having as its main components methane, ammonia and water, but in contrast to the present atmosphere containing little or no oxygen. A pool of organic materials, a prebiotic 'soup', could have been formed from these gases by the action of ultraviolet light from the sun, electrical storms, volcanoes, and heat and shock waves from the impact of meteorites. Oparin believed that life then originated through a series of chemical reactions of increasing complexity. The demonstration, initially by Miller and Urey, that such a mixture of organic molecules, including many similar to the monomers of current biological macromolecules, could have formed in these conditions is one of the major achievements of studies on the origins of life. The present challenge is to show how the first ordered macromolecules, and then primitive self-reproducing systems, could have evolved from simple organic molecules.

Among the thousands of organic molecules involved in biochemistry, the 20 naturally occurring amino-acids and the four or five nucleotides are particularly significant. The amino-acids are the monomers from which proteins are constructed, while the nucleotides are the building blocks of the nucleic acids that carry genetic information (see section 1.1). Miller and Urey initiated modern experimental studies on the origins of life with their work on the synthesis of amino-acids in non-living systems (**abiotic synthesis**). A mixture of methane, ammonia and water, Oparin's reducing atmosphere, was subjected to an electrical discharge in an apparatus that permitted the gases to circulate repeatedly through the discharge, while non-volatile products were trapped by dissolving them in water (Fig. 13.1). This process was designed to simulate the action of electrical storms on the atmosphere of the primitive earth. After the reaction was complete, the mixture of substances dissolved in the water was analysed. As much as 20% of the total carbon in the reaction mixture had been converted into a relatively small number of simple organic molecules, including substantial quantities of the amino-acids glycine, alanine and aspartic acid. Many thousands of organic molecules of comparable size are known, and there was no reason to expect anything other than an extremely complicated mixture of components.

These successful experiments were followed by many other syntheses of biochemical molecules from simple starting materials under prebiotic conditions, and by studies designed to discover the mechanisms by which they had been formed. Miller showed that the amino-acids obtained in his experiments were synthesised via simple aldehydes and hydrogen cyanide that formed in the electrical discharge. Oro showed that hydrogen cyanide alone, under very simple conditions, would react to give adenine, one of the important components of nucleic acids. The remaining components of nucleic acids were obtained in a similar manner from simple molecules like formaldehyde, cyanogen and cyanoacetylene.

Thus the most important molecules of living systems can almost all be readily formed via the simple reactive gases that are produced when a reducing atmosphere is subjected to electrical discharges, ultraviolet light or high temperatures. The most important of these reactive molecules are hydrogen cyanide, formaldehyde and cyanoacetylene, together with ammonia and water. There must be no free oxygen in the system, as this rapidly destroys the reaction intermediates and products; the appearance 2000 million years ago of molecular oxygen, from photosynthesis, brought about an irreversible change in the properties of the earth's atmosphere, and would have prevented further abiotic synthesis of organic compounds.

Biochemical work on the origins of life received substantial support from an unexpected quarter: radioastronomers discovered that interstellar dust clouds, where new stars are formed, contain large numbers of organic molecules. Among the most abundant are hydrogen cyanide, formaldehyde and cyanoacetylene. Furthermore, the analysis of newly fallen meteorites shows that these contain small amounts of amino-acids, suggesting that the synthesis of organic chemicals suitable for the evolution of life must be occurring throughout the universe. The extent to which organic chemicals present in the dust and gases which initially formed the earth, and those subsequently brought in by meteorites, contributed to the material from which life evolved is not known. The general principle that important biochemicals can readily be formed without living systems, both in interstellar space and in the earth's primitive atmosphere, is however well established.

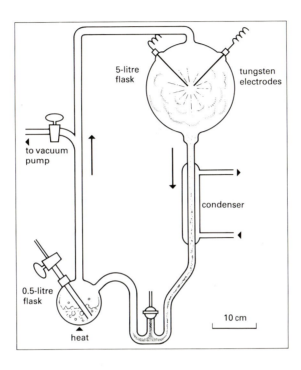

Fig. 13.1. The apparatus used by Miller to examine amino-acid formation in non-living systems and table of results.

molecules produced	μmoles	moles ratio
glycine	440	100
alanine	700	180
α-amino-*n*-butyric acid	270	61
α-aminoisobutyric acid	~30	~7
valine	19.5	4.4
norvaline	61	14
isovaline	~5	~1
leucine	11.3	2.6
isoleucine	4.8	1.1
allisoleucine	5.1	1.2
norleucine	6	1.4
tert-leucine	<0.02	–
proline	1.5	0.3
aspartic acid	34	7.7
glutamic acid	7.7	1.7
serine	5	1.1
threonine	~0.8	~0.2
allothreonine	~0.8	~0.2
α,γ diaminobutyric acid	33	7.6
α-hydroxy-γ-aminobutyric acid	74	17

Glycine and alanine yields, based on the carbon: 0.26% and 0.71%, respectively.
Total yield of amino-acids listed: 1.55%

Presumably, amino-acids and nucleotides could not have become the major components of our genetic system without being such abundant components of the prebiotic 'soup'.

Polymerisation and macromolecular organisation

Assuming that organic molecules, including amino-acids and the organic constituents of nucleotides, accumulated on the primitive earth, the next step is to explain the evolution from these of self-replicating organisms. Attempted reconstructions of this part of the evolutionary process are extremely tentative and the experimental evidence is, at best, fragmentary.

Both proteins and nucleic acids are 'optically active': their constituent monomers can exist in two forms, left-handed (L-) and right-handed (D-), which rotate the plane of polarised light to the left and to the right, respectively, and which are mirror images of each other but with otherwise identical chemical properties. However, modern proteins are composed only of L-amino-acids, and modern nucleic acids solely of D-nucleotides. Many important biological structures cannot be built up from a mixture of L- and D-compounds. A right-handed DNA helix, for example, can be built only with D-nucleotides, or the mirror-image left-handed structure only with L-nucleotides, but a mixture of L- and D-nucleotides would create a completely different structure or more likely no regular structure at all. The same is true of regular protein structures, and it is therefore both convenient, and also probably biologically necessary, to have a unique handedness in biological molecules. It is possible

that there is no particular reason why the system of D-nucleotides and L-amino-acids occurs, rather than the equally efficient mirror-image system of L-nucleotides and D-amino-acids, and that the D-nucleotide, L-amino-acid system was established at random.

Spontaneous polymerisation of amino-acids to give short polypeptide chains of random order can occur in a number of ways, but most first require evaporation to concentrate the solution of monomers. Sugars, nitrogenous bases and phosphate groups can also be combined to form nucleotides under prebiotic conditions, and random polymerisation of nucleotides to give short chains has been achieved in the laboratory. Thus, although the processes are crude and inefficient, synthesis under prebiotic conditions of short random polymers resembling proteins and nucleic acids is now a possibility. The major intellectual and experimental difficulties arise when considering the problem of the organisation of biological molecules that is so characteristic of living systems. The proteins and nucleic acids of living organisms are not random in the order of their constituent monomers, but are built up in many different precise orders, each of which is repeated from generation to generation. Replication (exact copying: see section 3.1) of biomolecules must have evolved at some stage, as must the genetic code which translates the order of bases in nucleic acids into an order of amino-acids in proteins. The development of a membrane surrounding self-replicating systems was also essential to prevent dilution or loss of the important intermediates.

Some progress has been made towards a demonstration of

315

replication in a non-enzymatic system. For example, a preformed chain of uracil-containing nucleotides, poly(U), will bind and then facilitate the chemical linking of the complementary adenine-containing nucleotides (A). Similarly, a preformed chain of cytosine-containing nucleotides, poly(C), will facilitate the polymerisation of the complementary guanine-containing nucleotide (G). Encouragingly, such reactions obey the pairing rules of Watson and Crick, so poly(U) has no effect on the polymerisation of G, and poly(C) has no influence on the polymerisation of A. Some striking examples of catalysis of these reactions by metal ions are known. The zinc ion, Zn^{2+}, is a remarkably specific catalyst for the polymerisation of G on poly(C). It permits the synthesis of polymers of G as much as 30 units long, while almost completely rejecting the other nucleotides. The lead ion, Pb^{2+}, is more efficient as a catalyst, but is not nearly so specific.

The ultimate objective of experiments of this kind is to develop a simple non-enzymatic system in which a polynucleotide of arbitrary sequence will facilitate the efficient synthesis of its own complement. This would represent a major step towards understanding how replication of nucleic acids could have evolved on the primitive earth. A number of serious difficulties remain to be overcome, but progress is being made.

Theoretical studies suggest that no great increase in biological complexity could have occurred until the system by which nucleic acids could produce copies of themselves became coupled to using nucleic acids to direct the synthesis of ordered chains of amino-acids (polypeptides). The original relationship may, of course, have been far less precise than that which underlies the modern genetic code (see section 3.1), but some primitive form of coding seems to be a necessity for the evolution of complex life structures. It is unclear whether there was any direct relation of shape or chemistry between the side chains of amino-acids and triplets of nucleic acid bases. Crick has suggested a 'frozen accident' theory, in which the first viable system to occur persisted, and this idea remains a possibility. At the present time, the origin of the genetic code is the most baffling aspect of the problem of the origins of life.

Localisation and membranes

A complex biological system requires some method of holding together its constituent macromolecules. Nowadays the cell membrane performs this function, so it is natural that a close analogue of the cell membrane has often been considered to be a necessary feature in the early development of life. However, this view is not without its difficulties.

All modern cell membranes are equipped with channels and pumps which specifically control the transport of nutrients, waste products, metal ions, and so on (see section 1.4). These specialised channels involve well-defined proteins, molecules that could not have been present at the very beginning of the evolution of life. A completely impermeable membrane, without specific channels, would equally have been a disadvantage,

since it would have excluded the useful components of the prebiotic medium. It seems likely that the macromolecular constituents in the earliest forms of biological organisation were kept together by self-aggregation, perhaps with the help of colloidal organic material or by being adsorbed on to mineral surfaces, in a form that permitted ready access to small soluble organic molecules and salts. The development of a continuous membrane was probably not the first step in the evolution of organisation, but occurred together with the evolution of more complex metabolic pathways to prevent dilution of the intermediates in these reactions.

13.2 PRECAMBRIAN LIFE-FORMS

By the end of the Precambrian era (570 million years ago), the fossil record shows a wide variety of invertebrates, and this implies a considerable period of prior evolutionary history. The potential of older Precambrian sediments for the study of the early development and diversification of organisms was revealed, however, only 20 years ago, with the description of the excellently preserved 1900-million-year-old Gunflint Chert microbiota from Canada. There are now reports of microorganisms from Archaean and Proterozoic sediments, and the oldest record is from Australian sediments of approximately 3500 million years old. The morphological descriptions of these organisms, and the accompanying ideas on their physiology, ecology and contribution to the evolution of the atmosphere, have made Precambrian biology an important research area of modern palaeontology.

Evidence for Precambrian life comes from three major sources. There are first the actual fossilised organisms, which are studied either embedded in cherts (a type of silicified sedimentary rock) or after extraction from sandstones and shales. Secondly, indirect evidence for life is obtained from the fossilised structures called **stromatolites**. The third type of evidence comes from the chemical analysis of organic compounds in Precambrian sediments. These **chemical fossils** include straight-chain hydrocarbons, isoprenoids, and porphyrins, lingering traces of the metabolism of early organisms; sometimes deposits of insoluble organic matter, called kerogen, are formed. Determinations of the ratio of stable carbon isotopes in such organic material have been taken to indicate that it was produced by photosynthetic activity.

Stromatolites are sedimentary structures of conical, columnar or hemispherical shape, and are laminated in vertical section, dark layers rich in organic material alternating with lighter layers where inorganic sediments predominate (Fig. 13.2). In fossiliferous stromatolites, the darker layers contain fossilised remains of unicellular or filamentous organisms. Modern examples are built by living communities of prokaryotic blue-green algae and/or bacteria in intertidal or subtidal zones, and occur in rather restricted habitats, such as the margins of the hypersaline lagoon in Sharks Bay, Western

a

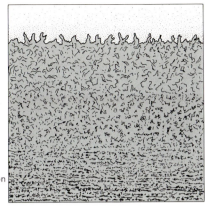

water:
   CaCO₃ precipitation

blue-green algae (aerobic):
   organic production

bacteria:
   organic decomposition

top of solid stromatolite:
   compaction and lithification

b

c

Fig. 13.2. (a) Diagrammatic section through a living stromatolite. (b) Cross-section through Precambrian stromatolite in the Wumishan Formation north of Beijing, People's Republic of China. (c) Cambrian stromatolite columns from Orr Formation, Utah. The upper surfaces are seen surrounded by calcareous sediment.

Australia, where the hostile environment reduces the activities of browsing invertebrates. Mats of microbial organisms, usually filamentous blue-green algae, trap sediment, which then becomes cemented by calcium carbonate precipitated as a result of the metabolism of the algae. The living blue-green algae are capable of limited gliding movements, and move towards the light to form a new surface layer; the dead remains left behind produce the dark layers of the stromatolite.

Archaean communities

Microbiotas in the Archaean (greater than 2500 million years ago) are rare, and have often been viewed with considerable and sometimes justified scepticism. The oldest assemblage comes from North Pole, Western Australia, is dated at 3400 million to 3500 million years ago, and comprises a variety of spheroidal structures. Such morphological simplicity poses major problems of identification and affinity, and indeed it is uncertain whether they are the remains of living organisms. In this case, simple statistical analyses of the range and distribution of sizes of the spheres, comparing the specimens both with living and with later Precambrian populations, suggest that these Australian structures are the remains of spheroidal unicellular organisms. Their biological affinities, whether to spherical blue-green algae or to bacteria, remain speculative. The discovery of non-fossiliferous stromatolites in the same area is further evidence for living organisms. In shape some resemble structures called *Conophyton*, a stromatolitic form typical of the late Precambrian, which was produced by gliding filamentous blue-green algae. However, since similar structures are today produced in hot springs by a green filamentous bacterium, *Chloroflexus*, these stromatolites should not be considered unequivocal evidence for the existence of filamentous blue-green algae some 3400 million years ago.

Similar assemblages of spheroids and stromatolites have been reported from slightly younger sediments in southern Africa. For some of these, such as the Fig Tree Series from South Africa, about 3200 million years old, geochemical studies have yielded porphyrins and isoprenoids consistent with a biological origin, while the carbon-isotope composition of

associated kerogen is indicative of some form of bacterial or blue-green algal photosynthetic activity.

Proterozoic communities

The early Proterozoic is marked by the widespread occurrence of stromatolites, and possibly contains the first direct microfossil evidence for blue-green algae. One of the earliest stromatolitic cherts to contain micro-organisms comes from the Transvaal in South Africa and is dated at about 2300 million years ago; spherical unicells are present, together with filaments in which are larger, darker cells, interpreted as nonmotile cells called akinetes (thick-walled storage cells serving in modern algae as a means of asexual reproduction). These are currently the oldest organisms which show cellular differentiation. Slightly younger stromatolitic cherts from Minnesota (the Pokegama Quartzite at about 2000 million years old) show filaments with occasional larger cells considered to be heterocysts. Heterocysts are the cells of modern blue-green algae which contain the enzyme system for fixation of gaseous nitrogen; oxygen inhibits this enzyme, and the thick walls of the heterocysts slow the diffusion of oxygen into the cells. The presence of apparent heterocysts in these fossil algae thus suggests that there was at least a little free oxygen present at this time.

The appearance of blue-green algae was crucial to the

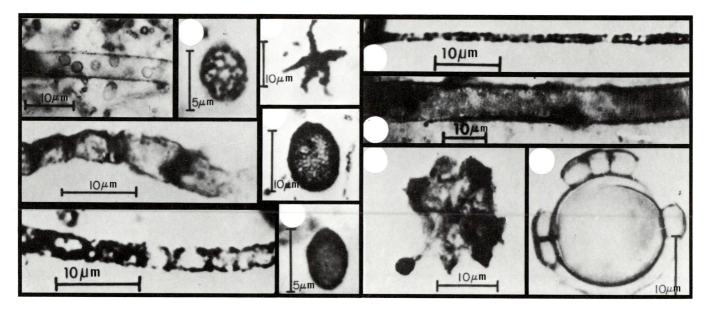

Fig. 13.3. Various Precambrian microfossils from the Gunflint Iron Formation in Canada. They are approximately 2000 million years old.

evolution of the atmosphere because, unlike bacteria, blue-green algae produce oxygen as a product of their photosynthesis. There was a reducing atmosphere in the Archaean, and the earliest organisms were probably anaerobic heterotrophs, growing on the soluble organic molecules accumulated during the previous thousand million years. The first oxygen produced by the earliest blue-green algae would have immediately reacted with reduced minerals and organic matter, and no oxygen would have escaped into the atmosphere. The presence of extensive oxidised iron deposits (banded iron formations) in rocks of the Archaean, occasionally associated with micro-organisms, suggests that oxygen-producing organisms were widespread in shallow water, the dissolved ferrous (Fe(II)) iron acting as an oxygen sink and being precipitated as ferric (Fe(III)) oxide. The appearance of terrestrial formations rich in oxidised iron (red-beds), and the disappearance of the readily oxidised mineral uraninite (pitchblende), at over 2000 million years ago, provides the first evidence for an atmosphere containing gaseous molecular oxygen, indicating that oxygen production was by then exceeding oxygen consumption.

It has been estimated that at the time of the Gunflint microbiota (about 1900 million years ago) the atmospheric oxygen concentration was about 1% of the present level. The Gunflint micro-organisms (Fig. 13.3) flourished in the shallow waters of an iron-precipitating basin, and several communities have been recognised. A marginal stromatolite-building community comprised the filamentous *Gunflintia*, which was probably a blue-green alga, associated with a spherical microbe called *Huroniospora*. Another spherical form, *Leptoteichos*, occurs sporadically throughout the non-stromatolitic chert-carbonate material thought to have been deposited in the quiet waters at the centre of the basin. *Leptoteichos* is interpreted as a planktonic blue-green alga. In some cases this non-stromatolitic material is dominated by a colonial micro-organism called *Eoastrion*, morphologically identical to the manganese-oxidising bacterium *Metallogenium* found today in habitats with very low concentrations of oxygen.

The appearance of free atmospheric oxygen would have had many effects on the evolving life on the earth. As free oxygen would have been highly toxic to the earliest organisms, they must either have retreated to persistently anaerobic environments such as deep-sea muds (which still contain obligately anaerobic bacteria), or have evolved physiological and biochemical mechanisms of tolerance. In addition, as the oxygen levels rose, a layer of ozone (another molecular form of oxygen) appeared in the upper atmosphere, shielding the surface of the earth from ultraviolet radiation and allowing the development of the more complex eukaryotic cell and the invasion of land. Eventually, cells evolved that could respire, actively employing oxygen in their metabolic processes and producing a great deal more energy to power their growth.

Diversification of blue-green algae

The Precambrian era is sometimes described as 'the age of the blue-green algae'. Well-preserved assemblages are recorded throughout the late Proterozoic, but the finest example illustrating the diversity of their organisation is the 800-million- to 900-million-year-old microbiota from Bitter Springs, central Australia. Again the microfossils are associated with stromatolites which developed in shallow warm water near the shore. The dominant organisms were filamentous blue-greens, some of which show remarkable similarities with living genera such as *Oscillatoria*, *Lyngbya* and *Spirulina*. In addition to these, spheroidal forms are found occurring singly, in pairs, or in larger colonies sometimes surrounded by envelopes considered to have been mucilaginous.

Although these micro-organisms appear morphologically more or less identical to modern blue-green algae forms, there is little evidence as to whether they were physiologically similar.

Proterozoic eukaryotic organisms

Somewhat larger spheres, up to 16 micrometres across, also occur in the Bitter Springs complex. These contain conspicuous material thought to represent degraded components of cytoplasm, nuclei or storage bodies, and are interpreted as the remains of eukaryotic unicells related to either red or green algae. Tetrads of such cells (groups of four) are also present, an arrangement usually associated with the meiotic production of spores (see section 1.5). Similar spheroids have been described from microbiotas as old as 1300 million years (the Beck Spring Dolomite) and, as is the case with their more recent counterparts, the eukaryotic nature postulated for them has been queried and much debated. There are, however, other lines of evidence which suggest that the origin of the nucleated cell, one of the most fundamental events in evolution, had occurred well before the time of the Bitter Springs assemblage.

All the organisms described above are present in hard cherts, and maceration of softer Precambrian shales has revealed different sorts of organisms. Common in late Proterozoic shales, particularly from the USSR, are spheroidal structures named acritarchs, which are 10 to 50 micrometres in diameter, with acid-resistant and occasionally ornamented walls. Their relationship to other organisms is unclear, but they are believed to be the reproductive stages or resistant spores or cysts of marine planktonic eukaryotic algae. Similar fossils from rocks from after the Precambrian era can sometimes be assigned to ornamented eukaryotic algae (dinoflagellates or prasinophyceans). Acritarchs of simple morphology have recently been found in the Roper Group of Australia at 1300 million years ago, further evidence for eukaryotic cells at this time in the Proterozoic.

The Beck Spring Dolomite also contains sparingly branched filaments in which occasional cross-walls mark off cells of larger diameter. These filaments are called *Palaeosiphonella*, and are again considered eukaryotic organisms allied either to green or to yellow-brown algae. Less impressive are the coalified ribbon-like films in shales from 1300 million years ago from Montana, which on the basis of their size (up to 2 millimetres in diameter) and regular shape are believed to have been macroscopic algae. Even older (from the McArthur Group in Australia at 1600 million years ago) are microscopic sheets, showing some indications of differentiation into various types of cell and bearing a superficial resemblance to cellular slime moulds. At the same locality occur small budding cells similar to modern yeasts. Further evidence for Precambrian fungi comes from the Bitter Springs assemblage, where there are extensive mycelium-like webs of unbranched tubular filaments, called *Eumycetopsis*, which have tentatively been related to the aquatic phycomycetes.

Collectively these various pieces of evidence suggest that the eukaryotic cell originated at least 1300 million years ago. This implies the existence at that time of an oxygen-containing atmosphere, as the vast majority of living eukaryotes are aerobic, requiring molecular oxygen for their respiration. It also implies that a layer of ozone had developed in the atmosphere and was screening the surface of the earth from ultraviolet radiation, since eukaryotes are unable to survive high doses of this. Bacteria and blue-green algae are much more tolerant than eukaryotes to short-wave radiation, as they possess effective mechanisms for the repair of their DNA, as well as systems such as pigments or mucilaginous sheaths for absorbing the ultraviolet radiation harmlessly. It seems likely that these protective measures appeared in the Archaean when oxygen was absent and prokaryotes flourished in less shielded subtidal or intertidal areas.

Studies on living organisms suggest that the earliest single-celled eukaryotes reproduced asexually by mitosis (see section 1.5). The point of appearance of meiosis, and hence the potential for eukaryotic sexuality, is problematical. Suggestive tetrahedral arrangements of cells (tetrads) are recorded from the Bitter Springs assemblage at 900 million years ago. The development of a sexual life-cycle would have led to a marked increase in diversity and rate of evolution, and is believed to have been essential for the emergence of multicellular and macroscopic organisms.

13.3 EVOLUTION OF MARINE INVERTEBRATES AND PLANTS

Precambrian protozoans and metazoans

The record of Precambrian animals is far shorter than is that of Precambrian micro-organisms, but it does show that a variety of soft-bodied forms had appeared before the end of that era. The earliest are from the Chuar Group of the Grand Canyon, at 750 million years ago, and are called chitinozoans. These tear-shaped and flask-shaped structures are probably resting cysts of marine planktonic protozoans (single-celled eukaryotic organisms), probably heterotrophs feeding on the phytoplankton, although it has also been suggested that they were the eggs or egg-cases of early multicellular invertebrates. The earliest evidence for benthic (bottom-living) metazoans (multicellular eukaryotes) comes from 700-million-year-old trace fossils, the tracks, burrows and other similar evidence of the activities of multicellular animals (see Fig. 12.3). Horizontal and vertical burrows suggest that the soft-bodied organisms which constructed them had already evolved a hydrostatic skeleton and were probably at the 'coelomate' level of organisation (see pages 73–4).

The 600-million- to 700-million-year-old Ediacara fauna from South Australia contains far more impressive evidence for metazoans. This is an assemblage of soft-bodied organisms of relatively simple body organisation, and contains representatives from several phyla (Fig. 13.4). Coelenterates include numerous jelly-fish (such as *Cyclomedusa* and *Mawsonia*), and soft corals called sea-pens with elongate feather-shaped bodies

Fig. 13.4. Reconstruction of Ediacara fauna with sea-pens,
jelly-fish and segmented worms.

(*Rangea* and *Pteridinium*). Three species of segmented worms,
which were possibly annelids, have been described in the
genera *Dickinsonia* and *Spriggina*, together with further diverse
forms of uncertain affinity which some authors assign to
arthropods or even echinoderms. Studies on the respiratory
system of living annelids indicate that such organisms can live
in oxygen concentrations as low as 6% of present atmospheric
levels, a figure which has been independently suggested for the
atmosphere at the end of the Precambrian. Ediacaran-type
faunas have also been recorded from late Precambrian strata in
Europe, USSR, North America and Africa. All the animals lack
hard skeletons, the development of which was the next major
evolutionary innovation.

The appearance of hard-bodied invertebrates

Most of the known groups of invertebrates appeared during
the Cambrian and Ordovician periods of the early Palaeozoic,
between 590 million and 438 million years ago. This radiation
may have been triggered by a significant improvement in
climate at this time, accompanied by a rise in sea-level due to
melting of the glaciers which had covered much of the world in
the late Precambrian. By the end of the Palaeozoic, however,
248 million years ago, many of the products of this initial
radiation had become extinct.

The end of the Precambrian is characterised by a great
increase in the diversity and complexity of trace fossils. Then
follows a sudden appearance of fossil shells, found in shallow
marine deposits, and these show all the variety of invertebrate
body-plans known today. The hard parts of an organism
fossilise much more readily than do soft tissues, and the
Precambrian–Cambrian boundary is effectively defined by the
appearance of abundant fossil shells. Although there was thus a
moderate diversity of soft-bodied Precambrian invertebrates,
there is no evidence for a previous long Precambrian history of
soft-bodied forms of most of the hard-bodied animals that
appeared in the early Palaeozoic. Why hard parts appeared in
so many animals at this time is also unclear. A change in the
chemistry of the atmosphere or of the ocean to favour the
secretion of the components of mineralised skeletons, such as
silica or calcium carbonate, has been postulated, but there is
little geochemical evidence for this. Hard exoskeletons would
however have provided mechanical support and protection
from predators which were probably rare in the previous
Precambrian. The **infaunal** habit (living in the sediment) was
also first seen at this time.

The ability to produce a mineralised skeleton appears to
have been acquired independently in a variety of early
Palaeozoic forms, including protozoans and algae, groups in
which soft-bodied forms had already existed for a long while.
The new groups included sponges, with hard spicules; brachiopods, bivalved filter-feeders, existing today as lantern shells;
many groups of primitive mollusc, including relatives of the
surviving *Nautilus*; conodontophorids, animals known mainly
from their unusual toothed microfossils containing calcium
phosphate as a skeletal material; archaeocyathids, sponge-like
animals now extinct; and various problematical extinct forms.
Later, there appeared larger invertebrates such as ostracods,
small bivalved crustaceans; various echinoderms distantly

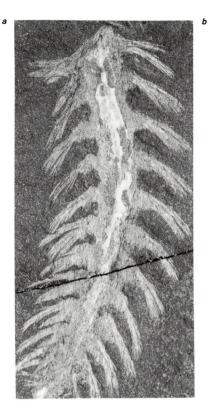

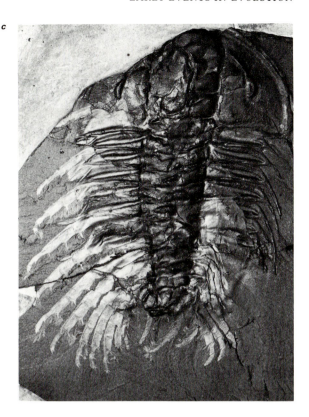

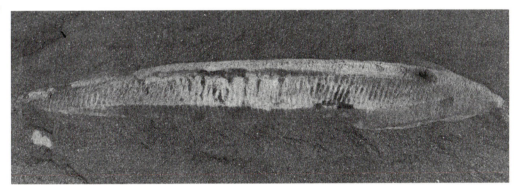

Fig. 13.5. Middle Cambrian fossils from the Burgess Shale, Canada.
(a) Burgessochaeta setigera, *a polychaete about 3 centimetres in length.*
(b) Sidneyia inexpectans, *about 14 centimetres long.*
(c) A trilobite, Olenoides serratus, *about 6 centimetres long. (d)* Pikaia gracilens, *a chordate, about 4 centimetres long.*

related to modern echinoderms such as star-fish and sea-urchins; and trilobites, the best known of the extinct invertebrates. Trilobites were a diverse and successful marine group of arthropods, which are the hard-bodied, jointed-legged invertebrates including modern insects, spiders and crustaceans. Trilobites persisted until the end of the Palaeozoic, and it is not known why they became extinct then. They bore a general resemblance to large woodlice, but showed considerable diversity of body size and form, which implies a similar but unknown diversity of habitat and lifestyle.

Early Palaeozoic faunas

Typical Cambrian faunas are dominated by shelled forms, especially trilobites. In certain exceptional faunas, however, such as the Burgess Shale fauna from Canada, where softer-bodied organisms are also preserved, forms such as worms and unmineralised arthropods greatly outnumber the mineralised fossils present (Fig. 13.5). This makes it obvious that our knowledge of fossil faunas (and floras) is usually biased

towards the types of animals and plants that are preserved easily. The Cambrian faunas are surprisingly diverse and contain a larger diversity of phyla, representing different basic body-plans, than have occurred either before or since. These include many short-lived groups, however, and the familiar present-day types of marine invertebrates are relatively rare.

The very rapid diversification of Cambrian invertebrates into these new phyla, and into many classes within each phylum, relates to the invasion of the many new ecological niches which became available. Deposit-feeders, suspension-feeders and grazers are all present, together with scavengers and predators. Many of the attempts at each of these modes of life were relatively inefficient, and became extinct in competition with more efficient forms.

At the end of the Cambrian there was a large extinction, involving all the archaeocyathids and certain lineages of brachiopods, molluscs and trilobites. Except for the appearance of the bryozoans, small colonial mat-forming animals related to brachiopods and still found today, the new radiation of shelled fossils in the Lower Ordovician represents a re-radiation of the

Fig. 13.6. Several individuals of the Early Jurassic crinoid Pentacrinus, *from Lyme Regis, Dorset, showing the main stalk and delicately branched arms.*

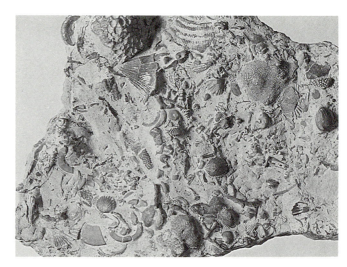

Fig. 13.7. A typical Late Silurian reefal limestone from Much Wenlock, Shropshire, showing fragmentory remains of various brachiopods, bryozoan colonies, colonial corals, rare gastropods, and crinoid plates.

surviving phyla, rather than the evolution of new phyla as had happened in the early Cambrian. Most important among the surviving groups were the brachiopods, which became the dominant benthic shelled forms for the rest of the Palaeozoic. Various molluscan groups appeared at this time, and these probably remained the major predators until the dominance of jawed fishes in the Devonian. These molluscs included the bivalves and cephalopods. Many of the cephalopods were shelled nautiloids, which survive today only as the pearly nautilus. Other important groups were corals, stalked crinoid echinoderms (Fig. 13.6), and planktonic animals such as the extinct graptolites. Trilobites were less important in the Ordovician than in the Cambrian, but were still diverse in deeper water.

The diversifications occurring during the late Cambrian and Ordovician produced more specialised forms than did the earlier evolution during the late Precambrian and early Cambrian. The groups that initially appeared filled more general ecological roles, having broad feeding and niche requirements, and colonised largely unoccupied habitats. Only in the late Cambrian and Ordovician did species with narrow individual requirements appear, but these were often able to replace their less-efficient predecessors.

At the end of the Ordovician there was another wave of extinction, with the disappearance of over half of the in-vertebrate fauna, although no major groups were completely extinguished. These extinctions were probably caused by a worldwide lowering of sea-levels due to glaciation in the southern hemisphere, and consequent drying out of shallow seas over the continental shelves, and were the most dramatic extinctions within the Palaeozoic. With the exception of terrestrial forms like insects and spiders, no major groups of invertebrates evolved after the Ordovician, and relatively few major groups became extinct.

Later Palaeozoic faunas

After the extinctions at the end of the Ordovician there was a rapid recovery of the invertebrate faunas in the Silurian, following a rise in sea-levels and the re-establishment of the shallow and productive continental-shelf seas. The fauna was basically similar to that in the Ordovician, but was more diverse, especially in terms of brachiopods which now comprised up to 80% of the fauna. Tropical reefs were common, formed not only by corals but also by stromatoporoids (an extinct group that were probably calcareous sponges), algae and bryozoans (see Fig. 13.7). Later Palaeozoic faunas are all of this basic pattern, which remained stable for 200 million years until the end of the era.

The major changes in the sea during this period were the appearance of coiled cephalopods called ammonoids, and of fish as the predominant carnivores. Following a major episode of extinction at the end of the Permian, involving most of the hitherto dominant groups of marine invertebrates, communities of essentially modern aspect were established in the Mesozoic.

Aquatic plants in the early Palaeozoic

The most important early Palaeozoic plants were calcareous algae. Some coalified compressions occur, presumably of soft-bodied sea-weeds, but these are impossible to relate to any major group as they lack details of anatomy, colour or reproductive stages. A large number of the calcareous forms are associated with reefs, but are not themselves the principal rock-

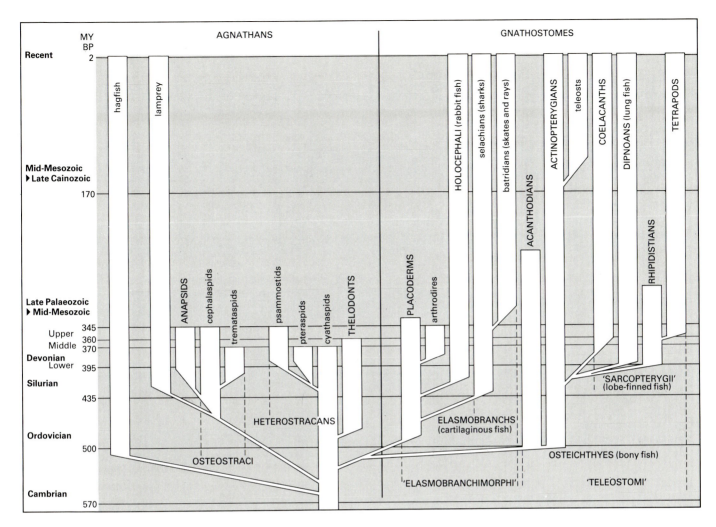

Fig. 13.8. Interrelationships of fish and distribution in time.

builders. The Cambrian reefs were mainly built by archaeo-cyathids, and together with the surrounding sediment these were frequently encrusted by small calcareous algae such as *Epiphyton* and *Frutexites*. The same algae occur on early Ordovician reefs, where the dominant rock-builder was *Calathium*. Far larger calcified forms are prominent members of later Ordovician and Silurian reefs formed by stromatoporoids associated with suspension-feeding bryozoans and tabulate corals (Fig. 13.7). The calcareous algae and filamentous blue-green algae could not colonise loose substrates, and attached themselves to hard skeletons as the reef developed. Good examples of this type of reef from the Ordovician are found in the USA, from the Silurian in the Welsh Borderland and Gotland (Sweden), and from the Devonian in Belgium and Germany, and they persisted until the early Carboniferous. Green algae were the commonest calcareous algae of open continental-shelf environments, where they formed gravels.

The fossilised reproductive structures of the green charophyte algae first appear in sediments in the late Silurian, and occurred in such profusion in the Devonian that they formed limy clays called 'Chara marls'. The fossil record of the charophyte green algae is of particular interest, as a survey of numerous characteristics of living forms indicates that, among all the families of green algae, these have most in common with terrestrial green plants.

13.4 EVOLUTION OF MARINE VERTEBRATES: THE FISH

Sites yielding the first fossil vertebrates are from the early Palaeozoic and are found in western Europe and North America. These areas were then part of the supercontinent Laurasia, situated over the equator, and the presence of coral reefs in these deposits suggests shallow warm tropical seas over continental shelves subject to little seasonal fluctuation. Later vertebrates are found in freshwater as well as in the sea.

Vertebrate ancestry is to be found among a group of marine invertebrates, sluggish filter-feeders without limbs or an obvious head, and including the tunicates (sea-squirts). The larva of a sea-squirt is motile and resembles a tadpole; it possesses many features seen in early vertebrates and in all vertebrate embryos. It has a dorsal rod, the notochord, which is the embryonic precursor of the backbone in higher vertebrates, and which supports the strong muscular tail used for swimming. It also has gill slits in the throat region which are used for filtering particulate food from the water, and which are similar in appearance to the gills of fish or the gill slits of the embryos of land vertebrates. When the tunicate larva becomes an adult it loses many of these vertebrate features, but if such an animal should become sexually mature while still a larva, a process

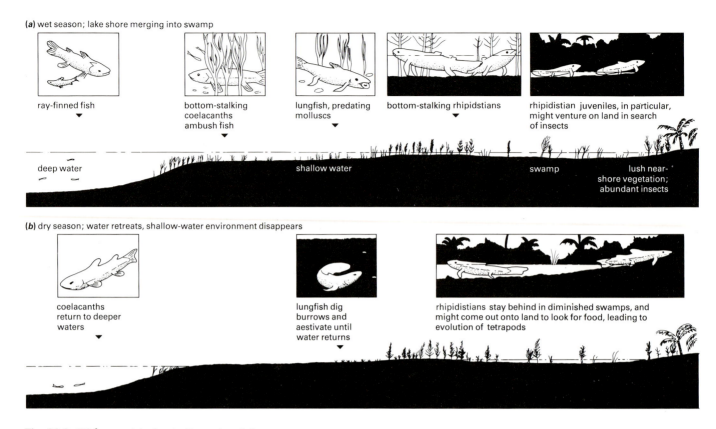

(a) wet season; lake shore merging into swamp

ray-finned fish ▼

bottom-stalking coelacanths ambush fish

lungfish, predating molluscs ▼

bottom-stalking rhipidstians ▼

rhipidistian juveniles, in particular, might venture on land in search of insects

deep water

shallow water

swamp

lush near-shore vegetation; abundant insects

(b) dry season; water retreats, shallow-water environment disappears

coelacanths return to deeper waters ▼

lungfish dig burrows and aestivate until water returns ▼

rhipidistians stay behind in diminished swamps, and might come out onto land to look for food, leading to evolution of tetrapods

Fig. 13.9. Niche partitioning in Devonian fish.

called **neotony** and which actually occurs in one species of tunicate, a new type of animal could result with no trace of the original adult phase. It is believed that this is how the first vertebrates arose.

Early vertebrates: the jawless fish

The earliest vertebrate remains are 500 million years old, from the late Cambrian. The Burgess shale formations from the mid-Cambrian contain the first creatures with recognisable vertebrate affinities: these come from the phyla Hemichordata and Chordata. The first true vertebrates are the early jawless fishes, the agnathans, fragments of which are known from the late Cambrian, but fossil fish remain rare until the late Silurian. In the Devonian the diversity of fossil fish reaches a peak, with the appearance and rapid radiation of many new forms. Fish faunas of today are rich in various adaptive types, but were more diverse taxonomically in the Devonian (Fig. 13.8).

From early on in vertebrate evolution there was a major division into two groups which used different methods for catching food, although both differed from the ancestral protovertebrates in being active predators rather than filter-feeders. The **agnathans** (jawless fish), probably specialised on soft-bodied prey, and the arches of cartilage supporting their gills were modified into a complex structure called a branchial basket. The larvae of these agnathans may have still been filter-feeders. In the other group, the **gnathostomes** (jawed fish), the front gill arches were modified into jaws, forming a large mouth bearing teeth. The gnathostomes were probably specialists on

hard-bodied or shelled invertebrates.

The agnathans were the more primitive fish, and appear earlier in the fossil record, but the adaptive radiation of fish in the Devonian included both gnathostomes and agnathans, suggesting that there were sufficient niches available for both types of feeding strategies. The decline of the agnathans after the early Devonian, and their virtual disappearance at the end of the Palaeozoic, was probably the result of a change in the ecology or anatomy of the animals on which they fed, or of competition from predatory invertebrates, rather than being due to direct competition with jawed fish. Living agnathans, the hagfish and the lamprey (Fig. 13.10), are highly specialised for scavenging or semi-paracitic ways of life, and bear little resemblance to the successful Devonian forms.

Bone was an early feature of vertebrates, but initially was found only in the external armour plates of the head and trunk region, characteristic of the Palaeozoic agnathans, and the internal skeleton was formed of cartilage. In some ancient agnathans these plates may have supported electrical sensing organs. There were three main lineages of Palaeozoic agnathans important in the Silurian and Devonian. The **heterostracan** lineage appeared earliest in the fossil record, was the most

a

b

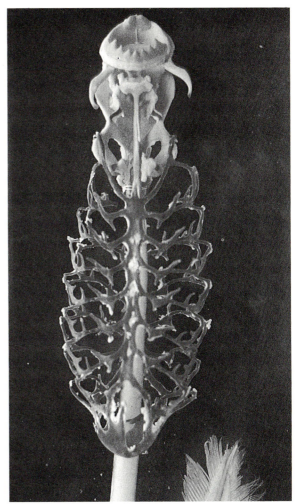

Fig. 13.10. (a–b) Agnathan (jawless) fish. (a) Hagfish, Eptatretus stoutii; *hagfish are scavengers feeding on dead and dying invertebrates and fish.* (b) Lamprey skeleton showing the skull and branchial basket; *fully formed vertebrae do not develop.* (c) A jawed fish, the Australian lungfish (Neoceratodus forsteri). *Lungfish live in freshwater and have, as their name suggests, functional lungs; their relationships to other fish groups and to tetrapods have long been matters for speculation.*

c

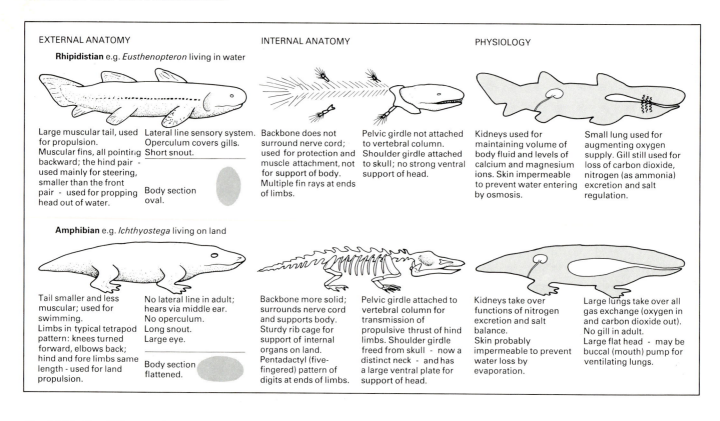

EXTERNAL ANATOMY | INTERNAL ANATOMY | PHYSIOLOGY

Rhipidistian e.g. *Eusthenopteron* living in water

Large muscular tail, used for propulsion. Muscular fins, all pointing backward; the hind pair - used mainly for steering, smaller than the front pair - used for propping head out of water.

Lateral line sensory system. Operculum covers gills. Short snout.

Body section oval.

Backbone does not surround nerve cord; used for protection and muscle attachment, not for support of body. Multiple fin rays at ends of limbs.

Pelvic girdle not attached to vertebral column. Shoulder girdle attached to skull; no strong ventral support of head.

Kidneys used for maintaining volume of body fluid and levels of calcium and magnesium ions. Skin impermeable to prevent water entering by osmosis.

Small lung used for augmenting oxygen supply. Gill still used for loss of carbon dioxide, nitrogen (as ammonia) excretion and salt regulation.

Amphibian e.g. *Ichthyostega* living on land

Tail smaller and less muscular; used for swimming. Limbs in typical tetrapod pattern: knees turned forward, elbows back; hind and fore limbs same length - used for land propulsion.

No lateral line in adult; hears via middle ear. No operculum. Long snout. Large eye.

Body section flattened.

Backbone more solid; surrounds nerve cord and supports body. Sturdy rib cage for support of internal organs on land. Pentadactyl (five-fingered) pattern of digits at ends of limbs.

Pelvic girdle attached to vertebral column for transmission of propulsive thrust of hind limbs. Shoulder girdle freed from skull - now a distinct neck - and has a large ventral plate for support of head.

Kidneys take over functions of nitrogen excretion and salt balance. Skin probably impermeable to prevent water loss by evaporation.

Large lungs take over all gas exchange (oxygen in and carbon dioxide out). No gill in adult. Large flat head - may be buccal (mouth) pump for ventilating lungs.

Fig. 13.11. *Key differences between lobe-finned fishes and amphibians.*

diverse and successful group, and may have given rise to the jawed fish. The heterostracans comprised both flattened bottom-dwelling forms and active middle-water fish. The other two agnathan lineages both possessed a bizarre distortion of the front of the head. The armoured **osteostracans** also contained bottom-dwelling flattened forms and middle-water forms, while the **anaspids**, confined to freshwater deposits from the late Silurian, resembled modern fish most in having a fine covering of scales rather than bony plates, and a small terminal mouth.

The lamprey shares the specialised distortion of the head with these agnathans, and probably has its ancestry among the anaspids. The first fossil lamprey is found in the Carboniferous, and is essentially the same as living forms. In contrast, the hagfish appears to be a much more primitive animal, and may be a very early offshoot from the vertebrate lineage.

Jawed fish

The jawed vertebrates first appeared in the late Silurian. They probably evolved in freshwater, not in the sea, as all living representatives have body fluids that are more dilute than sea-water. In those fish which have returned to the sea, a number of mechanisms have evolved for preventing or circumventing loss of water from the body by osmosis.

Gnathostomes (the jawed fish) differ from the agnathans not only in the possession of jaws, but also in that they have developed mobile paired fins and three semicircular canals in the middle ear, which suggests a greater ability to manoeuvre in three dimensions to catch prey. Living gnathostomes can be divided into two distinct types: **cartilaginous fish** (the Chondrichthyes) and **bony fish** (the Osteichthyes). These

differ in that only the bony fish have true bone in their internal skeleton; this replaces the initial cartilaginous skeleton during development. Various other aspects of their biology are also different. The cartilaginous fish (sharks, rays and rabbit-fish) are almost entirely marine, have no lung or swim bladder, and reproduce by means of internal fertilisation, producing a small number of large, yolky eggs. In contrast, the bony fish all have a lung or swim bladder (which is probably a modified lung), and are found in both marine waters and freshwater, and reproduce by external fertilisation, producing a large number of small eggs.

The earliest jawed fish, the extinct **placoderms** and **acanthodians**, probably occupied different niches. Lower Devonian acanthodians were apparently middle-water fish, and had stout spines on their fins which may have helped the fish cut through the water or may have been a means of defence. Later acanthodians were shaped more like eels, lacked teeth and developed specialised structures on the gills, called gill rakers, suggesting a filter-feeding habit. Such forms survived until the early Permian. Placoderms were mostly heavily armoured, flattened, apparently bottom-living forms, with ventral mouths and crushing tooth-plates. They flourished during the Devonian, and also developed in the middle and late Devonian into large mid-water predaceous forms up to 2 metres in length called **arthrodires.**

When the cartilaginous fish appeared in the late Devonian they rapidly radiated to replace the placoderms, the sharks taking the actively predaceous niche of the arthrodires, and the rabbit-fish the niche of the other placoderms as bottom-dwelling scavengers and mollusc-eaters. The rabbit-fish reached a peak of diversity in the late Palaeozoic, and were largely replaced during the Mesozoic by the skates and rays.

The early bony fish

Bony fish first appeared in the early Devonian. The early forms are divisible into two lineages: **ray-finned fish** (actinopterygians), and **lobe-finned fish**, including coelacanths, rhipidistians and dipnoans. The ray-finned fish have given rise to the common fish of today, while although lobe-finned fish are now much rarer, it is from this group that tetrapods (amphibia, and thus all land vertebrates) are believed to have evolved. Lobe-finned fish (Fig. 13.11) were found in equal numbers with ray-finned fish in the middle Palaeozoic, although the two types of fish apparently inhabited different environments. On the basis both of the fossil record and of the physiology of nitrogen excretion of the living forms, it has been suggested that lobe-finned fish initially diversified in the sea, with some forms returning to freshwater in the later Devonian, whereas the ray-finned fish diversified in freshwater and remained there throughout the Palaeozoic. The fleshy fin of the lobe-finned fish, with its sturdy internal skeleton, may have been used for walking on the bottom of shallow continental-shelf seas. In contrast, ray-finned limbs appear to be designed for manoeuvrability in fast-flowing rivers or freshwater lakes.

The **dipnoans** survive as modern lungfish, and have always been specialised for bottom-living, eating detritus or crushing molluscs with their large tooth-plates. This specialised dentition is thought to debar them from being ancestors to the tetrapods, despite many similarities between living lungfish and amphibians, such as the divided heart and the double circulation of the blood to the lungs and the body.

The **coelacanths** shared with the rhipidistians the specialised feature of a hinge joint in the skull, although this functions differently in each lineage and may therefore have been derived independently. This joint in coelacanths allows prey to be sucked into the mouth, and the coelacanths were probably ambush predators relying on stealth and concealment. Coelacanths survive today in the rare deep-sea fish *Latimeria*.

Rhipidistians were mainly freshwater fish, and their hinge joint appears to have allowed a more powerful bite once the jaws had closed on the prey, suggesting an actively predaceous mode of life. No rhipidistians survived past the Palaeozoic, but details of the internal structure of their limbs and of the roof of their skull suggest that the ancestor of the tetrapods may have been among these fish.

Fish evolution after the Palaeozoic

The taxonomic diversity of fish declined at the end of the Devonian when the extent of the shallow continental-shelf seas was reduced. Virtually all the groups of jawless fish became extinct, as did the placoderms, and the lobe-finned fish were severely reduced in numbers. Throughout the rest of the Palaeozoic and the early Mesozoic, gradual evolution of the ray-finned fish continued in freshwater habitats, and of the sharks in predominantly marine habitats. Little major change occurred until the middle Mesozoic, when the break-up of the giant continent of Pangaea opened up the Atlantic Ocean, and a host of new niches appeared in the marine environment, allowing the rapid evolution and adaptive radiation of ray-finned fish which occurred in the Jurassic. Most of the fish that successfully exploited this new environment were **teleosts**, a group which comprises most of the bony fish alive today. The key feature of their success was the modification of the jaws and the way these are suspended, allowing the evolution of many specialised types of feeding habits.

Further reading

Dickerson, R.E. Chemical evolution and the origin of life. *Scientific American*, 1978, **239** (3), 62–78.

Eigen, M., Gardiner, W., Schuster, P. and Winkler-Oswatitsch, R. The origin of genetic information. *Scientific American*, 1981, **244** (4), 88–118.

Miller, S.L. and Orgel, L.E. *The origins of life on the earth*. Englewood Cliffs: Prentice-Hall, 1974.

Moy-Thomas, J.A. *Palaeozoic fishes*. (2nd edn, revised by R.S. Miles) New York: Chapman & Hall, 1971.

Schopf, J.W. The evolution of the earliest cells. *Scientific American*, 1978, **239** (3), 84–102.

14 Origin and Development of the Land Flora and Fauna

14.1 THE PALAEOZOIC ERA

The appearance of plants on land

The earliest direct evidence for vegetation on land comes from the fossils of vascular plants from the late Silurian. However, the blue-green algae which flourished in the harsh intertidal environments of the Precambrian would probably have colonised all but the driest of land surfaces in the early Palaeozoic, contributing to the formation of the earliest soils. Modern terrestrial vegetation includes representatives from various groups of algae, as well as **bryophytes** (liverworts and mosses) and **tracheophytes** (all the vascular plants, including club-mosses, horsetails, ferns, conifers, ginkgos, cycads and mono-cotyledonous and dicotyledonous flowering plants: see section 2.2). Of these, only the vascular plants dominate the land; they are able to control the loss of water from their surfaces, thus remaining hydrated and able to photosynthesise even when water is in short supply.

The anatomical modifications that this has required are the development of conducting (**vascular**) tissue called xylem for transport of water up the plant, with thickened cell walls giving strength and rigidity to the plant body; and an impermeable **cuticle** to prevent desiccation but containing small pores (**stomata**), the opening and closing of which allow control of gas exchange (see section 2.2). Both xylem and cuticle require the synthesis of secondary metabolites, particularly lignin and cutin, and fortunately these complex polymers fossilise reasonably readily and persist in compression fossils when all other tissues have become coal. The preserved cuticle then provides information on the epidermis, and the xylem supplies direct evidence of the vascular nature of the fossil plant.

The ancestors of the earliest vascular plants were probably multicellular green algae of the same group as the modern *Chara*, and lived in shallow freshwater pools or lakes subject to periodic drying. The selection pressure to resist desiccation may well have resulted in the evolution of a cuticle and of thick-walled spores to facilitate dispersal between temporary bodies of water and survival through completely dry periods. In living and fossil bryophytes and vascular plants, the walls of the asexual spores and pollen grains are impregnated with sporopollenin, a polymer which prevents water loss and which filters out dangerous ultraviolet radiation. Development of the ability to synthesise sporopollenin must have been important for the evolution of land plants. Wind-dispersed spores require to be released into turbulent air, which in turn needs a plant body (main stem, or axis) some centimetres high and sufficiently robust to support the spore-producing organ, the **sporangium**, with its protective wall. The evolution of the ability to synthesise the hydrophobic polymer lignin would have allowed the development of supporting tissues in this larger plant, and a xylem system

conducting water to the tip.

Such a sequence of events is hypothetical as there is no direct **macrofossil** evidence for the ancestors of vascular plants, that is, no surviving fossils of large parts of the plant body. There is, however, a steadily accumulating body of **microfossil** evidence, in the form of spores and small pieces of cuticle lacking stomata, which suggests that the land was colonised in early Silurian and even Ordovician times. There is as yet no information on the identity of the parent plants, their level of organisation or indeed their relevance to the subsequent evolution of vascular plants.

The earliest vascular plants

The earliest example in the present northern hemisphere of a vascular plant with reproductive structures is *Cooksonia* (Fig. 14.1), which is found in late Silurian sediments deposited about 400 million years ago. This genus belongs to the simplest division of vascular plants, now extinct, called the Rhynio-phyta. The fossils are parts of very small plants, just a few centimetres high, with tufts of smooth symmetrically branching axes, each containing a central rod of primitive conducting cells sporadically thickened with lignin and called tracheids. At the tip of each axis was a single spherical or ellipsoidal sporangium containing small smooth-walled spores, each bearing a trilete or 'Y'-shaped mark indicating that they were produced in a tetrahedral group of four, and so presumably by meiosis (see section 1.5), and confirming the plant as a **sporophyte** (the diploid stage of the life-cycle producing haploid spores by meiosis, see page 38). Nothing is known about the **gametophytes** of these early plants (the stage of the life-cycle produced by germination of those haploid spores, and which gives rise by mitosis to structures containing male and female gametes, sperm and egg, which then fuse to give the zygote which grows into the next diploid sporophyte). These early plants, however, definitely contained transport (vascular) tissues, and were the first members of the **pteridophytes** (vascular plants, reproducing by spores not seeds, and showing this alternation of generations between separate gametophyte and sporophyte; see pages 107–9). Similar fossils have been found in older, mid-Silurian sediments (from the Wenlock Series, at 415 million years old) but these are poorly preserved and it cannot be decided whether tracheids were originally present or not.

Some rhyniophytes, such as *Hedeia*, were more advanced in that the elongated terminal sporangia were aggregated. They have recently been discovered, together with a lycopod called *Baragwanathia* originally described from the Lower Devonian of Victoria, Australia, in a new assemblage from late Silurian deposits contemporaneous with the Welsh deposits containing *Cooksonia*. The Lycopodiophyta is a division of plants with members such as the club-mosses, alive today; they were more complicated than other early plants in having distinct roots, and stems with small, spirally arranged leaves. Thus, although

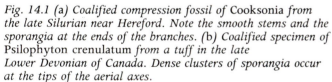

Fig. 14.1 (a) Coalified compression fossil of **Cooksonia** from the late Silurian near Hereford. Note the smooth stems and the sporangia at the ends of the branches. (b) Coalified specimen of Psilophyton crenulatum *from a tuff in the late Lower Devonian of Canada. Dense clusters of sporangia occur at the tips of the aerial axes.*

Wenlock sediments are the oldest yet discovered that contain erect, fertile plants resembling the early pteridophyte *Cooksonia*, the complexity of the slightly younger Australian plants suggests a much longer pre-history for vascular plants, perhaps extending into the early Silurian or even Ordovician.

At the end of the Silurian, assemblages containing *Cooksonia* and other simple rhyniophytes were preserved in marine, nearshore, and occasionally in freshwater river deposits, at a number of localities around the margins of the Old Red Land (Euramerica), a newly-formed land mass straddling the equator and resulting from the closure of the Proto-atlantic Ocean (see section 12.2). As for most fossils of land plants, these had been transported by rivers away from the places where they grew, so their original habitats remain obscure. Those found in brackish or freshwater sediments are often associated with fragments of scorpion-like arthropods called eurypterids.

The early (or Lower) Devonian saw the appearance worldwide of two other types of simple pteridophyte. *Zosterophyllum*, like *Cooksonia*, had smooth axes containing a simple central bundle of tracheids, but its sporangia were attached to the sides of the axis (lateral rather than terminal)

and were aggregated into a compact spike. The best-known examples of *Zosterophyllum* come from the Old Red Land, where it is thought that they lived, together with some rhyniophytes, on the dry shores of mountain lakes or on the banks of rivers running through plains nearer the sea. A period of diversification based on the *Cooksonia* and *Zosterophyllum* types of organisation then followed, together with the first occurrences of a plant called *Psilophyton* (Fig. 14.1). The finding of fossils preserved in various different ways has allowed the description of the internal anatomy of these plants, and this is used, together with the position of their sporangia, in the classification of these early simple vascular plants (excluding the lycopods) into three major groups, the Rhyniophyta, the Zosterophyllophyta and the Trimerophyta.

Psilophyton is the best-known genus of the trimerophytes, and had smooth or spiny stems which either branched equally, or produced a main axis and highly branched laterals. Some of the lateral branches terminated in bunches of elongated sporangia. The trimerophytes, which diversified late in the Lower Devonian, may have been derived from the rhyniophytes and ancestral to many Middle Devonian plants.

The Rhynie Chert

Perhaps the most famous Lower Devonian plant deposit is the Rhynie Chert from Scotland. This deposit is a petrified peat bog preserving the plants in exquisite anatomical detail in the place where they grew and died. The peat species include *Rhynia*, *Horneophyton*, *Nothia* and the pre-lycopod *Asteroxylon*, but the only plant preserved exactly in its growth position is *Rhynia gwynne-vaughanii*. The detail of preservation shows, for example, that the stomata of *Rhynia* were connected to an extensive intercellular system of air spaces, essential for the ventilation of a land plant, and that groundwater was absorbed through unicellular hairs on the horizontal stems.

The plant assemblage itself is interesting for the Lower Devonian in that its members are not recognised or recorded elsewhere on the Old Red Land. Some of the forms also present considerable taxonomic problems, in that several show intermediate characteristics and do not fit easily into existing groups. *Rhynia major*, for example, lacks conventionally thickened tracheids in the central tissue which nevertheless presumably served to conduct water, while *Asteroxylon* appears to be an intermediate between the rhyniophytes and the lycopods, since a vascular supply does not extend to the tips of the leaves, as occurs in modern lycopods. The presence of gametophytes in the chert is still controversial, and well-preserved gamete-producing organs have not yet been illustrated. Representatives of the algae include mats of filamentous blue-green algae, a charophyte green alga called *Palaeonitella*, and filamentous green algae. Wefts of fine, sparingly septate hyphae (see section 2.3), some terminating in vesicles, which occur within degraded tissue of vascular plants, are usually identified as a saprotrophic fungus (*Phycomycetes*), but thick-walled spore-like bodies superficially similar to those of endomycorrhiza (*Endogone*) (see section 10.1) suggest that the fungal hyphae lived in symbiotic association with the vascular plants.

It is impossible to determine how typical the Rhynie Chert flora was of the wetter areas of the Old Red Land. The other Lower Devonian assemblages contain plants with far greater amounts of thick-walled structural tissues, and are thus thought to have lived in places subjected to much drier periods.

Middle and Upper Devonian plants

The rest of the Devonian was a time of progressive innovation, with large numbers of lycopods, **sphenopsids** (a group surviving today as horsetails), early ferns, and a group called the **progymnosperms**, ancestors to conifers and seed-ferns (pteridosperms). The most readily recognisable plants were the lycopods with their small leaves spiralling along each stem. One of the most completely preserved was the herbaceous *Leclercqia* from Middle Devonian sediments. Its branched leaves were five-pointed and bore a ligule (a small, scale-like outgrowth), while the xylem resembled that of the primary xylem of the

huge Carboniferous tree-lycopods called *Lepidodendron*. *Leclercqia* produced only one type of spore, and homospory and the presence of a ligule are characters not found together in any living group, making *Leclercqia* an important 'link' fossil. The majority of Devonian lycopod remains are far more fragmentary, often comprising pieces of leafy stem or bark and lacking any reproductive organs, making identification within the lycopods difficult. However, some of the stems were of large diameter and their bark superficially resembled that of the Carboniferous tree-lycopods, implying that some, such as *Protolepidodendropsis*, were a few metres high, and by the end of the period the group probably included substantial trees, such as *Cyclostigma*.

In contrast, the recognition of sphenopsids and ferns poses considerable problems at least until towards the close of the Devonian. The arrangement of the sporangia-bearing organs of a plant called *Calamophyton* shared some similarities with that of sphenopsids, but on the basis of the anatomy of the xylem, *Calamophyton* is closer to ferns. The earliest unequivocal sphenopsid remains are complex cones from the Upper Devonian. The oldest fern in the modern sense, with large-leaved fronds bearing clustered sporangia underneath, occurred in the Carboniferous. The Progymnospermophyta includes plants reproducing like pteridophytes by producing freely released spores, but with gymnosperm (conifer-like) secondary xylem; these appear intermediate in organisation between the trimerophytes of the late Lower Devonian and the Carboniferous gymnosperms. Excellently preserved stems with secondary xylem, phloem and cork record the activities of lateral meristems, and apart from some differences in the arrangement of primary tissues their organisation is almost identical to that of the conifers which appear later. The older members of the group, such as *Rellimia* (also called *Protopteridium*), were bushy, woody shrubs with crowded branches bearing terminal, relatively unmodified, stem-like leaves. Later members such as *Archaeopteris* were trees with trunks at least a metre in diameter and with crowns of flattened frond-like structures composed of numerous small fan-shaped leaves.

The Devonian also saw changes in the reproductive strategies of the earliest pteridophytes. Lower Devonian plants were homosporous, producing by meiosis only one sort of haploid spore, and each spore giving rise to a separate independent plant, the free-living gametophyte generation (see pages 107–9). *Chaleuria*, a plant of uncertain affinity from the late Lower Devonian of North America, produced spores of two distinct sizes, and this heterosporous condition has been reported from several lines of Devonian pteridophytes, including the progymnosperms. It culminated in the retention of the larger megaspores on the sporophyte, with the smaller microspores being released and blown between plants. The unreleased megaspore developed into a female gametophyte containing the female gamete; one of the male gametes produced by division of the contents of a microspore fused with the female gamete, and the resulting zygote was contained within a seed. Thus the seed habit evolved. The appearance of gymnosperms occured in the late Devonian, when seeds within cup-shaped structures are recorded in an assemblage of 'ferns', lycopods and progymnosperms in the Famennian deposits from the USA.

Plant localities from Devonian sediments, particularly on Gondwanaland, are not numerous, but from the limited data available it appears that the Devonian floras were cosmopolitan. As yet, however, very little is known about their ecology. Differences in composition of two assemblages from the Middle Devonian of New York State, USA, one dominated by progymnosperms and ferns, the other by sphenopsids and lycopods, have tentatively been related to differences in habitats, with the second of these assemblages perhaps occupying a similar niche to the late Carboniferous swamp floras. It is possible, however, to generalise a little on the structure of communities. The acquisition of a lateral meristem, for example, allowed an increase in girth and hence greater height. This would have led to the development of a forest with many different layers of foliage and an increase in the types of habitat available for colonisation by animals. Some of these habitats would have been deeply shaded, and here the heterosporous condition and possession of seeds would have been advantageous, as the food reserves of the female gametophyte tissues in the seed would have allowed the young sporophyte to develop without the need for immediate photosynthesis. The seed habitat would also have allowed the colonisation of much drier environments.

Colonisation of land by animals

Terrestrial invertebrates

Fossil terrestrial invertebrates are unknown before the Silurian, perhaps because colonisation of the land was prevented by the lack of abundant food or by the more intense levels of ultraviolet radiation present before a protective layer of ozone had developed in the early atmosphere, or perhaps more simply because these invertebrates lacked fossilisable mineralised skeletons and did not inhabit regions of rapid sedimentation. The slow invasion of algae and lichens into humid lowland areas in the early Palaeozoic was probably accompanied by minute herbivorous and scavenging invertebrates equivalent to those of modern soil faunas. Larger forms may initially have made only nocturnal visits onto land to forage for vegetable detritus and soft-bodied prey, but later invasion of the land, facilitated by accumulated plant debris providing food and shelter from desiccation and radiation, probably occurred by several routes, such as directly from the sea over the shore, or more gradually via estuaries, lakes and streams.

The earliest recognised terrestrial macrofossils of invertebrates are several poorly preserved specimens of herbivorous millipedes from the early Silurian; they were probably not the only group present, but were preferentially preserved due to their calcified skin layers and burrowing habits. The Devonian record is also sparse, and contains sporadic millipedes and trace fossils, tracks, trails and burrows which cannot easily be assigned to specific groups, but it also contains three exceptional faunas dominated by arthropods.

The Rhynie Chert from the early Devonian in Scotland represents a petrified swamp containing small arthropods exquisitely preserved between the plant stems and within sporangia. These include a springtail (a primitive wingless jumping insect), several small mites, the first spider and numerous larger extinct mite-like arachnids called trigonotarbids. The trigonotarbids probably preyed on other arthropods while the insects and mites ate spores, leaf-litter, and micro-organisms or sucked plant sap, as the associated wounded plant stems suggest. The Alken fauna from Germany accumulated in a stagnant, brackish lagoon and contains a variety of amphibious and terrestrial arthropods, including many small eurypterids, now extinct forms resembling scorpions. These had spongy abdominal gills covered by plates, which could have functioned equally well in air or water, and their strong limbs and the contemporary trace fossils suggest they foraged on shore and in marginal vegetation for prey. Also present were xiphosurids (king-crabs), spiders, more trigonotarbids and large millipede-like herbivores called arthropleurids. The recently discovered Middle Devonian Gilboa fauna contains flattened fragments of trigonotarbids, centipede fangs, a spider, a mite and a bristletail, another wingless insect.

Thus the early fossil record of terrestrial invertebrates, although very sparse, indicates that the three dominant groups of land arthropods, **arachnids** (spiders, scorpions and mites), **myriapods** (predatory centipedes and herbivorous millipedes) and **insects** (although these were still flightless) had independently become established on land by the Middle Devonian (see Fig. 14.2). Several other arthropod groups, such as the king-crabs, eurypterids and arthopleurids, also began to colonise the land, but with less success, remaining amphibious or soon becoming extinct.

The appearance of tetrapods

The Devonian, the period of maximum diversity of fishes both in the sea and in freshwater, also marked the time when the first creatures with four limbs (**tetrapods**) evolved from the lobefinned fish and took up at least part of their life-cycle on land. The first amphibian skeletons are known from the late Devonian of Greenland, but other traces of Devonian fossil evidence, such as some tetrapod footprints and fragmentary remains from Australia, hint at a much greater distribution of Devonian amphibians than is currently revealed in the fossil record.

The warm, shallow, oxygen-depleted waters of Devonian inland lakes, surrounded by early plants, are believed to have provided an environment in which certain fish developed many of the essential features which would later be of use in a

Fig. 14.2. Early land arthropods. (a) Arthopleura; this specimen, about 4 centimetres in length, is the most complete known example of an extinct group of myriapod-like herbivores. Late Carboniferous, Montceau-les-Mines, France. (b) Plaster cast of the amphibious eurypterid Mixopterus, showing anterior grasping appendages and posterior swimming limbs. Late Silurian, Norway. (c) Xyloiulus, one of an extinct group of rigid, cylindrical millipedes. Late Carboniferous, UK. (d) Cryptomartus, a member of an extinct group of arachnids. Late Carboniferous, Mazon Creek, Illinois.

a

b

Fig. 14.3. (a) Reconstructions of living Lepidodendron *(left) and* Calamites. *(b) External mould of* Lepidodendron *bark covered in leaf bases, preserved in sandstone from the Upper Carboniferous.*

terrestrial mode of life. Lungs probably enabled the early bony fish to obtain extra oxygen by gulping air, a behaviour seen today in living ray-finned fish in tropical stagnant waters. For shallow-water fish, strong front limbs would have enabled the front end of the body to be lifted to raise the head above the water surface. Use of a kidney, rather than gills, for nitrogen excretion and maintenance of salt balance, may have resulted from the decreased use of the gills in stagnant waters.

Those ray-finned fish that come out on land today, such as the mudskipper, also live in shallow tropical waters, and emerge under conditions of high humidity to search for food. It seems likely that the first tetrapods came out of the water under similar conditions, following the development earlier in the Devonian of terrestrial plants and invertebrates to give a rich unexploited source of food in an environment free of predators. Those animals with the strongest limbs and the best capacity for breathing air would have been the most likely to survive. It is less likely that periods of drought were the driving force for emergence onto land, as was originally thought, with the early amphibians making their way overland to search for remaining pools of water. Living amphibians are found to congregate in the centre of diminishing ponds in times of seasonal dryness, instead of travelling in search of other sources of water.

Carboniferous plants

In the early Carboniferous (about 345 million years ago) the same type of vegetation, named the *Lepidodendropsis* flora, grew all over the world except in Siberia. The commonest fossils are from lycopods, sphenopsids and the foliage of the earliest gymnosperms, and many of the genera are also recorded later in the Carboniferous. The major botanical interest of the Lower Carboniferous lies in the initial large diversification of the earliest seed plants, the **pteridosperms**, a group in which the leaf resembles a fern frond but in which ovules are borne on stem-like organs or on the leaves themselves. Such ovules, each of which contains a single megaspore from which the female gametophyte and egg develop, are fertilised by the male gametes produced from microspores (pollen grains). Numerous petrified ovules, showing a wide range of types of construction, provide insight into the possible stages of evolution of the structures protecting the megaspore before and after fertilisation. The pteridosperms are thought to have lived on flood plains while the coastal swamps and lake margins were colonised by sphenopsids and lycopods, an ecological pattern that was to persist into the Upper Carboniferous.

Later in the Carboniferous there was a marked regional differentiation of world floras into four principal provinces: the Euramerican, Angaran (in Siberia), Gondwanaland and Cathaysian floras. Here the best known of these floras is considered, that of the Euramerican land mass, where the climate was tropical to subtropical, the palaeoequator passing through the present-day Appalachian coal fields and probably extending into those of northern Britain. The Euramerican flora was amazingly uniform both in species and in ecology, extending from Iowa in the USA to the Russian parts of Europe. The climate may have been a little cooler than in the tropics today, since in southern Gondwanaland there was a period of extensive glaciation.

There are two major sources of information on the plants: compression fossils, from shales between the coals, and, far more informative anatomically, the coal balls found at some horizons in bituminous seams. Coal balls are spherical masses of uncompressed peat petrified by calcium carbonate.

Carboniferous pteridophytes

The plants most unlike their modern representatives were members of the Lepidodendrales, tree lycopods up to 35 metres tall. The genus *Lepidodendron* was dominant in the swamps, and when it died and broke up it became the major peat-former (Fig. 14.3). This fragmentation of large plants prior to fossilisation, which also occurred during transport of plant fragments before burial, has meant that different generic names were given to organs or parts of organs of the same plant before fossilised connections between different parts were found in more complete fossils, thus creating considerable nomenclatural confusion. For example, the underground rooting system of *Lepidodendron* is called *Stigmaria*. Often, however, no such helpful connections are found, and the record consists of highly fragmented fossils.

Stigmaria is the commonest fossil of the peat earths or clays immediately below the coal seams and, as such rooting systems are normally in the position in which they grew, this suggests that *Lepidodendron* (Fig. 14.3) was a primary coloniser of open silted environments following flooding. Some of the axes still bear straight, radiating *Stigmaria* rootlets, although more usually there are only circular scars. The great numbers of rootlets in coal balls indicate that the peat was very thoroughly penetrated by the rooting systems of the lepidodendrids. Fragments of bark show the characteristic diamond-shaped leaf cushions bearing leaf scars. Loss of the cortex (the outer layer of the trunk) may remove these patterns, and such fossils are called *Knorria*. The tall unbranched massive trunks, up to 2 metres in diameter, terminated in a crown of branches bearing linear leaves (called *Lepidophyllum* or *Lepidophylloides*), which were shed from the older branches leaving small leaf scars on the leaf cushions. Despite the great dimensions of the trunk, very little secondary wood was developed, the main support coming from a layer of corky tissue in the outer cortex. It has been suggested that trees constructed in this way would have been short-lived and unstable, not remaining vertical for long.

Lepidodendron was heterosporous, producing both mega-spores and microspores by meiosis, and compact cones (known as *Lepidostrobus*) were borne terminally on the leafy twigs. Its microspores (called *Lycospora*) are often the most abundant spores in coals. Sometimes just one megaspore was contained in a sporangium, a condition also seen in some Carboniferous sphenopsids, and this may have been an approach to the seed habit. *Lepidodendron* exhibits many anatomical modifications characteristic of plants growing where the water table is high, such as a well-developed aerating system. Recent studies on the reproductive biology of the lepidodendrids suggest that the megaspores may have been dispersed by water. In some species, the cone producing the megaspores broke into units each containing a single sporangium and the leaf on which it was borne, and these are thought to have floated, being blown over open water by the wind to allow dispersal of the megaspores.

Lycopods similar to living herbaceous (non-woody) forms are difficult to recognise in the Carboniferous, because they are similar to the terminal leafy shoots of the Lepidodendrales. However there are a few records of herbaceous plants resembling modern *Selaginella*, and the profusion in certain coals of spores possibly derived from such plants suggests that they may sometimes have formed a wet heath type of vegetation.

Growth to a large size was not confined to the lycopods. An example from the sphenopsids is *Calamites* (Fig. 14.3), which may have reached a height of 20 metres and the trunk of which contained a far greater amount of secondary wood than did that of the *Lepidodendron*. The name *Calamites* was originally applied to common fossils which are in fact casts of the hollow stem of these plants. Both lateral branches and leaves were borne in whorls. The cones of *Calamites* showed a considerable diversity in form. The majority produced only one kind of spore, to which were attached elongate appendages with special thickenings. Such elaters are also found in the living herbaceous horsetail *Equisetum*. Although some *Calamites* is recorded in the *Lepidodendron* swamp vegetation, it dominated some coals and lake sediments, and may have formed dense stands, like reeds, around lakes and on river deltas. Another group of the sphenopsids (*Sphenophyllum*) formed part of the herbaceous understorey of the swamp forests. Their straggling stems with whorls of wedge-shaped, divided leaves resemble the modern bedstraws (*Galium*). *Calamites* survived into the Permian, but then soon disappeared, the herbaceous forms became extinct in the Triassic, and today the only representative of the sphenopsids is *Equisetum*.

The Carboniferous saw the first records of groups of ferns with living representatives. These are members of the Marattiales, a small group now confined to the tropics. The commonest Carboniferous example was *Psaronius*, a tree-fern about 10 metres high, the trunk of which was encased in rootlets and terminated in a crown of large, highly divided fronds. Some of these leaves carried sporangia on their undersurface. The vascular system of the trunk was highly complex, and the xylem has been compared to a set of interconnecting cylinders of lace. Such trunks are particularly abundant in late Carboniferous coal balls from Illinois, USA, where *Psaronius* is thought to have replaced *Lepidodendron* as the dominant plant of the swamp community, perhaps in response to a lowering of the water table.

Other ferns are less easy to classify. A group called the Coenopteridales were present throughout the Carboniferous. From coal balls, it seems that they were rather insignificant, but persistent, members of the understorey layer in swamp vegetation. Their leaves were rarely the flattened fronds typical of living ferns, comprising instead a three-dimensional branching system of structures superficially resembling stems but considered to be homologous to a single large fern leaf.

Fig. 14.4. Glossopteris *from the Permian of Australia. The leaf is simple with conspicuous indents and reticulate venation.*

Carboniferous gymnosperms

The **pteridosperms** (seed ferns) include more species than any other group of Carboniferous vascular plants, but they were only rarely dominant members of communities. Their fronds provide some of the most beautiful specimens in the whole of the plant fossil record, but reconstructions of entire plants are rare. The pteridosperms were recognised as a new group of gymnosperms at the turn of the century when seeds named *Lagenostoma*, often found associated with fern-like fronds (*Sphenopteris*) and stems (*Lyginopteris*), were shown to bear the same kind of epidermal glands as did these vegetative organs. The growth-habit of the complete plant is still unclear, but the *Lyginopteris* stems were small and it is unlikely that the plant attained any great height. *Callistophyton* was a pteridosperm with a scrambling habit, and *Medullosa* was a tree about 10 metres high. Its stem was buttressed both by long-lasting leaf-bases and by prop roots. The crown of *Medullosa* was composed of massive fern-like fronds; its seeds are quite common in peats and in shales, but are only rarely found attached to the leaves. Some seeds reached a considerable size (3 to 10 centimetres long), and contained a large amount of stored food in the female gametophyte; this would have been a high-energy nutrient source for any animal able to break through the hard outer layer of the seed coat. Trunks of *Medullosa* are found throughout North American coals, gradually increasing in numbers in swamps dominated by lycopods or by the gymnosperms called cordaites.

The assemblages of plants which are preserved in sediments between coal seams provide evidence for types of community outside the swamps. By far the most diverse come from the flood plains of rivers, from where are recorded ferns and pteridosperms, together with some sphenopsids, lycopods and occasional cordaites. The preservation of intact large fronds of pteridosperms suggests that they may have grown in stands on the banks of river bends, and were rapidly buried when these collapsed.

Other groups of gymnosperms which resemble the seed ferns are the cycads and bennettitaleans (cycadeoids), which appeared in the later Carboniferous or the Permian, and rose to prominence in the Mesozoic. Their ancestry probably lies within the pteridosperms.

The earliest members of the conifers belong to a group called the **cordaites**, first recorded from the early Carboniferous. These were trees with typically coniferous timber, having soft wood with considerable secondary activity (see section 2.2), and tufts of spirally arranged strap-shaped leaves, among which male and female cones occasionally hung. A complete tree has never been found, but some may have been up to 40 metres tall. Because of their similarities with conifers, the distribution of their pollen, and their scarcity at certain coal-ball horizons, cordaites are believed to have been colonisers of upland environments away from the major sites of coal and sediment deposition. In the USA, cordaites are found through-

out the Carboniferous and some types, with prop roots as in modern mangroves (see Fig. 7.6), may have replaced *Lepidodendron* as the dominant tree in the swamp vegetation, especially in coastal swamps subject to the influence of the sea. The cordaites became extinct in the Permian, not long after the first conifers appeared.

The earliest direct evidence relating to the vegetation of upland areas comes from Namurian assemblages in the USA. The commonest plants were gymnosperms (pteridosperms, cordaites, and true conifers) and a group of uncertain affinity called the noeggerathialians, but lycopods and ferns were rare. These upland areas may not have been particularly elevated, and are better called hinterland. They probably differed from the coastal lowlands in containing a much wider variety of ecological niches. The drier niches may not necessarily have resulted just from a cooler climate and more seasonal or lower total rainfall, but alternatively could have been due to well-drained soils and high rates of evaporation.

The Permian

Permian vegetation

In the major change in swamp vegetation, just before the end of the Carboniferous, the fern *Psaronius* and the seed fern *Medullosa* became more prominent, the swamp vegetation became more regionally diverse, and *Lepidodendron* and most other tree-lycopods disappeared. Since *Lepidodendron* appears to have been highly adapted to aquatic conditions, the swamps may have been becoming drier. However a similar range of coastal and swamp habitats, but with different assemblages of plants, is found in the Lower Permian of Germany, and so it was not until the mid-Permian that the lowlands of Euramerica became completely arid and the vegetation became dominated by gymnosperms. Of these, the conifers are particularly interesting in that it is possible to trace the stages which led from the extended female cone of the cordaites to the compact modern conifer cone.

During the Permian, conditions in Gondwanaland were improving and a flora dominated by the seed plant *Glossopteris* was rapidly spreading over some of the areas previously covered by ice. *Glossopteris* is best known from its simple entire leaves which occur in such abundance at certain horizons that the plant is considered to have been deciduous and adapted to seasonal cold (Fig. 14.4). Recent studies have indicated that it probably dominated coastal swamps. Ovules were borne on leaf-like structures, and hence *Glossopteris* is considered a pteridosperm even though its wood, which is rarely found, was conifer-like with growth rings. The habit of the whole plant may have been a shrub or small tree, with an irregularly branched crown. Although highly successful in the Permian, *Glossopteris* became extinct in the Triassic.

Amphibians

The adaptive radiation and diversification of the amphibians is not evident in the fossil record until the Carboniferous. All early tetrapods have a pentadactyl (5-digit) limb; there seems to be no particular advantage in having precisely five digits on each limb, which suggests that all the tetrapods diverged from a single ancestor that happened to have this type of limb structure, and thus that they derive from only one lineage of rhipidistian fish. The initial evolution of amphibians was followed by a period of rapid diversification as they took up the potentially available niches for large terrestrial and semiterrestrial animals that had been created by the earlier invasion of plants and invertebrates. Like their Devonian ancestors, all the known Carboniferous amphibians were found around the palaeoequator and were presumably dependent on a warm non-seasonal climate.

From the start of the radiation there were at least two distinct amphibian lineages: the small **lepospondyls**, which remained predominantly aquatic and probably occupied niches similar to those taken today by frogs and salamanders; and the large, diverse and more numerous **labyrinthodonts**, which were, in the main, more terrestrial forms, probably carnivorous or fish-eating, and with a niche similar to that occupied today by crocodilians. The labyrinthodonts showed a range of size similar to that of modern crocodiles and alligators, and are divided into two main lineages which occupied a diversity of terrestrial and semi-aquatic niches during the late Carboniferous and early Permian, one giving rise to the reptiles, and the other possibly containing the ancestors of modern amphibians. One early group in the first lineage consisted of

aquatic eel-like forms, and one specialised group in the second was of small terrestrial frog-like animals that may have given rise to modern frogs. Later Permian forms, such as the seymouriamorphs, greatly resembled reptiles and were for many years thought to be true early reptiles, until their larval forms were discovered to have possessed gills. These animals must thus have had a typically amphibian mode of reproduction in water although earlier members of this lineage may have been ancestral to true reptiles.

The appearance of reptiles

The first reptiles, found in the late Carboniferous, were small, probably insectivorous forms with a body length of about 10 centimetres. Reptiles did not increase in size nor did they form a significant component of the fauna until the early Permian, as the main available niches were semi-aquatic ones in a swampy environment and were colonised by amphibians. When the world climate changed at the end of the Carboniferous, however, the initially rare drier habitat of these early reptiles happened to become the dominant type of terrestrial environment. This explains the success of the early reptiles at the expense of the amphibians in the late Palaeozoic.

The origin of reptiles from the amphibians is obscure. They were for a long while supposed to have evolved from certain labyrinthodonts which resembled early reptiles in body form, but the middle ear of all known labyrinthodonts is too specialised for any of these to have been the actual reptile ancestor. The ancestry of reptiles is very old, and they probably branched off from the amphibians soon after these had evolved from fish.

The main difference between modern reptiles and modern amphibians is in their modes of reproduction. Reptiles and birds produce an egg with a series of membranes surrounding the embryo, outside which there is a leathery or calcareous shell, and the same series of membranes can be seen in the course of mammalian development. The advantage of this type of egg is that it can be laid in a dry environment without desiccation or damage, as the shell provides mechanical support while allowing the exchange of gases and water vapour. The development of this kind of egg was a vital step in the colonisation of drier and upland environments by early tetrapods, as it freed these animals from dependence on water during any part of the life-cycle. Carroll has suggested that the evolutionary steps preceding the initial development of such an egg could only have taken place in very small animals, making this strategy more likely for the early reptiles than for the larger contemporaneous amphibians, but once it was developed larger reptiles could evolve.

Permian faunas

In the early Permian the continents continued their northward drift across the palaeoequator, and fossil sites for this period are found further south than hitherto. **Pelycosaurs**, a group of reptiles that ultimately gave rise to the lineage leading to the mammals, dominated these faunas, radiating to fill fish-eating, carnivorous and herbivorous niches. They were of medium to large body-size, being up to a metre or so in length. Some lineages had large 'sails' on their backs, consisting of skin stretched between the elongated neural arches of the vertebrae, and which may have functioned as primitive thermoregulatory devices, suggesting that these animals lacked internal temperature regulation.

The **diapsid** reptiles, ancestral to the **lepidosaurs** (snakes and lizards) on the one hand, and to the **archosaurs** (dinosaurs, birds and crocodiles) on the other, were present as small-sized insectivorous forms and did not radiate out to fill any of the large-animal niches at this time.

Turtles and tortoises probably evolved from the earliest appearing reptiles, although they do not themselves appear in the fossil record until the Triassic. The marine reptiles of the Mesozoic, the ichthyosaurs and plesiosaurs, may also have been separate lineages from this time period, radiating from early, small, unspecialised reptiles.

Olsen has pointed out that there was a marked difference between the food-chains in these Permo-Carboniferous tetrapod communities and those of later on or of the present day. There were few truly terrestrial herbivores, and the base of the terrestrial food-chain was in aquatic plants, rather than in terrestrial ones. Large carnivorous pelycosaurs, such as *Dimetrodon*, would probably have eaten semi-aquatic herbivorous pelycosaurs and large fish-eating amphibians such as *Eryops*. A similar type of community, with a high proportion of carnivores and an absence of terrestrial herbivores, is seen today in some communities such as the Florida Everglades. The vegetation of the coal forest was largely lycopods, with some gymnosperms, and the herbaceous material was probably unavailable to terrestrial animals by being high in the canopy layer. A heavy canopy, and the numerous leaves of the lycopods, would also have discouraged the growth of smaller plants on the forest floor.

During the Permian the northward-drifting continent of Gondwanaland, carrying the cold-adapted *Glossopteris* flora, encroached on the land mass of Laurasia, and western Asia made contact with Euramerica. This opened up new habitats to the east and the south for any reptile able to adapt to the seasonal cold at latitudes away from the equator. The late Permian saw the radiation into Gondwanaland and western Asia of mammal-like reptiles called **therapsids**, the descendants of the pelycosaurs, and a rich fossil record for this period is found in South Africa and the Soviet Union.

Bakker has claimed that evidence from posture and bone histology of therapsids suggests that they had a mammal-like metabolic rate, and this is supported by their predator:prey ratios, although such quantitative data from fossil assemblages must always be interpreted with caution. The predator:prey ratio is the number of carnivores relative to the number of herbivores in an animal community. Endothermic mammals, whose high metabolic rate means that they must eat 10 times as much food per day as must ectothermic reptiles, have much lower predator:prey ratios in their communities. The therapsids were also distributed in high latitudes in the Permian. They may have been able to generate some body heat internally, and may have possessed a furry coat to cope with the presumed cold winters in Gondwanaland, but they probably did not have as high a metabolic rate as do living mammals.

Permo-Triassic faunas

The Permo-Triassic therapsids were fairly large animals, some carnivorous forms (theriodonts) reaching the size of a large bear, and some herbivorous forms the bulk of a small rhinoceros. The late Permian saw the first radiation of truly terrestrial herbivores, probably associated with the exploitation of the *Glossopteris* flora. At the start of the late Permian the dominant herbivores were all large animals, therapsids and **pareiasaurs** (a reptile unrelated to other major reptile lineages that paralleled other herbivorous reptiles, but which left no descendants). By the end of the Permian, the dominant terrestrial herbivores were the **dicynodonts**, a lineage of therapsids that paralleled herbivorous mammals in many ways, especially in the precise overlapping of the two jaws on closing the mouth, although they had turtle-like horny beaks and they were not directly ancestral to the mammals. Like present-day herbivores, the dicynodonts filled all herbivorous niches from that of rabbit-sized animals to that of rhinoceros-sized animals. The larger forms may have been more like giant ground sloths than like rhinos or hippos in their feeding behaviour.

The collision of Laurasia and Gondwanaland at the end of the Permian resulted in massive extinctions among the marine invertebrates, largely because the area of the coastal margin environment was effectively halved. Land faunas were also affected, but to a much lesser extent, with the main result being a decrease in faunal diversity rather than the complete extinction of many groups.

The Permo-Triassic communities that had a predominance of large herbivores were mainly a feature of the higher latitudes. The equatorial regions were still dominated by large semi-aquatic amphibians, suggesting the continuation there of swampy, non-seasonal environments. While the lowland non-equatorial communities were dominated by large herbivores, a parallel but less extensive community was evolving in environments away from the river margin, where the terrestrial vegetation was consumed by insects, which were then preyed upon by small insectivorous reptiles. Predominant in these communities were the small diapsid reptiles that were ancestral to present-day lizards, and **thecodonts**, the original archosaurs,

a

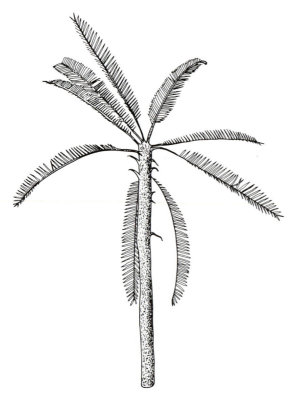

b

Fig. 14.5. (a) Reconstruction of the cycad Leptocycas gracilis. *(b) A living cycad,* Dioon spinulosum, *in Mexico, bearing a single cone. The tree is unusual in being branched: this occurs only in cultivation or when the plant has been damaged.*

ancestral to dinosaurs and crocodiles. In the middle Triassic the thecodonts started to radiate out from these restricted environments and increased in size, and by the end of the Triassic their descendants had taken over all the large tetrapod niches in lowland environments from the mammal-like reptiles and other reptilian types.

14.2 THE MESOZOIC ERA

The Triassic and Jurassic periods

Triassic and Jurassic floras

Triassic floras of Gondwanaland are characterised by seed ferns with leaves split into two parts and small leathery leaflets. These are called the *Dicroidium* floras, and came from historical latitudes that were higher than 30°S and probably cool to warm temperate. Little is known about tropical floras in the early Triassic, and records for the northern hemisphere are also infrequent. The Euramerican province is perhaps best characterised by conifers and the sphenopsid *Schizoneura*.

Later in the Triassic, new and diverse assemblages appeared which, by the mid-Jurassic, had evolved distinctly different floras in different latitudes. These groups were to last until the Cretaceous. In particular, the gymnosperms, including the **cycads**, were more varied and abundant than today. Cycads have survived until the present. The earliest convincing cycad, *Leptocycas*, is recorded from the late Triassic of North America. It had a slender trunk but was up to 1.5 metres high, with a

loose crown of leaves at the top. Divided leaves resembling those of cycads are common in these and younger strata, but many of these leaves came from bennettitalians (cycadeoids), plants from an extinct group allied to the cycads. Leaves of the two groups may be distinguished on the characteristics of their epidermis, particularly from the arrangements of cells in the stomatal apparatus. Although cycad leaves are fairly common in the Mesozoic, stems and reproductive organs are rare, so that reconstructions are based more on modern forms than on fossils: they were probably slender plants, with branched stems and well-spaced leaves (Fig. 14.5). Cycads bore male cones producing microspores (pollen), and female cones producing ovules containing megaspores (that were not released until fertilised by the pollen). The earliest bennettitalians were members of the family Williamsoniaceae, occurring from the Triassic to the Cretaceous. *Williamsonia sewardiana* was a small tree about 2 metres high, with a crown of divided leaves, and male and female cones; the male cones were cup-shaped and bore microsporangia.

The caytonialians were a small but widespread group of Mesozoic seed ferns which are of some importance because they have been considered possible ancestors to the angiosperms (flowering plants). The major type of leaf, called *Sagenopteris*, was a compound leaf with just four leaflets and with the leaf veins arranged in a net; stems with ovules are called *Caytonia*, and the male reproductive structures are *Caytonanthus*.

The Upper Triassic saw the first appearance of many modern **conifer** families, the Taxaceae (yews), Araucariaceae (monkey-puzzle trees), Cupressaceae (cypresses, junipers and *Thuja*) and

Fig. 14.6. Fossil of the bony fish Dapedius *from the Lower Jurassic of Lyme Regis, Dorset.*

Taxodiaceae (swamp cypresses and redwoods). Modern genera are first recorded from the Jurassic. In the Mesozoic the Araucariaceae occurred in both the northern and southern hemispheres, but today the family is confined to the southern hemisphere, while the Cupressaceae and Taxodiaceae are found only in the northern hemisphere.

Another group of gymnosperms, the **ginkgos**, is today represented by just one species, *Ginkgo biloba*, the maidenhair tree, thought to occur naturally in certain areas of China. The earliest member may have been *Trichopitys* from the Lower Permian, and in the Mesozoic the ginkgos were far more widespread than today, particularly in the high northern latitudes in Asia. The fan-shaped leaves characteristic of *Ginkgo* have remained unchanged morphologically since the Mesozoic, although other genera vary in the degree to which the leaf is divided.

Several families of ferns which still have living members appeared in the Mesozoic, including two important tropical families, the Matoniaceae and Dipteridaceae. Leaves from these families, such as those of the genus *Dictyophyllum*, were widespread, suggesting that the ferns formed lush ground-cover in the gymnosperm forests. There were also representatives of the Dicksoniaceae and Osmundaceae, ferns which first appeared in the Permian. The Marattiales declined at the end of the Triassic. The horsetail (sphenopsid) *Equisetum* was already present in the Mesozoic, growing in stands on the edges of Jurassic deltas, and except for its large size must have resembled certain modern aquatic species of *Equisetum*.

Lycopods were only an insignificant component of the Mesozoic floras of the northern hemisphere, but forms related to modern *Selaginella* and *Lycopodium* are recorded from the Jurassic. However a new group, the Pleuromeiales, is found in the Triassic of Eurasia and Gondwanaland, and is considered by many authors to be transitional between the larger Palaeozoic tree lycopods and living plants called quillworts (Isoetales). The Triassic *Pleuromeia* had a trunk about 1 metre high, with four root-bearing lobes at the base of the trunk, and with a terminal crown of elongated strap-shaped leaves. It seems likely that one or more cones were borne in the crown. Recent work in Australia suggests that *Pleuromeia* formed dense thickets around lagoons.

The mid-Jurassic assemblages from Yorkshire are particularly well known. They are characteristic of the area immediately to the north of the Tethys Sea in Europe, Central Asia and possibly America, although comparatively little is known of contemporaneous floras there. The climate was equable and tropical to subtropical. Siberian floras, from 40°N and higher latitudes, contained a much higher proportion of Ginkgoales, but fewer ferns and conifers. To the south, in Gondwanaland, seed-fern floras possessed a number of genera in common with the Europe–Central Asian province, but cycads were rare. These three floral provinces in different latitudes suggest that there was a more marked temperature and climatic gradient between the poles and the equator than earlier in the Mesozoic.

Triassic faunas

Although the climate in the upper latitudes was probably seasonally cold during the Permian and early Triassic, by the middle Triassic most of the global continental mass had drifted outside the polar regions, there was no build-up of ice at the poles, and the global climate was predominantly warm, arid and relatively non-seasonal. Under such conditions endothermic vertebrates, which have a high metabolic rate, requiring a high intake of food and oxygen to produce internal body heat, may be at a disadvantage to ectotherms which gain internal heat by absorbing radiant energy from the sun.

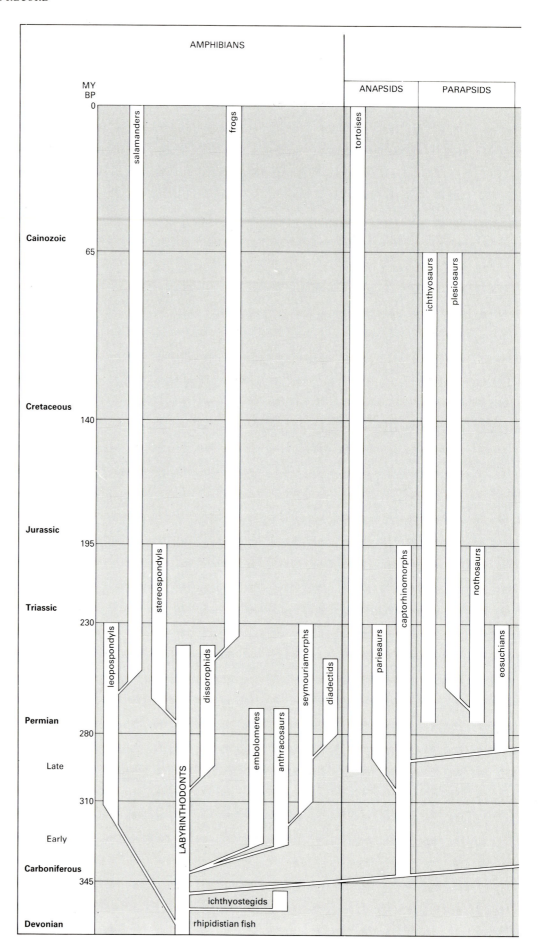

Fig. 14.7. Interrelationships
of tetrapods and distribution
in time.

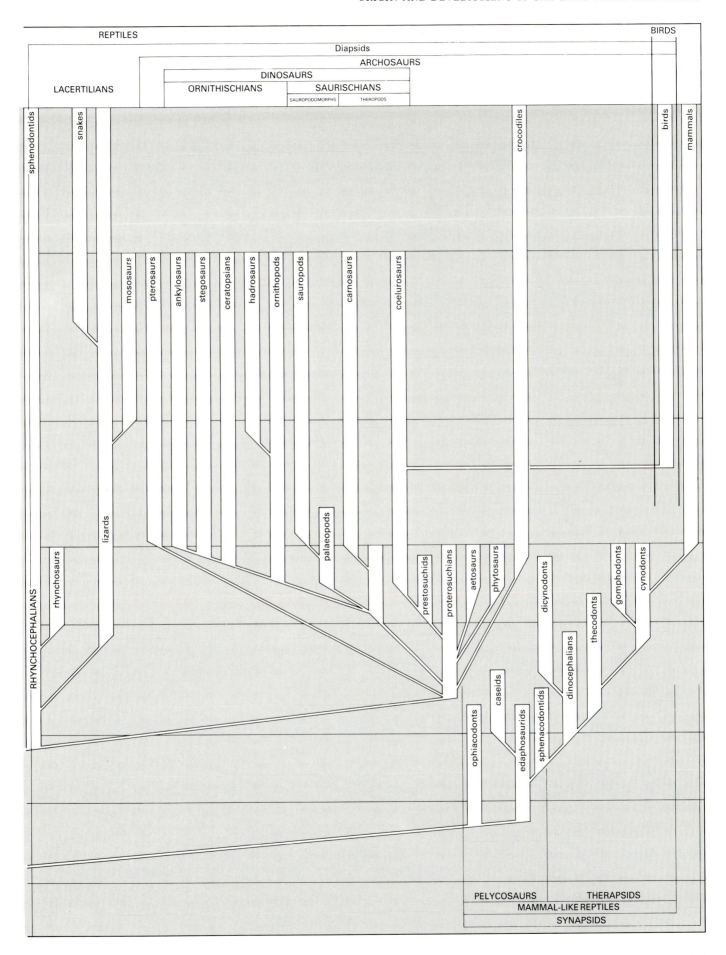

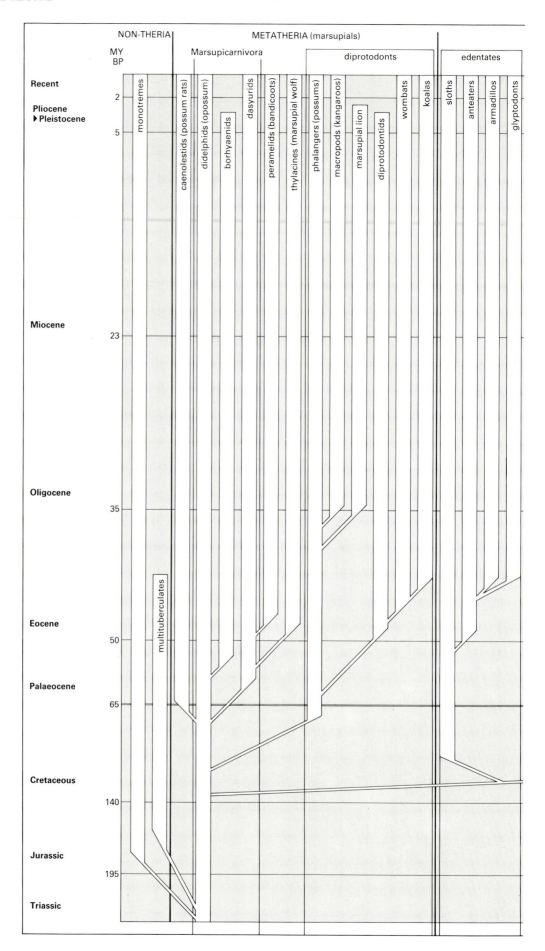

Fig. 14.8. Evolution of the major orders of mammals.

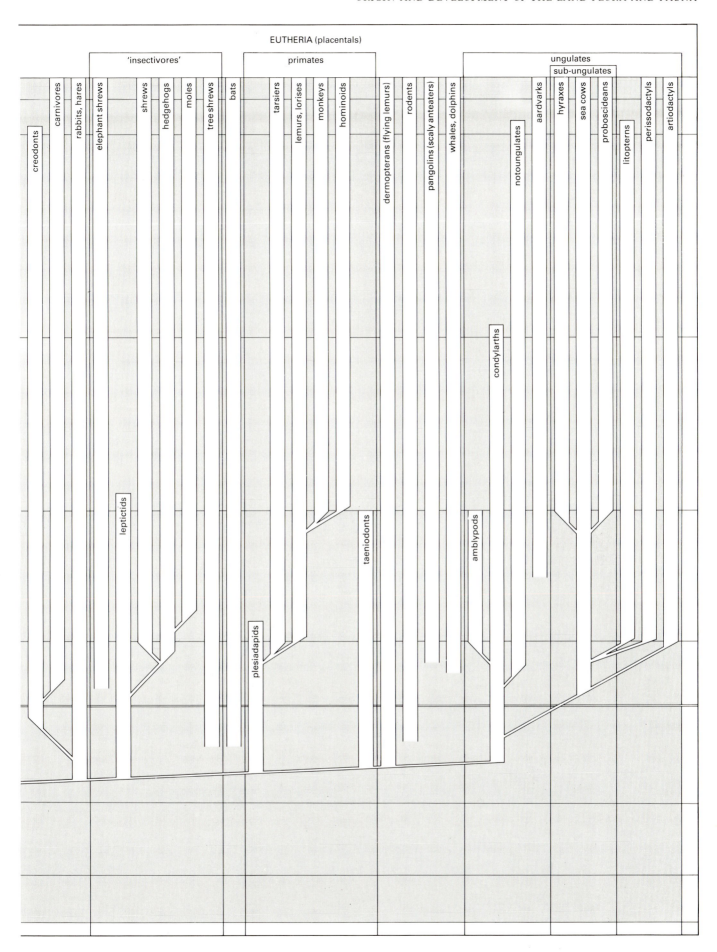

In the middle Triassic a group of archosaurian reptiles, the **thecodonts**, took over the niches for large carnivores; thecodonts were probably ectothermic. However, a great variety of mammal-like reptiles had become extinct at the end of the Permian, along with many other animals, and the apparent replacement of larger, mammal-like reptiles by thecodonts in Triassic faunas may have been fortuitous, rather than the result of any superior competitive ability of the thecodonts. Another Triassic group of mammal-like reptiles, the **cynodonts** (Fig. 14.7), may have had a higher metabolic rate, yet they held their own for most of the period in the smaller niches. Cynodonts may have been able to withstand thecodont competition because their high metabolic rate would have enabled a certain amount of sustained pursuit after active prey, whereas the thecodonts probably ambushed the larger slow-moving herbivores. The small size of cynodonts would have enabled them to avoid predation and the midday heat by hiding under bushes or in holes.

The small herbivorous niches were filled by other cynodonts, and the larger ones by **rhyncosaurs**, reptiles with parrot-like beaks that represented a third distinct radiation of the diapsid reptiles. The thecodonts invaded the herbivorous niche only in the equatorial regions. During the Triassic, some thecodonts partially ousted the surviving labyrinthodont amphibians from the freshwater semi-aquatic niches, relegating them to deep-water fully aquatic forms. One descendant lineage of the thecodonts, the crocodiles, still holds this river-bank niche today.

An abrupt and worldwide change in the tetrapod fauna occurred near the end of the Triassic, with the dramatic replacement of both cynodonts and thecodonts of all body sizes by **dinosaurs**, descendants of the thecodonts. This occurred at the same time as the extensive radiation of conifers, and suggests that dinosaurs did not replace the existing tetrapods by competition, but that the global floral changes resulted in the extinction of many specialised Triassic lineages. The first dinosaurs of the late Triassic were generalised animals that probably were able to react to the new environment with radiation into new forms in a way that the more specialised thecodonts and cynodonts could not.

The evolution of mammals

The mammal-like reptiles fared badly at the end of the Triassic, the sole surviving lineage being the very small true mammals. These presumably survived because they were able to occupy a niche unavailable to the dinosaurs, that of small nocturnal insectivores; the endothermic metabolism of mammals would have enabled them to be active at night. It is probably during this period that mammals developed their keen sense of smell and hearing, and their relatively large brains.

Some parental care of offspring was probably a feature of all mammal-like reptiles. No eggs have been found in association with these animals, although dinosaur eggs are known, and they may well have had a mode of reproduction similar to that of present-day monotremes (duck-billed platypuses and echidnas), where eggs are laid at a fairly advanced stage, and subsequently guarded and incubated by the mother. However, it was not until the early Jurassic that the characteristic mammalian mode of tooth replacement with only two sets of teeth appeared, derived from the pattern of continual replacement typical of reptiles. This suggests that lactation, freeing young mammals from the necessity of eating solid food early in life, did not evolve until this time. The retention of the young within the body, with the loss of the shelled egg, probably also occurred at this time in most lineages.

Mammals remained as small insectivorous animals until the end of the early Cretaceous. During the Jurassic two distinct lineages emerged, the **therians** and the **non-therians**. Therian mammals, with triangular interlocking cheek teeth, were the ancestors of all living mammals, with the probable exception of the egg-laying monotremes of Australia.

The radiation of the dinosaurs

The dinosaurs, descendants of the thecodonts, were the dominant large tetrapods from the late Triassic to the end of the Cretaceous. Other descendants of the thecodonts included flying reptiles, the pterosaurs, which also flourished during the Mesozoic, and the crocodiles, which still survive.

There were three main dinosaur lineages, probably derived from three different thecodont groups (Fig. 14.9). These were the bipedal carnivorous **theropods**, divided into large carnosaurs and small coelurosaurs, the herbivorous **sauropodomorphs**, divided into small, partially bipedal palaeopods and the much larger, quadrupedal sauropods, and the herbivorous **ornithischians**, which included small bipedal ornithopods as well as heavily armoured quadrupedal stegosaurs and ankylosaurs, and the duck-billed hadrosaurs and horned ceratopsians of the late Cretaceous.

Dinosaurs differed from thecodonts primarily in having longer legs held more closely under their bodies, and showed a distinct tendency towards bipedality (walking on two legs only). The smaller early dinosaurs were no bigger than thecodonts, but some forms rapidly achieved very large body sizes. Dinosaur radiation occurred at the same time as the global spread of conifers, presumably the predominant diet of the early herbivorous dinosaurs. Conifers are a poor source of nutrients, and are not eaten by any living mammal. However, a large animal requires relatively less food than does a small one, and the early dinosaurs may have become large precisely because they could then process conifers slowly and in bulk. The likelihood of predation was thereby also reduced, at least until large carnivores had evolved.

The earliest dinosaur faunas were similar all over the earth due to the closeness of the continental masses. They consisted predominantly of large herbivorous palaeopods such as *Plateosaurus*, the smaller herbivore niches being taken by small

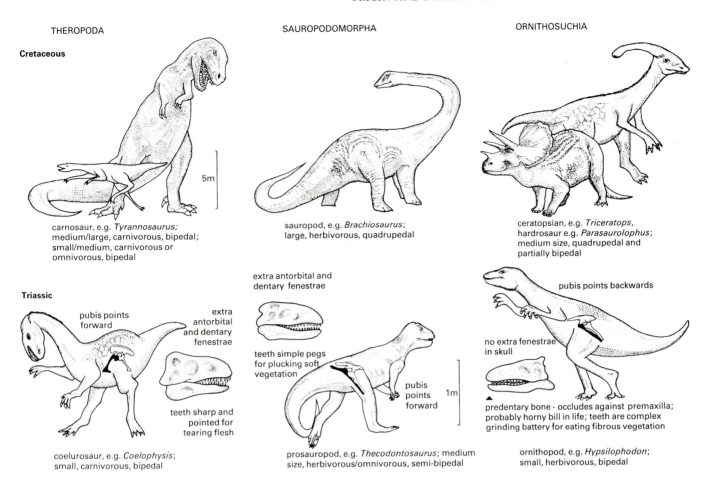

THEROPODA

Cretaceous

5m

carnosaur, e.g. *Tyrannosaurus*;
medium/large, carnivorous, bipedal;
small/medium, carnivorous or
omnivorous, bipedal

Triassic

pubis points
forward

extra
antorbital
and dentary
fenestrae

teeth sharp and
pointed for
tearing flesh

coelurosaur, e.g. *Coelophysis*;
small, carnivorous, bipedal

SAUROPODOMORPHA

sauropod, e.g. *Brachiosaurus*;
large, herbivorous, quadrupedal

extra antorbital and
dentary fenestrae

teeth simple pegs
for plucking soft
vegetation

pubis
points
forward

1m

prosauropod, e.g. *Thecodontosaurus*; medium
size, herbivorous/omnivorous, semi-bipedal

ORNITHOSUCHIA

ceratopsian, e.g. *Triceratops*,
hardrosaur e.g. *Parasaurolophus*;
medium size, quadrupedal and
partially bipedal

pubis points backwards

no extra fenestrae
in skull

predentary bone - occludes against premaxilla;
probably horny bill in life; teeth are complex
grinding battery for eating fibrous vegetation

ornithopod, e.g. *Hypsilophodon*;
small, herbivorous, bipedal

Fig. 14.9. Dinosaur types: anatomy and diversity.

ornithopods such as *Heterodontosaurus*. The large carnivore niches were still taken by advanced thecodonts, such as *Ornithosuchus*, which paralleled the later carnosaurs but were not directly ancestral to them. The small carnivores were the coelurosaurs.

Little is known of the land faunas of the early and middle Jurassic, but by the late Jurassic the dinosaur faunas were distinctly different from the early ones, although still similar in different continents. The carnosaurs, such as the North American *Allosaurus*, were now the predominant carnivores. Carnosaurs differed from coelurosaurs not only in their larger size, but also in the possession of a shorter neck, smaller front limbs and a more massive tail. The dominant herbivores were the massive sauropods, such as *Diplodocus*, together with the stegosaurs and small and large ornithopods such as *Iguanodon*. Sauropods were originally thought to be swamp-dwellers too heavy to support their own weight on land, but recently it has been suggested that they were high-level browsers, using their long necks like giraffes to reach tall vegetation (Fig. 14.10).

Origin and evolution of birds

Birds differ from all other animals in having feathers, and the earliest feathered animal known is the extinct *Archaeopteryx*. It was about the size of a crow, and lived in central Europe in late Jurassic times, about 140 million years ago. There is considerable knowledge of the structure of *Archaeopteryx* (Fig. 14.11), as several specimens fell into calm water, which preserved their skeletons almost intact, and were buried by fine sediments ensuring detailed impressions of their feathers. Although bird-like in possessing feathers, the animal resembled archosaurian reptiles in having a long bony tail, abdominal ribs, and teeth implanted in sockets in the upper and lower jaws; none of these latter features occur in modern birds. Both *Archaeopteryx* and modern birds resemble archosaurs in the pattern of holes in the skull, further suggesting a close relationship.

It is disputed whether *Archaeopteryx* was able to fly. Feathers would also have served for thermoregulation and insulation, probably their original function in birds before being used to assist flight. Birds may have evolved from arboreal reptiles that used the developing wing for gliding, or from fast-running predators that used their mobile forelimbs to catch prey such as insects, the feathers then functioning as a kind of net, or else from predators that leapt upon their prey and used their forearms for balance.

One group of archosaurs, the pterosaurs, flew, but they are not closely related to *Archaeopteryx* and their wings were constructed differently: they had a wing membrane formed of skin, rather than feathers. *Archaeopteryx* walked on its hind limbs with only its toes in contact with the ground, and this habit occurred among some thecodonts and many dinosaurs. As thecodonts were the early archosaur group, which gave rise to all other archosaurs, it is possible that birds too originated

345

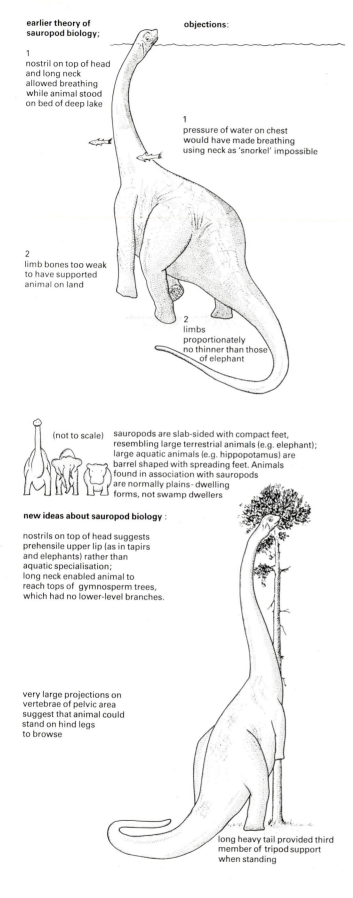

earlier theory of sauropod biology;

objections:

1
nostril on top of head
and long neck
allowed breathing
while animal stood
on bed of deep lake

1
pressure of water on chest
would have made breathing
using neck as 'snorkel' impossible

2
limb bones too weak
to have supported
animal on land

2
limbs
proportionately
no thinner than those
of elephant

(not to scale)

sauropods are slab-sided with compact feet,
resembling large terrestrial animals (e.g. elephant);
large aquatic animals (e.g. hippopotamus) are
barrel shaped with spreading feet. Animals
found in association with sauropods
are normally plains- dwelling
forms, not swamp dwellers

new ideas about sauropod biology :

nostrils on top of head suggests
prehensile upper lip (as in tapirs
and elephants) rather than
aquatic specialisation;
long neck enabled animal to
reach tops of gymnosperm trees,
which had no lower-level branches.

very large projections on
vertebrae of pelvic area
suggest that animal could
stand on hind legs
to browse

long heavy tail provided third
member of tripod support
when standing

Fig. 14.10. Sauropod biology.

directly from this group; several thecodonts were unique among archosaurs in having long, feather-like scales, and the skeletons of these thecodonts and *Archaeopteryx* are similar in general form. However, many skeletal details do differ markedly and it seems more likely that the similarities are in fact shared ancestral characters.

A more immediate bird-ancestor has been sought among the coelurosaurs, small agile carnivorous dinosaurs. These share with *Archaeopteryx* a long list of specialised characters, and except for one feature of the pelvic girdle and the typically fused collar bones of birds (forming the furcula or wishbone), every skeletal feature of *Archaeopteryx* occurs in more than one coelurosaur. However, most coelurosaurs post-dated the already bird-like *Archaeopteryx*, and the predominant evolutionary trend in the coelurosaurian lineage at that time was shortening of the forearm, whereas *Archaeopteryx* had elongated forearms. Nevertheless, there may well be an immediate common ancestor earlier in the Mesozoic for coelurosaurs and *Archaeopteryx*, and therefore for birds.

The radiation and success of insects

Most of the orders of insect that survived the extinctions at the end of the Palaeozoic are still present today. By the end of the Triassic, insect faunas were essentially modern, with most of the insects assignable to modern orders, including all major groups of wingless insects and most major groups of winged ones such as beetles, bugs, grasshoppers and cockroaches. Two major orders of insects first appeared in the Triassic: primitive members of the Diptera (flies) and of the Hymenoptera (modern forms of which include ants, bees and wasps). In the Jurassic there appeared more advanced types of dipterans, such as midges, and more advanced hymenopterans with a narrow 'waist' between the thorax and abdomen, ancestral to ants and wasps. Flies, beetles and lace-wings are the most common insect fossils from the Mesozoic.

The insect faunas of the Cretaceous were from families that mostly still exist today. A major radiation of two forms of insects at this time may have been correlated with the evolution of the flowering plants; in the middle Cretaceous social insects such as termites and ants appeared, and in the late Cretaceous the Lepidoptera (moths and butterflies) were first found. The only significant radiations of new insects in the Tertiary were those of the bees and social wasps in the Oligocene.

The insects are thus a diverse, ancient and highly successful group. Over half the species of all organisms living today are insects, about 1 million insect species having been described. Every year, roughly 20000 new species, more than five times the total number of living mammal species, are added to this list. Insects have colonised effectively every terrestrial habitat, including rainless deserts, snow on high mountain peaks, hot volcanic springs and upwellings of crude petroleum.

The insects are so successful essentially because, unlike any other group, they have developed an effective solution to the

Fig. 14.11. Reconstruction of Archaeopteryx.

problems of being a small animal on land. The most severe of these problems is loss of water. Small animals have a relatively large surface area compared to their volume, and the body store of water is lost rapidly in dry air. Insects are protected by a cuticle which has a surface layer of wax that is almost completely waterproof. Water loss also inevitably occurs during breathing, excretion and defaecation, but these potential losses of water are restricted too in insects. The respiratory system is constructed so that air is piped to the tissue surfaces, at which exchange of gases occurs, through waterproof tubes, called tracheae, lined with cuticle (see Fig. 2.19). The openings of the tracheae at the body surface, spiracles, can be tightly closed by muscular valves. The rectum, into which the final sections of both the excretory and the digestive systems open, has biochemical pumps which enable insects to reabsorb virtually all the water from their urine and their faeces, and to produce, if necessary, a completely dry and powdery excrement.

The second major problem for a small land animal is how to produce an efficient method of moving and of supporting the body. Insects inherited from their arthropod ancestors an external skeleton of cuticle, and have modified this to form a light, strong and highly adaptable mechanical system. The cuticle of insects has two basic components: chitin, a polysaccharide that provides tensile strength and flexibility, and protein, which when tanned to form sclerotin is tough and hard without being heavy. Insects have also developed a special protein, called resilin, which is the most perfectly elastic material known, and is present at joints and hinges where energy needs to be stored. The composition of cuticle can be modified for a variety of purposes, producing exceptionally hard mandibles even able to cut through sheets of metal, or a soft and extensible abdomen for accommodating a large meal of blood, or tough stylets able to penetrate the hide of elephants. Insect cuticle, being both light and strong, also provides ideal material for wings.

Flight is a key element in the success of insects. It enables them to colonise new habitats and to respond rapidly to environmental change. Insect wings are all constructed on a similar plan, and almost certainly evolved in a single common ancestor, during the mid-Devonian or earlier. For well over 100 million years, until the origin of pterosaurs and birds in the Jurassic, the insects had no competitors in the air. Although there are many insect fossils from the late Carboniferous onwards, these provide no direct evidence about the origin of wings. Wings may have evolved from lateral expansions of the thorax, enabling the insect to glide skilfully from tall vegetation and land neatly on its feet. Alternatively, wings may have evolved from modifications of the gill-plates in secondarily aquatic insects. Whichever way it occurred, the evolution of flight ensured the conquest of all terrestrial ecosystems by the insects.

The Cretaceous period

Cretaceous vegetation and the appearance of angiosperms

In the Jurassic, different latitudes had distinct climates and floras, and this zonation with its characteristic sets of species remained much the same into the Cretaceous. Subtropical communities flourished on the southern edge of the Laurasian land mass, the northern shore of the equatorial Tethys Sea. A profusion of ferns included representatives from many modern families. *Weichselia*, an important and typical fossil fern for the Lower Cretaceous, occurred on the north and south sides of the Tethys Sea, and possessed numerous features not seen in modern forms. Some of these features, such as a thick cuticle, recurved leaflets, and prop roots, were probably adaptations for survival in habitats similar to mangrove-swamps (see section 7.3). An enigmatic and spectacular fern, *Tempskya*, had a false trunk up to 6 metres high made of numerous minute intertwining stems, roots and leaf-stalks. Such trunks are preserved in their original position in sediments from peaty freshwater swamps, and may have formed thin coals.

Leaf remains from both cycads and bennettitalians (cycadeoids) occur in early Cretaceous floras, as do the distinctive, squat silicified trunks of *Cycadeoidea*; these are widespread, and the most famous come from the Black Hills of Dakota. They probably bore a crown of divided leaves, and attached to the trunk, between the leaf scars, were numerous bisexual globular cones. These have often been represented as open, coloured flowers like those of water-lilies, but there is no evidence that the whorl of microsporangiate organs around the ovules ever opened out to release the pollen. These plants may instead have been self-fertilised, although some cones are found to be extensively damaged, possibly by insects, and this may have resulted in some cross-pollination. *Cycadeoidea* has never been found in the position in which it grew, but from the type of deposits in which it is found it was probably a prominent plant along stream and river banks.

Conifers from the early part of the Cretaceous were members of several families, including the Araucariaceae, Cupressaceae, Taxodiaceae, and also the Pinaceae of which 200 species are alive today, including pines, spruces, larches, firs and cedars. Together these were dominant in the forest vegetation of flood-plain and upland environments. Conifers, such as some species of *Pseudofrenelopsis* of the extinct family Cheirolepidiaceae, may have formed coastal mangrove thickets around some parts of the Tethys Sea, as their pollen and twigs with reduced, succulent leaves, reminiscent of modern halophytes (salt-loving plants), are often recovered from sediments of coastal environments, and even from hypersaline lagoons; other species of *Pseudofrenelopsis* are interpreted as forest trees colonising the banks of freshwater streams and low-lying areas which were seasonally dry.

The Lower Cretaceous also contains the first fossils of **angiosperms**, or flowering plants. The earliest records are of typical angiosperm pollen grains with single grooves; subsequent sediments contain evidence for diversification, with pollen grains with three grooves. Although the plants producing the pollen are unknown, they spread rapidly over the globe; the rift valley separating West Africa and South America in north-western Gondwanaland has been suggested as a possible birthplace for the angiosperms. By the late Cretaceous, angiosperms dominated most terrestrial ecosystems. The sudden appearance of familiar leaf forms, resembling those of oaks or figs, together with the rapid rise to dominance of the angiosperms, has been taken to mean that the group had a history in upland areas earlier in the Mesozoic or even in the late Palaeozoic, in environments which did not favour fossilisation. Recent palaeobiological investigations of Cretaceous leaves, however, involving a detailed analysis of venation patterns and cuticular features, and studies on pollen, have affirmed that the angiosperms may have arisen in the Cretaceous, with these earliest leaves not being directly related to any living forms, and that during the Cretaceous there was a progressive increase in both numbers and diversity of angiosperm types.

In the absence of a good fossil record, ideas on the nature of the earliest angiosperms have come from studies on the comparative morphology and anatomy of living plants. These studies suggest that the subclass Magnoliidae of the dicotyledons (see section 2.2) contains in the magnolias and their relatives the most primitive surviving angiosperms, with wood containing tracheids rather than vessels, numerous spirally arranged floral parts not fused to each other, leaf-like stamens (containing the pollen) and open carpels (bearing the ovules). Simple unisexual flowers such as in catkins are in fact secondarily reduced forms, specially adapted for wind pollination.

The first leaves with typically angiosperm venation also occur in Cretaceous sediments of similar ages to those containing the pollen. The oldest leaves were very small (no more than 25 millimetres long) and elliptical. Younger records are far more diverse (although the vast majority of these leaves were still small and with primitive venation), and there was a range of shapes, some with lobed or serrated margins and many lacking a pronounced petiole (leaf-stalk). The earliest leaves were probably from magnolia-like forms, although probably not from robust woody trees, and later Middle Cretaceous forms

have been assigned to other plant subclasses, including the Rosidae, Nymphaeidae, Hammamelidales and to monocotyledons. This gradual progression of increasingly complex and diverse leaf forms parallels the progression seen in the pollen record, and is consistent with an evolutionary radiation beginning in the Cretaceous.

There are less records of flowers and fruits, but these are increasing in number and the critical study of Cretaceous flowers is just beginning. A very valuable contribution has recently come from the Upper Cretaceous of Sweden, where flowers turned to charcoal in a forest fire contain sufficient morphological detail to permit assignment to the orders Saxifragales and Juglandales, although they present a combination of characters not seen in modern forms (Fig. 14.12).

There is little direct evidence in the plant record for the co-evolution of insects and flowers in the Cretaceous, although insects are believed to have been of great evolutionary importance in the success of the angiosperms. Pollen studies do indicate that the earliest angiosperms were pollinated by insects; the first grains adapted for wind pollination appeared in the mid-Cretaceous, when angiosperms were becoming locally dominant.

It has been suggested that the angiosperms, with their more efficient strategies for and higher rates of reproduction, originated in response to arid conditions. The earliest angiosperm pollen grains, with single grooves, from equatorial Africa, are associated with other plants typical of environments with a seasonal variation of rainfall, and the layers of sediment in which they are found occur below, and thus were laid down before, layers of evaporated salt characteristic of very dry environments. A more diverse flora, marked by pollen grains with three grooves, then appears, indicating that the angiosperms began as rapidly growing and reproducing shrubs of seasonally dry environments, able to survive and diversify when conditions became generally more arid. The earliest angiosperms in Laurasia occur in sediments from disturbed habitats, and so it has been postulated that, following migration along the Rift Valley separating Africa and South America and crossing the Tethys Sea, they acted as opportunists, the equivalents of modern 'weeds', rapidly colonising disturbed habitats such as coastal swamps and river banks, and competing successfully with the existing communities of pteridophytes and gymnosperms.

The invasions and retreats of the sea, which began in the Lower Cretaceous, would have provided an abundance of such unstable environments, and angiosperm floras of this age from North America are associated with periods of marine influences: various types of community, containing angiosperms among other plants, are distinguishable, including those from mangrove-swamps, coastal stream sides, freshwater coastal swamps, fringing woodland with a ground cover of ferns, and lake margins. The flood plains were dominated by forests containing redwoods of the *Sequoia* type (family Taxodiaceae), and were little affected by the early angiosperms. However, the

Fig. 14.12. A carbonised flower of Scandianthus *from the Late Cretaceous in Sweden, showing how more or less complete flowers can be preserved. Although* Scandianthus *can be related to a living order, it presents a combination of characters not seen in modern genera.*

characteristic pteridophytes and gymnosperms of the marginal habitats, dominant in the early Cretaceous, decreased in abundance as the angiosperms increased, and many, including *Weichselia, Tempskya, Pseudofrenelopsis* and *Cycadeoidea*, did not survive the late Cretaceous. The success of the early angiosperms in such habitats, particularly mangrove-swamps and tidally influenced mud-flats, has recently led to the idea that some were adapted to tolerate physiological aridity, to which plants are subjected in such very salty environments. By the end of the Cretaceous, the angiosperms dominated the coastal lowlands and had also penetrated further inland, perhaps initially by way of the rivers.

The ancestry of the angiosperms remains highly conjectural. Almost all the groups of early Mesozoic gymnosperms have been proposed at some time as candidates since, together with their living representatives, they all show certain angiospermous characteristics. The trend for increased protection of the ovule, for example, which is perhaps associated with pollination by insects, is repeated in several widely separated lines, as is the development of net-like venation in leaves. The concept of a single origin for the angiosperms is based largely on evidence from modern plants, such as the structure of sieve-tubes and the embryo sac, the occurrence of double fertilisation, and the pattern of embryogenesis. This concept has some support from the Cretaceous fossil record, which also suggests that the small, primitive angiosperm leaves were derived from simply divided compound leaves. This points to an ancestry in the cycads, bennettitalians or pteridosperms.

Cretaceous dinosaur faunas

The start of the Cretaceous saw a significant change in dinosaur faunas, in addition to the change in the position of the continents and the change to a flora dominated by angiosperms. The dinosaurs of equatorial Gondwanaland remained much the same, with sauropods predominating until the end of the Mesozoic. In the more northern continent of Laurasia, however, a radiation among the ornithischians produced many new types of short-necked and short-legged dinosaurs that were considerably smaller than the sauropods. These ornithischians were probably low-level browsers on the newly emerging angiosperm vegetation and the simple reptilian peg-like teeth were united into complex dental batteries in some forms.

The carnivorous dinosaurs present were the very large carnosaurs, such as *Tyrannosaurus*, and ostrich-sized coelurosaurs such as *Deinonychus*. Another group of coelurosaurs partially succeeded to the omnivorous or herbivorous niches from the ornithopods. The ornithischians started to diversify at the start of the Cretaceous, but did not attain peak diversity until the late Cretaceous. One group prominent in the early Cretaceous was the heavily armoured ankylosaurs, which were somewhat smaller than their ancestral stegosaurs. Ankylosaurs had simple peg-like teeth, suggesting that they were not specialist feeders on tough vegetation, as were the hadrosaurs

and ceratopsians of the late Cretaceous.

Hadrosaurs were medium to large bipeds, with complex dental batteries. Their duck-like bills, webbed feet and laterally flattened tails suggest a semi-aquatic habit. Some types such as *Trachodon* had flat heads, but others such as *Parasaurolophus* had complex hollow crests on their heads. Since there is a difference between males and females in the development of these crests they may have been used in courtship, both for visual displays and for vocalisation. Other evidence for complex social behaviour in hadrosaurs comes from the colonies of closely grouped nests of baby hadrosaurs, suggesting the sort of parental care found also in birds.

Ceratopsians were medium-sized to large quadrupeds, with a turtle-like beak, complex shearing teeth, horns on the brow and nose in some genera, and an elaborate frill around the neck, as seen in *Triceratops*. This frill may have been used for defence, but also probably served as the origin for greatly enlarged jaw muscles, suggesting a highly fibrous diet.

It has recently been proposed that dinosaurs were endothermic, able to generate body heat internally, because their anatomy and bone histology resemble those of large mammals rather than those of lizards, which in turn suggests an ability to maintain high metabolic rates and levels of activity. Additionally, carnivorous dinosaurs are not very abundant compared to the herbivores, a ratio of predator to prey typical of endotherms. The advantage of endothermy is that it enables animals to live in environments that are cold or have fluctuating temperatures, and it allows the maintenance of a high level of activity. Sustained running or flight is impossible for ectothermic reptiles, which have a low metabolic rate, and hence a low blood pressure and low rate of oxygen supply to the tissues. The upright mammal-like stance of the supposedly endothermic reptiles and their highly vascularised bone, both certainly different from those of living reptiles, have however also been interpreted as being correlated with their size rather than with their physiology.

Some dinosaurs were so big, giving them a very low surface-area-to-volume ratio, that their body temperature would have changed only slowly. In a warm tropical or subtropical climate they would have had no need for additional mechanisms for the production of heat internally, that is, they may have been 'inertial homeotherms'. The initial radiation of dinosaurs occurred at the same time as an increase in global temperature in the late Triassic, and their extinction at the end of the Cretaceous was correlated with a drop in temperature. This is consistent with the hypothesis of dinosaurs being inertial homeotherms depending on a non-fluctuating warm climate to maintain a high body temperature. However, no large inertial homeotherms occur in the equatorial regions today, where the climate remains warm and non-seasonal. In addition, an inertial homeotherm would be incapable of sustained activity, while the limb anatomy of many dinosaurs evolved to a form similar to that of fast-running mammals.

Of course, all dinosaurs need not have had the same type of physiology. A large sauropod could have been an inertial homeotherm, and indeed would have had severe problems in dissipating body heat had it generated any internally, but the small, active and lightly built dinosaurs, especially those small coelurosaurs believed to be ancestral to birds, could not readily have had an ectothermic physiology like that of modern lizards, dependent on external sources of heat. The dentition of hadrosaurs and ceratopsians suggests a rate of processing of food similar to that of herbivorous mammals, and the rapid growth rate apparent in baby hadrosaurs would also have required a high metabolic rate. A range of metabolic rates is seen among living mammals, and the dinosaurs as a group could have possessed an equally wide or wider range of physiologies and of degrees of endothermy.

Radiation of Cretaceous mammals

The early Cretaceous was an important time in mammalian evolution. Changes in tooth structure in both therian and non-therian mammals suggest a divergence from the previous, fairly narrow range of primarily insectivorous diets, to a broader variety of omnivorous and herbivorous diets. This occurred at the same time as the appearance and spread of the angiosperm plants and the diversification of insects, which must have resulted in a much greater variety of available food. A group of now extinct non-therian mammals, called the **multituberculates**, became successful and diversified during the Cretaceous. They had teeth at the back of the cheek specialised for grinding, and those at the front of the cheek were blade-like for slicing. Multituberculates probably occupied a variety of terrestrial and arboreal herbivorous niches, taking a place similar to that of rodents in modern faunas.

The early Cretaceous also saw the splitting of the therian mammals into **marsupial** and **placental** lineages; the placental mammals were to become dominant over most of the globe. The first snakes also appeared and diversified during the Cretaceous. All modern snakes are carnivorous, and some are equipped with heat sensors to detect mammalian prey. Their evolution may have been in response to the increased number of small hole-dwelling mammals, especially as the early snakes appear to have been burrowers.

Mammal faunas, like those of the dinosaurs, were similar around the world during the Triassic and Jurassic, but were more regionally diverse during the Cretaceous as the continents moved apart. All Mesozoic mammals were of small body size. The multituberculates were ubiquitous, but for most of the period placental mammals were more or less restricted to Asia, and marsupials to North America. In the late Cretaceous, placental mammals became more common in North America, with the appearance of forms ancestral to modern insectivores, carnivores, ungulates (hoofed mammals) and primates. The radiation of the placental mammals that characterised the start of the Tertiary had thus begun before the end of the Cretaceous, and was not the consequence of the extinction of the dinosaurs.

Cretaceous extinctions

At the end of the Cretaceous, all land tetrapods with a body mass greater than about 10 kilograms became extinct, as did all marine reptiles. This extinction was important in terms of the total number of species involved, but even so was not as great as were the extinctions at the end of the Palaeozoic.

Many explanations have been advanced for the extinction of the dinosaurs at the peak of their diversity during the late Cretaceous, the most plausible being that it was a consequence of a gradual global change in climate. Dinosaurs did not become extinct simultaneously all over the world, but instead a wave of extinction spread from northern to southern regions over a period of approximately 1 million years. The pattern of extinctions of plants was similar, with the floras in equatorial regions little affected.

It is unlikely that the extinctions of dinosaurs were caused by an inability to consume the new angiosperms, as the complex dentition which evolved for this purpose in mammalian herbivores was paralleled in the ornithischian dinosaurs. Equally, as mammals had coexisted with dinosaurs throughout the Mesozoic, it is unlikely that the extinctions were caused by consumption of dinosaur eggs by mammals.

Dinosaur extinction may in fact have been a less dramatic event than it appears to our present perspective. Throughout the late Palaeozoic and all the Mesozoic there were cyclical extinctions and rebuildings of the tetrapod communities, associated with rising and falling sea-levels and with periods of mountain-building. Both these sorts of event affected the diversity of niches available on land and on the continental shelf. With each cycle the large and specialised tetrapods became extinct, and in the following period similar niches were filled again with new types derived from the surviving smaller and more generalised animals. For example, the sauropod and stegosaur fauna that became largely extinct at the end of the Jurassic was subsequently replaced by the hadrosaurs and ceratopsians which evolved from the small, early Cretaceous ornithopods. The end of the Cretaceous was different in that the radiation of angiosperms which had occurred favoured diversification of the mammals, rather than of small reptiles. The mammals thus provided the small and generalised animals from which the fauna of large tetrapods was rebuilt in the Tertiary.

14.3 THE TERTIARY PERIOD

The Tertiary period contains only the last third of the evolutionary history of the mammals, but during that time they radiated to fill the niches left vacant for large tetrapods at the end of the Mesozoic. The dominant Palaeocene mammals were forms that are largely extinct today, and only insectivores, primates and edentates are direct survivors from the groups living then. The first representatives of most modern mammalian orders appeared in the late Palaeocene or early Eocene, and the appearance of present-day families occurred largely in the Oligocene, with the radiation of mammalian faunas of a modern aspect first occuring in the Miocene.

By the start of the Tertiary the present continental land masses were largely separate, and so independent radiations of mammals took place in these relatively isolated areas (see Chapter 12). This allowed the well-known separate marsupial fauna of Australia to develop. Until the end of the Tertiary the faunas endemic to (only occurring in) South America were as isolated from the northern faunas as were those of Australia, but eventually several invasions occurred from the north, culminating in an almost complete replacement of the South American fauna when their land mass reconnected to North America at the end of the Tertiary. Until the middle Tertiary the faunas of Africa were also clearly distinct from those of Eurasia.

The second feature important for understanding Tertiary evolutionary events is that there was a dramatic deterioration in the climate at the end of the Eocene, with a drop in mean annual temperature of at least 10°C in the higher latitudes, accompanied by an increase in the annual temperature range from about 5°C to about 25°C. This climatic change had a particularly large effect on the land faunas because the main continental land masses were then in high latitudes in the northern hemisphere. The evolution of mammalian faunas after the Oligocene represents the radiation of animals and plants that were increasingly adapted to a climate with seasonal periods of cold and drought.

The early Tertiary

The Cretaceous–Tertiary boundary saw a significant drop in mean annual temperatures in the northern latitudes, with a change from an equable subtropical climate to a warm temperate one. This continued until the middle Palaeocene, when the floral diversity in the northern hemisphere reached its lowest point. Palaeocene forests in the northern hemisphere were dominated by trees of temperate climates, such as plane, aspen, poplar and redwood, and in the southern hemisphere a quite separate forest assemblage existed, dominated by *Nothofagus* (southern beech) and podocarps. In the equatorial regions the tropical floras were dominated by evergreen dicotyledons and palms, with a lesser representation of ferns and gymnosperms. Much of the temperate regions of the globe appear to have been covered by swampy forests.

Early Palaeocene faunas are only known from North America, although late Palaeocene deposits occur in Europe, South America and Asia. The Tertiary records from Africa and Australia do not begin until the Oligocene. Typical Palaeocene faunas had a high diversity of small animals, mostly smaller than present-day domestic dogs. A group of larger ungulates (hoofed animals), the amblypods, was also present, ranging from the size of a large pig to that of a hippopotamus, and many of these may have had a semi-aquatic mode of life in the temperate forest swamps.

The early Palaeocene of North America was dominated by insectivores (ancestral to present-day animals such as shrews and hedgehogs), prosimian primates, the now-extinct multi-tuberculates, and **condylarths**, which are the assemblage of ungulates ancestral to the living orders. The primates appear to have been more rodent-like in their adaptations than their modern relatives, resembling bushbabies rather than monkeys. The condylarths comprised carnivorous and scavenging forms, as well as more herbivorous and omnivorous types, and included groups ancestral to the perissodactyls (odd-toed ungulates) and to the artiodactyls (even-toed ungulates). Other mammals present included dermopterans, the 'flying lemurs' now confined to South-east Asia. Larger mammals included an extinct group called taeniodonts, large herbivorous bear-like animals with powerful claws.

The later Palaeocene saw the appearance of both orders of carnivorous mammals, the **Carnivora** and the now extinct **Creodonta**. Both the creodonts and the carnivores of the Palaeocene were small, long-bodied, short-legged forms that probably did not pursue their prey actively. Large flightless carnivorous birds, the diatrymaforms, were also present in the early Tertiary faunas of both Europe and North America, and may have been active predators on small mammals.

In the late Palaeocene a climatic shift occurred in the northern hemisphere, with a reversal to subtropical conditions, and this continued until the middle Eocene. The forests in the middle Palaeocene of North America were almost entirely deciduous, but by the late Palaeocene a third of the trees were evergreens, and this was correlated with the appearance of palms, cycads and other forms not tolerant of hard frost. In the early Eocene forest of North America the first subtropical elements appeared, such as lianas, and trees like avocado, bay laurel and cinnamon, and their abundance increased as the epoch progressed. Both animals and plants found today only in equatorial regions were present within the Arctic Circle during the early and middle Eocene. The typical lowland floras contained largely tropical plants, such as palms and swamp vegetation, but upland floras contained a greater variety of subtropical and warm temperate elements, such as beech and pine trees.

The unusual mixture of tropical and subtropical elements in the northern latitudes in the Eocene suggests that the mean annual temperature of these regions was not as high as in the present tropics, but that the flora was maintained by a greater rainfall than occurs in these northern latitudes today, with no pronounced seasonality in its distribution, and by the absence of winter frost.

The spread of tropical vegetation over northern latitudes in the Eocene brought about a radiation of an entirely new mammalian fauna. This may have been due to immigration from tropical zones in central America, rather than due to rapid evolution within the temperate zones. The land bridge between North America and Europe became more accessible at the start of the Eocene, resulting in considerable intermixing of the faunas, but this connection was broken by the middle of the epoch.

In the early Eocene a number of modern orders of mammals appeared, including bats, whales and, most notably, the **perissodactyls** (odd-toed ungulates such as horses and rhinos) and **artiodactyls** (even-toed ungulates such as pigs, camels and antelope). Until the end of the Eocene the artiodactyls were represented by small, omnivorous forms, but the perissodactyls rapidly radiated out into small to medium-sized leaf-eating forms, such as the horse *Hyracotherium* and the tapir *Homogalax*. Perissodactyls were the first mammals to exploit fibrous and leafy herbage, and it may have been that the Eocene forests, more arid than those of the Palaeocene, had more areas of open glades and breaks in the canopy cover, so that a significant amount of undergrowth was now available to be eaten by terrestrial mammals. Perissodactyls were common throughout the northern continents in the Eocene, but there were considerable regional differences.

The surviving herbivorous condylarths declined severely with the emergence of these new ungulate orders, and were extinct by the end of the Eocene. Some amblypod ungulates survived in North America until the end of the Eocene, with bizarre horned forms such as *Uintatherium*, which was like a rhinoceros but had sabre-like canine teeth. The hippopotamus-like *Coryphodon* was also common across the northern continents, but all amblypods were extinct by the end of the Eocene.

The predominant carnivores were hyaenodonts, creodonts

with relatively long limbs and compact feet. They may have been the earliest pack hunters, though they lacked the relatively larger brains characteristic of modern social carnivores. The carnivorous condylarths still occurred throughout the northern hemisphere.

The **rodents** first appeared in the late Palaeocene, but did not diversify until the Eocene. Rodents are characterised by chisel-shaped and continuously growing incisor teeth used for gnawing, and by grinding cheek teeth used by moving the lower jaw backwards and forwards rather than by rotating the lower jaw laterally as in ungulates. The radiation of both primates and rodents in the Eocene probably resulted in the extinction of the multituberculates, which had been successful and diverse in the niches for small omnivore/herbivores during the Cretaceous and Palaeocene. The modern superfamilies of rodents (squirrel-like types, mice and rats, and the South American caviomorphs) appeared at the start of the Oligocene. They have experienced great diversity and success, but have remained small animals up until the present and, with the exception of some South American forms, have been limited to the gnawing omnivore/herbivore niche.

The Palaeocene rodent-like primates were less successful after the radiation of true rodents. The Eocene saw the appearance of primates related to modern forms, the adapids (which probably gave rise to the lemurs) and the omomyids (which probably gave rise to all other higher primates).

The late Eocene saw the start of the climatic deterioration that was to characterise the rest of the Tertiary. The climate in northern latitudes changed from being essentially non-seasonal to being highly seasonal, with cold winters inhibiting plant growth. The causes of this change in the climatic zones of the earth are not known. It may have been due to a change in the tilt of the axis of the earth from the upright towards its present tilt of 23.5°, to a change in the output of solar radiation, or, following the arrival of the continents in their present northern positions, may have been due to the formation of a polar ice cap in the Arctic region coupled with a change in the warm ocean currents reaching northern continents.

This climatic deterioration caused the decline, and eventual disappearance at the end of the epoch, of the prosimian primates from northern latitudes. Primates require a non-fibrous herbivorous diet, and in general can only survive in non-seasonal environments where there is a year-round supply of young plant growth, fruits and nuts. In the Eocene the arboreal primates shared this herbivore/omnivore diet with the small terrestrial artiodactyls, but as the arboreal primates declined in the late Eocene the artiodactyls increased in body size and diversified into the various newly available terrestrial seasonal herbivore niches.

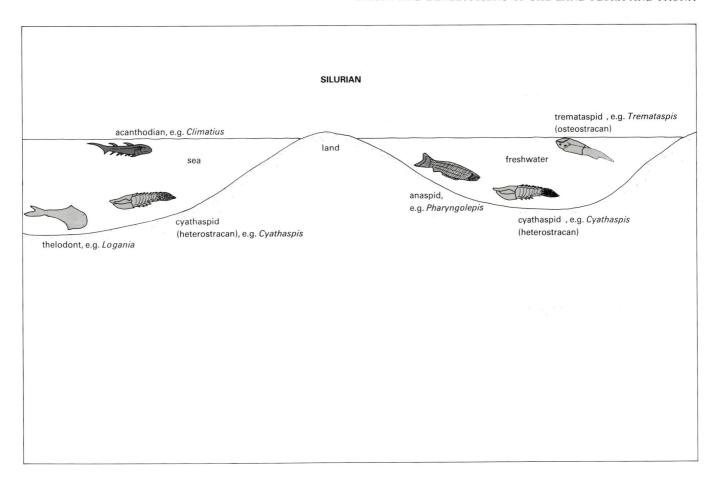

SILURIAN

acanthodian, e.g. *Climatius*

sea

land

freshwater

tremataspid , e.g. *Tremataspis*
(osteostracan)

anaspid,
e.g. *Pharyngolepis*

cyathaspid
(heterostracan), e.g. *Cyathaspis*

cyathaspid , e.g. *Cyathaspis*
(heterostracan)

thelodont, e.g. *Logania*

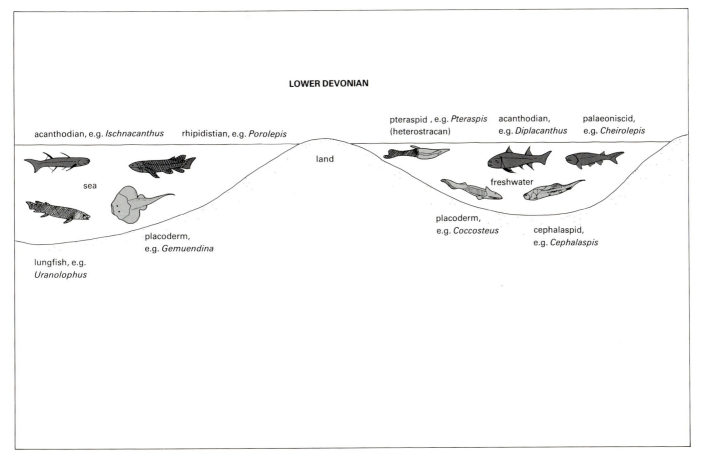

LOWER DEVONIAN

acanthodian, e.g. *Ischnacanthus*

rhipidistian, e.g. *Porolepis*

land

pteraspid , e.g. *Pteraspis*
(heterostracan)

acanthodian,
e.g. *Diplacanthus*

palaeoniscid,
e.g. *Cheirolepis*

sea

freshwater

placoderm,
e.g. *Gemuendina*

placoderm,
e.g. *Coccosteus*

cephalaspid,
e.g. *Cephalaspis*

lungfish, e.g.
Uranolophus

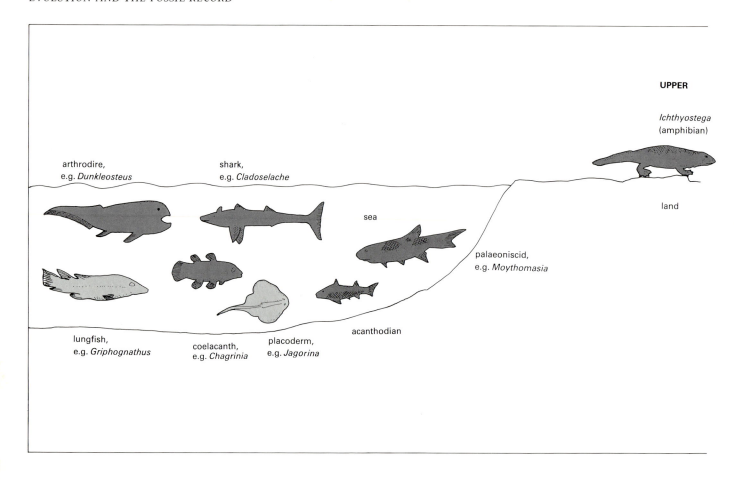

UPPER

Ichthyostega
(amphibian)

arthrodire,
e.g. *Dunkleosteus*

shark,
e.g. *Cladoselache*

land

sea

palaeoniscid,
e.g. *Moythomasia*

acanthodian

lungfish,
e.g. *Griphognathus*

coelacanth,
e.g. *Chagrinia*

placoderm,
e.g. *Jagorina*

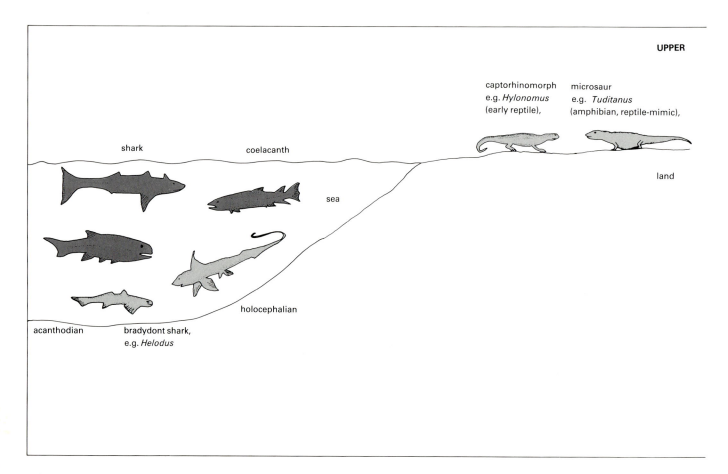

UPPER

captorhinomorph
e.g. *Hylonomus*
(early reptile),

microsaur
e.g. *Tuditanus*
(amphibian, reptile-mimic),

shark

coelacanth

land

sea

acanthodian

bradydont shark,
e.g. *Helodus*

holocephalian

DEVONIAN

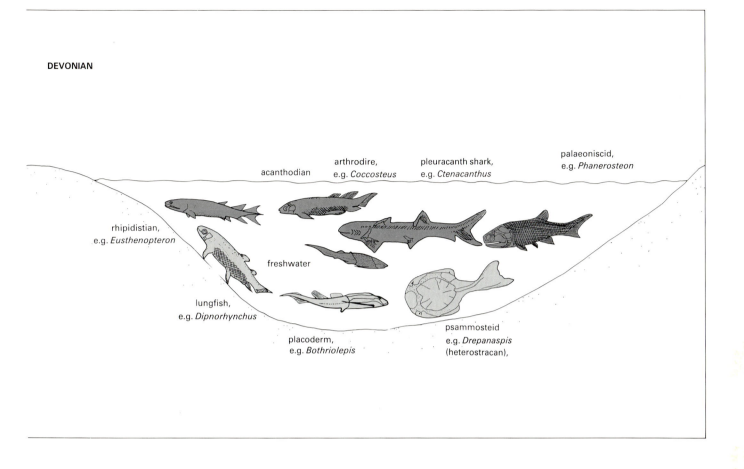

rhipidistian,
e.g. *Eusthenopteron*

acanthodian

arthrodire,
e.g. *Coccosteus*

pleuracanth shark,
e.g. *Ctenacanthus*

palaeoniscid,
e.g. *Phanerosteon*

freshwater

lungfish,
e.g. *Dipnorhynchus*

placoderm,
e.g. *Bothriolepis*

psammosteid
e.g. *Drepanaspis*
(heterostracan),

CARBONIFEROUS

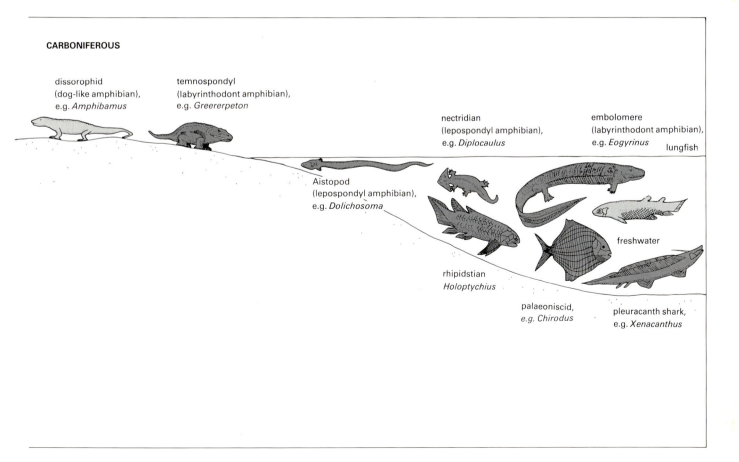

dissorophid
(dog-like amphibian),
e.g. *Amphibamus*

temnospondyl
(labyrinthodont amphibian),
e.g. *Greererpeton*

nectridian
(lepospondyl amphibian),
e.g. *Diplocaulus*

embolomere
(labyrinthodont amphibian),
e.g. *Eogyrinus*

lungfish

Aistopod
(lepospondyl amphibian),
e.g. *Dolichosoma*

freshwater

rhipidstian
Holoptychius

palaeoniscid,
e.g. *Chirodus*

pleuracanth shark,
e.g. *Xenacanthus*

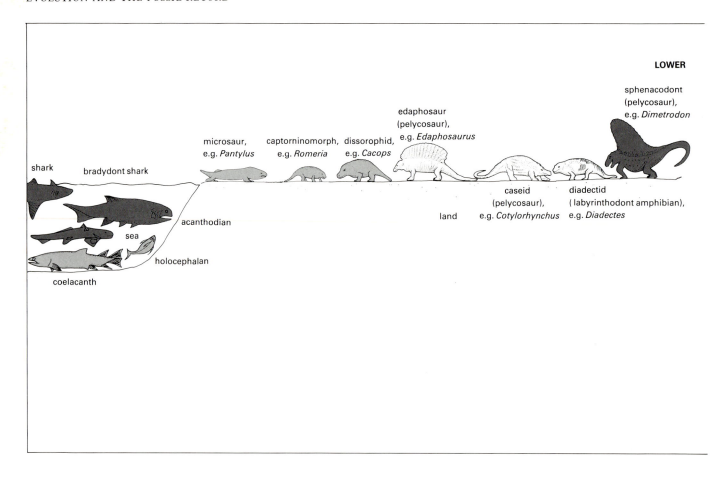

LOWER

sphenacodont (pelycosaur), e.g. *Dimetrodon*

edaphosaur (pelycosaur), e.g. *Edaphosaurus*

microsaur, e.g. *Pantylus*

captorninomorph, e.g. *Romeria*

dissorophid, e.g. *Cacops*

shark

bradydont shark

acanthodian

sea

holocephalan

coelacanth

land

caseid (pelycosaur), e.g. *Cotylorhynchus*

diadectid (labyrinthodont amphibian), e.g. *Diadectes*

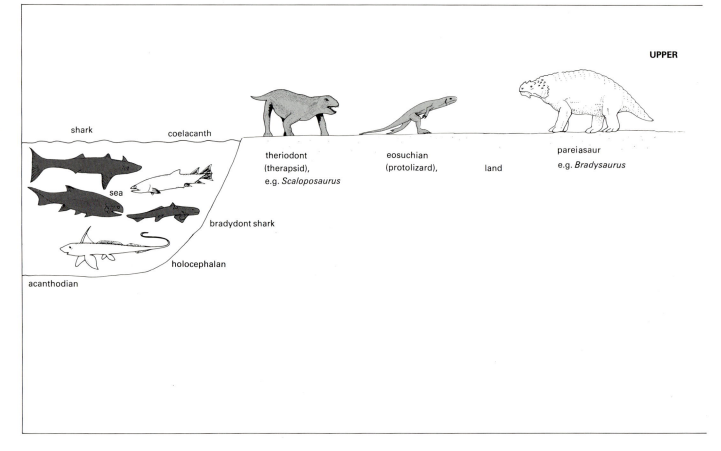

UPPER

shark

coelacanth

sea

bradydont shark

holocephalan

acanthodian

theriodont (therapsid), e.g. *Scaloposaurus*

eosuchian (protolizard),

land

pareiasaur e.g. *Bradysaurus*

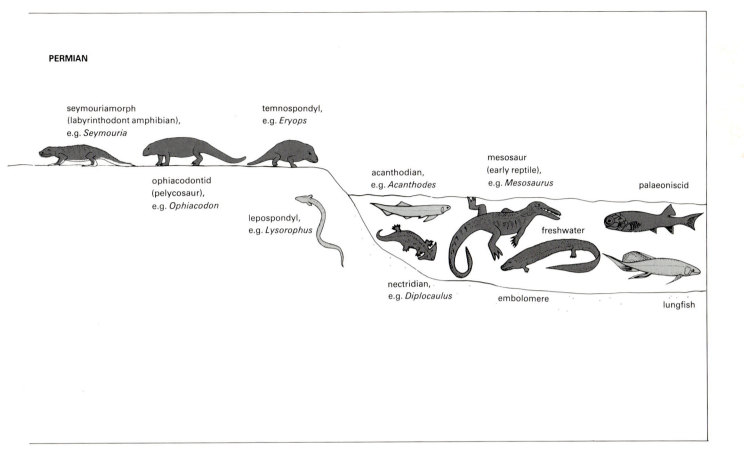

PERMIAN

seymouriamorph
(labyrinthodont amphibian),
e.g. *Seymouria*

temnospondyl,
e.g. *Eryops*

ophiacodontid
(pelycosaur),
e.g. *Ophiacodon*

lepospondyl,
e.g. *Lysorophus*

acanthodian,
e.g. *Acanthodes*

mesosaur
(early reptile),
e.g. *Mesosaurus*

palaeoniscid

freshwater

nectridian,
e.g. *Diplocaulus*

embolomere

lungfish

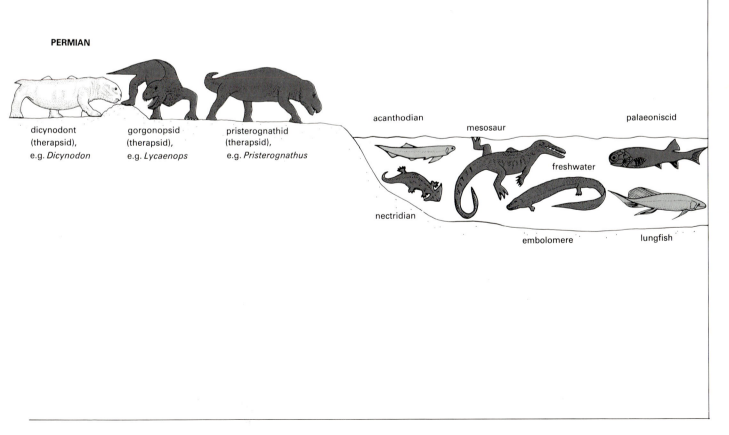

PERMIAN

dicynodont
(therapsid),
e.g. *Dicynodon*

gorgonopsid
(therapsid),
e.g. *Lycaenops*

pristerognathid
(therapsid),
e.g. *Pristerognathus*

acanthodian

mesosaur

palaeoniscid

freshwater

nectridian

embolomere

lungfish

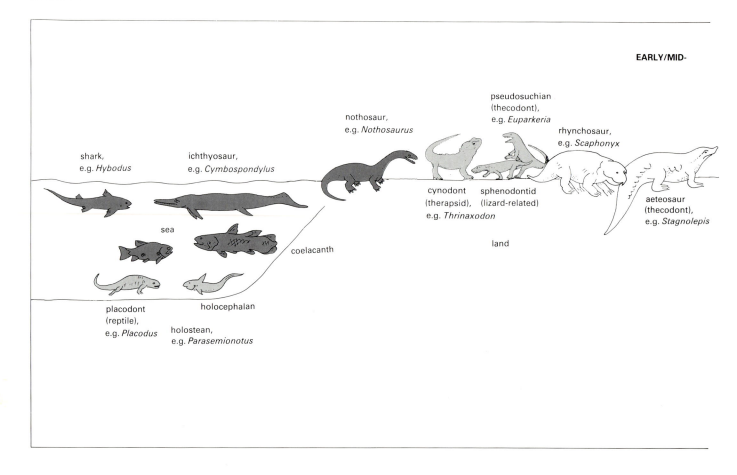

EARLY/MID-

shark,
e.g. *Hybodus*

ichthyosaur,
e.g. *Cymbospondylus*

sea

nothosaur,
e.g. *Nothosaurus*

pseudosuchian
(thecodont),
e.g. *Euparkeria*

rhynchosaur,
e.g. *Scaphonyx*

cynodont
(therapsid),
e.g. *Thrinaxodon*

sphenodontid
(lizard-related)

aeteosaur
(thecodont),
e.g. *Stagnolepis*

land

coelacanth

placodont
(reptile),
e.g. *Placodus*

holostean,
e.g. *Parasemionotus*

holocephalan

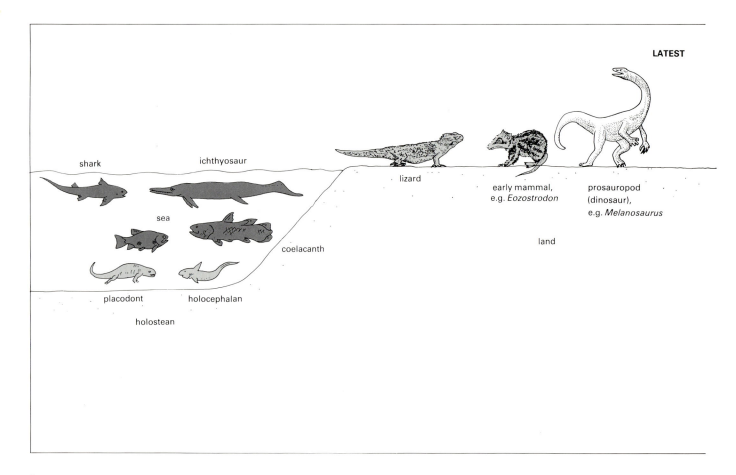

LATEST

shark

ichthyosaur

sea

lizard

early mammal,
e.g. *Eozostrodon*

prosauropod
(dinosaur),
e.g. *Melanosaurus*

land

coelacanth

placodont

holocephalan

holostean

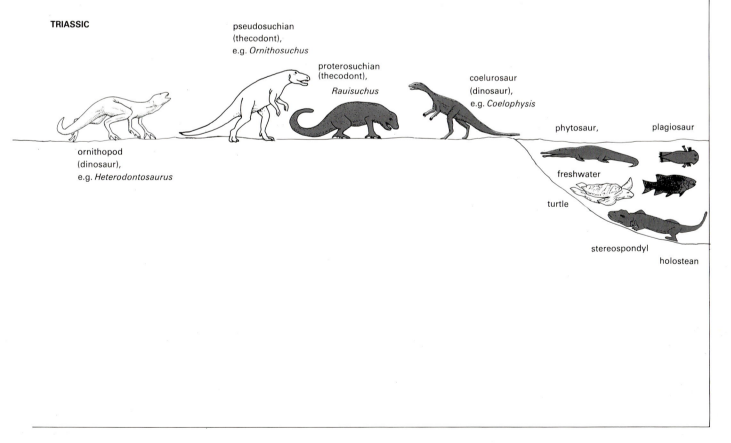

TRIASSIC

gomphodont
cynodont
(therapsid), e.g.
Diademodon

dicynodont,
e.g. *Lystrosaurus*

cynodont
(therapsid),
e.g. *Cynognathus*

proterosuchian
(thecodont),
e.g. *Chasmatosaurus*

lissamphibian
(early frog),
e.g. *Triadobatrachus*

Tanystropheus
(reptile)

phytosaur
(thecodont),
e.g. *Rutiodon*

plagiosaur
(labyrinthodont
amphibian),
e.g. *Gerrothorax*

turtle,
e.g. *Triassochelys*

stereospondyl
(labyrinthodont
amphibian),
e.g. *Capitosaurus*

holostean

TRIASSIC

pseudosuchian
(thecodont),
e.g. *Ornithosuchus*

proterosuchian
(thecodont),
Rauisuchus

coelurosaur
(dinosaur),
e.g. *Coelophysis*

ornithopod
(dinosaur),
e.g. *Heterodontosaurus*

phytosaur,

plagiosaur

freshwater
turtle

stereospondyl

holostean

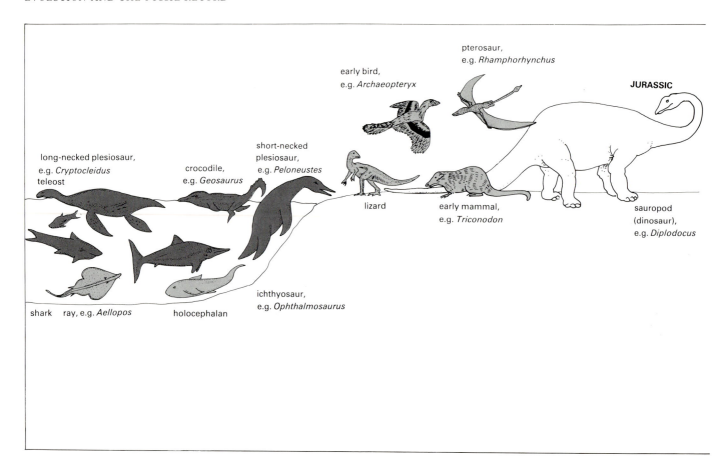

long-necked plesiosaur,
e.g. *Cryptocleidus*
teleost

crocodile,
e.g. *Geosaurus*

short-necked
plesiosaur,
e.g. *Peloneustes*

early bird,
e.g. *Archaeopteryx*

pterosaur,
e.g. *Rhamphorhynchus*

JURASSIC

lizard

early mammal,
e.g. *Triconodon*

sauropod
(dinosaur),
e.g. *Diplodocus*

shark   ray, e.g. *Aellopos*

holocephalan

ichthyosaur,
e.g. *Ophthalmosaurus*

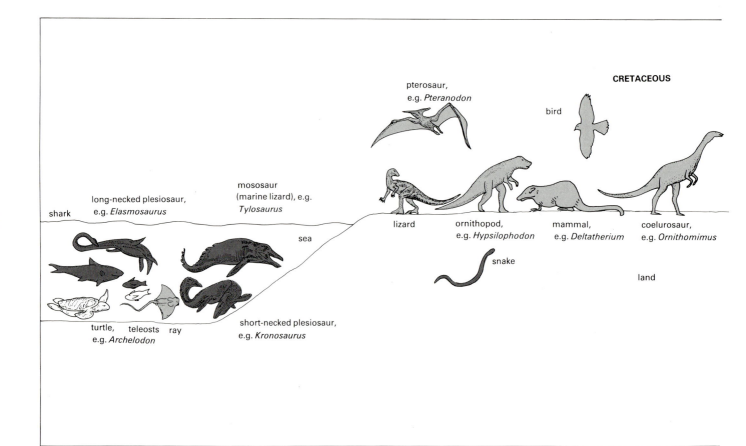

pterosaur,
e.g. *Pteranodon*

CRETACEOUS

bird

mososaur
(marine lizard), e.g.
Tylosaurus

shark

long-necked plesiosaur,
e.g. *Elasmosaurus*

sea

lizard

ornithopod,
e.g. *Hypsilophodon*

mammal,
e.g. *Deltatherium*

coelurosaur,
e.g. *Ornithomimus*

snake

land

turtle,   teleosts ray
e.g. *Archelodon*

short-necked plesiosaur,
e.g. *Kronosaurus*

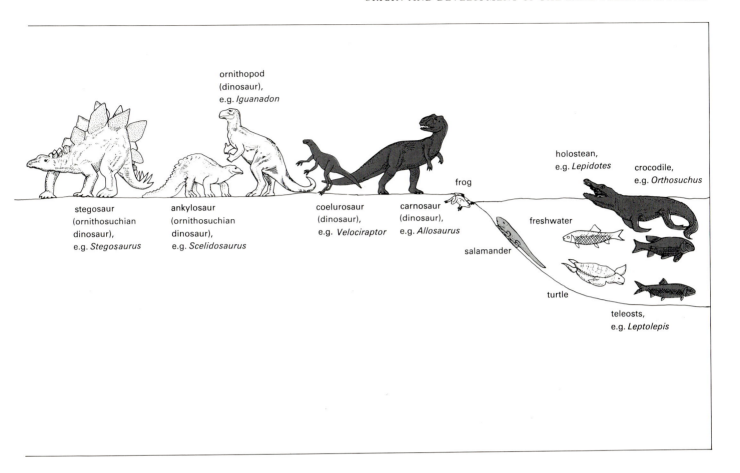

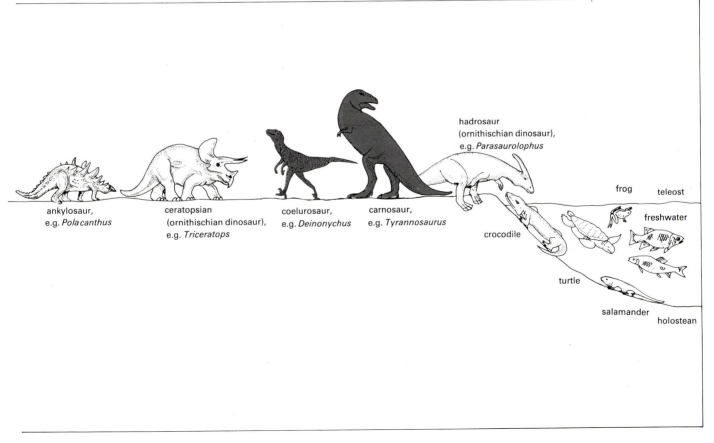

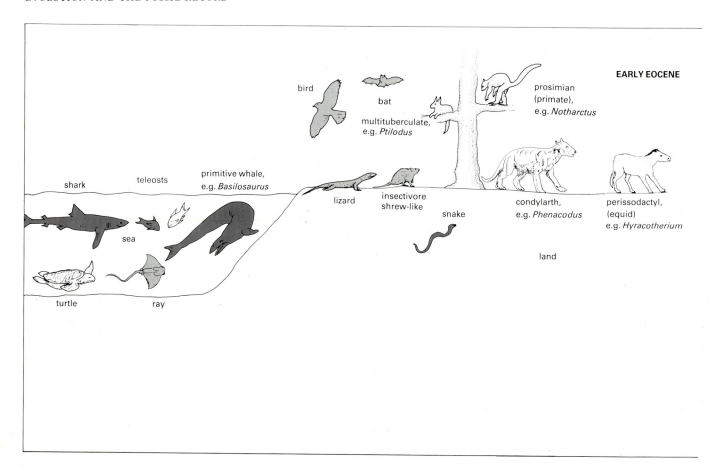

EARLY EOCENE

bird

bat

multituberculate,
e.g. *Ptilodus*

prosimian
(primate),
e.g. *Notharctus*

shark

teleosts

primitive whale,
e.g. *Basilosaurus*

lizard

insectivore
shrew-like

snake

condylarth,
e.g. *Phenacodus*

perissodactyl,
(equid)
e.g. *Hyracotherium*

sea

land

turtle

ray

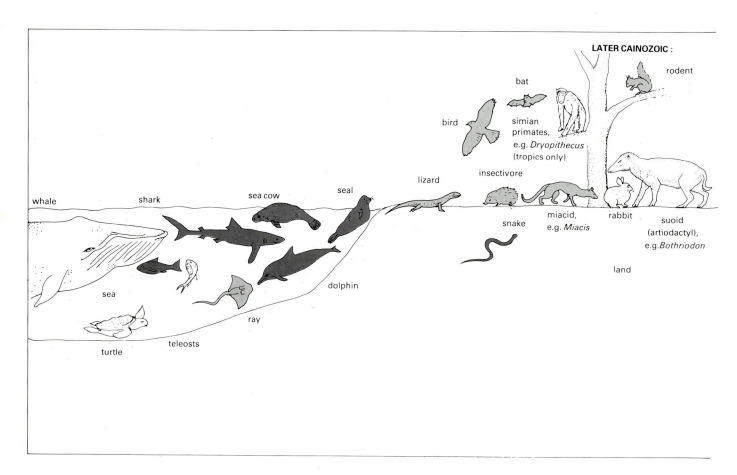

LATER CAINOZOIC :

rodent

bat

bird

simian
primates,
e.g. *Dryopithecus*
(tropics only)

insectivore

lizard

whale

shark

sea cow

seal

snake

miacid,
e.g. *Miacis*

rabbit

suoid
(artiodactyl),
e.g.*Bothriodon*

land

sea

dolphin

ray

teleosts

turtle

EARLY CAINOZOIC : early Eocene

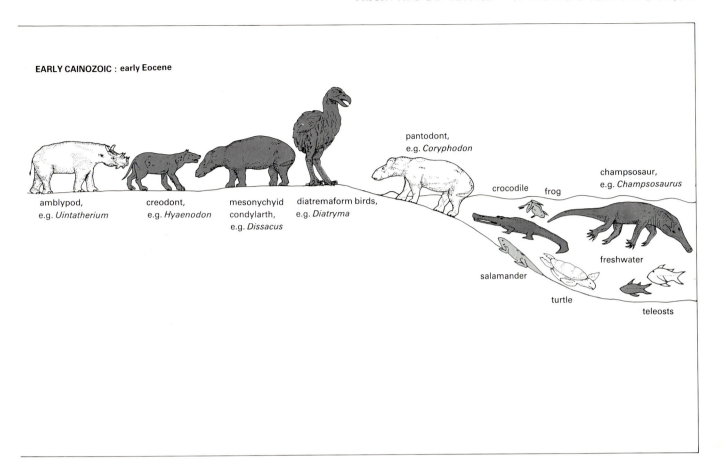

amblypod,
e.g. *Uintatherium*

creodont,
e.g. *Hyaenodon*

mesonychyid
condylarth,
e.g. *Dissacus*

diatremaform birds,
e.g. *Diatryma*

pantodont,
e.g. *Coryphodon*

crocodile

frog

champsosaur,
e.g. *Champsosaurus*

salamander

turtle

freshwater

teleosts

late Oligocene/early Miocene

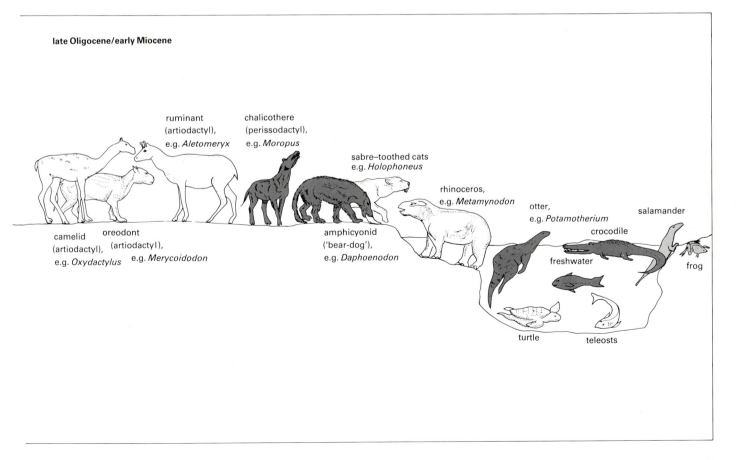

ruminant
(artiodactyl),
e.g. *Aletomeryx*

chalicothere
(perissodactyl),
e.g. *Moropus*

sabre–toothed cats
e.g. *Holophoneus*

rhinoceros,
e.g. *Metamynodon*

otter,
e.g. *Potamotherium*

salamander

crocodile

camelid
(artiodactyl),
e.g. *Oxydactylus*

oreodont
(artiodactyl),
e.g. *Merycoidodon*

amphicyonid
('bear-dog'),
e.g. *Daphoenodon*

freshwater

frog

turtle

teleosts

The Oligocene

The climatic changes at the end of the Eocene had caused dramatic changes in the vegetation in the northern hemisphere by the start of the Oligocene. The end of the Oligocene then saw a slight warming of the climate, but this was accompanied by drier conditions than those of the swampy warm temperate forests of the Palaeocene.

By the Oligocene, the major evolution and dispersal of modern types of angiosperms had occurred. The vegetation of the higher latitudes in the northern hemisphere changed from an essentially broad-leaved evergreen forest to a temperate mixed deciduous woodland of evergreen and broad-leaved trees. This type of woodland is seen today only in certain relict areas (regions containing surviving traces of previously dominant animals and plants), such as the North Island of New Zealand, and the tip of the South African Cape. The flora of North America consisted of a mixture of subtropical elements, such as cashews and *Litchi* (lychee trees), with temperate trees such as roses, beech and pine. Leguminous plants (the pea and bean family) were common, as were sedges, bulrushes and a variety of ferns. Grasses, which appeared for the first time as plants of water margins in the Eocene, became more common in open habitats.

North America was a stable land mass in the Oligocene, but Europe was cut into a series of islands, fluctuating in size and position throughout the epoch as sea-levels changed. A seaway spread from the North Sea to the Tethys Sea, which was in the same position as, but somewhat larger than, the present Mediterranean. These transgressions of the sea appear to have insulated Eurasia from the climatic changes of the late Eocene. The climate in North America became cooler, drier and more seasonal; both floral and faunal evidence suggest that this change was less dramatic in Eurasia. The European Oligocene retained a more prominent subtropical character, with palms, corals and crocodiles, but a general decrease was seen in the percentage of palms and other tropical plants, and an increase in the numbers of temperate trees and herbaceous plants such as grasses, rhubarb, sugar-beet and spinach.

The artiodactyls appeared to take over from the perissodactyls as the dominant medium-sized herbivores in the middle Tertiary. The omnivorous niches were filled by the pigs, which retained short legs and low-crowned teeth, and the leaf-eating niches in subtropical and temperate regions by the ruminants, many of which evolved long limbs and high crowned teeth in parallel with many perissodactyls. However, browsing perissodactyls, in particular certain equids (horse-like forms) and rhinoceros, remained a significant part of the fauna until the end of the Miocene.

Present-day ruminants (such as camels, deer, giraffes and cattle) have a complex fore-stomach, called the rumen, for the digestion of cellulose, a constituent of the plant cell wall. Vertebrates are not able to produce the enzyme that attacks cellulose (see section 5.4), and ingested plant material must be fermented with the aid of symbiotic micro-organisms in the gut. Ruminants also regurgitate their food and chew it several times ('chewing the cud'). This apparently evolved independently in the North American camels and in the Eurasian ruminants, and contrasts with the fermentation system in perissodactyls (such as horses and rhinos), where the food is only chewed once and then is fermented in a chamber in the large intestine or in the hind-gut. The type of system developed was dependent on the body size of the animal and consequently on the adoption of a fibrous diet. The gazelle-sized leaf-eating ruminants of the early Oligocene were considerably larger than the first Eocene leaf-eating perissodactyls and had the evolutionary 'option' for developing a rumen, which seems to be the system that works most efficiently for a medium-sized animal in most ecological circumstances. However, the hind-gut fermentation chamber of perissodactyls appears to be more efficient than a fore-gut system for animals (such as tapirs) eating tropical vegetation, for animals weighing over 1 tonne (as do rhinos) and for animals eating very fibrous vegetation (as do horses). This explains why the radiation of the ruminants did not result in the extinction of all perissodactyls. Proboscideans (elephants, mastodons, and so on) also have a hind-gut fermentation chamber, and have always been specialised for a large body size.

In the early Oligocene of Europe the endemic perissodactyls were forms related to horses and tapirs, and the endemic artiodactyls peculiarly specialised types possibly related to camels. In the middle of the epoch, the Turgai straits between Europe and Asia started to disappear, and these endemic forms were replaced by Asian perissodactyls (rhinos and chalicotheres) and artiodactyls (ruminants and pig-like forms). The predominant habitat appeared to be woodland.

In the North American Oligocene, animals of open habitats first appeared, such as the gazelle-sized camelid *Poëbrotherium*. The equids, such as the three-toed *Mesohippus*, appear to have been sheep-sized woodland browsers. Large rhino-sized brontotheres, perissodactyls with 'Y'-shaped nasal horns, were common in the early Oligocene, but had died out by the middle of the epoch. Tapiroids, common worldwide in the Eocene, became rare in the Oligocene. Rhinos were an emergent and highly successful group at this time. As well as members of the lineage of rhinos surviving today, such as the hornless cow-sized *Trigonias*, two other hornless rhinoceros lineages were present in both the Old World and the New World: the large hippopotamus-like amynodonts, and the pony-sized, long-legged hyracodonts which paralleled the equids in many respects.

The most common animals in Northern America were oreodonts, such as *Merycoidodon*, sheep-sized ruminants which probably wandered in mixed herds through woodland and open habitats. Pig-like artiodactyls included very large forms, such as *Dinohyus* which resembled a buffalo-sized warthog, as well as smaller peccaries. Rabbits, which originated in the Palaeocene of Asia, became common in both North America and

Europe during the Oligocene.

By the mid-Tertiary, the creodonts and the carnivorous condylarths had disappeared from the northern hemisphere, though some persisted in Africa until the end of the Tertiary. The predominant Oligocene carnivores belonged to two families of Carnivora that are now extinct, the amphicyonids and the nimravids. Amphicyonids or 'bear-dogs' were the size of modern wolves, but more heavily built. Most were probably scavengers but others, such as *Daphoenodon*, may have pursued their prey more actively. The sabre-toothed nimravids such as *Nimravus* and *Hoplophoneus* superficially resembled cats, and are often confused with true sabre-toothed cats such as *Nimravides* from the Tertiary and *Smilodon* from the Pleistocene, but in fact were probably an early offshoot of dog-like carnivores. Nimravids were all short-legged ambush predators, and can be distinguished from true cats by the presence of a bony flange on the lower jaw which protected the upper canine teeth. True dogs and cats were still small unspecialised animals during this period, and were to develop and radiate later.

Middle Tertiary African faunas

The first record of African Tertiary faunas comes from the early Oligocene, and contains a large number of endemic ungulates, such as a variety of proboscideans (the group including elephants) and hyracoid ungulates related to the modern hyrax. Other endemic animals included various rodents, insectivorous elephant shrews, aardvarks, and Old World primates including early apes such as *Aegyptopithecus*. Immigrants from Eurasia were also present at this time, including carnivorous creodonts and condylarths, and omnivorous anthracotheres, extinct animals related to pigs. Little is known of later Oligocene faunas, but the large expanse of the Tethys Sea in the Mediterranean region prevented free intermingling of European and African faunas, although some immigrations occurred.

The early Miocene African faunas suggest a woodland habitat, and the floral record shows that leathery-leaved ('laurophyllous') evergreen forest surrounded the Tethyan shores, and summer conditions were equable and wet. The large animals were predominantly rhinos, and proboscideans called deinotheres which had only lower tusks that curved downwards. All probiscideans were large animals possessing tusks and a long trunk, and there appear to have been three main groups distinguished by their feeding habits. Deinotheres ate leaves, mastodons were more omnivorous browsers, and the elephants of the later Tertiary were predominantly grazers. Other large browsers were the chalicotheres, a group of perissodactyls that had claws instead of hooves, and which they may have used to pull down higher branches while standing on their hind legs. A variety of smaller herbivores filled the terrestrial niches, and the arboreal niches were taken by prosimian primates and small hominoids (see section 14.4). The large carnivorous niches were taken by creodonts, and the

small ones by ancestors of modern mongooses and genets.

By the late Miocene, the Tethys seaway had been reduced in size, and considerable interchange of animals and plants had taken place between the Eurasian and African continents. The evergreen woodland that was present, with trees bearing small, hard leaves, indicates cooler and drier conditions, but the summers remained wet. The uplifting of the East African rift system during the Miocene reduced the rainfall on the eastern side of the continent, resulting in the spread of the open grassland habitats (savannas) seen in East Africa today (see section 8.10). The combination of the diverse and many-layered woodland with the newly formed savannas resulted in a greater variety of habitats than are seen today. Many large browsers were present, in contrast to present-day African savannas.

Middle and late Tertiary African faunas were dominated by bovid ruminants such as antelopes, and by a large diversity of giraffoids, including heavily built moose-like sivatheres that became extinct at the end of the Tertiary. Few mouse deer survived, and the remaining hyracoids were small, living among rocks and in trees. Hippopotamus appeared for the first time, and the creodont carnivores were replaced by cats and hyenas similar to modern forms. The diversity of hominoid primates was reduced by the late Miocene (see section 14.4), with only large knuckle-walking apes such as gorillas and chimpanzees remaining, together with the bipedal terrestrial ancestors of the human species. The small arboreal niches, originally occupied by early apes, were now taken by monkeys, able to eat leaves and unripe as well as ripe fruit.

Late Tertiary floras and faunas in the northern hemisphere

At the start of the Miocene, the subtropical elements began to disappear from the northern hemisphere, and temperate coniferous forests and grassy steppes appeared. In Eurasia, temperate trees, such as pine, alder, elm and beech increased, although subtropical elements were retained for longer into the Miocene than in North America, probably because of the presence of the Tethys Sea. Despite the cooling climate and spreading grasslands in North America, the trees present on the western side of the continent, such as sweetgum and tupelo, were characteristic of a higher level of rainfall throughout the year than occurs today.

The early Miocene saw the appearance in Eurasia of a number of families of horned ruminants, including cattle, deer and giraffes, in which bony horns were present in the males. In contrast, among the endemic North American ruminants only a group related to camels, called the protoceratids, evolved horns, and the dominant ungulates of North America in the mid-Tertiary were the hornless camels and horses. The evolution of horns in the Eurasian ruminants may have been related to male rivalry and combat in the acquisition and maintenance of woodland territories, whereas the habitat structure of the more open savanna of North America did not encourage the evolution of this type of behaviour in most of the endemic forms. A number of ruminants migrated across to North America, and the three-toed browsing equid *Anchitherium* moved across into Eurasia and Africa. Various rhinos and carnivores also appeared in North America from the Old World during the early Miocene. In this period a number of modern types of sea mammal also appeared, including whales, dolphins, seals and sealions.

While the Miocene of Eurasia was dominated by deer and various pigs, the early North American Miocene faunas were dominated by oreodonts, horses and camels. Recent immigrants from Eurasia in North America included several lineages of deer-related ruminants: small hornless forms; larger horned dromomerycids (some of which were notable in the possession of a third horn on the back of the head); and the small to medium-sized antilocaprids, which alone of these immigrants survives today as the pronghorn 'antelope' of the American west (see Fig. 8.16). Despite this diversity of horned ruminants in North America, they constituted only about 15% of the total ungulate fauna, in contrast to present-day Africa, where the horned antelopes make up 80% of the ungulates.

The middle Miocene faunas of North America contained a variety of woodland browsers and more open habitat browsers and grazers. Browsing forms included oreodonts, dromomerycids, clawed chalicotheres and small rhinos. The more open habitats were populated by equids, such as *Merychippus*, antilocaprids and camels. The camels filled a variety of herbivorous niches, similar to antelope in Africa today, and included small grazing gazelle-like forms, and larger browsing forms. Cat-like nimravids apparently inhabited the woodlands, ambushing the browsers, while amphicyonids ('bear-dogs') hunted or scavenged in the more open habitats.

This balance of habitat types was apparently disrupted by the arrival of the mastodons from Africa via Eurasia. (Of the other types of proboscideans, elephants did not reach North America until the Pleistocene, while deinotheres never left the Old World). The arrival of the mastodons during the middle Miocene was coincident with, and perhaps even a cause of, a profound change in the structure of the vegetational habitat, with the woodland being replaced by more open grassland. This decline of the woodland habitat resulted in the decline and the eventual extinction of the woodland fauna by the end of the Miocene. Large grazing rhinos, typical of open savanna habitats, appeared as recent immigrants from Eurasia, and replaced the smaller woodland browsing rhinos. The most dramatic event was the radiation of the open-habitat equids, producing many small and medium-sized grazers such as *Calippus* and *Neohipparion*, which came to dominate the faunas in terms of numbers. Some large woodland browsing equids, such as *Hypohippus*, did, however, remain until the end of the epoch.

One lineage of three-toed grazing equids, represented by *Hipparion*, migrated across to Eurasia and Africa in the late Miocene, coincident with the development of more open

grassland habitats in this continent too. The Old World fauna contained large numbers of this equid, together with large grazing antelopes, such as wildebeest, and browsing ungulates. In the Pleistocene, *Hipparion* and its descendants were replaced in the Old World faunas by *Equus*, the single-toed genus of the present day.

The camels increased in size but decreased in diversity in North American faunas of the late Miocene, some such as *Alticamelus* becoming very giraffe-like in size and proportions, while others such as *Megatylopus* were more heavily built but still considerably larger in size than modern camels. The scavenging and pack-hunting 'bear-dogs' were replaced in the late Miocene by dogs with domed foreheads, the borophagines. Ancestors of modern dogs were still the size of foxes at this time. The niche of active predators in the late Tertiary of the Old World was taken by hyenas, and both bears and true cats were now common in the faunas of northern latitudes.

The Pliocene brought a widespread climatic deterioration in the northern hemisphere, with the mixed hardwood forests being replaced by pines and herbaceous plants. Summer drought was now common in the western parts of what is now the USSR and North America, which carried steppe deserts. The faunal diversity of the northern latitudes decreased considerably with this change in climate. The variety of horses, camels and mastodons of the late Miocene was reduced to a few large representatives of each group, although the diversity of antilocaprids (the North American pronghorns) remained relatively high. Most browsing ungulates in North America, including the rhinos, became extinct, although some deer appeared as immigrants from Eurasia in the late Pliocene and have remained to the present day. True dogs, such as the wolves, became the dominant social carnivores across the northern hemisphere. The animals of more tropical woodlands, such as giraffes and deinotheres, became very rare in northern Eurasia during the Pliocene.

By the end of the Tertiary the zonation of climatic, vegetational and animal types was essentially similar to that seen today.

Southern hemisphere Tertiary faunas

The southern continents were the main areas of adaptive radiation of marsupials after the Mesozoic. Marsupials were common in North America until the end of the Cretaceous, and remained as small-sized components of the northern faunas until the Miocene. Medium and large forms, however, appeared only in South America and Australia, and they have remained the dominant animals in Australia until the present. The sole group of non-therian mammals, the egg-laying monotremes, occur today only in Australasia. This group comprises the ant-eating echidnas and the otter-like, semi-aquatic duck-bill platypus (Fig. 14.13).

The marsupials are now believed to have migrated to Australia from South America via Antarctica during the late

a

b

*Fig. 14.13. The two living monotremes. (a) The duck-bill platypus (*Ornithorhynchus anatinus). (b) An echidna (*Tachyglossus aculeatus).

Mesozoic or early Tertiary, before the southern continents had separated and Antarctica had moved to its present position over the south pole, with the formation of the polar ice-cap. It is not known why the placental mammals did not follow the same route, and the pattern of distribution of mammals suggests that the migration was difficult, with possibly only a few individuals arriving to colonise Australia.

Marsupials give birth at a very early stage of the development of their young, and subsequently carry them in a pouch until the offspring are large enough to fend for themselves. This feature cannot be recognised in fossil skeletons, and fossil marsupials are identified on details of the anatomy of their teeth and skull. The marsupial mode of reproduction was probably that of the ancestral therian mammals, with placental mammals subsequently evolving the strategy of carrying their young protected in the womb for a longer time. The marsupial mode of reproduction might, however, in certain circumstances, be at an advantage over that of placental mammals, as some marsupial species are able to retain partially developed young in their womb for several months or more. The embryos are effectively in a state of suspended animation, or diapause, and can recommence development when conditions are favourable. Marsupials can also eject half-developed young from the pouch when conditions are bad. Marsupials might thus be better suited than placentals to the harsh climate of Australia with its pronounced seasonal fluctuations.

One possible disadvantage of the marsupial reproductive system is that the newly born young must have well-developed front limbs so that they can climb up to the pouch immediately after birth. This might limit the amount of evolutionary selection that could act on the forelimbs, and this may be why no marsupials have reduced their forelimb digits or modified their claws into hooves, as have the placental ungulates. Instead, marsupial herbivores, the kangaroos, are hopping

bipeds, apparently having been able to adapt only their hind limbs for fast locomotion.

The Australian marsupials radiated into a similar diversity of niches as did the northern placental mammals (Fig. 7.18), although there are no marsupial equivalents of bats or whales, and the marsupial carnivores are not as adapted for running fast as are many carnivores in the northern hemisphere, having considerably shorter legs. The herbivore niches were taken by a variety of kangeroos and wombats.

The South American faunas also contained a large proportion of marsupials, but these only comprised insectivores, such as the opossum, or carnivores. The possum-rats were small marsupial carnivores, and the now extinct short-legged borhyaenids were larger carnivores. The borhyaenids evolved a sabre-tooth lineage, in parallel with placental carnivores. During the early Tertiary there was a radiation of terrestrial crocodiles, which were probably important predators on land mammals. The niche of the large active carnivore was taken during the later Tertiary by giant flightless diatrymaform birds. Three groups of placental mammals peculiar to South America filled the omnivore and herbivore niches: the edentates, the litopterns and the notoungulates.

The **edentates** retain many of the features of early mammals, but they also show certain specialised characteristics such as the tendency to lose or simplify the teeth, and the presence of double articulations on the vertebrae. Edentates are present in reduced numbers today, and include anteaters, armadillos and sloths. Sloths are now restricted to small tree-living forms, but during the Tertiary there was a diversity of ground-living forms, including the giant ground sloths of the Plio-Pleistocene.

The **litoptrans** were ungulates, derived from condylarths which migrated from North America. Their radiation included medium-sized forms similar to horses, larger forms like camels, and rhinoceros-like forms that may have been semi-aquatic.

The origin of the **notoungulates** is obscure. Fragmentary remains of notoungulates are also known from the Palaeocene of North America, and they were also reasonably diverse in China in this period. Notoungulates retained the squat bodies and short legs typical of early ungulates, but diversified into a number of feeding niches parallel to those of northern herbivores, with forms resembling rodents, rabbits, horses, gazelles, pigs, chalicotheres and rhinos.

Comparison of the South American ungulates with northern forms is interesting. Some forms, such as those resembling horses and gazelles, evolved high-crowned teeth much earlier in the Tertiary than did the northern forms, suggesting the earlier existence in South America of open savanna with widespread grasses. Few South American ungulates, however, evolved the elongated limbs typical of northern ungulates, and this may be related to the absence of fast-running carnivores in South America. A few animals may have had small horns similar to those of rhinos, but none of the South American ungulates had the elaboration of different types of horn characteristic of Old World ruminants. During the late Miocene, much of the savanna–woodland typical of the southern part of the continent became open prairie, as happened in North America in the Pliocene, and a large number of the indigenous South American ungulates and carnivores became extinct at this time.

Various faunal invasions into South America occurred from the north during the Tertiary. Caviomorph rodents (including guinea-pigs) and broad-nosed primates arrived at the start of the Oligocene, and occupied the terrestrial and arboreal niches for small herbivores. South American monkeys never evolved into ape-like forms, possibly because of the competition with the ground sloths already present. In contrast, the rodents radiated into the niches occupied by small ruminants in Africa, suggesting that the indigenous ungulates did not have the digestive physiology of ruminants. The middle Pliocene saw the arrival of carnivores such as the raccoons and coati-mundis.

By the Pleistocene, South America had re-established land contact with North America, and there was a considerable interchange of animals. The movement was primarily from north to south, with the migration into South America of horses, tapirs, peccaries, llamas, mastodons, deer, and carnivores such as dogs, cats and bears. The northern ungulates probably competed successfully with, and replaced, the remaining indigenous South American ungulates, but the borhyaenid carnivores were already all extinct. Armadillos, ground sloths, marsupial opossums and some large rodents, such as porcupines and capybaras, moved from south to north. By the end of the Pleistocene, horses, mastodons, elephants and ground sloths had become extinct in both continents, and camels and capybaras had become extinct in North America. Today tapirs in the New World survive only in tropical Central America, and peccaries and armadillos in North America are restricted to the southern part of the USA.

14.4 HUMAN EVOLUTION

There are two distinct types of evidence available concerning the evolutionary history of *Homo sapiens*, the human species. The relationships of human beings with other animals can be deduced from observation of the morphological features we share with them, and in particular with our closest living relatives, the **apes** (chimpanzees, gorillas, orang-utans and gibbons). It can be assumed that the greater the number of specialised features in common, then the more recently the two species being compared shared a common ancestor. The characters thus shared can be assumed to have been present in the common ancestor unless there is evidence for convergent evolution, and this type of comparison is the most direct evidence of ancestral conditions. The events which are considered major in human evolution, such as the development of bipedalism (walking upright on two legs), are those characters which now distinguish humans from the other living apes.

This evidence on presumed ancestral conditions can then be compared with the second source of evidence, the fossil record. The use of the fossil record involves considerable difficulty and uncertainty, as many species of ape, including human ancestors, are now extinct, and it cannot be assumed that every fossil species is on a direct lineage to the present. In addition, some fossil species are only known from small fragments of a skeleton, and we have little idea of how typical that individual was of the whole population at that time. Finally, the dating of many fossils is still only approximate (see section 12.2).

The apes

Modern apes

Unlike many orders of mammals, the primates have remained sufficiently unspecialised, in terms of anatomy, diet, and so on, to survive in a variety of habitats. They are distinguished from other mammals by possession of an opposable thumb or big toe, fingernails and toenails instead of claws, and four incisors (cutting teeth) in each jaw.

The primates comprise the prosimians, the New World monkeys, the Old World monkeys, and the apes (Fig. 14.14). The human species is placed in the apes (superfamily Hominoidea), because of basic anatomical similarities such as of dentition, the lack of a tail, and the possession of an appendix. The **lesser apes**, that is, the gibbons and siamangs, are distinguished by their very agile form of locomotion (brachiation), which involves swinging through the trees by the arms; their forearms, especially, have become greatly elongated and mobile to allow this. The other apes are called the **great apes**, and comprise the orang utan, chimpanzee, gorilla and the human species (see Fig. 14.15).

Recent work on the molecular structure of the proteins making up the body tissues, particularly the blood proteins such as haemoglobin, confirms these relationships, and has also

Fig. 14.14. The evolution and inter-relationships of primate groups.

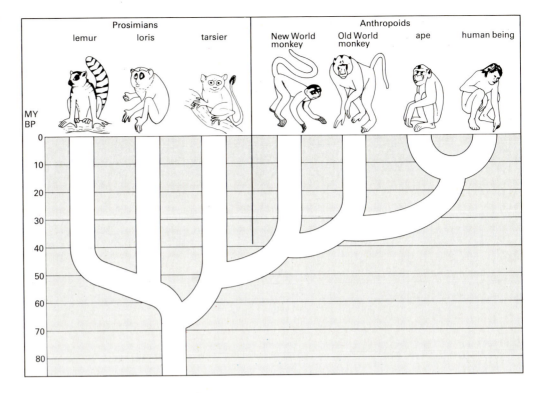

Fig. 14.15. Great Apes. (a) A group of mountain gorillas in Rwanda. (b) An adult male chimpanzee. Both gorillas and chimps are ground-living apes with present distributions limited to parts of Africa. (c) An orang utan hangs from a branch at the Ketarube Rehabilitation Station in Sumatra. Orang utans are tree-dwelling apes found in Sumatra and Borneo.

opened up certain new possibilities for relationships within the Hominoidea. Molecular similarities between proteins are most accurately assessed by direct analysis of the sequence of amino-acids in each protein (Fig. 14.16). By comparing the sequence of the same protein from different species it is possible to estimate the relatedness of these species on the basis of the fewest possible amino-acid substitutions, additions, or deletions needed to produce these different sequences of the protein from some postulated intermediate ancestral sequence. Since many genetic changes are expressed directly through protein sequence changes this method is accurate, but differences in amino-acids can also be estimated by a number of indirect techniques. Although easier and cheaper to perform, these only measure the effect of the protein sequence changes on some property of the protein molecule, such as its immunological or electrophoretic nature, and are thus less accurate than direct sequencing.

First and foremost, the molecular evidence has confirmed that the human species and the apes share a common origin and form parts of the same evolutionary lineage, and both anatomical and molecular approaches agree in the division between the gibbons and the great apes. The molecular evidence diverges from some of the anatomical evidence, however, in the relationships suggested within the Hominoidea. It used to be thought that there was a broad division within the great apes between human beings and the other species (chimpanzee, gorilla and orang utan), but the molecular evidence shows that the primary division is in fact between the orang utan on one hand and humans, chimpanzees and gorillas on the other. This reassessment comes about because the human species shares characters at the molecular level with chimpanzees and gorillas (the African apes) which are not shared with the orang utan, and it indicates that humans shared a common ancestor with the African apes after these had diverged from the lineage leading to the orang utan.

This implies that at least some of the characters shared by chimpanzees and gorillas with the orang utan, such as body hair, heavily browed faces with jutting jaws, and long arms, are either convergent for the two groups, or are primitive for the Hominoidea and have been subsequently lost in the human lineage. The common ancestor of humans and the great apes must therefore have been basically ape-like, and can be described as follows: the skull was robustly built, with moderately jutting jaws, a distinct buttressing of the brow region, a head crest on the skull of males, and massive cheek bones. The canine teeth were massive but not highly crowned, the central incisors broad and spatulate, and the molars and premolars small relative to jaw size but with thick enamel on the crowns. The limbs were adapted for four-footed climbing with mobile and fully extendable elbow joints, a mobile wrist, relatively long hands and feet, curved digits with strong tendons forming grasping hands and feet, and arms probably slightly longer than the legs. The ancestral hominoid was a social animal with a considerable degree of difference between the sexes, lived in tropical woodland, probably in Africa, and was omnivorous, with fruit and nuts from the trees, and seeds, roots and fungi from the ground, as the principal food sources. It would have lived partly in the trees and partly on the ground, much as chimpanzees do today, and in fact this whole outline differs from modern chimpanzees only in relatively minor details. The chimpanzee is the least specialised hominoid living today, and it provides a good model for the ancestral hominoid condition.

The fossil record for apes

There were at least 11 species of fossil ape in the early Miocene 18 million to 22 million years ago. These are grouped in the genera *Proconsul, Limnopithecus, Dendropithecus* and *Micropithecus. Proconsul* has certain specialised characters that debar it from the ancestry of the living apes and humans, but the other three genera retain mainly primitive features, and are all suitable for consideration as an ancestral hominoid.

All had limb bones adapted for living in trees, and the primitive dental characteristics of fruit-eaters. This agrees well with evidence on the other fossil fauna and flora of East Africa in the early Miocene, and with the palaeogeography, which together indicate much greater areas of tropical forest than are there at the present. It is likely that many of these early hominoids were primitive tree-living climbers, as they generally retained unspecialised limb bones and there is no evidence of even incipient bipedalism.

Fossil evidence is, however, available for changing dentition where none is yet available for other body parts. The fossil hominoids of the late Miocene, 8 million to 14 million years ago, show great resemblances in the morphology of jaws and teeth to the early australopithecines which were to appear less than 4 million years ago. *Ramapithecus punjabicus* from India and Pakistan is the species most similar in this respect to *Australopithecus afarensis*, and at 8 million years ago it is relatively recent, but there are problems in accepting *Ramapithecus* as a direct human ancestor. It is closely related to another Asian genus *Sivapithecus*, and it has been proposed that both are related to the orang utan due to a number of shared advanced characteristics of the face and dentition. This link to the orang utan is much more soundly based than are the few characters linking *Ramapithecus* with the human species, and so *Ramapithecus* may not be a direct human ancestor. Unfortunately there is no other obvious candidate in the fossil record of the Miocene.

One of the striking facts about fossil apes is their relative abundance compared with the number of living apes. Today there are just five species of great ape, including humans, and six lesser apes, and they are restricted (except for the human species) to the tropics of the Old World. In the early Miocene there were at least 11 fossil species from Kenya alone, and more if Uganda and Saudi Arabia are included; much of Eurasia has not been fully explored to add to these figures. The number

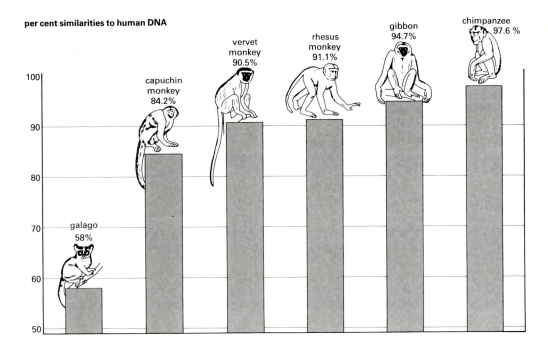

Fig. 14.16. DNA similarity between the human species and other primate groups.

diminished sharply towards the end of the Miocene, and no fossil hominoids are then found at all until the end of the Pliocene.

The observed decline in the diversity and geographical distribution of the hominoid apes during the Miocene can only be an indication of what took place. There must have been many Miocene species not represented in the fossil record, and the decline in numbers must have been correspondingly greater. As the hominoids of today are thus very few compared with past abundance, they can no longer be considered a successful group from an evolutionary point of view. Only one species, *Homo sapiens*, is an exception to this, being a specialised offshoot of this evolutionarily unstable group.

Human characteristics

There are four main sets of characters which distinguish the human species from the other apes and from the probable ancestral condition outlined earlier. These sets are called **structural complexes**, as evolution of a single functional change can cause changes in many bones. For example, the development of an upright walking position (bipedalism) has caused structural changes in the hip, knee and foot bones, the arms have become shorter than the legs, and the point of attachment of the backbone to the skull has shifted (see Fig. 14.17). This form of locomotion has freed the arms for other purposes, and the hands have evolved to be capable of both a powerful grip and a precision grip, with a fully opposable thumb. The second structural complex derives from the increased brain size in man, particularly of the parts controlling manipulative ability, and has resulted in an enlarged cranial vault relative to the face. The short, non-projecting face of humans thus caused is also related to the development of the teeth with a changing diet. The dental arcade (that part of the jaws bearing the teeth) is rounded, with reduced canines, two cusps (points) on the front premolars, and thick enamel on the molars. Finally, the skin is relatively hairless, although as soft parts are not conserved in the fossil record the development of this structural complex cannot be followed through evolution.

Any fossils showing some of these uniquely human specialisations can be linked in an evolutionary relationship to the human lineage, although they need not be direct ancestors of the modern human species.

Bipedalism

Despite the close relationship of the human species with the great apes, the structure of the hip bones, knees and feet in apes and humans are very different since human beings stand upright. The pelvis, in particular, has been shortened and widened, and the muscles attached to it realigned (Fig. 14.17). Changes in the knee allow stresses to pass through the outer side of the joint rather than through the inner; and the foot is no longer a grasping foot, but has the big toe in line with the others, forming a platform for transfer of weight to the ground, with arches to absorb the shock.

These anatomical characteristics are easily identified in the fossil record. The earliest direct evidence available so far comes from the Afar region of Ethiopia, where numerous limb bones have been recovered, including a partial skeleton known as 'Lucy'. This has the adaptations of hip, knee and foot that indicate upright bipedal walking, and this is confirmed by the sets of fossilised footprints discovered at Laetoli in Tanzania, which show that early humans from that site were capable of walking bipedally. The fossil species from the Afar and from Laetoli is known as *Australopithecus afarensis*, and the relevant deposits have been reliably dated at between 3.0 million and 3.75 million years ago, giving the earliest date yet for bipedalism. It is doubtful, however, whether the bipedalism was functionally identical to that of modern humans, for these earliest australopithecines differed from modern man in several primitive characteristics of hip and foot anatomy. The front, pubic, region of the pelvis, for example, was relatively longer, and the upper region relatively broader, than in modern humans. The toe bones of the foot were long and curved, as they are in the grasping feet of great apes. The upper bone of the forearm has some anomalous characteristics that support the view that these australopithecines were still efficient climbers.

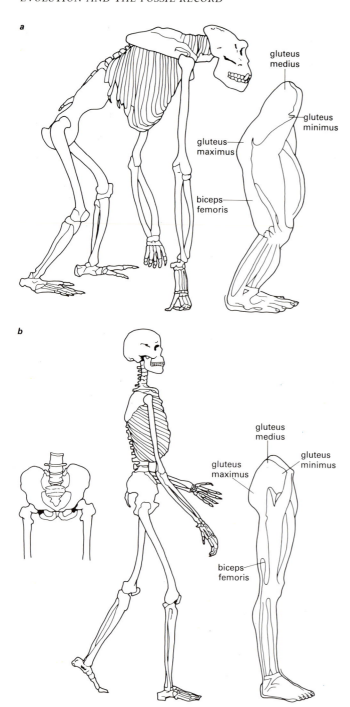

a

b

Fig. 14.17. Skeletons and lower limbs of gorilla (a) and human being (b), showing adaptations to different modes of locomotion. Long extensions on the neck vertebrae support the gorilla's heavy head; knuckle-walking needs long arms and powerful shoulders. In the human species, the leg muscles and pelvis have become adapted for upright stance and walking.

fully developed bipedal adaptations, and also adaptations for increasing the strength of the limbs. Both fossils from *Homo erectus* and, to a lesser extent, those from the earlier populations of *H. sapiens*, have limbs with thick shafts of bone. While this would have increased the inertia of the limbs, and so altered the rate of movement, there is no evidence that these early types were any less efficient bipeds than are modern humans. A fully modern skeletal form appeared relatively late in human evolution, with the appearance of upper Palaeolithic populations in the Middle East and Europe about 30000 years ago.

Brain size

Humans have a larger brain than do other apes of similar body size. The increase in brain size during human evolution can also be observed in the time sequence of the fossil record. There is, however, no clear relation between absolute or relative brain size and intelligence, technology or culture. Many large-bodied animals have similar-sized or larger brains than do humans, although when brain size is related to body size their relative brain sizes are much lower. Conversely, there are some smaller animals, including some prosimian primates, with relative brain sizes greater than those of humans, although in absolute terms their brains are of course much smaller. Porpoises have brains that are both absolutely and relatively larger than those of human beings. Thus, although we assume that the greater intelligence shown by the human species is in some way related to a larger brain, the quantitative nature of the relation is not clear, and it is difficult to measure arbitrarily the degree of complexity of the brain.

Both size and structure of the brain can be estimated through the study of endocasts, in-fillings of the inside of the brain case of fossil skulls. The endocasts of Plio-Pleistocene skulls from East and South Africa (2 million to 3 million years ago) show evidence of altered structure and reorganisation along human lines, before any increase in size had occurred and also well before any evidence for Stone Age cultures. The partial endocast of the fragmentary skull of *Australopithecus afarensis* from Ethiopia is reported to show some expansion and infolding of the cortical regions, so the reorganisation of the brain had commenced about 3.5 million years ago. These characteristics are more fully developed in *A. africanus* of 2 million to 3 million years ago.

There is, however, no evidence for any increase in the size of the brain until after 2 million years ago. Brain size in *A. africanus* varied from 420 to 500 cubic centimetres, and in *A. robustus* from 500 to 530 cubic centimetres. These values are roughly equivalent, in terms of body weight, because *A. robustus* had a greater estimated body size than did *A. africanus*. The value of brain size relative to body size for *A. afarensis* is also similar, as the value estimated from the single skull found is 400 cubic centimetres. After about 2 million years ago brain size increased rapidly, with values of from 590 to 800 cubic centimetres for *Homo habilis* (1 million to 2 million

The australopithecines of 2 million to 3 million years ago do not appear to have advanced far beyond the stage of *A. afarensis*. The ilium of the pelvis is still broad and the ischium elongate, and the toes of the foot are still relatively long. In slightly later deposits, however, to the east of Lake Turkana in Kenya, are fossils that may indicate the existence of a nearly modern bipedal adaptation. Unfortunately, the most relevant body parts, the pelvis and the foot, are not well represented, but some of the other leg bones, especially the femur (the thigh bone), are so modern in appearance compared with those of *A. afarensis* that it seems likely that the missing parts were modern also. The bones are generally assigned to the earliest species of *Homo*, *H. habilis*.

Later skeletal remains, both from Africa and Asia, show

Labels in figure a: gluteus medius, gluteus minimus, gluteus maximus, biceps femoris

Labels in figure b: gluteus medius, gluteus minimus, gluteus maximus, biceps femoris

Fig. 14.18. Skulls of an australopithecine and four species of Homo, *showing progressive modification.*

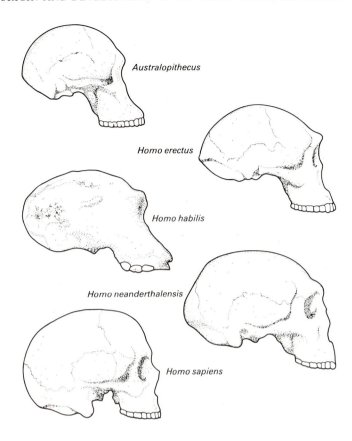

years ago), up to 1200 cubic centimetres for *H. erectus* (500 000 to 1.0 million years ago), and to *H. sapiens* with a mean of 1350 cubic centimetres.

Dentition and facial structure

The human dentition, both fossil and modern, has been much described, but it is a rather less useful source of information than are the other two structural complexes previously discussed. This is because the human dentition has retained until relatively recently many of the primitive hominoid characteristics.

The dentition of *Australopithecus afarensis* is of particular interest as it shows two of the distinctly human characters only incipiently developed. These are the partial reduction in the size of the canines with the associated rounding of the dental arcade, and the development of two cusps on the frontmost lower premolars. By the time of the later australopithecines, such as *A. africanus*, the dental arcade is well rounded and the anterior premolar is fully two-cusped. Apart from a general reduction in the size of the teeth, and of the canines in particular, there is little subsequent morphological change in the evolution of human teeth until the last few thousand years.

Conclusion

Taking an overall view of these concurrently evolving sets of characters, therefore, the human lineage is not known to have begun until *Australopithecus afarensis* at about 3.5 million years ago. In the preceding 4 million years fossil hominoids are extremely rare and fragmentary, and *Ramapithecus* at 8 million years ago shows no sign of these features. There is no real evidence, therefore, linking *Ramapithecus* directly with the human species.

The earliest evidence for the evolution of the human structural complexes, in *Australopithecus afarensis*, shows that they were present but not fully developed. The bipedal adaptations are combined also with adaptations of the arm, hip and foot for climbing, so bipedalism was only partial. Brain size had not started to increase, although some of the characteristically human structural modifications of the brain had appeared. The dentition retained basically primitive characters.

All these modifications were further developed in the later australopithecines of 2 million to 3 million years ago, and 1 million to 2 million years ago the first species of *Homo*, *H. habilis*, appeared. *H. habilis* shows much more fully developed bipedalism, a great increase in the size of the brain together with additional modifications in its structure, and a more modern appearance of the teeth.

H. erectus, of between 500 000 and 1.0 million years ago, is close to modern humans in many characters, although displaying other apparently unique ones. This is one of the problems in recognising *H. erectus* as a direct human ancestor; its skull possesses very thick bones and a keel on top, features which are not primitive but which are also not present in more advanced fossils nor in modern *Homo sapiens*. This excludes these populations of *H. erectus* from being directly ancestral to modern *H. sapiens*, although *H. erectus* may of course be closely related to some direct ancestor. The fossil record then contains a number of early types of *H. sapiens*, such as Neanderthal Man, and fully modern humans appear about 30 000 years ago.

Further reading

Charig, A. *A new look at the dinosaurs*. London: Heinemann and British Museum (Natural History), 1979.

Charig, A. and Horsfield, B. *Before the ark*. London: BBC, 1975.

Eisenburg, J.F. *The mammalian radiations*. Chicago: University of Chicago Press, 1981.

Feduccia, A. *The age of birds*. Cambridge, Mass.: Harvard University Press, 1980.

Kemp, T.S. *Mammal-like reptiles and the origin of mammals*. London: Academic Press, 1982.

Kurten, B. *The age of mammals*. London: Weidenfeld & Nicholson, 1971.

Lillegraven, J.A., Kielan-Jaworowska, Z. and Clemens, W.A. (Editors) *Mesozoic mammals: the first two-thirds of mammalian history*. Berkeley: University of California Press, 1979.

McFarland, W.N., Pough, F.H., Cade, T.J. and Heiser, J.B. *Vertebrate life*. New York: Macmillan, 1979.

Simpson, G.G. *Splendid isolation. The curious history of South American mammals*. New Haven: Yale University Press, 1980.

Vaughan, T.A. *Mammalology*. (2nd edn) Philadelphia: Saunders, 1978.

A reconstruction of the Late Carboniferous locality of Nýřany, Czechoslovakia, showing species known from coal measure freshwater swamp deposits. The coal swamps were densely forested by arborescent clubmosses (e.g. *Lepidodendron* and *Sigillaria*) with occasional shrubby seed ferns (e.g. *Alethopteris*). Open areas of water, sometimes stagnant, may have been fringed by stands of the arborescent horse-tail, *Calamites*. Small clearings in drier areas of the forest were colonised by the tree fern, *Psaronius*. The understorey layer comprised ferns, the scrambling herbaceous horse-tail *Sphenophyllum* and perhaps herbaceous clubmosses.

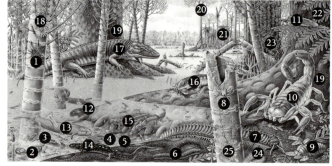

INVERTEBRATES
1. *trigonotarbid*
2. *king crabs*
3. *tubes of caddis fly larvae*
4. *bivalve molluscs*
5. *palaeocarid crustaceans*
6. Pleurojulus biomatus, *a cylindrical millipede*
7. Acantherpestes gigas, *a spiny millipede*
8. Promygale bohemica, *an anthracomartid*
9. Glomeropsis ovalis, *a pill millipede*
10. Isobuthus, *a scorpion*
11. *cockroach*
VERTEBRATES
12. Ophiderpeton, *an aistopod lepospondyl amphibian*

13. Microbrachis, *a microsaur*
14. Scincosaurus, *a nectridean lepospondyl amphibian*
15. Branchiosaurus, *a larval eryopid labyrinthodont amphibian*
16. Amphibamus, *a dissorophid labyrinthodont amphibian*
17. Cochleosaurus, *an edopoid labyrinthodont amphibian*
PLANTS
18. Calamites *(trunk) with* Annularia *(leaves)*
19. Lepidodendron *(trunk) with* Stigmaria *(roots)*
20. Lepidodendron
21. Psaronius *(tree-fern)*
22. Alethopteris
23. Sphenopteris
24. *fragments of the terminal leafy shoots from the crown of* Lepidodendron
25. Sphenophyllum *with cone*

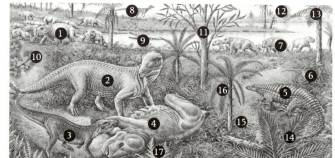

A reconstruction of the Late Triassic Ischigualasto locality of western Argentina. The animals shown are from the middle period of the fauna, which includes both dinosaurs and mammal-like reptiles. Ferns were the important ground-cover plants. Those shown here are members of the present-day tropical family Dipteridaceae. Arborescent types may have formed thickets. Unfortunately little is known about the habit of the seed-fern *Dicroidium* that characterises this flora, but other gymnosperms include shrubs or small trees of ginkgoalean (*Baiera*), cycad (*Leptocycas*, *Pseudoctenis*) and cycadeoid (*Williamsonia*) affinity. More dense forests in drier, inland and upland areas were probably dominated by conifers.

ANIMALS

1. Scaphonyx, *a rhynchosaur*
2. Saurosuchus, *a proterosuchian thecodont*
3. Venaticosuchus, *an ornithosuchid thecodont*
4. Ischigualastia, *a kannemeyeriid dicynodont*
5. Aetosauroides, *an aeturosaurian thecodont*
6. Pisanosaurus, *the earliest ornithischian dinosaur*
7. Exaeretodon, *a traversodont cynodont*
8. Herrerasaurus, *a prosauropod dinosaur*
9. Proterochampsa, *a crocodilian*

PLANTS

10. Baiera
11. Williamsonia *tree*
12. *conifers*
13. *dicksoniaceous tree*
14. Pseudoctenis *leaves*
15. *dipteridaceous leaves*
16. Leptocycas
17. Dicroidium *foliage*

A reconstruction of the (late) Early Miocene mammal fauna of Sheep Creek, Nebraska. The vegetation was probably substantially modern.

VERTEBRATES

1. Anchitherium, *an equid*
2. Miolabis, *a camelid*
3. Blastomeryx, *a palaeomerycid*
4. Archaeohippus, *an equid*
5. Sinclairomeryx, *a palaeomerycid*
6. Merycodus, *an antilocaprid*
7. Merychyus, *a merycoidodont*
8. Merychippus, *an equid*

9. Teleoceras, *a rhinocerotid*
10. Amphicyon, *a canid*
11. Aphelops, *a rhinocerotid*
12. Protolabis, *a camelid*
13. Protohippus, *an equid*
14. Pseudalticamelus, *a camelid*
15. Hesperhys, *a tayassuid*
16. Tylocephalanyx, *a chalicothere*
17. Bouromeryx, *a palaeomerycid*

15 Recent History of the Fauna and Flora

15.1 THE QUATERNARY CLIMATE AND FOSSIL RECORD

In this and the next two sections the history of the fauna and flora during the most recent period of geological time, the Quaternary, is discussed. The boundary between the Tertiary and the Quaternary is now placed at about 2 million years ago. The Quaternary can be divided into the Holocene (post-glacial or Recent) period, which covers the last 10000 years, and the Pleistocene, which is the rest of the Quaternary. Sometimes, however, the term Pleistocene has been used as synonymous with Quaternary.

Some mammals have shown considerable evolutionary changes during the Quaternary, but other animals and plants, as far as can be judged from fossil evidence, have changed very little. In general, changes in the fauna and flora of a locality through time have instead been brought about by migration in response to climatic changes.

The Quaternary is characterised by marked climatic oscillations superimposed on a long-term trend of global cooling. These climatic changes are reflected in the records of fossils in sedimentary rocks, and are used to define the different strata within the Quaternary. The generally accepted terrestrial sequences for Europe, Britain and North America are shown in Fig. 15.1. The sequence of Quaternary sediments is fragmentary, and there is still considerable controversy about the correlations between different older Quaternary deposits, even within a relatively well-known area such as North-west Europe. Certain more complete sequences have been found elsewhere in Europe, particularly in Greece, and also on other continents. Geographical differences in the fauna and flora mean, however, that it is difficult to say which part of one sequence corresponds to a particular part of another sequence when both are earlier than the limit of radiocarbon dating, which is about 60000 years ago (see section 12.1).

Climatic change in the Quaternary Period

The Quaternary Period witnessed great fluctuations in climate. There were several long cold periods, each lasting some 100000 years, with intermittent continental glaciation in high latitudes and corresponding depressions in the world sea-level. These alternated with shorter temperate phases, of about 10000 to 20000 years, when the climate and sea-levels were similar to those of today. These changes caused major changes in the type, distribution and stability of the vegetation, and may in part have been responsible both for the high rate of mammalian evolution and for the extinction of some species of both plants and animals. The Quaternary also saw the rise of the human species to become the dominant world animal, which has resulted in the modification of environments at an ever-increasing pace, especially following the beginning of farming about 10000 years ago in the Middle East.

The Middle and Upper Quaternary in much of Europe and North America was a period of predominantly cool, dry climate, interrupted on the one hand by relatively short periods of intense cold and extensive glaciation, and on the other by periods of temperate climate. The more marked temperate phases, in which temperatures equalled or exceeded those of today, are termed **interglacials**, while temperate phases of shorter duration and/or intensity are termed **interstadials**.

The causes of cyclic climatic changes of this magnitude are not fully understood. Both the overall trend of cooling throughout the world during the Tertiary and Quaternary and the climatic oscillations of the Quaternary remain to be explained in full. The general northward drift of the continents, the position of Antarctica over the south pole, and the widespread formation of mountain ranges, certainly provided favourable conditions for the growth of ice-sheets and glaciers. These terrestrial factors are, however, not sufficient to account for the extent and rapidity of the overall global cooling, which appears to have resulted from some extraterrestrial cause, most probably a decrease in the output of radiation from the sun. The Quaternary climatic oscillations have been plausibly related to cyclic variations known to occur in the earth's orbit around the sun, a theory especially associated with Milankovitch who first calculated these variations in detail.

Studies, using vertical cores taken through sediment on the ocean-floors, of the changes in the shells of Foraminifera, calcareous protozoans, and of the ratio of the stable oxygen isotopes (^{18}O: ^{16}O) in the calcium carbonate of their shells, yield evidence of the changing global temperatures. The ^{18}O: ^{16}O ratios are thought to reflect the amounts of global water locked up in ice-sheets and glaciers (see section 12.1). Since the last major reversal of the earth's magnetic poles about 700000 years ago, nine cold periods of comparable duration and severity to the last cold stage (called the Last Cold Stage or, in different areas, the Devensian, Weichselian, Würmian or Wisconsinian; see Fig. 15.1) have been identified. Several lesser climatic oscillations occurred before this time. Far fewer oscillations have been recognised in terrestrial deposits than in these marine deposits, and so far only the youngest part of the sequence from deep-ocean cores can be correlated with equivalent sequences on land.

Glaciers and ice-sheets have left prominent geomorphological evidence of their former presence in an area. The most characteristic glacial deposit is **till** (boulder clay), which is the debris carried by the ice and deposited where and when the ice melts. Till can form distinct features, called moraines, or it can be laid down as an irregular blanket sometimes traceable over tens or hundreds of kilometres. Glacial melting also produces deposits of material washed out from under the ice by melt-water, such as gravel fans and ridges (eskers). It also causes erosion, and overdeepened river valleys and gorges have been carved by large amounts of fast-flowing melt-water. Glaciers also erode the landscape directly, leaving glaciated 'U'-shaped

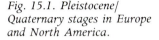

Fig. 15.1. Pleistocene/ Quaternary stages in Europe and North America.

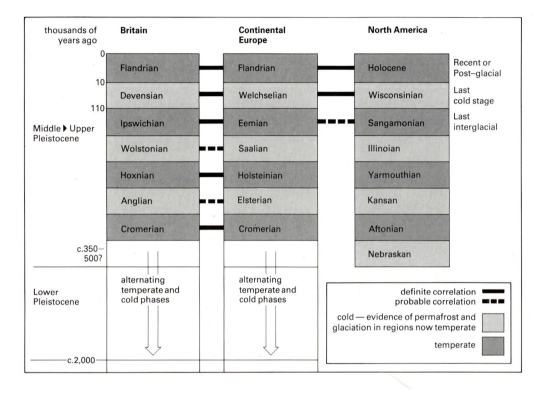

valleys and corries in mountains, and sets of parallel scratches (striations) on hard rock (see Fig. 5.5).

Tills can only be dated by radiocarbon dating, or indirectly, by tracing their relationship with non-glacial organic deposits which are datable by their fossil content. Two tills may be separated in time by an interglacial period, or they may result from two separate advances of ice during the same cold phase. In Europe, however, at least four major advances of ice have been recognised from the glacial evidence, both in the Alps and in north-western Europe.

During major phases of glaciation, much of the water that evaporated from the oceans was not returned to the sea via rivers. Instead it accumulated as ice, causing the world sea-level to fall by up to 100 metres, or sometimes more. The shapes of the land masses have been estimated for the last glaciation at 18 000 BP (years before present), together with sea-surface temperatures and the distribution of snow, ice, and vegetation (Fig. 15.2). The worldwide falls in sea-level exposed large areas of continental shelf, and caused formerly distinct areas of land to become united. For example, the British Isles became joined to Continental Europe across the dry bed of the North Sea, and Alaska became joined through the region of the Bering Straits to Siberia. These land bridges were very important for the migration of plants and animals, including the human species, during periods of cold climate. During the interglacials, the land masses were once again isolated as the ice melted and the sea-level rose.

Evidence of past environments from sediments

Evidence of past environments can be obtained from the sediments deposited then, and this is often of great value in aiding the interpretation of the fossil data. The composition of the sediment can reveal much information about the environment in which deposition was occurring, for example whether the landscape was being eroded, or whether warm conditions had allowed the development of vegetation which formed organic deposits. Organic sediments are deposited in relatively undisturbed environments such as peat bogs, fens, lakes, and forest floors. In contrast, inorganic sediments are often deposited in disturbed conditions. On land, deposits of loess are transported by wind, and gravels and boulder clays are deposited as a result of glaciation. In lakes, inorganic material is washed in by streams and rivers, as a result of soil erosion due to frost, forest clearance by human activity, or trampling by animals, or as a result of changes in water-level eroding the lake shores. Other types of Quaternary deposit include debris deposited in caves (cave-earths) and fissures, deposits on river terraces, and deposits of calcium carbonate (called travertines and tufas) from calcareous springs. Volcanic lavas and layers of ash have also been formed during the Quaternary. Inorganic material may also be precipitated from the water, for example calcium carbonate is deposited as marl after intense photosynthesis by aquatic plants in an alkaline lake. Sometimes this precipitation is seasonal, and annual layers may be formed, which can be useful in estimating the sedimentation rate; when analysed in detail, these laminations can give a yearly picture of environmental events.

The chemical composition of a lake sediment or peat can be used to interpret the palaeoenvironment. In the English Lake District, for example, the amounts of elemental carbon and of inorganic ions such as sodium, potassium, magnesium, iron and carbonate have been used to show that most of the sediment in these rather nutrient-poor lakes has been washed in by the rivers supplying the lakes. In more fertile lakes, much of the sediment may result from organic productivity in the lake itself. Eutrophication of a lake (see section 9.2) can often be traced by the increasing amounts of nitrogen, phosphorus and total organic matter in the sediment.

Sediments contain biological evidence in the form of plant and animal fossils. The most widespread and useful of these is pollen, which is usually present in sufficiently large amounts for characteristic charts ('**pollen diagrams**') of the frequency of different types of pollen to be obtained by analysing different levels in the sediment. These can be used for interpreting the nature of the environment and environmental changes, and characteristic pollen spectra can be used to correlate different sites within a small area. Other plant fossils, and fossils of animals such as beetles, molluscs and vertebrates, are usually less abundant than pollen grains, and are of a more local origin than pollen, which may be carried many miles by the wind; they therefore provide important information on the species that were present at the site at the time of deposition. From a knowledge of present-day ecological requirements of these plants and animals, a picture of past ecological and environmental conditions (**palaeoecology**) can be built up. In the case of a number of mammals which evolved relatively rapidly during the Quaternary, the conditions in which the extinct species lived can be deduced from the other fossil and sedimentary evidence.

Dating Quaternary sediments

General methods of correlation and dating of rocks are discussed in section 12.1. Radiocarbon dating can be used on organic sediments younger than about 60000 years and older than about 200 years. Dating Quaternary deposits older than 60000 years is difficult. Other radiometric methods, such as those using the uranium series or potassium:argon ratios, are generally rather inaccurate in such young rocks and/or are only possible on certain materials, such as stalagmites or volcanic rocks. Other absolute dating methods including thermoluminescence and amino-acid racemisation, are being actively investigated at present in an attempt to solve this problem.

Short-lived isotopes, particularly lead-210 (^{210}Pb), can be used to date recent lake sediments up to about 150 years old, which are too young for the radiocarbon method. Recent changes in the sediment and pollen can be dated and correlated with known events in the environment, such as forest clearance by immigrant Europeans in North America.

Palaeomagnetism can be used to date Holocene (post-glacial) lake sediments. The position of the magnetic north pole has moved in a known way during the Holocene, and magnetisable material in the sediments became orientated towards the pole at the time of deposition. If a core of known orientation is taken, the deviations from present north can be used to date the sediment, and to correlate the strata in different cores.

In a few cases, sediments have been discovered which contain layers each corresponding to one year of deposition. These annually laminated sediments have provided estimates of about 15000 to 16000 years for the duration of the Holsteinian interglacial in Germany, 4500 years for part of the Hoxnian interglacial in England, and about 11000 years for the Eemian interglacial in Germany. So far, the present temperate phase, the Holocene or Flandrian, has lasted about 10000 years (see Fig. 15.1).

Occurrence of fossil Quaternary vertebrates

Skeletal remains of Quaternary (Pleistocene) vertebrates occur as fossils in a variety of sediments deposited from a wide range of environments. Usually the sediments have a high content of calcium carbonate, which protects bones and teeth from being dissolved in acidic waters passing through the deposit. Vertebrate fossils from the Quaternary are mostly found in sediments laid down in limestone caves or fissures, in lake sediments, in wind-blown loess, and in river deposits. Marine deposits yield remains of fishes, whales, turtles and other marine vertebrates, and sometimes also non-marine material washed down by rivers.

It is very important when interpreting an assemblage of fossils to understand as far as possible the processes which have operated in deriving the fossil assemblage from a living assemblage (see section 12.1). These processes can result in a biased composition of the fossil fauna in comparison to the living community from which it was derived. For example, assemblages in caves generally show disproportionately high numbers of carnivore remains, because these animals lived and died in the caves. In contrast, assemblages from river deposits generally show roughly the relative abundance of fossil groups that one would expect from the relative population densities of these, or closely related, animals today, such as high numbers of small rodents, many large herbivores, and relatively scarce carnivores. Quaternary vertebrate assemblages contain animals which have died naturally (attritional mortality), or which have been killed in natural traps, or which have been killed by predators. The initial accumulations may remain in place or undergo subsequent transport, such as in a river, followed by redeposition.

In assemblages of fossils resulting from attritional mortality, bones and teeth of animals that died from a variety of causes

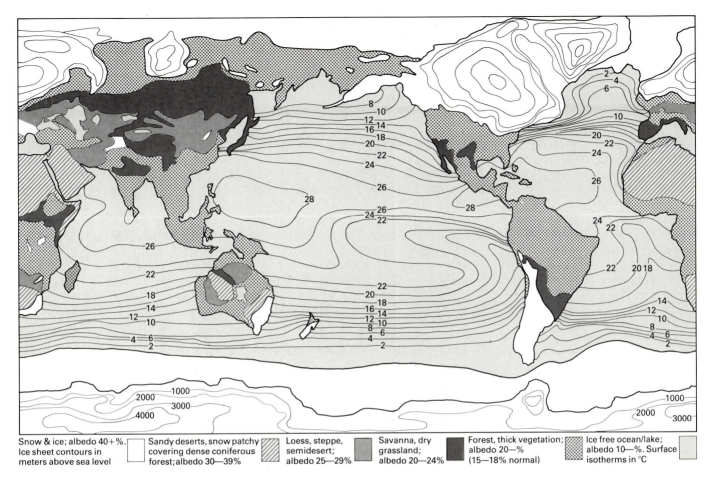

Snow & ice; albedo 40+%. Ice sheet contours in meters above sea level	Sandy deserts, snow patchy covering dense coniferous forest; albedo 30—39%	Loess, steppe, semidesert; albedo 25—29%	Savanna, dry grassland; albedo 20—24%	Forest, thick vegetation; albedo 20—% (15—18% normal)	Ice free ocean/lake; albedo 10—%. Surface isotherms in °C

Fig. 15.2. *Map showing sea-surface temperatures, ice cover and continental albedo (ratio of reflected to received radiation) for August, 18000 years* BP.

accumulate at sites over many years. For example, large numbers of bear remains are commonly found in European cave deposits (from the brown bear, *Ursus arctos*, and the extinct cave bear, *Ursus spelaeus*), and represent animals that died during winter hibernation. Also, a wide variety of vertebrates are incorporated in river deposits, most of the material having been washed in from the surface of the land, and all of it having experienced some degree of transport in the river after the death of the animal.

Natural traps can take many forms, and often the origin of an assemblage of fossils can be worked out from observations on modern animals. Large mammals from time to time became stuck in soft mud at the edge of a lake or river, and their bones were buried by the further deposition of sediment. Others appear to have drowned after breaking through thin ice on a lake or river, as may have happened in the case of numerous complete and partial skeletons of the extinct giant deer *Megaceros giganteus*, from late Pleistocene lake deposits in Ireland. Some cave assemblages appear to have resulted from animals falling through a hole in the roof. Extremely rare, but spectacularly rich in vertebrate fossils, are Pleistocene asphalt deposits ('tar pits') known from California (Rancho La Brea), South America and the Caucasus. Large mammals were possibly attracted to pools of water on the asphalt, and became caught in the sticky asphalt when they tried to drink. Predators and scavengers attracted to the scene were then trapped in their turn. Even more exceptional are the deep-frozen

carcasses of mammoth, bison, horse and other mammals preserved in the permafrost of Siberia and Arctic North America. Carcasses of woolly rhinoceros, naturally embalmed in salt and petroleum, have been found in Poland.

Skeletal remains of prey or of scavenged carcasses commonly accumulated where carnivorous animals lived. In Britain, in the Upper Pleistocene, the spotted hyenas (*Crocuta crocuta*) used many caves as dens, into which they dragged remains of mammals killed by the hyenas themselves, killed by other carnivores, or dead from other causes. Assemblages in these dens can be easily recognised since they mainly comprise isolated teeth, compact bones and characteristically shaped bone fragments: the sole materials remaining after having been chewed by the hyenas' powerful jaws and teeth. Humans similarly accumulated remains of prey when occupying caves, or at open sites generally by a lake or river. Assemblages of small vertebrates such as voles, mice and shrews, commonly comprising vast numbers of bones and teeth, and occurring especially in cave deposits, originate from the regurgitated pellets dropped by roosting owls and other predatory birds.

Plant fossils from the Quaternary

The evidence for the history of plants also comes from fossils. Where deposition has occurred in suitable environments, some plants or their parts can be well preserved: peat, for example, consists largely of plant remains, from which recognisable

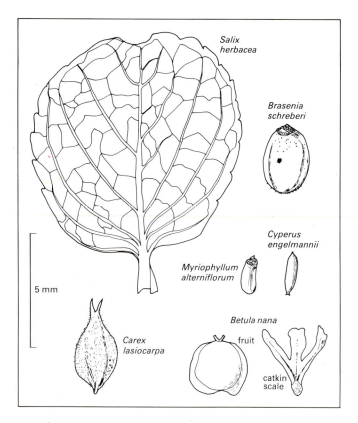

Fig. 15.3. Drawings of a range of plant macrofossils: leaves of Salix herbacea *(dwarf willow), typically found in sediments of cold periods; seeds of the aquatic plants* Myriophyllum alterniflorum *and* Brasenia schreberi; *fruits and catkin scales of* Betula nana *(dwarf birch); and fruits and seeds of marshland sedges,* Carex lasiocarpa *and* Cyperus engelmannii.

plant parts may often be readily extracted. Sometimes trunks and stumps of trees may also be preserved, and these remains form 'buried forests' along the coasts where sea-level changes have overwhelmed forests growing on peaty soils; good examples may be seen around the coasts of mid-Wales and the north-eastern USA. Tree stumps are also sometimes seen in eroded peat bogs, especially in Scotland, Ireland and Scandinavia, where peat growth has overwhelmed a forest growing either on mineral soil, or on an old dried-out peat surface.

Such large fossils, however, are comparatively rare. Smaller, but more numerous, are fossil fruits and seeds preserved in lake or bog sediments, and other plant parts such as cones, leaves, flowers and anthers may also be preserved (Fig. 15.3). The smallest, most numerous and most ubiquitous plant fossils are pollen grains. The resistant part of the pollen-grain wall consists of sporopollenin, an inert substance which decomposes very slowly, particularly in the anaerobic environments of bogs and lakes.

Fruits, seeds and pollen are produced by angiosperms (flowering plants) and gymnosperms (cone-bearing plants). Pteridophytes (ferns, horsetails and club-mosses) may be recognised from their spores (which also contain sporopollenin), from their sporangia (spore-bearing organs), and from impressions of fronds. Bryophytes (mosses and liverworts) commonly grow in bogs, fens and shallow water, and in the associated sediments leafy shoots of many mosses are preserved. Mosses, especially *Sphagnum*, sometimes form the bulk of a peat deposit, and 'brown mosses' characteristically accumulate in alkaline mires. Curiously, liverworts are poorly preserved and thus are rarely found as fossils. Some algae are fossilised: in particular, diatoms are frequently well preserved due to the tough siliceous shells of their single cells. Other algae, such as *Pediastrum*, may also be found if they have resistant cell walls.

Plant fossils may be conveniently divided into **microfossils**, which need a high-power light microscope in order to be seen, and **macrofossils**, which can be manipulated by hand and can generally be identified using a low-power dissecting microscope. Microfossils include pollen, spores and algae. Macrofossils include larger plant remains, such as fruits and seeds, leaves, wood, and bryophytes.

Pollen analysis

Pollen analysis is the most important and most generally used technique for reconstructing Quaternary floras. From the fossil flora (the list of species present), the type of vegetation and environment may be reconstructed.

Samples of sediment are taken from a suitable site: in an open section these can be taken directly from a clean face at measured intervals, or a column of material can be removed and sampled in the laboratory. Otherwise, a core of sediment is extracted from the peat bog or lake sediment, using a specially constructed device called a corer. The pollen grains, which can be very numerous in the sediment, can be extracted from it, as the resistant nature of sporopollenin allows the matrix material to be dissolved chemically, leaving behind the pollen. Pollen grains generally have a round shape, with each type having a characteristic number and arrangement of pores or slits (called furrows or colpi). These may be combined with a characteristically sculptured surface and wall structure, forming spines, nets and other shapes (Fig. 15.4).

The amount of each type of pollen is expressed as a percentage of the total, and the percentages plotted against the depth, or age, of the sediment levels to produce a **pollen diagram** such as that shown in Fig. 15.10. Pollen diagrams can be divided into pollen zones, which can be used for correlation with other pollen diagrams. The pollen spectrum at any particular time is a reflection of the vegetation around the site then, and can be used to study its palaeoecology. Changes in the pollen, and hence in the vegetation, with time can be used to investigate the nature of vegetational changes, such as the order in which different species invade and become established in vegetation, and how vegetation reacts to disturbance, such as forest fires or interference by humans. The environmental tolerances which the vegetation and its components are known to show today can be used to interpret environmental conditions in the past, including soil types and climate.

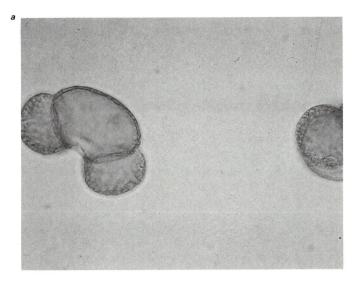

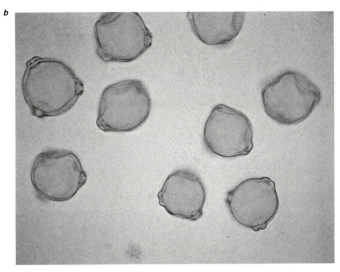

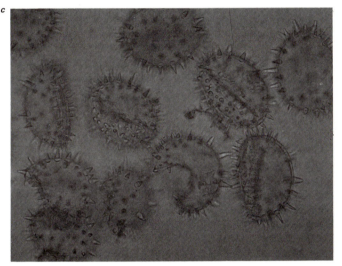

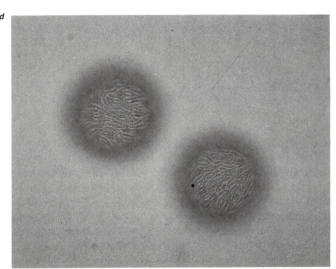

Fig. 15.4. Photographs of pollen grains showing some of the range in form. (a) Pine (Pinus): typical of many conifers, with a finely granular body (diameter 40–50 micrometres), bearing two coarsely sculptured air bladders. (b) Birch (Betula): smooth-walled spheres (diameter 25 micrometres), with protruding pores around the equator. (c) Yellow water-lily

(Nuphar lutea): bean-shaped grains (60 micrometres long), with one longitudinal furrow and a spiny surface sculpture. (d) Jacob's ladder (Polemonium caeruleum): spheres (diameter 45 micrometres), with numerous pores and a sinuate surface sculpture.

Plant macrofossils

Plant macrofossils are not chemically resistant like pollen grains, so they are separated from the sediment by gently breaking it up and passing it through a series of sieves of appropriate mesh size. The macrofossils are retained and the finer matrix material is washed through by a gentle stream of water. The concentrate is examined using a low-power light microscope, and the macrofossils picked out from any remaining sediment and from larger unidentifiable plant fragments. Depending on the abundance of macrofossils, the results of such analysis can be presented as a table, as a macrofossil diagram similar to a pollen diagram, or they can be plotted with pollen values from the same core or section, thus allowing a direct comparison to be made of the two types of fossil.

Macrofossils are of only limited use in the correlation of different strata, and their main use is in the interpretation of palaeoecological data; often macrofossils can be identified more precisely than can pollen grains. Because of their generally limited dispersal, in contrast to pollen which may travel great distances before becoming trapped in sediment, macrofossils of a species generally indicate that the species was present nearby at that time. This is particularly useful in the interpretation of pollen spectra which contain pollen from groups of plants with abundant and widely dispersed pollen, such as *Betula* (birch) and *Pinus* (pine). If macrofossils of these species are present too, it is certain that the trees grew in the vicinity. Similarly, macrofossils can indicate which species of tree within a genus produced the pollen, for example *Pinus* and *Picea* (spruce) species in the USA, and *Betula* species in Europe; this cannot be determined readily from their pollen grains.

Most macrofossils originate from wetland or aquatic plants growing near or actually at the site of deposition. Hence a macrofossil assemblage gives good palaeoecological information on the local environmental conditions. Changes in the macrofossils found through a stratigraphic sequence may be

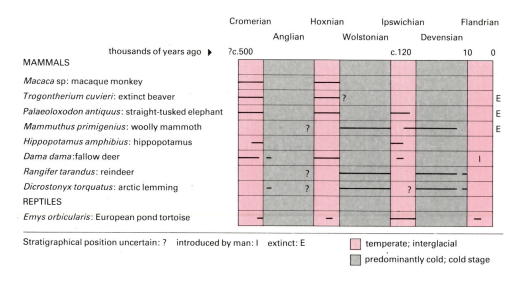

Fig. 15.5. The Pleistocene fauna of Britain.

Stratigraphical position uncertain: ?   introduced by man: I   extinct: E

temperate; interglacial

predominantly cold; cold stage

caused by local water-level changes or by widespread climatic changes causing either drying or flooding.

Diatoms

Fossil diatoms, often abundant in lake sediments, are also of value in reconstructing past environments. The sampling and preparation procedures for these organisms resemble those used for pollen grains. Since the microscopic diatom fossils consist of resistant siliceous cell walls, they can be concentrated by certain chemical treatments to remove the sediment matrix.

The assemblages of diatoms vary in different parts of a lake, and also between lakes. If the preservation is good each species can be identified, because the features of the fossil silica shells are just those used for identifying living diatoms. Diatoms respond to factors such as water chemistry, turbulence, the type of material on the bottom of the lake, and the presence of larger aquatic plants. Hence diatoms can be used to make detailed palaeoecological interpretations of lakes. However, diatoms are relatively insensitive to temperature, and are not good indicators of past climates.

15.2 QUATERNARY FAUNA

Quaternary invertebrates

Good fossil records are available for a number of Quaternary invertebrate groups, in particular foraminifers (shelled protozoans), marine and non-marine molluscs, and beetles (Coleoptera).

Foraminifers are often abundant in marine sands, silts and clays, and analyses of their distribution in sedimentary sequences from shallow-shelf seas and deep oceans have been used both to define the different strata, and to give climatic information. For example, in the North Atlantic, climatic changes are recorded by changing frequencies of species such as *Globorotalia menardie* which live in warmer water, and species such as *Globigerina pachyderma* which live in cooler water.

Molluscs are found in a wide range of marine sediments, including gravels. Non-marine molluscs, including both freshwater and terrestrial species, occur in a variety of lake and river sediments, but only where these are calcareous; deposits of

calcium carbonate formed by springs commonly preserve rich terrestrial mollusc faunas. Both marine and non-marine molluscs give much information on the climate, and especially on local ecological conditions. The occurrence of southern species of marine molluscs in the Holocene of the British Isles provides the first evidence for a warmer climate 5000 to 7000 years ago. In Britain, southern non-marine species, such as *Corbicula fluminalis* and *Belgrandia marginata*, are known from interglacials, while cold-stage faunas include species characteristic of cold climates today, such as *Columella columella*.

Beetles, usually remarkably well preserved, may occur in large numbers in freshwater sediments, and also in acid peats. Beetle faunas from the Quaternary have so far been studied mainly in Britain and North America. Most work has been done on radiocarbon-dated assemblages of Devensian (Last Cold Stage) age, with a few studies of earlier interglacial and cold-stage faunas. Ipswichian (Last Interglacial) faunas from England include southern and temperate beetle species. Faunas dated to various phases of the Devensian range from those of Arctic type and poor in species, to many dated around 42000 to 43000 years BP which contain temperate and southern species, indicating summer temperatures higher than those of today. There are few corresponding features detectable in pollen spectra of the same age, probably because there was insufficient time for the temperate plants to reach Britain from their cold-stage refuges in southern Europe.

European Pleistocene vertebrates

Lower Pleistocene vertebrate faunas cover a time range from about 2 million to 700000 years BP, and are known from relatively few sites, mostly in northern Italy, southern France, Spain and eastern Europe. Sparse remains of land mammals occur in the marine deposits, called 'crag', from Norfolk and Suffolk in England.

The first true horses (*Equus*, from North America) and elephants (*Archidiskodon*, from southern Asia) to appear in Europe are recorded from approximately the beginning of the Lower Pleistocene, but in general the Lower Pleistocene faunas have much in common with those of the Pliocene (see section 14.3) and lack many forms which are characteristic of later Pleistocene and modern faunas. The more prominent mammals include monkeys, primitive voles, sabre-toothed cats, mastodon (*Anancus*), tapir, zebrine horse (*Equus stenosis*), comb-

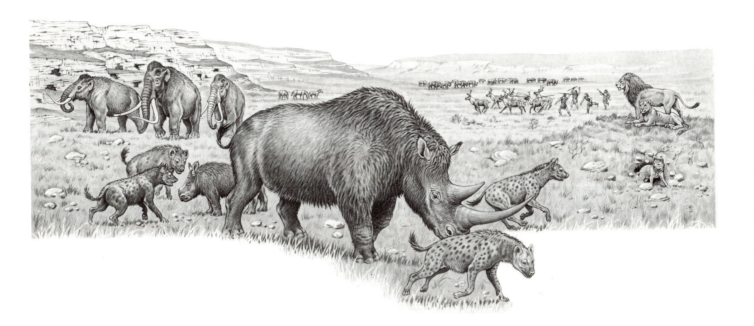

antlered deer, gazelles and the primitive ox *Leptobos*. There is no convincing evidence, either from skeletal remains or from artefacts, that humans were present in Europe at any time within the Lower Pleistocene. Although thère were extinctions in the later part of the Lower Pleistocene, such as some tapirs, gazelles and the mastodon, and new forms also evolved, such as voles with permanently growing molars, the general impression is of a relatively slow rate of change in the fauna in comparison with that occurring in the Middle and Upper Pleistocene.

Fossil vertebrates of Middle and Upper Pleistocene age, on the other hand, are known from numerous localities in most parts of Europe, and are especially plentiful in cave deposits dating from the Last Cold Stage and the Last Interglacial. The Middle and Upper Pleistocene were marked by an intensification of the climatic oscillations which occurred throughout the earlier part of the Pleistocene, resulting in phases of widespread glaciation in northern Europe and the Alps.

The history of the fauna during this period shows sharply increasing rates of turnover in the fauna, that is of evolution, immigration and extinction, with an overall trend towards decreasing diversity. These phenomena reflect the repeated stresses to which the fauna was subjected, the response to each change in climate being adaptation or migration. There was a sharp increase in the rate of extinction at the end of the Pleistocene. The record of humans in Europe, based both on artefacts and on skeletons, begins in approximately Cromerian times, and remains have been found at Mauer, near Heidelberg in West Germany, and Vertészöllös in Hungary.

Fig. 15.5 illustrates with a few examples the pattern of change in the British fauna during the Middle and Upper Pleistocene. Some species or groups are restricted to the interglacials, and others to cold stages.

Fig. 15.6. British fauna in the Devensian Last Cold Stage: the Mendip Hills about 35000 years BP.

Cold-stage faunas

Because much of the Last Cold Stage (called, in different parts of Europe, the Devensian, Weichselian or Würmian, see Fig. 15.1) falls within the range of radiocarbon dating, its faunas and faunal history can be reconstructed to a far greater extent than can those of the earlier cold stages.

For much of each cold stage, treeless vegetation dominated by herbs extended over northern and central Europe, and this was reflected in the presence as far south as the Alps and Pyrenees of animals found today in the Arctic, such as lemmings, Arctic fox, reindeer and the musk ox (*Ovibos*). Animals characteristic of temperate interglacial conditions in northern Europe, such as aurochs (*Bos*), fallow deer and the straight-tusked elephant (*Palaeoloxdon*), appear to have survived the cold stages in refuges in the Mediterranean area, and in South-west Asia.

More temperate climatic phases within the cold stages (interstadials) were accompanied by the northward spread both of trees and of temperate animals, such as aurochs in the late part of the Last Cold Stage in South-west France, and roe deer and beaver at about the same time in southern Germany. However, the typical cold-stage faunas of an area as far north as Britain show an intriguing mixture of zoogeographical elements, reflecting a combination of climatic and vegetational conditions not found anywhere at the present day. For example, faunas from the middle of the Last Cold Stage (Devensian) of England, dating from about 30000 to 40000 years BP, include animals nowadays extinct, animals now with an Arctic or northern distribution, animals now with an eastern steppe (continental grassland) distribution, southern or temperate animals, and animals now widespread over several ecological regions (Fig. 15.6). Faunas of similar age from

387

Germany show a much stronger component of steppe animals, with saiga antelope, birch mice and jerboa.

The widespread occurrence of a large form of red deer (*Cervus elaphus*) in cold-stage faunas is another reminder of the contrast between the environments of Pleistocene cold stages and that of present-day Arctic tundra. Red deer are now not only entirely absent from the tundra, but are also generally absent from taiga (boreal forest) as well (see section 8.4). Difficulties of foraging in winter snow may be the main factor in preventing the northward spread of red deer at the present day. Lion and spotted hyena are also present in these faunas, but probably are not genuine southern components since their absence from Europe today may well be due to human influences.

Interglacial faunas

During the interglacials, the improvement in the climate was of sufficient length to bring first birch and coniferous forests, and then temperate forests, to North-west Europe. These climatic and vegetational changes were accompanied by the immigration of temperate vertebrate faunas comprising a variety of zoogeographical elements, either currently extinct, or temperate, or southern, or widespread. The fauna known from the middle of the Last Interglacial (Ipswichian) of England is shown in Fig. 15.7. The warmest parts of each of the interglacials, including the current postglacial or Holocene, were a little warmer than the present day, and this is reflected in the occurrence in European interglacial deposits of fossil plants and animals which are hundreds of kilometres north of their present ranges. For example, the European pond tortoise (*Emys orbicularis*) is today absent from northern Europe because the summers are too cool and cloudy for its eggs to hatch. Abundant fossil records show, however, that it occurred as far north as England, Denmark and southern Sweden about 6000 years ago, and it is recorded from England in each of the interglacial stages.

Because of complex patterns of immigration, evolution and extinction the faunas of the last four interglacial periods differ. In England, for example, macaque monkeys and beavers do not occur after the Holsteinian/Hoxnian, while this stage is marked by the first appearance of aurochs and the absence of hippopotamus, which is also absent from the Holocene.

Faunal change within the interglacials is discernible in the detailed fossil records available for the Last Interglacial (Ipswichian/Eemian) of England and of East Germany. The English faunas show the horse (*Equus ferus*) and mammoth (*Mammuthus primigenius*) only in the second half of the interglacials, apparently correlated with a decrease in the forest cover.

It is also interesting to compare the faunas of the various interglacials in England and Germany. Those of the Cromerian and Holsteinian/Hoxnian are generally very similar in the two localities, but the Eemian/Ipswichian faunas are more different, with a more oceanic forest fauna in England including aurochs and hippopotamus and a more continental fauna in Germany, lacking these species but including steppe-dwelling species such as the tail-less hare (pika), ground squirrel and hamsters.

During interglacials, including the current one, animals widespread in cold stages have retreated into refuges either in the modern Arctic tundra, as have lemmings and the Arctic fox, or into both Arctic and mountain areas, as have the blue hare and ptarmigan.

North American Pleistocene vertebrates

Quaternary vertebrates have been found at numerous localities in North America, mostly in the USA and Alaska, but with the exception of the Late Pleistocene the faunal sequence can be only tentatively related to North American climatic stages. In the absence of a good framework of dated and correlated strata, the Quaternary land-mammal faunas have been grouped into three broad ages, following the practice with faunas of Tertiary age. These are the Blancan, covering the late Pliocene and Lower Pleistocene; the Irvingtonian, which is approximately Middle Pleistocene; and the Rancholabrean which is approximately Upper Pleistocene. Many Rancholabrean faunas can in fact be assigned either to the Sangamonian (Last Interglacial) or to the Wisconsinian (as the Last Cold Stage is called in North America), while the later Wisconsinian finds fall within the range of radiocarbon dating.

The most famous Pleistocene vertebrate locality in North America is Rancho La Brea, in Los Angeles, California, which gives its name to the most recent of the land-mammal ages. Here, sand and gravels impregnated with asphalt have yielded a spectacularly rich fauna of mammals and birds dating from the middle to late Wisconsinian. The fauna includes many species living today in North America, together with extinct forms such as the sabre-toothed cat, lion, ground sloths such as *Paramylodon*, a mammoth (*Mammuthus*), mastodon (*Mammut*), the camel-like *Camelops*, horse (*Equus*) and birds such as the giant condor-like *Teratornis*.

The Pleistocene and modern mammal faunas of North America can be divided into three broad components, endemic forms (found only in North America), forms of South American origin (which were able to migrate to North America following the formation of a land bridge between Central and South America in the Upper Pliocene), and forms common to both North America and Eurasia (Holarctic forms).

Endemic forms with a history in North America dating back well into the Tertiary include the white-tailed and mule deers, pronghorns such as *Antilocapra* and the extinct four-horned *Tetrameryx*, skunk, raccoon, and many rodents such as bog lemmings and the extinct giant beaver *Castoroides*. More spectacular extinct Pleistocene mammals include the camel-like *Camelops*, a tapir (*Tapirus*) and the American mastodon (*Mammut*).

South American forms include the living armadillo (*Dasypus*;

Fig. 15.7. British fauna in the Ipswichian Last Interglacial: Cambridge about 120000 years BP.

a member of a group of mammals called the edentates, see section 14.3), porcupine (a caviomorph rodent) and the opossum (a marsupial). Extinct edentates include *Glyptodon*, which was like a giant armadillo, and ground sloths such as *Megatherium* and *Mylodon*.

The numerous Holarctic mammals that are still found in North America include the red deer (wapiti), reindeer (caribou), elk (moose), bison, musk ox (now extinct in the Old World), brown bear, wolf, Arctic fox, beaver, lemmings and many voles. Holarctic animals now extinct in North America include the woolly mammoth (*Mammuthus*) and, perhaps surprisingly, the lion, which although now confined to Africa and a small area in India was present in the late Pleistocene across most of Eurasia and in both North and South America.

Land mammals were at times able to cross freely between North America and Eurasia via a land bridge from Alaska to eastern Siberia, across what is now the Bering Sea. The area, known as Beringia, was dry land during periods of major glaciation in the Pleistocene, when the sea-level was low. Some Eurasian mammals, including the saiga antelope and yak, travelled as far as Alaska in the Wisconsinian, but were probably prevented from colonising the rest of the continent by the presence of the vast ice-sheet which, while leaving Alaska largely ice-free, blocked all access to the south. Towards the end of the Wisconsinian, humans, having colonised much of Siberia, were able to reach Beringia and thus to enter the New World, and these human migrations probably occurred many times over a period of several thousands of years.

Late Pleistocene extinctions

It was realised in the last century that we live in a zoologically impoverished world from which many large and spectacular mammals have disappeared in the recent geological past. For example, the European fauna of about 20000 years ago included lion and spotted hyena (which are both still found in Africa), extinct species of elephant, rhinoceros and bison, and the extinct giant deer *Megaceros*. Faunas of a similar age from North America included mastodon, sabre-toothed cat, giant sloths, *Glyptodon* and horses, all now extinct in the New World, although horses have been reintroduced by man. Late Pleistocene faunas from Australia included such animals as the marsupial lion (*Thylacoleo*), giant short-faced kangaroos, and a herbivore called *Diprotodon* which was like a wombat but the size of a rhinoceros.

Radiocarbon dates on North American fossils indicate that the majority of the extinctions occurred between 12000 and 10000 years BP. A similar, although less marked, wave of extinctions occurred in Europe at about this time, but several late Pleistocene species died out well before this. Although the reality of a greatly increased rate of extinction in the late Pleistocene is firmly established, its causes are much in dispute. It needs to be explained why the extinctions were virtually confined to large terrestrial mammals, and why the extinctions were much more marked in some areas, such as North and South America, than in others, such as Africa and Europe.

It has been suggested that many species that were adapted to the steppe–tundra of the Last Cold Stage in the northern hemisphere were unable to adapt to the improving climate and the spread of forests at the beginning of the postglacial stage. Elsewhere, as in the south-west of North America and in Australia, a sharp increase in aridity in post-glacial times has been blamed. The hypothesis of climatic change as the cause of the extinctions is unsatisfactory, however, in that similar climatic changes took place at the beginning of a number of previous interglacial periods, and environmental conditions did not in any case remain stable for long within cold stages, so that the animals must have constantly been adapting to climatic changes without suffering mass extinction.

The alternative hypothesis attributes the late Pleistocene extinctions to excessive hunting ('overkill') by prehistoric humans, but this also runs into serious difficulties. The pattern of global extinctions was suggested to have followed the spread of the human species throughout the world, with the relatively recent arrival of humans in the New World correlating with the main period of faunal extinction there. However, similar, although less marked, extinctions occurred at the same time in Europe and Africa where humans had been present for very much longer, and moreover there is now accumulating evidence for the presence of humans in the New World well before 12000 years BP. The mass extinctions may instead, of course, have reflected the migration patterns of Upper Palaeolithic hunters, able to specialise in hunting large mammals by using relatively sophisticated weapons and hunting techniques. Two main objections however can be raised to this: there is little evidence that most of the species that became extinct were in fact ever hunted, and it is unlikely that small populations of humans, without firearms, could exterminate entire species of large mammals, when many other large mammals have survived more than 10000 years longer in the face of much larger human population pressures and more advanced weapons.

Evolution in Quaternary mammals

Plants, and those invertebrates with a good fossil record such as molluscs and beetles, show very little evolution throughout the whole of the Pleistocene. Of the vertebrates, however, many mammals have undergone considerable evolutionary change within the same period.

The abundant fossil record and the closely dated and correlated strata for the Pleistocene provide good material for the study of patterns of evolutionary change on time-scales from hundreds of thousands of years down to 1000 years or even finer. One difficulty, however, is that species were constantly shifting their ranges in response to climatic changes in the Pleistocene, which probably caused an increase in evolutionary rates, but which also confuses the interpretation of the fossil record in any one geographical area.

Size changes occurred regularly in many species in response to climatic changes, usually with larger forms in the cold phases and smaller forms in the temperate phases.

Broad evolutionary changes in Europe occurred in the elephant lineage, from *Archidiskodon meridionalis* (Lower Pleistocene) through *Mammuthus trogontherii* (Middle Pleistocene) to *M. primigenius* (Middle and Upper Pleistocene), with changes in the skull, tusks and molars. Trends in the elk

(moose) lineage include a shortening in the thickness of the antler beam relative to the spread, and decreases in the size of the whole animal, as shown from *Alces gallicus* (Lower Pleistocene) through *A. latifrons* (Middle Pleistocene) to *A. alces* (Upper Pleistocene and modern). Perhaps the best-studied lineage is that of the water voles (*Mimomys* and *Arvicola*). Originating from hamster-like ancestors with low-crowned, grinding molars in the Pliocene, *Mimomys* species from the Lower Pleistocene show progressive trends towards higher crowns and an increase in cement and enamel. Within the Cromerian Interglacial of the early Middle Pleistocene, permanently growing, rootless molars evolved, a major step enabling the animal to cope with more abrasive grasses in its diet and taken to mark the transition from *Mimomys* to *Arvicola*. Subsequent changes in *Arvicola* include a trend of increase in size and simplification of the enamel pattern on the first lower molar.

15.3 QUATERNARY FLORA

The cold periods

As we have seen (section 15.1), the Quaternary was a period of predominantly cool climate, with warmer interludes. At the onset of cooling in the late Tertiary, about 6 million years ago, plants migrated southwards to regions of favourable climate, or became extinct as conditions became too cold for their survival. Little is known about early Quaternary extinctions in North America, because suitable deposits are scarce. Much more is known from Europe, particularly from the Netherlands (Fig. 15.8), Germany, Poland, Greece and eastern England.

During each cold period, the area occupied by temperate species was reduced, but small populations survived in **refuges** ('refugia') of suitable climate. When the general climate improved, these species were able to recolonise their former areas. Their success in recolonisation depended upon the closeness of the refuges to the new favourable areas, the speed with which the species could migrate and recolonise, and their ability to compete with species already established. In some cases, a species was unable to survive the cold period in a suitable refuge area, and became extinct before the next improvement in climate. In other cases, a species was unable to migrate sufficiently fast from its refuge or to compete successfully, and it never regained its former abundance. As a result, **relict** populations remained close to the refugial areas, to which they subsequently retreated during the following cold period. These small populations tended to lose genetic variability, and this further impaired their ability to survive. An example of this in Europe is beech (*Fagus*), which appeared in decreasing abundance during successive interglacial periods. However, during the last cold phase, it seems that a vigorous genotype arose, and during the Holocene *Fagus* invaded and eventually became a dominant tree over much of North-west Europe.

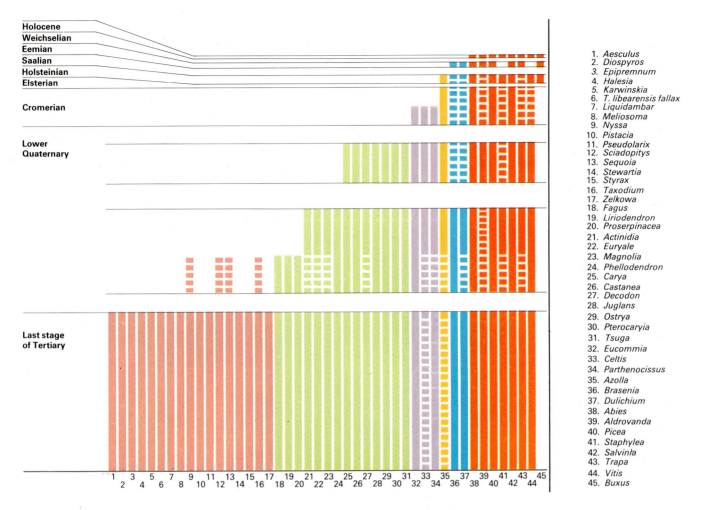

1. *Aesculus*	
2. *Diospyros*	
3. *Epipremnum*	
4. *Halesia*	
5. *Karwinskia*	
6. *T. libearensis fallax*	
7. *Liquidambar*	
8. *Meliosoma*	
9. *Nyssa*	
10. *Pistacia*	
11. *Pseudolarix*	
12. *Sciadopitys*	
13. *Sequoia*	
14. *Stewartia*	
15. *Styrax*	
16. *Taxodium*	
17. *Zelkowa*	
18. *Fagus*	
19. *Liriodendron*	
20. *Proserpinacea*	
21. *Actinidia*	
22. *Euryale*	
23. *Magnolia*	
24. *Phellodendron*	
25. *Carya*	
26. *Castanea*	
27. *Decodon*	
28. *Juglans*	
29. *Ostrya*	
30. *Pterocarya*	
31. *Tsuga*	
32. *Eucommia*	
33. *Celtis*	
34. *Parthenocissus*	
35. *Azolla*	
36. *Brasenia*	
37. *Dulichium*	
38. *Abies*	
39. *Aldrovanda*	
40. *Picea*	
41. *Staphylea*	
42. *Salvinta*	
43. *Trapa*	
44. *Vitis*	
45. *Buxus*	

Fig. 15.8. The occurrence of plant taxa in the late Tertiary and the Quaternary in the Netherlands, showing the progressive extinctions during cold intervals. Nearly a third of the Tertiary taxa were not present in the Quaternary, and nearly half the remainder did not survive beyond the lower Pleistocene. The temperate geological intervals are drawn in relation to their lengths; the cold intervals are not.

Evidence from pollen analyses shows that during the cold periods Europe and Asia were largely treeless, with steppe-like or tundra-like vegetation (see section 8.3). Southern Eurasia, around and to the east of the Mediterranean, was arid. In contrast, in North America, only a narrow band of treeless vegetation occurred adjacent to the ice margin, with larger treeless areas in Alaska and over the Bering Straits ('Beringia'). In eastern North America, there was then a broad belt of coniferous forest about 1000 miles wide, dominated by spruce (*Picea*) and also containing smaller amounts of pine (*Pinus*) and some deciduous trees such as ash (*Fraxinus*), elm (*Ulmus*) and maple (*Acer*). From the limited evidence available, the land to the south of this was arid, with predominantly treeless vegetation, even in the presently semitropical regions such as Florida.

In North America, the temperate species would have been able to migrate southwards, unhindered by barriers of west–east mountain ranges, such as occur in Europe. However, the aridity to the south was a barrier, and areas of suitable temperate climate were severely reduced. Evidence so far available suggests that temperate trees found refuges on the lower slopes of mountains and in river valleys. Many of the Tertiary species (see section 14.3 and Fig. 15.8) which became extinct in Europe survived successfully in North America and remain part of the rich flora today.

During the cold periods, the vegetation of most of the treeless northern European landscape, south of the ice sheets, was dominated by grasses, sedges, herbs and dwarf shrubs. The common features of these plants are that they can withstand cold winters, and that they require full sunlight, being unable to tolerate shading. In addition, many can tolerate soil disturbance, such as that produced by frost action and the melting of snow. The combination of species does not seem to match that found in any known vegetation today, but several groups can be recognised, based on their present-day behaviour and distribution. These are: Arctic and alpine species, confined to similar areas today, such as mountain avens (*Dryas octopetala*) and saxifrages (*Saxifraga*); steppe plants and plants of dry, south-facing slopes, including wormwood (*Artemisia*), members of the family Chenopodiaceae, and sea buckthorn (*Hippophae*); plants of disturbed habitats, which today we call 'weeds', including plantains (*Plantago*) and cornflower (*Centaurea cyanus*); and tall herbs which today grow in ungrazed damp and fertile habitats such as streamsides and cliff ledges, and which include valerian (*Valeriana*), meadowsweet (*Filipendula*), globe flower (*Trollius*), *Angelica* and willowherb (*Epilobium*).

The climate of the cold periods fluctuated, and there were warmer interstadials between periods of intense cold and extensive glaciation. In North-west Europe, several interstadials have been identified within the Last Cold Period, the Weichselian or Devensian, using evidence from fossils preserved in layers of organic sediments found between layers of sand or gravel. The most complete record comes from the Netherlands and Denmark, but it is known that there was a marked interstadial in England between about 20000 and 40000 BP. Evidence from beetle fossils suggests that parts of this interstadial were as warm as the present day, but trees failed to migrate into England at this time and the vegetation remained treeless. This is in contrast to the Allerød interstadial, which occurred throughout Europe between 12000 and 10800 BP, towards the end of the last glaciation. During Allerød times, birch (*Betula*) and larch (*Larix*) reached central Europe, and oak (*Quercus*) expanded its range in South-west Europe. A short 800-year cold spell, called the Younger Dryas, was severe enough to cause renewed glaciation, and this reduced the trees once more in North-west Europe. Only at the beginning of the Holocene, 10000 years ago, could trees extend their range unhindered by severe climatic reversals.

Although there were several interstadials in North America during the last glaciation, these do not correspond in time with the European ones.

The interglacial cycle in the warm periods

Those warm periods in the Quaternary during which forest developed in temperate latitudes all show a characteristic sequence of vegetational changes. A common general ecological pattern may be recognised and is called the **interglacial cycle** (Fig. 15.9). It is made up of four stages showing an ecological succession.

At the beginning of an interglacial, in the **protocratic** stage, the climate improved, and lush herb and shrub vegetation developed before the immigration of trees. The pioneer trees were usually birch, aspen (*Populus*) and pine (*Pinus*). These are light-demanding trees which can colonise treeless landscapes and relatively open soils. They mature rapidly and produce abundant wind-dispersed seeds, which enable them to migrate effectively to new treeless habitats.

During the protocratic stage, soils matured and their content of humus increased. Leaching removed many soluble minerals, particularly calcium carbonate, and the soils became fertile brown earths (see section 8.1).

As a consequence, conditions became favourable for the growth of deciduous forest trees in the next, **mesocratic** stage, particularly of elm (*Ulmus*), oak (*Quercus*), ash (*Fraxinus*) and lime or linden (*Tilia*). In any interglacial, the actual species present, the order of their arrival, and their relative abundance,

depended upon their rate of migration from their glacial refuges, their competitive ability, and upon chance processes of dispersal and establishment. This mixed deciduous forest persisted on well-drained soils for several thousand years. In poorly drained sites, willows (*Salix*) and alder (*Alnus*) were abundant, and marshes and lakes supported rich fen and aquatic vegetation associated with nutrient-rich water of relatively high pH (alkaline). Plants of open ground were restricted to areas beyond the tree-line, or to places within the forested areas which remained too open and unstable for tree growth, such as coastal sites and inland cliffs.

Gradually, as soil leaching progressed, soils became acidic and rather rich in humus, and podzols developed on well-drained sites (see section 8.1). This is the **telocratic** stage of the interglacial cycle. In less well-drained sites, the marshes became acidic, and were colonised by bog moss (*Sphagnum*) and converted into bogs. These soil changes were accompanied by the invasion of different species of trees, such as hornbeam (*Carpinus*) and the conifers spruce (*Picea*) and fir (*Abies*). Such trees may have been encouraged by the changes in the soil, and they certainly accelerated these changes by the addition of their own acid leaf litter. These changes away from the deciduous forests are termed **retrogressive succession**.

At the onset of cool climatic conditions marking the end of the interglacial, the **cryocratic** stage, trees of the protocratic stage became abundant once more, before giving way to open disturbed vegetation typical of the cold periods. The soil structure was destroyed by cryoturbation, a physical mixing of the layers which occurs with regular freezing and thawing.

The processes of the interglacial cycle occurred in all interglacials, in both Europe and North America. They also apply to the Holocene, which can be regarded as the present, unfinished, interglacial. During this period, the human species has come to dominate the world, and technological processes have altered much of the natural vegetation of the earth. However, although the processes of the interglacial cycle have been obscured, they are still continuing. In North-west Europe and North America, human activities have greatly accelerated retrogressive processes, particularly by forest clearance. This impoverishes soils, allowing acidic and leached podzols to develop. If, as a result, an impermeable layer called an iron-pan forms, the poor drainage encourages the growth of bog or, if drainage remains good, heaths develop. Human activity has also increased the rate of processes reminiscent of the cryocratic stage. Disturbed soils have led to the expansion of plants of open habitat, particularly weeds, and plants and animals of grassland.

Although the ecological processes occurring throughout any interglacial cycle were similar, the plants which made up the vegetation appeared in different combinations, orders and abundances in each individual cycle. For example, Tertiary species persisted during the first few interglacials of the early Quaternary, before becoming extinct in Europe at the onset of severe cold conditions during the pre-Cromerian cold period.

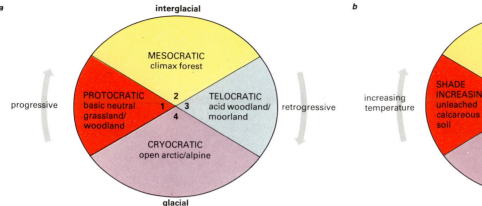

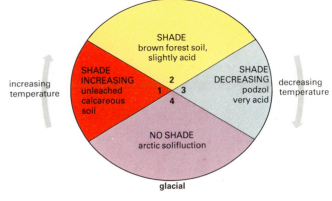

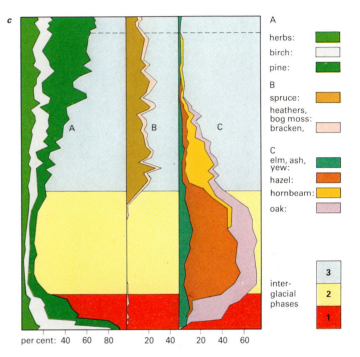

In the Eemian interglacial in North-west Europe, hornbeam (*Carpinus*) became abundant together with spruce (*Picea*) in the telocratic stage, but in eastern England spruce never arrived and *Carpinus* pollen is very abundant in the pollen diagrams. Beech (*Fagus*) has behaved very differently in the different interglacials.

The Holocene

The Holocene is an atypical interglacial because of the dominance of humans in its later part, but for this reason it is of great interest. In addition, it is the easiest to study, because so many fossil deposits are available in peat bogs, lakes, fens and soils, which have not yet been destroyed by the effects of a subsequent glaciation.

The forest history of the Holocene in Denmark has been studied using pollen diagrams. Humans first started seriously to affect the vegetation at about 5000 BP, when Neolithic people first practised farming. At this time, there was a fall in elm (*Ulmus*) pollen percentages, accompanied by the appearance of 'weed' and sometimes cereal pollen. There is no doubt that the latter two appearances are the result of cultivation, but there has been much discussion about the direct association of the decline of the elm with Neolithic culture. It is a widespread and almost synchronous phenomenon in North-west Europe, and it is hard to imagine Neolithic people having such a widespread effect. There is, however, archaeological evidence, and evidence from primitive farmers living today, that elm branches are used for cattle fodder, and that their cutting prevents the elm flowering. Other possible causes of the elm decline are a climatic change detrimental to elm, and the spread of a disease such as Dutch elm disease.

Because of the shifting nature of Neolithic agriculture, its effects noted in pollen diagrams tend to last for only a short period, followed by a period of regeneration of forest, and then perhaps by a further clearance. Later, Bronze Age and Iron Age farmers had a far greater impact, and made larger and more permanent clearings. Since then, humans have increasingly deforested North-west·Europe to produce the largely agricultural landscape of today.

The vegetation of North America seems to have been unaffected by humans until Europeans arrived and spread from the east coast. The modern technologies have managed to change the vegetation of North America so rapidly that today it has been almost as much modified as has that of Europe. The vegetational succession during the Holocene varied greatly across the North American continent. An example of a pollen

Fig. 15.9. The interglacial cycle: (a) phases and characteristic vegetation; (b) environmental changes. (c) Pollen diagram from Hollerup, Denmark, an Eemian interglacial site. A – light-demanding herbs and trees, characteristic of protocratic and cryocratic stages. B – pollen and spore curves for plants of acid soils, characteristic of the telocratic stage. C – plants of fertile soils, characteristic of the mesocratic stage. Hornbeam tends to reach maximum abundance in the telocratic stage.

diagram from Minnesota, in the northern mid-west, is shown in Fig. 15.10. This site is presently in a zone of deciduous woodland, but it has been covered by coniferous forest and prairie at different times in its history, as the climate changed and trees migrated. Only in the last 100 years has human activity affected the vegetation, and this is marked in the pollen diagram by a rise in ragweed (*Ambrosia*) pollen.

Plant migrations

As we have seen above, changes in climate during the Quaternary resulted in large changes in the distributions of plants. During the cold periods, plants of open ground, tundra, and steppe became widespread in Europe, and coniferous forest

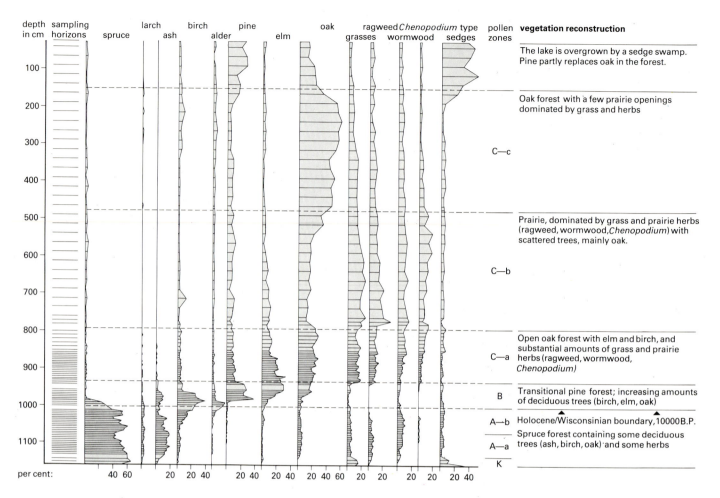

Fig. 15.10. Pollen diagram from Kirchner Marsh, USA, showing selected pollen types. Climatic changes largely controlled the vegetation changes indicated on the right. Spruce forest grew in the cool Wisconsinian climate. Warming at the opening of the Holocene allowed the development of deciduous forest. As the warming continued, forest gave way to prairie. Macrofossil evidence shows that the lake level fell at this time, in response to drought. A return to cooler, moister conditions allowed the redevelopment of oak forest, and the lake became deeper again. However, it eventually became filled with sediment and overgrown by sedges.

moved southwards to cover most of the eastern USA. Temperate species were forced southwards and, on both continents, encountered arid regions, which were a barrier to further migration. Therefore, temperate trees and their associated herbs and shrubs became restricted to suitably warm, moist areas, which in both cases were situated on the lower slopes of mountain ranges, such as the Appalachians and the Balkans.

When the climate improved, previously widespread plants tolerant of cold climates became restricted, either by climatic conditions or by competition from invading temperate species. The coniferous forest of America moved northwards to its present position, with some changes in its composition. Spruce and fir (*Abies*) were joined by various species of *Pinus* (pines), and deciduous trees other than birch and aspen (*Populus*) became rare. The plants of open tundra were also restricted to more northerly regions, although a few survived within the forested area in open unstable habitats, such as river banks, and rocky terrain such as that on the north shore of Lake Superior. This shows that tundra plants are not necessarily restricted by climate, but that competition from more vigorous plants in a warmer climate normally ousts them. In Europe, the plants of the treeless cold periods also moved northwards or up mountains, or became confined to treeless refuge areas within

the forests. Human activities have favoured the spread of many opportunist species tolerant of disturbed conditions, but other Arctic and alpine plants cannot compete in a warmer climate, and they remain at high altitudes and latitudes.

In North America and Europe there are sufficient dated pollen diagrams to study the migration routes and speeds of forest trees from their glacial refuges since the onset of the temperate Holocene climate about 10 000 years ago. In eastern North America these refuges were in the south-east. Each taxon shows its own pattern of migration, depending upon its ecological characteristics. For example, pines moved rapidly northwards and westwards, reaching southern Canada by 8000 BP. Hemlock (*Tsuga*) initially moved quickly until 8000 BP when it was slowed down by having to invade closed forest. At 5000 BP it suffered a disease which led to a population crash, similar in many ways to the European elm decline, but the hemlock recovered and continued to expand slowly westwards, perhaps in response to the moister climate in the mid-west during the last 4000 years (as shown at Kirchner Marsh, Fig. 15.10). Beech (*Fagus*) moved northwards at a relatively constant rate, always invading closed forest, for which it is well adapted. Chestnut (*Castanea*) spread slowly, also into closed forests, in which it often became dominant.

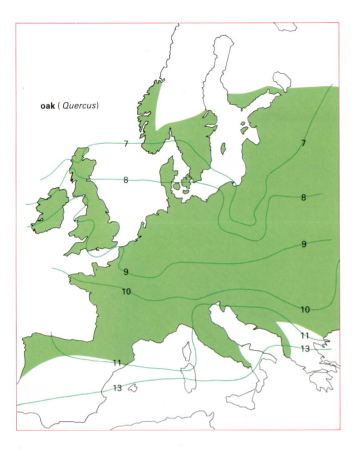

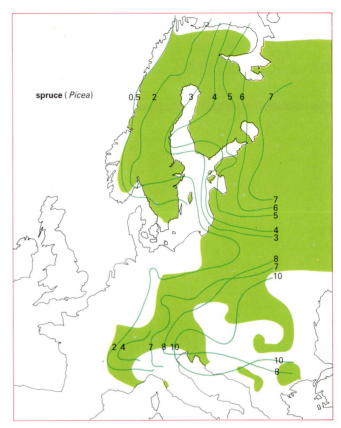

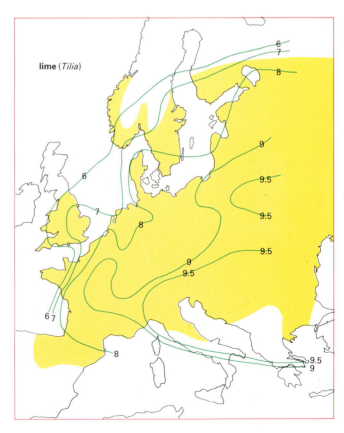

present-day ranges: oak   spruce   fir   lime

Fig. 15.11. *Migration maps of four trees in Europe during the Holocene and late glacial. The contours show where the tree taxon had arrived by that point in time. Because man has had a large effect on the distribution and abundance of trees, and* their ranges have contracted in many cases, only the time periods are shown during which the taxa were expanding in response to natural environmental factors. Their present ranges are coloured.

For Europe, and especially Britain, detailed pollen diagrams from which Holocene migration maps can be constructed are more numerous. These reveal nine main refuge areas in southern Europe, of which the Balkan peninsula was the most important. In contrast to North America, the trees had to pass the barrier of the Alps before colonising the plains beyond. Migration maps of four European tree genera are shown in Fig. 15.11. Oak (*Quercus*) and lime or linden (*Tilia*) spread steadily northwards from their refuges in southern Europe and reached their maximum extents by 7000 BP and 6000 BP, respectively. Lime spread further north than oak in Scandinavia, but oak reached farther north in Britain. In contrast, fir (*Abies*) spread northwards slowly during the early Holocene, only reaching central Europe by 4000 BP. It could not compete effectively with the deciduous trees in the lowlands, and became centred on the mountains. Spruce (*Picea*) spread slowly from its southern refuges, presumably restricted by the availability of suitable soils. It also moved westwards into Finland from Russia, and its frontier is still advancing southwards and westwards in Norway and Sweden today. Spruce can colonise closed deciduous forest, where it becomes dominant because the acidity of its leaf litter makes the soil unsuitable for the regeneration of other trees.

Recent history

Since 5000 BP, humans have been an important influence on the distribution and abundance of plants. The human species is mobile, and has been responsible for introducing many plants to areas where they did not naturally grow. For example, numerous European 'weeds', and southern trees such as sweet chestnut (*Castanea*), have been introduced further north. Also, many crops have been transported throughout the world from their native areas. In some cases, introduced plants become a nuisance, because effective competitors are absent.

Conversely, some species have become much reduced due to human activity, or have even become extinct. The most obvious effect is the reduction of tree cover by clearance of forests for timber and for agriculture. With the reduction in woodland habitats, many associated plants, such as the herbs of the woodland floor, have been reduced. In treeless areas such as natural steppes and prairies, the native plants have all been reduced by ploughing, burning and grazing. Many wetland habitats have become severely damaged by drainage or by water pollution, either by industrial chemicals or by water rich in nutrients draining from farmland and from towns (see Chapter 9). Several marsh and aquatic species have subsequently become rare, for example the insectivorous *Aldrovanda vesiculosa* in Europe. Peatlands have also been affected by human activity. In treeless areas, peat is used for fuel, and in Ireland, rich in peat bogs, peat is removed commercially for fuel or for horticulture. Burning of moorland to create better grazing has also caused the deterioration of many peatlands, particularly in the western British Isles. Humans have been a direct selective threat to rare and beautiful species by collecting them from the wild for growing in gardens. Orchids suffer especially, and many species have been severely reduced in tropical regions. In Britain, lady's slipper orchid (*Cypripedium calceolus*) has been reduced by collectors to a population of only one plant.

Changes controlled by climatic events have been the feature of the flora of the temperate regions during the Quaternary, involving extinctions and re-immigrations, but in these natural conditions equilibrium and diversity are maintained. The effects of human intervention, however, during the late Holocene, have been so great and so rapid that the vegetation has not had time to come to a new equilibrium, and as a result has declined in diversity with an overall loss or reduction of habitats. A study of the history of the flora leads to an appreciation of the antiquity of plant associations and of how these have changed and developed through time. The advent of humans has stopped the ancient experiment, and introduced so many new variables that we cannot now be certain how vegetation will react to future climatic changes.

Further reading

Birks, H.J.B. and Birks, H.H. *Quaternary palaeoecology*. London: Edward Arnold, 1980.

Dickson, J.H. *Bryophytes of the Pleistocene*. Cambridge: Cambridge University Press, 1973.

Godwin, H. *The history of the British flora*. (2nd edn) Cambridge: Cambridge University Press, 1975.

Godwin, H. *The archives of the peat bogs*. Cambridge: Cambridge University Press, 1981.

Huntley, B. and Birks, H.J.B. *An atlas of past and present pollen maps for Europe: 0–13000 years ago*. Cambridge: Cambridge University Press, 1983.

Imbrie, J. and Imbrie, K.P. *Ice ages. Solving the mystery*. New Jersey: Enslow, 1979.

Kurtén, B. and Anderson, E. *Pleistocene mammals of North America*. New York: Columbia University Press, 1980.

Pennington, W. *The history of British vegetation*. London: English Universities Press, 1974.

Sparks, B.W. and West, R.G. *The ice age in Britain*. London: Methuen, 1972.

Stuart, A.J. *Pleistocene vertebrates in the British Isles*. London: Longman, 1982.

Turekian, K. *The late Cenozoic glacial ages*. New Haven: Yale University Press, 1971.

West, R.G. *Pleistocene geology and biology*. (2nd edn) London: Longman, 1977.

A Classification of Living Organisms

INTRODUCTION

It has been suggested that between three million and ten million different kinds of organism are alive in the world today. Large numbers of other organisms have become extinct and are preserved as fossils. Schemes of classification have been devised to discern patterns and order in this seemingly infinite variety, and to enable biologists to communicate in a common language about individual organisms and groups of organisms.

Most modern schemes of classification are based upon the pioneering work of the Swedish biologist Carl von Linné (Carolus Linnaeus, 1707–1778), who established the practice of **binomial nomenclature**, by which all organisms are given two names, traditionally printed in italics. The first name is that of the **genus**, and is common to a group of closely related organisms. The second, the name of the **species**, is unique to a particular type of organism. Further, higher levels of classification show a hierarchy of relationships. Thus, just as species are grouped into genera, so genera are grouped into **families**, families into **orders**, orders into **classes**, classes into **phyla** (for animals) or **divisions** (for plants), phyla and divisions into **kingdoms**, and kingdoms into **superkingdoms**. The classification of the human species, *Homo sapiens*, in this way is shown in Table C.1. Intermediate levels of classification may be created by adding the prefixes 'sub' or 'super' to an existing group name, as in the case of subphylum in Table C.1.

The names used in most classification schemes are usually based on the classical languages, normally Latin but sometimes Greek. This creates an internationally recognised language of classification which can readily be understood by all biologists.

The analysis of the characteristics of organisms for the purpose of classification is known as **taxonomy**. The majority of classification schemes, including that given here, are based on morphological and anatomical characters, particularly those associated with reproduction. During this century, however, advances in methods of research have made possible the use of genetic, embryological and biochemical data, evidence from electron microscopy, and mathematical analyses, which increase the accuracy and precision of classification and reduce the intuitive or subjective elements of the process. The major effects of such developments have been in facilitating classification below the level of the species, in classifying populations of organisms, and, at the other end of the scale, in grouping organisms into kingdoms and superkingdoms.

During the nineteenth century most taxonomists recognised only two kingdoms: Plantae (plants) and Animalia (animals). Since then it has become clear that many intermediate organisms do not fit logically into either of these groups, and other kingdoms have been suggested to accommodate them. In the classification given here, four kingdoms are recognised: **Monera** (blue-green algae, prochlorophytes and bacteria), **Fungi** (mushrooms, toadstools and moulds), **Plantae** (algae [excluding the blue-green algae], liverworts, mosses, ferns, cone-bearing plants and flowering plants) and **Animalia** (unicellular and multicellular animals). Some taxonomists have suggested further classification at the kingdom level to deal with other intermediate organisms.

Research with the electron microscope and the techniques of modern biochemistry has produced compelling evidence for a more fundamental level of classification than that of kingdom, based upon the type of cell structure and metabolism. Thus, two **superkingdoms** are now recognised. The first of these is the **Prokaryota**, which includes all organisms that lack membrane-bounded nuclei, mitochondria and other cell organelles, while the second is the **Eukaryota**, in which cell organelles contained within membranes are present (see section 1.2). Only one kingdom, Monera, is placed in the Prokaryota. All the other kingdoms are placed in the Eukaryota.

The viruses have not been discussed so far. This is because they present a special problem for taxonomists. They are not composed of cells, but consist only of a core of nucleic acid (RNA or DNA) and a protein coat, and are entirely dependent upon the metabolism of the living cells of a prokaryotic or eukaryotic host for their growth and reproduction. Viruses may have evolved by reduction from prokaryotes and/or eukaryotes to their present 'simple' parasitic state, but this is not proven. In the classification scheme presented here they are dealt with as an entirely separate group, outside the main scheme.

Finally, it should be emphasised that classification schemes are simply cataloguing systems, devised by scientists to help them in their work. A classification therefore does not constitute proof of relationships between organisms, nor does it necessarily indicate a pathway of evolution, although classifications provide a conceptual framework for the discussion of these matters.

Table C.1 *The classification of the human species*

Superkingdom:	Eukaryota	(eukaryotic organisms)
Kingdom:	Animalia	(animals)
Phylum:	Chordata	(chordates)
Subphylum:	Vertebrata	(vertebrates)
Class:	Mammalia	(mammals)
Order:	Primates	
Family:	Hominidae	(hominids)
Genus:	*Homo*	
Species:	*sapiens*	

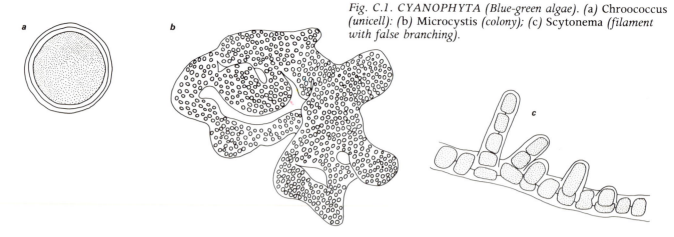

Fig. C.1. CYANOPHYTA (Blue-green algae). (a) Chroococcus (unicell): (b) Microcystis (colony); (c) Scytonema (filament with false branching).

SUPERKINGDOM 1: PROKARYOTA

Prokaryotes are organisms made of cells, and have a small range of cell size, approximately between 0.5 and 5.0 micrometres in diameter. The genetic material is in the form of a single strand of DNA, and is not separated from the rest of the cell by a membrane. Prokaryotic organisms have no internal membranes dividing the cell into compartments, as have eukaryotes, and their ribosomes are distinctly smaller than those of eukaryotes. When cell walls are present they are based on amino-acid–sugar groups. Flagella, if present, are built of a single protein strand which is rotated as a whole from the base. Prokaryotes may be unicellular, or form filaments or colonies of cells, but do not form tissues. Reproduction is normally by simple fission, and sexual systems are rare. Some prokaryotes are aerobic, requiring oxygen for metabolism, while others are anaerobic and may even be killed by the presence of oxygen. Some are photosynthetic or chemosynthetic autotrophs, using light energy or chemical energy to convert inorganic substances into food materials, while others are heterotrophic, requiring a source of preformed organic material, either from dissolved compounds in the growing medium (saprotrophs) or from another living organism (mutualistic or parasitic symbionts).

Only one kingdom is recognised, Monera, with three divisions (equivalent to phyla in animal classifications): the Cyanophyta (blue-green algae), the Bacteria and the Prochlorophyta (prokaryotic green unicellular algae).

Kingdom Monera

Division CYANOPHYTA (Blue-green algae) (Fig. C.1)

Cyanophytes may be unicellular, filamentous or colonial. Virtually all blue-green algae are photosynthetic, and their pigments include chlorophyll-*a*, unique carotenes and the characteristic phycobilins C-phycocyanin and C-phycoerythrin. Their photosynthetic membranes resemble those of eukaryotic plants, but are not separated into chloroplasts by bounding membranes. The chief reserve materials are a form of starch called myxophycean starch (an α-$(1\rightarrow4)$-linked glucose polymer) and cyanophycin (a protein). The cyanophytes have no flagella, but some are able to move by gliding over a surface. The cells are often embedded in a mucilaginous sheath. Gas vacuoles are present in some species. Reproduction is by simple fission of the cells or by formation of

spores; thick-walled resting spores called akinetes are produced by some species. Transparent, thick-walled cells called heterocysts are found in about 50 species, and contain the enzymes for fixing atmospheric nitrogen.

Blue-green algae are ubiquitous, being freshwater, marine (planktonic or benthic) or terrestrial. Some species form the algal component of many lichens. The cyanophytes are biochemically similar to the chloroplasts of some eukaryotic algae.

Division BACTERIA (Fig. C.2)

Bacteria are mostly unicellular, although some form short chains of cells and some are filamentous. Most bacteria are heterotrophs or are parasitic, but some are photosynthetic or chemosynthetic autotrophs. They are classified largely on cell shape, type of multiplication (division by simple fission or budding), wall characteristics, the presence and types of flagella, various chemical and physiological properties, and their reaction to stains. Bacterial cells may be spherical (cocci), short cylindrical rods (bacilli), or curved or twisted (spirilla). Some are non-motile, others have a single flagellum at one end,

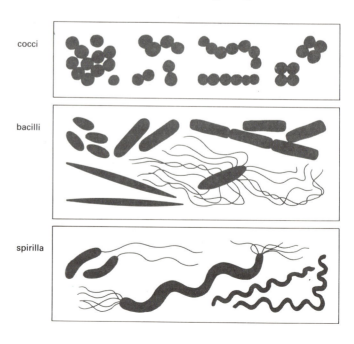

Fig. C.2. Morphological forms of BACTERIA.

Fig. C.3. PROCHLOROPHYTA: electron micrograph of a thin section of Prochloron didemni *(x 1500).*

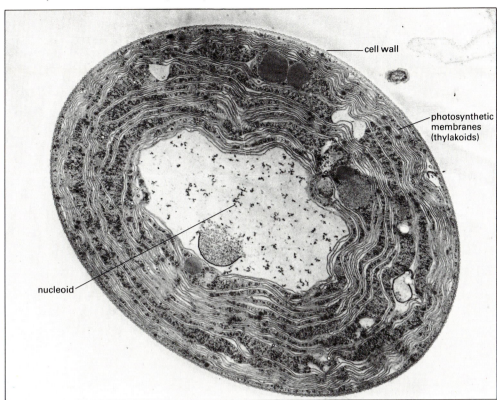

others have groups of flagella at both ends, and in others the cell may be uniformly covered by flagella. A stain called the Gram stain is widely used to investigate the properties of bacterial cell walls, and bacteria are classed as either Gram-positive or Gram-negative. Some bacteria form extremely resistant spores called endospores, usually one per cell.

The actinomycetes are difficult to classify, but they are best considered with the Gram-positive bacteria. They are pro-karyotic organisms with a filamentous organisation not unlike the fungi; but the filaments rarely exceed 1 micrometre in diameter. Actinomycetes reproduce by producing chains of dust-like spores, called conidia, by fragmentation of the web of filaments. Most live in soil, and they are responsible for the characteristic odour of soil after ploughing or wetting by rain.

Division PROCHLOROPHYTA (Fig. C.3)

Prochlorophytes are unicellular, non-motile, photosynthetic autotrophs which form extracellular associations with tropical and subtropical marine invertebrates. Prochlorophytes have many of the structural and biochemical characteristics of bacteria and are undoubtedly prokaryotes. Like eukaryotic green plants, however, they possess chlorophyll-*b* in addition to chlorophyll-*a*, their photosynthesis yields oxygen and they contain a linear, unbranched amylose-like starch. They do not seem to contain sucrose, the sugar synthesised by most green plants, but they do have small amounts of glucose. The Prochlorophyta resemble the chloroplasts of green plants.

SUPERKINGDOM 2: EUKARYOTA

Eukaryotes are organisms made of cells, and have a large range of cell size, mostly between 2 and 100 micrometres in diameter. The genetic material is in the form of chromosomes, which consist of DNA and proteins called histones and are contained in a membrane-bounded organelle, the nucleus. Eukaryotic cells also contain other membrane-bounded organelles such as mitochondria, Golgi apparatus and, in plants, chloroplasts. Their cytoplasmic ribosomes are larger than those of pro-karyotes. Mitochondria and chloroplasts contain their own separate DNA, and ribosomes of the prokaryotic type. Flagella, when present, are complex, consisting of eleven protein threads characteristically organised inside a membranous sheath; the energy for the movement of eukaryotic flagella is generated all along their length. Eukaryotes may be unicellular or filamentous, but many are multicellular with complex differentiation into tissues. Many forms of reproduction are known, including sexual reproduction, and involve two different types of nuclear division, mitosis and meiosis (see section 1.5).

In this classification three kingdoms are included in the Eukaryota: Fungi (mushrooms, toadstools and moulds), Plantae (plants) and Animalia (animals).

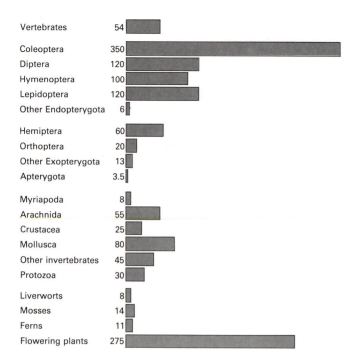

Fig. C.4. Histogram showing the numbers of species (in thousands) in different groups.

Vertebrates	54
Coleoptera	350
Diptera	120
Hymenoptera	100
Lepidoptera	120
Other Endopterygota	6
Hemiptera	60
Orthoptera	20
Other Exopterygota	13
Apterygota	3.5
Myriapoda	8
Arachnida	55
Crustacea	25
Mollusca	80
Other invertebrates	45
Protozoa	30
Liverworts	8
Mosses	14
Ferns	11
Flowering plants	275

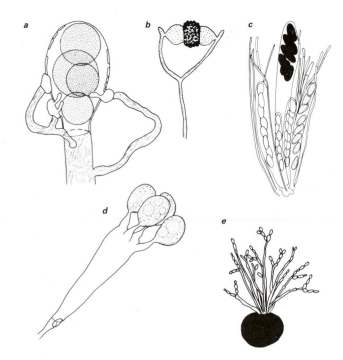

Fig. C.5. FUNGI: (a) Mastigomycotina; (b) Zygomycotina; (c) Ascomycotina; (d) Basidiomycotina; (e) Deuteromycotina.

Kingdom Fungi (Mushrooms, toadstools and moulds) (Fig. C.5)

The classification of the fungi used here is based on G.C. Ainsworth (Ainsworth, Sparrow and Sussman, 1973).

There are two divisions and five subdivisions of fungi. The classification of fungi is based largely on the morphology of their reproductive structures. Some fungi lack a cell wall, but the vegetative phase of the majority consists of thread-like walled filaments called hyphae, which extend by apical growth and branch profusely to form a web or mycelium (see section 2.3). The gross morphology of hyphae is of little diagnostic value, but the presence or absence and the form of septa (cross-walls), and the nature of the wall components, are important in distinguishing the various subdivisions. Fungi reproduce sexually, and often asexually, by spores. Subdivisions are based on the nature of the spores formed, especially the sexually produced ones, but the first major grouping of the fungi is based on the presence or absence of cell walls.

Division MYXOMYCOTA (Wall-less fungi)

The Myxomycota, as distinct from the Eumycota, lack a cell wall, and possess either a plasmodium or a pseudoplasmodium. A plasmodium is a mass of naked, multinucleate protoplasm which moves by amoeboid movement and feeds by ingesting particulate matter. A pseudoplasmodium is an aggregation of separate amoeboid cells. Both such structures are of a slimy consistency, and this has led to the Myxomycota being called 'slime-moulds', with those possessing a cellular pseudoplasmodium being referred to as the cellular slime-moulds (Acrasiomycetes), as distinct from the true slime-moulds (Myxomycetes). The plasmodia of the true slime-moulds are often brightly coloured, and eventually become converted into

delicate spore-producing organs of a wide variety of colour and form; they are cosmopolitan on moist decaying wood and other organic substrates. Members of one class of the Myxomycota, the Plasmodiophoromycetes, are biotrophic endoparasites, and cause economically important diseases such as club-root of plants of the cabbage family.

Division EUMYCOTA (True, walled fungi)

In the Eumycota ('true fungi', which have cell walls) it is customary to recognise five subdivisions. Almost 44000 species of true fungi have been described, 1100 in the Mastigomycotina, 610 in the Zygomycotina, 15000 in the Ascomycotina, 12000 in the Basidiomycotina, and 15000 in the Deuteromycotina; the total reaches almost 62000 if the fungi of lichens are included. Some 29% of all fungi are found in lichens; most of these are from the Ascomycotina, which is thus by far the largest subdivision. The Deuteromycotina is an artificial assemblage consisting of fungi related to the Ascomycotina or Basidiomycotina which have lost the ability to reproduce sexually, and fungi with a sexual state that has not yet been discovered or connected to the asexually reproducing state.

The Mastigomycotina is the only group of true fungi to produce motile flagellate zoospores, developing enclosed within a walled zoosporangium. This group, which includes many solely aquatic fungi, includes the non-mycelial chytrids (Chytridiomycetes) and hyphochytrids (Hyphochytridiomycetes), and also the water moulds and downy mildews (Oomycetes) which have a non-septate, diploid vegetative mycelium and cell walls containing cellulose among their polymers. These filamentous Mastigomycotina are like the Zygomycotina in possessing aseptate hyphae, but are distinguished on their cell wall components: the vegetative phase of Zygomycotina is mycelial and aseptate, but haploid, and the walls contain chitin-chitosan. The asexual spores of the Zygomycotina are non-motile, walled aplanospores enclosed within a sporangial wall, and their sexually produced spores are formed by the complete fusion of two gametangia (gamete-producing organs); in the Mastigomycotina, such as the Oomycetes, the antheridium, the male gametangium, is usually distinctly smaller than the oogonium, the female gametangium, where the sexual spores, oospores, develop after nuclear transfer from the male. The Zygomycotina include the pin moulds (Zygomycetes) and fungi parasitic on arthropods (Zygomycetes and Trichomycetes).

All other fungi have septate hyphae. The Ascomycotina have haploid vegetative mycelia, and septa with a simple septal pore connecting one cell compartment with another. The cell walls contain chitin and glucan. The group is subdivided on the nature of the ascocarp, the reproductive structure, and of the asci, the special sacs in the ascocarp containing typically eight sexually produced ascospores. The ascocarps may be completely closed spheres, open cup-like or saucer-like in shape, or flask-shaped; the asci may have one wall or two separable walls. Many Ascomycotina also reproduce asexually, by conidia. These are walled, but are not enclosed in a separate sporangial wall as in the Mastigomycotina and Zygomycotina. An enormous range of conidial morphology is found, with variation in shape representing adaptations to different methods of dispersal. The Ascomycotina includes the yeasts (Hemiascomycetes), the plant-pathogenic powdery mildews, and the blue and green moulds (Plectomycetes), the flask fungi (Pyrenomycetes), the cup fungi, truffles and lichen fungi (Discomycetes) and a heterogeneous group of plant pathogens and saprotrophs (Loculoascomycetes).

The vegetative phase of Basidiomycotina is mycelial and septate with complex perforated septa, and often has characteristic connections called clamp connections between adjacent cells in a hypha. The hyphal walls contain chitin and glucan. In the majority of Basidiomycotina the vegetative mycelium is not truly haploid, as it is in all the other mycelial fungi except the Oomycetes. Instead, each compartment (cell) of a hypha usually contains two compatible (in the sense that they will eventually fuse) haploid nuclei. This vegetative 'dikaryon' is unique to these fungi and, while functionally diploid, is genetically more flexible than a true diploid cell.

Most of the familiar large fungi are members of the Basidiomycotina: this group includes the mushrooms, toadstools, bracket fungi and jelly fungi (Teliomycetes), and the puffballs, earth-stars, stinkhorns and bird's nest fungi (Gasteromycetes). The group is usually subdivided on the nature of the reproductive structure, the basidiocarp, and of the spore-bearing basidia this contains. Basidiocarps are especially variable in size and shape, the most familiar being the fleshy agaric or toadstool, and the leathery and more durable polypore or bracket. One large class, the Teliomycetes, which includes pathogens causing the familiar rust and smut diseases of plants, lack basidiocarps. The spore-bearing basidium, which is

equivalent to the ascus of the Ascomycotina, may be a single cylindrical cell, undivided by septa and typically bearing four basidiospores on fine stalks on the outside, or it may be divided by transverse or longitudinal septa, or it may be forked. Asexual spores, which are rarely produced, are non-motile conidia.

The Deuteromycotina lack sexually produced spores, and are called the 'Fungi Imperfecti' because the sexual or 'perfect' state is absent. The only spores produced are asexual, non-motile conidia. The vegetative phase may consist of single cells which bud, or may form mycelia, with the conidia either borne directly on the hyphae, or partially or completely enclosed in some form of asexual reproductive structure.

Kingdom Plantae (Plants)

The cells of plants usually have a wall consisting largely of a variety of polysaccharides, including microfibrils of cellulose, a β-(1 → 4)-linked polymer of glucose. In some groups the walls of many cells also contain polyphenols, such as lignin, or lipid polymers, such as cutin or suberin. Mature plant cells usually have large central vacuoles filled with water containing dissolved solutes. Most plants are green and photosynthetic, containing chloroplasts, although a few are parasitic and have sometimes lost their chlorophyll. Various photosynthetic pigments may be present, but always include chlorophyll-a. As in most blue-green algae and in the prochlorophytes, water is used as a hydrogen-donor for photosynthesis and oxygen is produced.

The morphology of their reproductive structures is widely used in the classification of plants into major groups, although chemical data are also used in the classification of some types such as the algae. For convenience, the major divisions are here divided into three informal groups: the algae (7 divisions), the bryophytes (3 divisions) and the vascular plants (12 divisions).

The algae (Fig. C.6)

The term 'algae' for simple plants has been abandoned as a formal taxon in modern classifications of the plant kingdom, but is still used informally. As a group the algae include some of the smallest of plants as well as some of the largest. *Micromonas pusilla*, one of the Chrysophyta, is only about 1.5 micrometres long by 1 micrometre in diameter, whereas some of the giant kelps, members of the Phaeophyta, may attain lengths exceeding 60 metres.

In some unicellular algae the cell itself may function directly as a gamete. In other algae the gametes and spores are produced within specialised unicellular gametangia or sporangia or within multicellular ones where every cell is fertile. In this respect, algae are fundamentally different from the Bryophyta. Algae are, however, perhaps more easily defined on the

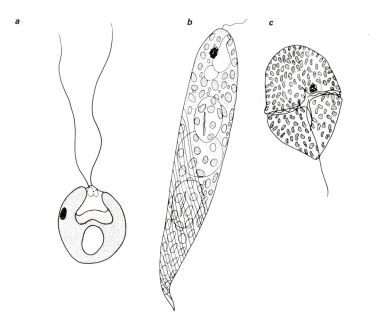

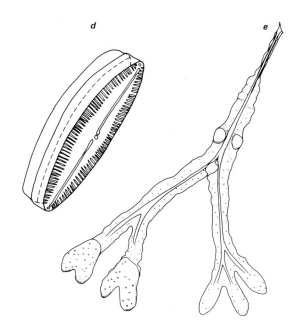

Fig. C.6. Algae: (a) CHLOROPHYTA: Chlamydomonas; (b) EUGLENOPHYTA: Euglena; (c) PYRROPHYTA: Gymnodinium; (d) CHRYSOPHYTA: Pinnularia; (e) PHAEOPHYTA: Fucus.

characters they lack. They never have xylem or its equivalent, or stomata, and very few possess a cuticle. Algae can conveniently be classified into seven divisions, with the green, brown and red algae being the most familiar.

The seven divisions are separated on fundamental biochemical characters, such as the nature of photosynthetic pigments, food reserves and cell walls, flagellation, and fine structure, especially the organisation of the chloroplasts. The assignment of divisional rank to all these groups of algae reflects the belief that they have been quite distinct from an early stage in evolution, and that only one, the Chlorophyta, is on the same line of evolution as the Bryophyta and the vascular plants. All the divisions have chlorophyll-*a* and *β*-carotene; they differ in the second chlorophyll present and in their other pigments. Each chloroplast encloses a number of flattened, sac-like thylakoids, the membranes of which contain the photosynthetic pigments. These membranes are found associated in groups, and the number in a group is characteristic of the division. There are three major types of food reserve: those with α-$(1\rightarrow4)$-linked glucose polymers, those with β-$(1\rightarrow3)$-linked glucose polymers, and those with oils rather than carbohydrates as the main storage products in their vegetative cells. The flagella vary in their position of insertion (apical, sub-apical or lateral), relative size (equal or unequal), number per cell (0, 1, 2, 3, 4 or many) and type (smooth, called whiplash, or with ultramicroscopic hairs, called tinsel). The divisions vary markedly in the degree of complexity of their vegetative forms, but this is not used in separating them, mainly because they show so many parallels in the evolution of their vegetative morphologies. However, considerable emphasis is placed on the development of parenchymatous growth as opposed to filamentous growth (see pages **000–00**).

Division CHLOROPHYTA (Chlorophytes: green algae)

This is a group with a very wide range of form, including unicellular flagellate and coccoid (non-motile sphere) types, palmelloid (non-motile cells, embedded in a common colloidal sheath) types, dendroid (branched tree-like) types, colonial, filamentous and parenchymatous types. Of all the algae they are biochemically the most like land plants.

Division CHAROPHYTA (Charophytes: stone-worts and brittle-worts)

These are plants with a main axis and whorls of lateral branches, with very large multinucleate internodal cells. They are often encrusted with calcium carbonate. Fossils are known from as far back as the Silurian period.

Division EUGLENOPHYTA (Euglenids)

The euglenids are mostly unicellular and flagellate. Thirty-six genera are known, of which only eleven contain chlorophyll; some are facultative saprotrophs, others feed like single-celled animals.

Division PHAEOPHYTA (Phaeophytes: brown algae, seaweeds)

The brown algae are almost entirely marine. They are multicellular, filamentous or parenchymatous, and are often very large. Many fucoids and kelps are structurally very complex, with leaf-like, stem-like and root-like organs exhibiting obvious differentiation into tissues.

Division CHRYSOPHYTA (Golden-brown and yellow-green algae, and the diatoms)

This is a diverse group with unicellular, palmelloid, dendroid and siphonaceous (multinucleate filaments with no cross walls) types. Carotenes and xanthophylls are present in greater quantity than are chlorophylls. The diatoms are by far the most numerous and economically important members of the divi-

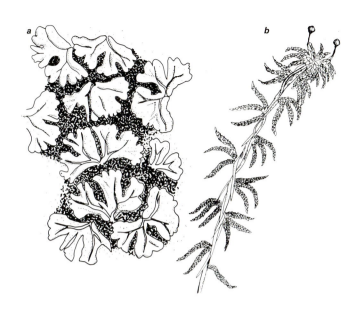

Fig. C.7. Bryophytes: (a) HEPATOPHYTA: Ricciocarpus; (b) BRYOPHYTA: Sphagnum.

sion. As members of the freshwater and saltwater plankton, they play a key role in the nutritional cycle of aquatic animals. The siliceous cell walls of diatoms preserve astonishingly well, and vast deposits of these, some dating from the Jurassic period, form diatomaceous earths.

Division PYRROPHYTA

This division includes the dinoflagellates. Carotenes and xanthophylls, some peculiar to the group, predominate over chlorophylls. The motile members of the Pyrrophyta are characterised by the arrangement of their flagella: one flagellum is elongated and extends behind, while the second is band-shaped and lies in a groove running around the cell; both flagella are of the tinsel type. When a wall is present it is often made of many cellulose plates. Many of these algae have spiny protrusions. The majority are planktonic, and marine 'blooms' of some genera such as *Gymnodinium* cause the 'red tides' that result in considerable destruction of fish populations.

Division RHODOPHYTA (Rhodophytes: red algae)

The red algae are almost entirely marine. The vast majority are multicellular, with filamentous growth, although they frequently appear parenchymatous because of the close aggregation of the constituent filaments. The only truly parenchymatous member, *Porphyra*, has been cultivated in Japan for many centuries for food.

The bryophytes (Fig. C.7)

The liverworts, hornworts and mosses are often classified together in one division, the Bryophyta. However, all these plants are only similar in one major unique characteristic: the form of their life-cycle. This involves a regular and well-marked alternation between a free-living haploid gametophyte generation, which is the dominant and long-lived phase, and a diploid sporophyte generation which is permanently attached to and nutritionally dependent on the gametophyte, even though in some mosses the sporophyte becomes relatively complex. The other characteristics common to all bryophytes, such as multicellular sex organs in the form of archegonia and antheridia, biflagellate male gametes, meiosis at spore formation, aerial spore dispersal and a terrestrial habitat, are significant but are shared with the algae or with vascular plants. The differences between the three types of bryophyte are such that each is classified here as a separate division, as follows.

Division HEPATOPHYTA (Thalloid and leafy liverworts)

Liverworts are the simplest existing land plants. The gametophyte generation is usually leafy, but sometimes thalloid (flattened and ribbon-shaped). Leaves are usually in three rows, two-lobed and one cell thick, and are always without a midrib. Rhizoids, the filaments attaching a liverwort to its substratum, may be present, and are unicellular. The sporophyte generation is short-lived, with poorly developed photosynthetic tissue, no stomata, no columella (central sterile tissue in the capsule) and, generally, no water-conducting tissue. The seta (stalk) of the sporophyte elongates when the capsule is mature and bursts through the gametophyte tissue. The capsule opens when mature by splitting into lobes, and elaters (sterile hygroscopic cells) are usually present in the capsule. The protonema, the filamentous phase of the gametophyte arising from the germinating spore, is short in duration or absent.

Division ANTHOCEROTOPHYTA (Hornworts)

The gametophyte generation of hornworts is a thallus, with one large chloroplast per cell, and sex organs sunken in the thallus tissue. Hornworts are never leafy, and their rhizoids are unicellular. The sporophyte generation is an elongated cylindrical structure, with a basal meristem, photosynthetic tissue with stomata, a central sterile columella and elaters. The capsule is not enclosed in any gametophyte tissue, and eventually gapes open into two valves at the apex, this split extending towards the base as development proceeds, with the columella appearing as a dark thread between the valves. There is no protonemal phase following germination of the spores.

Division BRYOPHYTA (Mosses)

The gametophyte generation of mosses is always leafy, and arises from a protonema that is of long duration. The shoots are usually radially symmetrical, and the leaves usually have a thickened midrib and are never lobed. The rhizoids are multicellular. The sporophyte generation of mosses is long-lived, usually with well-developed photosynthetic tissue and stomata at the base of the capsule. The seta is usually long and wiry, elongating before the capsule is mature and carrying some gametophyte tissue with it. The capsule has a central columella of sterile tissue, but no elaters, and opens when mature by a lid which exposes a single or double ring of often hygroscopic teeth. A simple water-conducting system is present in the gametophyte stem and sporophyte seta of most mosses. *Sphagnum*, the dominant plant in most bogs, is an unusual moss in having spirally thickened water-holding cells in its stems and leaves, and a capsule which releases its spores explosively.

The vascular plants

The vascular plants, that is those having conducting tissues of xylem and phloem, were formerly grouped as the Tracheophyta. The classification adopted here follows H.C. Bold *et al.* (1980), with some nomenclatural changes according to A. Cronquist *et al.* (1966), and has the living vascular plants divided into nine divisions. Four divisions are usually referred to informally as pteridophytes, four more as gymnosperms, and the last division as angiosperms or flowering plants. There are also four divisions of extinct pteridophytes, which are known only from fossils (see Chapter 14). These are the Rhyniophyta, Zosterophyllophyta and Trimerophyta, which all contain plants of very simple structure, and the Progymnospermophyta, which combine some of the characters of pteridophytes with some of the characters of gymnospermous seed plants. The divisions of the living vascular land plants are as follows.

The pteridophytes (Fig. C.8)

Division PSILOPHYTA

Plants in this division are rootless, with symmetrically branching rhizomes (underground stems) and aerial branches. The lateral appendages to these are scale-like or leaf-like, and more or less spirally arranged. The gametophyte generation is cylindrical in cross-section, subterranean and saprophytic. The male gametes (antherozooids) have many flagella. The sporangia (spore-producing organs) arise at the ends of very short lateral branches, have thick walls and are homosporous (producing spores of only one kind).

There are two living genera, *Psilotum* and *Tmesipteris*; *Psilotum* has two or three species, which are widespread throughout the tropics and subtropics, and extend to Florida and New Zealand, and *Tmesipteris* has two or more species in Australia, Polynesia and New Caledonia.

Division LYCOPODIOPHYTA (= MICROPHYLLOPHYTA, LYCOPSIDA) (Club-mosses)

These are plants with roots, simple or branched stems and small, spirally arranged leaves (microphylls). The sporangium is either borne on a fertile leaf (a sporophyll) or is associated with one; it is thick-walled, and is either homosporous (producing only one kind of spore) or heterosporous (producing two kinds of spore). The male gametes (antherozooids) have two or many flagella.

The division can be split into two classes. The first class includes the genus *Lycopodium*, with some 200 living species. These are mainly tropical, but several occur in Arctic and subalpine regions. Recent authorities suggest splitting *Lycopodium* into several genera, but no worldwide monograph has yet been published. The second class contains two main genera, *Isoetes* with about 70 species and *Selaginella* with about 700 species. These have a worldwide distribution.

Numerous fossil species are known in the two divisions, of which some 200 species of the order *Lepidodendrales* are the most striking (see section 14.1). These reached their greatest development in the swamps of the Upper Carboniferous, when they formed forests of trees 40 metres or more in height.

Division EQUISETOPHYTA (= ARTHROPHYTA, SPHENOPSIDA) (Horsetails)

These are plants with roots and stems, sometimes simple and sometimes with whorls of branches. The leaves are relatively small and are borne in whorls. Sporangia occur several together in terminal 'cones' and are thick-walled. Living species are homosporous, although some fossil species were heterosporous.

The only living genus is *Equisetum*, with some 14 species distributed throughout the world, except for Australasia. There are numerous fossil genera, and some species belonging to the order Calamitales were as tall as 20 metres.

Division POLYPODIOPHYTA (= PTERIDOPHYTA, PTEROPSIDA, FILICINEAE) (Ferns and their allies)

These are plants with roots and stems; the stems are mostly short and stock-like, or creeping with underground rhizomes, but sometimes form erect trunks. The leaves (megaphylls) are spirally arranged, and are often markedly subdivided (compound) and described as 'fronds'. The sporangia are often grouped in structures called sori, and are borne on the frond, either along the margin or on either surface. The male gametes (antherozooids) have many flagella.

The ferns have an enormous range of form and structure, and there are over 10000 living species, with a worldwide distribution, the greatest number and diversity being in the tropical regions. They range from small epiphytes with undivided fronds, to tree-ferns with broad trunks up to 24

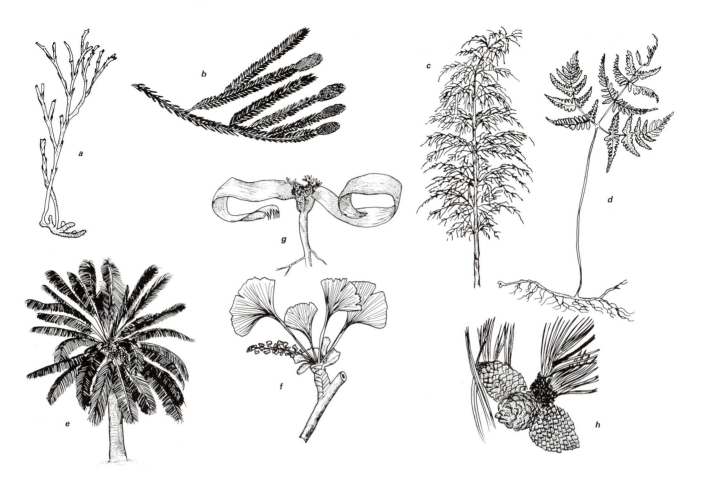

Fig. C.8. Pteridophytes: (a) PSILOPHYTA; (b) LYCOPODIOPHYTA; (c) EQUISETOPHYTA;

(d) POLYPODIOPHYTA. Gymnosperms: (e) CYCADOPHYTA; (f) GINKGOPHYTA; (g) GNETOPHYTA; (h) PINOPHYTA.

metres in height with highly compound fronds. In addition to living species, a great many fossil ferns have been described.

The gymnosperms

Division CYCADOPHYTA (Cycads)

These are woody plants, usually with unbranched stems. The xylem tissue has broad rays of parenchyma cells, and the pith and bark are extensive compared with the xylem and phloem. Leaves of cycads are large and in general singly compound. There are separate male and female plants, and reproductive organs are borne in terminal or lateral cones, except in females of *Cycas* species. The microsporophylls (small, spore-bearing leaves) are scale-like or peltate with pollen-sacs on their undersurface. The male gametes have a spiral band of flagella. The seeds are large.

There are nine genera and 65 species of cycads in central America, southern Africa, eastern Asia and Australia. There are also many fossil species in this division, including bennet-titaleans (cycadeoids) and pteridosperms (seed-ferns), and these had an almost worldwide distribution.

Division GINKGOPHYTA (Ginkgos)

Ginkgos are branching trees with two types of shoot, called long and short shoots. The xylem has narrow rays of parenchyma cells. The thick, leathery leaves are strap-shaped or fan-shaped, spirally arranged and are often deeply divided, with a symmetrically branching pattern of veins. There are separate male and female plants. Ovules are borne in pairs at the tips of short stalks, and male gametes have a spiral band of flagella.

At least 16 fossil genera are known, with numerous species once widely distributed in the northern hemisphere. The division is now represented by a single species only, *Ginkgo biloba*, with fan-shaped leaves, which originally came from south China but is now cultivated widely around the world.

Division PINOPHYTA (=CONIFEROPHYTA) (Conifers)

These are branching trees with long and short shoots. The xylem, which comprises the bulk of the stem, has narrow rays of parenchyma cells, and the pith and bark tissues are restricted. The leaves are simple, often scale-like or needle-like, and occasionally broad. They are arranged spirally or opposite, and occasionally in whorls. The reproductive organs of conifers are unisexual cones. The male cones are simple, with few to numerous microsporophylls bearing pollen sacs on their

Fig. C.9. Angiosperms: MAGNOLIOPHYTA: (a) Ursinia speciosa; (b) Quercus alba (white oak); (c) Lathyrus sylvestris; (d) Arum maculatum.

undersurfaces; the female cones are compound, with ovules usually on the surface of a scale.

This division includes some 50 genera and 550 living species of conifers, together with the extinct cordaites. Many conifers are large trees and form extensive forests in western North America and in parts of Europe and Asia. In the southern hemisphere they are abundant in temperate regions of South America, New Zealand and Australia.

Division GNETOPHYTA

These are trees, shrubs, lianes or stumpy plants with the woody stems partly below ground. Their simple leaves are opposite or whorled, and are broadly elliptical, strap-shaped or reduced to minute scales. Gnetophyta produce secondary wood with vessels. The reproductive organs, sometimes called 'flowers', are unisexual, normally on separate individuals, and are arranged in compound 'inflorescences'. Fertilisation involves a pollen tube with two male nuclei, and the embryo has two cotyledons.

This division is represented by three genera in three quite distinct families. *Gnetum* contains about 40 species from moist tropical forests in northern South America, western Africa and India to Malaysia. *Welwitschia bainesii* is restricted to about 600 miles along the coastal belt of south-western Africa. *Ephedra* contains about 40 species in both North and South

America, and in a broad belt from the Mediterranean to China. The species of this division approach more nearly the Magnoliophyta (angiosperms) than do those of any of the other divisions of gymnosperms.

The angiosperms (Fig. C.9)

Division MAGNOLIOPHYTA (=ANGIOSPERMAE) (Flowering plants)

This division includes annual, biennial and perennial plants which may be floating plants, submerged plants, herbs, shrubs, vines, lianes or trees, including epiphytes and colourless parasites. Magnoliophyta vary in size from small unattached water plants about 1 millimetre across, to trees up to 100 metres high. The xylem usually contains vessels. The plants are monoecious (both male and female reproductive organs are on the same plant) or dioecious (with the sexes on different plants), and have either unisexual or hermaphrodite flowers. The flower usually consists of four sets of structures arranged around an axis. The outer set is a series of modified bracts or leaves, called sepals, which together form the calyx. The sepals are usually green and probably have a protective function. The second set, the corolla, is formed of petals, which are usually coloured and sometimes serve to attract insects. Sometimes

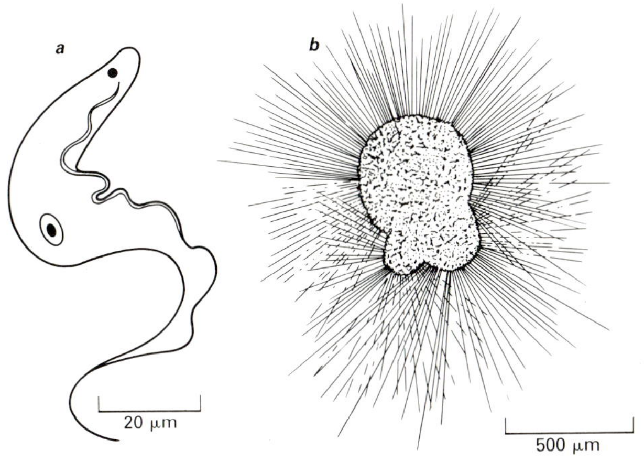

Fig. C.10. PROTOZOA: (a) Flagellata: Trypanosoma; *(b) Sarcodina: foraminiferan.*

both calyx and corolla are coloured and sometimes both are green; sometimes there is only one set of structures in place of the calyx and corolla. The pollen-bearing organs, known as the stamens, are the next set of structures, and the ovule-bearing organs, the carpels, complete the flower. After fertilisation the ovules develop into seeds. The major characteristic of the Magnoliophyta is that the ovules are enclosed.

The Magnoliophyta can be divided into two main groups. The class Magnoliatae (the dicotyledons) has embryos with two cotyledons. The vascular bundles of the stem are usually arranged in a single ring (when viewed in transverse section), and vascular cambium is usually present. The leaf veins are generally branched, and occasionally parallel. The flowers are typically arranged with four-fold or five-fold symmetry. The class Liliatae (the monocotyledons) has embryos with one cotyledon. The vascular bundles of the stem are arranged in an irregular fashion, and vascular cambium is usually absent. The leaves are usually parallel-veined. The flowers are typically arranged with three-fold symmetry.

Estimates of the number of species of the Magnoliophyta range from 220 000 to 250 000, which is at least ten times the number of any other division of plants. Their distribution ranges from the Arctic to the equator, from below sea-level to mountain tops and from tropical forests to the most arid deserts. Because they form the major vegetation of the landscape, flowering plants provide the habitats for most terrestrial animal life, as well as supplying a large part of the food of the human species. About two-thirds of the species of the Magnoliophyta are confined to the tropics and adjacent regions.

Kingdom: Animalia (Animals)

The animal kingdom is conventionally divided into about 30 major categories, known as phyla, equivalent to divisions in Monera, Fungi and Plantae. The animals contained in any one phylum share a common basic organisation and style of architecture, which makes them distinct from the animals in any other phylum. Naturally, opinions differ about the grouping of animals into phyla. For example, the six groups, from Rotifera to Nematoda, which are here treated as six separate phyla, are frequently classified as one phylum, the Aschelminthes. Conversely, the groups given here in the Arthropoda are often classified as a number of separate phyla.

The phyla of animals differ enormously in size, measured in terms of the number of described living species, from the Arthropoda with about 888 000 species to the Entoprocta with 6. The arthropods comprise about 77% of all described living animal species; a further 8 phyla, with between 10 000 and 100 000 species each, account for another 21.5%; and the remaining 1.5% of the known present-day species is spread over the other 22 phyla.

The animal phyla are sometimes grouped into three separate subkingdoms: Protozoa, Parazoa and Metazoa. The Protozoa is a highly diverse assemblage of organisms grouped together only because they are single-celled. The Parazoa contains one phylum, the Porifera (sponges), separated by virtue of their low level of cellular organisation. The Metazoa includes the remaining phyla of multicellular animals.

The Protozoa

Phylum PORIFERA (Sponges) (10 000 species) (Fig. C.11)

This phylum includes all single-celled animals, occurring either as solitary individuals or as colonies of individuals. There are several important classes of protozoans.

The Flagellata (or Mastigophora) are distinguished by their use of flagella for locomotion, and include zooflagellates such as *Trypanosoma*, the cause of sleeping sickness, and *Trichonympha*. The Euglenophyta, a division of flagellate algae which includes *Euglena*, *Volvox* and the dinoflagellates, are sometimes included here too.

The Sarcodina have flowing extensions of the body, called pseudopodia, for locomotion. They may be naked, such as *Amoeba*, or have a hard skeleton, such as foraminiferans and radiolarians. The class Sporozoa includes parasites of animals, such as *Plasmodium*, the cause of malaria. Members of the class Ciliata, such as *Paramecium* and *Vorticella*, have cilia and two nuclei.

The Parazoa

Phylum PORIFERA (Sponges) (10 000 species) (Fig. C.11)

Sponges are animals composed of aggregations of cells that retain considerable independence from one another. Their body is penetrated by pore canals and chambers through which water flows, but there is no differentiation of the body into organs. The adults are sessile (they do not move). Sponges are mostly marine, but some are freshwater.

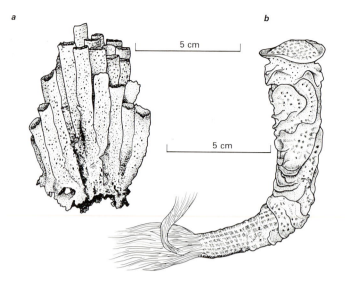

Fig. C.11. *PORIFERA: (a) Demospongia; (b) Hexactinellida.*

The class Calcarea includes sponges with calcareous spicules, such as *Leucosolenia*. Demospongia is the largest class, with a spongy skeleton and/or siliceous spicules; it includes bath sponges and freshwater sponges. The Hexactinellida includes the glass sponges with six-rayed, siliceous spicules.

The Metazoa

Phylum COELENTERATA (or CNIDARIA) (10000 species) (Fig. C.13)

Coelenterates are generally built on a radially symmetrical body plan. The body wall has two cell layers, an ectoderm and an endoderm, separated by a jelly-like layer called the mesogloea. There is only one body cavity, with a single opening at the mouth which is fringed with tentacles. The stinging organelles called nematocysts are unique to this phylum. Two basic morphological types of coelenterate are found, free-swimming medusae and sessile polyps, and both are often colonial.

The class Hydrozoa are mainly marine, such as *Obelia*, but some are freshwater, such as *Hydra*. There are usually both polyp and medusa stages in the life-cycle. The Scyphozoa are the jelly-fish, which are exclusively marine, and have the medusa as the dominant form. The Anthozoa are also an exclusively marine class, and have no medusa stage; they include sea-anemones, soft corals (such as *Alcyonium*), sea-pens, and reef-building corals.

Phylum CTENOPHORA (Comb-jellies) (80 species) (Fig. C.13)

Ctenophores are built on a radial plan like the coelenterates, with a single body cavity and a body wall of two cell layers separated by a jelly-like mesogloea. There are, however, no nematocysts, and comb-jellies are never sessile, never colonial, and always marine. They have eight rows of ciliary plates, called comb-plates, for locomotion, and comb-jellies such as the sea-gooseberry (*Pleurobrachia*) and *Beroë* are common in plankton.

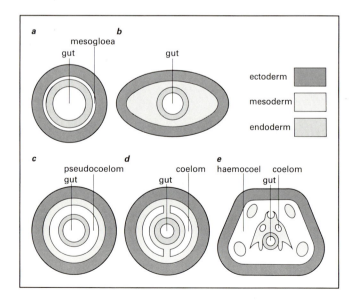

Fig. C.12. *Metazoan body cavities: (a) Coelenterata; (b) acoelomate; (c) pseudocoelomate; (d) coelomate; (e) haemocoel.*

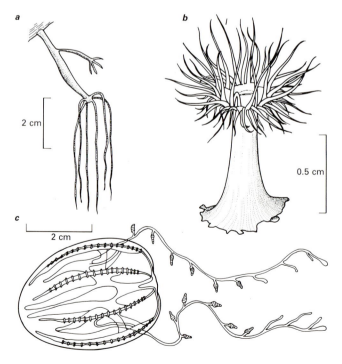

Fig. C.13. *COELENTERATA: (a) Hydrozoa:* Hydra; *(b) Anthozoa: sea-anemone. CTENOPHORA: (c) Pleurobrachia (sea-gooseberry).*

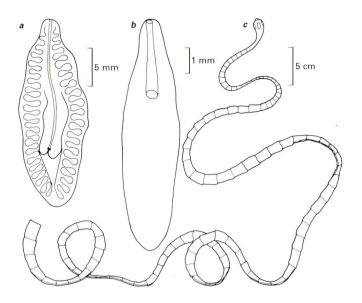

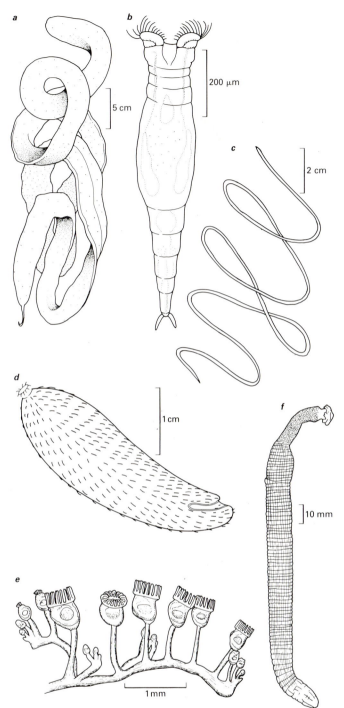

Fig. C.14. PLATYHELMINTHES: (a) Turbellaria: triclad flatworm; (b) Trematoda: liver fluke; (c) Cestoda: tapeworm.

Phylum PLATYHELMINTHES (Flatworms, flukes and tapeworms) (20000 species) (Fig. C.14)

Flatworms are bilaterally symmetrical worms that are dorsoventrally flattened. Their body has three layers of cells, a mouth leading to a blind-ending gut, but no body cavity, anus or circulatory system.

The Turbellaria are free-living flatworms, mainly marine but there are also many terrestrial and freshwater species. The class includes planarians and polyclads.

The Trematoda are the flukes, which include both ectoparasites and endoparasites such as the liver fluke of sheep (*Fasciola hepatica*) and human blood flukes (*Schistosoma*).

The class Cestoda are the tapeworms. Most of these are parasites of the vertebrate gut.

Phylum MESOZOA (50 species)

These are minute internal parasites of marine invertebrates, and have a body composed of two cell layers. The Mesozoa are thought by some zoologists to be degenerate flatworms.

Phylum NEMERTEA (Proboscis-worms) (800 species) (Fig. C.15)

The nemertines are bilaterally symmetrical worms, lacking a coelomic body cavity, but possessing a gut with an anus as well as a mouth; they also have a circulatory system, and a proboscis that can be everted from its tubular cavity dorsal to the gut. Most nemertines are marine, such as *Lineus* and *Tubulanus*, but some are freshwater, and there are also terrestrial species such as *Geonemertes*. They can be very long, and individuals up to 30 metres in length have been recorded.

Phylum ROTIFERA (Wheel-animals) (1500 species) (Fig. C.15)

The rotifers are aquatic, microscopic animals, less than 2 millimetres long, with their anterior end modified into a ciliary organ called a corona, the beating of which gives the impression of a rotating wheel. They have a pseudocoelomate body cavity. Most rotifer species are freshwater, but some are marine.

Fig. C.15. (a) NEMERTEA; (b) ROTIFERA; (c) NEMATOMORPHA; (d) ACANTHOCEPHALA; (e) ENTOPROCTA; (f) SIPUNCULA.

Phylum GASTROTRICHA (150 species)

These are aquatic, microscopic animals, less than 2 millimetres long, with cilia on their body, but these are not arranged in a corona. Their body cavity is a pseudocoelom, and the body surface has cuticular spines, scales or bristles, and usually one or more pairs of adhesive tubes. The Gastrotricha includes both marine and freshwater species.

Phylum KINORHYNCHA (100 species)

These are minute marine pseudocoelomate animals, less than 1 millimetre long, with a spiny body composed of 13 to 14 jointed sections. They lack cilia.

Phylum PRIAPULIDA (10 species)

The priapulids are marine, burrowing pseudocoelomate worms, with cylindrical, warty bodies that have superficial ring-like markings without any internal segmentation.

Phylum NEMATOMORPHA (Hair-worms) (250 species) (Fig. C.15)

These are very long, thin, pseudocoelomate worms, which are parasitic in insects and crustaceans as juveniles, and are free-living as adults. They are mostly freshwater and terrestrial, but one genus is marine.

Phylum NEMATODA (Roundworms) (15000 species)

Nematodes are unsegmented and more or less cylindrical pseudocoelomate worms. Their body is covered with a thick, non-chitinous cuticle, and cilia are absent. They occur free-living in all types of environment, and also as parasites of plants (for example *Heterodera*, potato root eelworm) and animals (for example *Ascaris*). In terms of numbers of individuals, nematodes are the most abundant group of multicellular animals.

Phylum ACANTHOCEPHALA (Spiny-headed worms) (300 species) (Fig. C.15)

These are pseudocoelomate, worm-like internal parasites of vertebrates. They have an evertible proboscis covered with recurved spines and used as an attachment organ.

Phylum ENTOPROCTA (6 species) (Fig. C.15)

The entoprocts are mostly marine, solitary or colonial pseudocoelomates with a terminal circle of ciliated tentacles. The adults are attached to the substrate by a stalk.

Phylum SIPUNCULA (Peanut-worms) (325 species) (Fig. C.15)

Sipunculans, such as *Golfingia*, are unsegmented marine worms with a coelomic body cavity. The front end of the body bears a long, slender proboscis, which can be introverted. They live in crevices or are burrowing.

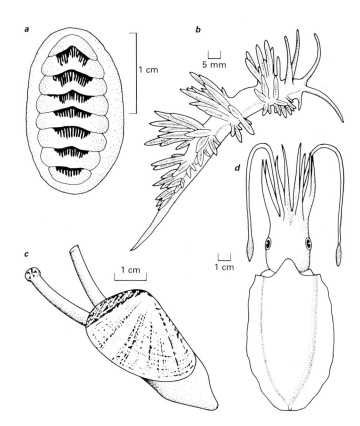

Fig. C.16. MOLLUSCA: (a) Amphineura: chiton; (b) Gastropoda: nudibranch sea-slug; (c) Bivalvia; (d) Cephalopoda: Sepia (cuttlefish).

Phylum ECHIURA (Spoon-worms) (130 species)

These are unsegmented coelomate worms, such as *Bonellia*, which burrow in marine deposits. Their proboscis is not evertible.

Phylum POGONOPHORA (100 species)

These are extremely slender, gutless, tube-living marine worms.

Phylum MOLLUSCA (Molluscs, including snails, clams and octopus) (100000 species) (Fig. C.16)

This is the second largest phylum of animals. Molluscs are soft-bodied, and are usually protected by a calcareous shell that is secreted by a fold of the body wall called the mantle. The coelom is a relatively small cavity surrounding the heart. The ventral body wall is modified as a muscular foot. Molluscs are predominantly marine, but there are a large number of freshwater and terrestrial species. There are five major classes of mollusc, and each contains animals very different in their appearance and habits from those of the other classes.

The class Amphineura includes the chitons, which have a shell divided into eight separate plates and a flattened adhesive foot. Chitons are mainly intertidal browsers. Gastropoda is the largest class of molluscs, and gastropods typically have a single spiral shell. Their head is well-developed, with tentacles, and the foot has a creeping sole. The shell may be reduced or lost, such as in sea-slugs and terrestrial slugs. Gastropods include

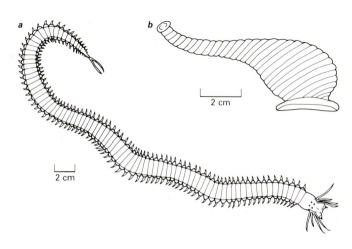

Fig. C.17. ANNELIDA: (a) Polychaeta: ragworm; (b) Hirudinea: leech.

limpets (such as *Patella*), marine snails (such as *Hydrobia*), sea-slugs (such as *Doris*), land snails (such as *Cepaea*), freshwater snails (such as *Lymnaea*) and land-slugs (such as *Arion*). The class Scaphopoda are tusk-shells, burrowing marine molluscs with a tusk-shaped shell open at both ends. The Bivalvia are molluscs with a laterally compressed body, and a shell made up of two valves, hinged dorsally. The head is rudimentary, but the gills are very large and generally bear cilia and are used for feeding. Bivalves are usually sedentary and are mostly marine, although some are freshwater. This class includes mussels, oysters, freshwater mussels (such as *Anodonta*), razor shells, and giant clams (such as *Tridacna*). Members of the fifth class, the Cephalopoda, are usually active rapid swimmers, with a funnel used in jet propulsion and highly developed sense organs. There is a circle of tentacles around the mouth. Cephalopods are marine and include the giant squids (*Architeuthis*) which grow up to 16 metres in length and are the largest of all the invertebrates. There are also many fossil groups of cephalopods, including the extinct ammonites and belemnites. The majority of living forms have their shell reduced or absent. Living members of this class include *Nautilus*, cuttle-fish such as *Sepia*, squids such as *Loligo*, and *Octopus*.

Phylum ANNELIDA **(Annelid worms) (14000 species)** (Fig. C.17)

Annelids are worms with a well-developed coelom, and with the body divided into a number of more or less similar segments. There are three classes of annelid. The Polychaeta are the largest class, and are marine worms with, on each segment, a pair of lateral, lobed appendages bearing strong projecting bristles. Polychaetes include ragworms (such as *Nereis*), lug-worms (such as *Arenicola*) and fanworms (such as *Sabella*). The Oligochaeta are sparsely bristled and without appendages.

They are terrestrial, freshwater or marine, and this class includes the earthworms (such as *Lumbricus*). The Hirudinea are the leeches, which are usually bristleless and are ectoparasitic or carnivorous. Leeches have adhesive suckers at each end of their body, and are mostly freshwater, but some are marine.

Phylum ONYCHOPHORA **(65 species)** (Fig. C.19)

These are soft-bodied, segmented animals with many paired but unjointed legs. They respire through tracheae: air-filled, tubular infoldings of cuticle. A fluid skeleton is used for locomotion and support. This phylum is confined to humid tropics, and includes *Peripatus*.

Phylum ARTHROPODA **(Crustaceans, arachnids, insects, centipedes, millipedes and others) (888000 species)** (Fig. C.18).

The Arthropoda is the largest animal phylum, with more species than all the other phyla and divisions of organisms combined. Arthropods are segmented animals, with a cuticle made of chitin and protein, and with paired, jointed appendages on some or all of their body segments. Parts of the

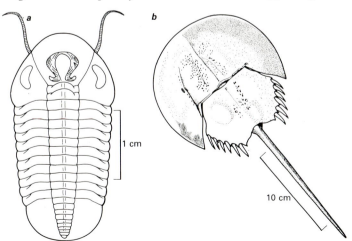

Fig. C.18. ARTHROPODA: (a) Trilobita; (b) Merostomata: Limulus *(horseshoe-crab);*

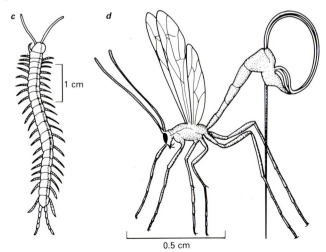

(c) Myriapoda: *centipede;* (d) Insecta: Hymenoptera *(parasitic ichneumon wasp).*

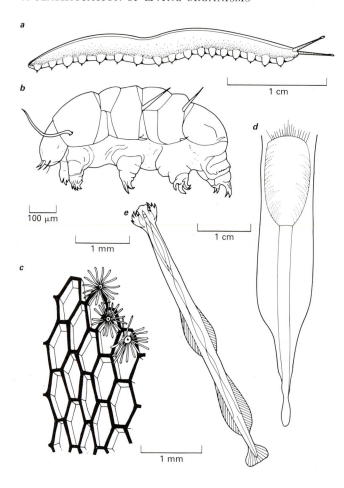

Fig. C.19. (a) ONYCHOPHORA: Peripatus; *(b) TARDIGRADA; (c) POLYZOA; (d) BRACHIOPODA:* Lingula; *(e) CHAETOGNATHA:* Sagitta.

cuticle are hardened (sclerotised) by the tanning of protein. The coelom is reduced or absent, and the body cavity is formed of enlarged blood spaces (a 'haemocoel'). Arthropods are abundant in all environments. There are five major living classes: the arachnids, horseshoe-crabs, crustaceans, myriapods and insects.

The Trilobita comprises the extinct trilobites, which were abundant and widespread in Palaeozoic seas. Their body had three regions, and the anterior region was covered by a dorsal, shield-like carapace. Trilobites had one pair of antennae, and a pair of two-branched appendages on all the post-antennal segments.

The Arachnida includes scorpions, spiders, harvestmen and Acari (mites and ticks). The body of an arachnid is divided into a prosoma and an abdomen. The prosoma has six pairs of specialised appendages and four pairs of walking legs. Arachnids are mostly terrestrial and carnivorous, but a few are secondarily aquatic. Horseshoe-crabs (*Limulus*) are placed in a separate class (Merostomata), closely related to the Arachnida and including many fossil species, such as the eurypterids.

Most of the Crustacea are aquatic and bear gills. The majority of planktonic animals are crustaceans, and have two pairs of antennae, three pairs of mouthparts, and usually a carapace. Crustaceans are divided into a number of subclasses. The Branchiopoda have leaf-like appendages, and include the

fairy shrimps (*Artemia*) and water-fleas (*Daphnia*). The Copepoda have no carapace, and adult copepods have a single central eye; they include important members of the zooplankton, such as *Calanus*. The Cirripedia are the barnacles, which are sessile as adults. The Malacostraca are the largest group of crustaceans, and include isopods (such as woodlice), amphipods (such as the freshwater shrimp *Gammarus*), euphausids (krill), shrimps and prawns, and lobsters and crabs.

The class Myriapoda includes centipedes and millipedes. These usually live on land in moist habitats, and have an elongated body with many segments bearing legs. Myriapods respire using tracheae, rather than gills.

The Insecta, with over 800 000 described living species, is by far the largest class of arthropods, and is the dominant group of land-living invertebrates. Insects are adapted for life on land, but a minor fraction inhabit freshwater; only very few are found in marine habitats. The body is divided into a head, with one pair of antennae; a thorax, with three pairs of legs; and an abdomen, which never bears walking legs. The thorax also bears two pairs of wings, except in primitively wingless groups (the Apterygota; including springtails and silver-fish) and in secondarily wingless groups (such as fleas and lice). Insects respire using tracheae.

The living winged insects, the Pterygota, are divided into about 25 orders, which are usually arranged in two distinct groups. The Exopterygota have a simple metamorphosis from juvenile through to adult, their wings develop externally, and the juveniles, called nymphs, generally resemble the adults in structure and habits. The Endopterygota form a much larger group and have a complex metamorphosis involving a re-organisation stage, the pupa, between the juvenile and the adult; their wings develop internally, and the juveniles differ from the adults in structure and habits.

The two major orders of the Exopterygota are the Hemiptera (the bugs, including cicadas, aphids, pond-skaters, and assassin bugs such as *Rhodnius*) and the Orthoptera (grasshoppers, locusts and crickets). Other important orders are Odonata (dragonflies), Ephemeroptera (mayflies), Plecoptera (stoneflies), Dermaptera (earwigs), Dictyoptera (cockroaches and mantids), Isoptera (termites), and Phthiraptera (lice).

The four major orders of the Endopterygota are the Coleoptera (beetles), with a staggering 350 000 described species, Lepidoptera (butterflies and moths), Diptera (two-winged flies, such as mosquitoes, horseflies, houseflies and the fruitfly *Drosophila*), and Hymenoptera (including sawflies, parasitic wasps, ants and bees). The four smaller orders are Neuroptera (lacewings and ant-lions), Mecoptera (scorpionflies), Trichoptera (caddis-flies) and Siphonaptera (fleas).

Phylum TARDIGRADA **(Water-bears) (400 species)** (Fig. C.19)
These minute animals, less than 1 millimetre long, live in films of water around mosses and other low terrestrial features. They have four pairs of stubby legs armed with terminal claws, and a chitinous cuticle that is periodically moulted to allow growth.

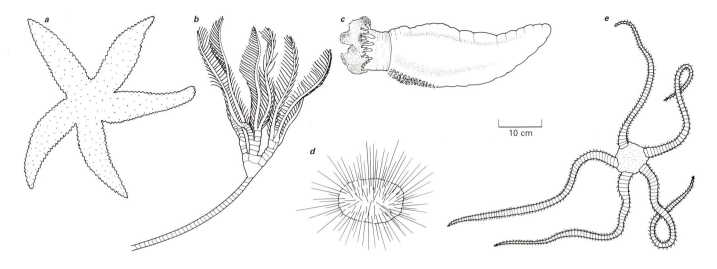

Fig. C.20. ECHINODERMATA: (a) Asteroidea: Asterias (starfish); (b) Crinoidea: sea-lily; (c) Holothuroidea: sea-cucumber; (d) Echinoidea: sea-urchin; (e) Ophiuroidea: brittlestar.

Phylum PENTASTOMIDA **(Tongue-worms) (70 species)**

These are parasites in the respiratory passages of air-breathing vertebrates, and have a chitinous cuticle that is periodically moulted to allow growth.

Phylum POLYZOA **(or** BRYOZOA **or** ECTOPROCTA**) (4500 species)** (Fig. C.19)

These are small, sessile, colonial animals with an extrusible ciliated proboscis called a lophophore. Each member of a colony lives permanently in a horny, gelatinous or calcareous case. They are mostly marine (such as *Membranipora* and *Flustra*), but some are freshwater (such as *Plumatella*).

Phylum BRACHIOPODA **(Lamp-shells) (300 species)** (Fig. C.19)

Brachiopods are bottom-living marine animals, with a shell with two valves, and a lophophore used in feeding and respiration. They have left an extensive fossil record, including about 30000 extinct species (such as *Lingula*).

Phylum PHORONIDA **(15 species)**

These are marine worms living in chitinous tubes, and have a horseshoe-shaped lophophore.

Phylum CHAETOGNATHA **(Arrow-worms) (50 species)** (Fig. C.19)

Arrow-worms, such as *Sagitta*, are small, slender torpedo-shaped marine planktonic animals. They are voracious carnivores.

Phylum ECHINODERMATA **(5900 species)** (Fig. C.20)

Echinoderms are exclusively marine, and most are bottom-dwellers. Typically, the adult body displays five-fold symmetry. A skeleton, made of calcareous plates, lies beneath the

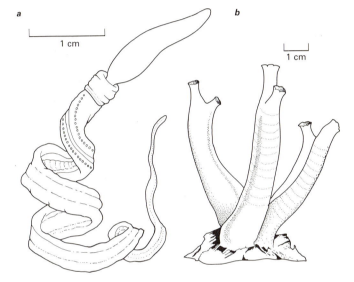

Fig. C.21. (a) HEMICHORDATA; (b) CHORDATA: Urochordata: sea-squirt.

skin, and spines and knobs often extend through the skin: hence the name echinoderm, meaning 'spiny skin'. Echinoderms have fluid-filled tube-feet which are used for locomotion and/or for feeding. Five classes of living echinoderms are generally recognised. The Crinoidea, which have a long fossil record, are the sea-lilies and feather stars, such as *Antedon*; the Asteroidea are the starfish, such as *Asterias*; the Ophiuroidea are the brittlestars and basketstars; the Echinoidea are the sea-urchins, including edible urchins (such as *Echinus*) and the sea-potato (*Echinocardium*); and the Holothuroidea are the sea-cucumbers.

Phylum HEMICHORDATA **(90 species)** (Fig. C.21)

Hemichordates, such as *Balanoglossus*, are marine and generally wormlike animals, with the body and the coelomic body cavity divided into three regions. Pharyngeal gill slits are generally present.

Phylum CHORDATA (Tunicates, lancelets and vertebrates) (48 000 species)

Chordates are distinguished by having the walls of their pharynx (that part of the body immediately behind the mouth cavity) perforated by gill clefts, plus a hollow dorsal nerve cord, and an axial skeleton in the form of a notochord lying immediately beneath the nerve cord. Most chordates have backbones and are called vertebrates, but two of the three subphyla are small invertebrate groups.

The subphylum Urochordata includes tunicates. These are exclusively marine, barrel-shaped and enclosed in a gelatinous or leathery cellulose-containing coat called a tunic. Most of the chordate characteristics are confined to the larval stage of urochordates. The group includes the bottom-living sea-squirts (such as *Ciona* and *Botryllus*), and the planktonic salps and larvaceans (such as *Oikopleura*).

The subphylum Cephalochordata includes the lancelets, such as *Branchiostoma* (once called *Amphioxus*). They are small, segmented fish-like invertebrates with a notochord but no vertebral column.

The subphylum Vertebrata contains animals with a notochord and a dorsal nerve cord, which is enclosed in a backbone of skeletal tissue. The brain is enclosed in a skull or cranium. The Vertebrata includes those animals commonly referred to as fish, amphibians, reptiles, birds and mammals. These groups have often been used in previous classifications, but recently the classification of vertebrates has emphasised more the evolutionary relationships within the subphylum. Much progress has been made in unravelling the complex evolutionary interrelationships of fish, and there has been increasing recognition that 'reptiles' is a diverse assemblage which is difficult to define.

The classification of vertebrates given here is a shortened version of one proposed by E.O. Wiley for living vertebrates, and makes use of taxonomic categories at somewhat unconventional levels. Three infraphyla are distinguished. The Myxinoidea (hagfish) and the Petromyzonta (lampreys) have often been grouped as Agnatha; the name reflects their lack of true jaws. They are eel-like in body form, with suckers, and are scavengers inhabiting the seas and freshwater. The evolutionary relationships of hagfish and lampreys to one another and to other vertebrates are uncertain. The third infraphylum, the Gnathostomata, includes all jawed vertebrates, and is divided into the superclass Chondrichthyes, the cartilaginous fish (sharks, skates and rays, with a skeleton composed of cartilage) and the superclass Teleostomi, which contains all the vertebrates with a bony skeleton.

The Teleostomi is then divided into two classes, the Actinistia, which contains the living coelacanth, which was first trawled off South Africa in 1938, and the Euosteichthyes. The Euosteichthyes is subdivided into two subclasses, the Sarcopterygii and the Actinopterygii. The Sarcopterygii includes the lungfishes, amphibians, and the amniotes with eggs adapted to development on land. Turtles, tortoises, lizards, snakes, crocodiles, birds and mammals are all amniotes. The Actinopterygii comprises a variety of groups of fish, including the teleost fish. There are some 18 000 living species of teleost fish compared, for example, to some 4500 species of living mammal and 888 000 species of arthropod.

VIRUSES AND VIROIDS

Viruses are obligate parasites of animals, plants and microorganisms (those infecting bacteria are commonly referred to as bacteriophages). Matthews has suggested the following definition:

> A virus is a set of one or more nucleic acid template molecules, normally encased in a protective coat or coats of protein or lipoprotein, which is able to organise its own replication only within suitable host cells. Within such cells virus production is (i) dependent on the host's protein synthesising machinery, (ii) organised from pools of the required materials rather than by binary fission, and (iii) located at sites which are not separated from the host cell contents by a lipoprotein bilayer membrane. To be identified positively as a virus [rather than, for example, a plasmid] an agent must be shown to be transmissible, and to cause disease in at least one host.

Various criteria are used in classifying viruses, the most important being as follows (after Matthews):

Structure of the nucleic acids: the basic genetic material may be single-stranded or double-stranded RNA or DNA, and the exact base sequence of this nucleic acid characterises the viral strain.

Organisation and strategy of the viral genome: the genome may be restricted to one virus particle (monopartite) or distributed between two or more particles (multipartite); the presence of another virus may be required for replication, and the genome may be used in replication in a number of different ways.

Viral proteins: the identity, properties and structure of the different kinds of proteins within the virus are used in its characterisation.

Structure of the virus: the virus particles may be symmetrical (isometric) or asymmetrical (anisometric); the particular nature of the symmetry, the arrangement of subunits in the protein coat, and whether or not the particle is surrounded by a lipoprotein outer layer (envelope), are also used in classification.

Physical and chemical properties of the virus: these include density, sedimentation coefficient, diffusion coefficient, electrophoretic mobility, absorption spectrum in ultraviolet light, and stability in different kinds of reagents.

Serological relationships of the virus: these concern the reaction

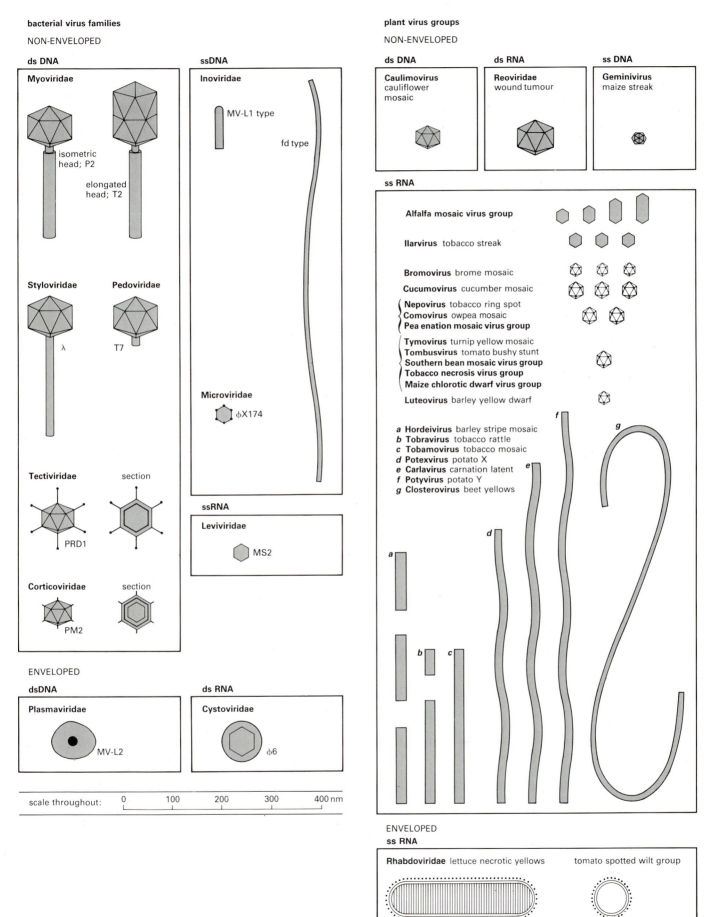

bacterial virus families

NON-ENVELOPED

ds DNA

Myoviridae

isometric head; P2

elongated head; T2

Styloviridae   **Pedoviridae**

λ   T7

Tectiviridae   section

PRD1

Corticoviridae   section

PM2

ssDNA

Inoviridae

MV-L1 type

fd type

Microviridae

φX174

ssRNA

Leviviridae

MS2

ENVELOPED

dsDNA

Plasmaviridae

MV-L2

ds RNA

Cystoviridae

φ6

scale throughout: 0   100   200   300   400 nm

plant virus groups

NON-ENVELOPED

ds DNA

Caulimovirus cauliflower mosaic

ds RNA

Reoviridae wound tumour

ss DNA

Geminivirus maize streak

ss RNA

Alfalfa mosaic virus group

Ilarvirus tobacco streak

Bromovirus brome mosaic

Cucumovirus cucumber mosaic

Nepovirus tobacco ring spot
Comovirus owpea mosaic
Pea enation mosaic virus group

Tymovirus turnip yellow mosaic
Tombusvirus tomato bushy stunt
Southern bean mosaic virus group
Tobacco necrosis virus group
Maize chlorotic dwarf virus group

Luteovirus barley yellow dwarf

a **Hordeivirus** barley stripe mosaic
b **Tobravirus** tobacco rattle
c **Tobamovirus** tobacco mosaic
d **Potexvirus** potato X
e **Carlavirus** carnation latent
f **Potyvirus** potato Y
g **Closterovirus** beet yellows

ENVELOPED
ss RNA

Rhabdoviridae lettuce necrotic yellows   tomato spotted wilt group

Fig. C.22. Classification of the VIRUSES.

animal virus families
NON-ENVELOPED

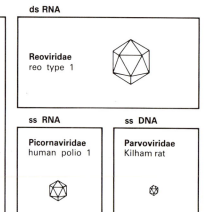

ds RNA

Iridoviridae
tipula iridescent

Adenoviridae
human adeno 2

Papovaviridae
Shope papilloma

ds RNA

Reoviridae
reo type 1

ss RNA

Picornaviridae
human polio 1

ss DNA

Parvoviridae
Kilham rat

ENVELOPED
ds DNA

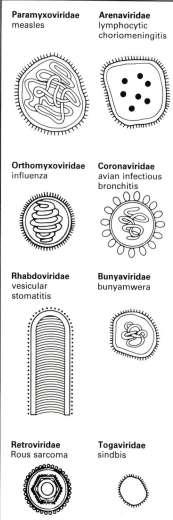

Poxviridae
vaccinia

Baculoviridae
nuclear
polyhedrosis

Herpesviridae
herpes simplex

ss RNA

Paramyxoviridae
measles

Arenaviridae
lymphocytic
choriomeningitis

Orthomyxoviridae
influenza

Coronaviridae
avian infectious
bronchitis

Rhabdoviridae
vesicular
stomatitis

Bunyaviridae
bunyamwera

Retroviridae
Rous sarcoma

Togaviridae
sindbis

of a virus with antibodies raised against it or against other viruses.

Viral activities in the host: these include the range of hosts infected, the symptoms produced, and the spread within the tissues.

Method of viral transmission: the virus may be transmitted from host to host by another organism (a vector); the nature and specificity of the virus–vector relationship are also used in classification.

Many schemes for the classification of viruses have been suggested (see Fig. C.22). Where sufficient information is available, as for most viruses infecting animals, then families, subfamilies and genera have been described and named. Where insufficient information is available to describe families precisely, as with most viruses infecting plants, the term 'group' is substituted. Species have not yet been fully defined; closely related strains of a virus which in practice constitute a species are usually referred to by their English common name (such as rabies virus).

Some viruses and virus-like agents remain unclassified because of lack of adequate information. The most important of these are the **viroids**, which are much smaller than the true viruses, and consist only of a single strand of RNA without any protein coat or envelope.

Further reading

Ainsworth, G.C., Sparrow, F.K. and Sussman, A.S. (ed.) *The Fungi: an advanced treatise.* 1973.

Barnes, R.D. *Invertebrate zoology.* (4th edn) Philadelphia: Saunders, 1980.

Barnes, R.S.K. (ed.) *A synoptic classification of living organisms.* Oxford: Blackwell Scientific, 1984.

Bold, H.C., Alexopoulos, C. and Delevoryas, T. *Morphology of plants and fungi.* (4th edn) New York: Harper and Row, 1980.

Buchanna, R.E. and Gibbons, N.E. *Bergey's manual of determinative bacteriology.* (8th edn) Williams and Wilkins, Baltimore: 1974.

Clark, R.B. and Panchen, A.L. *Synopsis of animal classification.* London: Chapman and Hall, 1971.

Cronquist, A. . . . 1966.

Heywood, V.H. *Flowering plants of the world.* Oxford: Oxford University Press, 1978.

McFarland, W.N. Pough, F.H., Cade, T.J. and Heiser, J.B. *Vertebrate life.* New York: Macmillan, 1979.

Margulis, L. and Schwartz, K.V. *Five kingdoms.* San Francisco: Freeman, 1982.

Matthews, R.E.F. 'Classification and nomenclature of viruses.' *Intervirology,* **12**, 129–296, 1979.

Matthews, R.E.F. *Plant virology.* (2nd edn) New York: Academic Press, 1981.

Primrose, S.B. and Dimmock, N.J. *Introduction to modern virology.* (2nd edn) Oxford: Blackwell Scientific, 1980.

Scagel, R.F., Bandoni, R.J., Rouse, G.E. *et al. Plant diversity: an evolutionary approach.* Belmont: Wadsworth, 1969.

Webster, J. *Introduction to fungi.* (2nd edn) Cambridge: Cambridge University Press, 1980.

Acknowledgments

We gratefully acknowledge all the help we have had from many sources with the artwork for this book. In particular, for assistance in preparing and providing illustrations, we thank the Botany School, University of Cambridge, the Department of Earth Sciences, University of Cambridge, the International Whaling Commission, Rothamsted Experimental Station; and for providing fossil specimens for photograph: the Sedgwick Museum, University of Cambridge. We also thank the following individuals for the photographs specified:

Frontispiece to Introduction copyright © L.M. McGowan; **Frontispiece to Part One** copyright © Brad Amos; **1.1**(*a*) A. Glauert; **1.1**(*b*) P.A. Wooding; **1.3** A. Glauert; **1.4**(*b*) E.A. Munn; **1.4**(*c*) P.A. Wooding; **1.6** T.N. Wreghitt; **1.14**(*a*) P.A. Wooding; **1.14**(*b*) N.J. Lane; **1.17**(*b,d,e*) P.A. Wooding; **1.17**(*c*) J.N. Skepper; **2.1**(*a,b*) F.E. Round; **2.1**(*d*) copyright © Brad Amos; **2.5** P.A. Wooding; **2.11, 2.13, 2.14** H.J. Hudson; **2.24**(*a*) copyright © Brad Amos; **2.24**(*b*), **2.30** copyright © John Mason; **4.4**(*a,b*) copyright © Tim Clutton-Brock; **4.4**(*c*) J. Warren; **4.5**(*a*) copyright © Tim Clutton-Brock; **4.5**(*b*) copyright © Prince and Pearson; **4.6, 4.7** copyright © Tim Clutton-Brock; **5.3**(*a*) copyright © Pat Morris; **5.3**(*b*) copyright © John Mason; **5.3**(*c*), **5.4**(*a*) copyright © J.M. Lock; **5.4**(*b*) copyright © L.M. McGowan; **5.5** copyright © John Mason; **5.8, 5.9** H.J. Hudson; **Frontispiece to Part Two** copyright © L.M. McGowan; **6.6** copyright © John Mason; **6.7** D. Allan; **6.9**(*a*) R. Price; **6.9**(*b*) C. Gilbert; **6.10**(*a,b,c,d*) copyright © John Mason; **6.10**(*e*) M. Burchett; **6.10**(*f*) D. Allan; **6.11**(*a*) H.J. Birks; **6.11**(*b*) D. Allan; **6.12** copyright © Pat Morris; **7.1** copyright © Gordon Langsbury; **7.2** R.S.K. Barnes; **7.3** copyright © Pat Morris; **7.5**(*a*) copyright © Pat Morris; **7.5**(*b*) copyright © John Mason; **7.6**(*a,b*) courtesy © J.M. Lock; **7.6**(*c*) P.F. Yeo; **7.8** R.S.K. Barnes; **7.10** Oleg Polunin; **7.11**(*a*) copyright © J.M. Lock; **7.11**(*b*) D. Allan; **7.12** Oleg Polunin; **7.13**(*a,d*) copyright © Pat Morris; **7.13**(*b,c*), **7.14** M. Burchett; **7.16** copyright © Pat Morris; **7.17** R.S.K. Barnes; **7.18**(*a*) copyright © Pat Morris; **7.18**(*b,c,d*) copyright © John Mason; **7.19, 8.2** copyright © Prince and Pearson; **8.3** D. Watton; **8.4, 8.5** copyright © Prince and Pearson; **8.7** copyright © Bryan Sage; **8.8** copyright © G. Halliday; **8.9** copyright © Bryan Sage; **8.10**(*a*) copyright © G. Halliday; **8.10**(*b,c,d,e,f*) copyright © Bryan Sage; **8.12, 8.13** H.J. Birks; **8.14, 8.16**(*a,c*) copyright © Pat Morris; **8.16**(*b*) copyright © John Mason; **8.16**(*d*) copyright © Tony Morrison; **8.17, 8.18**(*a*) copyright © John Mason; **8.18**(*b*) copyright © Marion Morrison; **8.19, 8.20** copyright © Tony Morrison; **8.21**(*a*) copyright © John Mason; **8.21**(*b*) copyright © Pat Morris; **8.21**(*c*) copyright © Marion Morrison; **8.23** copyright © John Mason; **8.24**(*a*) P.F. Yeo; **8.24**(*b*) copyright © J.M. Lock; **8.28** H.J. Birks; **8.29** copyright © Bryan Sage; **8.30** H.J. Birks **8.31**(*a*) copyright © Pat Morris, **8.31**(*b,c,d*) copyright © John Mason: **8.33** P.F. Yeo; **8.34**(*a,b*) H.J. Birks, **8.34**(*c*) Oleg Polunin; **8.35**(*a,b,d*) I. Spellerberg; **8.35**(*c*) copyright © Pat Morris; **8.37** copyright © Tony Morrison; **8.38**(*a,c*) copyright © L.M. McGowan; **8.38**(*b*) copyright © John Mason; **8.38**(*d*) H.J. Birks; **8.39** copyright © Tony Morrison; **8.40**(*a*) copyright © Pat Morris; **8.40**(*b*) copyright © Bryan Sage; **8.40**(*c,d*) I. Spellerberg; **8.41**(*a,c*) copyright © John Mason; **8.41**(*b,d,e,f*) copyright © L.M. McGowan; **8.42**(*a*) copyright © John Mason; **8.42**(*b*), **8.43, 8.45**(*a*) copyright © Tony Morrison; **8.45**(*b*) copyright © Pat Morris; **8.47**(*a,b*) copyright © J.M. Lock; **8.47**(*c,d*) copyright © L.M. McGowan; **8.48** copyright © Prince and Pearson; **8.49** copyright © Bryan Sage; **8.50** copyright © L.M. McGowan; **8.51** copyright © Bryan Sage; **8.52, 8.53** copyright © Tony Morrison; **8.54, 8.55**(*a*) copyright © John Mason; **8.55**(*b*) copyright © Pat Morris; **8.58** copyright © Tony Morrison; **8.59**(*a*) copyright © John Mason; **8.59**(*b*) copyright © J.M. Lock; **8.60** P.F. Yeo; **8.61** copyright © John Mason; **8.62** James P. Blair, © 1983 National Geographic Society; **8.63** copyright © Pat Morris; **8.64, 8.65** copyright © Tony Morrison; **8.66** copyright © Marion Morrison; **8.67**(*a*) copyright © Pat Morris; **8.67**(*b*) copyright © Tony Morrison; **8.68**(*a,b,c,e,g,h*) copyright © John Mason; **8.68**(*d*) copyright © L.M. McGowan; **8.68**(*f*) copyright © Tony Morrison; **9.1** copyright © John Mason; **9.2, 9.3** B.A. Whitton; **9.4** copyright © Pat Morris; **9.5** J.C. Chubb; **9.6**(*a*) I. Spellerberg; **9.6**(*b*), **9.7** copyright © Pat Morris; **9.9** B.A. Whitton; **9.10** copyright © L.M. McGowan; **9.11, 9.12, 9.13** copyright © Pat Morris; **9.14** copyright © John Mason; **9.15, 9.16** copyright © Tony Morrison; **9.17**(*a,b*) copyright © John Mason; **9.17**(*c*) copyright © Gordon Langsbury; **9.17**(*d*) copyright © Bryan Sage; **9.18** B.A. Whitton; **9.20** Oleg Polunin; **10.2** copyright © John Mason; **10.3**(*a*) C.A. Gilligan; **10.4**(*b*), **10.6**(*a*) J.A. Lucas; **10.6**(*b*), **10.7, 10.16** copyright © John Mason; **Frontispiece to Part Three** D. Bursell; **11.1** James Cadbury; **12.3**(*a,c,d*) D. Bursell; **13.3**(*b*) A.J. Stuart; **13.2, 13.4**(*a,d*) Simon Conway Morris; **13.4**(*b*) D. Bruton; **13.4**(*c*) H.B. Whittington; **13.6** D. Bursell; **13.7** A.J. Stuart; **13.10** copyright © Pat Morris; **14.1**(*a*) D. Edwards; **14.1**(*b*) J. Doran; **14.3**(*b*) D. Bursell; **14.4, 14.5**(*b*) D. Edwards; **14.6** D. Bursell; **14.12** E.M. Friis; **14.13** copyright © John Mason; **14.15**(*a*) D. Orchard; **14.15**(*b*) D. Chivers; **14.15**(*c*) copyright © Tim Clutton-Brock; **15.4** H.J. Birks; **C3** J. Whatley.

Species index

Subject index